ENCYCLOPEDIA OF
SOCIAL DEVIANCE

Editorial Board

ENCYCLOPEDIA OF
SOCIAL DEVIANCE

Edited by

Craig J. Forsyth
University of Louisiana at Lafayette

Heith Copes
University of Alabama at Birmingham

⑤SAGE reference

Los Angeles | London | New Delhi
Singapore | Washington DC

Los Angeles | London | New Delhi
Singapore | Washington DC

FOR INFORMATION:

SAGE Publications, Inc.
2455 Teller Road
Thousand Oaks, California 91320
E-mail: order@sagepub.com

SAGE Publications Ltd.
1 Oliver's Yard
55 City Road
London, EC1Y 1SP
United Kingdom

SAGE Publications India Pvt. Ltd.
B 1/I 1 Mohan Cooperative Industrial Area
Mathura Road, New Delhi 110 044
India

SAGE Publications Asia-Pacific Pte. Ltd.
3 Church Street
#10-04 Samsung Hub
Singapore 049483

Acquisitions Editor: Jim Brace-Thompson
Developmental Editor: Sanford Robinson
Production Editor: David C. Felts
Reference Systems Manager: Leticia Gutierrez
Reference Systems Coordinators: Laura Notton,
    Anna Villasenor
Copy Editor: QuADS Prepress (P) Ltd.
Typesetter: Hurix Systems Pvt. Ltd.
Proofreaders: Kristin Bergstad, Sally Jaskold
Indexer: Joan Shapiro
Cover Designer: Rose Storey
Marketing Manager: Carmel Schrire

Copyright © 2014 by SAGE Publications, Inc.

Printed in the United States of America.

Library of Congress Cataloging-in-Publication Data

Encyclopedia of social deviance / edited by Craig J. Forsyth, University of Louisiana at Lafayette, Heith Copes, University of Alabama at Birmingham.

pages cm
Includes bibliographical references and index.

ISBN 978-1-4522-4033-6

1. Deviant behavior—Encyclopedias. I. Forsyth, Craig J. II. Copes, Heith.

HM811.E53 2014
302.5'42—dc23   2013029359

14 15 16 17 18 10 9 8 7 6 5 4 3 2 1

Contents

List of Entries

MALE PROSTITUTION

Male prostitution includes any activity in which a male offers sexual services with the main purpose of receiving compensation (financial or not) from other males or females. The concept of prostitution has negative connotations and is influenced by medical and legal definitions. In the social sciences, the term *sex work* (*sex working/sex worker*) is preferred because it is considered more inclusive of all forms of selling sex, such as strippers and porn actors. This entry addresses male sex work in which the partner and potential client is another male. This is because homosexual *sex working* is a complex phenomenon that is underestimated and neglected not only by scientific research but also by social intervention and policy. In scientific literature, the social spheres of *sex working* and *sex workers* are often confused with a series of other phenomena, including child abuse, pedophilia, trafficking and exploitation, and drug consumption and addiction, which, while they may often be contiguous with sex work, have distanced the focus of research from its distinctive aspects and characteristics.

Male prostitution was not an uncommon phenomenon in ancient history and has been practiced in various cultures and civilizations. There are many accounts from ancient times and especially the classical age of individuals who prostituted themselves, such as the *pornoi* in ancient Greece and the prostitutes of ancient Rome. In both cultures, however, their activity was considered deplorable to the point that those who practiced it could not hold positions of public office. There are statistics and accounts relating to prostitution and the existence of male brothels in Paris and London during the 18th century, which were known as "Molly houses." These were secret meeting places for informal casual encounters between homosexuals or discreet places within female brothels, which were more widespread. In the United States in the late 19th and early 20th centuries, public and semi-public meeting places, specific neighborhoods, and underground cafes, theaters, and bars welcomed, protected, and contributed to the socialization, relationships, and recreation of their regulars. In New York, between 1890 and 1940, there were areas dedicated to homosexual male prostitution, specifically on Fourteenth Street at Union Square, which until the 1930s remained an area often frequented by prostitutes, until it was supplanted by Times Square. This new urban area was one of the most important places for male homosexual prostitution in the 1920s. Two specific groups of prostitutes competed for this territory: The first group, "well dressed" with "good manners," identified themselves as gay and usually met with requests from a middle-class clientele (including homosexuals). The second group included a more marginal/criminal element. There are also many accounts attesting to the existence of male prostitution throughout Italy between the end of the 18th century and the beginning of the 19th century. This was harshly repressed during the Fascist era, in part as it was considered the main criminal effect of the vice of pederasty. As homosexual liberation movements developed in the 1960s and 1970s, homosexual male prostitution flourished, together with other, indirect, activities (e.g., pornography and modeling), and street prostitutes or *call boys* were free to advertise in publications specifically aimed at and produced for the homosexual market. The period of sexual liberation and feminism coincided with the disappearance of *spontaneous* prostitution, almost a rite of passage that foresaw homosexual relations in highly homosocial contexts, and young *spontaneous* prostitutes gave way to marginal individuals, addicts, and immigrants.

Sociological Analysis of Male Prostitution

Though not purely sociological, initial analyses developed in Anglo-American contexts on the basis of indications drawn from the current of reformist social hygienism, of Victorian origin, which emphasized a strong link between homosexual conduct and a predisposition to deviant and delinquent behavior, significantly prostitution. Various studies at the time were aimed at repressing homosexual conduct, precisely to avoid delinquent behavior. These antecedents contributed to the stereotype of the runaway delinquent (and heterosexual) prostitute—the simple "hustler" and the adolescent prostitute running away from home. Therefore, it can be seen that male prostitution is strongly associated with the moral (and social) problem of homosexuality and protection of young people defined as innocent victims of the homosexual predator, who was usually thought to be older.

Various scholars connected with the Department of Sociology of The University of Chicago frequently produced unpublished material, such as PhD and MA theses, ethnographic notes, or simply life stories on "nonnormative sexual types." The first works were based on research on prostitution and marketed sex, commissioned by institutional bodies. The Vice Commission of Chicago, which included, among others, William I. Thomas and Charles R. Henderson, identified areas of the city where illegal sex was rife, as well as communities and typologies: immigrants, professional or occasional prostitutes, panders, female impersonators, and sex perverts. Research and reflections on the sexuality of young people had significant effects on the analysis of male prostitution. In theorizations of the 1950s and 1960s, male (homosexual) prostitution became a problem to be prevented and controlled because it mostly involved young heterosexual males. Representations of homosexuality and the analysis of young people at

risk of delinquency became the main research topics, following two main approaches: a sociological one based on the subcultures of delinquents or of homosexuals and a clinical one that pathologized male (homosexual) prostitution.

Social Structure, Typologies, and Social Spheres of Male Sex Work

Scholars often make a distinction between *direct sex work* ("organized" and "formalized" in places created expressly for the purpose, e.g., brothels) and *indirect sex work* (in which various professionals, e.g., masseurs, dancers, other individuals, and staff involved in running gay meeting places, supplement their income by performing sexual acts for payment). Scholars of deviance distinguish between *transactional sex* (sex-working activities not related to interactions and exchanges at a professional level but rather exchange agreements of material support characterized by involvement in relationships, friendships, romance) and *survival sex* (any sexual exchange practiced in conditions of extreme poverty and in response to contingent needs—this is not planned and occurs in contexts and conditions of deprivation, as in the case of drug addicts or young males with no fixed abode).

The two main types of sex work are *street hustling*, that which relates to other activities and services offered in a series of indoor locations such as bars and specialized nighttime venues, and *escorting*, which offers services through agencies and other organized channels. These two main types fall into a hierarchy, relating to the location of the act, the sexual practices involved, and the self-presentation of the sex worker. The *street hustler*, working on the street, has the lowest position and status within the social structure of the world of sex work; the *bar hustler* meets his own clients, mainly homosexuals, in bars and nighttime venues; the *call boy*, on the other hand, uses different forms of advertisement, from printed advertisements to the Internet and word of mouth; the *kept boy* is maintained by a single client for a variable period.

With the arrival of new technology, particularly the Internet, much of the sex market has moved online. There are in fact specialized sites and chat lines where escorts can publish their own profile, their physical characteristics and sexual practices, and through websites, they can attract their own clients, arranging meeting places themselves (*incall*) or according to the client's demands (*outcall*). With regard to the level of involvement and motivations, in sociological and criminological literature a distinction is made between (a) the *professional*, for whom sex work is the main source of income, supplemented by other minor commercial sexual activities; (b) the *amateur*, whose sexual activity is sporadic and depends on his need for money or the excitement derived from the activity; and (c) the *runaway*, the young person adrift, who has to sell his own body to survive. Male sex workers have greater independence and autonomy than their female counterparts, given that there are no intermediaries or male brothels—at least in the Western countries—which gives them greater mobility within the hierarchy of the male sex work sector. With regard to temporary involvement in sex-working activities, a distinction is made between full-time street hustlers and bar hustlers, between full-time call boys and kept boys, and between part-time hustlers (often students or workers, this is the largest group, whose main aim is to obtain financial resources) and peer delinquents, whose main aim is to find clients who become victims of their illegal activity (e.g., theft).

The types of employment are highly stratified: Street sex working is the most commonly stigmatized, and public opinion seems to be more tolerant of indoor types. Street activity is stratified in terms of ethnicity, sexual orientation, the relative construction of identity, and sexual practices (top vs. bottom); age and physical appearance; amount of payment requested; and the location in which the acts are carried out. There is some difference compared with female sex work regarding access to resources for protection, the possibility of refusing certain types of clients or refusing sexual acts and practices, and conditions of dependence and control by third parties. Escorts especially seem to have greater autonomy and control compared with street sex workers, though there are differences compared with female escorting: Men earn less than women. However, males are less stigmatized by their own families and within the gay community for their activities.

The results of sociological research suggest that sexual acts are particularly well compensated by clients if offered by individuals whose physical characteristics are associated with hegemonic masculinity: Older escorts are cheapened, as are those who are too thin or too fat (characteristics associated with femininity); "muscular" individuals, on the other hand, are particularly rewarded, as this is seen as a sign of masculinity and dominance. The sexual acts carried out are also seen in terms of the implications for hegemonic masculinity: Top has greater significance than bottom, as top denotes dominance and bottom submission. The intersection between ethnicity and sexual behavior shows that blacks, Hispanics, and whites gain advantage if they are top, but it is black men who are most rewarded: They would, however, be stigmatized for being bottom, not just within their own ethnic group but also by the homosexual and nonhomosexual communities.

Males are usually transitorily involved in sex work, and they abandon it sooner than do females. While they depend less on prostitution as a source of income or for survival, unlike females, they are at times obliged to define their sexual orientation. Most sex workers are relatively young: According to some studies, their age varies between 18 and 40 years, and the period of sex working is about 8 years. There are also long-term sex workers (*long-term survivors*) who have spent up to 20 years on the streets, and these individuals are more reticent when it comes to programs for reduction and prevention of the risk associated with sexually transmitted diseases. Two other groups are "chickens," adolescent sex workers, and "pin feathers," still younger (between 6 and 16 years old), who carry out these activities with their family's consent, contributing to the family income.

The majority of male sex workers are not forced to prostitute themselves; this suggests that they have greater control over their working conditions and also obtain greater gratification from the sexual contact with their clients. This is not the case with marginal individuals in the social sphere of sex working—that is to say drug addicts, young people with no fixed abode, individuals with HIV (human immunodeficiency virus) or AIDS (acquired immune deficiency syndrome), those who don't normatively adhere to dominant representations of masculinity (transgender or particularly effeminate sex workers), those who do not have sufficient economic resources following their acts, and foreign immigrants (especially illegal ones). For all these groups, the social spheres of sex work act as an informal social network for support and protection of essential needs, which are often not provided by official and "normal" networks. Male prostitution is a matter of great interest for the study of deviant activities because it enables observation of how individuals find themselves in informal work and exchange systems (of drugs, sex, money, other gratuities, and proceeds from illegal activities and other resources) in a range of contexts and together with a variety of participants.

Cirus Rinaldi

See also Deviant Career; Homosexuality; Public Sex; Sex Tourism; Street Hustling

Further Readings

Humphreys, L. (1970). *Tearoom trade: Impersonal sex in public places.* Chicago, IL: Aldine.

Leap, W. L. (Ed.). (1999). *Public sex/gay space.* New York, NY: Columbia University Press.

Luckenbill, D. F. (1985). Entering male prostitution. *Journal of Contemporary Ethnography, 14*(2), 131–153.

Rinaldi, C. (2012). Il sex work maschile (omosessuale): Rappresentazioni, mondi sociali ed analisi [Male (homosexual) sex work: Representations, social worlds and analysis]. In C. Cipolla & E. Ruspini (Eds.), *Prostituzioni visibili e invisibili* [Visible and invisible prostitutions] (pp. 189–222). Milan, France: Franco Angeli.

Tewksbury, R. (1996). Cruising for sex in public places: The structure and language of men's hidden, erotic worlds. *Deviant Behavior, 17*(1), 1–19.

Weinberg, M. S., & Williams, C. J. (1975). Gay baths and the social organization of impersonal sex. *Social Problems, 23*(2), 124–136.

Weitzer, R. (2009). Sociology of sex work. *Annual Review of Sociology, 35,* 213–234.

Malicious Software

The term *malicious software*, or malware, refers to computer programs used by hackers and computer attackers to compromise systems. There are various forms of malware that have increased in complexity in keeping with the evolution of technology over the past two decades. Malware has myriad functionality and is designed to automate attacks against systems and simplify the process of hacking overall. At the same time, malware exists in a nebulous legal space, as there are no specific laws against the creation of malicious software. Many malware writers argue that they create tools to better understand the limits of computer and network security. The use of these tools in computers without permission from the system owner is, however, illegal. Thus, individuals who write malicious codes but do not use it on their own may have minimal legal culpability for the way that it is used by others. The lack of standards for legislation against such cyberattacks has also enabled the formation of safe havens where malware writers and hackers can operate with minimal risk of extradition and prosecution.

Malicious software programs operate by affecting vulnerabilities or flaws in computer software or hardware. Every program has some design flaws, and there are literally hundreds or thousands of vulnerabilities that have been identified in systems like Microsoft Windows and the web browsers individuals use every day. The presence of a vulnerability allows an attacker to understand and gain initial access to a target system in some way. Many security professionals attempt to identify vulnerabilities to help secure computer systems, though this information is typically released to the public through open forums or e-mail lists. As a result, attackers can immediately use information on vulnerabilities to their advantage.

Once a vulnerability is identified, a malware writer can then create an exploit, or program, that can take advantage of vulnerabilities to give the attacker deeper access to a system or network. The creation of exploit codes serves as a way to compromise a computer system, and there are myriad tools available to exploit existing vulnerabilities in computer software. Various forms of malicious software can be used to engage in attacks that can be acquired for free from web forums or purchased from vendors in online black markets. Most malware is used to disrupt e-mail and network operations, access private files, steal sensitive information, delete or corrupt files, and generally damage computer software and hardware. As a result, the dissemination of malware across computer networks can be costly for several reasons, including the loss of data and copyrighted information, identity theft, loss of revenue due to customer apprehension about the safety of a company's website, time spent removing the programs, and losses in personal productivity and system functions. The interconnected nature of modern computer networks also allows an infected system in one country to spread malicious software across the globe and cause even greater damage. Thus, malware infection poses a significant threat to Internet users around the globe.

Types of Malicious Software

The most common forms of malware include computer viruses, worms, and Trojan horse programs that alter functions within computer programs and files. Viruses can conceal their presence on computer systems and networks and spread via e-mail attachments, downloadable files, instant messaging, and other methods. A virus cannot spread on its own, and therefore, it requires some user intervention to be installed on a system and to activate its payload. To that end, viruses are often used in conjunction with Trojan horse programs. Much like the Trojan Horse from Greek history, this sort of malware arrives as a downloadable file or attachment that people would be inclined to open, such as photos, video, or documents with misleading titles such as "XXX Porn" or "Receipt of Purchase." When the file is opened, it executes some form of malicious code. Worms are a unique form of malware that can autonomously spread on their own, though they do not necessarily have a payload. Instead, they use system memory to spread and self-replicate and deteriorate system functionality.

There are now also blended threats, which combine multiple aspects of viruses, Trojans, and worms into a single piece of malicious code. For instance, one of the most prevalent and problematic forms of malware today are botnets. This form of malware combines aspects of Trojan horse programs and viruses, in that the code may be sent to a victim through an attachment or other mechanism. Once the program is executed, it then installs a bot program, meaning that the computer can now receive commands and be controlled by another user through Internet Relay Chat channels. The infected machine then surreptitiously contacts a preprogrammed Internet Relay Chat channel to wait for commands from the bot operator. Multiple machines that are infected with this malware will contact the channel, creating a botnet, or a network of zombie machines. The size of botnets enables their operators to engage in a wide range of cybercrimes, including the distribution of spam and other malware. Botnets can also be used to perform Distributed Denial of Service attacks, where each computer in the network attempts to contact a computer or server. The target system becomes flooded with requests and cannot handle the volume, resulting in a loss of services to users. This is an extremely costly form of cybercrime for companies, as they can lose millions of dollars in revenue if customers cannot access their services.

Similarly, malware writers have recently developed tools that can infect web browsers and thereby enable remote takeovers of computer systems. These programs are called exploit packs and must be installed on a web server to attack individuals visiting a website. The exploit pack malware contains multiple common vulnerabilities for the most prevalent web browsers and its associated exploits. The program then detects the type and version of browser software that an individual is using to go to that website and cycles through these vulnerabilities and exploits until it can infect the user. This type of attack exponentially increases the ease of infection by operating surreptitiously and without the inherent challenges that may be present in Trojan horse or virus infections. In addition, web browsers often store sensitive information about a user such as passwords and common sites visited, thereby increasing the risk of identity theft, data loss, and computer misuse.

In light of this global problem, a small body of research has considered the individual-level motivations for malware creation. Research on virus writers and hackers suggests that they may have a deep interest in technology, though they are motivated by various interests, including destruction, political beliefs, and revenge. Both hackers and malware writers also have shifting ethical beliefs about the consequences of their actions. Individuals differentially perceive hacking or virus creation as wrong, and they can justify and rationalize their actions in a number of ways. For instance, the evolution of malware and the growth of sophisticated attack infrastructures via botnets in the computer underground have revolutionized cybercrime and hacking.

An online marketplace has emerged in forums and Internet Relay Chat channels for the sale and distribution of malicious software, stolen data, and hacking tools that enable less skilled actors to gain direct access to services that extend their abilities. Examinations of these online markets indicate that hackers can now buy and sell resources to facilitate attacks or sell information acquired through a compromise. In fact, hackers regularly sell credit card and bank accounts, PIN numbers, and supporting customer information obtained from victims around the world in lots of tens or hundreds of accounts. Individuals also offer cash-out services to obtain funds from electronic accounts or ATMs offline, as well as checking services to validate whether an account is active and has any available balances. Spam- and phishing-related services are also available, including bulk e-mail lists to use for spamming and e-mail injection services to facilitate responses from victims. Some sellers also offer Distributed Denial of Service services and web hosting on compromised servers.

Detecting and Countering Malware Attacks

While there is a good deal of research on the technical processes of malware and their functionality, less is known about the factors that affect the likelihood of infection or victimization. This is due in part to the challenge of determining when someone has been attacked. Some individuals may not recognize their system has been compromised until either their information has been removed or corrupted because malware infections can mimic general errors and system crashes. In addition, limited research on the correlates of malware infection suggests that there are no real age, race, or gender relationships present. This may be a reflection of the desires of malware writers and hackers to affect as many targets as possible. To be effective, hackers cast wide nets to compromise thousands, if not millions, of computer users because they may only infect a small proportion of all machines. Thus, it may be difficult to discern any unique demographic trends in the risk of victimization.

One of the only real predictors of hacking and malware victimization is individual participation in certain forms of cybercrime, like digital piracy and viewing pornography. Malware writers are aware that individuals will click on files that they download to view a film or image. As a result, they may insert malicious code into what appears to be a music or media file in the hope that someone will download the item and execute the code. Additionally, peer offending also increases the risk of victimization. In virtual environments, the activities of one person expose others to harm directly or indirectly. For instance, if an individual's computer is infected with malware, some programs will attempt to replicate and spread by sending infected files to others through the distribution of spam messages.

The high risk that malware poses to computer users has led to the emergence of an entire industry dedicated to detecting and removing malware. The antivirus and computer security industry have created various products to protect computer systems from compromise through automated scans. These programs work by creating signatures of known malware that can be used to detect the presence of malicious codes or files on a computer. Antivirus vendors must, however, diligently identify new variants of malware to create these signatures. Thus, when new malware is released, there is a lag in the likelihood that their software will detect malicious code.

As a consequence, it is important to recognize that the defensive power of security software against random attacks is moderated by the system owners and operators. For example, protective security tools must be regularly updated and run to ensure that the user is protected. Simply having antivirus present on a system does not mean that it is working. Instead, the user may have to configure and direct the program to scan his or her system in order to detect the presence of malware. Thus, many individuals are victimized despite the presence and use of antivirus software and other protective programs to defend their system against the random nature of damaging computer attacks.

Thomas J. Holt

See also Digital Piracy; Hacking; Phishing

Further Readings

Bossler, A. M., & Holt, T. J. (2009). On-line activities, guardianship, and malware infection: An examination of routine activities theory. *International Journal of Cyber Criminology, 3,* 400–420.

Chu, B., Holt, T. J., & Ahn, G. J. (2010). *Examining the creation, distribution, and function of malware on-line* [Online]. Washington, DC: National Institute of Justice. Retrieved from https://www.ncjrs.gov/pdffiles1/nij/grants/230111

Denning, D. E. (2011). Cyber-conflict as an emergent social problem. In T. J. Holt & B. Schell (Eds.), *Corporate hacking and technology-driven crime: Social dynamics and implications* (pp. 170–186). Hershey, PA: IGI-Global.

Holt, T. J., Soles, J. B., & Leslie, L. (2008). *Characterizing malware writers and computer attackers in their own words.* Proceedings of the 2008 International Conference on Information Warfare and Security, Peter Kiewit Institute, University of Nebraska Omaha.

The Honeynet Project. (2001). *Know your enemy: Learning about security threats.* Boston, MA: Addison-Wesley.

Kapersky, E. V. (2003). *The classification of computer viruses.* Bern, Switzerland: Metropolitan Network BBS.

PandaLabs. (2007). *Malware infections in protected systems.* Retrieved from http://research.pandasecurity.com/blogs/images/wp_pb_malware_infections_in_protected_systems.pdf

MARDI GRAS

Mardi Gras ("Fat Tuesday," literally translated from French) has long been considered an epicenter of social deviance in modern American life. The days that lead up to this famous Tuesday before Ash Wednesday of each year are all part of the Carnival, which stretches from the 12th night of Christmas (e.g., the evening of January 6) until Lent begins. As this should signal to the reader, the Carnival has its roots in Catholic traditions as a period of celebration before a time of introspection and soul-searching, which Lent beckons. Areas with densely Catholic populations have been renowned to have extravagant festivities planned throughout the Carnival, with the most notable being on Mardi Gras; many of these festivities are peppered with bohemian, raunchy, and racy activity likened to the masquerades of the famous Moulin Rouge in Paris, at its height of notoriety. Provocative costumes, binge alcohol and drug consumption, sexual promiscuity, and outlandish behavior all seem to be inseparable from the common conception of the Carnival. It truly seems as though the Carnival is an incubator for social deviance wherever it is observed around the world.

The State of Louisiana, the City of New Orleans in particular, has enjoyed a rich history of Carnival tradition that dates back to the late 17th and early 18th centuries. The vast majority of festivities revolve around social clubs whose various get-togethers do not center on social deviance at all. Carnival goers, on the other hand, have long been depicted in their hedonistic displays of deviance. In old local newspapers, for example, one can find coverage of public nudity dating back to the late 1800s. In contemporary times, the majority of deviant and transgressive behavior is concentrated in a few key areas in the City of New Orleans on Mardi Gras and the roughly 10 days that precede it. These areas include the French Quarter and Marigny (pronounced *mare'-in-ee*), where many revelers seek out lewd and lascivious behaviors, especially after dusk. In these areas, law enforcement tends to concentrate on public order rather than strictly enforcing local rules and regulations, and this relaxation of formal social control (up to a point) is widely accepted and anticipated. As such, displays of public nudity (e.g., exposure of women's breasts and male genitals) and public intoxication are commonplace after dark as Mardi Gras approaches. Since the 1970s, most of this behavior has concentrated along Bourbon Street where the core entertainment district is located, which houses many of the city's bars and almost all of its strip clubs and risqué establishments. The vast majority of these establishments and the local hotels offer up their balconies facing Bourbon Street to Carnival goers who throw beads and other trinkets to individuals below in exchange for public displays of nudity. Face-to-face encounters on the streets below may offer different exchanges such as kissing, groping, and fondling, and perhaps sexual favors (sometimes in public, which is not tolerated by law enforcement).

These exchanges are frequently controlled through informal means outside the French Quarter where families tend to congregate to enjoy the parades that also make the New Orleans Carnival famous. In this regard, Carnival goers across the State of Louisiana (including the more rural parishes and bayou countryside) enforce rules largely through informal means, while law enforcement takes a more relaxed approach to ensure everyone's safety. Meanwhile, it is well-known among the locals that certain parades, locations, and times are reserved for adult-only Carnival goers. Krewe du Viuex (pronounced *crew doo voo*) is a recent example of a string of social clubs that form to create a raucous parade that travels through the Marigny and the French Quarter late in the evening roughly 2 weeks before Mardi Gras. This parade offers satirical floats that graphically depict political figures sodomizing citizens, bondage and sadomasochism, and many other common taboos. This parade attracts drug use (in particular, marijuana and hallucinogens, e.g., psilocybe mushrooms and LSD), while alcohol consumption remains persistent, as with a large proportion of Carnival festivities across the state.

It seems as though the vast majority of social deviance tied to the Carnival is strongly correlated with binge alcohol consumption. Previous sociological research points to the relaxed morality of the New Orleans Carnival; however, it appears that individual levels of self-control may play a role in who seeks out risky and indulgent behaviors (e.g., self-selection). Contemporary research of the social deviance at the Carnival stretches back to the 1980s and is prominently qualitative in methodology. Most of the discourse in interviews with parade goers depicts an escape from reality and the doldrums of daily life as a part of a renewal of sorts. Other themes involve peer pressure, the feeling of a rush, as well as citing intoxication as the fundamental reason to engage in deviance during the Carnival. While less prominent in scholarly research, heavy alcohol consumption and high-density crowds also seem to fuel violence in the form of assaults and handgun-related injuries and deaths. Every year, since the turn of the century, at least one individual has been injured or has died from gunshot wounds while attending the Carnival in New Orleans (in specific, on Mardi Gras or the 10 or so days leading to it while being near or on a parade route or in the French Quarter). These incidents have been well documented by the New Orleans Police Department as well as by local, regional, and sometimes national news outlets. In general, the New Orleans Police Department has displayed mastery of crowd control; yet these incidents have never ceased to haunt the law enforcement agency each year the Carnival arrives. This level of violence does not seem to plague the parishes outside of the Orleans Parish; however, frequent problems of alcohol-related injuries are noted each year no matter where the festivities occur.

Despite the accounts of violence, the allure of the Carnival brings upward to 1 million revelers to New Orleans every year. These events account for a large proportion of the city's tourism dollars, thus the local government does its best to protect Carnival festivities from anything that may bring about a change to this special event. Many of the Carnival's nuances have not changed for over two centuries, including the tolerance of social deviance; this pattern seems likely to remain in effect long into the future. The festival of music, food, culture, shared history, freedom from slavery, and many more long-ingrained traditions will no doubt be continued by generations of Louisianans to come.

David N. Khey

See also Bead Whores

Further Readings

Forsyth, C. J. (1992). Parade strippers: A note on being naked in public. *Deviant Behavior, 13,* 391–403.

Huber, L. (1972). The great traditions of Mardi Gras. *New Orleans Magazine, 6,* 36–65.

Jacobs, T. (2010, February). The evolution of Mardi Gras rituals. *Pacific Standard* www.psmag.com/culture/unmasking-mardi-gras-deviants-8972/

Mitchell, R. (1999). *All on a Mardi Gras day: Episodes in the history of New Orleans Carnival.* Cambridge, MA: Harvard University Press.

Redmon, D. (2003). Examining low self-control theory at Mardi Gras: Critiquing the general theory of crime within the framework of normative deviance. *Deviant Behavior, 24,* 373–392.

MARGINALITY

A general definition of marginality includes the core concept of exclusion from mainstream society and its activities and processes. The principal construct of marginality is the removal of an individual or individuals from the broad center of society to the edges or fringes. Individuals who are marginalized are the outliers of society. In 1928, Robert Park first put forth the idea of marginality with his concept of the Marginal Man. This Marginal Man was the product of increased human migration, which resulted in the loosening of social structures and increasing the individualization of the person. In this construct, marginality is created when two cultures or societies come into sustained contact with one another. Individuals who successfully navigated these frontiers became marginal men who identified with neither group.

The construct of marginality has changed considerably over the past 80 years. Other researchers have taken a more psychological interest in the state of marginality. In a related manner, Abraham Maslow's hierarchy of human needs places belonging and acceptance as a crucial aspect of human need immediately after physiological and safety needs, but before self-esteem needs. This highlights the potentially negative implications of marginalization. Different research has focused on situational marginality—that is, contexts where an individual may experience social exclusion or marginalization.

Types of Marginality

Initially, sociologists studied marginality as a cultural construct. These scholars claimed that individuals were marginal when they straddled two or more cultures. This can be seen in mixed-race individuals who often self-report being excluded from all racial groups. Another level of marginality is social or community marginalization. This occurs when individuals are left out of relevant social activities by a group or community. Examples include children excluding one of their classmates from play or refusal to eat or make physical contact with patients with HIV/AIDS (human immunodeficiency virus/acquired immune deficiency syndrome). A related construct is political marginalization, where excluded individuals are prevented from engaging in ordinary community activities through rules or regulations. This occurred extensively in America through the now defunct Jim Crow laws designed to prevent blacks and other minorities from voting, as well as past school policies that prevented children with disabilities from receiving a free and appropriate public education. A final conceptualization of marginality is the idea of psychological marginality. This concept refers to the distinctiveness that an individual may possess or appear to possess such as high intelligence or obesity. In this case, there are several means by which an individual may become marginalized. Some of these are situational; that is, a person may be marginalized only in certain social settings. For example, a female legislator may be marginalized in some legislative bodies that are predominantly male. While she may be a member of mainstream society outside her role as a legislator, she may be a marginalized member in the legislature.

The ways and means for a person to be marginalized from mainstream society are numerous and may be roughly categorized as follows:

Concealed versus observed: An initial means of categorizing marginalizing characteristics is on whether the characteristic is apparent or not. For example, physical disabilities such as paralysis or amputation are usually readily apparent, while mental illnesses such as depression or obsessive–compulsive disorder are often not.

Positive versus negative: It should also be noted that any trait or ability that places the individual outside of mainstream society is a cause for marginalization. People of extremely high as well as low intelligence may be marginalized from society. Other positive traits subject to marginality are athletic prowess, fame and celebrity, wealth, and beauty. On the other end of the spectrum, poverty, physical disfigurement, and shyness can be marginalizing conditions as well. These negative conditions are often referred to as stigmatizing.

Internal versus external: While many individuals are forcibly marginalized from society, there are others who voluntarily withdraw to the fringes of society. Some famous examples of voluntary withdrawal include Emily Dickinson, Greta Garbo, and Howard Hughes. Other individuals form marginalized subgroups—a few examples being illegal immigrants, the homeless, and teenage runaways.

Implication of Marginalization

The implications of marginality for individuals are as unique as each person and can be either positive or negative. While all marginalized people are excluded at some level from mainstream social processes and activities, the effects will be different. Some more positively marginalized people (athletes, celebrities) will use their outsider status to improve themselves or the world around them (e.g., Olympic athletes, philanthropists, etc.). Some negative traits commonly linked to marginality include depression, anxiety, and anger. Anger can be seen often in the victim-turned-perpetrator scenario. Recent research has focused on the loss of purpose in life or meaning following social exclusion. Interestingly, some research has shown that people who have experienced social rejection are less self-aware, while other research focuses on the increased mindfulness of the marginalized in novel social contexts. A common stereotype is that marginalization often leads to criminal activity. While there is little evidence to attribute causality between marginality and criminal deviance, there has been research demonstrating a negative cyclical effect of incarceration and marginality. At a minimum, marginality sets the stage for social deviance, either positively or negatively.

Holly Howat

See also Conformity; Norms and Societal Expectations; Outsiders; Positive Deviance; Social Disapproval; Stigma and Stigma Management

Further Readings

Dickie-Clark, H. F. (1966). *The marginal situation.* London, England: MW Books.

Frable, D., Blackstone, T., & Scherbaum, C. (1990). Marginal and mindful: Deviants in social interactions. *Journal of Personality and Social Psychology, 59,* 140–149.

Park, R. (1923). Human migration and the mindful man. *American Journal of Sociology, 33*(6), 881–893.

Stillman, T., Baumeister, R., Lambert, N., Crescioni, W., DeWall, C., & Fincham, F. (2009). Alone and without purpose: Life loses meaning following social exclusion. *Journal of Experimental Social Psychology, 45*(4), 686–694.

MARIJUANA

Marijuana refers to the dried flowering tops and leaves of the hemp plant, *Cannabis sativa*, and its relative, *Cannabis indica*; it also refers to the plant itself. The female of the species is rich in the sticky psychoactive resin that coats its upper parts; cultivators exclude the male plant to prevent pollination and seeding. Cannabis is a wild (or feral) and hardy weed; it grows in every country of the world and in every state in the United States. Though THC (tetrahydrocannabinol) is its principal psychoactive agent, the plant contains more than 400 chemicals, called cannabinoids, unique to itself. Different batches of marijuana contain varying proportions of THC, from plants growing by the side of the road, which contain 1% to 3% THC to cultivated *sinsemilla* (seedless plants) and hydroponic plants (grown in a nutrient-rich aquatic solution) containing more than 10% to as much as 20% of the psychoactive ingredient. Not only do batches vary by potency, users affirm that varying batches induce qualitatively different *kinds* of effects as well. Hashish contains only the resin and pollen (and some flowering buds) of the plant; processors press this material into solid or crumbly form. Hash usually contains a higher THC content than the average batch of marijuana. Unlike drinking alcohol, cannabis use is *by definition* the attempt by users to introduce a psychoactive substance into their body—to get high or intoxicated. However, intoxication is manifested in degrees, from "getting a buzz on," a mild high, to "getting wasted," a more extreme state.

Historical evidence suggests that, for millennia, societies have cultivated cannabis for its psychoactive properties and possibly for a far longer stretch of time. Archaeologists have found charred cannabis seeds in 3,000-year-old burial sites in Romania, China, Nepal, the Middle East, and Central Asia. Currently, the use of cannabis for euphoric purposes is common in North Africa, the Middle East, India, Southeast Asia, and Latin and North America. In 2004, the United Nations estimated that 4% of the world's adult population—162 million people—took marijuana at least once during the prior year, and 0.6% (or 22.5 million) used it daily; worldwide, it is the most commonly used illicit psychoactive substance. In the United States, natural marijuana is most commonly smoked in the form of cigarettes or joints, though also often in a small pipe through a tin foil, or in a bong or water pipe. Some users take it by means of a vaporizer, which releases the substance's smoke without igniting it—that is, active ingredients without combustion thereby throwing off fewer toxins.

In some regions of the world, cannabis is brewed into a tea.

Shifting Social Attitudes and Patterns of Marijuana Use

In the United States, in most social circles and social contexts, the regular use of marijuana is regarded as deviant; moreover, such use tends to be statistically co-occurrent with even more deviant acts, including the use of harder or more dangerous drugs. In 1937, with the passage of the Marihuana Tax Act, the federal government criminalized the possession and sale of cannabis. In 1970, Congress superseded this act with the passage of the Comprehensive Drug Abuse Prevention and Control Act, which categorized substances according to "schedules" on the basis of their abuse potential and their "accepted medical use." Federal law classifies marijuana as a Schedule V drug—with a high potential for abuse and "no accepted medical use." Likewise, all states outlaw the possession of a stipulated quantity of marijuana. In 2010, roughly 850,000 persons were arrested on marijuana charges in the United States. Though the courts incarcerate virtually no offenders for simple, small-quantity marijuana possession, the risk of imprisonment imperils every user, and repeat offenders often receive jail or prison time.

Marijuana use has undergone something of a roller-coaster ride with respect to its deviant status. In the 1920s, few Americans had even heard of the drug. But during the 1930s, moral entrepreneurs stigmatized marijuana as the "weed of madness," the "killer weed," and "a sex-crazing drug menace." A popular film distributed in the 1930s, *Reefer Madness*, graphically expressed this panic. But during the 1940s and 1950s, use was extremely low, as were the awareness and condemnation of the use of the drug. During the 1960s and 1970s, attitudes toward marijuana softened, use increased, and the consumption of cannabis came to acquire the mantle not of respectability or conventionality, but at least not of complete condemnation or stigma. In 1979, Monitoring the Future's yearly survey of 8th, 10th, and 12th graders indicated that only a quarter (24%) of high school seniors thought that using marijuana should be a crime, only a seventh (14%) believed that occasional users risked harming themselves, and under half (45%) said that they disapproved of occasional use. But beginning with the election of conservative Ronald Reagan as president in 1980, the more-or-less tolerant attitude toward marijuana use that had been growing in the 1960s and 1970s began to dissipate, and a more condemnatory mood set in. By 1991, student belief that marijuana use should be a crime doubled (49%), the belief that occasional use represented a risk of harm more than doubled (to 41%), and the proportion who disapproved of occasional use increased to four fifths (79%). But in the 1990s, once again, a more accepting sentiment began to settle in, and disapproval declined; during the early 2000s, attitudes toward marijuana use have more or less remained at a plateau. These student attitudes paralleled or reflected the views of the general public, as measured by the National Survey on Drug Use and Health.

According to the ongoing national survey conducted in the United States, in 1960, lifetime use of marijuana among young adults between 18 and 25 years of age—the highest drug-using segment of the population—stood at only 4%. By 1967, this had increased to 14%, and it continued to increase into the 1970s. In 1979, lifetime use for young adults was an astounding 68.5%—and 35% for use during the *past month*. Use has substantially declined since then. In 2010, this survey indicated that 17.4 million people in the United States who were 12 years or older—7%—used marijuana once or more in the prior month. For young adults, this figure was 18.5%. Monitoring the Future (MTF) found that 22.6% of 12th graders, 17.6% of 10th graders, and 7.2% of 8th graders had used marijuana or hashish once or more in the prior 30 days. For both the national survey and MTF, marijuana was *by far* the most common illicit drug used. Six out of 10 illicit drug users (60%) took *only* marijuana, and three quarters of all episodes of illicit drug use were specifically with marijuana.

Numerous researchers have interviewed cannabis users about their marijuana experiences. Users describe their "high" or intoxication largely or overwhelmingly in positive terms. The drug, they say, makes them feel calmer, more relaxed, more peaceful, more sensitive, more perceptive, have more intellectually profound thoughts, laugh more, experience time in a more slowed-down manner, feel "good" or pleasant, think in a more stream-of-consciousness fashion, feel lethargic or lazy, have memory lapses, feel the stimulation of their senses in a more powerful and sensitive way, feel hungrier, and appreciate music more. The positive, pleasant, enjoyable sensations outweigh the negative ones by a factor of roughly 10 to 1. For most who take it, marijuana use is a hedonistic experience, though

many have found unusual intellectual or emotional insights as well, and a minority say that they have felt uncomfortable, paranoid, delusional, depressed, or even terrified under its influence. During the most recent year, the Drug Abuse Warning Network—a federal data collection estimate of drug-related visits to emergency departments around the country—recorded 376,000 reactions to marijuana (usually along with one or more other drugs) that required hospital intervention.

The most controversial issue surrounding the use of marijuana, especially among the young, is the extent to which cannabis functions as a "gateway" or "stepping stone" to the consumption of harder, more dangerous substances—and, specifically, whether such a progression is *etiological* in nature: When it happens, does the marijuana use itself *cause* the subsequent use of drugs such as methamphetamine, cocaine, and heroin? Contemporary research indicates that marijuana use per se does not increase the user's risk of later, hard drug use. The factors that play the strongest role in this progression, when it does occur, is the *predisposition* or "proneness" of the user to abuse drugs, the drug use of one's peers, their subcultural approval of hard drug use, the opportunities peers give to the marijuana user to try and to use more dangerous drugs, whether the user is employed, and whether or not the user experiences life stresses. In and of itself, evidence indicates, by itself, that the consumption of marijuana contributes very little to this process. It is possible that smoking cigarettes and drinking alcohol more effectively serve as "gateway" drugs than the use of cannabis.

Studies suggest that, at higher levels of use, cannabis use correlates with lower school performance and higher dropout rates, but a close examination of the evidence indicates that both tend to be outcomes of a common cause—a general pattern of deviance, risk taking, drug proneness, and unconventionality. Users are more likely to be alienated from conventional institutions, including organized religion, even before their first puff of marijuana; hence, the contribution of the use of the drug seems to play a weak to nonexistent independent role in this process. The MTF surveys of schoolchildren and the national surveys indicate a decrease in, and a growing disapproval of, drug use since the late 1970s and early 1980s, a trend compatible with the growing tendency of the American public to be concerned with health, diet, and exercise, which has resulted in the drastic decline of smoking and the more moderate declines in alcohol consumption, and in the use of illicit drugs, generally.

Current Trends

Contrarily, MTF's data indicate that over the past 5 years (2007–2012), the use of marijuana has increased slightly year by year because students see a declining risk in, and express a declining level of disapproval of, cannabis use. Since the 1970s, 13 states have *de*criminalized the possession of cannabis—that is, one cannot be arrested according to state law for possessing less than 1 ounce of marijuana, the penalty entailing a small fine and the confiscation of one's stash. In addition, 16 states and the District of Columbia have legalized the medical use of marijuana to relieve intraocular pressure and combat glaucoma; to combat nausea attendant on taking AIDS and cancer medication; as an appetite stimulant; to relieve chronic pain; and to relieve the symptoms of multiple sclerosis. Hence, in the 16 states with medical marijuana laws, state law contradicts (but does not contravene) federal law, which allows no medical marijuana; federal agents continue to raid marijuana shops in states that permit medical marijuana. Nonetheless, given the current antidrug climate in the United States, the legalization of marijuana does not appear to be a political option; even the expansion of decriminalization to more states seems unlikely in the foreseeable future. The Netherlands, where the distribution of cannabis is technically illegal but tolerated de facto, has recently passed laws forbidding the sale of cannabis to foreigners, thereby clamping down on "marijuana tourism." Possibly, with the attainment of the political maturation of the current American generation of teenagers and young adults, the future will bring greater tolerance in the form of relaxed marijuana laws and widespread social acceptance of the drug, but observers have been making this prediction for decades.

Erich Goode

See also Changing Deviance Designations; Decriminalization and Legalization; Defining Deviance; Drug Policy

Further Readings

Booth, M. (2003). *Cannabis: A history.* London, England: Bloomsbury.

Chapkis, W., & Webb, R. J. (2009). *Dying to get high: Marijuana as medicine.* New York: New York University Press.

Earleywine, M. (2002). *Understanding marijuana: A new look at the scientific evidence.* New York, NY: Oxford University Press.

Morral, A. R., McCaffrey, D. F., & Paddock, S. M. (2002). Reassessing the marijuana gateway effect. *Addiction, 97,* 1493–1504.

Novak, W. (1980). *High culture: Marijuana in the lives of Americans.* New York, NY: Knopf.

MARITIME PIRACY

In waterways around the world, armed gangs of pirates wreak havoc with trade routes, interfering with the delivery of cargo, fuel, and relief supplies. They hold crews for ransom and steal millions of dollars in goods every year. Dormant for generations, the crime of piracy, one of the world's most enduring criminal plagues, has returned.

The European colonization of the Americas, with much of its wealth exposed on the sea, led to what has been termed the *golden age of piracy*, 1660–1730. This was the era of Blackbeard, Captain Kidd, and other notorious pirates of the Caribbean. The era ended only after seafaring nations expanded their navies to deal with the threat. In modern times, the 1960s saw a rise in acts of piracy; characteristically, these pirates attacked ships at anchor and stole cargo or ship's stores. Today, piracy is once again flourishing and is recognized as another contemporary form of organized crime.

Preventing piracy is challenging because of four general problems: (1) prosecuting pirates is particularly difficult, because many of the attacks take place outside the territorial waters of any state; (2) pirates seek sanctuary in countries whose judicial system is ill equipped to prosecute them; (3) few countries have ratified any international laws regarding the problem; and (4) in many parts of the world, piracy, although illegal, is an accepted aspect of the culture, providing the citizenry with supplemental income and the means of survival. In many places, particularly the East African nation of Somalia, private groups who claim to fight piracy actually engage in acts of piracy instead. In areas such as Somalia and Sri Lanka, the stimulus seems to be the political, military, and economic failures of a region and the complacency of local authorities. Pirates do not lurk in the waters of the United States because of the proactive stance taken by the U.S. Coast Guard and U.S. Navy.

Piracy has been grouped into three types based on their respective routine scenarios of attack. The most common are pirates who rob the crew and the ship and then depart. They prefer to take items that enable an easy escape. The second type of piracy targets people, cargo, and perhaps the vessel. The third, and perhaps most sophisticated type of piracy, entails stealing the vessel to steal cargo and/or haul illegal contraband or drugs. No type of vessel is immune to a pirate attack: cargo ships, fishing boats, tug boats, tankers, container vessels, passengers/ cruise ships, yachts, or sailboats. Any ship whose crew is small, including privately owned yachts, can become a victim. The human cost of piracy is much more dramatic. Crew members are often wounded, killed, or simply lost at sea. In some cases, hostages are taken.

Modern pirates have modern tools at their disposal. They use cellular telephones, automatic weapons, speedboats, and global positioning systems to find their prey and radar to avoid any would-be pursuers. Their raids are also well planned. Armed crews on targeted vessels are rare. Although crews use preventive measures and evasive maneuvers to prevent boarding, such efforts are not always successful. The chief problem is that crews do not remain constantly alert to the potential problem. Once pirates are on board a vessel, the crew tends to retreat to quarters. At sea, a captain has the following means of deterrence: evasive maneuvers, fire hoses, bright lighting, mustering, LRAD (long range acoustic device), and broadcasting for assistance. Pirates are known to attack when the fewest crew members are on duty, usually when the day workers are off duty and sleeping, between the hours of 10 p.m. and 6 a.m. Therefore, a ship at anchor is an attractive target for piracy and should be made to look as though a full crew is on board. As Jim Gray and colleagues recommend, night watches need to remain visible on deck with lights over all sides of the ship.

Several factors have caused the resurgence of piracy: downsizing of naval forces since the end of the cold war, the availability of weapons, and the ever-increasing amounts of cargo being moved across the world's oceans. Some researchers attribute the recent rise in piratical activity to the downturn in the global economy and the increase of Third World poverty.

The case of the Philippines requires particular attention. By the early 1990s, as noted by Paul Chapman and Craig J. Forsyth, Filipinos represented more than two thirds of the world's merchant seamen. This was due to the poverty in the country and the lack of a viable industry for its population to work. Subsequently, the Philippines began to export labor. This arrangement was facilitated by labor contractors, who sell labor to shipping companies for a fee. Such contractors are known to have engaged in many exploitative labor practices, thereby fostering conditions under which aggrieved workers have sought to redress injustices by committing acts of piracy. Poverty, a generalized hatred of the shipping industry that has exploited them, nautical skills, and knowledge of merchant ships serve as the motivational and opportunity factors that enable crimes of piracy in the area of the Philippines. Similar factors contributed to piracy with other peoples worldwide.

The high seas have been the locale for some of humankind's nastiest businesses: rum running, slave trading, and piracy. Those responsible for these acts have fled to the oceans. Many ships are registered under flags of convenience, which have led to a lack of standards on ships and a decline in responsibility of ship owners to the crew. It is not surprising that the sea is the domain of independent adventurers and pirates because it is the setting for an industry that falls far outside the influence of the law. The oceans are a symbol of exploitation for many seamen. Eighteenth-century piracy represented an attempt on the part of seafarers to revenge and/ or overcome some of the abuses of shipboard life. Piracy in the past was a deliberate rebellion against the oppressive structure of the cargo ships of the time. Obviously, pirates of the past and present have plundered to enrich themselves.

In the Caribbean, hundreds of vessels have disappeared in the past 40 years. In the South China Sea, hundreds of thousands of refugees have been robbed, abused, and killed by pirates. In the waters off Somalia, large vessels are being attacked. The Gulf of Aden is a gauntlet between Somalia and Yemen, about 550 miles long by 200 miles wide, where ships sailing to and from the Suez Canal cross. The pirates there are drawn by the concentration of prey and nourished by the freedoms that exist along both shores, especially in Somalia, where formal government has long since collapsed. More than 20,000 commercial ships traverse the Gulf yearly, going to or coming from the Suez Canal.

Six locations account for most of the pirate attacks in the world since 1995: South China Sea, Malacca Strait, Indian Ocean, East Africa, West Africa, and South America. The situation in two African nations, Somalia (East) and Nigeria (West), has gotten much worse over time and are the primary contributors to piracy statistics generated in their locations. The South China Sea was the leading location of piracy until 2007. In 2008 and 2009, the South China Sea had the second highest number of pirate attacks. During both 2008 and 2009, East Africa became the leading place for piracy; recording the highest in 1 year for any location recorded in 2009. The greatest reduction in piracy has occurred in the Malacca Strait, which has gone from the second highest location for piracy in 2000 to no reported acts of piracy during 2009. The Malacca Strait would be a good location for the study of both the cause and prevention of piracy. In 1998, there were only six reported acts of piracy; this grew almost 1900% in 2 years and then decreased to nothing over the next decade. Similar to statistics on land-based crime, it is estimated that half of all attacks go unreported.

Somalia has entire villages along the coast engaged in piracy. Unemployed young men provide the manpower, fishermen offer boats and knowledge of the coastline, and foreign businessmen provide the money for technical equipment and arms. The pirate's chief weapon is the element of surprise and planning. The main difference between pirates and shipping is that most ships are not equipped with deadly weapons. Modern pirates have many opportunities because 95% of international commerce occurs via maritime shipping.

Many pirate attacks take place at choke points. Major shipping routes take cargo ships through narrow bodies of water, such as the Malacca Strait, the Gulf of Aden, the South China Sea, and the oil-rich Niger Delta. Ships have to lower cruising speeds to allow for navigation, making them prime targets for piracy. Pirate ships are capable of disguising themselves as fishing vessels or cargo vessels when not carrying out their crimes, to avoid detection. Pirate groups have informers in London who are in regular contact with control centers in Somalia where decisions on which vessels to attack are made. These insiders provide information on a ship's cargo and course. The pirate's information network reportedly extends to Yemen, Dubai, and the Suez Canal. The national flag of a ship is also taken into account when choosing a target, with British and American vessels being increasingly avoided. They also have apparently cultivated an insider at London shipbrokers. This enables pirates to know which ships are in demand and can be sold quickly.

Pirates often operate in the waters of developing countries along international trade routes. Such countries typically have relatively small navies

and limited capability to deter piracy. Locations where conditions of political unrest exist are ripe for piracy. Following the U.S. withdrawal from Vietnam in 1973, Thai piracy was aimed at the many Vietnamese who took to boats to escape. Following the disintegration of the government of Somalia, warlords in the region attacked ships. After the cold war, navies of powerful nations decreased in size and number and in frequency of patrols, while trade increased, and with it, the number of targets increased and so also the vulnerability. Modern pirates are sometimes linked with organized-crime syndicates, but often, they are small groups. These small groups/crews are used for tactical/logistic reasons but are generally linked with syndicates. Few of these pirate crews operate independently. Pirate crews may consist of 8 or fewer pirates, if going after a ship's safe or cargo, or the personal belongings of the crew, or up to 70 pirates, depending on the size of the target ship and its crew, if the plan is to seize the whole vessel. In other cases, the pirates force the crew off the ship and then sail it to a port to be repainted and given a new identity through false papers often purchased from corrupt officials.

York A. Forsyth

See also Robbery; Routine Activity Theory; Transnational Terrorism

Further Readings

Burnett, J. S. (2002). *Dangerous waters: Modern piracy and terror on the high seas.* New York, NY: Dutton Press.

Chapman, P. K. (1992). *Trouble on board: The plight of international seafarers.* Ithaca, NY: Cornell University Press.

Forsyth, C. J. (1999). Some unsettling maritime terms: The interpretation of found, cargo, ballast and voyage. *Maritime Policy & Management: An International Journal of Shipping and Port Research, 26*(1), 61–68.

Forsyth, C. J., Gisclair, K. H., & Forsyth, Y. A. (2009). Waterborne crime: Examining contemporary piracy. *Deviant Behavior, 30*(8), 669–679.

Forsyth, Y. A., & Forsyth, C. J. (2010). Using a routine activities approach to explain the resurgence of piracy. *International Journal of Crime, Criminal Justice and Law, 5*(1–2), 23–29.

Gray, J., Monday, M., & Stubblefield, G. (1999). *Maritime terror.* Boulder, CO: Vantage Press.

Mueller, G. O. W., & Adler, F. (1985). *Outlaws of the ocean.* New York, NY: Hearst Marine Books.

Rediker, M. (1987). *Between the devil and the deep blue sea: Merchant seaman, pirates, and the Anglo American maritime world, 1700–1750.* Cambridge, England: Cambridge University Press.

MARXIST THEORY

Karl Marx and Friedrich Engels conceived the materialist conception of history in the mid-19th century as a response to idealist philosophy and a critique of liberal political economy. Marxist historians, philosophers, revolutionaries, and scientists elaborated the theory in the decades that followed. Variations of Marxism remain a major intellectual and political force in many, if not most, contemporary societies. In light of history, one could argue that there is not one but multiple Marxist theories. Nonetheless, there are elementary assumptions and concepts running through the various schools and permutations that differentiate Marxism from other critical theoretical standpoints and, more broadly, the conflict perspective. The application of Marxist theory to crime and deviance studies is likewise manifold; yet, here too, an intellectual core shapes the work in a similar way. This entry sketches the foundation of Marxist theory and, in broad strokes, surveys the crime and deviance literature employing this approach, what often goes under the label of "radical" or "critical" criminology.

Foundations

From the standpoint of historical materialism, a human being is understood as a thing realized through social action, principally acts embedded in and surrounding the production of material life. Human essence lies at the intersection of the totality of social relations in which individuals emerge as social beings. Dialectically, individuals collectively objectivate society through social action and, in turn, realize their humanity in the process. However, in segmented societies, especially those marked by social class, individuals become alienated from their essential activities, from the objects they bring into existence, and from others and themselves. For Marxists, the fundamental problem to explain and overcome in history is the fact that the majority has lost control over the act of creating the world and the world it created, a condition that denies "species-being"—that is, the power of self-activity and self-actualization. This problem focuses on both

Marxist theory and political practice. Indeed, the political demand this approach entails is inseparable from the theory that explains it, which Marx envisioned in his youth as an epistemological position transcending the "is-ought" dichotomy that limits positivist thinking and liberal politics, both related expressions of bourgeois, or capitalist, idealism.

The solution to the problem of alienation, Marxists contend, is the achievement of substantive freedom for all members of society, which requires popular control over society's productive forces, a state of affairs requiring—and justifying—the revolutionary transformation of the existing conditions. Empowered, the proletariat, or working class, collectively shapes the direction of history. Thus, socialist revolution lays the foundation for a more just social order and a more complete humanity. Crucially, this standpoint conceptualizes freedom not in liberal terms of limited political democracy, which is necessarily constrained by the capitalist imperative to accumulate property and usurp wealth, what Erich Fromm calls "negative liberty," but in the radical terms of economic democracy, or socialism—with communism, a stateless and classless social order of self-actualizing individuals, envisioned as the final goal.

The concrete character of work, the objects on which work is performed, and the instruments produced by and used in that work constitute the labor process that moves history. Objects of labor may be things producers find in nature or things already worked up by prior labor activity. Some of these objects become instruments of labor, such as tools and machines that concentrate a worker's activity on an object. The objects and instruments make up the means of production. Taken together, objects, instruments, and human labor power make up the forces of production, constituting the practical and technological basis of a given social formation.

Underpinning this conceptualization of production is the *labor theory of value*, a foundational concept in both classical liberal political economy and the Marxist critique. Marx incorporates into his theory of capitalist production the distinction between, on the one hand, use value, which is value imputed from biological needs and historically conditioned wants, and, on the other hand, exchange value, which represents the quantum of labor contained in a commodity. He demonstrates in *Capital* (Volume I) that human labor is the sole source of exchange value. It follows that workers are entitled to that value. However, since the labor process is necessarily a collective one, that entitlement is social in character. In demonstrating the validity of the labor theory of value, Marx not only makes a major contribution to the field of political economy but also identifies the material underpinning of the struggle for social justice.

The question of control over the labor process raises the matter of the character of the social relations in which the production forces are embedded. Marxists define the social relations of production primarily in terms of property relations and the authority that attaches to them. Social class is paramount, defined as an individual's relationship to the means of production, a position that she or he shares with other individuals bound by the same or similar relations. Taken together, the forces and the social relations of production constitute the mode of production, what the philosopher Georg W. F. Hegel calls "civil society." In the popular base-superstructure metaphor, civil society is the foundation, or "base" of society. Marxists theorize that contradictions within the base, such as class antagonisms, drive social transformation.

On the base arises a "superstructure," or political society, comprising state, law, and ideology, which functions to protect the prevailing property relations either by force, if need be, or, more efficiently, through ideas that legitimize the prevailing relations by embodying notions of right and wrong, good and bad. Political power and ideas are thus theorized to be rooted in the material control of the forces of production, expressed by Marx and Engels in the famous dictum: "The ideas of the ruling class are in every epoch the ruling ideas, i.e., the class which is the ruling material force of society, is at the same time its ruling intellectual force" (Marx & Engels, 1976, p. 67). The character of the superstructure ultimately reflects, albeit not always in an immediately discernible way, the interests of the dominant economic class. Ultimately, the conditions under which people produce their material life stamp an entire society with a particular class consciousness.

Marxists conceptualize history as a series of revolutionary transformations in modes of production, classified as stages, which include primitive communism, ancient society, feudalism, and capitalism. Under primitive communism, typified by hunter-gatherer societies, there are no social classes. The forces of production are collectively controlled, and the community share the social product based on need. With the appearance of large-scale agricultural production, occurring roughly 5,000 to 7,000 years

ago, and with it the generation of substantial social surplus, it becomes possible for some families to live without working. Over time, the means of production are divorced from the laboring masses and concentrated in the hands of a nonproductive class, which forces the majority into subservience. The families freed from labor become a ruling class who, served by functionaries (managers, intellectuals), steer segmentally organized modes of production in their favor. This state of affairs is characteristic of all social formations up to the present, each successive stage of development in segmentation leading to greater inequality between those who produce the social surplus and those who appropriate it.

To illustrate how contradictions internal to production modes fuel the transformational moments that impel history through its stages, consider the periodic crises of overproduction/underconsumption that mark the capitalist mode of production. The contradiction exists by virtue of the fact that capitalist firms strive to maximize surplus value by rationalizing production through automation, mechanization, and wage suppression, which in turn displaces, impoverishes, and marginalizes workers. The immiseration of workers undercuts the opportunity for capitalists to realize surplus as profit in the market. What constitutes rational behavior at the level of the firm becomes irrational at the level of the system. The bourgeoisie, or capitalist class, strives to overcome the irrationality in various ways: the destruction of productive forces through war, the conquest of new markets through imperialism, the exploitation of old markets, state intervention in the economy, and promotion of finance capital. However, while adaptation may temporarily lift the economy from a slump, it sets the stage for deeper crises in the future.

Working from this model of historical change and social formation, Marxists approach the subject of crime and deviance in two basic ways. In the first, scholars theorize that the categories of deviant behavior that draw official sanction are products of the imperative to secure and entrench exclusive property and related forms of oppressive social relations and, more specifically, manage labor markets. Because the character of the superstructure reflects the interests of the ruling class, it is these that shape the deviance-making process and the content of the categories used to control individuals and groups. Moreover, since the structure changes over time, the character of the deviance-making enterprise and its products is temporally variable. These ideas express the dialectical theorization of societal development.

In the second, Marxists focus on the criminogenic character of class-based social structures, theorizing in particular that the discontents of capitalism, a system marked by alienation, immiseration, inequality, and injustice, produce the criminogenic conditions requiring the criminal law and necessitating its aggressive enforcement.

The historical record supports the theory that the economic imperative and the attendant political character of a concrete mode of production shape the control machinery and its deviant categories. At the stage of primitive communism, where there is neither social class nor state and law, one finds scant evidence indicating the existence of formal and coercive social control machinery. Instead, control of deviance appears as being informal and not particularly punitive. The emergence of the state and law coincides with the appearance of social class and patriarchal relations, which are associated with the arrival of large-scale agriculture. At this point, social control as an institutional force appears. Each successive stage of development in segmentation leads to greater inequality in wealth and power; with each stage, the control machinery becomes more extensive and elaborate.

Capitalism represents the highest stage of exploitative relations and therefore reaches the highest level of coercive and ideological control. It is in this context that advanced police and carceral structures appear, accompanied by a scientifically framed intellectual system, principally the disciplines of criminology and penology. Other historically unique control systems also emerge, such as the mental health industry, with its intellectual justifications (psychiatry and psychology) in tow. Noting that this machinery is far more extensive than past arrangements, Marxists theorize that the chronically alienated state of the working class and the problem of managing the fallout from the periodic crises associated with capitalism require an extraordinary control apparatus operating at the boundaries of the structure of workplace rules. The latter concern especially flows from Marx's theory of the general law of capitalist accumulation, presented in *Capital* (Volume I), wherein the rising organic composition of capital, defined as the ratio of variable capital to constant capital, swells the ranks of the unemployed, or the industrial reserve army.

Marxist Literature on Crime and Deviance

The interest in the relationship between wage labor and carceral control is long-standing in the Marxist literature on crime and deviance. Perhaps, the paradigm of modern Marxist penology is Georg Rusche and Otto Kirchheimer's landmark *Punishment and Social Structure* based on Rusche's article "Labor Market and Penal Sanction." Rusche posits a relationship between labor supply and rates, types, and intensities of punishments. Harsh physical punishments are associated with economic downturns, a function of the concomitant rise in surplus laborers; since one's labor is attached to one's person, the less valuable one's labor, the less valuable one's person. In contrast, rehabilitation and prison labor, publicly appealed to as enlightened reform, take priority during periods of economic expansion. Again, supply and demand plays a crucial role: The need for labor shrinks the supply of labor, thereby making each laborer more valuable. Stripped of complexities, the pendulum swinging between repression and reform is a function of the rhythms of capitalism.

Punishment and Social Structure expands on this idea and, inspired by Marx's analysis of primitive accumulation in *Capital* (Volume I), explores the history of carceral control. Rusche and Kirchheimer compare the capitalist epoch with the epoch it superseded. There was no centralized state or bureaucracy under feudalism. Conflicts were, for the most part, resolved privately. Moreover, social arrangements were not such as to require repressive public control. Consequently, punishments were not severe. However, by the latter Middle Ages, private criminal law yielded to greater levels of state control and punishment. Capitalism required the destruction of relations protecting labor under the feudal system: The lord was dispossessed of political and economic power, the master craftsman of the guilds transformed into unattached skilled proletarian, and serf and peasant were forced off the land via enclosure for use as cheap labor. Elites achieved this, in part, through measures criminalizing guilds and unions with the charge of conspiracy, as well as statutes and ordinances expanding the scope of foraging, poaching, trespassing, and vagrancy laws. Theft naturally increased with manufacturing, as objects once owned by those who made them became the property of those who owned the land and the means of production. Subsequent works by several scholars, including William Chambliss and Christopher Adamson, have sustained Rusche and Kirchheimer's thesis.

In the area of legal theory, Evgeny Pashukanis demonstrates that the criminal law (and law in general) embodies an ideology that functions to perpetuate the rule of the bourgeoisie. For example, the principle of equal treatment obscures the reality of class inequality and exploitation by projecting an image of the law with the outward appearance of neutrality and universality. Bourgeois morality becomes common morality, concealing the true operation of criminal justice as an apparatus managing the working class for the sake of reproducing the unequal division of property. A leading modern exponent of this view is Jeffrey Reiman, who, in *The Rich Get Richer and the Poor Get Prison*, argues that whereas the pretense to universalism legitimizes the use of force by government, the state's failure to manifest equal justice makes its coercion analogous to criminal violence.

The second way Marxists approach the subject of crime and deviance is by focussing on the criminogenic conditions generated by the capitalist mode of production. This emphasis emerges early in the development of Marxist theory. Engels argues that the degrading working conditions prevailing under industrial capitalism demoralize the proletariat, leading to a loss of social control among workers and their children. The discontents of capitalism provide workers with the temptation to engage in deviant behavior and wear down their moral capacity to withstand temptation. Capitalism thus generates the social conditions that turn some members of the working class into criminals. Engels characterizes crime among the working class as a form of "primitive rebellion," which, because of its expression at an individual level, is not only suppressed by the state but also condemned by the working class. Engels and Marx are thus skeptical that working-class criminals could be of much use to the revolutionary efforts. They write that the conditions of capitalist society make more probable that working-class rogues will play "the part of a bribed tool of reactionary intrigue." Marx and Engels describe street criminals as "social scum, that passively rotting mass thrown off by the lowest layers of the old society" (Marx & Engels, 1988, p. 65).

Marxists do not see the street criminal as the only criminogenic consequence of capitalism. Engels theorizes that capitalism encourages crime among the bourgeoisie as well and, furthermore, observes that class location shapes the character of crime control. Willem Bonger, credited with the first full Marxist criminological work of the 20th century, echoes Engels's argument, theorizing that the tendency of capitalism to reduce everything to a cash nexus, pitting worker against worker in unforgivingly competitive markets, and promoting egoism over altruism constitute a criminogenic milieu. This allows Bonger to account for crime across the class structure.

A critique emerged in the late 1970s wherein proponents, most notably Jock Young, took issue with "left idealism," identified as the tendency to treat criminals as something of working-class heroes. The left idealist, so goes the critique, romanticizes working-class criminals, depicting rogues as revolutionaries, a portrayal that stands in stark contrast to that painted by Marx and Engels. In one notable example, David Greenberg characterizes proletarian criminals as the "vanguard of the revolution." This view of crime, according to the "left realist," rationalizes the behavior of workers who turn to crime, explicitly justifying behavior harmful to working-class interests. Given that most victims of street crime are proletarian, if Marxist criminologists are to represent working-class interests, then they must take the problem of working-class crime seriously. Left realist arguments were influential in the United Kingdom during the 1990s, where they played a role in the development of New Labor's crime control policies. However, Young himself was critical of these policies as New Labor jettisoned class analysis and shifted blame to capitalism's victims.

What of Marxism as the transformational political project? A piece of the project manifests today in the revolutionary act of overthrowing bourgeois definitions of crime. Developing her own conception of crime, the politically committed Marxist indicts capitalism and the associated problems of alienation, imperialism, poverty, racism, and sexism. Herman and Julia Schwendinger argue that the capitalist mode of production represents the systematic violation of human rights as understood from the radical democratic and egalitarian standpoint, or, using Erich Fromm's distinction, "positive liberty." The Schwendiners distinguish between personal rights necessary for continued personal existence, such as the right to clean water and nutritious foods, and those necessary for dignified human existence, for example, the right to democratic freedoms, an education, and housing standards. Marxists believe that capitalism is incapable of fulfilling these rights, as it rests on the exploitation of human labor and the unequal division of the fruits of that labor.

It is in the rejection of bourgeois definitions of crime and the redefining of criminal conceptions along radical egalitarian lines that Marxists most clearly differentiate their project from that of the conflict theorist. Seeing crime and deviance as social problems resulting from inadequate social institutions and the struggle over cultural values and partisanship inherent in a pluralist society, public issues that can in turn be addressed with a more equitable distribution of income and engaged citizenry, conflict theory is ultimately reformist in character. The conflict social scientist's failing is that he or she does not begin with a critique of the material foundation of the social order. His conception of power is rather more idealist; it is the struggle over social power that generates conflict. In contrast, the historical materialist sees conflict as emanating from the mode of material life, with class antagonisms and the property arrangements serving as fuel. Power emanates from the prevailing socioeconomic arrangement. Criminogenesis in both its senses is ultimately the manifestation of the underlying class struggle that pervades capitalist societies: The criminal justice apparatus is, by design and by historical development, a structure to secure bourgeois rule over the proletarian masses; the impoverished and conflict-ridden conditions generated by capitalism imperil the working family, while, at the same time, they encourage the pursuit of profit at the expense of the public good. The Marxist critique strikes at the roots of modern capitalist society as an unjust system that humankind cannot reform but must instead abolish.

Andrew Austin

See also Conflict Theory; Social Control; White-Collar Crime

Further Readings

Adamson, C. (1984). Toward a Marxian penology: Captive criminal populations as economic threats and resources. *Social Problems, 31*(4), 435–458.

Bohm, R. (1982). Radical criminology: An explication. *Criminology, 19*(4), 565–589.

Engels, F. (1943). *The condition of the working class in England in 1844*. London, England: Allen & Unwin. (Original work published 1845)

Greenberg, D. F. (Ed.). (1993). *Crime and capitalism: Readings in Marxist criminology*. Philadelphia, PA: Temple University Press.

Lynch, M. J., & Stretesky, P. B. (Eds.). (2011). *Radical and Marxist theories of crime*. Denver: University of Colorado.

Marx, K. (1970). *Preface and introduction to a critique of political economy*. New York, NY: International. (Original work published 1859)

Marx, K. (1992). *Capital: A critique of political economy capital* (Vol. 1). London, England: Penguin Classics. (Original work published 1867)

Marx, K., & Engels, F. (1976). *The German ideology*. Moscow, Russia: Progress Publishers. (Original work published 1845)

Marx, K., & Engels, F. (1988). *The Communist manifesto*. New York, NY: W. W. Norton. (Original work published 1848)

Pashukanis, E. (2001). *The general theory of law and Marxism*. St. Louis, MO: San Val. (Original work published 1924)

Phillips, P. (1980). *Marx and Engels on law and laws*. Oxford, England: Martin Robertson.

Taylor, I., Walton, P., & Young, J. (1975). *Critical criminology*. Boston, MA: Routledge & Kegan Paul.

MASOCHISM

See Bondage and Discipline; Sadism and Masochism

MASTURBATION

Masturbation, or the practice of solo sexual pleasure, is often considered a safe sexual activity that can improve both the health of the practitioner and his or her sex life with a sexual partner. For many adolescents, masturbation is the first type of sexual activity that they engage in. It serves as a way for adolescents to explore their own sexuality and to become familiar with their body. Many clinicians have recommended masturbation as a way for individuals to fulfill their sexual needs in the absence of a sexual partner. In addition, masturbation serves as a way for men to treat premature ejaculation and for women to improve their ability to attain orgasm. What now is considered an acceptable practice was at one time a sexually deviant taboo, a sin that goes against the natural order. Masturbation even caused a panic to break out in Europe during the 18th century. This entry provides a brief history of masturbation, the evolution of the practice from taboo to acceptable, the prevalence of the practice, and commonly accepted masturbation practices.

Historical Background

Although masturbation is thought of in a positive light in the modern medical era, for much of recorded history, it was considered a shameful practice and was highly stigmatized. It is believed that the word *masturbator* originated in the Roman Empire between the years 84 and 85 and 103 CE. Although the exact origin of the word is unclear, scholars believe that the word is derived from a combination of *manus* meaning "hand," *sturprum* meaning "a debauch or a defilement," and *perpetrare* meaning "to penetrate." There are ancient artworks depicting the gods, and human men and women, engaging in masturbation. In addition, the Book of Genesis, in the Hebrew Bible, tells the story of two brothers, Er and Onan. Er married a woman named Tamar, but he died an early death for angering God. Onan married Tamar out of brotherly duty, but when it came time for the couple to produce a child, Onan avoided conception by spilling his seed on the ground each time that he and Tamar consummated their marriage. Onan's actions also angered God, causing his early death just like his brother. Religious scholars identify two reasons why Onan angered God—first, he masturbated and second, he engaged in *coitus interruptus*, meaning that Onan withdrew from Tamar's body prior to ejaculation in an attempt to avoid inseminating his wife. For many years, masturbation was only referred to as "onanism"—a term that was taken from a pamphlet called *Onania*, first published in London in 1715. This pamphlet warned against the dangers of masturbation, including the medical consequences of engaging in solitary sexual activity. Doctors viewed masturbation as a chronic disease that would lead participants toward sickness, insanity, blindness, impotence, and, even in some cases, loss of limbs or internal organs. Physicians completed well-documented case studies in which the frequent use of masturbation transformed healthy, robust individuals into emaciated, malnourished, deformed shells of their former selves. Some even believed that early death was an inevitable outcome for the masturbator. A French doctor in 1828 is reported as saying that masturbation was the cause of more deaths than war, plague, or the pox combined—a bold statement about a sexual activity that many health professionals now advocate their patients to engage in.

From Taboo to Accepted Practice

The extremely conservative nature of Victorian England and many other European nations during the same era made masturbation out to be a stigmatized behavior that only base, carnal individuals

engaged in. Civilized people could control themselves, but those who could not would succumb to the temptations of self-pleasure. With the advent of the 20th century, these conservative viewpoints remained, but slowly a change was beginning to take place. Medical advancements made it clear that a person would not become extremely ill from chronic masturbation, nor would anyone die from the practice. In the 1940s and 1950s, Dr. Alfred Kinsey's studies about sex would reveal that masturbation was a common practice that occurred more often than the general public believed. Kinsey was able to provide a scientific explanation for the behavior and explained that all types of individuals masturbated—poor and rich, educated and uneducated, men and women alike. He went on to explain that masturbation did not detract from couples having children nor did it weaken a marital relationship. Many of the Kinsey findings were considered suspect, and his work did not bring about an immediate change in public attitudes.

The late 1960s and early 1970s ushered in a period of social change in the United States. A sexual revolution was taking place throughout the country, and with it, many sexual taboos were being eliminated. Some, although not a majority, adopted the idea of free love that is often associated with the counterculture, but at a minimum, people started to break free from the conservative outlook that had constrained sex. Sex stores began to open across the country and allowed for easy access to pornographic material, sex toys, and other masturbatory aids. One of the country's most famous sex stores, Good Vibrations, was established in California in 1977 and continues to prosper through the sale of sex products. Masturbation has even made its way into popular culture—movies and television shows have depicted the practice on multiple occasions. However, there is still a certain sensitivity surrounding the idea of masturbation. Although many people engage in the practice, not everyone is willing to talk about it.

Prevalence and Frequency

Masturbation is a common practice. At very young ages, many children touch their own genitals or the genitals of other children, mainly out of curiosity rather than for sexual pleasure. Once puberty strikes, these innocent explorations cease, and adolescents start touching themselves with sexual arousal in mind. These experimentations with masturbation begin as youths learn about sexuality and develop into sexually active people. Self-pleasure allows the adolescent to experiment in a safe manner without the risk of exposure to HIV and other sexually transmitted diseases, or of pregnancy. In comparison to how masturbation was viewed in the past, the current generation of adolescents is growing up in a time when most Western cultures are accepting of masturbation as a healthy and beneficial practice. Not only does masturbation provide a starting point for many sexually innocent young people, but it also has been associated with removing some of the sexual guilt that can occur in those who have experienced very conservative or highly religious upbringings. This type of guilt can sometimes be a hindrance when having sex with a partner. By becoming personally acquainted with their bodies and what actions cause pleasure, adolescents can alleviate that guilt, boost their self-esteem, and increase their sexual health and satisfaction in a positive manner.

Although masturbation is more widely accepted than ever before, some individuals are still reluctant to discuss such a personally intimate sexual activity. Sex therapists and physicians believe that masturbation is a very widespread and frequent occurrence, but it is difficult to determine actual prevalence and frequency. For all age-groups, masturbation is thought to be the most common of sexual practices. In 2010, the National Survey of Sexual Health and Behavior reported frequency rates among 20- and 24-year-olds as high as 92% for males and 77% for females. In other studies, males reported higher rates of masturbation over the course of their lives—74% of males compared with 48% of females. Many researchers have concluded that masturbation is a healthy and safe alternative to sexual activity with a partner and can aid in the sexual satisfaction of the participant. However, other researchers have stated that masturbation is not as satisfying in the long term. Studies focusing on a variety of heterosexual sexual behaviors indicate that it is the frequency of penile–vaginal intercourse that creates the most sexual satisfaction among individuals. Solitary masturbation and even mutual masturbation—or masturbation committed with a partner, as a substitute for intercourse—can aid in that satisfaction, but there is still a great desire to engage in intercourse with a partner.

A Commonly Accepted Practice

More often than not, masturbation is a solitary action. Many people do use some sort of masturbatory aid when they engage in self-pleasure, such as the use of pornography or a sex toy. Just as masturbation is a centuries-old practice, so is the use of these aids. Ancient Japanese art depicts individuals masturbating with erotic books nearby. English, French, and Italian paintings created between the late 1600s and the 1800s also depict individuals (mainly women) masturbating with books nearby or resting in one hand. This was a common occurrence for people to be depicted in such scenes—the paintings were tasteful, but they represented the use of pornographic materials, even at a time when masturbation was considered to be a chronic disease. Today, people still use pornography as a masturbatory aid, but the variety of pornography available has increased substantially. Virtually any style of pornography is available to interested viewers—ranging from the most basic sexual acts to fetish porn, to porn focusing on specific body types, and can be highly graphic when incorporating more hard core sexual elements. But for every type of pornography, there is an interested viewer and a production company willing to create a product to meet that demand.

The use of sex toys is also common. As with the pornography industry, there is a large market of sex toys available for purchase. Some are more basic in nature—vibrators are a commonly used item—while others are more extreme; anal beads and plugs, for instance, are less commonly used. There are vibrators available for both internal and external use, but traditionally, they are associated with female masturbation. Women frequently use a vibrator or a dildo (both phallic in shape), in addition to digital stimulation while masturbating. In contrast, artificial vaginas have been developed for male masturbation. An array of devices may be used for solitary masturbation, but some may also be used with a partner. Although many of these items can be obtained from sex stores and online, many people turn to household items as masturbatory aids. Of these, some items can cause injury if the user is careless; however, it is not uncommon for people to use things such as vacuum cleaner attachments, showerheads, and even vegetables as masturbatory aids.

Conclusion

Beliefs about masturbation have changed significantly over time. Masturbation was once considered a base and carnal activity that people only engaged in if they could not control themselves. It was commonly supposed that such activity would lead to extreme sickness, blindness, insanity, and eventually death—a notion endorsed by physicians during the conservative Victorian age. Today, medical professionals no longer believe that masturbation will cause sickness and death but rather that it is a healthy sexual outlet.

Jennifer L. Klein

See also Corruption; Erotica Versus Pornography; Fetishes; Pornography; Solitary Deviance; Taboo

Further Readings

Gerressu, M., Mercer, C. H., Graham, C. A., Wellings, K., & Johnson, A. M. (2008). Prevalence of masturbation and associated factors in a British national probability survey. *Archives of Sexual Behavior, 37,* 266–278.

Herbenick, D., Reece, M., Schick, V., Sanders, S. A., Dodge, B., & Fortenberry, J. D. (2010). Sexual behavior in the United States: Results from a national probability sample of men and women ages 14–94. *Journal of Sexual Medicine, 7*(5), 255–265.

Kaestle, C. E., & Allen, K. R. (2011). The role of masturbation in healthy sexual development: Perceptions of young adults. *Archives of Sexual Behavior, 40,* 983–994.

Laqueur, T. W. (2003). *Solitary sex: A cultural history of masturbation.* New York, NY: Zone Books.

Stengers, J., & Van Neck, A. (2001). *Masturbation: The history of a great terror.* New York, NY: Palgrave.

MEDICALIZATION OF DEVIANCE

Medicalization is the process by which previously considered nonmedical concepts become conceptualized and treated as medical problems. Medicalization of deviance, then, is conceptualized as a process by which deviant behavior (e.g., alcoholism, homosexuality), appearance (e.g., obesity, dwarfism), and belief systems (e.g., racism) are subsumed under medical jurisdiction. The medicalization argument introduced by Irving Zola saw medicalization of deviance as a mechanism for health professionals to define and control an array of social problems, by redefining social problems as medical ones. Scholars note that because illnesses are constructed as social and moral judgments, they are subject to ambiguity and, in turn, largely socially and culturally interpreted, defined, and treated. Thus, it is important to mention that social behaviors, appearances, and belief systems that are medicalized as illness often reflect dominant social and cultural values.

Illness, Deviance, and Social Control

Historical roots of medicalization of deviance trace to Parsonian models that define illness as deviant because it disrupts social cohesion and, in turn, the stability of social systems. Although criminal behavior and illness are both violations of social norms, the labels and sanctions are often prescribed differently. Deviant behavior is seen as purposeful, and therefore, the social response imposed on deviant behavior seeks to alter behavior in the direction of conformity. However, nonpurposeful deviance is regarded as an illness and, in turn, is treated with the goal of altering the conditions that restrict conformity to social norms. It is in this regard that Talcott Parsons developed the "sick role" model. While this model sees illness as a deviance, Parsons clearly differentiates between deviance and illness and develops a framework for the medicalization of deviance.

For Parsons, the sick role consists of four elements: Two of the elements exempt individuals from their normal social responsibilities (i.e., work obligations) and two present new requirements for the individual. First, those in the sick role are exempted from their social roles and responsibilities. Second, the individual in this role is not held responsible for his or her condition and cannot be expected to recover by an act of will. Third, the individual must recognize that his or her ill state is undesirable and is, therefore, obligated to seek wellness. Fourth, the sick person is required to seek competent help and cooperate with the process to get well.

For illness, then, the institution of medicine is an "appropriate" institution in which behavior can be socially controlled and regulated by holding the sick accountable to ensure that social norms are maintained. Furthermore, the institution of medicine legitimizes the illness, and physicians, institutions, and organizations function as agents of medical social control. This line of thinking implies that behavior that is not considered socially acceptable is deemed as illness. Thus, like criminal behavior, illness is often defined within social, cultural, and ethnic contexts—not medical frameworks. Although medicalization of deviance draws on medical terminology and frameworks to treat problems, the process by which problems are medicalized or medically controlled may or may not involve the medical profession.

In the medical profession, the greatest social power lies in the ability to define certain behaviors and individuals. Thus, the key to social control is definitional. Social control is conceptualized as the means by which society ensures conformity to social norms; specifically, how it reduces, eliminates, or normalizes deviant behavior. Social control can operate formally or informally. Formal social controls are institutionalized and include social agents such as the criminal justice system, correctional facilities, and medical institutions. Informal social controls are less structured and include self-controls and relational controls. Self-controls (i.e., conscience) usually are internalized and reside within the individual. Although self-controls are internal sources, they are created and maintained by external forces, such as society's norms, values, and beliefs. Relational controls are conceptualized as face-to-face interactions of everyday life. They include praise, gossip, ostracism, support, and alienation.

In the context of medicalizing deviance, Peter Conrad explores four types of formal medical social controls: (1) medical ideology, (2) collaboration, (3) medical technology, and (4) medical surveillance. Medical ideology is the accrued social and ideological benefits of medical models. Collaboration involves physicians' assistance as claims makers, gatekeepers, and technicians. Medical technologies are social controls imposed through technology such as drugs, surgery, and genetic screening. It is important to note that physicians can assist through the usage of medical technologies. Therefore, these categories (i.e., collaboration and technological controls) often overlap. Medical surveillance involves complete control over a behavior or condition (i.e., hospitalization). The classic example of medical surveillance is childbirth. Scholars note a substantial increase in the medicalizing of social problems and, in turn, medical social controls.

The Process of Medicalization

As conceptions of deviance shift from "badness to illness," social responses to illnesses have also transformed. Simply put, social problems that initially were controlled by religious authorities and defined as sin, immoral, weakness, and crime are medicalized and are now defined as illness and controlled by medical professionals. Scholars argue that these transformations were not natural evolutions but rather a social response to social conditions. These social conditions were influential in shifting power from religion to medicine.

By the mid-19th century, we saw considerable reductions in the incidence and mortality of infectious diseases. These improvements raised optimism for medical practice. Although these dramatic improvements in public health were perceived as advancements in medicine, the results had little to do with improved medical procedures or technologies. Rather, social conditions, such as a rising standard of living and better nutrition and housing, engendered lower mortality rates and incidence of infectious diseases. Despite the absence of medical interventions and technologies, medicine was largely credited with improved health outcomes. The consequence of medicine's new image was an expansion of medical jurisdiction, whereby medical professions gained the power to construct, label, and treat behaviors that are socially unacceptable.

As demonstrated above, social conditions greatly influenced the expansion of medical jurisdiction; however, social conditions alone do not explain how medicalization has been perpetuated over the past century. For Conrad, the perpetuation of medicalization occurs at three distinct levels: (1) conceptual, (2) institutional, and (3) interactional. At the conceptual level, medical models and terms are used to define social problems. Furthermore, medical professionals/academicians are not needed, and medical treatments are not necessarily applied. At the conceptual level, medicalization usually takes the form of professional journals, official professional reports, and/or professional conferences. At the institutional level, organizations may adopt or develop a medical approach to understanding and treating social problems in which the organization specializes. Physicians may be the gatekeepers for such organizations (i.e., drug rehabilitation facilities), however; nonmedical professionals accomplish day-to-day functions. At the interactional level, physicians are directly involved. Medicalization occurs as part of the doctor–patient interaction in which the physician medicalizes a social problem by diagnosis (e.g., physician diagnoses a patient with depressive disorder) and/or medical treatment (e.g., the physician prescribes medication).

Agents of Medicalization

To further understand the process by which social problems (e.g., deviant drinking) shift to meanings of medicalization (alcoholism), it is also important to remember the influence of social agents. Advocates can be physicians, social movements, organized lay groups, medical technology industries (e.g., pharmaceutical companies), or patients. Early studies of medicalization primarily focused on physicians, social movements, and moral entrepreneurs; however, contemporary studies have shifted to include corporate interest (i.e., pharmaceutical industries and consumers) in medicalization models.

Physicians historically served as the primary gatekeepers to medically define and treat problems. Physicians were involved as "claims makers" with respect to hyperactivity, aging, and menopause. Claims making is usually in the form of medical journals, official professional reports, and special services. As previously mentioned, organized lay groups and medical industries are also agents of medicalization. For example, scholars note that extreme forms of drinking have been defined as sin, moral weakness, crime, and, most recently, illness (alcoholism) by social movements (e.g., Alcoholics Anonymous). Pharmaceutical industries also serve as agents of medicalization (i.e., medicalization of attention-deficit/hyperactivity disorder) by promoting pharmaceutical treatments. By and large, pharmaceutical companies disseminate information to the various sectors that eventually reach the public.

The Dark Side of Medicalization of Deviance

Critics of medicalization of deviance question the expansion of the medical jurisdiction and posit that the growth of medicalization of deviance has engendered an "overmedicalized society." Conrad points to several negative consequences of medicalizing deviance. First, theorists contend that overmedicalized societies can undermine conceptual understandings of health and illness and, in turn, give complete control to medical professionals. Although the public may have their own conceptual understandings of deviant behavior and whether or not it constitutes an illness issue, medical definitions tend to dominate public understandings. Additionally, the medical language used widens the gap between the public's accessibility and, in turn, the public's ability to participate in decisions related to health and illness.

Second, the expansion of the medical jurisdiction increases medicine's capacity to socially control behavior. Medicalization of deviance influenced a fundamental shift from individuals being viewed as responsible agents acting in and on the social world to the social and biological forces acting on

responsive agents. The consequence of this shift is that it dislocates responsibility from the socially deviant individual. Simply put, medicalization of deviance diminishes the responsibility of individuals and shifts control to medicine.

Third, although medical frameworks assume that illness is embedded in biological and psychological abnormalities, medicine is heavily influenced by moral judgments. Thus, the assumption that medicine and treatment are value free and objective misrepresents reality, allowing behavior to be controlled by medical jurisdiction.

Concluding Remarks

As conceptions of deviant behaviors increasingly shift from "badness" to "illness," scholars contend that medical definitions and treatments will be defined and/or redefined. These shifts have been influenced by changes in the medical profession and social policy. Most notable of the changes in medicine is its growth. Medicine has become increasingly specialized. For example, in the 1920s, only 20% of physicians specialized. However, by the early 1970s, nearly 80% of physicians considered themselves specialized. The expenditures for medical care nearly doubled from 1950 (4.6% of the gross national product) to 1970 (which accounted for 8.3% of the gross national product). Medicine has been one of the fastest growing institutions and one of the most expansive segments of our economy. Peter Conrad and Joseph W. Schneider contend that (a) increases in spending indexes result in increases in medicalization of deviance or (b) increases in economic resources engender a substantial pool of money to be allocated to medical solutions and problems. It is important to note that these increases in expenditures might influence demedicalization simply because medical treatments have become too costly.

The insurance industry has not only influenced the rising cost of medical care but also gained jurisdiction in deciding whether and how deviant behaviors, appearances, and belief systems should be treated. Consequently, then, modifications in policies by insurance companies can drastically affect the types and/or amount of deviance medicalized.

The medical industry has also witnessed a rising number of physicians. Between 1970 and 1990, there has been an 80% increase in physicians. One consequence of the influx in medical personnel could be in supply creating demand. In other words, the influx of physicians may increase medicalization as physicians seek to develop new areas of medicine.

In sum, the changes in medicine (i.e., medical expansion, influence of insurance industries, and the influx of physicians) have indeed increased the potential for medicalization. Acknowledging *only* the "dark" or "bright" side of medicalization without fully considering both its negative and positive consequences creates parochial models that, in turn, fail to inform effective social policy and limit improved strategies to effectively understand social behavior.

Claire Norris and Christopher A. Faircloth

See also Defining Deviance; Epidemiology of Crime and Deviance; Normalization

Further Readings

Conrad, P. (1979). Types of medical social control. *Sociology of Health & Illness, 1,* 1–11.

Conrad, P. (1992). Medicalization and social control. *Annual Review of Sociology, 18,* 209–232.

Conrad, P., & Schneider, J. W. (1992). *Deviance and medicalization: From badness to sickness.* London, England: Mosby.

Parson, T. (1975). The sick role and the role of the physician reconsidered. *Health Society, 53,* 257–278.

Zola, I. K. (1972). Medicine as an institution of social control. *Sociological Review, 20,* 487–504.

MENTAL ILLNESS

Worldwide, approximately one in four adults has a mental illness. Mental illness is a major source of disability, affecting one's thoughts, feelings, and behaviors. These thoughts, feelings, and behaviors are considered abnormal, and the persons who experience them are often viewed as deviant. In the United States, the most common mental illnesses are anxiety (22%, at a 12-month prevalence rate) and major depressive disorders (6.7%, at a 12-month prevalence rate). Other forms of mental illness, which are less prevalent, but that are more often associated with dehumanizing stereotypes by the general public, include schizophrenia (1.1%, at a 12-month prevalence rate) and bipolar disorder (2.6%, at a 12-month prevalence rate).

Mental illness as deviant behavior can be traced back to prebiblical times. Persons with mental illness were believed to be under the control of evil spirits.

Prior to the 18th century, Christians commonly believed that persons with mental illness were possessed by demons or were witches. In the late 19th and early 20th centuries, social views of persons with mental illness varied—with some believing that mental illness was a character flaw and others that it was a result of poor parenting. Current views of mental illness are consistent with a biological/medical model of disease.

What do you think when you pass a person on the street talking to himself or herself? Is this deviant behavior? Experts agree that symptoms of mental illness are context specific and socially determined. What is classified as abnormal/deviant behavior in one context may not be classified as such in another context. An example is auditory hallucinations. In a psychiatric setting, such an experience may be indicative of a mental illness caused by a disorder of the brain or mind; however, in other contexts such voices may be indicative of a religious experience. And in the example above, the person may simply be using a wireless mobile phone headset to engage in a conversation with his or her mother.

This entry on mental illness as a social deviance is divided into four sections. Three popular, but ideologically different, views on the etiology and consequences of mental illness are presented—(1) the social constructionist framework, (2) the labeling theory, and (3) the biological/disease model. The concluding section explores the consequences of mental illness.

Social Constructionist Framework of Mental Illness

The social constructionist view of mental illness pits the validity of observation against the expectations of the observer. Is mental illness a real medical disorder, or is it based on societally held norms of what constitutes abnormal behavior?

Thomas Szasz, a psychiatrist, famously theorized that mental illness *does not exist* as a separate medical condition. Diseases of the body, such as diabetes, can be attributed to actual biochemical or structural abnormalities. Diseases of the mind (not to be confused with diseases of the brain), including aberrant behavior, thoughts, or feelings, cannot be objectively diagnosed. For example, a blood test can be used to diagnose syphilis; however, there is no blood test for diagnosing depression. Yet mental illnesses are treated as medical illnesses. Szasz emphasizes that mental illness has been wrongly medicalized when it really is a societally constructed phenomenon.

According to Szasz, mental illnesses are really mechanisms of social control of deviant behavior. The diagnosis separates "normal" people from "others." Psychiatrists are granted the authority to define and label deviant behavior. Furthermore, psychiatrists help persons comply with societal norms by prescribing psychotropic medications and/or psychotherapy. Psychiatrists can institutionalize those believed to need physical separation from society.

Persons ascribing to the social constructionist view of mental illness do not question that certain persons do exhibit behavior that deviates from what society deems "normal." However, constructionists caution against ascribing physical causes to socially constructed deviant labels. Rather than seeing mental illnesses as socially defined forms of deviance, treating mental illness as a medical problem highlights the individuals responsible for the deviant behavior and not society's role in classifying such behavior as aberrant.

Labeling Theory

A specific theory under the social constructionist umbrella is labeling theory. Thomas Scheff, a sociologist, was among the first to apply labeling theory to mental illness. Rather than being concerned with the etiology of mental illness, labeling theorists concern themselves with the societal response to the label of mental illness. Persons learn early in life about mental illness from the popular media, friends, family, and other sources. Far from being benign, these views portray persons with mental illness as objects to be feared and pitied.

Central to the labeling theory of mental illness is the label. Labeling is not a simple process. Persons with mental illness often display signs of mental illness before an unofficial or official label of mental illness is conferred. Two types of deviance are part of the labeling process: primary deviance and secondary deviance. Primary deviance is the periodic breaking of social norms that does not lead to official labeling. For example, a person may display signs and symptoms of mental illness, which are violations of social norms (e.g., talking to oneself). These early symptoms are often ignored or explained away by family members and friends. To varying degrees, most people engage in primary deviance. In most instances, primary deviance is transient and does not evoke a negative social response or result in a label.

Secondary deviance is the sustained breaking of social norms that result in an official label. Persons with mental illnesses, such as schizophrenia, continually break social norms. Family members and friends are unable to explain away the bizarre behaviors, and the person is officially labeled as mentally ill. Unlike other social roles (parent, spouse, employee, etc.), persons labeled with mental illness take on the role of mental illness. Mental illness becomes self-defining—and persons with mental illness use the label as a "master status" and act in accordance with the label. Similarly, members of the public use the label as a means of defining and reacting to the person with mental illnesses. The negative beliefs learned early in life become the rationale for the negative social reaction.

The sociologist Erving Goffman, a contemporary of Szasz, also highlighted the blurry line between physical illness and mental illness. He contended that no matter the label, whether "physical disorder" or "mental disorder," persons shared a common experience of devaluation. The societal role of being "mentally ill" was/is constructed in interaction. Persons with mental illness play the role of being mentally ill, and others accept the role as legitimate and respond in kind. As a result, labeled individuals are limited in their participation in society. For example, persons with schizophrenia are not expected to engage in normal human activities, such as employment or romantic relationships.

Biological/Disease Model of Mental Illness

A radically different view of mental illness from the social construction of mental illness and the labeling theory is the biological theory of mental illness. The advent of psychopharmacological treatments for mental illness and a classification system for diagnosing mental illness ushered in a new era in societal views of mental illness. Deviant behavior was the result of biochemistry, genes, and brain structural abnormalities; these abnormalities could be treated with biological agents (antidepressants) and psychosurgical procedures (prefrontal lobotomies and electroshock therapy). Mental illnesses, as a form of deviant behavior, were now to be understood as medical diseases.

The discovery of biochemical treatments for mental illness occurred serendipitously. In the early 1950s, chlorpromazine, which was used to potentiate anesthetics, was discovered to have a calming effect on persons with psychosis. The discovery of the antipsychotic effects of chlorpromazine was the beginning of the psychopharmacological industry, which is today a multibillion dollar industry. Biochemical treatments for other psychiatric disorders soon followed, including the development of antidepressants (tricyclics), mood stabilizers (e.g., lithium), and anxiolytics (benzodiazepine and barbiturates). The discovery of psychopharmacological medicines set the groundwork for post hoc hypotheses about biomedical processes of mental illness, including the dopamine hypothesis of schizophrenia and the serotonin hypotheses for depression, based on idiopathic variations in blood levels of these neurotransmitters

Parallel to the development of psychiatric drugs was the development of an official system for classifying mental illnesses. In the early 1950s, the American Psychiatric Association developed the first *Diagnostic and Statistical Manual of Mental Disorders (DSM)*. The manual grouped together behavioral, emotional, and cognitive symptoms under syndromes and diagnostic classes. The manual, which is soon to be in its 5th edition, is the diagnostic handbook used by mental health professionals to diagnose mental illnesses. Unlike other medical classification systems that rely on biological or observable tests for illness, such as a blood sugar test for diabetes, the classification of mental illnesses is done through a process of expert consensus. The *DSM* is a nosology of mental illness and not a "scientifically" based classification system. Together, the advent of psychopharmacology and the development of a classification system of mental illnesses solidified psychiatry as a legitimate specialty in medicine and set the groundwork for a medically based view of mental illness.

The medical establishment and many mental health advocacy groups, such as the National Alliance on Mental Illness, embraced the medical model as a promise for treatment of mental illness and a way to change public perceptions of mental illness. After all, mental illness was now similar to any other physical condition and could be treated. Recent research suggests that the general public has embraced the medical model of mental illness. However, with this embrace came a desire for greater social distance from people with mental illness. People believe that persons with mental illness suffer from a biological illness, and they want to keep away from persons with mental illness, just as they would from a person with a contagious virus. However, people are not afraid of catching

mental illness; rather, they are fearful that persons with mental illness are dangerous. To members of the general public, persons with mental illness still engage in deviant behavior and must be avoided.

The medical model places an emphasis on the biological and genetic factors associated with mental illness. However, even the most ardent adherents of the medical model recognize that environmental factors play a role in the onset of a mental illness and the life trajectory of a person living with a mental illness. One theory that has been used to explain the interchange between biological factors and the environment is the diathesis–stress model. The diathesis–stress model postulates that some people are predisposed to a particular mental illness and that exposure to a certain amount of stress activates a biological process that leads to mental illness.

Conclusion

No matter how one understands mental illness, one common reality is the stigmatization of, and discrimination against, persons with it. The public stigmatizes persons with mental illness by denying them access to basic rights, such as housing, jobs, and relationships. Persons with mental illness self-stigmatize by viewing themselves through common stereotypes of mental illness and by self-discriminating. Bruce Link and Jo Phalen developed a sociological theory of mental illness stigma as a process that consisted of six interrelated components that, when combined, result in negative effects. The first component is *labeling* the individual as different or "other." The second component is *stereotyping*. The individual is reduced to negative views associated with the label. The third component is *separating*. Persons put a social distance between themselves and persons identified as mentally ill. The fourth component is *discriminating*, which involves overt/covert behaviors that result in loss of social status by persons with mental illness. Two overarching factors are part of this process—*emotional reactions* and *power*. The stigmatizer (and the stigmatized) experiences negative affective responses to the label, including fear, pity, and embarrassment. Power is absolutely necessary for discrimination to occur. Only individuals with power can label, stereotype, separate, and discriminate against others.

Despite the devaluation of persons with mental illness, hope remains for a future where persons with mental illness are not social lepers. At the end of the 20th century, a new paradigm has emerged for viewing mental illness—recovery in mental health. Spurred on by research that suggests that persons with even the most debilitating mental illness can get better, the recovery movement promises to find new pathways for integrating persons with mental illness into mainstream society with the hope of recovery. However, the view of persons with mental illness as deviant remains strong.

David Kondrat and Brittany Wilkins

See also Culturally Specific Mental Illnesses; Deinstitutionalization; *Diagnostic and Statistical Manual*

Further Readings

Becker, H. (1964). *The other side: Perspectives on deviance.* New York, NY: Free Press.

Corrigan, P. W., & Watson, A. C. (2002). The paradox of self-stigma and mental illness. *Clinical Psychology: Science and Practice, 9*(1), 35–53.

Goffman, E. (1961). *Asylums: Essays on the Social situation of mental patents and other inmates.* Garden City, NY: Anchor.

Lemert, E. M. (1962). Paranoia and the dynamics of exclusion. *Sociometry, 25,* 2–20.

Link, B. G., Cullen, F. T., Struening, E., Shrout, P. E., & Dohrenwend, B. P. (1989). A modified labeling theory approach to mental disorders: An empirical assessment. *American Sociological Review, 54,* 400–432.

Link, B. G., & Phelan, J. C. (2001). Conceptualizing stigma. *Annual Review of Sociology, 27,* 363–385.

Pescodolido, A., Martin, J. K., Long, J. K., Median, T. R., Phhelan, J. C., & Link, B. G. (2010). "A disease like any other"? A decade of change in public reactions to schizophrenia, depression, and alcohol dependence. *American Journal of Psychiatry, 167,* 1321–1330.

Scheff, T. J. (1974). The labeling theory of mental illness. *American Sociological Review, 39,* 444–452.

Szasz, T. S. (1960). The myth of mental illness. *American Psychologist, 15*(2), 113–118.

MENTAL RETARDATION

The term *mental retardation* (MR) is currently one of two terms widely employed that refers to a disability in individuals based on three diagnostic criteria: (1) significant limitations in intellectual functioning, (2) limitations in adaptive behavior as expressed in conceptual, social, and practical adaptive skills, and (3) origination of these limitations before the age of 18. The other term, one that has replaced *mental retardation* in many areas in recent years, is *intellectual disability* (ID). Both the *Diagnostic and Statistical Manual of Mental Disorders–Fourth Edition-Text Revision (DSM-IV-TR)* and the World Health Organization's forthcoming *International Statistical Classification of Diseases and Related Health Problems—10th Revision (ICD-10)* still employ the term *mental retardation.* However, the American Association on Intellectual and Developmental Disabilities (AAIDD)—formerly the American Association on Mental Retardation (AAMD)—and numerous other organizations (e.g., the International Association for the Scientific Study of Intellectual Disabilities and the President's Committee for People with Intellectual Disabilities) have switched to the term *intellectual disability.* Nearly all of the classification systems and the major professional organizations now treat these two terms as synonymous. In keeping with the current trend but recognizing the more familiar term, this entry will hereafter refer to the term as *mental retardation/intellectual disability (MR/ID).*

MR/ID is also classified as one of the various *developmental disabilities* (DD). This is primarily due to the passage of the Developmental Disabilities Act in the United States, which employs the term *developmental disability* for severe chronic disability involving criteria similar to those employed for MR/ID. The differences are generally the age of onset (DD is onset before 22 years of age), the severity of limitations (DD refers to only severe levels of impairment), that DD may be based on physical as well as mental impairment, and the fact that the DD definition does not refer to an IQ requirement. The term *global developmental delay* may be attached to severely impaired children less than five years of age, since these children often cannot undergo normative intelligence testing.

The Three Diagnostic Criteria

The three criteria employed to determine MR/ID are essential to defining the diagnostic term. These criteria aid in explaining the term, providing characteristics that clearly differentiate this disability from others, providing characteristics that are foundational for the concepts of disability and MR/ID, and providing some direction for assistance and intervention. Although many terms have been employed to describe what we now refer to as MR/ID (including *cretin, idiocy, moron, feeblemindedness, imbecile, mental deficiency*, *mental disability*, *mental handicap*, and *mental subnormality*), two essential characteristics have formed the foundation for the construction of the concept—intellectual limitation and social impairment.

The dimension of intellectual limitation is the first diagnostic criterion, and it refers to impairment of one's intelligence. Intelligence itself is defined as a general mental ability that is multifactorial in nature and that gives rise to abstract thinking, reasoning, problem solving, learning, comprehending complex ideas, and planning. However, there are currently no documented psychometric instruments that can effectively measure the several multifactorial constructs that have been proposed. Consequently, the current method of determining intellectual limitation is based on a psychometric approach through the administration of one of several intelligence tests. These tests are designed to measure intelligence as a general or global factor that yields an intelligence quotient (IQ score) as a measure of intellectual functioning. Through this psychometric approach, intellectual impairment is frequently subcategorized by the severity of the impairment based on IQ levels derived from the intelligence tests that generally designate a mean IQ score as 100 with a standard deviation of approximately 15 points. With these tools, an IQ score ranging from approximately 70 to 55–50 is considered a mild impairment, 55–50 to 40–35 is considered a moderate impairment, 40–35 to 25–20 is considered a severe impairment, and an IQ score below 25–20 is considered a profound impairment.

The AAIDD has raised several points regarding intelligence and its measurement. These include the belief that subaverage intellectual functioning must be considerably below what is expected in the average individual, so such a designation must be based on scores at least two standard deviations below the mean (hence the 70 cutoff score); that when using psychometric instruments, there should be stringent adherence to psychometric principles (e.g., tests must demonstrate strong reliability and validity, be appropriately norm-referenced and administered, and interpretation should include employment of the standard error of measurement); that there should be careful consideration of the impact of experiential, language, and cultural diversity during test score interpretation; that the IQ score is a necessary but insufficient singular criterion to establish a diagnosis of MR/ID; and that testing should be conducted on an individual basis

and carried out in strict compliance with acceptable professional practice.

The second dimension, social impairment, is a key identifying variable, and it gives rise to the second diagnostic criterion. Historically, individuals were identified as exhibiting MR/ID based on their inability to adapt socially to their environment. They were seen as having maturation problems with poor learning that resulted in poor social adjustment. Eventually, these observed characteristics were conceptualized as poor ability to adapt, and in 1961, the AAMD's *Manual on Terminology and Classification in Mental Retardation* employed the term *adaptive behavior* to categorize these earlier social descriptions. In the 2002 modification of the AAMD's Manual (*Mental Retardation: Definition, Classification, and Systems of Supports*), adaptive behavior was defined as "the collection of conceptual, social, and practical skills that have been learned by people in order to function in their everyday lives." This definition focused on the expression or performance of a set of skills relevant to adaptation across the three areas. For example, the conceptual skills of relevance included language proficiency, literacy ability, money concepts, and self-determination; the social skills included following contextual rules, interpersonal proficiency, a developed sense of responsibility, self-esteem, and avoiding victimization; and the practical skills were concerned with adequate activities of daily living. Identification of limitations within these skills is based on either an acquisition deficit wherein the individual does not know how to perform these skills or performance deficits such as not knowing when to use learned skills or having a lack of motivation that affects the expression of these skills.

Similar to the measurement of intelligence, determination of significant limitations in the adaptive criterion is generally based on standardized measures normed on the general population. Significant variance is also operationally defined as performing at least two standard deviations below the mean in at least one of the three types of adaptive behavior or an overall score on a standardized measure involving skills across all three of the adaptive behavioral types. The AAIDD have also raised points concerning the measurement of the adaptive skills. Chief among these are the understanding (a) that adaptive behavior is a multidomain construct across the three previously discussed skill types; (b) that no existing tool effectively measures all adaptive behavior domains; (c) that since adaptive behavior limitations are generally noted across all three skill types, it is assumed that if even one skill type meets the operational definition that this is sufficient to meet criterion; (d) that some adaptive behaviors are difficult to measure with rating scales or existing standardized measures, so one must sometimes go beyond the formal testing situations; (e) that maladaptive behaviors are not necessarily indices of acquisitional or performance deficits by themselves; and (f) that contextual factors like developmental life span and cultural variables must be considered during interpretation.

The third criterion for diagnosis involves the age of onset of the intellectual and adaptive limitations. To differentiate between MR/ID and other disabilities (dementing conditions, e.g., *multiple infarct dementia* and *Alzheimer's disease* or later occurring traumatic brain injury) and to ensure a more developmental focus, onset must be before 18 years of age.

History of MR/ID

Although the earliest reference to what we refer to as MR/ID dates back to around 1500 BCE in Egypt, and it was also recognized by other cultures throughout history, the first detailed discussions and activities associated with MR/ID most likely occurred in 19th-century France. Jean-Marc Itard, recognized as a founder of special education, worked to educate a feral child with intellectual limitations, and Eduoard Seguin, influenced by this work, established what might have been the first training program for the "feebleminded" at Saltpetrière Hospital in Paris. When Seguin emigrated to the United States, he continued his work with this population and published a book on MR/ID in 1866 (*Idiocy and Its Treatment in Physiological Methods*) that helped usher in innovations in the treatment of individuals with MR/ID. Samuel Howe established the first public training facility for persons with MR/ID in the United States within a wing of the Perkins Institute for the Blind in Boston in 1848 (seven years after a similar residential training facility, Abendberg, was opened by Guggenbühl in Switzerland). While other residential and training facilities were opened in the latter part of the 19th century, the focus on treatment and the optimism regarding further development of individuals with MR/ID received a serious setback around this time due to social pressures derived from the ending stages of the Industrial Revolution and the increased urbanization that accompanied it.

At this time, society was beset with many problems due to overcrowding and poor economic and social planning. Based on Darwinian theory, Sir Francis Galton and a group of scholars and social reformers advocated a social philosophy that addressed social ills due to urbanization and intended to improve human hereditary traits by reproductive engineering. In the two books that he authored during this period (*Hereditary Genius* in 1869 and *Inquiries Into Human Faculty and Its Development* in 1883), Galton helped create a different narrative for individuals with MR/ID. These reformers, referred to as eugenists, advanced the idea that since heritability likely determined personality and intellect, society would be better served if those individuals who were "feebleminded" were isolated and not allowed to reproduce so that their undesirable intellectual and personality traits—some of which they believed were responsible for the social disintegration—were eliminated from the gene pool. Two books (both now discredited), *The Jukes: A study in Crime, Pauperism, Disease and Heredity* and *The Kallikak Family: A Study in the Heredity of Feeble-Mindedness*, provided additional impetus for the ideas of this eugenics movement. As a response to eugenics in the United States, the state of Indiana passed the first sterilization law in 1907 for "imbeciles" and other individuals who had been diagnosed as "unimproveable." Other states followed Indiana so that by 1944 30 states had sterilization laws. According to estimates, from 1907 to 1963 approximately 64,000 individuals were sterilized in the United States in an attempt to eliminate the presumed genetic sources of diseases, including MR/ID. Similar methods were employed in Nazi Germany with the passage of a compulsory sterilization law, and although Great Britain did not favor sterilization, the Mental Deficiency Act of 1913 emphasized segregation of males and females with MR/ID in institutions. This law remained in effect until 1959. The primary outcome of these reactions to the eugenics movement was to segregate individuals with MR/ID into institutional settings in order to protect society and control their reproductive lives. Between 1848 and 1970, more than 200 residential institutions were established in the United States for individuals with MR/ID.

Eventually, the narrative regarding individuals with MR/ID became more positive. Several trends occurred to establish this change. First, there were legislative and legal initiatives that helped change opinions and that protected the legal rights of individuals with disabilities—especially including those with MR/ID. In the United States, laws were passed at the federal and local level that protected the civil rights and provided services for all disabled individuals. The Social Security Act of 1935 set a context for more compassion to those citizens in need of societal support, and by the early 1950s, 46 of the 48 states had passed legislation to educate children with mild MR/ID. Then, in the mid-1950s, Congressman John Fogarty chaired a subcommittee on the 1956 appropriations that funded several U.S. Department of Health, Education, and Welfare initiatives to more effectively address MR/ID; Fogarty also marshaled legislation promoting enactments of the Social Security Amendments of 1956 authorizing income maintenance benefits and disability insurance for adults disabled in childhood.

In the early 1960s, the U.S. president John F. Kennedy, who had a sister with MR/ID, established the President's Panel on Mental Retardation (1961) and encouraged and extended congressional actions that arose out of the Fogarty Hearings. Backed by Kennedy, federal legislation was enacted on comprehensive state planning, maternal and child health, and maternity and infant care, which assisted in reducing etiological factors and provided other services to mothers and infants, including those with MR/ID. In 1963, Public Law 88–164 authorized construction of 12 research centers and University Centers of Excellence in Developmental Disabilities. After Kennedy's death, President Lyndon Johnson's Great Society legislation (1964–1968) and authorization of the 1971 Medicaid Intermediate Care Facility/Mentally Retarded program, class action litigation on the right to habilitation in the least restrictive environment, and the Education for All Handicapped Children's Act in 1975 provided finances and opportunity for innovative changes in care and education. Similar changes were occurring at the governmental level in many developed countries around the world and culminated with the United Nations passing the *Standard Rules on Equalization of Opportunities for Persons with Disabilities* in 1994, which provided an international standard for policies and laws dealing with all disabilities. The World Health Organization's *Atlas on ID* provides additional data on worldwide trends.

A second trend was the progressive change over the past four decades regarding residential arrangements for individuals with MR/ID. Up until the 1970s, many individuals with MR/ID—especially the profoundly to moderately impaired—resided in large and centralized institutions. These have been replaced by alternative residential opportunities that are less isolated. In real numbers, state-operated institutional census of individuals with MR/ID declined from approximately 195,000 in 1967 to 52,801 in 1998, and 118 U.S. institutions have closed. At present, many individuals with MR/ID reside either in community-based and supervised residential settings with 15 residents or less (the majority in settings with 6 or less individuals) or in the family home. From 1993 to 1998, for example, the number of residents in larger public and private settings for 16 or more persons declined by 21%, while in 1998, 237,796 individuals with MR/ID or other DDs lived in out-of-home residential placements with 6 or fewer residents (57% of the total number of identified MR/ID in the United States.). These changes were possible because of the health and educational support provided by federal and local legislations. Although family homes are important residential locales for children with MR/ID, the likelihood of out-of-home residential placement greatly increases when these individuals reach adulthood and their caretakers (usually parents) age. While residential placements outside of centralized institutions increased the presence of individuals with MR/ID in society and provided greater access to community services and opportunities, recent research suggests that these individuals are still quite socially isolated.

The third historical trend involved changes in identification and classification approaches. Early definitions and identification of individuals as MR/ID were based on a social approach. These individuals were set apart due to failure to adapt socially in their environments. With the rise of modern medicine and its medical model, identification and classification shifted to a focus on one's symptoms complex and determination of a clinical syndrome wherein organicity, heredity, and pathology were emphasized along with the social criterion. Another shift in identification and classification was based on the psychometric revolution in the early 20th century. With the emergence of intelligence as a viable construct and the development of intelligence tests, the emphasis changed to intellectual functioning as measured by an intelligence test and reflected in an IQ score. Finally, the AAMD advocated a dual-criterion approach in 1959, which focused on both intellectual functioning and adaptive behavior. With the inclusion of age of onset, this is the current approach to diagnosis.

The final historical trend was one that arose in the early 20th century as societal progressivism was established in the United States and other countries and as a reaction to eugenics. Despite the trend toward isolating the MR/ID population, advocates for these individuals started organizing. This movement enabled a more compassionate and inclusionary approach to MR/ID. Without question, this trend and the increased presence of advocacy groups for individuals with MR/ID was an impetus for the legislative innovations noted earlier in this section. For example, the National Association of Parents and Friends of Mentally Retarded Children (now known as *Arc*) established in 1950, the National Disabled Student Union (NDSU), and professional organizations like the Council for Exceptional Children and the AAMR (now the AAIDD) effectively influenced the Kennedy legislation and the subsequent passage of both the Medicaid Intermediate Care Facility/Mentally Retarded program in 1971 and the Education for All Handicapped Children's Act in 1975.

Epidemiology

Because MR/ID is partially determined based on IQ scores, prevalence figures should be similar to what is expected in normal distribution of intelligence across the population. This suggests that approximately 2.3% of the population (>2 *SD* below the mean) should be diagnosed as MR/ID with approximately 80% of individuals so identified being classified as having a mild level of severity. However, there is considerable variation in demographic studies around this figure (general figures are approximately 1.3% in the United States and Australia and about 0.5% in the United Kingdom). In some studies, MR/ID has a different prevalence figure overall (both higher and lower figures have been cited), and the severe category tends to represent a larger proportion of this distribution than expected. Several reasons for this involve the degree of effort placed on identification, the subjective nature of employing labels even with diagnostic criteria, the variability of scoring interpretations (it is interesting that the AAMR definition before 1973 required an IQ score of >1 *SD* below the mean, which would have included approximately 16% of the total population), and poor administration and interpretation of intelligence tests (e.g., not accounting for socioeconomic, language, or cultural diversity). The ratio of males to females with MR/ID in the demographic studies is approximately 1.4:1.

As a heterogeneous group of disorders that are typically described by behavioral criteria, there are a number of known etiological causes for MR/ID, and for approximately, 70% and 24% of children with severe MR/ID and with mild MR/ID, respectively, there is a known cause. Prenatal conditions account for the largest percentage of known causes of MR/ID (up to 15% of all diagnosed MR/ID). These conditions include genetic factors, maternal behaviors and exposures during pregnancy, and intrauterine infections. While there are more than 500 genetic diseases known to be associated with MR/ID, most are very rare. The most frequently identifiable of the chromosomal abnormalities are Down syndrome (trisomy 21), accounting for up to 22% of those cases with a known etiology; Fragile (X) syndrome, accounting for 1% to 6% of cases with known etiology; and Prader–Willi syndrome and Angelman syndrome, accounting for up to 0.6% of known cases. Relatively heavy and prolonged maternal alcohol usage during pregnancy can result in fetal alcohol syndrome, which results in MR/ID in approximately 45% of fetal alcohol syndrome cases, and high dosages of environmental contaminants like methylmercury or polychlorinated biphenyls can result in serious neurological damage in fetuses that can cause MR/ID. The most frequent intrauterine infections that might result in MR/ID are toxoplasmosis, human cytomegalovirus, and rubella. While there is a worldwide increase in HIV infections in women resulting in more than 1 million children with AIDS (acquired immune deficiency syndrome) due to intrauterine infection, the contribution of HIV infection as a cause of MR/ID is still not determined.

Other etiological factors for MR/ID involve postnatal conditions (accounting for approximately 3% to 15% of those MR/ID cases with known etiology), such as heavy exposure to environmental contaminants like lead, methylmercury, or polychlorinated biphenyls, and postnatal infections like bacterial meningitis due to *Haemophilus influenza*, *Streptococcus pneumonia*, and *Neisseria meningitides*. Finally, injuries such as closed-head trauma due to child battering, motor vehicle accidents, and falls account for 52% of MR/ID cases due to postnatal causes.

Ryan L. Nelson and Holly L. Damico

See also Autism Spectrum Disorders; *Diagnostic and Statistical Manual*; Mental Illness

Further Readings

American Psychiatric Association. (2000). *Diagnostic and statistical manual of mental disorders* (4th ed., text revision). Washington, DC: Author.

Bigby, C. (2008). Known well by no-one: Trends in the informal social networks of middle-aged and older people with intellectual disability five years after moving to the community. *Journal of Intellectual & Developmental Disability, 33*, 148–157.

Braddock, D. (2007). Washington rises: Public financial support for intellectual disability in the United States, 1955–2004. *Mental Retardation and Developmental Disabilities Research Reviews, 13*, 169–177.

Braddock, D., Emerson, E., Felce, D., & Stancliffe, R. J. (2001). Living circumstances of children and adults with mental retardation or developmental disabilities in the United States, Canada, England and Wales, and Australia. *Mental Retardation and Developmental Disabilities Research Reviews, 7*, 115–121.

McConkey, R. (2005). Promoting friendships and developing social networks. In G. Grant, P. Goward, M. Richardson, & P. Ramcharan (Eds.), *Learning disability: A lifecycle approach to valuating people* (pp. 468–490). Maidenhead, England: Open University Press.

Murphy, C. C, Boyle, C., Schendel, D., Decouflé, P., & Yeargin-Allsopp, M. (1998). Epidemiology of mental retardation in children. *Mental Retardation and Developmental Disabilities Research Reviews, 4*, 6–13.

Schalock, R. L., & Luckasson, R. (2004). American Association on Mental Retardation's *Definition, Classification, and System of Supports* and its relation to international trends and issues in the field of intellectual disabilities. *Journal of Policy and Practice in Intellectual Disabilities, 1*, 136–146.

Schalock, R. L., Luckasson, R., Shogren, K. A., Borthwick-Duffy, S., Bradley, V., Buntix, W. H. E., . . . Yeager, M. H. (2007). The renaming of mental retardation: Understanding the change to the term intellectual disability. *Intellectual and Developmental Disabilities, 45*, 116–124.

Switzky, H. N., & Greenspan, S. (Eds.). (2003). *What is mental retardation? Ideas for an evolving disability in the 21st century.* Washington, DC: American Association on Intellectual and Developmental Disability.

METAL CULTURE

Heavy metal is a genre of music and an associated subculture that initially developed in Britain and the United States during the 1970s. The music, imagery, and mythologies of heavy metal have attracted an audience that primarily consists of working-class, white male youths growing up in postindustrial societies. The social deviance and moral panics surrounding metal music and metal subculture have mostly centered on suicide, drug use, explicit sex, and religious occultism.

Heavy metal music originated during the 1970s with the bands Black Sabbath, Led Zeppelin, and Deep Purple; other bands followed. Metal music is primarily characterized by high volume and distortion, fueled by the use of power chords on the guitar. Radio stations typically judged the music as too vulgar for airplay, but metal bands were able to sell albums and build loyal audiences through touring and live performance. Metal concerts were spectacles of power and theaters of horror, as pioneering groups like Alice Cooper, KISS, and Iron Maiden used elaborate stage sets, light shows, and costumes in their performances.

Metal subculture emerged in the 1970s as a mixture of the hippie counterculture and the more hypermasculine styles inherited from outlaw biker gangs and other working-class forms of rebellion. While the utopian dreams of the late 1960s were fading away, antiauthoritarian attitudes and behavior endured in metal subculture. As a style of dress, metal subculture mixed the hippie attire of long hair and blue jeans with the codes of masculine power embodied in leather attire and motorcycles. The worldview of metal subculture was also shaped by the cultural collision between the hippie ethos and the enduring ideologies of militarism, patriarchy, and xenophobia that persisted in many working-class subcultures.

During the 1980s and early 1990s, heavy metal became embroiled in moral panics that charged its music with responsibility for spreading drug use, antisocial behavior, sexual promiscuity, and Satanic worship. The popularity of metal music continued to increase as American politics underwent a sharp turn to the right during the administrations of Ronald Reagan and George H. W. Bush. Along with rap music, the lyrics and imagery of heavy metal became central targets for political figures who blamed music for the social problems of youth. In 1985, these efforts led to the formation of the Parents Music Resource Center—founded by Tipper Gore and a handful of other "Washington wives"— along with hearings in the U.S. Senate about sexually explicit lyrics, videos, and album covers in heavy metal, rap, and other forms of popular music. A list compiled by the Parents Music Resource Center of the 15 most objectionable songs (the "filthy fifteen") included ones by the heavy metal bands Judas Priest, Mötley Crüe, AC/DC, Twisted Sister, Def Leppard, W.A.S.P., Black Sabbath, Mercyful Fate, and Venom. The U.S. Senate hearings of 1985 gave several musicians an opportunity to testify as opposing witnesses and make anticensorship statements, including the long-haired and defiantly dressed lead singer of Twisted Sister, Dee Snider.

During this same period, a few prominent metal musicians were directly implicated in lawsuits that alleged that their music had influenced young listeners to commit or attempt suicide. In 1986, the singer Ozzy Osbourne was sued by the parents of a teenager who had committed suicide, the allegation being that Osbourne's song "Suicide Solution" contained subliminal messages that provoked the teen to shoot himself in the head; the case was eventually dismissed, with Osbourne cleared of all charges. The band Judas Priest was also sued by the parents of two young men who had attempted suicide together in Nevada, with a similar charge that subliminal messages hidden within the music had incited their suicide attempts. Metal music and metal subculture also came under widespread scrutiny in 1987 following the group suicide of four young people from Bergenfield, New Jersey, who were known to be members of the local metal subculture and avid metal fans.

Young people involved with metal subcultures have often found themselves labeled and treated as deviants by a host of authorities and moral entrepreneurs. For example, the Back in Control Center was founded in the 1980s to serve distressed parents of metal fans, offering to "deprogram" their children with the same methods used on members of religious cults. During the 1980s, there was also a dramatic increase in the number of teenagers, many of them connected with metal subculture, institutionalized within psychiatric hospitals or rehabilitation centers, often diagnosed with conduct disorder or oppositional-defiant disorder. The moral panic surrounding metal subculture was most visible during the sensational trial of three teenage boys for the 1993 murder of three children near West Memphis, Arkansas. Prosecutors charged that the murder was part of a satanic ritual and successfully convicted the teenage defendants by playing up their involvement with religious occultism and metal music, despite a lack of physical evidence linking them to the crime.

Since the mid-1980s, metal music and metal subculture have expanded to become international entities while spinning off into a multitude of subgenres

such as death metal, doom metal, and grindcore. The deviance and moral panics provoked by these forms of metal have mainly involved attacks on Christianity. Most infamously, members of the local death metal scene in Norway took part in the burning of more than 50 Christian churches between 1992 and 1996. Different forms of metal music achieved widespread popularity among youth across Europe in the later decades of the 20th century, but more recently, the music and subculture have gained even larger followings among young people in Latin America and Asia. As various styles of metal continue to expand their global reach, controversies and conflicts with organized religion are likely to continue.

Ryan Moore

See also Moral Panics; Satanism; Subculture; Suicide

Further Readings

Gaines, D. (1991). *Teenage wasteland: Suburbia's dead-end kids.* Chicago, IL: University of Chicago Press.

Kahn-Harris, K. (2007). *Extreme metal: Music and culture on the edge.* New York, NY: Berg.

Moore, R. (2009). Hell awaits. In R. Moore (Ed.), *Sells like teen spirit: Music, youth culture, and social crisis* (pp. 75–113). New York: New York University Press.

Weinstein, D. (2000). *Heavy metal: The music and its culture.* Cambridge, MA: Da Capo.

METHAMPHETAMINE

Methamphetamine, commonly referred to as meth, is a white, odorless, and tasteless crystalline powder that produces a powerful and long-lasting high. Following the crack cocaine scare of the 1980s, meth became the most feared illicit drug in the United States, especially in rural areas. A recent National Geographic documentary film described meth as "The World's Most Dangerous Drug," and the Public Broadcasting Service (PBS) has described it as "The Most Dangerous Drug in America." Additionally, other popular media outlets frequently describe the spread of meth in apocalyptic medical terms such as a plague or epidemic. Meth is largely a drug of rural areas and small towns. Young, adult white users are the most common.

For as long as there have been mood-altering substances, there have been occasional moral panics about these substances. In the 1800s, British citizens were fearful of the dramatic spread of gin among the lower and working classes. In the 1980s, crack cocaine became a major media story. The increasing use of meth in the same decade gave rise to the next moral panic. Current evidence suggests that since then, meth use has dramatically declined and is likely to continue to decline in the coming years.

Brief History

Meth is a derivative of the chemical known as ephedrine. Ephedrine is a stimulant that activates various receptors in the brain, providing a period of increased energy. The history of meth is one that mirrors others in the amphetamine family. First synthesized in 1893 by the Japanese chemist Nagai Nagayoshi, meth is a derivative of methyl alpha-methylohenylethylamine. Meth is not naturally crystallized but was turned into a solid by another Japanese pharmacologist, Akira Ogata, via reduction of ephedrine using red phosphorus and iodine.

Meth was a popular drug during the Second World War. Notably, both Allied and Axis forces used meth to provide energy to pilots flying long missions. Hitler might have been a user of liquid meth to treat his Parkinson's disease. In a three-month period in 1940, 35 million 3-milligram doses were distributed to the German military. After World War II, a large surplus of meth existed, and its use spread rapidly to the civilian population. Japan had one of the largest surpluses and thus suffered one of the first meth epidemics. This epidemic spread to the U.S.-controlled islands in the Pacific and eventually to the West Coast of the United States.

Modern use of meth is varied, depending on the country's laws. In the United States, meth only had two approved medicinal uses, one being for treatment of attention-deficit/hyperactivity disorder and the other for exogenous obesity. However, illegal use of meth rose steadily during the 1970s and 1980s but has steadily declined since the late 1980s. In the late 1970s and early 1980s, use of the drug among urban males increased, and the drug became a "party drug" especially among the homosexual populations of large urban centers. Motorcycle gangs had been using amphetamines since the early 1960s. One of the early names for meth was "crank" because many gang members hid the drugs in their motorcycle's crankcase. By the 1980s, much of the domestic production of meth came from the West Coast motorcycle gangs. The drug quickly spread to rural areas of the American Midwest and South.

By the mid-1980s, Mexican drug cartels supplanted the motorcycle gangs in meth production; the gangs became transporters and distributors of Mexican-produced meth.

Making Meth

One aspect that makes meth unique in the drug world is that it can easily be made. Nearly anyone can make meth with simple household containers and available household chemicals. Meth is most commonly "cooked" with the following chemicals: ephedrine/pseudoephedrine, iodine, red phosphorus, ether, and several other chemicals. A motivated person will most often learn to cook meth through an informal mentoring system. Clandestine laboratories are scattered across the country. Meth cooking is related to the older craft of moonshining, the illicit distillation of alcohol that became especially prevalent during the Prohibition era. Many grandchildren of moonshiners became meth cookers since the business is much more profitable than moonshining. About $100 worth of supplies produce about $1,000 worth of meth. Meth labs may range from small retail operations to less common middle-size operations. With meth's increasing popularity, Mexican drug cartels created large industrial laboratories, from which much of the U.S. supply originates.

Securing these chemicals, called precursor chemicals, has become a difficult task for the meth cooker. Cookers obtain red phosphorus by buying thousands of matches, cutting off the heads, and crushing the resulting match heads. Ephedrine/pseudoephedrine is found in over-the-counter cold medicines. In the mid-2000s, states began to pass laws limiting the availability of such cold medicines. The federal government passed the Combat Methamphetamine Epidemic Act in 2005. Before such laws, cookers would simply go to the nearest drugstore and buy every available box of the cold medicine. For larger operations, the cooker would send out customers to buy up all the medicine from all the nearby stores. The laws have had a modest effect, and the large production of meth has moved to Mexico; however, local labs are still quite common.

Meth production has several significant problems: explosion, toxicity, and secondhand exposure. The most noteworthy is that meth labs are liable to explode. The process of making meth is volatile, and resulting explosions are common. These explosions can easily destroy small homes, mobile homes, and outbuildings. Frequently, the cooker and others in the location are killed in the explosion.

Meth is toxic. After the meth is produced, the cooker is left with toxic waste that is routinely hazardously disposed of in the nearest sewer or ditch. This leads to wider exposure to the poison through community sewer systems, groundwater, or incidental contact. Residues of all the chemicals used to create meth remain in the drug. As a result, the user and those nearby are exposed to dangerous and often carcinogenic substances. For example, meth often has benzene, methylene chloride, trichloroethane, and toluene in it. All of these substances are toxic and are directly related to cancer. Smoking meth effectively introduces these caustic and carcinogenic chemicals into the body. One notable result is "meth mouth." The chemicals in meth erode the enamel of the teeth and particularly the front teeth, which quickly discolor and rot.

A third problem is secondhand exposure. Since local users in their home often make meth, children and other nonusing family members are exposed to the toxic chemicals. Beyond the consequences of meth user's behavior, the children and nonusing family members breathe and ingest the caustic, carcinogenic, and toxic chemicals. The children are of particular concern. In areas where meth is the dominant drug of abuse, child protective and foster care services are often overwhelmed by the needs of children of meth users and cookers. The long-term health consequences for the children remain unknown; however, public health officials are fearful of cancer and other health consequences.

After law enforcement agents seize a lab, many public agencies have to deal with the toxic site. Law enforcement officers are exposed in the arrest and evidentiary collection process. Child protection workers may enter the home to rescue the children. These workers too are exposed. Finally, someone has to clean up the site. Very strict hazardous material management procedures must be followed, and as a result, site cleanup is expensive. This is particularly onerous for small towns and rural counties that frequently lack the budgets for such a cleanup.

Meth Use and Effects

Meth is a powerful stimulant. The drug can be injected, snorted, or smoked. Once ingested, the drug increases the release of dopamine and blocks the reuptake of dopamine. As a result, the users feel a great sense of energy and pleasure. When smoked or injected, the user will feel an intense rush. After the rush, the user feels a general sense of euphoria and a sense of unlimited energy, depending on dose, and individual tolerance. The euphoric feeling can last from several hours to as long as 12 hours.

Meth provides a relatively cheap, long-lasting high that is readily available and is therefore highly addictive. Meth users are likely to have poor physical appearance, compromised health, and are likely to ignore basic hygiene. Furthermore, meth represses appetite and sleep; regular users are likely to appear gaunt or emaciated and generally unhealthy. Since meth users frequently inject the drug, they may be exposed to and are likely to contract HIV/AIDS (human immunodeficiency virus/acquired immune deficiency syndrome), tuberculosis, and hepatitis. Through casual sexual contact and prostitution, meth users spread these diseases to a larger population.

As with all addiction, meth becomes an obsession, and the users will spend much of their day finding money for the drug, seeking the drug, experiencing the drug, and recovering from the use. Therefore, normal human relationships, behaviors, and tasks become less important. Addicted users are likely to experience profound relationship problems with nonusers, lose employment, engage in minor criminal behavior, and generally experience a low quality of life. With continued use, the users will continue to experience profound disruptions in normal social functioning. Prolonged and repeated use of meth frequently leads the user to a paranoid and agitated state with periodic hallucinations and delusions. This state is sometimes referred to as becoming "sketchy" or "sketching." During this time, the user is volatile, potentially violent, and unpredictable.

One long-term effect is anhedonia and depression. The continued use of meth leads to a depletion of pleasure neurotransmitters. Without these transmitters, the individual loses the ability to feel and may experience deep feelings of emptiness. Stopping the drug use does not lead to a return of emotions, and former users may experience years of missing or diminished senses of pleasure and enjoyment.

As with other addictive substances, meth is strongly associated with crime and violence. The source of some crimes is found in the users securing the funding for more meth; however, according to Hunt, Kuck, and Truitt (2006), when compared with cocaine and heroin, meth is less likely to lead to economically based crimes. There is some but limited violence related to the meth marketplace.

Since meth is a powerful stimulant, the psychopharmacological effects of the drug may promote individual acts of violence like assault. Sketchy users are likely to misinterpret social cues and see threats and aggression in otherwise ordinary behavior.

Mitchell B. Mackinem and
Christopher B. Mackinem

See also Cocaine; Drug Dependence Treatment; Drug War (War on Drugs); Race/Ethnicity and Drug Use

Further Readings

Ardus, P. V. (2011). *Methamphetamine laboratories.* New York, NY: Nova Science.

Haight, W. L. (2009). *Children of methamphetamine-involved families: The case of rural Illinois.* Oxford, England: Oxford University Press.

Hser, Y.-I., Huang, D., Chou, C., Teruya, C., & Anglin, D. M. (2003). Longitudinal patterns of treatment utilization and outcome among methamphetamine abusers: A growth curve model approach. *Journal of Drug Issues, 33,* 921–938.

Hunt, D., Kuck, S., & Truitt, L. (2006). *Methamphetamine use: Lessons learned* (99-C-008). Washington, DC: U.S. Department of Justice.

Oser, C., Leukefeld, C., Staton-Tindall, M., Duvall, J., Garrity, T., Stoops, W., & Booth, B. (2011). Criminality among rural stimulant users in the United States. *Crime & Delinquency, 57,* 600–621.

Pennell, S., National Institute of Justice (U.S.), & San Diego Association of Governments. (1999). *Meth matters: Report on methamphetamine users in five Western cities.* Washington, DC: U.S. Department of Justice, National Institute of Justice, Office of Justice Programs.

Roll, J. M. (2009). *Methamphetamine addiction: From basic science to treatment.* New York, NY: Guilford Press.

Swetlow, K. (2003). *Children at clandestine methamphetamine labs: Helping meth's youngest victims* (NCJ 197590). Washington, DC: U.S. Department of Justice.

Taylor, B. G., Brownstein, H. H., Mulcahy, T. M., Fernandes-Huessy, J., Woods, D. J., & Hafford, C. (2011). The characteristics of methamphetamine markets and their impact on communities. *Criminal Justice Review, 36*(3), 312–331.

MILITARY DEVIANCE

Discipline and order are key characteristics of any military. Such characteristics suggest that the military as a social institution would employ sufficient controls and sanctions to inhibit deviant behaviors. It is this very discipline and order that makes deviance among military personnel unique and yet similar to other "total institutions." As a total institution, with its own norms, laws, and sanctions, we can consider military deviance as behaviors that violate the expectations of the institution and as individual deviant behavior committed among those in the military. This entry provides an overview of what is known about deviance *in* the military and about deviance *among* those in the military.

Deviance in the Military

The military is an example of what the sociologist Erving Goffman referred to as a total institution. Total institutions are those where people are situated in a fixed place for both work and residence and that which is somewhat isolated from the larger community. In total institutions, a person's private and work life often become inseparable and are highly regulated. Goffman's typology of total institutions included the military, and his other examples are paramilitary, thus suggesting that the military is the archetype of total institutions.

The military has rigid norms of behavior that are enforced through informal sanctions among all members of the military and enforced formally through occupational sanctions. Furthermore, the U.S. military has its own legal code, known as the Uniform Code of Military Justice (UCMJ). The UCMJ criminalizes behavior addressed by most national criminal justice systems, including rape, murder, and theft. The UCMJ also criminalizes behavior that may be considered deviant but not criminal in some societies (i.e., drunk on duty, sodomy, and adultery), and others where the deviance/criminality is only defined as such by the military (i.e., insubordination, absent without leave, and conduct unbecoming).

These examples of military-specific deviance provide an understanding of the core values of the military and consequently the ways in which deviance occurs in the military. Deviance in the military can be thought of as behaviors against the institution and behaviors against the expectations for the soldier.

Deviating From the Military

Effective military operation depends on discipline, including unquestioning adherence to rules and respecting a clear and rigid hierarchy of authority.

As such, many of the written and unwritten rules in the military revolve around following orders. In fact, one of the articles in the UCMJ is "failure to obey order or regulation." This same value is seen in other articles, including absent without leave, desertion, insubordination, missing movement, contempt/disrespect of officers, and mutiny. The rules are clear: A soldier owes respect to the institution and its processes, and any behavior that deviates from these expectations will be negatively sanctioned.

Deviating From the "Soldier"

In addition to discipline, effective military operation—and effective operation of any institution—depends on uniformity. As such, the military has a strict standard for the soldier, a standard that includes expectations ranging from appearance to behavior. Military personnel can be punished for not meeting the regulations of hair length, facial hair, uniform, and clothing accessories. Military personnel can also be sanctioned for general violations such as misconduct, misbehavior, drunk on duty, and conduct unbecoming. The last can include behaviors ranging from dishonesty to cruelty and injustice. This standard of soldiering shows that the total institution of the military defines not only acceptable behavior but also acceptable identity. While this is not unique to the military—all of society has norms about appearance and behavior—the socialization of these norms in military personnel and the sanctions of those who violate these norms are significantly more intense in the military compared with the larger society.

Deviance Among Military Personnel

The previous section discussed how the violation of the standards of military discipline itself is deviant. Following is a discussion of how military personnel engage in deviant behaviors beyond military-specific deviance. It should be noted that the following discussion is not suggesting that all or even most military personnel engage in these types of deviance, only that when military personnel engage in deviance, it comes in these forms.

Theft

One of the areas of deviance for military personnel is theft of military property and theft while deployed. This behavior walks a line of crime and deviance, as it is technically criminal and socially deviant; however, according to the norms of the military—especially individual units—this theft can be considered acceptable.

Military personnel are issued a variety of property ranging from socks and items for hygiene to resources for battle. Many of these items are expected to be returned on completion of assigned use; however, it is common for soldiers to keep military property. Military personnel will either never officially sign for the items or will claim the items lost. Either way, the behavior amounts to theft of military property.

The historical notion of "to the victor go the spoils" is relevant for understanding theft while military personnel are deployed. Military personnel will take what they call "souvenirs" from foreign lands, including from the homes of civilians. True to the quote, soldiers will deny it as theft and will instead claim some entitlement to money or artifacts. This behavior has been occurring as long as there has been war and military occupation, and however acceptable within the institution, it is still considered theft.

Substance Use

As with other forms of deviance among the military, it is important to separate substance use while deployed with substance use in normal military life. It is also important to consider the range of substances, including those that are legal (alcohol and steroids) and those that are illegal (marijuana, cocaine, and other illicit drugs).

Alcohol is not only legal, but alcohol consumption is also very normative in military culture. Officer's Clubs and Non-Commissioned Officer's (NCO) Clubs are popular facility attractions, as are bars that are off facility. With that said, alcohol use among military personnel could be considered deviant by the larger society given the frequency and extent of alcohol consumption among military personnel. It would seem that drinking is a pastime for military personnel, a very common way of spending one's time when off duty. Research suggests that alcohol use, along with other substances, is used as a way to cope with military life both while deployed and at noncombat duty stations.

Although steroid use is legal, it is not normative. Recent research shows increasing use of anabolic steroids by military personnel while in combat and noncombat duty. The most common explanation for steroid use while in combat is to provide energy and strength, while the explanation for using steroids during normal duty is strength—but specifically to achieve some hypermasculine standard of strength and appearance.

The final area of substance use is the use of illegal substances. The most common types of illegal substances used by military personnel are marijuana, cocaine, and heroin—although there are cases of using methamphetamines, MDMA (3,4-methylenedioxy-N-methylamphetamine), and other illegal substances. There is evidence of all substances being used in noncombat settings, with marijuana being used with the most prevalence (no difference from the civilian population). There is an increased use of cocaine in recent combat settings, with soldiers claiming the benefits of energy and fearlessness as an explanation for using cocaine (Bucher, 2012). As noted with alcohol, the primary explanation for using marijuana and heroin either when deployed or in normal duty is to cope with various stressors.

Violence and Aggression

Abu Ghraib

In 2004, the world learned of prisoner mistreatment that occurred at Abu Ghraib, a military-run prison for convicted and alleged criminals. Abu Ghraib is located in Iraq and was staffed by U.S. military personnel. In what amounts to the infamous Zimbardo experiment coming to life, prisoners were humiliated, tortured, and otherwise abused by military personnel. The deviance at Abu Ghraib became much more than a violation of the UCMJ (prisoner abuse) and received significant negative social sanction given the extreme nature of the abuse. The graphic images supplied by the media intensified the social reaction, thereby intensifying the perceived deviance. Another aspect of this occurrence that contributes to the deviance is the participation of female soldiers. The behavior itself is considered deviant; however, as with many forms of deviance, the behaviors at Abu Ghraib were masculinized forms of deviance, thereby making female participation further deviant.

Rape and Murder While Deployed

Similar to the events at Abu Ghraib, the media have provided examples of egregious crimes such as rape and murder committed by military personnel against foreign civilians. While these are relatively rare, they are significant in extent. The same mentality discussed regarding theft (pillage) while in combat is the mentality that drives civilian violence (including rape)—the belief that military presence and occupation indicates entitlement. Furthermore, much like theft while in combat, violence, while obviously officially criminal and socially deviant, may be socially acceptable within certain units. The military has long been accused of supporting a culture that places female soldiers at risk of being sexually assaulted; this same culture could support the assault and other nonsanctioned violence against foreign civilians.

Domestic Violence

The U.S. Army Crime Records Center shows domestic violence to be one of the most prevalent forms of violent/personal crime committed by military personnel. The prevalence is compounded given the understanding that domestic violence is an underreported crime. Some of this violence manifests in spousal homicide and consequently receives media attention similar to the deviant behaviors discussed earlier. It can be argued that the less extreme, but no less significant, forms of domestic violence that do not result in death are equally deviant.

Influences

The focus of this entry has been on the forms of deviance that can take place in the military and among military personnel. Given that the military is a total institution, it is important to consider the factors that may explain different forms of deviance.

Social Learning

An easy explanation for military deviance, especially violence, is that the military supports a culture of violence. Whether it is the basic training of soldiers to kill or the acceptance of other forms of violence, there is a logical argument that the military itself is a factor in violent deviant behavior in the military. Violence is not only taught but also encouraged, celebrated, and defended when the acceptability of it is questioned by those inside and outside of the military. While these are all basic conclusions drawn from basic logic, it is possible that military deviance is, at least in part, learned.

Stress/Coping

In the previous discussion of types of deviance, especially substance use, it was suggested that military deviance can be explained as a way to cope with stress. The rigid work environment that other occupations have creates certain kinds of stress, while the nature of combat creates unique stress only experienced by a few occupations, including police officers, fire fighters, and emergency room medical personnel. Military personnel who are unable to effectively and legitimately cope with these stressors may engage in deviant behaviors as a result.

Masculinity

Finally, when discussing social learning or stress as possible influences on military deviance, the role of masculinity should be considered. The U.S. military, and most military throughout history, is hypermasculine and as such holds military personnel, including women, to rigid standards of masculinity. Masculinity could factor in the learning of violent deviant behaviors given the association of violence and masculinity; it could explain some of the deviant ways soldiers cope given the association between excess substance use and masculinity and the dissociation between masculinity and legitimate coping mechanisms (i.e., talking about one's problems), and it could also be considered a stress itself given the emphasis on being masculine (those who cannot meet the standard experience stress). Not only does this potentially explain some of the deviant behaviors discussed throughout this entry, but it also suggests a possible unique phenomenon of military deviance among female personnel.

Jacob Bucher

See also General Strain Theory; Normalization; Occupational Criminality; Social Learning Theory; Total Institutions

Further Readings

Bryant, C. D. (1979). *Khaki-collar crime.* New York, NY: Free Press.

Bucher, J. (2011). General issue (G.I.) strain: Applying strain theory to crime among the military. *Deviant Behavior, 32*(9), 846–875.

Bucher, J. (2012). Soldiering with substance: Substance and steroid use among the military. *Journal of Drug Education, 42*(3), 267–292.

Enloe, C. (2004). Wielding masculinity inside Abu Ghraib: Making feminist sense of an american military scandal. *Asian Journal of Women's Studies, 10*(3), 89–102.

Grossman, D. (1995). *On killing: The psychological cost of learning to kill in war and society.* New York, NY: Back Bay Books.

MONITORING THE FUTURE

Substance use by American adolescents is a continually changing and rapidly evolving phenomenon and as such requires frequent measurement and assessment to accurately report trends and prevalence of substance use among the nation's youth. Initially titled the National Senior High School Senior Survey, Monitoring the Future is an ongoing, large-scale study of 8th, 10th, and 12th graders in the United States and is the most powerful and reliable data source for the measurement of attitudes and behaviors among this population. Monitoring the Future has been collected on an annual basis by the University of Michigan's Institute for Social Research since 1975 and is funded through the National Institutes of Health. Data gathered through Monitoring the Future is disseminated through a wide range of public venues. Findings have often appeared in national news programs, magazines, and a variety of prestigious scholarly journals. Due to such wide dissemination and its representative nature, Monitoring the Future is the leading resource for assessing and measuring drug use and abuse among the nation's youth.

Purpose and Scope

The main purpose of Monitoring the Future is to study the changes in beliefs, attitudes, and behaviors related to drug use among adolescents in the United States. Questions about licit and illicit drug use, the survey's principal target, make up approximately 50% of the total survey. Monitoring the Future measures everything from personal use and drug-related problems to attitudes about their drug use by others and beliefs about the perceived harmfulness of drug use. As of 2011, the survey included these measures in relation to more than 50 different classes and subclasses of drugs. This survey encompasses more types of drugs than any other nationally representative survey in the United States. Since its inception, every few years a new set of drugs has been added to the survey as new alternatives for mood-altering substances available to adolescents have grown exponentially, a trend that is expected to continue as new drugs continue to flood the market. In addition to measuring attitudes about substance use, the survey also measures a variety of related factors, including (but not limited to) personal lifestyle choices, high school experiences, views about social institutions, health, leisure activities, victimization, home environment, and life satisfaction.

The majority of the data collected through Monitoring the Future are cross-sectional, meaning that they provide researchers with information collected at one specific point in time, a snapshot view of current incidence and prevalence of drug use. In addition to the cross-sectional data collected annually, the survey also includes a longitudinal study of a subsample of each graduating class, which allows researchers to track individual changes in behaviors and attitudes across a long period of time. Beginning in 1976, researchers began gathering longitudinal data on this subset, conducting follow-up surveys every other year. This longitudinal sample is then divided into two subsamples, students who went on to college after high school and those who did not. Data gathered through Monitoring the Future provide the public with a picture of changing trends. The combination of both cross-sectional and longitudinal components allows for the measurement of specific types of changes: (a) historical trend changes that are common to all age cohorts, (b) changes across the life span of those enrolled in the survey follow-up, (c) enduring cohort differences that change from one graduating class to the next, and (d) the follow-up data that were collected on individuals into their 50s, which allow for the measurement of the differential impact of post–high school environments (e.g., college, workforce, and military), major life course changes (e.g., marriage and parenthood), and individual characteristics.

Sampling Design and Survey Administration

Initially the survey was administered only to high school seniors, but in 1991, the survey expanded to include nationally representative samples of 8th and 10th graders. Adding 8th- and 10th-grade students allows researchers to survey students who might drop out of school before their senior year. Each year, the survey is administered by University of Michigan personnel to approximately 50,000 public and private secondary school students in their normal classroom settings during the spring semester. Because the survey addresses a number of sensitive topics, 8th- and 10th-grade surveys are completed with total anonymity—no identifying information is collected. For 12th graders, the survey is confidential; names and addresses are collected to allow for follow-up surveys to be sent to those chosen for the longitudinal subset.

To ensure a nationally representative sample, a multistage sampling design is employed. The first stage of sampling involves identifying the primary geographic units to survey. Monitoring the Future uses the sampling units developed by the University of Michigan's Survey Research Center, which include the nation's 28 largest metropolitan cities and 136 smaller primary sampling areas. The second stage involves the identification of schools to participate in the survey. In the 28 largest metropolitan cities, two or more schools are chosen for inclusion, and only one school is chosen from from the smaller primary sampling areas. The final stage in the sampling process involves the selection of individual students to participate in the survey. Within each school, approximately 350 students from each grade are selected. Furthermore, a small subset of graduating seniors is chosen from larger schools through random sampling techniques for annual follow-up surveys.

Kristi L. Stringer

See also Drug Abuse Warning Network; National Youth Survey

Further Readings

Bachman, J. G., Johnston, L. D., O'Malley, P. M., & Schulenberg, J. E. (2011). *The Monitoring the Future Project after thirty-seven years: Design and procedures* (Monitoring the Future Occasional Paper No. 76). Ann Arbor: University of Michigan, Institute for Social Research, Monitoring the Future.

Johnston, L. D., O'Malley, P. M., Bachman, J. G., & Schulenberg, J. E. (2012). *Monitoring the Future, national results on adolescent drug use: Overview of key findings, 2011.* Ann Arbor: University of Michigan, Institute for Social Research.

MORAL ENTREPRENEURS

Moral entrepreneurs are those who take the lead in persuading society to create rules or policy based on particular moral viewpoints; they often aim to control personal behavior and definitions of morality. Such crusades for the betterment of society generate greater social concern, which may culminate in the establishment of long-standing social changes and enforcement institutions. Moral entrepreneurs have been cited as playing roles in redefining moral boundaries regarding a variety of issues, including drugs and alcohol, crime, terrorism, medicalization, immigration policy, perceptions of ethnic groups, and even witchcraft. This entry begins with a discussion of rule creation within society and goes on to define and elaborate on the role moral entrepreneurs play in this process. It continues with a discussion of the process of moral reform, highlighting what have been found to be essential requirements for its success. Next, moral panics, which often arise from efforts of moral entrepreneurs, will be defined. The entry concludes with a discussion of rule enforcement as an outcome of successful moral reform.

Rule Creation and Moral Entrepreneurs

Rule creation has been a sustained topic of interest for scholars of social deviance. Symbolic interaction and constructionist theorists point to the socially manufactured nature of deviance and suggest that social morality is continually redefined within societies rather than the implementation of a fixed social consensus. This plays to the subjective nature of morality construction—that the meanings attributed to morality are not necessarily bound by an objective reality. In other words, whether something is considered beyond social–moral boundaries may not be as contingent on the act itself so much as on those defining the boundary. This leads to the question not only of how morality is structured and periodically restructured but also of how morality and social norms become elevated to such importance that society requires formal enforcement to regulate or end acts defined as immoral. Howard Becker's concept of the moral entrepreneur has been useful in illuminating the process whereby a new element of the moral constitution of society is created and put into effect.

Moral entrepreneurs, or moral crusaders, are individuals or groups who campaign for new social regulation to control what they deem to be socially deviant and ultimately negative to society. This process is not to be understood simplistically by viewing these individuals as intrusive nuisances forcing their own will on others. Such moral entrepreneurs often have strong humanitarian ideals and view their crusades as righteous. In many cases, this view is held not only by the moral entrepreneurs themselves but becomes seconded by others outside of the crusade. The Women's Christian Temperance Union, an early movement for prohibition of alcoholic beverages, can be seen as an example of this. This organization was one of the first to highlight the ills brought into the domestic sphere by the abuse of alcohol. This cause was seen by others as honest, and eventually, its calls for social reform were answered in the passing of the Eighteenth Amendment to the U.S. Constitution, which banned the sale and consumption of alcohol. Moral entrepreneurs see themselves on a didactic crusade that will benefit society if they accomplish their goal of having others conform to what they see as "right." They are singularly interested in the content of rules and are very often involved in what they truly see as justified moral reforms.

The Process of Moral Reform

The methods moral entrepreneurs use to achieve social reform have been theorized to be partially dependent on the perceived moral mind frames, status, and social actions of the "deviants" who are the objects of reform. Depending on the perception of the deviant, the moral entrepreneur's ambition is for either assimilative or coercive reform. If the deviant group is seen as defiant toward the views of the moral entrepreneurs, the method of social reform utilized by social regulators will be coercive. However, if the deviant group is seen as being morally unaware, it will be perceived in a sympathetic light, and moral entrepreneurs will seek integrative efforts aimed at helping those who are deviant to understand and willingly accept the proposed reform. Coercive reform is sought through punitive measures using formal social control institutions. Here, social moderators will often seek affirmation by turning to formal social control mechanisms, such as the law, or will employ force to accomplish their goals. Since those that are argued to need reforming are seen as enemy deviants, they are demonized and labeled as outsiders or threats. This dichotomous relationship focuses the rhetoric on the goals of reform and away from the ones who are the targets of reform.

Integrative reform turns the focus on those deviant members of society more willing to be educated regarding their noncompliance with social norms. It is thought that the repentant deviant will conform to the new moral boundaries advocated since, once enlightened, he or she will acknowledge it as the correct thing to do. In this sense, moral entrepreneurs see themselves as helping others achieve a higher social status, which can only be attained through assimilation. These integrative tactics are employed through educative rather than punitive strategies.

Requirements for Successful Moral Reform

The ability for moral crusaders to accomplish their task relies on various factors: their social power and position within the social hierarchy, whom they enlist to help them accomplish their goals, and the ability for them to generate interest within society regarding the importance of their moral agenda.

Moral reform tends to succeed when the moral entrepreneurs come from dominant classes within society and target their crusade toward those less favorably situated in the economic and social structure. Howard Becker formulated the concept of "hierarchies of credibility," which postulates that one's position in the moral-social order dictates one's credibility, with those maintaining higher positions being perceived as more credible. An examination of the Prohibition movement in the United States can be used as an example of this. Many temperance leaders were native-born, middle-class, nonurban Protestants, which established them among the higher social strata. This group felt threatened by the social drinking culture of the new working class, mostly Catholic immigrants migrating to urban areas within the United States. Furthermore, temperance leaders became concerned when younger generations of these immigrants started to compete outside of the working-class labor market. Owing to their social position, these temperance leaders were able to stigmatize this incoming group, by having the power and resources to do so. Furthermore, the absence of power often prevents moral entrepreneurs from achieving their goals. This has been illustrated in the inability of antipornography groups to get restrictive legislation passed or in the failure of antiabortion groups. Both groups have been largely framed as being formed from among the socially marginalized (see, e.g., Erich Goode and Nachman Ben-Yehuda, 1994).

The second factor in a successful moral enterprise is finding individuals or groups to help in the crusade. Since there are no existing rules to deal with the new threat to society, moral entrepreneurs must construct the impression that they are necessary. In doing so, they draw on the testimonials of "experts" in the field, such as doctors, scholars, clergy, and others with specific knowledge of the situation. One such example would be the key role psychiatrists have played in the recent "epidemic" of attention-deficit/hyperactivity disorder. These expert testimonials are disseminated to society through the media as "facts." The media play a crucial role in this process by selectively sensationalizing certain issues and focusing public attention on them while ignoring others. An example of the importance of this type of collaborative efforts is the key role that media mogul William Randolph Hearst played by utilizing various Hearst publications to bring attention to and exaggerate the dangers of marijuana. These relationships take on a symbiotic nature. Moral entrepreneurs advance their moral crusade by forming alliances with those who may be motivated by other needs and desires. In relation to marijuana regulation, Hearst was well aware that sensational headlines sell more newspapers. Similarly, Prohibition lobbyists often looked for help within the private sector, enlisting business owners to speak of the problems of alcohol consumption. As Joseph Gusfield has argued, the concern of such business owners was not the moral evil of drink but the practical need for a sober work force to increase productivity and hence profitability.

Politicians are also often vital players in this process. Their occupation designates them to the court of public opinion and thus they must present themselves as purveyors of the moral high ground. Thus, they often ally themselves with the press and the moral entrepreneurs in a fight against the evils propagated by the norm violation. Furthermore, these testimonials by all experts are instrumental not only in getting the attention of society but also in their acceptance of the said cause as a legitimate threat.

This leads to the third key to successful moral enterprise, or gaining the public's support and agreement on the necessity of social regulation. Most literature on this step highlights the ability of moral entrepreneurs and interest groups to get the public into a panicked frenzy. These moral panics have been documented around drug legislation, immigration policies, and even witchcraft. Within these panics, it is the incentive of the moral entrepreneur to legitimate their claim of a subversive threat that was until recently unknown or unregulated. First, they proclaim to the public the intensity of the threat. While establishing the intensity of the threat, it is often linked to other unrelated social ills. Temperance leaders routinely linked the detrimental effects of industrialization in the United States to overdrink. These proclamations garner public attention while also misleading the public into viewing complex societal problems from a simplest narrow focus. Eventually, this panic moves the public to ask for help in protecting themselves from the social "evil."

Some movements will additionally link the societal threat to an individual or group. These folk devils or scapegoats typically maintain lower rungs within the social stratification system. These folk devils are deviant stereotypes identifying the enemy or the source of the threat. They are labeled as selfish, wrong, or evildoers who are responsible for the trouble. Examples of this have been shown in moral panics dealing with drug legislation. The antiopium movement has been documented to be an extension of an already progressing anti-Chinese movement in the West, early cocaine legislation was aimed at African Americans, and the Prohibition movement is often looked at as an attack on working class, urban, Catholic immigrants. These subpopulations are made to appear deviant through "stigma contests," which spoil their identities. These stigma contests utilize propaganda to control public opinion. This allows moral entrepreneurs to use their power and network resources to their advantage. These moral panics lead the general population to accept the new rules and their subsequent enforcement. However, this process leading to legislation depends on what the moral entrepreneurs of legitimate groups are able to link to their crusade.

Moral Panics

The calls of attention of the public to the societal moral infractions by moral entrepreneurs often lead to the creation of moral panics. Simplistically, moral panics are a social response to beliefs about a threat from moral deviants. These panics occur when the reaction of the media, law enforcement, politicians, action groups, and the general public are out of proportion to the real and present danger a given threat poses to society. Once this moral panic is established, sensitization occurs. This is when behavior that was previously ignored is noticed and linked to offending agents. Moral panics are defined by at least five crucial elements or criteria: (1) concern, (2) hostility, (3) consensus, (4) disproportionality, and (5) volatility.

A moral panic requires a heightened level of concern over the behavior (or supposed behavior) of a certain group and the consequences of that group. There must also be an increased level of hostility toward the category of people seen as engaging in the threatening behavior. A certain minimal level of agreement in the society as a whole or in designated segments of society that the threat is real, serious, and caused by the wrongdoing of the group members must be ascertained. This concern must be out of proportion to the nature of the threat. These moral panics are often short lived and lose media and public interest quickly. Even though these panics are volatile, the effect they have in creating formal social control institutions is not.

Who Starts Moral Panics?

Social movements based on moral panics are stated to originate from three different social actors. These actors range from the general public to various interest groups to powerful elites within the social structure. These models should not be thought of as competing arguments toward all social movements but as three different possible starting points for various moral crusades.

The grassroots model posits that panics originate spontaneously within the general public. The general public is the first actor to become concerned and angry with what they see to be a widespread social problem or moral deviance. This concern is misplaced anxiety arising from other widespread social stresses that are displaced and directed toward social deviants, who become collective scapegoats regarded as the cause for concern. Due to this concern, other social actors and institutions (e.g., politicians, news media, social institutions) become involved in the movement and essentially reflect public opinion about the reality of the problem. These actors provide the vehicle that allows the grassroots movement to become widespread throughout the larger general public. The ability for the social problem to be accepted depends on deeply felt attitudes and beliefs on the part of a broad sector of the society, that a given phenomenon represents a real and present threat to their values, their safety, or even their very existence.

The elite engineered model argues that a powerful group or set of groups can deliberately and consciously undertake a campaign to generate and sustain fear, concern, and panic on the part of the public over an issue they recognize not to be terribly harmful to the society as a whole. This campaign is intended to divert attention away from the real problems in society to which the solution would threaten the interests of the elite group. This power elite manufactures the threat and utilizes various institutions of society (e.g., mass media, religion, formal social control institutions) to influence public opinion.

The final model states that moral panics are the latent consequences of moral crusades launched by specific interest groups. Activists of these groups attempt to focus public attention on moral evils that they truly perceive to be threats to society. The motivation for the rule creators and moral entrepreneurs who launch these moral crusades is to make sure that certain rules take hold and are enforced. As these groups become increasingly successful in implementing and enforcing policy, they stimulate dissension among other interest groups.

Rule Establishment and Subsequent Enforcement

Once this crusade is accomplished, the final step is the establishment of rules and the creation of new or adapted enforcement agencies to implement the rules. It is here where moral entrepreneurs are often excluded or pushed away from the process. This does not garner resistance from moral entrepreneurs since they are only interested in the rules themselves and not their enforcement.

Once the laws are set in place, the power is completely taken out of the hands of the moral entrepreneurs. The process of labeling the deviance and deviants becomes independent of the moral entrepreneur and establishes that the rule enforcer becomes the most important actor. This enforcer is most likely detached from rule enforcement. For the enforcer, the humanitarian goal is not important or valued, just the objective enforcement of the rule on the books. The establishment of new formal social control institutions can institutionalize and bureaucratize rule enforcement. This institutionalization promotes the likelihood of the rule to be enforced in the future. This is due to the incentive of the rule-enforcing agency to remain in practice. This places the agency in a counterintuitive dilemma in justifying themselves. They have to convince others that the problem still exists, while, in turn, legitimating their attempts at enforcement as being effective and worthwhile. This often leads to claims of increasing and more dramatic threats.

Timothy C. Brown

See also Constructionist Definitions of Social Problems; Labeling Approach; Medicalization of Deviance; Moral Panics; Symbolic Crusade; Symbolic Interactionism

Further Readings

Becker, H. S. (1963). *Outsiders*. New York, NY: Free Press.

Ben-Yehuda, N. (1980). The European witch craze of the 14th to 17th centuries: A sociologist's perspective. *American Journal of Sociology, 86,* 1–31.

Ben-Yehuda, N. (1986). The sociology of moral panics: Toward a new synthesis. *Sociological Quarterly, 27,* 495–513.

Cohen, S. (2004). *Folk devils and moral panics*. London, England: Routledge.

Conrad, P. (1975). The discovery of hyperkinesis: Notes on the medicalization of deviant behavior. *Social Problem, 23,* 12–21.

Goode, E., & Yehuda, N. B. (1994). *Moral panics: The social construction of deviance*. Oxford, England: Blackwell.

Gusfield, J. R. (1955). Social structure and moral reform: A Study of the Woman's Christian Temperance Union. *American Journal of Sociology, 61*(3), 221–232.

Gusfield, J. R. (1963). *Symbolic crusade: Status politics and the American temperance movement*. Chicago: University of Illinois Press.

Reinarman, C. (2006). The social construction of drug scares. In P. Adler & P. Adler (Eds.), *Constructions of deviance* (pp. 139–150). Belmont, CA: Thomson Wadsworth.

Tuggle, J., & Holmes, M. (1997). Blowing smoke: Status politics and the Shasta County smoking ban. *Deviant Behavior, 18,* 77–93.

Victor, J. (1998). Moral panics and the social construction of deviant behavior: A theory and application to the case of child abuse. *Sociological Perspectives, 41,* 541–565.

Zurcher, L. A., Jr., & Kirkpatrick, G. R. (1976). *Citizens for decency: Anti-pornography crusades as status defense*. Austin: University of Texas Press.

MORAL PANICS

In Siberia, Russians distribute a newsletter accusing Jews of kidnapping Christian children, bloodletting them to perform the Passover Seder, and tossing their victims' bodies onto garbage dumps. In Australia, politicians and the media allege that immigrants are fomenting a crime wave and call for restrictions on the migration of new residents from Asia. Everywhere that videogames have become popular, parents and the media contend that their producers and distributors corrupt the young, causing them to engage in delinquent behavior. How do we make sense of such episodes? Some observers dismiss such outbreaks of irrational fears as trivial and exotic marginalia, social and historical delusions of little or no sociological significance. Others argue that these accusations, allegations, charges, claims, and expressions of concern share a common thread: All embody the moral panic.

A moral panic is an outbreak of moral concern about the menace from an agent of corruption—a designated "folk devil"—whose imputed threat is out of proportion to its actual danger or potential harm. Such concerns are not always entirely bogus, since the named threats may be genuine, but the claims of impending or ongoing injury are substantially exaggerated regarding the seriousness, extent, typicality, or inevitability of the specified harm or danger. Empirically assessed, the concerns stirred up by ritual murder, immigration, and videogames are out of proportion to their objective threat. For such episodes, the society (or a sector of the society) *overreacts* to a seeming danger in its midst. There is, in other words, a *delusional* aspect to the moral panic. Any time a substantial number of people make a false claim of harm, or raise an exaggerated alarm, about a threat posed by a supposed deviant—a category of people who, presumably, menace the society's culture, way of life, and central values—we have a moral panic on our hands. And such concerns signal significant social and cultural rifts or insecurities to which sociologists should pay close attention. The moral panic is perhaps the most influential and widely disseminated concept devised in the 20th century by a sociologist.

In the collective behavior literature, researchers and scholars are careful to point out that what they refer to as a "panic" does not necessarily or usually imply irrational, self-destructive headlong flight away from an imaginary or trivial threat. The term *panic* is used by the moral panic literature as a metaphor; it borrows from but does not rigidly apply this stereotype drawn from the disaster literature. There is a major and obvious difference between the threat from a disaster and that from the moral panic: In a disaster, the threat tends to be immediate, physical, and genuine. In the moral panic, the threat is usually more slow moving, largely symbolic and cultural, and, more than occasionally, nonexistent.

Historically, the first analyses that specifically named the concept "moral panic" were conducted in the early 1970s by the sociologists Jock Young, who conducted a study of the exaggerated fear of drug use in England, and Stanley Cohen, who analyzed the public's attitudes toward "mods" and "rockers," two youth groups who inflicted relatively minor acts of vandalism on an English seaside town. At the time, Young and Cohen were left-wing, recent PhDs from the London School of Economics; they noticed the inappropriate and exaggerated attention paid to and concern expressed by key actors in the drama of designating folk devils and their threat. How do we know we have a moral panic when we see one? We know this when social actors express exaggerated concern about or become unduly riled up about a supposed threat by a designated wrongdoer or "folk devil."

The folk devil is the deviant or villain in this drama. Not all "deviants" are innocent as charged, and not all harm by actors who have attracted condemnation is imaginary or exaggerated—but much of it is. When scholars and researchers carefully, soberly, and systematically weighed the evidence, it became clear that, contrary to charges made in the 1970s and 1980s, satanic ritual abuse—the kidnap, torture, and murder of children by Satanists—did not take place, and certainly not in the numbers that activists claimed—that is, in the tens of thousands; that "snuff" movies, in which women were supposedly murdered on camera for the pornographic delight of male viewers, was the stuff of urban legends, not reality; that horror comics did not make a major contribution to juvenile delinquency. But even if such claims were approximately true, the moral panic assertions about such deeds are grossly exaggerated with respect to the number of victims, the cost to society, how widespread the harm is, and the inevitability of the causal sequence from lesser to greater harm.

Agents of Moral Panic

Who are the actors who play out the drama of moral panics?

The Press. The media have become the most effective generators and conveyors of moral panics in history. Whenever the media address a story about wrongdoing with exaggerated attention, exaggerated events, inventions, distortions, and stereotyping, it's evident that there's a moral panic brewing. In Cohen's case, the media accorded the scuffles and minor acts of vandalism that took place far out of proportion to their objective importance. The media sensationalized the harm and the events depicted, repeatedly using phrases such as "riot," "orgy of destruction," and a "screaming mob." In the past generation or so, however, the sources and diversity of the media have proliferated and ramified to the point where we find competing claims about a supposed threat; indeed, what we see in the media is competing moral panics. Not all media agree with one another, and a diversity of panics often break out among different media audiences.

Law Enforcement. In addition to the press and the general public, the actions of the social control culture demonstrate that a moral panic is taking place. In no sector is this principle more clearly evident than in what the police and the courts—law enforcement—believe they ought to be doing about the perceived threat. Officers make efforts to broaden the scope of law enforcement, increasing its intensity; they justify punitive and overly zealous actions they've already taken on the basis of the enormity of the threat the society faces. Today, we see such forces at work in alerted measures that the police take against illegal immigration and the possibility of terrorism.

Politicians and Legislators. In a moral panic, legislators get into the act, proposing bills to curb the threat. In 1986, Congress enacted a series of laws designed to control the use of illicit substances; some of them remain in place today. In 1988, the Anti-Drug Law called for the death penalty for major drug traffickers as well as anyone causing someone's death during the course of committing a felony. Clearly, in the late 1980s, politicians jumped on the moral panics bandwagon with respect to the drug threat. Legislation often emerges from moral panics.

Action Groups. During moral panics, interested parties issue appeals, launch campaigns, and finally, form full-fledged action groups to address newly existing threats. Such parties are what sociologists call moral entrepreneurs, who believe that existing remedies are insufficient. Action groups are germinal social movements. The emergence of such social action groups in the heat of the moment is one sign that a moral panic is brewing.

The Public. For a classic moral panic to break out, some latent potential must exist on the part of the public to react to an issue, some raw material out of which a media campaign about a given issue can be built. The issue must have resonance with at least some sectors of the public. In September 1989, following a series of speeches by President Ronald Reagan pumping up several proposed drug bills, a New York Times/CBS poll revealed that nearly two thirds (64%) of the American public thought that drug abuse was the number one problem facing the country at that time. Given the objectively more serious problems the country faced (social inequality, poverty, the prospect of a Gulf War), this was an assertion that tapped into subjective concerns rather than objective conditions—a huge exaggeration of a relatively less serious problem.

The hallmark of moral panics is the attempt at moral regulation. The five actors, spoken of earlier, attempt to *regulate and reaffirm the moral order*—to control drug use and, hence, excessive hedonism; to ensure that women are not debased, demeaned, exploited, or subject to free, open, and easy sexual temptation; to attest to the hegemony of Christianity; to affirm the superiority of patriotic values over those of foreign cultures; to endorse adult over teenage values; to ensure capitalist values over communism; and to protect humanity from subversion or annihilation by creatures from other planets.

Still, social panic actors do not always have the same moral order in mind when they engage in claims-making activities; the morality that one set of actors supports is often contested by another. Today, moral orders that different panics affirm may compete against one another. Moral panics have traditionally argued against threats to the *dominant* moral order; however, contemporary panics increasingly oppose threats to a *range* of moral orders—each of concern to particular audiences. The earliest model, based on the notion that the unit of analysis of moral regulation encompasses the society as a whole, has to be supplemented by an awareness that the regulatory ends to which panics are oriented include claims and counterclaims distinctive to particular social circles, subgroups, interest groups, and settings as well.

Explanatory Models of Moral Panic

Researchers and scholars of the moral panic have advanced three theories or explanations to account for their outbreak and proliferation—(1) the "elite-engineered" model, (2) the interest-group model, and (3) the "grassroots" model.

According to the *elite-engineered* model, the most powerful or influential sectors of the society fabricate, orchestrate, and/or engineer a panic to gain something of value or divert attention away from issues that, if addressed, would threaten their dominance. This is a *top-down* model—the most powerful members of the society stir up moral panics to advance their own class or power interests. In contrast, advocates of the *interest-group* theory hold that occupants of the middle levels of power in a society act independently of the elite to express or maximize their morality or ideology and/or seek material or status advantage. The interest-group model argues that moral panics originate neither from the top nor from the bottom rungs of a society but from somewhere in society's middle and growingly powerful strata: professional associations, religious groups, social movement organizations, educational institutions, middle-level associations, organizations, groups, and collectivities of every description. Last, the *grassroots* model argues that moral panics are initiated and generated from the bottom up, as more or less spontaneous eruptions of fear and concern on the part of large numbers of people about a given threat or putative threat. In this model, the influence of large numbers of unorganized, lower-ranking members of the society generates widespread concern about a putative threat; such panics are not necessarily valorized by the media and don't always become translated into law.

No theorist would argue that all panics can be explained by a single model. Still, observers of and commentators on scares or panics usually lean in one direction or another and favor one theory over another to explain most, or the most important, panics.

Erich Goode

See also Changing Deviance Designations; Defining Deviance; Urban Legends

Further Readings

Cohen, S. (Ed.). (1971). *Images of deviance*. Middlesex, England: Penguin Books.

Cohen, S. (1972). *Folk devils and moral panics*. London, England: MacGibbon & Kee.

Critcher, C. (2003). *Moral panics and the media*. Buckingham, England: Open University Press.

De Young, M. (2004). *The day care ritual abuse moral panic*. Jefferson, NJ: McFarland.

Hier, S. P. (Ed.). (2011). *Moral panic and the politics of anxiety*. New York, NY: Routledge.

Krinsky, C. (Ed.). (2012). *The Ashgate Research Companion to moral panics*. Burlington, VT: Ashgate.

Thompson, K. (1998). *Moral panics*. London, England: Routledge.

Young, J. (1971). *The drug takers: The social meaning of drug use*. London, England: MacGibbon & Kee.

MOTOR VEHICLE THEFT

Motor vehicle theft is the theft or attempted theft of a motor vehicle. The Federal Bureau of Investigation's Uniform Crime Reporting (UCR) program defines a motor vehicle as a self-propelled vehicle that runs on land surfaces and not on rails. Motor vehicles include automobiles, sport utility vehicles, trucks, buses, motorcycles, motor scooters, snowmobiles, and all-terrain vehicles. Although considered larceny, thefts that involve farm equipment, construction equipment, airplanes, and water craft are not classified as motor vehicle theft. Because of the volume and seriousness of the offense, the UCR Program has monitored motor vehicle theft separately from larceny since 1933.

Prevalence and Trends

Motor vehicle theft is considered one of the most reliably reported offenses. The most recent National Crime Victimization Survey shows that more than 90% of completed motor vehicle thefts were reported to police in 2010, the highest reporting rate among all crimes. According to the UCR, motor vehicle theft began to decline in 1991 after steadily rising through most of the 1980s. Between 1991 and 2010, motor vehicle theft rates dropped by 64% in the United States. Nearly 740,000 vehicles, one of every 330 registered vehicles, were reported stolen to police in 2010, resulting in an estimated total property loss of $4.5 billion, or an average loss of $6,150 per stolen vehicle. About 56% of the value lost to motor vehicle theft was later recovered. The Federal Bureau of Investigation has reported that the chance of recovery of a stolen vehicle decreases considerably over time. That is, the longer the vehicle is in the possession of offenders or away from the owner, the smaller the chance of recovery.

Automobiles, such as sedans, coupes, station wagons, sport utility vehicles, and minivans, accounted for 73% of all stolen vehicles in 2010, while trucks and buses constituted 17%. However, regional variation exists in the patterns of motor vehicle theft. For example, 86% and 5% of vehicles stolen in the northeastern states were automobiles and trucks/buses, respectively. In the southern states, automobiles made up 65% of stolen vehicles, and trucks and buses constituted 21%. In general, the number of auto thefts is higher in states with more registered vehicles, while the number of truck thefts is higher in states with more trucks on the road. At present, motor vehicle theft rates are the highest in the west (425/100,000 registered vehicles), 1.4 times higher than in the South (305), 1.9 times higher than in the Midwest (225), and 2.3 times higher than in the northeast (187). From 1965 through 1991, however, the northeast had the highest motor vehicle theft rates.

Location and Time

Motor vehicle theft is not evenly distributed throughout the social landscape, but rather, it tends to cluster in certain locations. Official data and victimization surveys indicate that motor vehicle theft rates are as much as four times higher in urban areas than in rural areas. The most common location for this crime is the owner's home (e.g., garage, driveway) or the street near the owner's home, followed by parking lots and garages. However, when taking into account the length of time vehicles are parked, they are at highest risk of theft while parked in public parking lots and at lowest risk while parked in private garages or driveways. Single, ground-level parking lots, large lots with more than 100 stalls, lots without security features, trolley station lots, and lots close to a freeway have been found to be especially susceptible to motor vehicle theft. While the majority of motor vehicle thefts occur at night, motor vehicle thefts in parking lots are more likely to take place during daytime hours than during the nighttime.

Certain types of land uses are also prone to motor vehicle theft. Schools and business districts are found to be susceptible to this crime because they attract large numbers of vehicles and people, some of whom could be offenders. Downtown row-type apartments (those with retail stores on the ground floor), shopping malls, movie theaters, stadiums, and bars are found to have high levels of motor vehicle theft, not only because they attract a large number of people and vehicles but also because these land uses promote more anonymity and less direct supervision by managers and property owners. In addition, areas with more vacant lots and warehouses tend to be at higher risk of theft because of little guardianship provided to the site. Empirical literature has shown that motor vehicle theft rates are higher in low-income neighborhoods and in neighborhoods with a higher percentage of single-family households.

Victims and Vehicles Targeted

Motor vehicle theft tends to be more prevalent with certain people and vehicle models. The National Crime Victimization Survey indicates that households headed by persons less than 20 years of age; headed by African Americans; with an annual income less than $7,500; multiunit dwellings; and households whose residents had lived in their home for less than one year are more likely to be the victims of motor vehicle theft than are other groups. Official data show that young males tend to be the most susceptible to motor vehicle theft.

The risk of theft associated with vehicles varies according to their make, model, and year. In general, older vehicles are most at risk of theft. The most recent indices from the United Kingdom and Australia show that the risk of theft (the number of theft per 1,000 registered vehicles) increases as vehicles become older. For example, vehicles that are 15 years old faced the highest risk of being stolen in the United Kingdom, while vehicles less than 3 years old faced the lowest risk of theft. In Australia, vehicles that were between 20 and 24 years old were most at risk of theft in 2008. Furthermore, vehicles that were more than 9 years old accounted for 78% of all vehicles stolen in Australia, while these vehicles made up 54% of all registered vehicles.

In the United States, older vehicles also constitute the majority of stolen vehicles. According to the National Insurance Crime Bureau, the nation's top 10 most frequently stolen vehicles between 2001 and 2011 were, on average, 14 years old when they were stolen. Specifically, early 1990s Honda Civics, Accords, and Toyota Camrys have continued to dominate the list of the top 10 stolen vehicles since the early 1990s, being among the top three for many years. The vulnerability of old vehicles to theft is found to be associated with their availability, their lack of security, and attractiveness to thieves. For example, as vehicles become older and lose value on the used car market, they are more likely to be owned by people in poor neighborhoods where likely thieves generally reside. Vehicle security also wears out as vehicles age.

While limited in scope, other data sources also illustrate variation in risks among newer vehicle models. According to the National Highway Traffic Safety Administration's theft index, which draws on thefts of car models in the first year of manufacture, in 2009, the Dodge Charger had the highest theft rate among models with more than 10,000 vehicles produced, followed by Mitsubishi Galant, Chrysler 300, and Dodge Avenger. In 2009, the Dodge Charger was about 81 times, 56 times, and 28 times more likely to be stolen than Mercury Mariner, MINI Cooper, and Honda CR-V, respectively. Similarly, data from the Highway Loss Data Institute shows that the 2007 Cadillac Escalade ESV had the highest theft claim rate (calculated as the number of theft claims divided by the number of vehicles insured) between 2005 and 2007, followed by Ford F-250 pickup and Dodge Charger. The Cadillac Escalade ESV theft rate was 26 times higher than Buick Terraza, which had the lowest rate.

Vehicle Thieves

Offenders of motor vehicle theft tend to be young males living in low-income urban neighborhoods, just like their victims. According to the UCR, 83% of those arrested for motor vehicle theft in 2010 were male, 22% were less than the age of 18 (54% were less than 25), and 38% were African Americans. Historically, motor vehicle theft used to be a mundane activity dominated by juvenile joyriders. In 1993, 46% of persons arrested for motor vehicle theft were juvenile, while juveniles made up around 16% of those arrested for all other crimes. The percentage of juvenile arrests for motor vehicle theft dropped to 22% in 2010. Conversely, persons arrested for motor vehicle theft are, increasingly, adult offenders who are more likely than juveniles to be involved in professional theft. The declining rates of recovery of stolen vehicles and clearance over the past decades also indicate an increasing involvement of more skilled and adroit thieves.

Motor vehicle theft is described as a crime that is most likely to involve chronic offenders or repeat offenders. For example, one study found that only 6% of 33,319 offenders accounted for 78% of all vehicle thefts (10,927 thefts). One professional auto thief who had operated a "chop shop" business in California once testified that his auto theft ring, which involved around 40 individuals, was responsible for more than 2,000 auto thefts in a single year. Another study based on interviews with 100 thieves shows that the average number of cars stolen per thief is 45 for those less than 18 years old and 94 for older thieves. About one third of offenders interviewed reported that they had no experience of offenses other than car theft. On the other hand, for those who have committed other crimes, nearly all of them reported that they had reverted to car theft because it was more attractive than other crimes. The most common reason for committing car theft was reported as being the ease of stealing cars. Other reasons included excitement and release from boredom. It was also found that thieves' motivation tended to shift toward financial gains as their criminal career developed.

Motor vehicle theft is considered a debut crime involving the highest risk for the development of chronic criminal career. For example, of those whose first conviction is for auto theft, 55% subsequently become either repeat offenders or chronic offenders who commit nine or more offenses over the course of their criminal career.

Method of Offending

Vehicle thieves are thought to be able to get into a vehicle without a key and drive away within a matter of seconds. Conversely, in many cases, vehicles are left unlocked with the key in the ignition. Hotwiring, which starts the engine by connecting the power and ignition wires, is a classic way to steal vehicles. For less secure vehicles without immobilizers, such as 1980s and 1990s Chevrolet, Ford, Honda, and Toyota models, master keys are available. These keys used to be available online at $25 each with complete instructions. As vehicles are increasingly equipped with new vehicle security systems, especially electronic immobilizers, thieves have to continually develop and employ new ways to defeat those systems.

Transponder systems, the most common immobilizers used worldwide, employ a transponder to activate the immobilization unit, in which case, the car will not start unless a transceiver located near the ignition switch detects a unique signal from the transponder embedded in the key. While some of the techniques used by thieves include modern technology (e.g., rewiring immobilized components or bypassing or cloning a transponder signal), there tend to be rather straightforward ways of circumventing the antitheft devices. For example, electronic immobilizers may be overcome simply by obtaining the vehicle keys. Thieves first obtain the vehicle identification number of vehicles they target and then work with an accomplice at dealerships, who then access their computer system and generate a duplicate key. Thieves may break into a house, steal a vehicle key and drive off in the vehicle located in the driveway, or they may rob a driver to obtain the key or the vehicle itself.

Types of Motor Vehicle Theft

There are many different types of motor vehicle theft, each involving some differences in the modus operandi of the thief, his or her purpose for stealing, the types of vehicles he or she targets, and the types of intervention required. Different factors (e.g., vehicle make and models, their appurtenances and attachments, and their lack of security) are more or less important in different types of motor vehicle theft. It has become common to distinguish temporary and permanent theft measured by recovery status. Temporary theft, where a stolen vehicle is eventually recovered, is a proxy for nonprofessional theft, often committed by amateur (opportunistic) thieves. This includes joyriding, transportation, and use in another crime. Permanent thefts generally mean those thefts where the vehicles are not recovered and those that are most often conducted by professional thieves for economic gain. This includes stripping vehicles for parts, retagging for resale, exporting stolen vehicles, and insurance fraud. It should be noted, however, that particular cases of motor vehicle theft could easily fit into more than one category.

Joyriding offenders, often young males, steal vehicles for fun, thrills, and excitement. For those joyriders, being successful at the crime provides a pleasurable feeling or a sense of accomplishment. It has been estimated that this type of theft accounts for the majority of temporary theft, which constitutes between 70% and 80% of all motor vehicle thefts. These offenders tend to target cars that are easy to steal, familiar cars that they feel comfortable driving, and sporty cars with high performance. Thieves often first target insecure old cars and then move on to sporty/higher performance cars as they gain experience.

Some offenders steal vehicles for a more personal reason: travel. They may steal a car for a quick ride home or to their destination. Natural targets would be vehicles that are widely available and have lower levels of security, such as older cars, because neither the performance nor the monetary value of these vehicles matters to offenders.

Offenders also steal vehicles to commit other crimes, including another vehicle theft, burglary, robbery, and drive-by shootings. By using a stolen car, offenders can conceal their identity while engaging in other crimes. Types of vehicles offenders target depend on types of crimes that they are about to commit. For example, offenders may steal a high-performance car, such as a Honda Civic that can make sharp turns and move at a relatively high speed, to commit robberies and assist in evading police detection. They may steal vans/minivans to transport stolen vehicle parts because these vehicles are suited not only for transporting bulky parts but also for riding with co-offenders.

Some offenders, particularly professional thieves, steal vehicles for their parts, which are then used to replace damaged parts from another vehicle, upgrade a vehicle, or resell. Although opportunistic thieves may engage in this type of theft, stealing minor components or "come across" goods, their involvement is not close to the magnitude of thefts that are committed by professional thieves. Both newer and older vehicles can be targets of this type of theft. Offenders may target newer luxury vehicles that have expensive components (e.g., exotic wheels and tires, headlights, global positioning systems). On the other hand, certain older vehicles are particularly susceptible to theft for their parts, specifically body replacement parts and engines that have compatibility with a wide variety of models and model years as well as great resale value. The demand for stolen parts is greater when legitimate parts are difficult to obtain because of manufacturers ceasing to produce or when replacement parts for a low-value old vehicle are too costly in relation to the value of the vehicle.

Offenders, namely, skilled professional thieves, also steal vehicles and use them to rebuild wrecked ones intended for resale. In other instances, professionals known as retag operators replace vehicle identification numbers of a stolen vehicle with legitimate numbers that can be obtained from a wrecked vehicle of a similar type from insurance auctions or salvage yards. Alternatively, offenders can alter the vehicle identification number using the numbers that are not likely to be listed as stolen and then reregister the revived vehicle with fraudulent documents. Although any type of vehicle can be retagged, vehicles that are in high demand tend to be natural targets.

Some vehicles are stolen to be exported to other countries. In some cases, vehicles stolen in the border areas of the United States, including Arizona, Southern California, and Texas, are exported to Mexico. Consequently, these jurisdictions have low recovery rates of stolen vehicles. Vehicles targeted for this type of theft are generally thought to be relatively new luxury sport utility vehicles or otherwise desirable models that are not readily available in destination countries. However, older vehicles of all types are exported from Miami to Caribbean destinations. Vehicles stolen in the United States and driven to Mexico are often those that are also manufactured and commonly owned in Mexico.

Finally, some cars are stolen to commit insurance fraud. This type of theft occurs when a vehicle owner disposes of or fraudulently reports his vehicle stolen to collect insurance money. To ensure that the vehicle is a write-off, the owner may burn it, submerge it in a lake, or bury it underground. Some owners may arrange to have their vehicle stolen or leave it unprotected in a high-theft area, and others may report the vehicle stolen and hide it for 30 days, which is long enough to settle the claim. Theft for insurance fraud often involves either leased vehicles with high mileage whose turn-in costs are high or purchased vehicles whose owners no longer desire to make the monthly payments.

Shuryo Fujita

See also Larceny; Property Crime

Further readings

Cherbonneau, M., & Wright, R. (2009). Auto theft. In M. Tonry (Ed.), *The Oxford handbook of crime and public policy* (pp. 192–221). New York, NY: Oxford University Press.

Clarke, R. V., & Harris, P. M. (1992). Auto theft and its prevention. In M. Tonry (Ed.), *Crime and justice* (Vol. 16, pp. 1–54). Chicago, IL: University of Chicago Press.

Maxfield, M. G., & Clarke, R. V. (2004). *Understanding and preventing car theft* (Crime Prevention Studies, Vol. 17). Monsey, NY: Criminal Justice Press.

Sallybanks, J., & Brown, R. (1999). *Vehicle crime reduction: Turning the corner* (Police Research Series Paper 199). London, England: Home Office.

National Crime Victimization Survey

The National Crime Victimization Survey (NCVS) is one of the primary sources of data about the nature and extent of crime in the United States. Started in 1973 as the National Crime Survey, the NCVS uses a random sample of households in the United States, and respondents are asked about their experiences as victims of criminal behavior. When compared with the Uniform Crime Reports (UCR; the oldest and best known source of official crime data in the United States), the overall trends reported by the two sources are more alike than they are different (e.g., the "crime drop" of the 1990s was seen in both the UCR and NCVS). The rate of crime estimated by the NCVS is almost always higher than the rate of crime measured by the UCR, because the NCVS includes criminal incidents that may have never been reported to authorities and thus do not appear in official reports. Understanding the methodology of the NCVS is important to understanding its strength as a measure of crime. There are important strengths and weaknesses of the NCVS that should be noted.

An advanced statistical design known as a stratified multistage cluster design is used to select a sample of households that participated in the U.S. Census. This design ensures that the sample includes households from various parts of the United States and that specific households within each geographical area are randomly selected. This approach allows generalizations to be made from the sample to the broader U.S. population. The only requirement for participation once contacted is that respondents need to be at least 12 years old. Because of the size of the NCVS sample (more than 40,000 households in the sample at any given time), the interviews are conducted on a continuing basis throughout the year. Individuals who are selected to participate in the NCVS remain a part of the sample for three years and participate in interviews every six months, for a total of seven interviews (two in person, five over the phone) per individual participant. Each interview focuses on the six months preceding the interview date. Following completion of the final interview, the participant is removed from the survey and a new respondent is selected (using the statistical procedure discussed above) to replace the participant who is removed.

The survey begins with a series of demographic characteristics about the victim (age, race, marital status, level of education, etc.). After answering the demographic questions, respondents are asked whether they have been the victim of certain crimes in the past six months. The NCVS includes questions about various crimes, including robbery, burglary, motor vehicle theft, assault, and rape/sexual assault. A sample question reads, "In the last six months, since [date] was something belonging to you stolen?" If respondents report that they have been victims of any of the crimes that they are asked about, a series of follow-up questions will be asked to gain additional information about each criminal incident. Some of the follow-up questions focus on the incident itself: when it took place, where it took place, and whether witnesses were present. Some of the questions focus solely on the offender(s), for example, whether it was an individual offender or a group, whether the victim knew the offender, whether the offender was armed, and demographic characteristics of the offender (as perceived by the victim). Other questions focus on the victim, for example, whether the victim was injured, whether the victim reported the crime to the police, and whether the victim employed any self-protective strategies during the incident.

Collecting data about these contextual characteristics helps provide a better understanding of criminal behavior. Most important, the crimes that individuals report to the NCVS may have never been reported to the police and therefore are not counted in any official data sources. Speaking directly to victims helps uncover some of these otherwise unknown crimes. The trends of certain types of crimes that are known to be underreported (specifically, rape and sexual assault) are believed to be more accurately recorded by the NCVS than the UCR.

However, not all crimes are included in the NCVS. Because the methodology relies on contact with living victims, homicide is not included in the NCVS. Drug use is also not covered in the survey, because many drug users do not consider themselves "victims" of drug use. Furthermore, there are three primary concerns regarding the accuracy of those criminal incidents that are reported. Because of the fact that respondents are asked to report their own experiences, it is possible that they may be incorrectly identifying an incident as a crime when, in fact, the incident does not meet the legal criteria necessary to be considered as a crime. It is also possible, despite the fact that their responses are confidential, that respondents are too embarrassed or otherwise unwilling to share victimization experiences that they may have had. This concern is especially relevant if the victim has an intimate or personal relationship with the offender. Finally, it is possible that respondents report criminal incidents that they have actually experienced but that took place more than six months prior to the interview. Although these are shortcomings to the NCVS, the overall picture of crime painted by the NCVS is believed to be a useful indicator of crime in the United States.

Sarah Koon-Magnin

See also Crime Statistics; Quantitative Methods in Studying Deviance; Uniform Crime Reports; Violent Crime

Further Readings

Cantor, D., & Lynch, J. P. (2005). Exploring the effects of changes in design on the analytical uses of the NCVS data. *Journal of Quantitative Criminology, 21*(3), 293–319.

Catalano, S. (2006). *The measurement of crime: Victim reporting and police recording*. New York, NY: LFB Scholarly.

Lynch, J. P., & Addington, L. A. (2007). *Understanding crime statistics: Revisiting the divergence of the NCVS and the UCR*. New York, NY: Cambridge University Press.

U.S. Department of Justice, Bureau of Justice Statistics. (2010). *National Crime Victimization Survey, 2010* (Collection Year Record-Type Files). Ann Arbor, MI: Inter-university Consortium for Political and Social Research.

NATIONAL INCIDENT-BASED REPORTING SYSTEM

The National Incident-Based Reporting System (NIBRS) is a federally operated criminal database listing incident-level offenses reported by local, state, tribal, territorial, and federal law enforcement agencies annually. Before the creation of NIBRS, the Federal Bureau of Investigation's (FBI) Uniform Crime Reports (UCR) provided the only nationwide statistics for criminal offenses. UCR limitations include inaccessibility to more incident-level characteristics of crime, hierarchical crime reporting, and limited victim and offender information. In 1982, a research initiative was begun to address UCR limitations, which resulted in the development of NIBRS to expand the UCR database by allowing for the reporting of incident-level crime characteristics. Between 1992 and 1995, the implementation of the NIBRS database became official. To become certified to report crime data, states are required to participate in a preliminary testing phase in NIBRS. Once the requirements set forth for participation are met, the agency/state is deemed NIBRS certified. Being NIBRS certified means the incident-based data submitted during the NIBRS certification process was consistent with FBI UCR Program standards.

By 1995, 9 states had become certified to report crime data, and by 1999, 18 states had completed the certification process. It is important to note that not all law enforcement agencies within an NIBRS-certified state will necessarily report criminal incidents to the FBI, since participation is voluntary. Much of the data required for NIBRS are already collected at the agency level by officers preparing incident and arrest reports. However, data extracted from such reports for NIBRS are more detailed and, therefore, require increased time for data entry and data processing. NIBRS reporting is still going through developmental stages in uncertified states, while a few states show no intention of reporting to NIBRS.

As of June 2012, 32 states were certified and 15 states were submitting incident-based data covering 100% of their state agencies. In addition, 7 states or territories were in the developmental phases, 7 states were in the testing phase, and 6 states had no formalized plan to report incident-based data. Although NIBRS is not representative of crime in the United States, it covers approximately 29% of the population, representing 27% of the nation's reported crime and 43% of law enforcement agencies. As of 2013, NIBRS represents the most detailed criminal database available. A complete listing of states and the number of participating agencies can be found on the Justice Research and Statistics Association's website: http://www.jrsa.org/ibrrc/background-status/nibrs_states.shtml.

Content

The accumulated NIBRS database for all years contains tens of millions of cases and continues to grow at an accelerating rate as the coverage of the U.S. population expands. The 2010 NIBRS, for example, added approximately 5 million criminal incidents that were voluntarily provided by participating law enforcement agencies to the total files. Information available through NIBRS is gathered and classified primarily by crime type and contains case-specific incident numbers, as well as state, county, and city information. This identifier information can be used to run analyses specific to various community levels including states, cities or Metropolitan Statistical Areas, counties, and regions. NIBRS data contains six data segments. These include administrative, offense, victim, offender, property, and arrestee data. In total, 57 data elements are captured in this process. Group A incident data are reported within 22 offense categories constituting 46 specific crimes. Additionally, there are 11 Group B crime categories, which are specific to arrest information. Examples of Group A offenses include arson, assault, burglary, drug/narcotic offenses, homicide, kidnapping, and

sex offenses. Group B offenses include, but are not limited to, disorderly conduct, drunkenness, voyeurism, runaway, and trespassing. Specific details of each incident such as weapon used, location of incident, and demographic information on victims, offenders, and arrestees are some examples of data available in NIBRS.

Strengths and Limitations

NIBRS was implemented to provide law enforcement agencies with information that could be used to identify when and where crime takes place, what form it takes, and the characteristics of victims and perpetrators. NIBRS is capable of delivering such incident-based data due to the detailed incident submissions, which differ greatly from the summary data made available from its predecessor system, the UCR. Since its initial implementation, NIBRS has continued to develop through definitional alterations and amendments. Included in these changes are new offense definitions, new UCR offense codes, the creation of a new crime category (crimes against society), and the elimination of the hierarchy rule. Furthermore, compared with the UCR, NIBRS offers the ability to determine the victim-to-offender relationship for additional offense categories, correlations among variables (e.g., offense, property, victims, offenders, and arrestees), whether an offense was attempted or completed, and additional offense circumstances. Therefore, NIBRS is capable of producing more detailed, accurate, and meaningful data than those produced by the UCR.

As with any database, NIBRS comes with limitations. As previously mentioned, NIBRS is not a nationally represented sample. Since law enforcement agencies report on a voluntary basis, the amount of information can vary from year to year. NIBRS provides participating agencies with a multitude of data entry options, but it is up to the reporting agency to completely fill in these categories. Owing to this discrepancy, not all data may be entered into the database. Additionally, as NIBRS is an expansive database, it may be cumbersome for new users. Tasks, such as merging database segments, rely on the understanding of which primary keys should be used depending on what data from which segments are being combined.

Regardless of these limitations, NIBRS offers the most comprehensive source of criminal incident data. As the database is still expanding, it is difficult to describe all the potential benefits to eventually come from its implementation. Its ability to capture specific incident-level data makes it a database that surpasses the abilities of the UCR. NIBRS data are made available through the Interuniversity Consortium for Political and Social Research's website: http://www.icpsr.umich.edu/icpsrweb/landing.jsp.

James C. McCutcheon, Melissa J. Tetzlaff-Bemiller,
and Mindy Weller

See also Crime Statistics; Uniform Crime Reports

Further Readings

Addington, L. (2010). Studying the crime problem with NIBRS data: Current uses and future trends. In M. D. Krohn, A. J. Lizotte, & G. P. Hall (Eds.), *Handbook on crime and deviance* (pp. 23–42). New York, NY: Springer.

Akiyama, Y., & Nolan, J. (1999). Methods for understanding and analyzing NIBRS. *Journal of Quantitative Criminology, 15*(2), 225–238.

Chilton, R., & Jarvis, J. (1999). Using the National Incident-Based Reporting System (NIBRS) to test estimates of arrestee and offender characteristics. *Journal of Quantitative Criminology, 15*(2), 207–224.

Federal Bureau of Investigation. (n.d.). *National Incident-Based Reporting System (NIBRS): General information.* Retrieved from http://www2.fbi.gov/ucr/faqs.htm

NATIONAL SURVEY OF DRUG USE AND HEALTH

The National Survey of Drug Use and Health (NSDUH), formerly the National Household Survey of Drug Abuse, is the most comprehensive data set measuring substance use and treatment in the United States. The NSDUH is funded and compiled by the United States Department of Health and Human Services, Substance Abuse and Mental Health Services Administration, Office of Applied Studies. The NSDUH is a nationally representative, cross-sectional survey, aimed at estimating the prevalence and incidence of drug, tobacco, and alcohol use by persons 12 years and older in the United States. To date, the NSDUH is the federal government's primary source of information on drug use in the United States. Each year, the survey recruits approximately 70,000 individuals and administers questions concerning the recency and

frequency of use and attitudes toward the use of alcohol, tobacco, and drugs. The NSDUH also collects data on substance abuse treatment history, perceived need for treatment, and mental health services utilization.

The NSDUH's target population includes noninstitutionalized individuals; residents of households, shelters, and dormitories; and civilians residing in military bases. To gain a representative sample, the NSDUH survey employs a multistage, 50-state sampling technique. The first stage of selection begins with the construction of a sample frame for each census tract in the population. The second stage of sampling consists of dividing the census tracts into smaller segments. After segments are selected, the third stage of selection consists of selecting households within each segment. Finally, individuals are selected within households based on the age-group composition of the household residents.

First administered in 1971, the NSDUH was initially developed in response to the same 1970 legislation that created the national Commission on Marijuana and Drug Abuse. This commission is responsible for measuring and reporting the extent of illicit drug use to the U.S. Congress and the president. During the 1970s and 1980s, the survey was collected sporadically, every two to three years. Due to an increase in demand for data, and additional funding support for the measurement of substance use in the United States, the survey began to be conducted on an annual basis, increased its sample size, and widened its scope of questions. The NSDUH has also been modified over the years to represent current trends in drug use and drug-using behavior. For example, in 1982, questions were added to the survey to measure the recreational use of prescription medications, in 1985, the survey adopted questions related to tobacco use and the various ways that cocaine can be administered, and in 1988, questions were included about the use of crack cocaine.

The NSDUH has always been conducted using face-to-face interview techniques at the respondent's home; however, the mode of administration has changed drastically over the years. Prior to 1999, the NSDUH was conducted using paper-and-pencil interviewing. At that time, the survey consisted of a questionnaire booklet completed by an interviewer and a set of individual answer sheets completed by a respondent. All sensitive questions, including those related to substance use and treatment, appeared on answer sheets, which allowed the respondent some privacy in answering sensitive questions. Less sensitive questions were asked aloud by the interviewer and recorded in the questionnaire booklet.

Since 1999, interviewers have adopted the use of handheld computers to assist with data collection. To ensure confidentiality, questions about substance use and mental health are now completed as a computer-assisted interview in which information is obtained through computer audio interviewing technology. Less sensitive questions are completed through an in-person computer-assisted interview in which interviewers verbally ask questions and record respondents' answers using the handheld computer. The methodological changes began in 1999 and were fully implemented by 2002. Although these changes have ultimately made the survey more accurate, data collected prior to 2002 cannot be accurately compared with the data collected before these changes were implemented.

The NSDUH's greatest advantage is the representativeness of its sample. To date, the NSDUH is the most comprehensive and representative survey of the U.S. population measuring substance use. Data gathered through the NSDUH is used to inform a variety of policy decisions affecting both public and private institutions. The U.S. government uses the data to measure the effectiveness of the National Drug Control Policy and to measure the extent to which administration has been successful in reducing illicit drug use and addressing barriers to treatment. Additionally, NSDUH data are used by government at the state and local levels to identify areas of need and to develop treatment programs aimed specifically at populations where the need is greatest. Finally, data from the NSDUH are used by funding institutions and universities to develop research and intervention strategies to treat and prevent substance use. In general, the NSDUH is an excellent source for data examining the prevalence and incidence of drug use in the U.S. population. However, one criticism of the NSDUH is that it may underestimate the use of more serious drugs, such as heroin and cocaine. This underestimation is due to its sampling design, which excludes individuals who are likely to experience serious drug problems, such as individuals in prisons and homeless individuals. Despite possible underrepresentation of these populations, the NSDUH remains the most accurate measure of drug use in the United States available to date.

Kristi L. Stringer

See also Drug Abuse Warning Network; Monitoring the Future; National Youth Survey

Further Readings

Kennet, J., & Gfroerer, J. (Eds.). (2005). *Evaluating and improving methods used in the National Survey on Drug Use and Health* (DHHS Publication No. SMA 05–4044, Methodology Series M-5). Rockville, MD: Substance Abuse and Mental Health Services Administration, Office of Applied Studies.

Substance Abuse and Mental Health Services Administration. (2011). *Results from the 2010 National Survey on Drug Use and Health: Summary of national findings* (NSDUH Series H-41, HHS Publication No. SMA 11–4658). Rockville, MD: Author.

NATIONAL YOUTH SURVEY

The National Youth Survey (NYS) used a multiple cohort sequential design to collect 10 waves of data from 1976 to 2002. The study was subsequently expanded to become the National Youth Survey Family Study (NYSFS) with the inclusion of additional family members in surveys conducted in 2003 and 2004. The NYS and the NYSFS have collected self-reports of legal and illegal and deviant and nondeviant behavior, plus related sociodemographic characteristics, attitudes and beliefs, and patterns of interaction in social contexts such as the family, school, and work, on a national probability sample of individuals who were adolescents in the mid-1970s, plus their spouses, parents, and children in the early 2000s. NYS and NYSFS data have been used to examine the distribution and correlates of crime and deviance, ranging from minor thefts, minor assaults, sexual behavior, and status offenses to serious assaults (including partner violence), serious property offenses, marijuana and other illicit drug use, and to test theories of crime and deviance, including an integrated theory that combined elements of strain, control, and learning (and later social disorganization) theories. The NYS and NYSFS have also been used to examine patterns of criminal victimization, including physical abuse and other forms of victimization, in adolescence and adulthood and the consequences of adolescent victimization on adult outcomes. Most recently, they have been used to examine molecular genetic relationships with substance use and antisocial behavior and to study both life course developmental and intergenerational variations in delinquent, deviant, and criminal behavior.

Survey Design, Participation, and Retention Rates

The original survey sample was based on a probability sample of households in the continental United States selected using a multistage cluster sampling design. The sample was drawn in late 1976 and contained 2,360 eligible youth respondents between ages 11 and 17 at the time of the initial interview. Of these, 1,725 (73%) agreed to participate in the study and were interviewed in 1977. One parent (usually the mother) of each of these youth respondents was also interviewed in this first wave. Retention rates over Waves 2 to 4 (collected 1978–1980) were more than 94%, 87% for Waves 5 (1981) and 6 (1984), 80% for Wave 7 (1987), 83% for Wave 8 (1990), and 78% for Wave 9 (1993).

In Wave 10 (2002), the original respondents were again interviewed, and family data were collected to help locate and interview their surviving parents, current spouses or partners, and adolescent and adult children for subsequent waves of the NYSFS. Additional deaths among the respondents were identified during the Waves 10 to 12 data collection, reducing the total eligible sample (including hard refusals) to 1,677. Of these 1,677, a total of 1,266 or 75% were interviewed in Wave 10 and 1,173 or 70% in Wave 11. In Waves 11 (2003) and 12 (2004), attempts were made to identify eligible (living and in sufficient physical and mental health to complete an interview) spouses and partners, parents, and children of the original respondents. Of the known eligible parents, spouses, and children, in Wave 11, a total of 881 or 71% of the parents, 679 or 71% of current spouses or partners of the original respondents, 802 or 77% of their adolescent children (age 11 to 17 years), and 464 or 66% of their 707 adult children (age 18 and above) were interviewed. In Wave 12, only the children of the original respondents were interviewed; of the known eligible respondents, 815 or 78% of the adolescent children and 491 or 70% of the adult children were interviewed.

Representativeness, Reliability, and Validity

Repeated age, sex, and race comparisons between nonparticipating eligible youth and participating youth indicated that NYSFS respondents appeared to be representative of the total 11- through 17-year-old youth population in the United States as established by the U.S. Census Bureau for 1976 and continued to be representative in subsequent years. NYSFS participation and attrition rates appear reasonable in comparison with other surveys, particularly in light of substantial increases over time in rates of nonresponse and refusal to participate in surveys, both in the United States and internationally. Analyses of the effects of attrition suggest that the level of attrition in the NYSFS has little or no impact on substantive findings. While questions have been raised concerning the possibility that there are panel conditioning, testing, or maturation effects in NYS measures of crime and victimization, it appears that the variation in the results for different offenses is less consistent with panel conditioning than with real period trends that vary by offense.

Tests of reliability and validity of NYS data indicated that test–retest reliabilities over a 4-week interval were about 70% to 90% for the self-reported offending *items* in the total sample, and test–retest reliability for *scales* involving serious crime was .81 to .99. Reliability is better for low-frequency offenders than high-frequency offenders; the pattern of the difference suggests that high-frequency offenders simply do not remember each of their many separate offenses with the same accuracy that low-frequency offenders remember each of their few offenses. There also appears to be memory loss associated with length of recall; recall periods of more than one year produce substantially lower rates of offending than one-year recall periods. Analysis to determine whether trivial events were being included in the reporting of serious offending found that approximately two thirds of the felony assault and felony theft items and all the hard drug sales items were appropriate and nontrivial, according to respondents' reports of details on follow-up questions about these incidents. For minor assault, by contrast, more than half of the items reported were considered trivial (unlikely to provoke an official response, even if they are technically illegal). Overall, the NYS/NYSFS results have suggested that self-reports can provide reliable and valid data on deviant and criminal behavior, and the NYS has been used as a model for other self-report data collection efforts, including the International Self-Report Delinquency Study.

Scott Menard

See also Delinquency; Integrated Theories; Self-Report Surveys

Further Readings

Elliott, D. S., Huizinga, D., & Ageton, S. S. (1985). *Explaining delinquency and drug use.* Beverly Hills, CA: Sage.

Elliott, D. S., Huizinga, D., & Menard, S. (1989). *Multiple problem youth: Delinquency, substance use, and mental health problems.* New York, NY: Springer-Verlag.

Menard, S. (2012). Age, criminal victimization, and offending: Changing relationships from adolescence to middle adulthood. *Victims and Offenders, 7,* 227–254.

Menard, S., & Elliott, D. S. (1993). Data set comparability and short-term trends in crime and delinquency. *Journal of Criminal Justice, 21,* 433–445.

Menard, S., Morris, R. G., Gerber, J., & Covey, H. C. (2011). Distribution and correlates of self-reported crimes of trust. *Deviant Behavior, 32,* 877–914.

NECROPHILIA

Necrophilia involves sexual intercourse with a corpse. It comes from the Greek words *nekros* (meaning dead body) and *philia* (meaning love or friendship). Psychiatrists classify it as a paraphilia, which involves sexual arousal to an object that is not a part of standard stimulation. In some instances, violators murder a victim and subsequently engage in sexual activity with the dead body. Arousal related to necrophilia can come from simply viewing a dead body. It may also occur when a necrophiliac visits a social context associated with dead bodies. This includes funeral homes and cemeteries.

History of Necrophilia

In ancient Egypt, officials would keep fresh corpses from embalmers, fearing they would exploit the dead bodies sexually. Historically, various legends involve necrophilia. King Herod, who ruled a dynasty in Palestine during the time of Jesus, allegedly had sex with his wife for seven years after her death. Reflecting current pop culture on vampires, there has always been a cultural attraction to the mythology of a dead bloodsucker penetrating the living with his fangs in a bodily fluid–extracting frenzy. However, this is the opposite of necrophilia, which involves a living person victimizing the dead. Ideas on cannibalism imply that eating the body of the dead transmits life power to the consumer. In some instances, eating humans carries a sexual tone. Popular fairy tales even reflect necrophiliac desires.

Consider themes associated with the story of Snow White or Sleeping Beauty. The desire to have sex with a partner who is sleeping is somnophilia, a condition some researchers link to necrophilia.

Forms of Necrophilia

Necrophiliacs tend to be intelligent males with otherwise normal personalities, with a mean reporting age of 34 years. Around 80% are heterosexual, 13% bisexual, and the remaining homosexual. Victims are typically female. Similar to sexual deviants who engage in telephone sex, scholars believe most necrophiliacs experience discomfort and rejection from females in whom they have a sexual interest. Still desiring sexual contact, necrophiliacs substitute a corpse for a living sexual partner. Since the corpse is not a willing participant, analysts characterize the sexual contact as an act of masturbation. Three varieties of necrophiliacs exist. Not all involve firsthand contact with a corpse.

The pseudonecrophiliac merely has an attraction to corpses but never engages in sexual contact with them. They typically only go as far as acting out fantasies based on corpse-related sexual gratification. For example, a pseudonecrophiliac might ask a living partner to dress in funeral-related attire, apply cosmetics to the skin to simulate the appearance of a dead body, or lie still during sexual activity, since movement has a tendency to decrease sexual arousal. Some pseudonecrophiliacs enjoy it when partners take cold showers to remove the typical level of body heat given off by a living person. Research implies that pseudonecrophilia relates to extreme forms of sadism. The sadist enjoys giving pain to sexual partners and having elevated amounts of social control during sexual encounters. Forcing a partner to play the dead role may be the ultimate form of sadism. Studies show that 78% of necrophiliacs have previously engaged in sadist sexual practices. Some scholars classify people who murder others and then have sex with them as pseudonecrophiliacs. However, this rests on the condition that the perpetrator did not have a chronic desire for sex with the dead but just spontaneously took an opportunity to do so.

The genuine, or regular, necrophiliac follows the standard model of someone who engages in sexual encounters with the dead. To feed their preoccupation, some seek employment in areas that provide them with high levels of access to corpses. Reflective of routine activity theory, elevated access paired with necrophiliac motivation, low supervision, and non-responsive targets allows regular necrophiliacs to flourish in occupations related to morgues, funeral homes, and medical examiner work.

The third type of necrophiliac is the necrosadistic offender. This form murders with the intent of having sex with the victim postmortem. Often mutilation of the corpse occurs. Analysts believe mutilating the corpse provides a sense of psychological ease for the necrosadistic offender. It lowers the symbolic worth of the body and reduces it to something less than human. This objectification increases a necrosadistic offender's comfort with the process while simultaneously permitting arousal. The sex with the corpse is more important than the homicide. The pleasure is not in the killing as much as it is with the sexual contact occurring afterward. Cases exist where people with necrosadistic tendencies kill animals to have sex. In some of those cases, this practice is a precursor to the killing of a human for sexual purposes.

Legal Aspects

The legal system connects a variety of famous killers, from Ted Bundy to Jeffery Dahmer, to aspects of necrophilia. This creates the perception that necrophilia is clearly against the law, but that is not the case. For example, recently in Wisconsin, three young males attempted to dig up the body of a deceased girl to have sex with her. Prosecutors initially pushed for sexual assault charges; however, defense attorneys pointed out that the dead body was not a victim but merely an object since she was not living. Prosecutors moved forward with theft and property damage charges. However, the Wisconsin Supreme Court shortly thereafter ruled sex with a corpse does fall under legal provisions and overturned the lower court ruling. Although necrophilia-related cases such as this are rare, recent legal cases imply that pornography on the Internet can prime a pseudonecrophiliac for future actions involving physical harm to others. Most individuals have the ability to distinguish reality from fantasy when viewing such material. However, necrophiliacs suffering from other psychological problems may lack that ability.

Jason S. Ulsperger

See also Animal Cruelty; Bondage and Discipline; Cybersex; Pedophilia; Phone Sex; Routine Activity Theory; Sadism and Masochism

Further Readings

Aggrawal, A. (2011). *Necrophilia: Forensic and medico-legal aspects*. Boca Raton, FL: CRC Press.

Burg, B. R. (1982). The sick and the dead: The development of psychological theory on necrophilia from Krafft-Ebing to the President. *Journal of the History of Behavioral Sciences, 18*, 242–254.

Laws, D. R., & O'Donohue, W. T. (2008). *Sexual deviance: Theory, assessment, and treatment*. New York, NY: Guilford Press.

Rosman, J., & Resnick, P. (1989). Sexual attraction to corpses: A psychiatric review of necrophilia. *Bulletin of the American Academy of Psychiatry and the Law, 17*, 153–163.

Neutralization Theory

In the 1950s, the criminologists Gresham Sykes and David Matza sought to explain how juveniles who commit delinquent acts are able to do so while still accepting conventional social values and norms. They concluded that juveniles would be able to commit such acts only if they could temporarily overcome their sense of a moral obligation to obey the law by using one or more of the mental techniques of *neutralization*, mechanisms to block the potential guilt and negative self-image associated with violating social norms. By using these techniques, individuals could engage in criminal behavior and still maintain a positive self-concept.

Techniques of Neutralization

According to neutralization theory, juveniles who commit delinquent acts overcome the demands for conformity by learning how to neutralize society's norms and values prior to violating them. In so doing, delinquents redefine their behavior to make it acceptable. Even though the juveniles know that delinquency is essentially bad, they later claim that their criminal behavior was justified or excused based on one of the neutralization techniques. In their original article, citing interviews with offenders, Sykes and Matza identify five techniques of neutralization. These include (1) *denial of responsibility*, (2) *denial of injury*, (3) *denial of the victim*, (4) *condemnation of the condemners*, and (5) *appeal to higher loyalties*. While there may be five techniques of neutralization, not all five may be used. There may be different variations of techniques that could be used, based on individual traits and on the nature of delinquent act. Therefore, certain techniques could be more crime specific. While the original techniques were discussed in the context of an investigation of juvenile delinquency, other scholars later tested the theory with various offenders such as white-collar criminals, street offenders, rapists, and identity thieves.

Denial of Responsibility

Juveniles can deny responsibility for delinquent acts by claiming that they were not in control of their actions or that what happened was an accident. The delinquent can even go so far as to place blame on their environment, their peers, or their parents. By not accepting responsibility, the individual sees himself or herself more as a victim than as a delinquent. As a result, the juvenile is able to accept the delinquent act and denounce society's conventional moral beliefs without feeling remorse.

Denial of Injury

The next technique focuses on the results of the delinquent act as it is related to injury or harm toward others. While juveniles do not always fully understand the consequences of their delinquency, they still evaluate the "wrongness" of their actions. When using this technique, juveniles attempt to justify their actions based on whether or not anyone was directly hurt by their actions. An individual may see graffiti as not hurting anyone because it was only vandalism and no one was physically hurt. Similarly, embezzlers contend that they were not stealing but merely borrowing the misappropriated money. Although individuals accept responsibility for their actions, they use the technique to justify their actions on the grounds that no one was hurt.

Denial of Victim

In contrast to denial of injury, this technique is used when the individual is aware that there *is* a victim and *accepts* responsibility. However, in this situation, when the delinquent inflicts injury, it is not seen as wrong because the individual believes that it is justified. The juvenile's rationale is that he or she believes that the other person deserved the injury. It could be perceived as a righteous retaliation toward someone (e.g., for a punishment from a parent or teacher). Denial of victim can be divided into four categories: (1) close foes: individuals who have directly injured them; (2) those who engage in deviant behavior (e.g., homosexuals, drunkards);

(3) members of groups with tribal stigmas (racial and ethnic minorities); and (4) distant foes: politicians and remote authority figures. Consequently, individuals who claim this technique do so, because they feel that their victims "had it coming to them" based on the victim's perceived conduct or social status. They may perceive the other person or institution as the wrongdoer who thus "deserved what they got."

Condemnation of the Condemners

In using this technique, the individual admits to the delinquent act but attempts to justify the behavior as being acceptable because others also commit the same or even worse acts. Here, juveniles state that they are not the only ones committing the delinquent act, and furthermore, others are not caught and punished for similar acts or are even praised for such acts. Therefore, they attempt to shift the focus from their own delinquency to others who commit the same delinquency. By questioning why they are being condemned when compared with others, they attempt to illustrate how their delinquency is acceptable since "everyone is doing it." They feel as if they are "being singled out" or "being made an example of" for something that is common among their peers.

Appeal to Higher Loyalties

The last technique discussed by Sykes and Matza is the appeal to higher loyalties. The individual understands that his or her activity is wrong; however, the individual excuses and justifies his or her actions in an attempt to reduce feelings of guilt or shame on the basis of his or her motivation: namely, because it served the purpose of a group (or sometimes an individual) to whom they owe allegiance. The individual feels forced to make a decision: either break a law or reject his or her allegiance to the group. Some individuals claim that they "had to do it" for their friends, or their gang. This behavior reflects the need of juveniles to seek attachment and a sense of belonging, as reflected in such statements as "I didn't want to chicken out" or "I didn't want to rat on a friend."

In addition to the original five techniques of neutralization, others have introduced and expanded neutralization theory. Over the years, other scholars have made contributions to neutralization theory by suggesting other justifications and excuses such as the metaphor of the ledger, defense of necessity, justification by comparison, the claim of entitlement, and the claim of normality.

Causal Order

Sykes and Matza argued that while some juveniles are committed to delinquency, they are also able to retain a commitment to conventional society and its standards of behavior. They presume that delinquents knew right from wrong while committing the delinquent act. Moreover, most juveniles believe in the dominant value system of society. In fact, if juveniles are asked about their delinquency, they would readily admit that their delinquent acts are wrong. By this account, if juveniles could not justify or excuse their delinquency, thereby reducing guilt, they would not engage in it. It is important to note that these techniques of neutralization are often made before the individual commits the delinquent act so that the individual can free himself or herself of guilt and/or shame.

There have been numerous empirical studies of techniques of neutralization and criminal activity; however, much of this research has been criticized for not properly taking temporal order into account. This research has found it difficult to establish what happens cognitively prior to an individual committing a crime. Researchers are often not present when an individual decides to commit a crime; therefore, most previous research has only investigated their decision making after the criminal activity has occurred. As a result, causal order is difficult to identify.

Moreover, neutralizations do not always occur, nor do all neutralization techniques have to be used by everyone who commits a crime. Research has shown that each person may or may not fully accept the neutralization technique. Some scholars argue that if the individual accepts more neutralization techniques, he or she will participate in more criminal activity than those who do not accept neutralizing beliefs. Additionally, just because neutralizations are not present, it does not mean that they were not used at some point by the individual. Consequently, neutralizations could occur prior, during, or after criminal acts and could possibly act as rationalizations for future criminal acts. This rationalization could contribute to a hardening process, potentially leading in turn to future criminal acts. The use of neutralization techniques over a prolonged period can eventually result in a diminished need to use them to reduce feelings of guilt. In essence, prolonged exposure to criminal activity reduces the chance of the individual feeling guilty.

Techniques of neutralizations could be necessary for certain offenders and not others. Therefore, neutralizations are used more often when an individual has a strong belief that a criminal activity would violate his or her own moral convictions. So if the individual does not have any strong moral convictions or strong agreement to society's moral beliefs, then techniques of neutralizations would not be necessary. Essentially, the extent to which the techniques of neutralization are used are based on the individual's level of commitment to conventional values and norms.

Conclusion

Sykes and Matza do not state that delinquents fully renounce their allegiance to conventional norms and morals. Instead, they argue that delinquents do acknowledge conventional norms and morals but claim that their delinquent acts are based on extenuating circumstances and are therefore justified and excused. When delinquents believe statements such as "They had it coming to them," "I didn't mean to do it," or "I didn't do it for myself," they are using techniques of neutralization to denounce their feelings of regret, guilt, and shame, thereby preparing themselves to commit the delinquent act. According to Sykes and Matza, many juvenile offenders *do* appear to feel regret, guilt, and shame for their delinquent acts; however, they use techniques of neutralization to temporarily deflect their own internalized feelings and beliefs by justifying and excusing their actions.

In the end, there may not be an adequate way to solve the causal order problem of neutralization theory, since decision making occurs at the same time as the criminal activity. There is a need to understand why some techniques of neutralization are used more frequently for certain types of crimes and not others. Therefore, further research is needed to grasp a better understanding of the constructs of the techniques as they relate to juvenile offenders' relationship to a system of beliefs and attitudes.

Arthur G. Vasquez

See also Accounts, Sociology of; Control Theory; Differential Association Theory

Further Readings

Maruna, S., & Copes, H. (2005). What have we learned from five decades of neutralization research? *Crime and Justice, 32,* 221–320.

Minor, W. W. (1981). Techniques of neutralization: A reconceptualization and empirical examination. *Journal of Research in Crime and Delinquency, July,* 295–318.

Scully, D., & Marolla, J. (1984). Convicted rapists' vocabulary of motive: Excuses and justifications. *Social Problems, 31,* 530–544.

Sykes, G. M., & Matza, D. (1957). Techniques of neutralization: A theory of delinquency. *American Sociological Review, 22,* 664–670.

Topalli, V. (2006). The seductive nature of autotelic crime: How neutralization theory serves as a boundary condition for understanding hardcore street offending. *Sociological Inquiry, 76*(4), 475–501.

NORMAL DEVIANCE

Deviance is a violation of the social norms, the consequence of which is societal disapproval or censure against the rule breaker or the behavior. Historically, there has been disagreement among sociologists concerning how to use the term accurately. Additionally, public perceptions about what constitutes deviant behaviors or situations further complicate researchers' abilities to develop meaningful, acceptable, and workable definitions.

Sociological theories of deviance usually emphasize how social structures and social environments exert strain on people pressuring them to engage in deviant behaviors. Émile Durkheim's early theory of deviance argues that since deviant behavior is present in all societies, it must fulfill some needs of the society for its survival. According to Durkheim, the deviant actor serves a positive role in society by helping define and publicize laws and social rules for others, thus creating social cohesion. The deviant individual functions as an outsider, someone whom the collective members of society can react against. Such reaction can lead to social change, ultimately providing a positive function in every society. Durkheim, along with American proponents of social disorganization theory, viewed the rapid social changes in society as a variable central to rates of deviance.

Proponents of symbolic interactionism, tracing their approach to the writings of the University of Chicago philosopher George Herbert Mead, stress the interpretive adjustment of humans to the real or imagined reactions of others, interpreting or defining others' actions instead of merely reacting to them. The reaction theorist Howard Becker asserts that a given act cannot be assumed to be deviant simply because it is commonly regarded as such. Researchers must observe the process by which that common definition arises—labeling. Becker's approach evaluates behaviors through (a) the concrete interactions between labelers and the potential targets of labeling and (b) the historical construction of labels themselves. Deviant labels emerge as the product of enterprise and conflict and are designated by groups with the social position and power to enforce rules, whether legal or otherwise. Described as *moral entrepreneurs,* these politically and socially powerful entities describe deviance through a society's political struggles within government, between interest groups, in the media, among social scientists, in law enforcement, and among those labeled deviant.

Becker's model of deviance unfolds over time, with patterns of behavior developing in sequence, such as what might be seen in the progressive stages by which an individual becomes a deviant drug user. At each stage of the process, the potential deviant experiences myriad social forces that influence whether or not there is an advance into further nonconformity. In the case of the deviant drug user, such forces might include availability of drugs, the environment in which to use drugs, access to money for drugs, and the associates with whom to use—all social factors contributing to the individual's increasing deviance.

People may initially deviate for biological, psychological, or sociological reasons. Gagnon and Simon, in their research on human sexuality during the 1960s, strayed from the traditionally biological and behavioral view of human sexuality and sexual deviance popularized by Sigmund Freud and Alfred Kinsey and approached their subject from a sociological perspective. Writing initially on the cusp of the 1960s "sexual revolution," and during a period of second-wave feminism (during debates about sexual violence, pornography, and women's sexuality) and Stonewall (the symbolic start of a global gay and lesbian movement), Gagnon and Simon took a constructionist approach to human sexuality, identifying three categories of sexual deviance: normal, pathological, and sociological. Borrowing heavily from the social critic and philosopher Kenneth Burke, who described humans as symbol-using creatures, the authors viewed human sexuality as language, symbol, and metaphor, making sexuality different from that of the world of other animals.

From Erving Goffman, they borrowed the concept of *scripting*, identifying sexual life as dramatic, performed, improvised, and created through interpretation and presentation.

Like Mead, Gagnon and Simon saw human sexuality as located in the worlds of self, shared communications, significations, and significant others. For Gagnon and Simon, human sexuality and sexual deviance could not be limited to biological urges; they must be examined within the broader context of interactional and cultural–historical realms.

Normal sexual deviance, as described by Gagnon and William Simon, occurs often, across cultures globally, and among large numbers of people. Behaviors labeled as normal sexual deviance include oral sex, masturbation, premarital sex, and extra-marital sex—normal because of their widespread practice and generally low social visibility. Only few people are sanctioned for practicing these behaviors. In fact, statistically speaking, normal sexual deviant behaviors are fairly standard and must be considered within a broader, socially constructed domain. For example, is masturbation a response to sexual deprivation or to a stressful day? Is sexual intercourse outside of marriage a perceived means to a better career?

Thus, according to Gagnon and Simon, there is no "essential" sexuality that is biologically based and separate from the social. Nor are there any permanent significant truths about sexuality or sexual deviance. The study of sexual deviance must always be grounded with wider cultural and social forces. Human sexualities are always socially produced, organized, maintained, and transformed through economic, religious, political, familial, and social conditions.

Margot Hasha and DeAnn Kalich

See also Masturbation; Norms and Societal Expectations; Premarital Sex; Symbolic Interactionism

Further Readings

Durkheim, É. (1966). *The rules of sociological method.* New York, NY: Free Press.

Gagnon, J. H., & Simon, W. (1967). *Sexual deviance.* New York, NY: Harper & Row.

Gagnon, J. H., & Simon, W. (2009). *Sexual conduct: The social sources of human sexuality* (2nd ed.). Piscataway, NJ: Aldine Transaction.

Little, C. B. (1983). *Understanding deviance and control.* Itasca, IL: F. E. Peacock.

NORMALIZATION

Analysis of the concept of normalization and its effects in various economic, political, and cultural contexts is crucial in the study of the production of deviant behavior and in defining policies and practices of control and contrast. An initial etymological analysis of the term shows that the concept can generally be used as a synonym of standardization, from which the adjective *normal* is also derived. Normalization, in this sense, relates not only to what is considered and perceived as normal but also to making something (an individual, behavior, or belief) normal, natural, and acceptable and ensuring it conforms to a certain standard. This definition implies that there is someone who defines the standard, the norm, that this is decided on and then used to assess other individuals or behavior and that the process of normalization is verifiable and measurable through the distribution and determination of a series of "normalities." Closely linked to the subject of normalization, and considered its opposite, are the subjects of deviance and exclusion, concepts that are used as a litmus test to explore conditions of social order and reveal the close links between normalization and power.

The term *normalization* implies policies, rules, strategies, and rituals of construction of standards to which individuals are forced to adhere because of the *normalities* they represent, in terms of statistical distribution, moral imperatives, or distribution of powers. Regarding the historical and philosophical use of the concept, much attention is paid to the works of Georges Canguilhem and his student Michel Foucault; while the former mainly stresses the standardizing/normalizing activities and practices intertwined with the production of social normalities that emerged with the rationalization of political and economic means during the rise of modern industrial societies (especially in the realm of biology and medicine), the latter reflects on the political use of normalization in terms of exerting power in modern society. Modern societies are identified strongly with the proliferation of discipline, mostly in the realm of knowledge, as a form of power whose methods of exertion in schools, hospitals, prisons, and the military are directed to the production of *normal* people as opposed to *abnormal* (and so deviant, criminal, sick individuals). Specialists and professionals, according to Foucault, are the individuals in charge of normalizing people through the creation of standards, classificatory systems, diagnoses, measures, and examination, with which people must be made to conform. In philosophical terms, normalization works as a practice whose aim is mainly directed to the homogenization and standardization of social parameters and patterns used to distinguish directly and clearly what is normal and what is not in order to erase, stigmatize, and annihilate the abnormalities. The defined standardizing process is firmly connected to specific economic, political, and governmental strategies that mainly contribute to the construction of specific subjectivities: A process of normalization always implies the production of a subject who conforms to the needs of a given social system.

A direct consequence of normalization is *naturalization*, which mainly refers to the rendering of states of conditions, identities, and personal traits in a standardized idiom (biological, medical, or even judicial) to render them unproblematic, self-evident, and so to speak *natural*. If the systemic and macrosociological perspectives take into account the connection between power and institutional and political practices, a microsociological analysis allows thorough comprehension of the everyday manufacturing of normalization. The latter perspectives are grounded mainly in phenomenological and symbolic interactionist research, interested in the revelation of the microrealities on which the macrofoundation is based.

Microsociological Applications

Processes of normalization refer, therefore, in everyday interactions, to all those practices that individuals use to control their own interactions to "appear normal," or practices that in some way reassess previously stigmatized behavior, conduct, or conditions. In microsociological analyses of the concept of normalization, processes that challenge social expectations (deviance) and the consequent instruments of censure and normalization, such as processes of stigmatization, must be considered. The order of social interactions is thus constructed on the perception of trust, built through appearances and normal occurrences, which contribute to its predictability,

reliability, and legibility. Social actors are therefore involved in processes of construction of normality, on the basis of which they routinely plan and conduct everyday interactions. The definition of normality is based on the repetition and strengthening of these routine practices of normality, familiar to individuals in the form of tacit knowledge, aimed to demonstrate to themselves but especially to others that "everything is as it should be." These issues relate to activities that re-create the (legitimate) order of appearances and normality, aiming to avoid loss of face, as Goffman asserts; that is, they are typified, and they come to constitute the normal reality: The representation of normality and its "organized" construction become collective activities supported by interactional rituals.

When behavior (or characteristics, habits, personality traits) is considered inappropriate to a situation, the normal course of events is challenged and others are driven to sense that "something must be done." Processes of stigmatization can be interpreted as instruments used by "normal" individuals to highlight the "abnormality" of individuals who possess "alarming" traits, conditions, and characteristics, to bring them back to the norm, if feasible, as in the case of young delinquents or drug addicts in rehabilitation centers. Precisely because of the need to maintain and legitimate the order, the concern with normality and appearing normal becomes a goal for the stigmatized individuals themselves who, often when it is feasible, tend to "pass for normal" to avoid being discovered and ruined or becoming further stigmatized. This prompts reflection on how normality is a precarious condition, continuously negotiated within performances by individuals aiming to come across as reliable and to "pass for normal."

Cirus Rinaldi

See also Conformity; Defining Deviance; Norms and Societal Expectations; Stigma and Stigma Management

Further Readings

Canguilhem, G. (1991). *The normal and the pathological*. New York, NY: Zone Books.

Foucault, M. (1975). *Discipline and punish: The birth of the prison*. New York, NY: Random House.

Goffman, E. (1963). *Stigma*. Englewood Cliffs, NJ: Prentice Hall.

Goffman, E. (1971). *Relations in public: Microstudies of the public order*. New York, NY: Basic Books.

Norms and Societal Expectations

Norms and societal expectations are the basic principles of human behavior that govern a society. As rules of behavior, they determine what actions are acceptable, or unacceptable, by a set of individuals and serve to produce and maintain order in a society. The framework of societies, social institutions, formal and informal groups, and the daily lives of individuals are built on norms and societal expectations. How such norms and expectations are managed, as well as the ways in which they are violated, expose the values of the social groups that are regulated by, create, and enforce such principles. At the same time, social deviance arises with the violation of norms and societal expectations.

Norms and societal expectations guide the everyday lives of members of cultural groups. They are important to social and cultural groups because they mandate uniformity of individual behavior, which makes life for all individuals more predictable and manageable. Institutionalized norms are those that are widely accepted by members of a society and are often adopted and exercised automatically. These expectations are those that mandate the most common of behaviors, such as sitting down at a vacant desk when entering a classroom or turning around and facing doors when entering an elevator.

Many norms and societal expectations are acquired through the process of socialization or acculturation. The process of introducing guidelines about acceptable behavior is especially important in the early stages of childhood development. By teaching children what is socially acceptable, or normative, a society or culture is perpetuating the beliefs and values of the group as a whole. For example, when children are taught to eat with their mouths closed, they are being prepared to function successfully in larger society. Individuals within a group abide by these norms and expectations because they have been socialized to believe that such behavior is expected, if not morally imperative.

Proscriptive norms and expectations prohibit certain behavior, such as drug use or violence. Conversely, prescriptive norms and expectations guide individuals by emphasizing socially desirable behavior, or what members of society should do. For these norms and expectations to effectively influence members of a society, however, failure to comply with such principles must result in social sanctions.

Violation of Norms and Societal Expectations

Violations of norms and societal expectations can cause difficulties for both violators and society. Social deviance may lead to community disorder, reduced trust, and increased fear among individuals. Likewise, when two groups with differing sets of norms and expectations meet, conflict may surface between individuals and groups. Although all individuals are adhering to the norms and expectations of their respective group, they may be violating the norms and expectations of another.

The violation of certain norms and expectations can be seen as problems affecting the larger society. For example, drug use is often considered a norm violation, but prolific drug use among society members is also regarded as a social problem. As a result, violations of proscriptive social norms often result in sanctions, or punishments. Generally, sanctions involve punishment or penalty for those engaging in deviant behavior. However, sanctions can also involve positive rewards for engaging in normative behavior. Positive and negative sanctions can be informal and executed by society members or formal and imposed by officials tasked with authority.

Types of Norms and Societal Expectations

Norms and societal expectations are generally classified into folkways, mores, and laws. These principles that guide the behavior of individuals are often classified in relation to the degree of significance a society attributes to the behavior that norms and expectations attempt to regulate. Thus, norms and societal expectations vary in their ascribed importance and associated sanctions, and they include both formal and informal principles of behavior.

Considered to be informal principles of behavior, folkways are types of norms and societal expectations that may be violated without serious consequences. Folkways outline rules for proper social conduct; however, these principles of behavior are often mildly enforced and are not regarded as necessary for a society to survive. In American culture, folkways include wearing age- and gender-appropriate clothing and eating food with one's mouth closed. Although violation of this behavior would likely generate disapproving stares, it does not result in more serious consequences.

Unlike folkways, mores—another type of norms and societal expectations—are considered to be necessary rules of behavior for a society to survive. Mores are folkways of critical importance, which embody the fundamental moral attitudes and beliefs of a society. When these norms and societal expectations are violated, they evoke severe repercussions. Mores are founded on cultural values, and they are regarded as critical to a society's stability. As a result, violators of mores experience more negative consequences than those who do not adhere to folkways. Cannibalism and incest in the United States are examples of violations of mores.

Laws are a third type of norms and societal expectations. Although they are not necessarily regarded as more important, the primary difference is that these norms and expectations are formalized, or have been made "official." Laws are rules of behavior that are designed, maintained, and enforced by the governmental authority of a society, including legislatures, police, and courts. They act as vehicles to maintain the social acceptance of other norms and societal expectations, encouraging individuals to adhere to them. For instance, when society responds to criminals, it is restating its expectations for citizens.

David Patrick Connor

See also Conformity; Informal Social Control; Social Control

Further Readings

Bicchieri, C. (2005). *The grammar of society: The nature and dynamics of social norms.* Cambridge, MA: Cambridge University Press.

Kiesler, C. A., Kiesler, S. B., & Pallak, M. S. (1967). The effect of commitment to future interaction on reactions to norm violations. *Journal of Personality, 35*(4), 585–599.

McKirnan, D. J. (1980). The identification of deviance: A conceptualization and initial test of a model of social norms. *European Journal of Social Psychology, 10*(1), 75–93.

Posner, E. A. (2002). *Law and social norms.* Cambridge, MA: Harvard University Press.

NUDISM

Sometimes considered deviant, nudism is normative for more than 30 million people worldwide. *Nudism* and *naturalism* are sometimes used interchangeably to describe people who prefer to be clothing-free; however, persons describing themselves as naturalists are more likely to be spiritual and engage in clothing-free activities for the purported health benefits. The term *nudism* was first used in 1929; earlier clubs and groups practicing a clothing-free lifestyle were referred to as naturalists. True nudism is ostensibly nonsexual in nature; however, some nudists believe sex is one way of embracing nature and humanism. Nudists may also have political, cultural, and/or social agendas. In keeping with its original conception as a lifestyle in harmony with nature and as a means of establishing social equality, some naturist movements may espouse environmentalist or political causes.

Nudism can be personal/family or social. Personal/family nudity is practiced in the private sphere. Social nudism is practiced in a social setting, with others outside the immediate family. Social nudism can be practiced at home with friends, at a club, beach, resort, or other public space. Some individuals use nudity as a political tool or as a prank; this is not true social nudity. Social nudity is not intended to be deviant; rather, it is intended to be normative. Streaking and events such as the University of Michigan's "Naked Mile" run are not considered social nudity; in these cases, nudity is not intended to be normative but to be deviant and to attract attention.

Nonsexual nudity has its antecedents in ancient human history. Greek Olympic athletes competed naked until 393 CE, when Emperor Theodosius I banned the Olympics. Theodosius, a Christian, considered the Olympics a pagan ritual. Concurrently, a Christian sect (the Adamites) practiced holy nudism, described as an attempt to return to the "pure state of innocence" of Adam and Eve. Some early baptismal practices required complete nudity, and several Christian sects (Adamites, Adamianis, Carpocrations, Aquarii, and Marcosians) practice social nudity (nudity in public and private locations).

Until the early Victorian era, most swimming was done naked, as clothing of the time was voluminous and likely dangerous to the swimmer. Beaches and swimming areas were segregated by sex. The invention of the bathing suit (or swimming costume) in the 1870s put an end to the practice of "skinny dipping" as normative, and social nudity, for the most part, ceased to exist. A private club for nudists was established in India in 1891 by a British civil servant;

however, the first true nudist club was opened in Hamburg, Germany, in 1903 by Paul Zimmerman. Known as the Freilichtpark (Free-Light Park), this park was inspired by "The Cult of the Nude," published in 1900 by Heinrich Pudor, a German sociologist.

The years leading up to World War II saw the establishment of a number of nudist and naturist societies, as well as organized protests in support of the nudist movement. Several naturist and nudist clubs were founded during this time period, including Fiveacres Country Club in Bricket Wood, Hertfordshire. During this time, proponents of social nudity protested, published, and were persecuted in Canada, the Soviet Union, France, and the United States. A town for nudists, Heliopolis (off the coast of the Riviera) was founded in 1931. The first permanent nudist communities in the United States, Sky Farm and Rock Lodge Club, were founded in New Jersey in 1932; both clubs are currently active. Ironically, Germany (the birthplace of contemporary social nudity) banned nudist organizations in 1933; however, these groups were redefined as sports groups and legalized.

Social nudity remained underground from the 1930s to the 1960s. In 1968, John Lennon and Yoko Ono released the record album titled *Two Virgins*, with a photo of themselves naked on the cover, reinvigorating the nudist movement. Danish beaches became clothing optional after a 1969 demonstration by 300 nude Danish citizens at a Danish beach in 1969. Social nudism also became more common in many Western nations, both at beaches and festivals. Nudism is currently widely practiced in many European nations; however, even in Europe, culture seems to affect approaches and attitudes toward nudism. For example, German nudists are what H. W. Smith (1980) refers to as "low-context" nudists: more body conscious, more sexualized, and more modest. The French, according to Smith, are "high-context" nudists: less body conscious, less sexualized, and less modest.

Regardless of context, a number of options to practice nudism are open to persons wishing to engage in clothing-free activity. Nude (or free) beaches are clothing optional. Clothing-optional status may be de facto (not legitimized but tolerated by local authorities) or de jure (formally designated by the state). Nude beaches offer the casual nudist anonymity and can be found throughout Europe: all beaches in Denmark are officially clothing optional. Many other countries allow naturist sunbathing not only on designated beaches but also in designated areas in public parks.

Nudists may also choose to join a naturist club. These are of two types: landed (members') clubs and nonlanded (travel) clubs. Landed clubs are permanently based, while nonlanded clubs meet at a variety of locations. Unlike nude public beaches, clubs are private organizations and as such can determine their own membership criteria, up to and including criminal background checks.

Holiday centers and naturist resorts, while sharing many of the characteristics of naturist clubs, do not have membership requirements. A holiday center is a commercial organization providing housing or campus facilities for paying visitors. European resorts are less a vacation spot and more a housing development where nudism is the norm; houses, apartments, and condos may be purchased or leased.

Nudists also participate in nude recreational activities outside of beaches, clubs, and holiday centers. Sporting activities are particularly popular, including nude sky-diving, watersports, hiking, cycling, and even team sports, such as volleyball.

Pamela Black

See also Changing Deviance Designations; Public Sex; Taboo

Further Readings

Descamps, M.-A. (1987) *Vivre Nu: Psychosociologie du Naturisme* [Living naked: Social-psychology of naturism]. Paris, France: Trismégiste.

Hill, T. L. (1996). The problem with non-nudists. *Society-Société, 20*(1), 23–25.

Smith, H. W. (1980). A modest test of cross-cultural differences in sexual modesty, embarrassment and self-disclosure. *Qualitative Sociology, 3*(3), 223–241.

OBESITY

Obesity is a rapidly growing phenomenon in the United States; because it involves health issues, some observers have referred to it as an epidemic. The Centers for Disease Control and Prevention report that in 2010, 36% of adults and 17% of children were obese. Since 1980, obesity rates have doubled for adults and tripled for children. The overall prevalence of obesity in men and women is virtually the same. However, the obesity rate for adolescent boys (19%) is higher than the obesity rate for adolescent girls (15%), and women at least 60 years old have higher rates of obesity (42%) than do their male counterparts (32%). Both African Americans and Mexican Americans have a considerably greater prevalence of obesity than do whites.

For adults, obesity is defined as a body mass index (BMI) greater than or equal to 30 kilograms of body mass per height in meters squared (kg/m^2). Nevertheless, much research on obesity includes "overweight" individuals with a BMI range of 25 to 29.9 kg/m^2. The terms *obesity* and *overweight* are often used interchangeably. Children are considered overweight if their BMI is greater than or equal to the 95th percentile of children, controlling for age and sex.

Being obese is especially problematic because it is linked to several physical health problems, including cardiovascular disease, various cancers, dyslipidemia, stroke, osteoarthritis, reproduction problems, metabolic syndrome, and respiratory problems. In addition, being overweight is linked to mental health problems such as impaired cognitive function, depression, and feelings of stigmatization. In fact, the prevalence of weight discrimination or obesity stigmatization has increased by 66% over the past two decades.

Stigmatization is the result of linking a negative trait to a perceived disposition that disqualifies an individual from certain interactions. Stigmatized individuals are associated with a wide range of imperfections (e.g., lazy, sloppy, unintelligent, and/ or unattractive). The sociologist Erving Goffman maintained that individuals might be stigmatized for their physical traits, social identity, or a perceived weakness of character. Obesity is doubly stigmatizing, because it is a physical trait and often attributed to a lack of willpower. The severity of stigmatization may increase if there is a perception that an obese individual could lose weight, but she or he is perceived as not trying to maintain a healthy weight. Weight bias tends to be stronger than other commonly recognized stigmas (e.g., sexual orientation and racial minority status).

Obesity is thought to affect an individual's ability to reason, think logically, or focus. Obesity stigma among children is linked to low self-esteem, self-perceptions of physical appearance, athletic competence, and cognitive ability. Persistent low self-esteem among obese children increases the likelihood of future low self-esteem, as well as other risky behaviors such as smoking and alcohol use. Obese children often develop eating disorders such as anorexia and bulimia. Overweight girls are twice as likely to develop an eating disorder as are normal weight girls. Eating disorders occurring among obese children are often attributed to teasing by other children and parents.

Employment

Obese individuals are frequent targets of disparaging humor and pejorative remarks in the workplace. Obesity stigma is particularly common among women, and it is imputed by coworkers, supervisors, and employers. Overweight and obese people are much more likely to experience discrimination than are people of normal weight. One study showed that severely obese individuals were 100 times more likely to experience discrimination in the workplace than were normal-weight individuals. Obese individuals report experiencing a variety of weight-related discrimination, including not being hired, receiving more negative job evaluations, not receiving promotions, and being wrongfully terminated. Several studies have shown that obese individuals experience significant wage disparities compared with others. While statistics vary, some studies show that obese men earn as much as 20% less than normal-weight men, and obese women earn as much as 24% less than normal-weight women. Women tend to experience discrimination at lower weight levels than do men, and professionals are more likely to report weight-related discrimination than are other workers.

Health Care Professionals

Physicians, nurses, dietitians, exercise professionals, and mental health professionals routinely make stigmatizing comments to and about obese patients (e.g., they are lazy, noncompliant, undisciplined, and lack willpower). In one study, physicians tended to expect that obese patients would have low self-esteem and poor health. Studies conducted in France, England, and Australia show similar patterns of obesity stigma and discrimination. There are physicians from around the world who attribute obesity to overeating, unhealthy diet, lack of exercise, low motivation, or weakness of personal character.

Studies show that normal-weight nurses tend to evaluate obese patients more negatively than do overweight nurses. One study showed that the perceptions of medical students are that health care professionals routinely use derogatory humor about obese patients, and it occurs frequently during surgeries and in obstetrics–gynecological settings. Furthermore, medical students complain that obese patients create more work for them than do normal-weight patients. Obese children were also the targets of disparaging remarks, and the medical students did not consider their derogatory humor to be inappropriate. Even dental students report stigmatizing attitudes about obese patients. One study reported that one third of dental students thought obese patients were lazy. The dental students also stated that they were uncomfortable examining obese patients and felt little empathy for them.

Exercise professionals and dietitians tend to attribute obesity to lack of motivation and/or laziness. Exercise professionals who have never been overweight are particularly likely to have a negative bias toward overweight/obese people. Young white females who have never been overweight tend to be among the most weight biased. Dietitian students not only share the negative attitudes of exercise professionals but also tend to believe that obese individuals eat too much junk food and that they are responsible for their weight. Unfortunately, psychological stress caused by stigmatization is significantly associated with increased caloric intake and fewer calories burned through physical activity.

Exacerbating the problem is that health care professionals often believe that treating obese individuals is ineffective. Studies show that physicians spend less time with obese patients than with normal-weight patients. Nevertheless, one study showed that physicians tend to set more strict weight loss standards than they do for normal-weight patients. Physicians also report discussing weight with their patients far more than they would like and declining to discuss weight with some patients even though it is warranted. Obese patients report that their own physicians are the second most common source of stigmatization (after family members) and that physicians routinely make inappropriate comments about patients' weight. Similarly, nurses, dietitians, and exercise professionals tend to believe that they are ill-prepared to treat obesity, that treatment is futile, and that treating obese patients/clients is generally unrewarding.

Given the severity of obesity stigmatization imputed by health care professionals, obese individuals tend to avoid and/or ignore preventative care. Several studies have shown that weight-stigmatized individuals are less likely to seek breast, cervical, or colorectal cancer screenings. Also, stigmatizing experiences are inversely associated with frequency of exercise and with obese individuals' perceptions of physical activity competence.

Education

European studies have revealed that obese individuals tend to attain lower levels of education than do normal-weight individuals. Studies utilizing the National Longitudinal Study of Adolescent Health show that obese women are about one half as likely to attend college as normal-weight women. Obesity stigma is especially severe in social contexts in which obesity is not the norm. Studies by Rebecca Puhl and Janet Latner indicate that obesity stigma may influence teachers' negative attitudes toward obese children in elementary school, continuing through high school and even in college. Teachers have lower expectations for obese students, including perceptions that obese students have poorer social, reasoning, physical, and cooperation skills. Studies of middle school and high school teachers reveal that they frequently report believing that obese students are untidy, relatively unlikely to succeed, overly emotional, and have family problems, including a lack of love and attention. Furthermore, many teachers believe that most normal-weight people are uncomfortable with interactions with the obese. Male educators seem to impute stigma and discriminate on the basis of weight more than do women educators.

Interpersonal Issues

Obese individuals tend to experience less social support than normal-weight people. Family tends to be the primary source of obesity stigma for women, with mothers being the most common sources. Obese parents are just as likely as normal-weight parents to impute obesity stigma or discriminate based on weight. Obesity stigma is also frequently imputed by both friends and spouses. Obesity is linked to decreased popularity among peers. Obese women are less likely to date than are normal-weight women and are often described as less sexually attractive, sexually skilled, or responsive.

Peers and parents routinely stigmatize obese children. In fact, obese children as young as three years of age have been identified as having experienced weight-related discrimination. The same types of negative characteristics attributed to very young children often persist and even get worse for obese adolescents and college students. Parents are likely to make disparaging remarks about their children's overweight/obesity, especially of their daughters. Obese daughters also tend to receive less financial support for college than do normal-weight daughters. Studies have reported that parents feel frustrated, angry, and guilty about their children's obesity.

Grandparents, aunts, uncles, and cousins are all potential sources of weight-related teasing for obese children and adolescents. Family members report that they engage in stigmatizing and discriminating behaviors against the obese as a means to urge them to lose weight. However, studies have shown that obesity stigma only exacerbates the difficulty of losing weight and discourages the obese from engaging in nutrition and exercise programs that might help them achieve a healthy weight.

Race and Sex

Obesity stigma is common across race and ethnicity, and it occurs globally; however, there are different cultural standards that promote stigmatization. White women are the most likely racial group in the United States to be stigmatized for being overweight. The level of overweight at which stigma is likely to occur is much lower for white women than that of other groups. African American men are less likely to be stigmatized for being overweight than are African American women or whites. African Americans are less likely to impute stigma than are whites. Whites, especially women, are more concerned about being overweight than are African Americans. Hispanic children are just as likely to have weight bias as are white children and both groups are more likely to discriminate based on weight than are African American children. Native American and Asian American boys are more likely to be teased by family members about their weight than are white boys.

Media

Weight-related stigmatization is perpetuated by media portrayals of the overweight and the obese. Overweight women are more likely to be negatively portrayed on television comedies than are their normal-weight counterparts, and those negative portrayals are often the bases of the comedies. Obese women are dramatically underrepresented on entertainment television. Children's programs, especially cartoons, depict overweight characters as unattractive, unintelligent, unhappy, and friendless. Overweight female characters are often depicted as evil, unfriendly, and cruel, whereas thin female characters are portrayed as sociable, kind, happy, and successful.

There is a disproportionate amount of advertising on television for weight loss systems and aids.

A typical marketing strategy for weight loss systems and aids is to portray overweight people as generally unhappy and unattractive. The news media frame obesity as the responsibility of the individual, with women being the targets of stereotypical comments. Even Internet images of the obese tend to be negative. Online photos frequently depict the obese as unprofessional, nonathletic, and slovenly. Experimental studies show that individuals who view stigmatizing media images of the obese may hold stronger social distance attitudes and more negative attitudes than do individuals who view positive images of the obese.

Rose M. D. Carter and W. Craig Carter

See also Abominations of the Body; Eating Disorders; Physical Characteristics as Deviance; Stigma and Stigma Management

Further Readings

Carr, D., & Friedman, M. A. (2005). Is obesity stigmatizing? Body weight, perceived discrimination and psychological well-being in the United States. *Journal of Health and Social Behavior, 46*, 244–259.

Goffman, E. (1963). *Stigma: Notes on the management of spoiled identity.* Englewood Cliffs, NJ: Prentice Hall.

Latner, J. D., O'Brien, K. S., Durso, L. E., Brinkman, L. A., & MacDonal, T. (2008). Weighing obesity stigma: The relative strength of different forms of bias. *International Journal of Obesity, 32*, 1145–1152.

Muennig, P. (2008). The body politic: The relationship between stigma and obesity-associated disease. *BMC Public Health, 8*, 1–10.

Puhl, R. M., & Brownell, K. D. (2006). Confronting and coping with weight stigma: An investigation of overweight and obese adults. *Obesity, 14*(10), 1802–1815.

Puhl, R. M., & Heuer, C. A. (2008). The stigma of obesity: A review and update. *Obesity, 17*(5), 941–964.

Puhl, R. M., & Heuer, C. A. (2010). Obesity stigma: Important considerations for public health. *American Journal of Public Health, 100*, 1019–1028.

Puhl, R. M., & Latner, J. D. (2007). Stigma, obesity, and the health of the nation's children. *Psychological Bulletin, 133*(4), 557–580.

OCCUPATIONAL CRIMINALITY

Occupational criminality is a broad concept. Edwin Sutherland first proposed a reconceptualization of crime in 1940, which sought to broaden the definition of crime to include behaviors such as fraud and insider trading. These behaviors have become collectively known as *white-collar crime.* In an address to the American Sociological Society, Sutherland spelled out various examples of behaviors that had not been thought of as criminality, owing to the social status of the actors. It was his goal to convince social scientists to adopt an expanded view of criminality to include violations of law that were committed by people of high social status in the course of their occupations. Until that point, criminologists viewed crime as behaviors engaged in almost exclusively by lower-class individuals. Until that time, research and theory in the field of criminology had principally been done only with regard to lower class, uneducated individuals.

Since Sutherland's speech, many criminologists have become interested in the concept of white-collar crime. One issue within the study of white-collar crime is the question: What exactly is white-collar crime? There are now different typologies of white-collar crime, which range from public versus private employment, corporate level versus individual level, and legal violation behaviors versus norm violation (i.e., deviance). To be certain, there are forms of occupational deviance that come close to violations of legal codes, but there are also examples of occupational norm violation that do not even border on law violation (i.e., rate busting by employees).

All of the efforts to reconceptualize and redefine white-collar crime have successfully brought a much needed expansion of our understanding of crime. However, it is still likely that the average person does not include white-collar crime in their cognitive conceptualization of crime. Those who research and theorize about crime are now forced to distinguish between conventional and white-collar crimes. Furthermore, it is now probable that criminologists are forced to distinguish between different varieties of white-collar criminality.

There is an ongoing debate among criminologists over what is the true definition of white-collar crime. Some have separated corporate crimes (e.g., polluting the environment, manufacturing of unsafe products, or exposing workers to unsafe work conditions) from individual-level crimes (e.g., performing unnecessary surgeries, excessive billing by lawyers, or employee theft). These discussions that have thrived in criminology journals and textbooks have created great confusion over all of the possibilities of criminality that exist in the course of people's occupations. Several researchers in this area of criminology have called for a replacement of the term *white-collar crime* with *occupational criminality*.

The status of the offender is often taken into consideration when discussing white-collar crime or occupational crime. It has been stated by several theorists that these crimes are most likely to be committed by people of upper- or middle-class standing. However, there is no complete agreement on this, and many believe that even employees at lower levels are provided opportunities to engage in occupational crimes. For instance, employee pilferage is thought to be quite extensive in most businesses and organizations. Theft of small items such as pens or paper clips has been estimated to add up to billions of dollars lost in the course of a year. Furthermore, theft by lower-level employees can exist in the form of time theft where an individual intentionally or accidentally misrepresents the actual amount of hours worked, therefore, being paid wages that were not earned.

Another important consideration in regard to this form of criminality is the victim. Who are the victims of occupational crimes? One obvious answer is the employer for whom these individuals work. Theft from employers adds up to huge losses for private companies, government agencies, and even nonprofit organizations. However, a broader view would suggest that the general public is victimized by occupational crime. When employers incur losses from employee theft, they are likely to pass those costs on to the consumer in order to generate profits. At least part of the higher prices paid for goods and services by consumers can be directly attributed to occupational criminality. Furthermore, the effects of this type of crime can be felt throughout the economy in terms of investor confidence and business failure, leading to layoffs and unemployment.

Of concern to many criminologists is the lack of official response to many forms of occupational crime. The lower rate of detection is one reason for the minimal official actions taken against occupational criminals. However, even when detected, there is often little official prosecution. One of the reasons given for this is the desire on the part of companies to avoid negative publicity. If an employee is exposed for malfeasance, it can reflect negatively on the company that hired this individual and the lack of control that the company has over internal workings. Therefore, the preferred method of dealing with the occupational criminal is to simply terminate employment of the guilty party. This is thought to be a serious problem with regard to deterrence. The low likelihood of being prosecuted for occupational crimes means little inhibition on the part of employees.

Another major problem with prevention and detection of occupational criminality is the mind-set of people in our society. It is common for employees to believe that they are entitled to take things from their workplace. There is a general belief among many workers that the value of small workplace items (e.g., pens, paper, envelopes) amounts to a "perk" of the job. More evidence of this is the fact that many employees often recognize that there are limits to what can be taken from an employer. Larger items (e.g., a laptop computer or expensive merchandise) are considered off-limits, but smaller, less expensive items are seen as acceptable to pilfer. There is also a generally accepted belief that since the employer will not notice the theft of small items, they are not worthy of consideration as true theft. Even if an individual is directly told that he or she is not permitted to take items home for personal use, it is unlikely that the individual will see this as criminal behavior. Furthermore, it is also possible that some supervisors use discretion when responding to minor forms of employee theft as to not jeopardize employee morale.

Another common motivation for employee theft is to get even with the employer. Workers who feel that they are not being fairly compensated or otherwise mistreated by their employer often feel that taking items will balance the scale, or make up for shortcomings in pay and/or benefits. Some research does find that newer and younger employees who are likely to be paid less than more experienced and older employees are more likely to engage in employee theft. Furthermore, it is likely that these employees have less loyalty to the company than do more experienced employees.

Lower-level employee theft is only one form of occupational crime. There are many possible avenues for occupational crime to occur among higher-level employees, such as kickbacks on contracts, judges taking bribes, and accountants or stockbrokers embezzling funds from a client or employer. These forms of occupational criminality are engaged in by employees who are entrusted with more responsibility to carry out functions in the course of their occupations but may be no different from the feelings held by lower-level employees. The belief that these are accepted practices in the occupation, or are not truly criminal, is quite common.

Another consideration is to determine where the boundary lines of occupational criminality lie. Simply because an offense occurs in the workplace does not necessarily make it occupational criminality. For instance, an employee using illicit drugs while at work does not necessarily constitute occupational criminality. It is a question of whether this type of behavior is parallel to employee theft, or simply a criminal offense that happens to take place at someone's workplace rather than at home or on the street corner. To be certain, an employer would be highly motivated to remove such a person from his or her payroll and possibly report the offender to authorities (or encourage them to seek counseling), but would there be a different response if this same employer found out that the employee was using illegal drugs away from work? Furthermore, there would probably be a different response if the employer found that the employee was stealing money from the company's cash register versus showing up to work under the influence.

Likewise, there are certain circumstances that border on occupational crime but in many theorists' minds need to remain outside of this concept. Workers may be exposed to criminal victimization while in the course of their work. A convenience store employee being assaulted by a robber, or a jilted husband seeking out his estranged wife at the workplace to take his revenge would be seen as different incidents than one employee assaulting another employee during work hours. These are examples of criminal acts that take place in the workplace and even target a person in the course of his or her work. While both of these types of offenses would be viewed by law enforcement officials as criminal incidents, the criminological theorist most likely would view them as different types of crime.

There have been many theories used to explain occupational criminality. Most of the theories have also been applied to conventional criminality. For instance, Sutherland himself advocated for his *differential association theory* to be used to explain white-collar crime. This theory explains crime as being the result of learning criminal behaviors from others. Hence, the occupational criminal is understood to be the product of his or her environment, especially coworkers who are engaging in similar behaviors. More recently, Michael Gottfredson and Travis Hirschi have suggested that their *general theory of crime*, which claims that low self-control is the underlying cause of all crime and deviancy, be used to explain white-collar crimes. Therefore, it is quite common in the field of criminology to believe that the motivations for occupational crime are similar, if not identical, to the motivations for street crime.

Data on occupational criminality can be difficult to find, owing to the fact that very little official data are collected by any governmental agency. The most used source of official crime statistics in the Uniformed Crime Report does not provide much information on these types of crimes. Some offenses such as embezzlement are included in the report but are not as frequently reported as other types of crime. In fact, the Uniformed Crime Report states that white-collar crimes are less common than street crimes, which criminologists understand to be a product of underreporting.

What is known about occupational criminality is gained from self-report surveys or estimated by other entities, such as trade organizations. Most of the estimates of occupational crime state that the cost of occupational criminality far exceeds the costs of street criminality. Surveys find that, for instance, one third of all employees admit to stealing from their employer. Looking at the literature on occupational crime, costs range from a low of \$5 billion/year to as high as \$400 billion/year. Either the low or the high end greatly exceeds the estimates for street-level crimes.

John McMullen

See also Corporate Deviance; Fraud; White-Collar Crime

Further Readings

Clinard, M. B., & Quinney, R. (1973). *Criminal behavior systems: A typology.* New York, NY: Holt, Rinehart & Winston.

Friedrichs, D. O. (2002). Occupational crime, occupational deviance, and workplace crime: Sorting out the difference. *Criminal Justice, 2,* 243–256.

Geis, G. (1982). *On white-collar crime.* Lexington, MA: Lexington Books.

Green, G. (1990). *Occupational crime.* Chicago, IL: Nelson-Hall.

Hollinger, R. C., & Clark, J. P. (1983). Deterrence in the workplace: Perceived certainty, perceived severity, and employee theft. *Social Forces, 62,* 398–418.

Jensen, G. F., & Hodson, R. (1999). Synergies in the study of crime and the workplace. *Work and Occupations, 36,* 6–20.

Parilla, P. F., Hollinger, R. C., & Clark, J. P. (1988). Organizational control of deviant behavior: The case of employee theft. *Social Science Quarterly, 69*, 261–280.

Sutherland, E. H. (1940). White-collar criminality. *American Sociological Review, 5*, 1–12.

Wright, J. P., & Cullen, F. T. (2000). Juvenile involvement in occupational delinquency. *Criminology, 38*, 863–896.

OCCUPY MOVEMENT

What became globally known as "Occupy" or "the Occupy Movement," and more popularly in the United States as "Occupy Wall Street," emerged as an international social and economic justice movement involving hundreds of thousands, or depending on how counted, several million people. Although Occupiers followed the law in wide measure, they were frequently defined and treated as deviants by the state because of their fundamental opposition to governing political, economic, and social control institutions.

Occupy arose in response to the global economic crisis of 2007–2008, which resulted in large downturns of stock markets and the worst economic collapse since the Great Depression of the 1930s. Internationally, Occupy is connected to burgeoning democratic movements claiming inspiration from the Arab Spring, and aligning itself with popular European resistance to crippling austerity policies imposed by grossly indebted states, such as Spain and Greece. In the United States, Occupy provided an outlet for outrage at the government's response to the financial crisis. The state chose to bail out large private financial institutions even as these same institutions issued evictions and foreclosures on homes and businesses. The state failed to provide protections to a public unable to bear the costs of devalued houses or to maintain small businesses in the face of growing unemployment and trillions of dollars of lost consumer wealth.

Occupy took hold in the United States with coordinated protests in the financial districts of multiple American cities on October 17, 2011. The protests were prompted by a call to action by *Adbusters* magazine with media attention focusing on Zuccotti Park in lower Manhattan near to Wall Street itself. The movement spread quickly and, with its quintessential slogan of "We are the 99%," called for a class war against the wealthiest 1% of society. The latter were portrayed as the owners of greedy economic entities responsible not only for the economic collapse but also for the wide national gap in wealth, for the government's failure to protect its citizens from the housing bubble, and for the corporate media who looked to sales and profits instead of warning the public about a deregulated capitalism let loose and a war on Iraq that was misleadingly achieved and extraordinarily costly.

The Occupy movement quickly defined itself by the use of nonviolent resistance and protest; the occupying (encampment) of public spaces (parks, squares, etc.); and the symbols of tents (in encampments), general assemblies (organizational governance by consensus), and the "human mic" (group repetition of a speakers' statements to ensure all can hear). State resistance to Occupy soon filled America's television screens with scenes of riot police inflicting harm on citizens exercising constitutional rights of protest. Two important incidents—virally disseminated on the Internet—included footage of the violent expulsion of the Occupy Oakland encampment, in which an Iraq war veteran protester was critically injured, and footage showing a small group of University of California, Davis Occupy students being heavily pepper sprayed as they sat in quiet resistance to a police demand that they disperse. Such scenes raised public sympathies and evoked memories of Civil Rights and Vietnam-era antiwar protests, which had included both the occupying of buildings and state violence against citizens.

Although nationally decentralized and without any key figures as leaders, Occupy soon had encampments in most major cities and within months had spread to smaller towns, universities, and neighborhood campaigns. Occupy created and promoted a clear class message that centered on protesting economic injustice through key critiques of neoliberal democracy's defense of the wealth divide, the government-led economic rescue of corporations rather than, and at the expense of, the populace, and the abuse of legal protections of "corporate personhood" that directly prevented accountability for the economic collapse. The inequities of this latter concept were underscored by vivid contrasts: Bankers who were responsible for the loss of trillions of dollars not only walked free but also continued to receive multimillion-dollar salary bonuses subsidized by taxpayer "rescue" dollars even as thousands of nonviolent protesters were arrested and incarcerated for peaceable assembly.

After a year of Occupy, a series of critiques came to define media logic about the movement. Dominant among these were characterizations of

Occupy as a public nuisance (encampments), as a disorganized entity (rudderless and without agenda or common ground), and as a series of unmet expectations and disappointments. In some circles, these critiques originated in disappointed hopes and unmet expectations that a political party would emerge to forward arguments about dominant economic inequities. In other circles, they emerged from an unfulfilled hope that Occupy would exert the kind of political influence other social movements had achieved, such as the Tea Party. The deeply disappointed argued that, after a year of Occupy and a costly public campaign expelling them from public spaces, nothing had changed.

Occupiers responded with observations about the corporate-owned media carrying these critiques. First, they argued, the media were perpetuating their failure to inform the public—notably on the corporatization of American democracy—and were instead diverting attention by selling out the people's movement (Occupy). Second, the media had failed to distinguish Occupy as a critique of institutional politics, not more of it. Finally, the media had misinterpreted Occupy as a reform effort, when in fact, it was a rejection of the system.

Politically speaking, when the public that had been inspired by President Obama's "Dream" campaign realized that it was just more political rhetoric, they refused to abandon the vision and in part gave rise to Occupy. In turn, the class consciousness raised by Occupy helped the Obama administration to pass universal health care law. Also, despite the damage done by extreme deregulation without which the financial crisis would have never happened, it was in this context that labor unions and public education finally found a voice to counter the "useless," "inflated," and "incompetent" labels. Last, while accountability for the economic collapse has yet to find many faces, it has served to further embolden the progressive work of the social justice movement, the economic justice movement, and the environmental movement.

In the United States, the Occupy movement's distinction, "99%," has powerfully raised the issue of class and economic inequities in a society notorious for not wanting to have such conversations. A genuine progressive taxation system is now discussed, unions can enter partnerships without strictly negative labels, and culturally a wider perception of "doing it without the corporates" exists: the co-ops, the community gardens, the strikes against student debt, and the global issue of jobs now live on.

Finally, Occupy has marked the social landscape in the United States. In 2011, *Time* magazine selected "The Protestor" as Person of the Year, signifying the global impact of a social movement defined by protesting economic injustice. Importantly, Occupy grew as an idea that in the end sends a message more than it does a program—that people have the power to occupy and live out of alternate spaces of economic justice, social control, and community.

Michael J. Coyle

See also Civil Disobedience; Conflict Theory; Corporate Deviance; Governmental Deviance

Further Readings

Brand, U. (2012). Contradictions and crises of neoliberal-imperial globalization and the political opportunity structures for the global justice movements. *Innovation: The European Journal of Social Sciences, 25,* 283–298.

Goodman, A. (2012). *The silenced majority: Stories of uprisings, occupations, resistance and hope.* Chicago, IL: Haymarket Books.

Marcus, D. (2012). The horizontalists. *Dissent, 59,* 54–59.

Pickerill, J., & Krinsky, J. (2012). Why does Occupy matter? *Social Movement Studies, 11,* 279–287.

ONLINE DATA COLLECTION

See Collecting Data Online

ORGANIZED CRIME

Organized crime is defined as the illegal activities of the members of an organized association engaged in supplying illegal goods or services. The services involved include prostitution, loan-sharking, labor racketeering, narcotics, and gambling. Some add that these groups must also be *highly* organized and disciplined.

Piracy

Pirates have been considered the earliest organized crime groups. Concentrated in areas bordering the Indian Ocean, heavily armed gangs of pirates in fast boats interfere with shipping. But this is nothing new, as pirates have been causing problems even before the rise of the English Sea Dogs in the 16th century. The European colonization of the Americas, with much of its wealth exposed on the sea, led to what has been termed the golden age of piracy, 1660–1730. This was the era of Blackbeard, Captain Kidd, and other famous pirates of the Caribbean. The era ended only after seafaring nations expanded their navies to deal with the threat.

In the 1960s, piracy returned. These pirates mostly attacked ships at anchor and stole cargo or ship's stores. By the 1990s, the problem had grown to such a level that the Piracy Reporting and Rescue Centre was established in 1992. In the waters off Somalia, large vessels continue to be attacked. The Gulf of Aden is a connection between Somalia and Yemen that is about 550 miles long by 200 miles wide and a necessary crossing point for ships sailing to and from the Suez Canal. The pirates are drawn by the concentration of ships and the lack of control, especially in Somalia, where formal government is nearly nonexistent. The scope of contemporary maritime piracy is now costly, massive, growing, and horrific. Piracy in this region is now considered a form of transnational organized crime. Since 2010, the United Nations has tracked the financial profits of pirates and of those who support and finance piracy.

The Mafia

While piracy is indeed a form of organized crime, it is not what most Americans think of when imagining it. Instead, what most Americans traditionally think of as organized crime is the Mafia. The roots of this group were secret societies in Italy, which have existed for hundreds of years. During the 19th century, the Italian Camorra became known for acts of murder and extortion. The Camorrian code demanded total silence. Italian criminal organizations that came to the United States with the wave of European immigration during the late 19th and early 20th centuries included the Black Hand and the Mafia. The Black Hand specialized in extortion and focused on the intimidation of Italian immigrants. The Black Hand became powerful in New Orleans, Detroit, Kansas City, and St. Louis. The Mafia, with roots in Sicily, were organized in the Italian ghettos of large industrial American cities.

Secret societies in Italy barely survived during the Fascist reign of Mussolini, which ended after World War II. The surviving Mafia members were aligned with American and allied intelligence services during the war and assumed their traditional positions of power within Italian society after the war. Links between American criminal organizations and those in Italy expanded after World War II.

Although the Mafia was the first group to gain center stage in the world of organized crime in the United States; Italians were not the first group of criminals to organize. In fact, Irish and Jewish gangs flourished in many cities prior to the arrival of the Italians. The Irish mob has been in existence since the early 19th century when large numbers of Irish came to the United States. Internationally, the history of Irish organized crime can be traced to England, Scotland, and Ireland. When Irish immigrants arrived in the United States, they were not welcomed, and there was no infrastructure to take care of the needs of their large numbers. In response, they reverted to their traditional tribal structure, which took care of their survival needs. They also soon converted their huge numbers into political power. This power resulted in political machines that took over local governments and used political patronage to maintain this power. These machine organizations, such as Tammany Hall, were corrupt but provided services and jobs to Irish immigrants. They gained control of large cities such as New York and Boston. The Irish mob emerged and took advantage of political power, community loyalty, and the chaos in the fast-growing cities of the United States and Canada. The Irish mob organized gambling, prostitution, and protection rackets in urban immigrant communities. The families of the Irish mob never achieved the success of the Mafia but operated alongside them in Boston and Chicago. The Gustin Gang emerged in Boston during Prohibition. Infighting between Irish gangs and with the Mafia eventually allowed the Italians to take over in the 1960s. The Winter Hill Gang emerged during the 1960s as the most powerful Irish organized crime group. Perhaps, the most violent Irish mob was the Westies, which operated out of New York. The gang formed an alliance with the Gambino Mafia family. During the 1980s, the fortunes of the Westies grew with their involvement in narcotics and sports betting. Jimmy Coonan, the leader of the Westies for about 20 years, was finally convicted under Racketeer Influenced and Corrupt Organization Act (RICO) in 1988 and sentenced to 75 years in prison.

Jewish organized crime groups emerged in the United States during the late 19th and early 20th centuries, with a large wave of Jewish immigrants from Eastern Europe. The Five Points Gang was perhaps most notable, as well as gangsters such as Arnold Rothstein, Abe Bernstein, Meyer Lansky, and Bugsy Siegel. During Prohibition, Jewish organized crime groups played major roles in the distribution of alcohol and the spread of organized crime throughout the large cities of the United States. After Lucky Luciano murdered the Old World Sicilian Mafia bosses in 1931 and took control of the Italian Mafia, he formed associations with Jewish gangsters. Alliances with Jews were forbidden before Luciano. The building of Las Vegas was done by combining the Jewish and Italian Mafia into a national organized crime group. Arnold Rothstein is credited with transforming organized crime from a group of thugs into a large, well-run corporation. Rothstein is allegedly responsible for fixing the 1919 World Series. Meyer Lansky was involved in organized crime's gambling interests in both Cuba and Las Vegas.

The term *ethnic succession* has been used to describe the continuing process whereby one ethnic group succeeds another through the assumption of a particular position in society. Just as Jewish and Irish gangs were replaced by Italians, in a similar way African American, Hispanics, and Asian Americans moved into the drug trade and other illegal activities in many parts of the United States. But even with the intrusion of other groups into organized crime, any discussion has to recognize the dominance of Sicilian American involvement. The terms *Mafia* and *La Cosa Nostra* have been used interchangeably since 1963 when Joseph Valachi, a member of the Genovese crime family, testified before the McClellan committee, which was holding hearings on organized crime.

The influence of the Mafia had been extended to most American cities by 1919. But the advent of Prohibition gave the Mafia the financial power to expand its grip. Prior to Prohibition, the activities of the Mafia were concerned mostly with gambling, protection rackets, and loan-sharking. Mafia operations were generally considered small time. In 1919, the U.S. Congress passed the Eighteenth Amendment to the U.S. Constitution, which prohibited the sale, transportation, and manufacture of alcoholic beverages. The period that followed lasted 14 years and is known as Prohibition. Section 1 of the Eighteenth Amendment to the U.S. Constitution reads as follows:

> After one year from the ratification of this article the manufacture, sale, or transportation of intoxicating liquors within, the importation thereof into, or the exportation thereof from the United States and all territory subject to the jurisdiction thereof for beverage purposes is hereby prohibited. (MaGruder & Claire, 1933, p. 343)

This Mafia had two characteristics that would make it rich: (1) the ability to manufacture low-cost, high-proof, untaxed alcohol and (2) the national and international organization to get it to markets. Prohibition gave the existing Mafia families the opportunity to accumulate enormous wealth. But Prohibition also institutionalized the heritage of official corruption. It began or extended corrupt relations between some illegal enterprises, local police, and politicians. Even today, organized crime only exists when these relationships are present. During Prohibition, a series of gangland wars took place (these were not unlike the murders and other violence that now characterize urban youth gangs). Leaders of organized crime fought over the huge profits from the sale of illegal alcohol and also sought to consolidate their power. This warfare reached a peak in 1931, and by the end of that year, a peace had been reached. By the end of 1931, the Mafia had become a large series of corporations across the United States linked together into a cartel. The Mafia was now an integrated criminal organization able to settle most disputes internally and capable of hiding its operations from the police. In 1933, the Eighteenth Amendment was repealed. Through World War II, there was little interest in organized crime; Mafia activity was out of sight, and investigations of Mafia operations were nonexistent. In 1951, the Kefauver Committee brought organized crime back into the spotlight. The special committee was headed by Senator Estes Kefauver and was focused on investigating organized crime in interstate commerce. The committee came to the following conclusions:

1. A nationwide crime organization, known as the Mafia, exists. The center of this organization is found in large cities.

2. The Mafia in America has international links that are particularly apparent in the trafficking of narcotics.

3. Leaders of the Mafia are in control of the most lucrative illegal enterprises in the cities in which they are located.

4. There is a centralized control in the illegal enterprises, and leadership is vested in a group.

In 1957, there was a meeting of Mafia in upstate New York. There was a raid on the meeting by the Federal Bureau of Investigation, which led to an investigation. The investigation produced the 1967 President's Commission report that for the first time described in great detail the organization of the Mafia. According to the commission, the Mafia was an Italian American crime organization. It consisted of 24 crime families that operated in the Unites States under the leadership of a commission. The commission's membership consisted of the bosses of the nation's most powerful crime families. The core of the organization at this time consisted of 24 groups that operated as crime cartels in large cities across the nation. The membership is exclusively Italian. The functioning of the organization is insured by a national body of overseers, who are in frequent communication with each other. The most influential and wealthiest core groups operated in states including New York, Illinois, New Jersey, Nevada, Florida, Michigan, Rhode Island, and Louisiana. Nationwide membership was placed at 5,000; membership in each of the 24 families varied from a high of 700 to as few as 20. Only three American Cities were found to have multiple families—New York with as many as five families and Chicago and Philadelphia with at least two families each.

The organization of each family consisted of a *Boss*, whose chief functions were maintaining order and maximizing profits; an *Underboss*, who collected information for the boss and relayed messages from and to him; a *Counselor* (*Consigliere*), who served as an advisor to the boss, but who was not in the line of leadership; several *Lieutenants* (*Caporegima*), who, depending on the size of the family, served as leaders of operating units; and the *Soldier* (*Soldati*; the lowest level of membership in a family), who operated a specific crime enterprise. Beneath the level of soldier were a number of people employed by the Mafia, who were not considered members of the family and were not necessarily of Italian descent. These individuals do the actual work in a criminal enterprise. A strict but unwritten code of conduct called *omertà* (*manliness*) controls the behavior of members of families. The code demands silence and loyalty of family members. Members are formally introduced to the code through an initiation ritual. The code of *omertà* operates to concentrate power in the bosses of families and also functions to ensure their protection. The most important aspects of the code are the prohibition against appealing to outside authorities for justice, while at the same time demanding great respect, honor, and loyalty to the family. This code, obey your superiors and keep silent, is the reason why power is concentrated in the hands of a few bosses, and men in lower status positions are exploited by these same leaders.

The Mafia is now said to be involved in large-scale drug trafficking, the fencing of stolen goods, loan-sharking, the establishment and control of both legalized and illegal forms of gambling (e.g., wagering on athletic events, bets on horse racing, lotteries, and bookmaking), infiltration of legitimate businesses (e.g., labor unions and corporations that can be used as fronts for money laundering and other activities), and labor union racketeering, by which legitimate businesses are intimated through the threat of work stoppages, strikes, walkouts, and sabotage.

Other Organized Crime Groups

The Mafia is not the only large organized criminal group in the United States. There are many other notable criminal organizations in the United States. Each of these groups has been referred to under various terms, and it is difficult to discuss/categorize such a diversity of groups with any consistency. Such groups have been referred to as the Cuban Mafia, the Haitian Mafia, the Russian Mafia (Mafiya), and various groups of Asian criminals. Other notable groups are Dominican, Mexican, Colombian, and Cuban cartels, which are often importers of cocaine and other drugs.

Outlaw biker groups, otherwise known as one-percenters, have probably been the most publicized but are not necessarily associated with organized crime but rather with the destruction of property, fighting, and other disruption activities. But these groups who have entered the world of organized crime now consist of clubs with local, regional, national, and international status. They are dominated by the "Big Four" clubs—the Hells' Angels (HA, HAMC or "Angels"), the Outlaws, the Bandidos, and the Pagans. The term *Big Four* dates to the early 1970s and is equated with one-percenters by some observers. The term, and especially its equation with the one-percenters subculture, is extremely problematic. The Angels, Bandidos, Outlaws, and Pagans have been the largest, most powerful groups in the subculture for many years. The term is somewhat arbitrary, however, depending on whether membership, geographic spread, reputation, or sophistication are used as criteria for inclusion. Valid arguments can be made for reference to the "Big Three" or the "Big Six," but neither of these groupings are widely accepted.

The Pagans lack many traits of the other three: They are significantly smaller in number, control only parts of the mid-Atlantic region, are less conventionalized, and have put little effort into public relations. Conversely, the HAMC is significantly larger, wealthier, and more sophisticated than the rest of the subculture. The Mongols and Sons of Silence share many traits with the so-called Big Four, especially the more purist-oriented Pagans and Outlaws. The Sons have a large but sparse, geographic spread, with a fairly small membership that tends to keep a fairly low profile. The Mongols are rapidly expanding across North America and claim a few international chapters; they may lack the criminal and social sophistication of the "Big Three" but have an especially fierce reputation.

While reference to the "Big Four" is traditional and most common, some speak of two "superpowers, the HAMC and the Outlaw–Bandito coalition; a few have dropped the Outlaws from this pair and simply describe the HA and Banditos as subcultural superpowers. Others use the term *Big Three* excluding the Pagans, while some want to add the Mongols or Sons of Silence to the "Big Five." Size, power, reputation, and geographic spread result in different groupings. Outlaw biker organizations have spread into Canada, Germany, the United Kingdom, and Australia. Their chief crimes have been drug related, and they have associations with other organized crime groups. RICO has been used to control these biker gangs.

The world's major crime organizations have been identified as the Hong Kong–based Triads, South American cocaine cartels, Russian Mafiya, Japanese Yakuza, Italian Mafia, and the West African crime groups. Each of these extends its criminal activities beyond its home country. The most notable of these is the Russian Mafiya. Russian organized crime grew quickly following the collapse of the Soviet Union. Already involved in the drug trade, they quickly expanded into banking through money laundering, the investment of profits, intimidation, fraud, and murder. Estimates are that Russian organized crime controls a majority of private businesses in Russia and nearly half of the country's wealth. Over the past 20 years, several hundred thousand Russian citizens have immigrated to the United States. As federal law enforcement officials now realize, many of these people were criminals released from Soviet prisons, which included former black market profiteers.

Russian organized crime groups are operating out of as many as 17 American cities. The Federal Bureau of Investigation believes that there are 15 separate Russian organized crime groups consisting of 4,000 members operating in the Unites States. Their activities include automobile theft, loan-sharking, money laundering, smuggling, narcotics-related activities, human trafficking, credit card and telecommunications fraud, illegal sale of arms, and counterfeiting of popular American goods.

The involvement of a small percentage of recent immigrants in organized crime creates a lasting stereotypic image of deviant immigrants who corrupt the morality of a nation. Organized crime was and continues to be a complex set of relations between recently arrived groups and those already established. The most important piece of federal legislation that specifically targets the activities of organized crime is the RICO.

Craig J. Forsyth

See also Biker Gangs; Gangs, Street; Maritime Piracy; Symbolic Crusade

Further Readings

Abadinsky, H. (1994). *Organized crime.* Chicago, IL: Nelson Hall.

Barzini, L. (1965). *The Italians.* New York, NY: Atheneum.

Haller, M. H. (1990). Illegal enterprise: A theoretical and historical interpretation. *Criminology, 28*(2), 201–212.

Katcher, L. (1994). *The big bankroll: The life and times of Arnold Rothstein.* New York, NY: DaCapo Press.

Magruder, F. A., & Claire, G. S. (1933). *The constitution.* New York, NY: McGraw-Hill.

Pietrusza, D. (2003). *Rothstein: The life, times, and murder of the criminal genius who fixed the 1919 world series.* New York, NY: Carroll & Graf.

Potter, G. W. (1994). *Criminal organizations: Vice, racketeering, and politics in an American city.* Prospect Heights, IL: Waveland Press.

President's Commission on Law Enforcement and Administration of Justice. (1967). *Task force report: Organized crime.* Washington, DC: Government Printing Office.

Simpson, A. E. (1977). *The literature of police corruption.* New York, NY: John Jay Press.

Special Committee to Investigate Organized Crime in Interstate Commerce, U.S. Senate, 82d Cong. (1951).

OUTSIDERS

An outsider is a person who is not accepted by, and does not belong to, a particular group. Outsiders are excluded by particular groups owing to such reasons as socioeconomic status, race, ideology, and gender. Howard S. Becker defines outsiders as individuals labeled as rule breakers or deviants who see themselves in contradiction with the general tendencies of conventional society.

Exclusion from society can be observed in varying degrees with populations such as the physically disabled, the elderly, criminals, and the unemployed. Many of these outsiders depend on involuntary membership for their marginalized status and are sometimes referred to as the falsely accused. Prejudices and thinking that one's values are superior to others lie at the heart of the exclusion of others by individuals or groups. Overidealizing one's own ethnic, religious, or ideological identity and isolating others by reducing them to stereotypes constitutes the simplest form of marginalization. Outsiders are often considered to be a main source of problems in the society; thus, they are generally regarded as those individuals who threaten the established order, who should be rehabilitated, and against whom protective measures should be taken.

The process of marginalization entails a vicious circle. On one hand, those who deviate from social norms are labeled as outsiders, and on the other hand, outsiders regard those who exclude them as outsiders in return. Excluded individuals or groups react against those who exclude them and cut their ties with the society, positioning themselves at the opposite pole of the society as radicalized structures. Therefore, those who adapt to social norms and act accordingly, and those who position themselves against such norms constantly become alienated from each other, which results in social crises for those labeled as outsiders.

Society compels its members to behave in accordance with the norms and values adopted by the majority. However, once those who deviate from such norms and values are excluded and labeled as outsiders, they are now expected to display behaviors that fit their labels. When several members of a minority group are labeled due to an incidence of theft, resulting generalization causes the entire group to be associated with acts of theft. Development of a reactionary and generalizing approach in the society against the outsider compels those individuals seen as deviants to behave according to the pattern forged for them. Frequently, the reaction displayed against outsiders by the society hinders those measures to be taken for deterring the individual from behaviors regarded as deviant, and consequently, the individual maintains such behaviors.

Social exclusion brings about many adverse consequences. Along with consequences such as cutting of ties with, and hostility toward, mainstream society, as well as loss of self-respect from the perspective of outsiders, an increase in crime and other deviant behaviors and social problems is expected to occur. Types of deviation suggested by Becker shed light on the process of exclusion. Whereas those who display deviant behaviors or commit crimes are so labeled in the society, there are others who are not evaluated as criminals or deviants though they act against the law or violate social norms.

The first type consists of "pure" deviants. Those individuals who display rule-breaking behaviors by acting against the law or otherwise violating social norms are consequently labeled by the society as deviants. The second type consists of those who do obey the rules. These individuals are accepted by society since they conform to expectations. A third type consists of individuals who are labeled as deviant even though they too conform to society's rules. For instance, although the law prohibits discrimination by skin color as a basis for citizens' enjoyment of human rights and freedoms, the social categorization of people on the basis of skin color creates a framework for those of minority status to be defined, and thus seen, as deviant. Although these individuals may display no behavior contrary to social norms, there exists a perception of their being deviant, and they may be stigmatized accordingly. The fourth type consists of secret deviants, those individuals who are not perceived and labeled by society as deviant although they repeatedly violate social norms. A popular entertainer, for example, may also privately engage in illicit drug use or collect child pornography but behave perfectly normally in public.

Nurullah Altun and Yavuz Kahya

See also Identity Work; Labeling Approach; Norms and Societal Expectations; Secret Deviance

Further Readings

Becker, H. S. (1966). *Outsiders: Studies in the sociology of deviance*. New York, NY: Free Press.

Bordua, D. (1970). Recent trends: Deviant behaviour and social control. In C. Bersani (Ed.), *Crime and delinquency* (pp. 453–468). London, England: Macmillan.

Goffman, E. (1963). *Stigma: Notes on the management of a spoiled identity*. New York, NY: Simon & Schuster.

Kitsuse, J. (1962). Societal reaction to deviance: problems of theory and method. *Social Problems, 9*(2), 247–256.

PARTICIPANT OBSERVATION

Participant observation is a method used by social science researchers to learn more about various groups of people, including those engaged in taboo or deviant behaviors. More specifically, researchers can use participant observation to acquire firsthand knowledge about how individuals in groups interact with one another as well as with their surrounding environment. For example, researchers who want to learn about how street-level drug transactions are performed (from initial contact between the buyer and seller to the exchanging of goods), how public sexual encounters occur (e.g., the verbal and non-verbal cues used to initiate such encounters), or how drag show performers interact with one another both on- and offstage can use participant observation to temporarily become a part of those groups and acquire an insider's view of the settings.

Participant observation provides a rich understanding of a particular group that may be difficult to attain using other methods such as using surveys to inquire about peoples' perceptions of various groups about whom they may have no intimate knowledge. Participant observation also helps the researcher gain knowledge about groups in which no official data sources with information about a group exist. In addition, with participant observation research, the researcher often gets more than one opportunity to interact with members of a particular group or to be part of a setting. If a researcher is interviewing one or more members of a group only one time, the knowledge that can be acquired is limited in comparison with that which can be obtained when the researcher can go back to a group on multiple occasions.

Participant observation research falls into two distinct categories: overt and covert. Overt participant observation occurs when a particular group is aware of the researcher's presence in the group and is aware that the group is being examined for research purposes. This typically involves research subjects who are willing and consenting participants in a study. Conversely, covert participant observation occurs when a particular group may be aware of the researcher's presence (or may not be aware of his or her presence) but does not know the true identity of the researcher and is unaware that the group is being examined for research purposes. Covert research is practical in attaining information about groups who may never agree to be knowingly researched because they frequently engage in illegal or nonconventional activities or in situations where there is no other way to acquire the desired knowledge about a group using other methods.

Researchers who perform participant observation research experience a number of practical and ethical challenges. In terms of practical challenges, the researcher must initially gain trust among a group's members and take steps to blend within the group. The researcher must also be cognizant of his or her personal safety when researching groups that are known to be dangerous, such as drug dealers or outlaw motorcycle gangs. Also, the participant observer must try to not become too much a part of the group as doing so may cause the researcher to lose sight of the goals of a particular project, which may, in turn, have negative effects on the knowledge gained from a project.

With regard to ethics, especially for the covert participant observer, it may be unfair to engage in research in which people are unaware that they are being examined for research purposes. This may be viewed as an invasion of the individuals' privacy. In addition, should groups later learn that they were the subject of a research project without their knowledge, it may cause a degree of psychological harm or embarrassment to the individuals. This harm could, as a result, lead to increased distrust of outsiders among a group's members, which may hinder the ability of future researchers to study the group. Finally, the participant observer (particularly the covert participant observer) may be in a position in which breaking the law is necessary to avoid being identified as a true outsider (e.g., buying, selling or using drugs to blend in with the group being studied) or be in a position to not disclose violations of the law to the police.

In sum, participant observation allows researchers to acquire deeper knowledge about specific groups of individuals that is difficult to attain using other research methods. This knowledge, then, can be shared with other researchers with similar interests, the public, policy makers, or leaders in various types of organizations who may use such knowledge to address assumptions about particular groups or adjust future research and organizational policies. In spite of the inherent practical and ethical challenges that must be addressed by the participant observer when proposing and undertaking a project, participant observation is a valuable tool in all types of social science research, including the fields of criminology, sociology, anthropology, and psychology.

Corey Burton

See also Dramaturgy; Edge Ethnography; Ethics and Deviance Research; Institutional Review Boards and Studying Deviance

Further Readings

Berg, B. L. (2009). *Qualitative research methods for the social sciences* (7th ed.) Boston, MA: Allyn & Bacon.

Miller, J. M. (1995). Covert participant observation: Reconsidering the least used method. *Journal of Contemporary Criminal Justice, 11*(2), 97–105.

Miller, J. M., & Tewksbury, R. (2006). *Research methods: A qualitative reader.* Upper Saddle River, NJ: Pearson.

Simpson, J. F. (2007). *More than simply "hanging out": The nature of participant observation and research relationships.* Durham: University of New Hampshire.

Tewksbury, R. (1995). Adventures in the erotic oasis: Sex and danger in men's same-sex, public, sexual encounters. *Journal of Men's Studies, 4*(1), 9–24.

PAWNBROKERS

A pawnbroker is a licensed dealer who lends money on personal property at a regulated rate of interest. If the loan is not repaid in the agreed-on time, the pawnbroker has the right to take possession of the item and sell it. Although pawnbrokers may not be viewed on the whole as taboo, they are, and have been, a necessary fixture of a deviant subculture of American society. Before any laws were established to regulate the industry, pawnbrokers served the credit needs of low-income households, criminals, and those with gambling addiction or other vices. Many of the transactions of pawnbrokers and their clients stigmatized the occupation as deviant—a stigma that still holds true today regardless of the new regulations placed on them.

Early pawnbrokers in America lent to individuals who could not obtain a loan from a bank because these prospective borrowers were deemed high risk due to their low income. Pawnbrokers of the 17th and 18th centuries were not regulated by any governing body, and they could charge a customer an interest amount well above that of the banks. However, individuals in dire need of quick, short-term loans were able to obtain them by pawning assets, such as cattle, plows, and clothing. Tavern owners and innkeepers also became pawnbrokers in a sense, allowing patrons to pawn items and receive money in exchange for the opportunity to continue drinking. Proprietors of these establishments not only made money by way of interest but also on the sale of alcohol. In the early 19th century, government officials began receiving complaints about these tavern activities and shut down many of them because of a belief that men should not be borrowing money and spending it on alcohol. Rather, they should spend on the needs of their family. Pawnbrokers were viewed as a means for individuals to continue their self-destructive behaviors.

The many complaints received by the government gave rise to the visibility of pawnbrokers and began the implementation of the stigma placed on pawnbrokers. Pawnbrokers had increased their visibility by relocating their shops to areas that had the possibility of offering countless business opportunities by way of low-income households. With the increase in pawnbrokers and the increasing visibility and stigma placed on them, the government passed regulations to help impede the growing industry. The eventual model used to control the dealings of pawnbrokers was passed in 1812 by the New York City Council. The ordinance required pawnbrokers to pay a $50 fee and apply for a license and to keep records of all transactions and a description of all patrons, and it no longer allowed pawnbrokers to conduct business with minors or slaves. Hence, the government was able to oversee business deals between legitimate pawnbrokers and society. However, not all pawnbrokers chose to conduct business within the watchful eye of the government and found ways to circumvent the regulations placed on them.

When pawnbrokers chose to operate so as to avoid government surveillance, it was often because the business conducted was criminal. Some pawnbrokers became the primary means for the selling of stolen property by burglars. Pawn tickets have often been found on the arrest of suspects in these crimes, linking the pawnbroker to criminals. The knowledge that criminals were able to steal items and have the items resold through a pawnbroker or his establishment added to the stigma already placed on the pawnbroker. Many believed that the locations of the pawnbrokers' establishments encouraged criminals to commit crimes of theft in hopes that they could sell the stolen goods through the more accessible pawnbrokers. With an increase in links between criminals and pawnbrokers, the government, beginning in the 20th century, sought to obtain more control over the industry and establish a need for regulations that would impinge on pawnbrokers across the country.

The 20th and 21st centuries presented a fluctuating economy for all Americans, including pawnbrokers. Much like the early pawnbrokers who lent money so that their patrons could purchase alcohol, pawnbrokers of the 20th century gave visibility to a not-so-new vice, money for a variety of addictions. Today, pawnbrokers are much more visible due to several reality shows on cable television, which depict interactions with patrons needing money for their vices. One show, titled *Pawn Stars*, is located in the heart of Las Vegas, Nevada. As seen on the television show, many of the patrons pawning and selling items admit to needing the money so that they can continue gambling at nearby casinos.

Because these admissions are televised, the public view of pawnbrokers has changed very little since the time of their predecessors. Although this television show often reflects on the rarity and value of the items being pawned, it also offers insight on the negotiations between the pawnbroker and the patron. The pawnbrokers retain their deviant status because of the difference in price that is offered to the patron versus the value at which the item has been appraised. Pawnbrokers rationalize this discrepancy as a function of operating costs and salary for employees.

Another popular television series, *Hardcore Pawn*, set in Detroit, Michigan's 8 Mile area, also depicts the value discrepancy between offer and appraisal as well as the "hardness" of both the pawnbroker and the patron. This show counters the stereotype that pawnbrokers fence stolen property by depicting how the pawnbrokers legitimize the item and the validity of the ownership before allowing the sale or pawn. Television viewers are also able to see how pawnbrokers interact with patrons trying to pawn or sell items to support a drug habit or other taboo vices. While this show focuses less on the value of the items being pawned, it helps alleviate some of the stigma that labeled pawnbrokers as deviant since their inception.

Christina Newgebaver, Margot Hasha, and DeAnn Kalich

See also Deviant Career; Gambling Addiction; Occupational Criminality; Stolen Goods Network

Further Readings

Banerjee, S. (2010). Urban technology and changing forms of crime in early colonial Calcutta. *Social Scientist, 38,* 25–36.

Hudson, M. (1996). *Merchants of misery: How corporate America profits from poverty.* Monroe, ME: Common Courage Press.

Woloson, W. A. (2007). In hock: Pawning in early America. *Journal of the Early Republic, 27,* 35–81.

PEACEMAKING CRIMINOLOGY

Peacemaking criminology is a set of diverse traditions (religious, feminist, and critical) that share a critique of a culture permeated by an obsession with competition and oppression. While only recently appearing as a formal theory in academia, it builds on the philosophy and actions of historical peace-makers from the 19th and 20th centuries, such as Mahatma Gandhi and Martin Luther King Jr. These key figures belonged to and led communities of activists who highlighted spiritualism, human rights, and nonviolence. Currently, peacemaking criminologists use these guiding principles to examine how crimes and social harms are embedded in institutional practices and legitimated by cultural beliefs at every step of the criminal justice system, in the making and breaking of laws, and in society's response to lawbreaking.

Proponents of peacemaking criminology argue that from the definition of crime to enforcement practices, the criminal justice system violently maintains an unjust social order and thereby perpetuates crime and social harm. Examples of violence in the system include the death penalty, long prison terms, harsh treatment of prisoners, and incarceration of nonviolent drug offenders. In addition, repressive social control is aimed at the poor or powerless individual offender while ignoring institutional practices that benefit the powerful and are ostensibly more harmful (e.g., corporate harms/crimes such as toxic waste dumping, institutional discrimination, poverty/inequality, and racism). Because the criminal justice system is charged with maintaining an unjust social order, the criminal justice system is seen as criminal. This entry summarizes the commonalities; draws distinctions between the spiritual, feminist, and critical peacemaking traditions; and gives examples of applications, contributions, and critiques of peacemaking criminology.

Peacemaking criminologists share a critique of objective knowledge, arguing that theory cannot be unbiased or objective because it is impossible to separate values from any research agenda. Researchers who claim objectivity by eschewing activism are not remaining neutral but rather choosing the side of the status quo. For example, the data sets generally preferred by mainstream criminologists tend to favor quantitative data (e.g., Uniform Crime Report and National Crime Victimization Survey) that are considered objective (albeit with data collection problems). However, these data focus on the crimes of the poor and powerless at the exclusion of crimes of the powerful (e.g., state and corporate crime). Indeed, there is no systematic data collection of state and corporate crimes even though they are more harmful (physically and monetarily) than are widely reported Index crimes (i.e., crimes included in the Federal Bureau of Investigation's annual crime index—willful homicide, forcible rape, robbery, burglary, aggravated assault, larceny more than $50, motor vehicle theft, and arson). This is given as an example of the political bias (e.g., activism) embedded in quantitative data specifically and objective science generally. Because all research is seen as activism, there is an overt and unapologetic commitment to using research to further social justice goals. The source of crime is examined with the purpose of offering empathy, harmony, and social justice to those classified as deviant or criminal.

Proponents tend to use a wide variety of methodologies including quantitative, qualitative, cross-cultural, and historical. Cross-cultural and historical methodologies are particularly important because of the goal to generate alternatives to current practices.

For example, proponents highlight the works of Mahatma Gandhi and Martin Luther King Jr. as examples of nonviolent actions that further social justice. Others compare the U.S. and Norwegian criminal justice practices to show the repressive nature of the U.S. system and advocate for more restorative justice practices.

Spiritual and Religious Peacemaking Traditions

Gandhi's philosophy of Satyagraha is an example of spiritual and religious influences on peacemaking criminology. Traditionally, the purpose of violent and nonviolent conflict is to assert one's will on another or to thwart, interpersonally or at the nation-state level, the goal of others. The goal of Satyagraha is to convert the opponent. In Satyagraha, it is impossible to separate the process (means) and the goals (ends). A successful outcome is cooperation with the opponent to meet a just end. In this way, the goal is to seek elimination of antagonisms and to transform and thereby purify the antagonist. A lasting peace could never be achieved through violent or coercive means.

While Satyagraha is seemingly focused on individual enlightenment, peacemaking criminologists note the blocks to compassion and kindness found in societal arrangements. For example, the social contract model of community based on self-interest discourages compassion. Any act to aid another comes at the expense or sacrifice of self-interest. A social order based on self-interest will facilitate conflict and crime, because it requires alienation and exclusion of the other. Examples of social order that encourage compassion such as "mutuality" in the

Hutterite community and the law of *agapē* in the Mennonite community, which decrees "you shall love your neighbor as yourself," are used to show the impact of societal arrangements on the ability of individuals to care for others. Specifically, the social contract encourages self-interest and punishes caring, while alternative examples of social order encourage and reward trust and interdependence.

Feminist Peacemaking Traditions

Peacemaking criminology and feminist theory share a basic critique of structures of domination. Feminist peacemakers argue that women and their values are important and that social institutions have suppressed women's perspective. Because historically institutions and practices were created by men, the social structure itself is built on and reflects the values men have historically been taught to embody (hierarchy, domination, competition, aggression, and violence). Conversely, institutions and social practices have excluded, delegitimized, even demonized, those values historically associated with women (egalitarianism, equality, cooperation, caring, and compassion). Women have only entered the public sphere by adopting the values associated with men. Therefore, institutions and practices have not changed and remain oppressive (for both men and women). The goal is not to have women equal with men on men's terms, by becoming like men, but that women change societal institutions and practices to incorporate and reflect values traditionally associated with femininity. Because women have been taught (and are more likely) to exist in a web of relationships where they define themselves in relation to others, including women's values and skills in social institutions can aid in the creation of a just society.

Critical Peacemaking Traditions

Peacemaking criminologists operating in the critical tradition see the major source of crime as power over others and the related unresponsiveness power engenders. Unresponsiveness occurs when an actor (individual, organization, and/or nation-state) pursues his or her agenda regardless of how others are affected. Unresponsiveness is built into the social structure and furthers domination of the oppressed. While law and government tend to hold the underclass responsible for social disorder, they also tend to limit the responsibility of the corporate elite. Laws limit the liability of investors, large monopolized

markets ignore the welfare of customers, and legal practice is unresponsive to the social harms caused by large corporations. Societal practices (from the individual to multinational corporations and the nation-state) require responsiveness such that actions (intent) continue to be adapted and changed to take into account those affected. Change requires persistent attention to outcomes of actions and responsive dialogue between parties with competing interests. The solution is conflict resolution based on collaborative problem solving aimed at the root of the problem. The goal is not to manage or settle the conflict temporarily but to eliminate the sources of conflict by meeting the needs of all parties involved. A forced or coerced peace is a temporary solution because resentment lives in the heart of the defeated, and conflict will return in the future.

Contributions

Peacemaking criminology has offered several contributions to criminology. Perhaps the most important contribution is in current epistemological debates between positivism and postmodernism. Generally, the positivist perspective postulates that a real objective world can be discovered without recourse to philosophical speculation. The use of scientific methods disconnects the researcher from the object such that universal principles can be discovered through unbiased observations. In this way, words and things have direct correspondence. In contrast, postmodern critiques argue that it is not possible to objectively view the world because it is always filtered through the perception of the subject. Words do not directly represent objects but are a reflection of the particular viewpoint of the subject. Therefore, multiple truths exist, and there is no possibility of universal objective truth or reality. In both cases, peacemaking criminology is left out of the "legitimate" production of knowledge and theory. While positivists claim that to seek justice, love, and peace through research is biased, postmodernists claim that justice, love, and peace are not "real."

Peacemaking criminology moves past the debate between positivist adherence to and postmodernist critiques of objectivity, arguing that just because pure objectivity is problematic, and multiple truths exist, does not mean there is no reality, no suffering, no war or peace. The goal is not objectivity as in traditional positivist views of criminology or continual deconstruction of and death of meaning as in postmodern criminology. Rather proponents work toward an intersubjective working truth that is continually assessed and refined by seeking out multiple diverse perspectives.

Finally, peacemaking criminology reveals the importance of including multiple levels of analysis by showing that individual behavior is deeply rooted in social structures. For example, proponents show the importance of examining traditional masculinity as embedded in cultural beliefs and social structure and as an integral part of individual identity. This is used in the prison abolition movement to challenge traditional masculinity as the cause of oppression and violence in individual inmates, the prison system, and the larger culture or social structure. Insights gained have been used at multiple levels of analysis to address and improve international issues, the interconnections between nations and the environment, economic systems and religions, interactions between individuals, and how individuals treat themselves.

Critiques

Critics argue that peacemaking criminology is not a criminological theory. First, it is not criminology, because it focuses on the broader culture and structure of society. Proponents agree but see this as a strength, arguing that the criminal justice system is embedded in the culture and structure, and to analyze it in isolation is to misrepresent reality. Second, critics argue that there is a lack of conceptual clarity, which prevents the refinement of a coherent theory. Proponents see the diversity of approaches as a strength that maintains the dynamism necessary to build an intersubjective truth and allows the flexibility to study multiple phenomena.

Critics also argue that peacemaking criminology is utopian, unrealistic, and soft on crime. Proponents see this critique as a reflection of the deeply embedded cultural values of punishment and oppression. Perhaps the most frequent critique is that there is no evidence to support the assertions of peacemaking criminology. Rather, violence is necessary to stop evil from spreading in the world. The most common given example to prove this point is the "good" war (World War II), when violence was needed to stop Hitler's bid for dominance and ethnic cleansing. Proponents argue that while World War II got rid of Hitler, they question whether even this war was necessary or successful. Rather, it is seen as a temporary peace. A total of 50 to 70 million deaths, countless injuries (physical and psychological), and uncountable suffering in World War II not only did not "work" but also served to increase militarism, the justification for the use of arms, and the subsequent nuclear arms race. Proponents argue that there is no evidence that this or any other war "works" in the long term because it does not address the underlying conflict and because resentment lives on in the hearts of the defeated.

Tina Hebert Deshotels

See also Positivist Definitions of Deviance; Racism; Social Control; White-Collar Crime

Further Readings

Avruch, K., Scimecca, J. A., & Black, P. W. (Eds.). (1991). *Conflict resolution: Cross-cultural perspectives.* Westport, CT: Greenwood Press.

Barak G. (2005). A reciprocal to peacemaking criminology: Between adversarialism and mutualism. *Theoretical Criminology, 9*(2), 131–152.

Fuller, J. R. (1998). *Criminal justice: A peacemaking perspective.* Needham Heights, MA: Allyn & Bacon.

McEvoy, K., & Newburn, T. (Eds.). (2003). *Criminology, conflict resolution and restorative justice.* New York, NY: Palgrave Macmillan.

Pepinsky, H. E. (1998). Empathy works, obedience doesn't: Criminal justice. *Policy Review, 9,* 141–167.

Pepinsky, H. E., & Quinney, R. (Eds.). (1991). *Criminology as peacemaking.* Bloomington: Indiana University Press.

Quinney, R. (1993). A life of crime: Criminology and public policy as peacemaking. *Journal of Crime and Justice, 16,* 3–9.

Wozniak, J. (2008). Poverty and peacemaking criminology: Beyond mainstream criminology. *Critical Criminology, 16*(3), 209–223.

PEDOPHILIA

Pedophilia is generally considered to be the sexual attraction to children who have not yet reached puberty. Pedophilia is a paraphilia, which is a sexual dysfunction. The most commonly used definition comes from the *Diagnostic and Statistical Manual,* fourth edition (*DSM-IV*) published by the American Psychiatric Association. The *DSM-IV* imposes age limits on pedophilia, requiring that the diagnosis apply only to persons who are age 16 years or older and are at least 5 years older than the child, unless the person in question is an adolescent. In the case of an adolescent, age difference and sexual maturity of both parties are considered. To be diagnosed as a pedophile under the *DSM-IV*, the person must have had recurring intense sexual fantasies or urges involving sexual behavior with a child under the age of puberty for at least 6 months, and the individual has either acted on the fantasies or the urges have caused distress or interpersonal difficulty.

While some pedophiles are attracted to any prepubescent child, pedophiles generally report being attracted to children within a particular age range. Some pedophiles are attracted only to children, while others report occasionally being attracted to adults. Some pedophiles report being sexually attracted to both male and female children, but many report that their attraction is limited to either male children or to female children. Pedophilia involving female victims is considered to be more common, but the recidivism rate for pedophiles with male victims is higher.

This entry begins by denoting the differences among pedophilia, hebephilia, and child molestation and then discusses the acceptance of pedophilia in some cultures. Next, the entry examines the theories of causes of pedophile and other research issues. The entry concludes with a discussion of various treatment programs.

Hebephilia

While pedophilia refers to a sexual preference for a prepubescent child, the term *hebephilia* refers to a sexual preference for a pubescent child. Pubescent children are generally those from age 11 or 12 years to age 14 or 15 years. Pubescence is dependent on the start of physical, sexual development, such as the first stages of pubic hair growth, the appearance of breast buds in females, and the initial changes in the penis, testicles, and scrotal skin in males. Prepubescent children have not started physical sexual development. Research indicates that hebephilia is relatively common compared with other forms of sexual interest in children. Hebephilia is not currently included as an official diagnosis in the *DSM-IV*; however, there has been significant discussion about including it in the next edition.

Child Molesters and Pedophiles

It is important to note that not all pedophiles act on their sexual urges for children. It is equally important to note that there are individuals who do sexually molest children who are not pedophiles. Child molesters may be pedophiles, but they may also be individuals who sexually abuse children as a substitute for their preferred sexual partner, because they lack the social skills to attract an adult partner, or because they have the opportunity to explore their sexual interests with a nonthreatening or nonjudgmental child. Child molesters who are not pedophiles have engaged in sexual activity with a child but do not have a sexual preference for children. For example, if a man is married to a woman with a 10-year-old daughter, and he prefers to have sex with the daughter, he is a pedophile. However, if he prefers to have sex with his wife, but she refuses to have sex with him, so he has sex with the daughter as a substitute, he is a child molester, but not a pedophile. While pedophile is a clinical term, child molester is a social/legal term.

Females as Pedophiles

Very few females are identified as sex offenders or as pedophiles. It is believed that pedophilia is rare among women. While the number of cases of females sexually abusing children is significantly lower than that of males, it is probable that some cases of females having sexual contact with children go undetected, because it may occur during regular caregiving activities, such as bathing or dressing a child.

The socialization of men and women may explain the difference in rates of pedophilia. Men are socialized to be more sexually aggressive and to seek partners who are smaller, weaker, and less powerful. Women are socialized to be the primary caregivers for children and may be less likely to sexually exploit the child because they are more sensitive to the child's needs. In addition, women are often perceived to be harmless and nonthreatening in sexual matters. Even in publicized cases where women have engaged in sexual activity with adolescent males, though hebephilia not pedophilia, it is sometimes seen as a rite of passage for the adolescent male victim rather than as genuine victimization.

Other Cultures

While behavior associated with pedophilia is negatively sanctioned in most cultures, it is not considered deviant in all cultures. There is evidence that sex between an adult and a child has been accepted by a variety of cultures throughout history, including during some periods in Rome. The Sambia tribe in New Guinea has an initiation rite of passage for males where prepubescent boys perform fellatio on pubescent boys, because semen is seen as necessary to bring about maturity for the younger boys.

For centuries, men in parts of Afghanistan have used boys, usually between the ages of 9 and 15 years, as sexual partners. Some Pashtun tribal members in southern Afghanistan are *bacha bazi*, their term for a man with a boy lover. Here young boys dress up as girls, wear bells, and dance at parties for groups of men who throw money at the boys. After the dancing is over, each man often takes one of the boys home with him. While Islamic law forbids homosexuality, men who participate in this activity claim that it is not homosexuality, because they are not in love with the boys.

What Leads to Pedophilia?

The cause of pedophilia is unknown, but significant research is being done, and there are many theories about what may lead to it. The prevailing theory suggests that pedophilia is a form of sexual orientation, much like heterosexuality or homosexuality. This theory suggests that because pedophilia is a sexual attraction to children discovered in early adolescence and remaining stable over time, it is simply another form of sexual orientation. Those who propose this theory recognize that even if pedophilia is a form of sexual orientation, it is unlikely to gain social or legal acceptance in Western culture because the behavior that accompanies the preference involves the sexual exploitation of children who are not legally able to consent.

Studies of personality traits of pedophiles indicate that pedophiles often suffer from feelings of inferiority, powerlessness, isolation and loneliness, emotional immaturity, and anger or hostility. Pedophiles also have difficulty with interpersonal relationships, particularly mature age-appropriate relationships. Some have severe personality disorders or major psychiatric disorders. Low self-esteem is a trait commonly found in pedophiles. Impulsivity is sometimes, but not consistently, found in studies of pedophiles and is debated in the literature. Those who argue against impulsivity generally argue that because sexually molesting a child is usually planned and not a spontaneous act, it indicates that pedophiles do have impulse control.

Another theory about pedophilia is that persons who were abused as children, particularly sexually abused, are more likely to be pedophiles. Studies indicate that those who engage in homosexual child sexual abuse are more likely to have been sexually abused as a child than persons who engage in heterosexual child sexual abuse. However, it must be noted that the majority of individuals who are molested as children do not sexually abuse children when they are adults.

Some studies indicate that pedophiles have neuropsychiatric differences from the general population. These differences include lower intelligence, a slight increase in left-handedness, and abnormal brain function. Neurochemical differences, particularly relating to serotonin function and metabolism as well as hormonal responses, have also been found in pedophiles. There is also some discussion in the literature that a genetic link may lead to a predisposition for pedophilia. It is important to note that while there are varying theories about what may lead to pedophilia, there is no known cause for it.

Research Issues

The limitations on research make it difficult to estimate how prevalent pedophilia is in the general population, or even among child molesters. There are very few studies on adults who have a sexual interest in children that represent the social composition of society as a whole. Because most known pedophiles and child molesters are male, the research centers on males. Most research is done on incarcerated sex offenders or patients who are seeking treatment, often because of a court order. This group is not considered representative of child molesters, because many cases of child sexual abuse probably do not come to the attention of the criminal justice or the mental health systems. It is difficult to study persons from the general population, because they are likely to be reluctant to identify themselves as sexually attracted to children, or as having had a sexual relation with a child for fear of what consequences might follow. Child molesters who are participating in research studies may be unwilling to admit to sexual fantasies about children, thus making it difficult to differentiate between someone who has engaged in sexual activity with a child based on opportunity rather than because of sexual fantasies and urges that involve children.

Assessment Methods Used in Research

There are various assessment methods used to research pedophilia. One assessment method used during research includes surveys and interviews where participants report their own sexual fantasies, urges, and behaviors that involve children. This method is dependent on the honesty of the participant, which is why it is often paired with another form of assessment. The sexual behavior offense history of survey and interview participants is often used to provide verification of the participants' truthfulness. The measurement of psychophysiological responses is another assessment tool that may be combined with survey and interview research or used as an independent measurement.

There are three types of psychophysiological response assessments. The first is polygraphy, also known as a lie detector. Polygraphy assesses changes in heart rate, blood pressure, skin conductance, and respiration while subjects are asked a series of questions about their behavior. The belief is that deceptive answers concerning self-reported information about sexual interests and behavior will produce physiological responses that can be differentiated from those associated with nondeceptive answers. The reliability of the polygraph is still a controversial topic in the scientific community.

Another psychophysiological response assessment method used is referred to as viewing time. Subjects are given photographs of male and female adults and children. In the photographs the subjects are clothed, semiclothed, or nude. Nude photographs generally come from medical books and are not erotic in nature. This avoids any legal prohibition against possessing child pornography. Subjects are asked to rate each photograph according to attractiveness and interest. Subjects are unaware that the length of time they spend with each photograph is the key measure, which is then compared with their self-reported interest in children. Researchers have had more success in identifying pedophiles who prefer boys and hebephiles who prefer girls than other types of sexual dysfunction. It is important that subjects are unaware that viewing time is what is being measured to minimize manipulation by the subjects.

The last psychophysiological response assessment is the phallometric testing procedure. The phallometric procedure involves fitting an apparatus to the subject's penis that will measure changes in circumference or blood volume while the subject is presented with photographs, videos, and/or audio depictions of sexually explicit material involving female adults, male adults, female children, male children, female adolescents, and male adolescents. The greater the change in penile circumference or blood volume, the greater the sexual arousal to the stimulus is considered to be. Subjects' faces are also monitored to determine whether the subject is paying attention to the stimuli during the test to determine whether the subject is attempting to manipulate the testing.

Historically, phallometric testing has been the most reliable means for determining pedophilia. It measures strictly sexual arousal rather than physiological responses that could be explained by other circumstances and has accurately distinguished between sex offenders with child victims, sex offenders with adult victims, and nonoffending males. It is believed that levels of sexual arousal can be used to differentiate between pedophiles and other offenders with child victims. However, there are problems with this method. Phallometric testing is invasive, requires expensive equipment, does not work on females, requires functioning male genitalia, requires sexually explicit images of children, the possession of which is illegal in the United States, and can be manipulated by the subject thinking about something other than the images he is being shown.

Treatment

There are a variety of treatment programs for pedophiles, but the effectiveness of each type has been questioned. Treatment is only effective when pedophiles are motivated and committed to changing their behavior. The majority of treatment programs are aimed at preventing pedophiles from sexually abusing a child rather than at changing their sexual orientation. The current thought is that the treatment of pedophiles has better outcomes if psychotherapy is combined with drug treatment.

Pedophiles often rationalize, justify, and minimize their behavior. One way is by suggesting that their actions were educational to help the child learn about sexuality from a caring adult. Others claim that the child encouraged and/or started the sexual encounter and that the child derived as much pleasure from the activities as the pedophile. Others simply deny that they did anything wrong. Overcoming these beliefs is one of the major obstacles to treating a pedophile.

Psychotherapy for pedophiles is aimed at enabling patients to recognize and overcome their rationalizations, developing empathy for the child, and at developing techniques to control their sexual impulses. A series of behavioral therapies have been designed to help pedophiles change their attitudes and beliefs along with their behaviors. Aversion therapy is a treatment program that forces the pedophile to associate sexual fantasies and urges toward children with an unpleasant sensation such as a shock, unpleasant smell, or nausea. Aversion therapy was once a popular way to treat pedophiles, but positive results have proven to be short term at best.

Desensitization exercises teach the pedophile muscle relaxation techniques to help tolerate discomfort from suppressing a sexual urge. Another technique is teaching pedophiles to imagine the negative consequences of a sexual encounter with a child as a substitute for engaging in fantasies. Negative consequences include arrest, prosecution, imprisonment, public humiliation, and losing employment, family, and friends. Victim empathy training teaches pedophiles how sexual abuse feels from the victim's perspective. Relapse therapy teaches the patient to recognize the types of situations that lead to sexually abusing a child and how to avoid those situations and helps the patient find better ways to handle those situations. The literature is inconsistent about the success of relapse therapy programs, but it is thought that patients in all types of programs need relapse prevention therapy and continued monitoring to help them continue with the techniques they have learned, to help avoid urges, and to maintain support for abstinence.

Drug treatment has gained popularity in treating sex offenders, including pedophiles. Drug treatment is essentially chemical castration that reduces or eliminates sexual urges. Chemical castration is preferred over physical castration because those who have been physically castrated can take testosterone and reoffend, and because physically castrated offenders rarely receive long-term follow-up visits, continuous monitoring, or continuing psychiatric evaluation and treatment. Pedophiles undergoing drug treatment generally receive all of these continuing forms of monitoring. The best outcomes in preventing sexual offenses against children by pedophiles have come from a combination of psychotherapy and drug treatment. Critics claim that drug treatment is expensive and has side effects for some who receive it. Proponents argue that the dose of the drugs can be adjusted to control side effects and that the economic cost is less significant than the cost of harm to children.

Conclusion

Pedophilia is the sexual attraction to prepubescent children that is accompanied by persistent fantasies and urges and either sexual activity with a child or distress at not acting on the urge to have sex with a child. Sexual attraction to pubescent children is hebephilia. While both pedophilia and hebephilia are clinical terms, acting on either impulse with a child is illegal in the Western culture. Child molesters not only include pedophiles and hebephiles who engage in sexual activity with a child but also include those who are not sexually attracted to children but participate in the activity because of opportunity, curiosity, or inability to find a willing adult partner. Pedophiles are generally male. The cause of pedophilia is unknown, but it is currently believed to be a sexual orientation. The prevalence of pedophiles in society and among child molesters is unknown, because the crime is likely underreported, and research has many limitations. There is no cure for pedophilia, but there are a variety of treatments aimed at helping pedophiles control their urges, fantasies, and behaviors.

Diane M. Daane

See also Abuse by Clergy; Child Sexual Abuse; Defining Deviance; *Diagnostic and Statistical Manual*; Homosexuality; Incest

Further Readings

American Psychiatric Association. (2000). *Diagnostic and statistical manual of mental disorders* (4th ed., text revision). Washington, DC: Author.

Blanchard, R., Lykins, A. D., Wherett, D., Kuban, M. E., Cantor, J. M., Dickey, R., & Klassen, P. E. (2009). Pedophilia, hebephilia, and the *DSM-IV*. *Archives of Sexual Behavior, 38*, 335–350.

Brinkley, J. (2010, August 29). Afghanistan's dirty little secret. *The San Francisco Chronicle*, p. E8.

Denov, M. S. (2001). A culture of denial: Exploring professional perspectives of female sex offending. *Canadian Journal of Criminology, 43*, 303–329.

Hall, R. C. W., & Hall, R. C. W. (2007). A profile of pedophilia: Definition, characteristics of offenders, recidivism, treatment outcomes, and forensic issues. *Mayo Clinic Proceedings, 82*, 457–471.

Lanning, K. V. (2010). *Child molesters: A behavioral analysis* (5th ed.). Alexandria, VA: National Center for Missing & Exploited Children.

Seto, M. C. (2004). Pedophilia and sexual offenses against children. *Annual Review of Sex Research, 15*, 329–369.

Seto, M. C. (2012). Is pedophilia a sexual orientation? *Archives of Sexual Behavior, 41*, 231–236.

Smiljanich, K., & Briere, J. (1996). Self-reported sexual interest in children: Sex differences and psychosocial correlates in a university sample. *Violence and Victims, 11*, 39–50.

PEOPLE FOR THE ETHICAL TREATMENT OF ANIMALS

The nonprofit group People for the Ethical Treatment of Animals, or PETA, describes itself as the largest animal rights group in the world. PETA takes an "uncompromising" stance on animal rights, arguing that animals' lives have inherent value, apart from their usefulness to human beings. As documented on PETA's website, PETA president and cofounder Ingrid Newkirk has said, "When it comes to pain, love, joy, loneliness, and fear, a rat is a pig is a dog is a boy. Each one values his or her life and fights the knife." This statement in itself represents an act of deviance through its contrast with dominant views about animals, which portray them as existing for human purposes and pleasures. PETA's motto asserts that "animals are not ours to eat, wear, experiment on, or use for entertainment," indicating four domains in which animals undergo sustained confinement and suffering. Thus, PETA's campaigns focus primarily, but not exclusively, on industrial (or factory) farming, fur farming, animal testing, and animals in entertainment (e.g., circuses and rodeos). Many campaigns use controversial tactics to make people aware of animal abuse. PETA illustrates how social practices taken for granted in one era, such as the routine abuse of animals in laboratories and on farms, can become unacceptable over time. It also shows how a once deviant philosophy, such as animal rights, can move into the mainstream.

Founding of the Organization

PETA's origins date to 1980 when, along with Alex Pacheco, Newkirk started the group to educate people about the concept of animal rights. Although a lifelong animal lover, the British-born Newkirk consumed meat and did not contemplate animal rights until adulthood. In her early 20s, she began working in an animal shelter, and then in law enforcement and animal protection in Maryland and Washington, D.C. She served as Poundmaster of Washington, D.C., and spearheaded legislation to establish the District of Columbia's first spay and neuter clinic. She also served as Director of Cruelty Investigations for the Washington Humane Society. After reading Peter Singer's *Animal Liberation*, which argues against discrimination based on species membership, Newkirk wanted to start a group that would take action against cruelty. Pacheco and Newkirk met at a Washington, D.C., animal shelter, where Pacheco volunteered at the time. He had been involved in animal rights activism since visiting a slaughterhouse as a teenager. He had tracked whaling operations while on the crew of the *Sea Shepherd*, the first vessel of the nonprofit Sea Shepherd Conservation Society. In 1980, Pacheco and Newkirk launched PETA as a more radical alternative to existing avenues for animal advocacy.

The Silver Spring Monkeys

The campaign that brought PETA to national and international attention lasted for more than 10 years. In 1981, Pacheco began working as a volunteer at the Institute of Behavioral Research in Silver Spring, Maryland, to observe firsthand what took place in animal research laboratories. At the Institute, the psychologist Edward Taub studied neuroplasticity, using monkeys as experimental subjects. Taub's research involved deafferentation, or surgically severing nerves in the monkeys' spinal cords that send signals between the brain and the arms. Taub then restrained the monkeys' limbs in an attempt to retrain them to use the deafferented arms. Proponents point out that primate research on neuroplasticity has led to techniques that enable paralyzed individuals to regain the use of limbs after injury or stroke.

Pacheco found that the monkeys lacked veterinary care and lived in conditions he considered deplorable. He told Taub that he wanted to work at night, which allowed him to photograph the conditions in the lab. Pacheco reported violations of Maryland's Prevention of Cruelty to Animals law to the State Police of Montgomery County. They raided the laboratory in September 1981. Taub faced more than 100 counts of animal cruelty and failure to provide veterinary care. The case represents the first charges of this sort brought against a scientist in a U.S. research laboratory. Taub claimed that Pacheco had staged the conditions in the lab. After several trials and appeals, the court acquitted Taub in 1982, claiming that Maryland's cruelty laws did not apply to researchers.

Battles over custody of the monkeys lasted for more than a decade and ignited national debate about the treatment of animals used in research. The Maryland State Police had given the monkeys to PETA during the raid, but the court remanded them to Taub. PETA filed suit to regain custody, and two sanctuaries had offered to house the monkeys.

Because the laboratory at the Institute of Behavioral Research received funding from the National Institutes of Health (NIH), they retained custody of the monkeys and criticized PETA's efforts as a publicity stunt. Courts repeatedly denied PETA's claims for custody on grounds that the group had no legal standing. Five of the monkeys went to zoos. The others went to Tulane University's Delta Regional Primate Research Center. The remaining monkeys were euthanized in 1991.

Publicity of the case helped facilitate the 1985 passage of a revision of the Animal Welfare Act, which introduced guidelines for the use of animals in research, including the requirement that institutions receiving federal funding have an Institutional Animal Care and Use Committee to oversee the treatment of animals in laboratories under their purview. The case also brought animal rights and PETA to public attention. By 1991, the organization that had started with Newkirk, Pacheco, and a few other people had more than 350,000 members, a paid staff of more than 100, and an annual budget of more than $7 million. Pacheco left the organization in 1999. Newkirk remains president of PETA. In 2013, the organization claimed to have more than 3 million members.

Campaign Tactics

Both Newkirk and Pacheco stated the need to use potentially controversial tactics to make people aware of the suffering of animals in its four focus areas. Throughout PETA's history, the group has pursued media attention through celebrity endorsement, consumer boycotts, direct action, and street theater. In antifur campaigns, PETA activists have thrown red paint on store windows and catwalks at fashion shows. Through its Shareholder Resolution Campaign, PETA purchases stock in publicly traded companies, including McDonald's, Monsanto, YUM Brands, and 3M. After becoming a shareholder, the group then introduces resolutions promoting the cruelty-free treatment of animals.

PETA often uses graphic images to make the treatment of animals visible where it would ordinarily be hidden from view, such as in laboratories and on factory farms. One of the controversial photos taken by Pacheco in Taub's lab became readily associated with PETA. The image depicts a monkey, named Domitian, with his head and all four limbs restrained in a homemade contraption referred to as an "immobilizing chair." The photo was, and

remains, widely published in PETA's literature, with the caption, "This is vivisection. Don't let anyone tell you different." Other images use less violent images that still have shock value. In PETA's antifur campaign, for example, many celebrities have posed nude to protest the fur industry in photos featuring the caption, "I'd rather go naked than wear fur." Activists have attended fur and fashion shows wearing leg-hold traps to call attention to the methods used by commercial fur trappers to capture animals.

PETA makes astute use of social media and online marketing to raise funds, educate the public about the treatment of animals, and promote cruelty-free alternatives. Many campaign videos have gone viral. Mobile apps, e-cards, and online games have allowed the group to reach the age 13 to 24 years demographic, in particular, through its youth division, peta 2. PETA Prime targets audiences above the age of 50, and PETA Kids reaches children through middle school.

Use of Undercover Investigations

Following the Silver Spring Monkeys case, PETA has routinely used undercover investigations to document animal abuse. PETA investigators gain access by visiting, posing as volunteers, or becoming employees in animal industries. Video and photographic evidence obtained undercover has often led to legal action against the offenders.

In 1984, PETA circulated a film titled *Unnecessary Fuss* to media outlets and the U.S. Congress. The film revealed the gross mistreatment of baboons at the University of Pennsylvania's Head Injury Clinic. Newkirk and Pacheco compiled the film from video footage taken by the researchers themselves and stolen from the lab during a raid by a group identifying itself as the Animal Liberation Front. After reviewing the unedited tapes, a panel of veterinarians from the American College of Laboratory Animal Medicine, commissioned by the Office for Protection from Research Risks, found numerous violations of animal care standards. Although the NIH initially defended the research, a 4-day PETA sit-in at NIH headquarters brought negative publicity. The Head Injury Clinic's grants were suspended, the university incurred fines, and within a few months, primate research at the clinic ended. Together with the Silver Spring Monkeys case, the University of Pennsylvania's Head Injury Clinic case brought attention to the ethics of animals used in research.

Undercover investigations have also revealed abuse in PETA's other areas of focus. In 2010, PETA's undercover investigations at a product-testing facility in North Carolina resulted in 14 felony charges of cruelty to animals. Investigations at the training compound for elephants that perform in Ringling Brothers and Barnum & Bailey circus revealed numerous instances of noncompliance with the Animal Welfare Act. In 2011, the circus's parent company, Feld Entertainment, incurred fines of $270,000, the largest settlement of its kind in U.S. history. Feld denied any violations of the act. A three-month investigation at a North Carolina pig farm in 1999 resulted in the first indictments for animal cruelty on a U.S. factory farm.

Praise and Criticism

More than any other animal rights organization, PETA has raised awareness of animal abuse and shifted public opinion. It has brought media and legislative attention to many issues once considered insignificant. Opinions remain divided on the extent to which the group ultimately helps or hinders the cause of animal rights.

Relationships With Grassroots Animal Advocacy Groups

PETA is one of several animal protection groups that appeared in the 1980s. PETA's public relations efforts, which brought it national and international stature, overshadowed many smaller organizations. Critics argue that people who would have supported local grassroots animal rights groups now donate to PETA instead. Others claim that PETA cooperates with local organizations, providing advice, research, staff, and literature, and helps generate publicity. PETA is often aware of and on the scene at sites of animal abuse before local organizations.

Promoting Animal Rights While Advancing Animal Welfare

Although PETA describes itself as an animal rights organization, some critics claim that the group actually promotes animal welfare. The animal rights position holds that animals have the right not to be used as a means to an end; their lives have intrinsic meaning. The animal welfare position approves of the use of animals, as long as people treat them humanely. Those who claim that PETA is not an animal rights group point to the organization's

willingness to work with targeted animal industries to introduce reforms and regulations. Proponents support negotiation with industries as necessary for improving the treatment of animals by ensuring compliance with existing welfare regulations.

Controversial Use of Nudity

PETA's frequent use of full or partial nudity in protests, videos, and print ads has drawn criticism, both from animal rights activists who argue that it trivializes the cause, and from feminists, who claim that it objectifies and degrades women. PETA supports the use of any tactic necessary to bring attention to the suffering of animals. In response to claims that the ads objectify women, PETA points out that men have also disrobed for the cause.

Terrorist Watch List

Following the attacks of September 11, 2001, the Federal Bureau of Investigation (FBI) placed PETA, and several other environmental groups, on its Terrorist Watch List based on what it referred to as "troubling" practices. The U.S. Justice Department later found that the FBI acted without evidence. Critics of the FBI's actions point out that the targeting of groups engaged in nonviolent protest diverts resources from investigations of actual terrorist threats. PETA's opponents argue that Newkirk has publicly stated her support for direct action and allege financial ties between PETA and militant animal rights groups, such as the Animal Liberation Front.

Leslie Irvine

See also Animal Cruelty; Cockfighting; Dogfighting; Vegetarianism and Veganism

Further Readings

Finsen, L., & Finsen, S. (1994). *The animal rights movement in America: From compassion to respect.* New York, NY: Twayne.

Hall, L. (2006). *Capers in the churchyard: Animal rights advocacy in the age of terror.* Darien, CT: Nectar Bat Press.

Jasper, J. M., & Nelkin, D. M. (1992). *The animal rights crusade: Growth of a moral protest.* New York, NY: Free Press.

Newkirk, I. (2000). *Free the animals: The amazing story of the Animal Liberation Front.* New York, NY: Lantern Books.

Regan, T. (1983). *The case for animal rights.* Berkeley: University of California Press.

Scully, M. (2003). *Dominion: The power of man, the suffering of animals, and the call to mercy.* New York, NY: St. Martin's Press.

Singer, P. (1975). *Animal liberation.* New York, NY: Avon Books.

Website

People for the Ethical Treatment of Animals (PETA): http://www.peta.org

PERFORMANCE-ENHANCING DRUGS

While often described with reference to anabolic steroids or their precursors, the phrase performance-enhancing drugs (PEDs) applies broadly to include a variety of hormones, diuretics, stimulants, as well as blood, oxygen, and genetic manipulation used to improve physical performance. Defining PEDs is problematic as distinctions between natural and artificial drugs or between those used for performance enhancement or for therapy are rarely clear and often depend on context and dosage. Furthermore, certain performance-enhancing substances such as anabolic steroids are near-universally banned, while other enhancing substances such as vitamins and various supplements generally are not. While the use of PEDs in competitive sport is widely condemned as deviant, the difficulty of distinguishing in an objective and definitive way between natural and artificial drugs and between drugs used for enhancement or for therapy suggests that the problem of PEDs and their use in competitive athletics is socially constructed. In general, a substance is banned if it meets two of the three criteria: (1) the potential for enhanced performance, (2) being detrimental to the athlete's health, and (3) a violation of the spirit of sport. Some ethicists argue that these subjective criteria could also justify banning all types of innovative sport products, such as lightweight and aerodynamic clothing and equipment.

Reliable information regarding prevalence and volume of PED use is hard to come by given the stigma and legal ramifications as well as increased sophistication of PEDs, but research suggests that PED use is widespread, and consumption varies considerably from one sport to another. Consumers are male and female, young and old, from all countries, and in all sports and at all levels. This entry discusses the history and testing of PEDs and explores reasons for their use.

History

All types of stimulants, including caffeine, herbs, and hallucinogenic funguses, were used in ancient Greece in hopes of enhancing athletic performance. Although PED use is as old as sport itself, consumption has only been viewed as a medical or social problem for roughly the past century. During the early 20th century, athletes ingested a range of substances including mixtures of alcohol, opium, strychnine, cocaine, and caffeine. Athletes began using cortisone and stimulants (e.g., amphetamines) as they became more available. Fueled in large part by cold war competition, athletes from both superpowers (the United States and the Soviet Union) began injecting muscle-building anabolic steroids derived from the hormone testosterone. As early as the 1960s, endurance athletes experimented with blood manipulation or "blood doping" and, in the 1980s, the use of oxygen-boosting drugs, including erythropoietin, to increase performance and endurance. While erythropoietin, cortisone, human growth hormone, and a range of "designer steroids" are currently some of the most popular PEDs among elite athletes, new substances and methods including so-called gene doping, which holds the potential to modify one's genes, are constantly emerging.

Testing

Antidoping legislation in competitive sports is frequently advocated for reasons of fair play and concern for the health of athletes. The deaths of a few high-profile athletes along with changing conceptions of sport and health precipitated antidoping advocacy following World War II. Early antidoping advocates often employed the rhetoric of "pure" competition and "dirty" cheating to frame PED use as a moral and public health issue. Although some sports began drug testing earlier, the first Olympic testing occurred in Mexico City in 1968. Early testing was often inconsistent, heavy handed, and, in some cases, carried out by police rather than medical professionals. As testing became more rigorous, unannounced and out-of-competition tests were instituted. Early antidoping efforts lacked uniformity as nations and sporting federations often adopted their own banned substance lists, testing protocols, and sanctioning procedures. In 1999, the World Anti-Doping Agency (WADA) was created to harmonize, coordinate, and monitor antidoping efforts for most Olympic sports. Out-of-competition testing for most Olympic sports is conducted by the WADA, while in-competition tests are overseen by various international sports federations. Currently, non-Olympic sports, including American football and baseball, have adopted their own testing and sanctioning procedures, which are generally less severe than WADA's guidelines. The majority of global PED testing is conducted on elite and professional athletes in Olympic sports, but testing also occurs in all major North American National Collegiate Athletic Association and some high school sports.

The WADA utilizes a strict liability standard for adjudicating positive drug tests. In general, sanctions mandate a two-year ban and event disqualification for the first offence and a possible lifetime ban for the second. The Court for Arbitration of Sport provides a venue for athletes to appeal their sanctions; however, there is no guaranteed legal representation.

Although most antidoping resources are devoted to testing for banned substances, the advent of the Athlete Biological Passport in 2009, which collects longitudinal and biological information from athletes, marks a significant shift and may represent the future of drug testing. Traditional tests register a positive result only for a single episode of substance use, whereas with the Biological Passport, athletes can now be found guilty of doping based on inferences drawn from "suspicious" biological fluctuations observed over time.

Explanations

Behavior often identified as deviant by society, such as drug taking, is frequently portrayed as an individual decision made by unethical, immoral, or "addicted" people. However, studies indicate that far from being an individual or private activity, PED use at the elite level represents a form of institutional or organizational deviance since consumption frequently requires a network of sport actors working collectively to facilitate, optimize, and justify consumption and avoid detection. Complementary explanations point to a broader set of values and norms within sport exemplified by the Olympic motto *Faster, Higher, Stronger* that can encourage PED use among athletes by viewing consumption as an expression of commitment to core sport values. These values also pervade many Western societies that are increasingly defined by competition, innovation, and performance enhancement and extol the regular use of all manner of enhancing substances, such as beta blockers, Ritalin, and Viagra. From this perspective, PED use in sport can be understood

as but one instance of a practice common in many other institutional arenas.

Ophir Sefiha

See also Designer Drugs; Drug Normalization; Occupational Criminality; Socioeconomic Status and Drug Use

Further Readings

Atkinson, M., & Young, K. (2008). *Deviance and social control in sport*. Champaign, IL: Human Kinetics.

Dimeo, P. (2007). *A history of drug use in sport: 1876–1976, beyond good and evil*. New York, NY: Routledge.

Hoberman, J. (2005). *Testosterone dreams: Rejuvenation, aphrodisia, doping*. Berkeley: University of California Press.

Moller, V. (2010). *The ethics of doping and anti-doping: Redeeming the soul of sport?* New York, NY: Routledge.

Waddington, I. (2000). *Sport, health and drugs: A critical sociological perspective*. London, England: Routledge.

Waddington, I., & Smith, A. (2009). *An introduction to drugs in sport. Addicted to winning?* London, England: Routledge.

PHENOMENOLOGICAL THEORY

Phenomenology is rooted in philosophy and involves the study of perception, conscious experience, and interpretation or meaning ascribed to interaction with a specific phenomenon or object. The study of consciousness was the source of considerable debate among early social scientists, particularly psychologists like Wilhelm Wundt and Edward Titchener who were interested in the elements of conscious experience. Although both men were pure experimentalists who had no intention of expanding their theory beyond the laboratory, they paved the road, albeit unintentionally, so that the study and understanding of consciousness could make a significant contribution to the understanding of human behaviors.

According to phenomenologists, reality is socially constructed and experienced through interactions with the external world. Therefore, conscious experience is subjective based on one's constructed view of reality. Social deviance is considered to be behaviors that are outside the norms set forth by a society or culture. For example, fetishes are considered by many to be abnormal or deviant forms of behaviors. However, some experience this as a normal part of reality. In essence, you have two sides of the same coin. Deviant behaviors are socially constructed, interpreted, and experienced differently by each individual. In addition, what is considered deviant in one society may be the norm in another society. Therefore, deviance as a construct is highly subjective and open to interpretation.

Background

Although the mind–body problem and dualism were discussed extensively by René Descartes, the 18th-century philosophers like Immanuel Kant focused exclusively on mental states, specifically perception and how our interactions with objects are organized into meaningful representations. According to Kant, the mind did not perceive objects as bits and pieces that are mechanically organized into meaningful objects. Instead perception is the basis for the mind to organize elements into a meaningful experience. From this perspective, knowledge is not simply the by-product of a combination of sensory processes but the product of experiencing an object or a phenomenon.

Franz Brentano and Carl Stumpf were late-19th-century psychologists who attempted to infuse Kant's transcendental philosophy into a psychological method for understanding consciousness. Both argued that mental activity should be the focus of psychology and rejected Wundt's hypothesis that mental processes could be reduced to elements. Brentano is often credited with being the father of phenomenology because of his focus on mental activities (the act of seeing) rather than the contents (what is being seen). Although Brentano developed empirical methods to study mental acts, his greatest contributions to modern phenomenological theory were his use of descriptive methods and his observation that consciousness is intentional or directed toward objects. The latter would be an essential component to modern phenomenological philosophy and theory.

Although Stumpf is not cited as often with phenomenology theory as Brentano, his work in the area of phenomenology was influential to modern phenomenologists and the philosophical tenets of modern phenomenology. Stumpf, like Brentano, believed that psychology should be the study of phenomena and was one of the first social scientists to describe phenomenology in terms of rigorous research method. Stumpf believed that phenomenology is the study of the unbiased experience as it occurs. A keyword in Stumpf's definition is the term *unbiased*, which would be incorporated into modern phenomenology theory and philosophy.

During the early part of the 20th century, the science of psychology changed drastically. Mentalistic concepts like consciousness were rejected in favor of a more objective science—the science of behaviorism. John Watson's famous "Behaviorist Manifesto" officially ushered in the era of positivism and observable behavior as the primary study of psychology. Although Brentano and Stumpf's influence would eventually reemerge in the form of Gestalt psychology, the phenomenological torch would be carried on by 20th-century European philosophers like Edmund Husserl and Martin Heidegger, both of whom incorporated concepts related to conscious experience espoused by Brentano and to a lesser degree by Stumpf.

Husserlian Phenomenology

Although some scientists credit Brentano as the father of phenomenology, most philosophers and phenomenologists consider Husserl to be the father of modern phenomenological theory. While Brentano attempted to incorporate the study of mental activity as the standard focus of psychology, Husserl continued to represent phenomenology as a philosophical movement that deals with the questions surrounding the nature of appearances. Husserl was a prolific writer and spent a great deal of his life pioneering concepts related to his form of phenomenology called transcendental phenomenology. Philosophers like Heidegger and Maurice Merleau-Ponty expanded on many of Husserl's views and ideas to formulate their own brand of phenomenology. In some instances, Husserl's concepts were completely rejected by his contemporaries. However, the central tenets of phenomenology (consciousness and experience) remained constant.

A complete discussion of the works of Husserl is far beyond the scope of this entry; however, there are three concepts that are central to transcendental phenomenology and to a small degree to other forms of phenomenology (i.e., hermeneutics), which will be discussed later. Husserl's greatest contribution and perhaps his most complex is the conceptual framework that underlies his brand of phenomenology. Three central components to Husserl's phenomenology are intentionality, noema, and noesis.

The beginning of modern phenomenology theory can be traced to Husserl's 1901 book *Logical*

Investigations. In this book, Husserl defined phenomenology as the science of consciousness as experienced by the individual and described his phenomenological theory of intentionality. Although there are disagreements among phenomenologists surrounding the experience of consciousness, intentionality and consciousness are considered the cornerstones to phenomenological theory.

Although Brentano introduced the concept of intentionality by proposing that consciousness is intentionally directed toward an object, Husserl disagreed with Brentano's belief that an object must exist for experience to occur. According to Husserl, the perceptual experience of an object could be real or imaginary. Therefore, the act of consciousness and the object of consciousness are intentionally related whether the object is real or nonexistent. Husserl's conceptual framework of phenomenology represents a break from the mentalistic concepts of psychology and a move toward the logic and abstract thinking associated with philosophy.

Husserl expanded his conceptual framework beyond intentionality. Humans are not simply perceivers of objects of our intention. Knowledge is rooted in the meanings individuals ascribe to their conscious experience. Therefore, one epistemological assumption of phenomenology is that meaning is constructed through intentional experiences of consciousness and the noema and noesis of what is experienced.

Noema and noesis work in unison with intentionality and refer explicitly to meanings. All three concepts provide the philosophical basis for explaining the relationship between the mental act, its content, and the external world. Noesis represents one side of intentionality and refers to the perceiving, remembering, feeling, or reflecting on what experience or meaning has been associated with an object or a phenomenon. Husserl referred to the other side as noema, or the act of perceiving, which varies depending on variables like spatial representation, noesis (previous experience), or other properties. Noema is not simply the perception of the object but the perception of the object as it "appears" at that moment in time.

Husserl's phenomenological theory infuses psychology and philosophy into a descriptive method of exploring experience as it occurs in the first person. From the psychological perspective, Husserl explains consciousness as a by-product of mental activity or experience. However, he uses logic as a method to describe his theory of meaning or types

of experiences (noema and noesis). Husserl also added the concept epoche as part of the theoretical framework of phenomenology. Epoche or bracketing occurs when the individual sets aside any presuppositions related to experience with an object or a phenomenon. This allows the phenomenon to be experienced freshly and undisturbed. Husserl's belief that bracketing was essential to uncover new meaning as it appears in consciousness for the first time created an approach to phenomenology commonly referred to as transcendental phenomenology.

Heideggarian Phenomenology

Heidegger was a student of Husserl who agreed that phenomenology could best be explained and understood through philosophy. However, he disagreed with Husserl's emphasis on epistemology and the phenomenological connection through conscious experience. Heidegger was much more interested in the ontological aspects of phenomenology. Part of his emphasis on the nature of being can be traced to his existential beliefs surrounding two forms of existence: A state of forgetfulness of being (inauthentic) and a state of mindfulness of being (authentic). The key question for Heidegger was how one exists or one's "Dasein" (being in the world).

Inner subjectivity is the central tenet for all forms of phenomenology. All knowledge is constructed through interaction with the world and its objects. Therefore, meaning that is ascribed to experience is subjectively based on the description or interpretation of the interaction. Although Heidegger agreed with Husserl that phenomenology was the appropriate method to examine the "lived experience" of interaction with objects in the world, he disagreed with Husserl's emphasis on conscious experience or what individuals know consciously.

Heidegger adopted hermeneutics as his approach to explaining phenomenology. According to Heidegger, hermeneutics goes far beyond the descriptive concepts of Husserl's transcendental phenomenology. Hermeneutics focuses on finding the meanings embedded in reality or in the world in which an individual lives (appearances) and interpreting those meanings. This philosophical stance is congruent with Heidegger's position that phenomenology as a philosophy or theory seeks to answer ontological questions, because reality is the by-product of the world in which the individual lives. Language and text are important components to hermeneutic theory, because they provide phenomenologists with an important description of conscious experience. However, description alone is insufficient when trying to extrapolate meaning. Hermeneutic phenomenology calls for a reflective interpretation of text to uncover the intention and meaning behind appearances.

Descriptive and Interpretive Phenomenology

Phenomenologists who follow Husserl's concepts view phenomenology as a descriptive method to understanding consciousness and experience. They adhere to Husserl's theory of intentionality and that knowledge occurs through a state of consciousness that happens when the mind is directed toward an object: physical or imaginative. Epoche or bracketing is essential to describe phenomena because it allows consciousness to be expressed without adding or subtracting to the experience that is occurring in the moment.

Individuals who follow Heideggarian (hermeneutics) phenomenology theory are considered interpretivists. Interpretation of text facilitates the extrapolation of meaning or being associated with experience and how subjective meaning influences choices. Heidegger's existential background is firmly rooted in hermeneutic phenomenology.

Transcendental (descriptive) and hermeneutic (interpretive) phenomenologists differ on many aspects beyond philosophical tenets or how best to study and analyze conscious experience. Perhaps the greatest disparity surrounds the concept of bracketing the natural world. Criticism of this technique is not only confined to quantitative researchers. Hermeneutic phenomenologists believe that bracketing as a technique is not achievable because many preconceptions are hidden and that separation from conscious experience or "being" is simply not feasible. Husserlian phenomenologists counter the criticism by professing that bracketing is achievable if the researcher is aware of his or her presuppositions. There is no denial that prejudgments or knowledge exists; however, one can suspend personal opinion and describe conscious phenomena without interference or biasness.

Conclusion

Phenomenology is rooted in philosophy. However, researchers have developed methods that allow them to incorporate transcendental or hermeneutical concepts into rich studies that provide insight into the lived experience of a specific phenomenon. Despite the advances in phenomenological research, phenomenologists tend to fall into one of two camps: the descriptive (Husserlian) or interpretive (Heideggarian). Although Husserl's concepts and philosophy contributed greatly to phenomenological theory, his philosophy is very abstract and difficult for many to interpret. Heidegger's approach is considered by many to be more concrete, perhaps due to its ontological focus and infusion of existential concepts.

Husserl and Heidegger remain the dominant figures in phenomenology; however, contributions to phenomenology theory have been made by philosophers like Jean-Paul Sartre and Maurice Merleau-Ponty. The former expanded on Heidegger's existential concepts to include free will and the capacity to choose; the latter expanded Husserl's theory of consciousness into the existential realm by theorizing that consciousness is oriented toward the lived experience or existence in the concrete world. Sartre and Merleau-Ponty's existential phenomenology is considered a branch of hermeneutic phenomenology because of its orientation toward the nature of reality or ontological truth and emphasis on the experience of free will and creating meaning in a meaningless world.

Although there is some disagreement among phenomenologists surrounding the definition of phenomenology, all agree that phenomenology is the study of conscious experience that involves analyzing the structure and conditions that influence experience and the meaning of the experience. Therefore, phenomenology is both a philosophy and a theory of the mind.

When studying social deviance from the phenomenological perspective, one must consider how the behavior is consciously experienced. Deviant behavior as a construct contains a strong element of subjectivity as evidenced by the different norms that exist in different societies. Social deviance that is criminal in nature is more complex. How a society individually and collectively experiences or interprets a crime can have a profound effect on the saliency of a deviant behavior. Strong social agreement (similar experiences) about a deviant form of behavior can lead to more severe consequences than deviant behaviors with little social agreement (divergent experiences).

Ray Biggar

See also Positivist Definitions of Deviance; Qualitative Methods in Studying Deviance; Structural Functionalism

Further Readings

Annells, M. (1996). Hermeneutical phenomenology: Philosophical perspectives and current use in nursing research. *Journal of Advanced Nursing, 2*, 705–713.

Bernet, R., Kern, I., & Marbach, E. (1999). *An introduction to Husserlian phenomenology* (3rd ed.). Evanston, IL: Northwestern University Press.

Berrios, G. (1989). What is phenomenology? A review. *Journal of the Royal Society of Medicine, 82*, 425–428.

Creswell, J. (2007). *Qualitative inquiry & research design: Choosing among the five approaches* (2nd ed.). Thousand Oaks, CA: Sage.

Moustakas, C. (1994). *Phenomenological research methods.* Thousand Oaks, CA: Sage.

Schultz, D., & Schultz, S. (2004). *A history of modern psychology* (8th ed.). Belmont, CA: Wadsworth/ Thompson Learning.

Sokolowski, R. (2008). *Introduction to phenomenology.* New York, NY: Cambridge University Press.

Phishing

Phishing is a form of social engineering (a general term that describes gaining advantage through the use of deceptive manipulation) in which a victim is contacted by a person or group masquerading as a legitimate entity to obtain personal information. Victims are typically contacted via electronic communication by an assumed trustworthy or known source and lured into disclosing personal information directly or by clicking a link that redirects users to bogus sites that captures information or installs malicious software. This has been a growing problem that is estimated to have cost more than $687 million in the first half of 2012 alone.

The term *phishing* is derived from an earlier form of hacking, which is a general term describing the practice of modifying a piece of equipment from its original intended use or purpose. Hackers in the 1960s and 1970s manipulated telephone systems to obtain illegal free calls, called *phreaking*, a play on the words *phone freak*. Phishing uses similar wordplay to metaphorically describe "fishing" for information. Similar to actual fishing, scammers first bait prospective victims with false information before hooking and capturing information.

This entry begins with a discussion of the escalation and anatomy of phishing attacks, followed by a description of popular forms of phishing. Finally, this entry examines the detection and policing of phishing incidents.

Escalation of Attacks

The numbers of phishing incidents have risen significantly in the past few years. According to the computer security firm RSA (Ron Rivest, Adi Shamir, and Leonard Adleman), there was on average 36,980 unique phishing attacks per month worldwide from August 2011 to August 2012, an increase of nearly 55%. A 2009 PhishTank study of 3 million banking customers over a 3-month period revealed that 45% of bank customers who were redirected to phishing sites divulged their bank login information. In 2011, the Federal Bureau of Investigation (FBI) received nearly 28,000 victim complaints of a type of phishing attack called advance fee frauds.

The escalation in phishing attacks can be attributed in part to the growing range of potential victims. Attackers are increasingly targeting users of smartphones, computer tablets, and other portable computing devices, which are increasingly used for online banking and e-commerce. In addition, social network users are being targeted by phishing scams. For example, one Facebook phishing scam baits users to click on a link, such as a viral video, which redirects the user to a phony account security verification page that solicits personal information.

Phishing attacks can be potentially more harmful in nature with the installation and spread of unauthorized software. Malicious software, or malware, is a broad term used to describe a variety of unauthorized computer code, such as viruses, worms, spyware, and adware that can compromise personal computer systems and networks. Computer viruses, for example, are self-replicating software that can spread to other computer systems, where they can steal sensitive information (spyware), propagate unwanted advertisements (adware), and disrupt larger networks. For example, an attacker can take control of a network of infected "zombie" computers, known as a "botnet," that can be used for a variety of nefarious purposes, ranging from sending unsolicited advertisements (spam) to executing a distributed denial-of-service attack that disables websites by overwhelming their servers with requests or gaining access to networks, where information can be collected and sent to attackers.

Anatomy of the Attack

Attackers often appeal to potential victims into cooperating by employing emotional prompts. Attackers often create a sense of urgency in their message, appeal to the potential victim's greed with outlandish offers, make false accusations posing as federal agencies, and even scare victims into believing that they have been a victim of fraud by falsely representing a financial institution. Ironically, even phishing and Internet scam enforcement groups have been emulated by fraudsters. For example, scammers have impersonated representatives of the Better Business Bureau's Complaints Department, which deals with phishing scams.

Once trust is established, victims often disclose information directly to a scammer or indirectly via a link that redirects them to a legitimate-looking website. For example, many phony websites contain official company images and logos to create realistic-looking pages that are often indistinguishable from legitimate sites. More sophisticated attackers may employ a "man in the middle"–type attack, whereby information is intercepted before redirecting the victim to the legitimate website.

Popular Forms of Phishing

Spear Phishing

Spear phishing is a targeted phishing attack against an individual or an organization using specific information about the target to gain a victim's trust. In comparison, more generalized phishing casts a broader general lure, such as a generic e-mail to multiple recipients simultaneously. Spear phishers, however, obtain some specific information about the target before implementing their attack. For example, scammers can impersonate the victim's company technical help desk to convince the potential victim to provide personal information. A scammer can also gather information from a company's website, the victim's social networking page or personal blog, or even an organization's computer network through a previous hack, before contacting the potential victim.

A specific type of spear phishing that targets more lucrative upper managers is referred to as "whaling." In 2008, the FBI investigated a large-scale whaling scheme where 20,000 corporate executives received a fake FBI e-mail subpoena to click on a link that installed software that captured and sent their passwords to the attackers.

Clone Phishing

Clone phishing involves an attacker sending a spoofed, or fraudulently copied, e-mail to make it appear as if it was sent by the original sender. The attacker extracts information from an authentic e-mail, such as the content and e-mail path, before sending a subsequent fraudulent e-mail. A scammer can resend a duplicate of an original e-mail message and replace only an attachment or link. Unsuspecting victims opening the attachment or link believing it was sent from the real sender may unwittingly install malware or be subjected to disclosing personal information. Attackers can also steal e-mail login information by sending the legitimate e-mail owner a password reset link.

Advance Fee Scams

Advance fee scams solicit advanced payment in some type of proposal that falsely promises larger returns in the form of money, products, or services. The most infamous Internet advance fee frauds are Nigerian 419 scams, named after the Nigerian felony penal code for defrauding victims under false pretenses. These 419 scammers initially contact victims with business proposals promising unrealistically large rewards for their assistance. For example, scammers often masquerade as official bank agents or beneficiaries of a very large fund who need the victim's advance fee to "release" the money. Some victims are often further coaxed by religious appeals and sympathy for victims of recent disasters.

Victims who respond often face an endless cycle of escalating fees and further victimization. Some victims who have paid tens of thousands of dollars attempting to collect their promised rewards received nothing more than pieces of black paper purported to be cash concealed with a protective coating of black ink. Many pay extra for supposed special chemicals that remove the black ink. In some cases, this black cash is presented in potentially dangerous face-to-face meetings with scammers. The U.S. State Department has 15 documented cases of murdered or missing individuals related to Nigerian advance fee scams from 1992 to 1995. In 2009, two men in New York were gunned down at home during a meeting with scammers.

Ransomware

Victims of phishing attacks may unknowingly install ransomware to their computer, a type of malware that extorts victims by locking them out of their computers or encrypting their data. The victim must pay a ransom to an attacker to receive a code that unlocks or decrypts their information. Some attackers threaten to destroy or disclose sensitive information. In most cases, however, a fake government notification informs the victim that an illegal activity was detected on their computer and ordered to pay a fine in order to avoid prosecution and restore the computer to its full functionality.

Detecting Phishing and Victimization

Phishing remains a significant problem despite affecting a relatively small fraction of total Internet users. The growing number of Internet users coupled with the ease and low cost of carrying out phishing attacks have exposed virtually every e-mail user to phishing attacks. According to Internet security firm Symantec, nearly 1 in every 508 e-mails was identified as phishing in January 2013.

While phishing victims are often criticized for being gullible to obvious scams, many informed Internet users are fooled by increasingly clever and sophisticated attacks. For example, even highly educated and intelligent individuals fall prey to phishing attacks. In 2005, internationally renowned psychiatrist Dr. Louis Gottschalk lost nearly $3 million over a 10-year span to a Nigerian scammer, believing he would be receiving $20 million in return trapped in African bank accounts.

Sophisticated phishing detection and filtering technologies employed by companies, such as Microsoft, Google, and Yahoo!, have not prevented victimization. Since phishing is a form of social engineering that works by manipulating the trust of individuals, many electronic security measures are circumvented by end users who authorize malware installation by clicking on links and opening attached files contained in e-mails. Furthermore, once malware is introduced into a home or organization's computer network, it can potentially allow attackers to victimize other users, steal private information, and disrupt entire network operations.

Policing Phishing

The enforcement of phishing has been very limited. As such, most organizations, including law enforcement organizations, mainly focus on prevention through public awareness. Most federal agency websites, such as those of the FBI, Securities and Exchange Commission, and Internal Revenue Service, warn users on how to protect against phishing scams. The FBI and National White Collar Crime Center run the Internet Crime Complaint Center, where victims can file a complaint. Due to the high volume of complaints, only a small percentage is fully investigated by law enforcement. Moreover, victims rarely get any of their money back.

Several key groups police phishing. First, private companies employ various technologies to stop phishing. Free webmail service providers, such as Google, Microsoft, and Yahoo!, employ filtering technologies. In addition, operating systems, web browsers, and antivirus software have become more sophisticated in detecting and preventing malware. However, as mentioned, many end users can still circumvent these safeguards by ignoring these warnings and permitting its installation.

Second, some private organizations focus specifically on phishing. For example, the Anti-Phishing Working Group collects and analyzes phishing attacks submitted by Internet users. The 419 Eater group targets Nigerian scammers by engaging in time-wasting dialogues with scammers.

Third, public–private alliances have formed to defend against phishing attacks. The Internet Crime Complaint Center, for example, has sustained partnerships with public and private organizations, such as the Business Software Alliance, eBay, the Federal Trade Commission, and Microsoft.

Finally, international governments have stepped up their efforts in fighting phishing. Arrests have been made in Nigeria, Zaire, Ghana, and India in the past few years. Nigeria's Economic and Financial Crimes Commission has been aggressively policing Internet cafes and other phishing hot spots and launched a public awareness campaign to fix the country's image of tacitly accepting phishing as an industry.

Johnny Nhan

See also Cybercrime; Digital Piracy; Fraud; Spamming

Further Readings

Dyrud, M. A. (2005). "I brought you a good news": An analysis of Nigerian 419 letters. *Proceedings of the 2005 Association for Business Communication Annual Convention.* Retrieved from http://businesscommunication.org/wp-content/uploads/2011/04/07ABC05.pdf

Federal Bureau of Investigation. (2009). *Spear phishers: Angling to steal your financial info.* Retrieved from http://www.fbi.gov/news/stories/2009/april/spearphishing_040109

Federal Bureau of Investigation & National White Collar
Crime Center. (2011). *Internet crime complaint center
2011: Internet crime report*. Retrieved from http://www
.ic3.gov/media/annualreport/2011_ic3report.pdf

Jaishankar, K. (2008). Identity related crime in the
cyberspace: Examining phishing and its impact.
International Journal of Cyber Criminology, 2(1),
10–15.

Shun-Yung, K. W., & Huang, W. (2011). The evolutional
view of the types of identity thefts and online frauds in
the era of the Internet. *Internet Journal of Criminology,*
1–21.

Symantec Intelligence. (2013). *Symantec intelligence report:
January 2013*. Retrieved from http://www.symantec
.com/content/en/us/enterprise/other_resources/
b-intelligence_report_01–2013.en-us.pdf

U.S. Department of State Bureau of International Narcotics
and Law Enforcement Affairs. (1997). *Nigerian advance
fee fraud*. Retrieved from http://www.state.gov/www/
regions/africa/naffpub.pdf

Websites

Anti-Phishing Working Group (APWG): http://www
.antiphishing.org

419 Eater group: http://www.419eater.com

Internet Crime Complaint Center (IC3): http://www.ic3
.gov/default.aspx

PHONE SEX

Phone sex is the sexually explicit conversation between two (or more) adults that occurs via telephone wire or other electronic means. When a person is paid or pays to engage in phone sex it becomes part of the larger category known as sex work. Although sex work has been around for centuries, phone sex is a relative newcomer to the field, having emerged in the 1980s. There are several events that occurred which made its appearance possible. One such event is the U.S. government–mandated 1982 breakup of AT&T; as a result, "Ma Bell" and the "Baby Bells" were looking for sources of revenue and began selling access to information lines, also known as "Dial-It" lines. These proved very lucrative and when the lines were auctioned off to entrepreneurs, an adult magazine bought the rights to one and started offering sexually explicit messages. It immediately began receiving 500,000 calls per day. The magazine effectively gained access to a new distribution network—the nation's phone system,

and for the first time, individuals interested in listening to sexually explicit material could do so instantly from home. This was, then, the beginning of the phone sex industry, and within the first 13 years, profits went from $0 to between $750 million and $1 billion. This entry examines the phone sex industry, including its structure and revenues, the workers and the callers, and the calls' content.

Structure of the Industry

At first, a prerecorded message was the principal type of phone sex available. However, companies soon realized that there was a vast untapped market in the form of live conversation. Phone sex is a business that is transacted both internationally (through 900 numbers) and domestically (using 800 numbers). Domestically, 800 numbers remain popular and are often advertised according to type of caller preference or desire. Because phone sex, in theory, can be produced at and distributed from any location coupled with easy access to distribution channels, low production costs, low advertising costs, reliable billing methods, and a large pool of potential employees, entrepreneurs can run a successful phone sex operation with little capital investment. More recently, the Internet has leveled the playing field between small phone sex agencies and larger ones by enabling small agencies to operate like larger agencies—such as providing descriptions and photos of phone sex workers, audio samples, links to other sites—without huge advertising costs.

Callers may be billed for calls in different ways: a flat rate for a specified amount of time, a per-minute charge, and international call billing, each typically paid by a credit card. Additionally, the cost for services depends on where the worker is located, that is, whether the worker is located in the United States or in another country.

Revenues and Earnings

In 1997, the phone sex industry's revenues were estimated to be approximately $1 billion annually and an estimated 250,000 people each evening used the telephone to engage in phone sex. Although the most recent figures are more than 15 years old, phone sex is ubiquitous and is advertised in virtually all men's magazines, many newspapers, television commercials, and on the Internet. It is likely therefore that revenues are much higher today and higher yet if money spent on international lines is included.

Estimates of workers' earnings vary, but estimates suggest that women earn from $8 to $15 per hour doing phone sex calls, which in some areas is well above minimum wage. In addition to wages, workers can receive gifts from callers, and workers can augment their earnings by selling photos, videos, and other items, such as lingerie.

The Workers

Workers can work from home and calls can be dispatched to them from a central location or switchboard, or they can work at the equivalent of a call center with other women or sometimes with men impersonating women. The phone sex industry is aimed primarily at heterosexual men with very few men offering phone sex to either women or other men, and those agencies and workers have not been the focus of research to date. Like most sex workers, phone sex operators have a work persona—a fictitious name and physical description—to protect their personal identity.

Demographic information on those who staff the phones is sparse and based on qualitative research, so it is difficult to characterize workers' demographics. However, some data do exist and suggest that workers' ages range from 21 to 46 years, they are thin to normal weight, many have boyfriends or are married, and some have children; for some agencies, workers are diverse in terms of race; for others, the workers are predominantly white. Additionally, there is a range of social class: Some workers are working class, some are middle class. Educational level varies from high school graduates to college educated, and many phone sex workers are students. Sexual orientation is also diverse, including heterosexuals, bisexuals, and lesbians. These demographics are not generalizable, but they nonetheless call into question the images of phone sex workers in media portrayals and social stereotypes such as cartoons that depict phone sex workers as middle aged, overweight, and unattractive or films that portray workers as falling in love with their callers.

Although phone sex is legal in all jurisdictions in the United States, it still falls under the category of sex work and therefore carries with it the same stigma. Consequently, workers often identify ways of managing that stigma especially in terms of who they tell about their work. Workers may sometimes feel degraded by both callers and persons who learn of the work they do and, therefore, may develop ways of maintaining a high sense of self-esteem,

including focusing exclusively on the economic aspects of the job. The economic aspect of the job is the key for many phone sex workers, and in fact, the recruitment of workers oftentimes suggests that they can participate in the high earnings of the sex industry without being exposed to the dangers traditionally associated with the industry such as arrest, mistreatment, and violence at the hands of pimps or customers.

Some phone sex workers are referred to as phone actresses, especially in help wanted advertisements on the West Coast, and many workers report being aware that they are acting out a fantasy with callers. To the extent that phone sex is acting, it is largely improvisational with some "psychotherapy" thrown in since callers often want to talk about their lives and personal troubles. Learning the work occurs largely on the job, because many phone sex workers receive no formal training. However, phone sex operators who work in a central location for a large service bureau may receive informal training by watching and hearing other operators handle calls.

The Callers

Little demographic information is known about those who call phone sex lines. Callers may also adopt a persona just as many workers do, so it is possible that callers' descriptions are part of the fantasy of the call. Sometimes, callers describe themselves in stereotypically masculine ways: as tall, relatively young, well-muscled, and white collar or professional. While there is no way to confirm that the callers' descriptions are accurate, workers nonetheless often categorize the callers, including their reasons for calling. Although the categories identified by phone sex workers differ, they share some consistencies. The first and most populous category is the "regular guy" for whom phone sex is just another type of sex material, such as books or movies. This category also includes men who have called numerous times but do not form an attachment to any one worker. Also included here are the callers who offer little or no conversation and ask for fast descriptions of specific sex acts. Men who are first-time callers and simply call out of curiosity also are in this category. The second category is the "cheaters" who, because they think they can't tell their wives or girlfriends their sexual fantasies, use the phone lines to engage in their fantasies. The third category is the "the loser," for whom the phone lines, workers assume, may be their only contact with women. Some of these callers are regular callers who form fantasy relationships with particular workers and may make plans for the future and even offer marriage. The fourth category is the "sick ticket" or "psycho." These men are interested in violence, dominance, torture, and pedophilia. It is evident in the research that although workers' category labels may vary, workers' opinion of the callers seemed consistent and was often stigmatizing to the callers.

The Calls

Sometimes, callers explicitly tell the worker what type of fantasy they want to hear, but other times, the actual content of the call is emergent. Typically, however, phone sex fantasies are standard in terms of what callers say and what sort of acts they want to be described to them. Although callers enjoy an illusion of great freedom and adventure, their fantasies are considerably constrained because the content of phone sex depends on typifications and stereotypical images provided by traditional sex materials and society in general. Although calls may follow patterns, the exact imagined settings, content, and direction of the fantasy can be constructed for a particular call.

The content of calls typically includes discussions of straight sex, lesbianism, rape, and anal sex. Less common are other types of fantasies such as of incest, sex with underage girls, sadomasochism, bestiality, violent sex, and fetishism. Moreover, callers sometimes make specific requests for women with particular physical characteristics. A small number of calls are nonsexual and involves callers talking about their lives and troubles. The phone sex industry primarily involves heterosexual encounters and female operators. Few calls come from couples and even fewer are from women; however, more recently phone sex lines advertised on the Internet are being marketed as lesbian or bisexual phone sex "*by* women *for* women."

Finally, some researchers have investigated the calls from a linguistic perspective, including how workers consciously produce language that is stereotypically feminine and is associated with powerlessness. This style shifting is based primarily on gender and secondarily on race, class, and geography. So when on the telephone, the worker switches into a definable conversational style that the worker associates with "women's language" or characteristics she assumes typifies the caller and the caller's preferences.

Conclusions

Little is known about phone sex agencies and their workers, especially relative to other forms of sex work. To date, only a handful of researchers have explored the topic. Their conclusions should be seen as tentative because their samples are not random and thus are not considered generalizable to all phone sex workers or companies. Nonetheless, the few studies available provide valuable insights and starting points for future research.

Christine Mattley

See also Cybersex; Masturbation; Sexting; Sexual Addiction

Further Readings

Guidroz, K., & Rich, G. J. (2010). Commercial telephone sex: Fantasy and reality. In R. Weitzer (Ed.), *Sex for sale: Prostitution, pornography, and the sex industry* (2nd ed., pp. 139–162). New York, NY: Routledge.

Hall, K. (1995). Lip service on the fantasy lines. In K. Hall & M. Bucholtz (Eds.), *Gender articulated* (pp. 183–216). New York, NY: Routledge.

Lane, F. S., III. (2000). *Obscene profits: The entrepreneurs of pornography in the cyber age.* New York, NY: Routledge.

Mattley, C. (2002). Voicing gender: The performance of gender in the context of phone sex lines. In P. Gagne & R. Tewskbury (Eds.), *Gendered sexualities: Advances in gender research* (Vol. 6., pp. 79–102). London, England: JAI/Elsevier Science.

Mattley, C. (2005). Aural sex: The politics and moral dilemmas of studying the social construction of fantasy. In R. T. Wright & D. Hobbs (Eds.), *The handbook of fieldwork* (pp. 141–156). Thousand Oaks, CA: Sage.

Rich, G. J., & Guidroz, K. (2000). Smart girls who like sex: Telephone sex workers. In R. Weitzer (Ed.), *Sex for sale: Prostitution, pornography, and the sex industry* (pp. 35–48). New York, NY: Routledge.

Weitzer, R. (2009). Sociology of sex work. *Annual Review of Sociology, 35,* 213–234.

PHYSICAL CHARACTERISTICS AS DEVIANCE

Societies have long considered physical characteristics as predictive of or attesting to the character, abilities, and morals of the individuals possessing or exhibiting them. Some physical characteristics, such as physical beauty or great strength, have been seen as positive and indicative in greater or lesser degree that an individual who holds these traits is to be accorded respect and honor. There are also physical characteristics that, in some cultures, have been seen to indicate that the person should be viewed as deviant; those so judged may be treated with disparagement, denial, and dishonor.

In this entry, the word *deviant* is used to refer to physical characteristics or individuals who are *perceived* as different from what is regarded as normal and whose difference or differences are evaluated negatively in a particular cultural context. Importantly, then, it is incorrect to speak of physical characteristics or individuals as being essentially and always deviant. Rather, "deviant" is a label conferred on certain physical characteristics and individuals in specific societies at a specific time.

Deviant physical characteristics include, but are not limited to, vision disabilities; a motor disability that marks the person as different or requires that the person use an assistive device; an absent limb or part of a limb; greater than average fatigability; epilepsy; Down syndrome; cerebral palsy; stammering or stuttering; stature very much under or over the average; or having one's body covered with tattoos or decorated with piercings and plugs.

This list of conditions suggests that some conditions can be thought of as affecting a person's ability to perform activities of daily living, whereas others are conditions that affect a person's ability to get and keep a job; some are physical characteristics that limit the individual's ability to undertake certain occupations; a person with very low visual acuity, for instance, would not be qualified to pilot a jetliner. Of course, many people with deviant physical characteristics function quite well in their daily and work lives. Beethoven, for example, continued to compose and score music after becoming deaf; Helen Keller, deaf and blind from childhood, learned to read and write Braille and became a successful author. Similarly, Franklin Delano Roosevelt, who had poliomyelitis, is widely regarded as among the greatest U.S. presidents. Steven Hawking, a Nobel Prize–winning physicist, has a degenerative neurological disorder that impairs his ability to speak and move on his own.

The ability of persons with "deviant" physical characteristics to perform their jobs well raises another set of issues. Interestingly, regardless of whether those with deviant physical characteristics can function well in their daily and work lives, some mainstream individuals question whether such individuals should have a job at all, believing that they rob "normal" people of available jobs.

An individual may have more than one of these characteristics, increasing the degree of deviance he or she is thought to have and suggesting to some that he or she is even more incapable of performing daily living and work activities and is thus in need of societal support. Regardless of the many changes that have been wrought by recent social changes in disability activism and advocacy and in legislation, some still view those with deviant physical characteristics as individuals who are at best dependent on society to meet their needs.

Besides these representative deviant physical characteristics, there are some arrangements that can signal a deviant physical characteristic even when no deviance is perceptible. This is the case for the use of assistive devices like wheelchairs, crutches, or red-tipped white canes or the use of personal assistants or service animals. Even though the arrangements themselves appear to say little about the person using them, they can announce that the person has a disability.

Physical Characteristics as Stigma

The original use of the term *stigma* dates from ancient Greco-Roman world, where a stigma was a mark, such as a brand, that signaled that its wearer had engaged in seriously deviant activities, such as theft or adultery. Thus, stigmas were originally physical attributes that signaled that the bearer was deviant. The sociologist Erving Goffman (1922–1982), who first examined stigma as a form of deviance, defined stigma as an attribute of a person or a group so deeply discrediting as to result in what he called a "spoiled identity."

In his classic work *Stigma: Notes on the Management of Spoiled Identity* (1963), Goffman presents a typology that divides stigma into three categories. The first, *blemishes of moral character*, included criminal activity or evidence of a serious mental disorder. The second, *abominations of the body*, refers to deviant physical characteristics, sometimes termed as disfigurements and deformities, and also included physical differences that were not immediately evident, such as deafness, blindness, or sometimes paralysis of a limb, but could have a notable effect on the person's social abilities with those who are "normal." Extremes like clinical obesity or skeletal thinness are also included here.

The third, *tribal stigma*, are stigma that result from membership in a devalued group, such as a devalued racial or ethnic minority or an outcast religion. Stigmatizing attributes, and stigmatized persons, are by definition deviant. They are seen as violations of norms about what is normal, rewarding, and desirable. Many, if not most, deviants are so classified because of what they *do*. Persons with deviant physical characteristics violate norms as to what a person should appear like or *be*.

Because people with some physical characteristics are discriminated against, they may be reluctant to trust others who do not have the deviance characteristics, believe they must strategize when dealing with "normal" people, and sometimes try to pass as normal themselves. Up until very recently, lesbians and gay men would often try "passing" as straight men and women to avoid the discrimination and violence that might befall them should their "real" identities be revealed.

The Importance of Context in Designating Physical Characteristics as Deviant

To most sociologists of deviance, deviance is regarded as relative rather than absolute. To them, it is important to recognize that a person with a deviant or devalued physical characteristic may receive different types of treatment on the basis of the same characteristic in different situations. This is to say that the meaning of the physical characteristic is not fixed but varies according to the context within which it is displayed. Thus, a child with severe epilepsy in mainstream U.S. society would be aggressively medically treated; a child with severe epilepsy in the Hmong immigrant subculture in the United States would be adored and respected as a shaman, for the Hmong consider epilepsy a sign of divine favor.

Discredited and Discreditable Identities

Another important contextual feature relative to deviant physical characteristics is whether or not they are publicly displayed. In his discussion of stigma, Goffman distinguished between persons who were *discredited* as a result of their stigma, and those who were *discreditable*. Some physical characteristics discredit a person's identity immediately on being perceived, while others have only the *potential* for identity spoilage. Thus, some characteristics are immediately discrediting, such as being confined to a wheelchair, while others may only exercise a stigmatizing effect when they become known. A person

with a criminal record, then, will not be stigmatized until and unless that record becomes known to his or her various audiences. Physical characteristics that are immediately visible, however, can act to discredit the individual as soon as they are perceived. The color of one's skin, the shape of one's eyes, the fact that a person is using a wheelchair are all directly observable; to the extent that such characteristics are viewed as stigmatizing and deviant, the person possessing these characteristics will find that his or her identity has been spoiled in the eyes of others before interaction can even begin.

The Normalization of Physical Deviance

Beginning in 1973, with the passage of the Rehabilitation Act by the U.S. Congress, and continuing through 1994, a number of pieces of legislation have mandated the provision of services and the protection of the rights of persons with mental and physical disability. A disability is defined in such a way that education and work are protected categories, among a number of others, so that there is now legal recourse in the case of job discrimination and failure to provide a "least restrictive environment" (e.g., through mainstreaming in the case of public education). One such piece of legislation is the Americans with Disabilities Act of 1990, which protects people with both mental and physical disabilities and also people who have aesthetic norms that do not fall into either of these categories but who, nonetheless, experience hiring discrimination. Thus, persons' scarifications, or altered appearance after accidents or burns, are therefore protected along with people with more traditionally defined disabilities.

Carol Gardner and William Gronfein

See also Blindness; Deafness; Physical Disabilities; Stigma and Stigma Management; Tribal Stigma

Further Readings

Deshen, S. A. (1992). *Blind people: The private and public life of sightless Israelis.* Albany: State University of New York Press.

Fadiman, A. (2012). *The spirit catches you and you fall down: A Hmong child, her American doctors, and the collision of two cultures.* New York, NY: Farrar, Straus & Giroux.

Goffman, E. (1963). *Stigma: Notes on the management of spoiled identity.* Englewood Cliffs, NJ: Prentice Hall.

Groce, N. E. (1985). *Everyone here spoke sign language: Hereditary deafness on Martha's Vineyard.* Harvard, MA: Harvard University Press.

Link, B., & Phelan, J. (2001). Conceptualizing stigma. *Annual Review of Sociology, 27,* 363–385.

Lomgmore, P. K. (2003). *Why I burned my book and other essays on disability.* Philadelphia, PA: Temple University Press.

PHYSICAL DISABILITIES

According to the International Classification of Functioning, Disability and Health (ICF), *disability* is an umbrella term for health impairments, activity limitations, and participation restrictions. Disability refers to the negative aspects of the interaction between individuals with a health condition (e.g., cerebral palsy, Down syndrome, and depression) and personal and environmental factors (e.g., negative attitudes, inaccessible transportation and public buildings, and limited social supports). Due to the interaction between the debilitating health condition, the environment, and other personal factors, it is difficult to isolate a disability, physical or otherwise, from the other unique traits of an individual and the environment in which he or she functions. This is a departure from previously accepted definitions of disability that focused on physical and mental impairments, abnormalities, handicaps, and other restrictions in abilities. While terms such as *cripple, spastic, invalid,* and *freak* were commonly used in the past to label people with disabilities, these terms are now considered derogatory. In many places in the world, "person first" language is the preferred terminology (e.g., person with Down syndrome; person with a visual impairment). This entry provides information on the classification of physical disabilities, laws related to people with physical disabilities, and barriers to full inclusion in the society. Furthermore, while this entry focuses on physical disabilities, it is sometimes impossible to separate physical, cognitive, and mental disabilities due to comorbidity (e.g., Fragile X syndrome has physical impairments, cognitive impairments, and often mental impairments).

The World Health Organization's inaugural *World Report on Disability* in 2011 published the most accurate up-to-date global estimates on disabilities. The report estimated that 15.6% (785 million people) of people aged 15 years and above have some type of disability (physical, mental, and/or cognitive) with 2.2% (110 million people) having a "severe disability." A related survey of children (birth to 14 years) estimated that 5.1% (95 million) have a disability. According to the Centers for Disease Control and Prevention, 15.6%, or 35.8 million, U.S. adults (18 years and older) report having a physical functioning difficulty.

Categorizing Physical Disabilities

As seen from the definition of disability, the term *physical disabilities* represents a broad and complex set of physical impairments, restrictions, and limitations. An exhaustive list of physical disabilities is beyond the scope of this entry, and there are multiple ways to organize the varied disabilities a person may have. Various simplistic organizational systems divide disabilities into two categories: physical structural impairment and physical functioning impairment. Some professions use a medical model for classification of physical disabilities, often by the impairment's origin or prognosis.

In keeping with the World Health Organization and the ICF, many classify disabilities by the physical impairment (the affected body structure or function), the activity limitations, and the participation restrictions. For example, a person with the physical impairment of paraplegia (paralysis of the legs) may have mobility activity limitations and potentially some activity restrictions such as walking, driving, or standing. The International Classification of Diseases 10th Revision, which is a companion to the ICF, provides 22 classifications primarily based on the specific body system. Relevant ones include the following:

- Blood and circulatory conditions, such as hemophilia
- Digestive conditions, such as Crohn's disease
- Endocrine conditions, such as Turner's syndrome
- Eye and ear diseases, such as blindness and deafness
- Genitourinary conditions, such as kidney stones
- Infectious conditions, such as Lyme disease
- Musculoskeletal conditions, such as fibromyalgia
- Neoplasms, which are tumors
- Nervous system diseases, such as multiple sclerosis
- Respiratory diseases, such as asthma
- Skin diseases, such as leprosy

The ICF provides a simple classification system for the severity of the disability: mild, moderate, severe, and complete. There are a variety of scales and instruments that can be used to determine the severity level of the disability. Most often, the negative impact of the disability is evidenced by the person's activity limitations and participation restrictions. Generally, the following categories are used to evaluate any limitations and/or restrictions:

- Ability to learn and apply knowledge
- Communication
- Mobility
- Self-care
- Community and social life
- Activities of daily living
- General tasks and demands

Laws Related to Physical Disabilities

In many countries around the world, lawmakers and advocacy groups have come together to enact legislation designed to improve the quality of life for people with a disability. This entry focuses on several crucial laws passed in the United States. In 1973, the Rehabilitation Act (PL 93–112) was enacted by the U.S. Congress. This law extended or replaced rights afforded in the earlier Vocational Rehabilitation Act. In this law, an emphasis was placed on providing services to people with severe disabilities and to expand research and programs for all individuals with disabilities. It also charged the U.S. Departments of Health, Education and Welfare to coordinate programs and services. Two years later, President Gerald Ford signed the landmark law regarding the education of students with disabilities. Public Law 94–142, the Education for All Handicapped Children Act, required all school districts that received federal funds to allow equal access to public education for children with physical and/or mental disabilities. Today, this concept, the right to a free and appropriate public education, is a benchmark of all public special education. Additional salient aspects of this law were to protect the educational rights of children and their families, to provide federal support for state and local education agencies to educate students with disabilities, and to assess the effectiveness of such efforts. This law was amended in 1984 after the Supreme Court case *Smith v. Robinson* to state that parents have the right to seek judicial intervention and that parents may collect attorney fees if successful.

This law was further amended in 1990 under President George H. W. Bush and renamed the Individuals with Disabilities Education Act. The last amendment to this act occurred in 2004 under President George W. Bush. Some of the changes over the past 35 years include, but are not limited to, establishing early intervention programs for children from birth to kindergarten entry, transition programs from high school to the workforce, creation of Individual Education Plans and Individual Family Service Plans, the concept that children should be educated in regular education environments as much as possible (least restrictive environment), and procedural policies and safeguards.

A third prominent law related to people with disabilities is the Americans with Disabilities Act of 1990. Also signed by President George H. W. Bush, this law sought to protect the individuals with disabilities from discrimination and to create societal conditions for such individuals to function successfully in mainstream society. The Americans with Disabilities Act provides accommodations in public transportation, commercial buildings, and telecommunications as well as offers protections from discrimination in employment. This law was most recently amended in 2008 under President George W. Bush.

Barriers for People With Disabilities

Individuals with disabilities face many obstacles in their lives in addition to their physical condition. There are often physical barriers such as broken sidewalks, lack of accommodating transportation, and food restrictions that cannot be accommodated in public. Systemic barriers are also present in an individual with a disability's life. These may include limited or no access to public venues and no opportunities for social and civic interaction. These types of barriers seem to be decreasing with advances in technology and medicine as well as a host of federal, state, and local laws designed to increase access to mainstream society for individuals with disabilities. Meanwhile, attitudinal barriers for people with disabilities continue to exist. These attitudinal barriers serve to create unintended social isolation and marginalization. Common negative attitudes about disabilities include the following:

Backlash: The belief that individuals with disabilities have an unfair advantage over others; that these individuals are taking advantage of their employers and not working as hard as those without disabilities.

Denial: Some disabilities are visible (e.g., paralysis, limb amputation), while other disabilities are not (e.g., congenital heart defect; missing kidney). This can lead to the belief that a person does not have a physical disability unless it can be clearly observed.

Fear: The belief that people with a physical disability are to be regarded with suspicion and apprehension. Until recently in the United States, children and adults with disabilities were often hidden from society, so people had little contact with them. Many times, people react in fear because they do not know what to do or say around a person with a disability.

Hero worship: This springs from the belief that a person with a disability functioning well in society must have special characteristics that set him or her apart. They are not seen as real people but as individuals endowed with extraordinary gifts.

Inferiority: The opposite belief is that a person with a disability is less than a real person or someone who does not have the same rights and responsibilities of other citizens.

Ignorance: Due to a lack of interaction with people with disabilities, there is a lack of understanding regarding the physical disability, including capabilities and limitations.

Pity: The belief that individuals with disabilities expect pity and sorrow over their condition. This is often seen as patronizing by these individuals who want to be treated like everyone else.

Spread effect: This is the belief that if a person is disabled in one aspect, all aspects of that person are to be treated as disabled. An example of this attitude is to speak loudly or in a childlike manner to a person with blindness.

Stereotypes: The belief that all people with a specific disability will act in the same manner. All people with disabilities are unique with individual strengths and limitations.

These barriers cannot be overcome by legislation or system change; it must come about from a shift in thoughts, ideas, and feelings about people with disabilities.

Many individuals with disabilities may feel isolated from mainstream society despite legal, systemic, and societal actions to remove barriers. Some groups of people with disabilities eventually shun mainstream society and form their own communities. One example is evident in the emergence of Deaf culture over the past 50 years. Deaf culture has

its own language (e.g., American Sign Language), social mores, and beliefs. Fundamental to the Deaf culture is the belief that deafness is not a physical disability but a difference in the human experience. From that standpoint, many members of the Deaf community oppose medical and technological advances to increase oral communication skills (speaking and hearing). It is imperative to emphasize that not all individuals with deafness are members of the Deaf community, nor must one be deaf to be a member of the Deaf community. However, this community within a community celebrates its differences from mainstream society.

Holly Howat

See also Deafness; Discrimination; Mental Retardation; Physical Characteristics as Deviance

Further Readings

Abberley, P. (1987). The concept of oppression and the development of a social theory of disability. *Disability, Handicap & Society, 2*(1), 5–19.

Padden, C., & Humphries, T. (2005). *Inside Deaf culture.* Cambridge, MA: First Harvard Paperback Press.

Schiller, J., Lucas, J., Ward, B., & Peregoy, J. (2012). Summary health statistics for U.S. adults: National Health Interview Survey, 2010. *Vital and Health Statistics, 10*(252). Retrieved from http://www.cdc.gov/nchs/data/series/sr_10/sr10_252.pdf

Smith v. Robinson, 468 U.S. 992 (1984).

Torres-Corona, S. (2009). *Attitudes toward people with physical disabilities and accommodations.* Ann Arbor, MI: ProQuest.

U.S. Office of Special Education Programs. (2000). *History: Twenty-five years of progress in educating children with disabilities through IDEA.* Washington, DC: U.S. Department of Education.

World Health Organization. (2010). *International classification of functioning, disability and health.* Geneva, Switzerland: Author.

World Health Organization. (2011). *World report on disability.* Geneva, Switzerland: Author.

PICA

Pica is the recurrent craving or consumption of nonnutritive items. The name was reportedly introduced in the 6th century by Aetius of Amida, a Byzantine physician, in reference to the magpie—*pica pica*—known for its propensity to gather all sorts of objects, albeit to build its nest not to consume as food. The practice has long been documented in the medical literature from Hippocrates and Galen in Antiquity, to Ambroise Paré and Jean Liebault in the 16th century, and throughout the 18th and 19th centuries when developing modern medicine turned its attention to European peasants and enslaved or subjugated populations in the Americas and Africa. Along the centuries, several other terms have been used to describe pica: malacia, cachexia africana, or mal d'estomac. This entry presents the major dimensions of the practice, including the products consumed, the scope of the phenomenon, the categories of people known to engage in pica, and the causes and consequences of the behavior.

Items consumed by pica patients constitute a long and diverse list. Soil or clay (geophagia), raw starch (amylophagia), feces (coprophagia), ice and freezer frost (pagophagia), paint chips (plumbophagia), wood, bark, and twigs (lignophagia), cigarette butts (tobaccophagia), and hair (trichophagia) are the most commonly noted in the literature. Ingestion of other soft (paper products, soap, fabric, clothing, and ashes) and hard nonorganic products (nails, bolts, coins, paper clips, crayons, and plastic items) has also been documented.

In most circumstances, pica is considered an eating disorder and is most commonly observed in individuals with developmental disabilities. However, geophagy, the consumption of soil, is culturally sanctioned in many societies, including the United States, and is mostly practiced by pregnant women and young children. Geophagy is found around the world with incidences varying from the very rare in northern Europe, to 5% in Tanzania, to more than 50% of pregnant women in Kenya, Ghana, and India. In the United States, rates have ranged from 14% to more than 50% among African American mothers, the most likely consumers of earth. In 2001, the Agency for Toxic Substances and Disease Registry of the Centers for Disease Control and Prevention estimated that 33% of American children ingest more than 10 grams of soil 1 or 2 days a year. Rates tend to be much higher in other regions of the world, between 29% and 75%.

Geophagy has been thought to help with nutrient supplementation (especially iron and calcium) during pregnancy and food shortages, with the adsorption of toxins in cases of poisoning, and with the relief of gastrointestinal discomfort. It was also thought to act against hunger by filling the stomach, to fulfill religious functions, especially in Central America, or to provide psychological comfort. However, recent research has challenged most of these explanations and has retained the detoxification hypothesis as the most likely. Still, researchers point to the relevance of integrating the biological, physical, cultural, and symbolic dimensions of geophagy to adequately understanding the behavior.

The situation is quite different for other forms of pica. An eating disorder, it is frequently observed in individuals with developmental difficulties such as autism, severe intellectual disability, and Prader–Willi syndrome, a genetic disorder associated with compulsive eating. The prevalence of pica within this population in the United States ranges from 9% to 25%. As it is the case for geophagy, the etiology of pica is difficult to establish. Nutritional factors such as anemia; environmental factors such as stress, poverty, or limited human interaction; sensory factors (pleasure generated by the smell, texture, or taste of ingested material), as well a variety of mental health factors from depression to schizophrenia have been associated with pica behavior.

The frequent co-occurrence of pica with developmental disorder, especially in early childhood, has led the American Psychiatric Association to set four criteria for a diagnosis of pica in its 2000 *Diagnostic and Statistical Manual of Mental Disorder*, fourth edition, text revision (*DSM-IV-TR*): (1) the persistent eating of nonnutritive items that lasts for at least a month (thus excluding simple mouthing or inadvertent ingestion); (2) the eating of nonnutritive items is inappropriate to the developmental level; (3) it is not culturally sanctioned; and (4) if the eating behavior occurs along with a mental disorder, it must be sufficiently severe to warrant independent clinical attention.

There are serious risks associated with pica. They include toxicity, especially lead poisoning; malnutrition, especially iron deficiency (although it remains unclear if iron-deficiency anemia is a cause or a consequence of pica); parasitic infection (intestinal worms); oral and dental problems such as laceration and gum disease; and gastrointestinal obstructions and perforation resulting from the ingestion of sharp objects and indigestible items.

Several approaches are recommended by physicians to treat pica. The kind and variations of treatments hinge on whether individuals have developmental disabilities or not. They include a range of behavioral treatments. For instance, psychological treatments involve only individuals—and their parents in case of minors—without developmental disabilities. Nutritional treatments—mostly iron and zinc supplementation—and medications have been reported to treat pica in individuals with and without developmental disabilities. Behavioral interventions are almost exclusively used with patients with mental disorders and range from intrusive measures (overcorrection, physical restraints and face masks, use of mist, ammonia pills, or acidic juices) to less aversive procedures such as differential reinforcement, discrimination training, and ecological precaution (removing pica material). Treatments are reported to be quite successful but come with significant ethical and safety considerations, especially for patients in institutional settings.

Jacques Henry

See also Culturally Specific Mental Illnesses; *Diagnostic and Statistical Manual*; Mental Illness

Further Readings

Agency for Toxic Substances and Disease Registry. (2001). *Summary report for the ATSDR soil-pica workshop.* Atlanta, GA: Author.

MacClancy, J., Henry, J., & MacBeth, H. (Eds.). (2007). *Consuming the inedible: Neglected dimensions of food choice.* New York, NY: Berghahn Books.

Parry-Jones, B., & Parry-Jones, W. (1992). Pica: Symptom or eating disorder, a historical assessment. *British Journal of Psychiatry, 160,* 341–354.

Stiegler, L. (2005). Understanding pica behavior: A review for clinical and education professionals. *Focus on Autism and Other Developmental Disabilities, 20,* 27–38.

Young, S. (2011). *Craving earth: Understanding pica.* New York, NY: Columbia University Press.

PICKPOCKETING

Pickpockets are thieves who steal wallets, passports, and other valuables from people's clothing and bags as they interact in public places. Often included in the category of larceny, the key feature of pickpocketing is that it involves stealth but does not involve force, the threat of force, or deception. Larceny/theft is the attempted or completed unlawful taking, carrying, leading, or riding away of property from the possession or constructive possession of another. Larceny/theft is a miscellaneous, catch-all category that includes acts such as shoplifting, pickpocketing,

purse snatching, the theft of contents from automobiles, and bicycle theft. It excludes property crimes that involve deception, including embezzlement, fraud, and forgery.

The dying art of pickpocketing is interesting to examine because of both the high skill involved and its recent decline in the United States. The pickpocket is among those deviants who have disappeared almost entirely over the past several decades. In fact, some researchers consider pickpockets to be nearly nonexistent in the United States. There was once estimated to be 23,000 pickpockets in New York City alone. That number has decreased to a level that the New York City police department now considers it a vanishing breed of criminals, and it no longer keeps statistics on pickpocketing.

Many European cities are home to large numbers of pickpockets, but the United States, which once harbored a large and very active criminal trade of pickpockets, no longer fosters and nurtures this mass of thieves. This change is likely due to the increased use of credit cards and traveler's checks, and enhanced security factors among cities and airports in the United States. Once a lucrative criminal career in the United States, Europe is now the harbor and training ground for this dying art in the United States. This change in the prevalence of pickpocketing can be seen in the demographic makeup of pickpockets in different countries. Those who still engage in the practice in the United States tend to be middle-aged males. In Europe, the average age of pickpockets is between 23 and 35 years. Another possible reason pickpockets are disappearing in the United States are the felony charges attached to such crimes and the longer sentences imposed by courts. The picketpocket offense currently brings with it a felony charge not subject to financial consideration, meaning any amount stolen is deemed to be a felony. Most established pickpockets in the United States are known to the police because many of them have been arrested at least once. Law enforcement officials are now able to track these known criminals easily through electronic communication, media, or billing or any use of identifying numbers such as social security or driver license; hence, catching these men or women is always near at hand, which further reduces the workforce in this criminal professional. While the crime of pickpocketing is seen as becoming a lost art and dying out among the entrepreneurial and skilled sector of criminals, other crimes, like piracy, which were once said to have had the same fate, have returned with a violent vengeance, with perpetrators possessing high levels of organization, skills, and technologies.

Pickpockets frequent crowded areas such as airports, train stations, athletic games, conventions, and other large crowded events that are likely to produce potential victims. In crowds, a thief can easily blend in the crowd to avoid detection. The practice and performance of a pickpocket is deployed to distract, such as dropping money accidentally or starting an argument or fight. Prostitutes, who are often pickpockets as well (dual deviance) often physically touch men offering their services, while frisking and probing for a pocket hit (usually a wallet or money that is easily taken) or a smaller trophy to sell or barter. Tools for facilitating pickpocketing include a razor for opening pockets or cutting a strap on a purse or carry bag and tongs that reach around the waist or over the shoulder to prevent the victim from noticing.

Many pickpockets operate in teams. One may distract, while another does the deed and hands the stolen items off to a third party who then departs the scene. If the first thief is apprehended, he or she will not be in possession of stolen goods to justify an arrest and/or charge. When pickpockets do not operate as individuals, they function as something between the informal organization of street corner gangs and the formal organization of units like the Cosa Nostra (the Mafia). The fundamental form of organization among pickpockets is the team, tribe, or troupe, which is typically composed of two to four members. The tasks of each position are finely dictated and established beforehand. There is a position for the team member whose duty it is to locate the prospective victim and distract his or her attention. The second position is the most highly skilled as it calls for a specialist highly proficient in removing the wallet or other goods from the victim's pocket or purse. A third position requires skills in receiving the stolen items from the person who took it. The fourth position involves the disposal of the stolen goods.

Pickpockets are professional thieves or criminals. Certain types of crimes can be committed without any prior experience or skill (e.g., homicide). A professional criminal has had training and is a member of a highly skilled occupation whose crimes are planned with unusual care. He or she is differentiated from amateur, occasional, and opportunistic criminals. The safecracker (i.e., "boxman") was once considered the most skilled criminal by other professional thieves; hence, he or she is at the top

of his or her profession. Professional thieves make a regular business of theft. They use techniques that have been developed over a long period. These techniques have been transmitted by traditions and personal associations that usually involve apprenticeships. A good example is the Bhamptas, who are still a tribe in India. The Bhamptas were once highly skilled pickpockets and thieves. They were trained for careers in crime from their earliest childhood. They specialized in railway stations. The children were initiated into their profession by lessons in the stealing of any items that they may come across. If they were not good at it, they were beaten during their training. They soon became adept. Adults usually worked in gangs of three or four. The first role of children was to play the "beaten child" in public whereby the child rushes to the protection of a well-to-do person who has already been spotted. As a member of the team argued with both the child and the victim, the victim's wallet or purse is stolen, and the thieves disappear.

The professional thief is generally characterized by (a) *skill*—a complex of techniques that exists for committing crimes; (b) *status*—has a position of high prestige in the criminal world, hence, *high recognition*; (c) *consensus*—shares common values, attitudes, beliefs, and a esprit de corps among members of the thievery profession; (d) *differential association*—associations are with other professional criminals to the exclusion of other criminals and the law-abiding public; and (e) *organization*—criminal activities are pursued in terms of common knowledge and through an informal assistance and information network. The process of acquiring recognition as a professional thief includes several necessary elements: (a) *contact*, (b) *selection*, and (c) *training*. *Contact* is a requisite for both selection and training. Professional thieves come in contact through their association with other criminals. Once an informal agreement or arrangement is reached, *selection* takes place. Selection means the skilled and experienced pickpocket has agreed to take on the apprentice pickpocket as a partner. After the selection process is complete, *training* begins. This involves the learning of attitudes, values, skills, and techniques. This learning takes place while engaging in criminal activity. During this period of apprenticeship, the thief assimilates standards of group morality (not snitching and honesty among thieves), learns methods of stealing and the disposing of goods, and becomes acquainted with other thieves. The professional thief knows those who are the most skilled in his or her specialty and indirectly confers recognition and status on these individuals. Gradually he or she hopes to become and be accepted as a top tier professional thief.

Craig J. Forsyth

See also Check Forgery; Deviant Career; Larceny; Maritime Piracy

Further Readings

Clinard, M. B., & Quinney, R. (1973). *Criminal behavioral systems.* New York, NY: Holt, Rinehart & Winston.

Cressey, P. F. (1936). The criminal tribes of India. *Sociology & Social Research, 20,* 503–511.

Maurer, D. W. (1964). *Whiz mob.* New Haven, CT: College and University Press.

Sutherland, E. (1937). *The professional thief.* Chicago, IL: University of Chicago Press.

POACHING

Poaching—the unlawful taking of wildlife resources—is a deviant practice that has existed for centuries. Historically, in England and Europe, the nobility and elite members of society owned the wildlife, and poaching laws were used to keep members of the lower class from killing their game. In the United States, extensive and unregulated market hunting in the 19th century was having a destructive effect on wildlife populations. As a result, game laws and regulations were enacted beginning in the late 19th and early 20th centuries to protect wildlife populations.

Poaching occurs when individuals hunt or fish illegally and takes a variety of forms. The term *poaching* is generally associated with the illegal killing of game that occurs outside of prescribed hunting seasons. However, poaching encompasses a variety of offenses that may occur outside of as well as during established hunting and fishing seasons. For example, deer poaching is a common offense. It occurs when someone illegally kills a deer before the hunting season begins. It would also be poaching if someone killed a deer during nighttime hours with the aid of a spotlight within the time frame of an open hunting season. Poaching also includes exceeding bag limits of fish or game. Thus, it is considered poaching if a hunter takes an over limit of deer even if it is during hunting season. Another type of poaching offense is party hunting, which occurs when a hunter illegally takes a deer for another hunter during the hunting season.

Whatever the particular form it takes, poaching is a timely topic since considerable social change is occurring at the present time with respect to the value placed on animals by different segments of society. Given increased concern for the environment in the context of an increasing human population and rapid urbanization occurring in modern society, poaching is considered a serious social problem because it depletes fish and game populations. This entry discusses poaching in contemporary society and gives an overview of the topic that includes information about locations of poaching, characteristics of poachers, reasons for poaching, and why enforcement of poaching is difficult.

Locations of Poaching

Poaching activities occur all over the world wherever wildlife is found and generally take place in sparsely populated rural areas where wildlife species are abundant. These remote and isolated locations most often comprise wooded areas or agricultural regions that provide good habitat for wildlife species.

Specific geographical locations where poaching frequently occurs include large areas of North America and Africa that are rich in wildlife resources. States in rural America that contain large populations of trophy big game such as Alaska, Montana, and Wyoming are prime locations for poaching activities. Countries in Africa have a diversity of large trophy game animals, and poaching has been a problem for decades in these locations.

Characteristics of Poachers

Hunting is a male-dominated activity, and with this being the case, it follows that the overwhelming majority of poaching is committed by males. Some females do participate in poaching activities, but their level of involvement tends to be minimal when compared with that of males. With respect to stage in the life cycle, poachers can come from any age category. However, as with offenders who commit other types of crimes, the majority of poachers are young. Poaching is most often committed by individuals who range in age from the teenage years through their 30s. In terms of socioeconomic status, poaching is committed by members of all social classes. Most of the poaching in contemporary society is committed by working-class individuals who are employed in blue-collar jobs. Individuals of higher socioeconomic status (upper middle and upper class) are more likely to engage in specific types of poaching, including the poaching of trophy animals.

Reasons for Poaching

Research on poachers has found support for differential association theory in that poaching behavior appears to be learned from family members or close friends. Studies have also found that poachers often use a variety of rationalizations, or neutralization techniques, to account for their wildlife law violations.

It is important to note that there are different types of poachers and motivations for poaching. While many poaching activities are planned, others are spontaneous. There are a variety of factors that can exert an influence on poaching activities that include the type and volume of wildlife species that are present in a given area, the number of law enforcement agents as well as their effectiveness in enforcing the law, the economy and culture of a community or region, public access to wildlife habitat, and the availability of cover for escaping detection. Individuals engage in poaching for a variety of reasons, and several of the common ones are discussed here.

In some instances, economically disadvantaged individuals poach wildlife because they are in dire circumstances and need the food. These poachers consume the meat from wildlife they take illegally. While there are still some individuals who participate in the activity in modern society, this type of subsistence poaching has generally given way to other forms of poaching.

Some individuals are opportunists who engage in poaching simply because an opportunity presented itself to them and they may decide to kill an animal because it is fun or exciting. Unlike other types of violators, opportunist poachers do not plan their crimes beforehand. As a result, this type of poacher is generally more likely to get caught than other types of poachers.

Some poachers devote their attention to trophy animals. These individuals selectively seek out and kill trophy wildlife, especially animals that possess large antlers or wildlife that is rare. Those who engage in this type of poaching do so because they want to impress others, and they think that possessing trophy animals will enhance their status as a hunter. An example of trophy poaching is when someone kills a deer with exceptional antlers that can be displayed on the wall for others to see.

Another reason that individuals kill wildlife illegally is because they are able to profit economically from the activity. These commercial poachers take wildlife illegally for the purpose of selling the animal parts for money on the black market. Similar to the illegal drug trade, this type of poaching can be a lucrative business enterprise for some individuals. In North America, a common type of poaching is when individuals kill black bears and take the gall bladders, which some consider to have medicinal qualities, to sell on the black market. Internationally, poachers kill elephants in Africa for their ivory tusks, which are valuable commodities on black market.

Enforcement of Poaching

In the United States, laws protecting wildlife exist at both the state and federal levels. Each state is responsible for managing its fish and wildlife resources, and as a result, most poaching offenses are violations of state law. Federal laws also protect wildlife species. In 1900, the Lacey Act was enacted to control the market hunting of wildlife, and it makes it a federal offense to bring illegally taken wildlife across state lines. The Endangered Species Act of 1973 protects species that are in danger of going extinct.

The apprehension of poachers is difficult given the vast geographical areas where the crimes occur as well as the relatively small number of law enforcement officers that enforce this type of crime. Game wardens, also known as conservation officers, are the law enforcement officers who are responsible for enforcing wildlife laws and apprehending poachers. When compared with the number of traditional police officers in society, the number of game wardens is extremely small. Because poaching offenses generally occur in remote rural areas with small human populations, enforcement is difficult. Game wardens rely on information and tips from the public to solve crimes, and many states have poaching hotlines that citizens can call to report poaching offenses. In some situations, game wardens participate in undercover operations to catch poachers.

Individuals who are convicted of violating poaching laws face a variety of sanctions, including fines and short jail terms. In an attempt to prevent poaching, some states revoke hunting privileges for periods of time ranging from one year up to a lifetime. Some states impose mandatory restitution on poaching offenders that is associated with the type of animal killed, which pertains mostly to trophy wildlife. In some instances, habitual poachers have been sentenced to prison.

The trend in recent decades in the United States is toward the increased criminalization of poaching offenses. Most poaching offenses are misdemeanors, but in some states, the illegal killing of wildlife now constitutes a felony offense, especially if trophy wildlife is involved.

Stephen L. Eliason

See also Differential Association Theory; Folk Crime; Neutralization Theory; Sport and Deviance

Further Readings

Eliason, S. L. (1999). The illegal taking of wildlife: Toward a theoretical understanding of poaching. *Human Dimensions of Wildlife, 4*(2), 27–39.

Eliason, S. L. (2008). Wildlife crime: Conservation officers' perceptions of elusive poachers. *Deviant Behavior, 29*(2), 111–128.

Eliason, S. L. (2012). From the king's deer to a capitalist commodity: A social historical analysis of the poaching law. *International Journal of Comparative and Applied Criminal Justice, 36*(2), 133–148.

Eliason, S. L. (2012). Trophy poaching: A routine activities perspective. *Deviant Behavior, 33*(1), 72–87.

Forsyth, C. J. (2008). The game of wardens and poachers. *Southern Rural Sociology, 23*(2), 43–53.

Forsyth, C. J., & Marckese, T. A. (1993). Thrills and skills: A sociological analysis of poaching. *Deviant Behavior, 14*(2), 157–172.

Muth, R. M., & Bowe, J. F. (1998). Illegal harvest of renewable natural resources in North America: Toward a typology of the motivations for poaching. *Society & Natural Resources, 11*(1), 9–24.

POLICE DEVIANCE

Police have four basic functions: (1) maintaining order, (2) crime prevention, (3) criminal investigation, and (4) public service. While performing these functions, police have a limited right to restrict fundamental freedoms of individuals, which can result in adversarial relations with citizens. Juvenal, a Roman poet who lived between 60 and 140 BCE, first asked the question, "Who is policing the police?" (*Quis custodiet ipsos costodes?*). Lord Acton, a British historian, once said that "power tends to corrupt, and absolute power corrupts absolutely." To prevent its corruptive effects, the powers given to the police are controlled by oversight institutions and various accountability mechanisms.

Criminologists and scholars in policing have tried to classify deviant police behaviors. Their efforts are clustered around the concepts of police deviance, police misconduct, police corruption, police crime, police brutality, police abuse, police ethics, and police integrity. There is no consensus on what term to use to describe police deviance. Likewise, there is no agreement on how to define it or what particular behaviors constitute it. In this entry, police deviance is used as an umbrella term for all police wrongdoings, as it is the most encompassing term.

Categorizations

According to Maurice Punch, police deviance consists of three subcategories: (1) corruption, (2) misconduct, and (3) crime. He describes police corruption as behaviors of commission or omission associated with taking money or gifts from an external corruptor. Punch defines police misconduct as violations of administrative rules and procedures that are internally investigated and penalized by the police organization. Police misconduct includes behavior such as sleeping on duty, coming to work late, drinking or having sex while on duty, being disrespectful to superiors, neglecting one's duties, reporting sick when healthy, and missing work excessively. These forms of deviance usually do not transgress criminal laws but do violate the disciplinary rules of the department. Punch defines police crime as illegal behavior committed by officers while in uniform; it can include both police misconduct and police corruption. According to Punch, police crime occurs when officers violate the law such as using excessive violence, discriminating against certain races, sexually harassing suspects or fellow officers, using or dealing in illegal drugs, and violating human rights.

Tom O'Connor classifies police deviance as (1) police gratuity, (2) police shakedowns, (3) police perjury, (4) police brutality, (5) police profanity, (6) police sex while on duty or duty related, (7) police sleeping while on duty, (8) police drinking and abusing drugs while on or off duty, and (9) police misuse of confidential information. Jeffrey Ross provides a multidimensional taxonomy of police crimes based in part on whether the act was violent, motivated by profit, or perpetrated on behalf of an individual or an organization.

Some researchers suggest using only two major categories to characterize police deviance: (1) police misconduct and (2) police corruption. Both concepts cover general abuses of police authority, but the term *police misconduct* is often used for less serious cases and *police corruption* for more serious cases. Under this dichotomy, police misconduct includes inappropriate actions performed by police officers within official capacities. It can consist of violent or nonviolent actions without considering any personal gain. Police misconduct can be defined as a less obvious wrongdoing such as drinking while on duty or threatening to harm suspects if they do not cooperate with the police. Police misconduct may involve violent or nonviolent practices. Some police scholars and academics use the term *police brutality* or *police use of excessive force* instead of violent police misconduct. Nonviolent police misconduct ranges from graft and corruption to perjury to fixing fines. Although all types of police misconduct are serious, some types of misconduct are taken more seriously than others by the public. For instance, citizens may be most interested in police use of excessive force when making arrests of public protesters. In the same manner, people are more concerned about police officers who commit perjury in court or who engage in sexual harassment of civilians than those who sleep on duty. The term *police corruption* refers to abuse of police authority for personal or institutional gain. Corruption may involve profit or any type of material benefit gained illegally as a consequence of the officer's authority such as taking bribes, opportunistic theft, kickbacks, and shakedowns.

Police Misconduct

Police misconduct occurs when police officers use their power in a manner that is inconsistent with the law and professional standards, codes of conduct, and ethics. Police misconduct comprises illegitimate, unlawful, illegal, or unethical behaviors. It includes any behavior that violates departmental rules and policies, administrative procedures, professional ethic code, and civil and criminal law. Dean Champion provides the following examples of police misconduct: accessing police records for personal use; abusing sick leave; lying to supervisors and managers; committing perjury on reports and in court; committing a crime; falsifying overtime records; using excessive force; drinking while on duty; being involved in off-duty firearms incidents;

failing to complete police reports; accepting gratuities; providing recommendations for an attorney, towing service, or bail bond service; failing to report misconduct of a fellow officer; failing to inventory recovered property or evidence; sleeping while on duty; cheating on a promotional examination; and sexually harassing or performing other such improprieties.

As can be seen from this list, the concept of police misconduct refers to a wide range of procedural, criminal, and civil violations. In a general manner, police misconduct means abuse of authority by police officers. Abuse of authority erodes public confidence in law enforcement and criminal justice systems worldwide. Police misconduct may also have grave consequences; for example, as a result of police misconduct, innocent citizens may be arrested, prosecuted, and convicted of crimes they did not commit, commonly termed *miscarriages of justice*. Officers can perform police misconduct actively or passively. In other words, police misconduct can be the result of an *act* or *omission* made by an officer.

Although all types of police misconduct are serious, the public considers some misconduct behaviors more serious than others. For instance, citizens may be more concerned with police use of excessive force when making arrests in public protests, police officers who commit perjury in court, or police who engage in sexual harassment with civilians than they are with an officer who sleeps while on duty.

Police Corruption

The second major category of police deviance is police corruption. The United Nations defines police corruption as engaging in proscribed behaviors to gain profit or advantage for oneself or for another. Police corruption can be classified into four subcategories: (1) straightforward corruption, (2) strategic corruption, (3) predatory corruption, and (4) noble cause corruption. Straightforward corruption occurs when a certain act is engaged in or avoided with the goal of receiving payment (in money or services). Conventional understanding of this sort of corruption is usually referred to as "grass-eating," as officers usually do not seek out such gratuities or bribes but accept them when they are offered. Strategic corruption occurs when police and organized crime actors engage in a stable, long-term agreement. Police and organized crime may regulate illegal markets like gambling and prostitution. This stable and strategic cooperation creates regular payoffs for the police and provides protection from arrest for criminals. Predatory corruption occurs when police manage crime, extort money, and organize graft. Here, police take an active role in the corruption and are often referred to as "meat-eaters." Finally, noble cause corruption involves using illegal means for institutionally and socially confirmed ends. To secure convictions, police may pay informants illegally, obtain drugs, falsify testimonies, plant evidence, intimidate witnesses, and so on. The primary purpose is not personal gain. The motivation is doing good, but the means are bad because police violate the law to uphold the law. Such corruption is often referred to as the *Dirty Harry* problem, in reference to the 1971 film of the same name in which the title character, Inspector Harry "Dirty Harry" Callahan, uses morally questionable means to achieve a morally good result.

John Kleinig provides eight broad types of corrupt behavior: (1) corruption of authority, (2) kickbacks, (3) opportunistic theft, (4) shakedowns, (5) protection of illegal activities, (6) fixes, (7) direct criminal activities, and (8) internal payoff. In the corruption of authority, officers receive gain by virtue of their position without violating the law, such as free drinks, meals, services, and discounts. Kickbacks refer to officers receiving money or other valuables from those who provide services to the clients of the police (e.g., towing companies, ambulances, and garages) for sending work their way. Opportunistic theft involves stealing unprotected property or stealing property from arrestees, victims, and crime scenes. Shakedowns occur when officers take money, goods, or other valuables from criminals as payment for not arresting them or allowing their criminal enterprises to continue. Protection of illegal activities involves police accepting money from vice operators or companies who are operating illegally. Fixes include quashing prosecution proceedings to protect those involved in illegal behaviors. Direct criminal activities are any behaviors that are criminal offenses in their own right (regardless of whether the offender is a police officer). Finally, internal payoff is when officers sell work assignments, off days, holidays, evidence, and promotions to other officers.

Prevalence and Scope of Police Deviance

Policing is an occupation at high risk for misconduct due to the high level of authority granted to officers. The problem of police deviance has existed since the beginning of law enforcement agencies. In fact, the issue of police misconduct has been discussed since the inception of the first modern police, which was founded in 1829 in London by Sir Robert Peel. In the first three years (1829–1831), Peel asked for 6,000 police officers' resignations, and more than 5,000 police were fired because they abused their authority.

The prevalence of police deviance is a much debated statistical issue all over the world. It is difficult to assess the extent of police deviance because of the lack of reliable data. There are no exhaustive statistics available on crimes committed by law enforcement officers and only a limited number of studies providing specific data on police crimes. However, there is some evidence that police deviance among police departments all over the world is pervasive. For instance, a survey of 1,151 police departments in cities with populations of 10,000 or more showed widespread police misconduct and numerous public allegations of it. In this study, it was shown that tort actions filed against police officers in the United States in 1990 resulted in awards to citizens in excess of $2 million depending on the jurisdiction.

Further evidence of the pervasiveness of police deviance throughout the world are the numerous police scandals that have emerged with regularity. In New York City, it appears that roughly every two decades, commissions are formed to counter police corruption. Some of the major committees in New York include the Lexow Committee (1894), the Curran Committee (1913), the Seabury Committee (1930), the Harry Gross Committee (1950), the Knapp Commission (1971), and the Mollen Commission (1994). In the context of examining police corruption, Los Angeles and Chicago have also established commissions such as the Webb Commission (1998) in Chicago and the Rodney King (1992) and Bostic (2000) commissions in Los Angeles. Australia has seen a large number of commissions established to assess police deviance. In the 1970s, serious investigations were conducted in New South Wales, Queensland, and Victoria. Major commissions to assess police deviance in Australia include The New Fitzgerald Commission (1987) and the Queensland and Wood Commission (1997). The United Kingdom also witnessed major police scandals, including the Birmingham Six, the Guildford Four, and the Carl Bridgewater Affair. All of the scandals mentioned here were scandals of police corruption around the world.

Measuring police misconduct is a difficult task. To overcome this problem, David Packman developed the National Police Misconduct Statistics and Reporting Project in the United States. According to its 2010 report, 4,861 unique reports of police misconduct were tracked, involving 6,613 sworn law enforcement officers (354 were agency leaders, e.g., chiefs or sheriffs) and 6,826 alleged victims; 247 fatalities were associated with tracked reports; and $346,512,800 was spent on misconduct-related civil judgments and settlements, excluding sealed settlements, court costs, and attorney fees. Of the 6,613 law enforcement officers involved in reported allegations of misconduct, 1,575 were involved in excessive force reports, which was the most prominent type of report at 23.8% of all reports. This was followed by sexual misconduct complaints at 9.3% of reports and then theft/fraud/robbery allegations involving 7.2% of reports.

Police may commit deviant acts as individuals, as part of groups, or as members of an organization. In the policing literature, the rotten apple metaphor implies that police deviance is an individual matter. The claim is that the vast majority of officers do not engage in any types of deviance, and it is only a few "rotten apples" who do. Those who take this perspective assume that when a number of officers in a unit or department engage in deviance, it is because one or two deviant officers slip into bad ways and then contaminate other good officers. In contrast, some take a "rotten barrel" perspective, which implies that police deviance is systemic throughout the department. Punch coined the concept of rotten orchards to emphasize police deviance at an organizational or systemic level. Police departments have the tendency to explain police deviance by using the rotten apple theory to minimize public backlash, whereas outsiders (e.g., academics) often promote the rotten barrel perspective.

Ercan Balcıoğlu and Osman Dolu

See also Abuse by Clergy; Governmental Deviance; Military Deviance; Police Profiling

Further Readings

Champion, D. J. (2001). *Police misconduct in America: A reference handbook.* Santa Barbara, CA: ABC-CLIO.

Dean, G., Bell, P., & Lauchs, M. (2010). Conceptual framework for managing knowledge of police deviance. *Policing & Society, 20,* 204–222.

Kleinig, J. (1996). *The ethics of policing.* Cambridge, England: Cambridge University Press.

Newburn, T. (1999). *Understanding and preventing police corruption: Lessons from the literature* (Police Research Series 110). London, England: Home Office, Policing and Reducing Crime Unit, Research, Development and Statistics.

Prenzler, T. (2009). *Police corruption: Preventing misconduct and maintaining integrity.* Boca Raton, FL: CRC Press.

Punch, M. E. (2000). Police corruption and its prevention. *European Journal on Criminal Policy and Research, 8,* 301–324.

Punch, M. E. (2009). *Police corruption: Deviance, accountability and reform in policing.* Portland, OR: Willan.

Sherman, L. W. (1978). *Scandal and reform: Controlling police corruption.* Berkeley: University of California Press.

Skogan, W. G., & Meares, T. L. (2004). Lawful policing. *Annals of the American Academy of Political and Social Science, 593,* 66–83.

POLICE PROFILING

In recent years, police profiling has been a much debated issue not only in the United States but also across the world. Also known as racial profiling, police profiling includes actions of police authorities based on the perceived race of a person rather than on legal cues. In other words, racial profiling is the use of race as a key factor by law enforcement officers in targeting citizens for surveillance and questioning. The criminologists Scott Wortley and Julian Tanner provide one of the broadest definitions of racial profiling. Specifically, they say racial profiling exists when members of specific racial groups are targeted for greater levels of surveillance than are members of other races. It includes behaviors such as when police stop and search some races more than others, when there are increased patrols in minority neighborhoods, and when sting operations target particular ethnic groups. According to a 1999 Gallup poll, 60% of Americans believe that racial profiling exists. The popularity of phrases such as "driving while black" and "driving while brown" indicates the public concerns that ethnicity and race play an important role in police discretion.

There is a consensus among citizens, advocates, and even police officers that police profiling based on ethnicity and race is not acceptable, even though some believe that profiling minorities is a pragmatic decision that many law enforcement agencies have to make to get better results in crime fighting. On the other hand, there is no doubt that police, scholars, and the public have different beliefs and opinions about the ways in which racial police profiling occurs. This entry examines the sources of such disparity and myths regarding profiling, and explores measures to combat racial profiling.

Sources of Disparity

One explanation for racial profiling is that it occurs due to the actions of racist law enforcement officers toward minorities. Some people believe that profiling is merely the problem of racist individuals, not the systematic problem of organizations. From this perspective, individual discriminatory actions by police, judges, correction personnel, and prosecutors are seen as the main cause of profiling, and individual discriminatory actions based on race and ethnicity should be dealt with by harsh policies and punishing the people who are involved. However, others claim that individual discriminatory actions account for a small fraction of the overall problem. The "bad apples" explanation does not adequately explain the overrepresentation of minorities at the different stages of criminal justice system. Some people believe that racial profiling is not a problem in which a few bad apples in law enforcement engage, but rather, it is a systematic and accepted belief within law enforcement that minorities are more likely to commit crime than are Whites.

Another argument for racial profiling made by some scholars and practitioners is the cognitive stereotyping of law enforcement agencies that, based on the premise that minorities are more likely to commit crime, targeting minorities for offenses may result in uncovering many other violations. Racial profiling is done not with the idea of discrimination, but with the idea of efficient use of resources by law enforcement to get the maximum benefits from their actions. Therefore, some law enforcement agencies identify hot spots in their geographic jurisdictions—that is, locations where the majority of the crimes occur—and they try to intervene in those places to combat crime. This tactic is considered a cost-effective allocation of law enforcement resources.

Another important issue is that cognitive stereotyping or contextual discrimination plays an important role in the judgments of officers. The utilitarian argument made by proponents of racial profiling is that minority members have been found to be disproportionately responsible for the commission of certain crimes. The premise behind this argument is that minorities are more likely to be involved in some offenses than others. Therefore, for many law enforcement agencies, crime prevention strategies are designed to focus on certain minorities with the aim of minimizing the expenses of crime prevention.

Another important reason that makes law enforcement officers engage in racial profiling may be related to the organizational deployments of officers, which may not be directly associated with race. For instance, some predominantly minority communities where the majority of crimes occur may be targeted by law enforcement agencies for organizational deployments and policing with the aim of fighting crime.

Stereotypes that influence the judgments of law enforcement officers subconsciously are claimed as an important reason for the practice of racial profiling. Racial and ethnic factors may affect the attitudes of law enforcement officers without their conscious awareness.

Myths About Profiling

Some false assumptions about racial profiling are often accepted as true. For example, some have argued that police should stop more Black drivers in the United States because African Americans are more likely to be drug users. In fact, this assumption is untrue; the number of White drug users is greater than that of African Americans.

After the attacks of September 11, 2001, in which 19 men from various Arab countries hijacked four planes, crashing two into the World Trade Center in New York City, one into the Pentagon outside of Washington, D.C., and another in a field in Pennsylvania, some people have assumed that Americans of Arab origin are likely to be terrorists. This assumption has led some law enforcement agencies to use Arab ethnicity as a pretext for interrogations. The fact that most Arab Americans are neither terrorists nor terrorist sympathizers makes this assumption false.

Actions to Counter Racial Profiling

A number of practitioners and academicians have recommended some measures to help end racial profiling. Providing training to law enforcement personnel about racial diversity and cultural awareness is recommended to end or at least decrease the number of incidents of racial profiling. Following the establishment of written organizational policies that strictly prohibit discriminatory actions, law enforcement agencies are advised to see that all personnel attend racial profiling training. Training about cultural awareness and diversity could be a good strategy to share information related to the issue and an important step to affect people's attitudes toward discriminatory actions.

Because most complaints against racial profiling come from traffic stops, setting up standards for data collection and analysis for traffic stops might help alleviate the problem. This strategy could help not only identify the problematic officers who use racial or ethnic background to interrogate but also highlight the problematic organizational policies that may lead to racial profiling. This strategy also provides police chiefs the opportunity to create more ethical and impartial public safety policies that involve the public.

Many police departments have faced civil lawsuits due to incidents of racial profiling by their employees, and such litigation has been recognized as a serious problem for law enforcement agencies. It has been recommended that to protect their agencies against such civil actions, managers of police departments have been advised to implement effective data collection and analysis systems in addition to establishing clearly defined organizational policies that forbid discriminatory activities of their members.

Bias-based activities on the part of police officers can easily undermine the public's trust of law enforcement agencies. Therefore, another recommendation is for governments to create and maintain an effective and fair citizen complaint system. The intent is to establish a valid procedure for reviewing complaints of racially based conduct by law enforcement officials, thereby ensuring that the rights of citizens are equally protected and that the facts of such incidents are thoroughly investigated and brought to light in an efficient way. Law enforcement agencies have the responsibility to ensure that their personnel are trained and supervised in the actual day-to-day requirements of providing fair and impartial police services.

Sedat Kula

See also Discrimination; Drug Policy; Drug War (War on Drugs); Police Deviance; Racism

Further Readings

Barlow, D. E., & Barlow, M. H. (2002). Racial profiling: A survey of African American police officers. *Police Quarterly, 5*(3), 334–358.

Engel, R. S., Calnon, J. M., & Bernard, T. J. (2002). Theory and racial profiling: Shortcomings and future directions in research. *Justice Quarterly, 19*(2), 249–273.

Gross, S. R., & Livingston, D. (2002). Racial profiling under attack. *Columbia Law Review, 102*(5), 1413–1438.

Persico, N. (2002). Racial profiling, fairness, and effectiveness of policing. *American Economic Review, 92*(5), 1472–1497.

Petrocelli, M., Piquero, A. R., & Smith, M. R. (2003). Conflict theory and racial profiling: An empirical analysis of police traffic stop data. *Journal of Criminal Justice, 31*(1), 1–11.

Reitzel, J., & Piquero, A. R. (2006). Does it exist? Studying citizens' attitudes of racial profiling. *Police Quarterly, 9*(2), 161–183.

Wilson, G., Dunham, R., & Alpert, G. (2004). Prejudice in police profiling. *American Behavioral Scientist, 47*(7), 896–909.

Withrow, B. L. (2006). *Racial profiling: From rhetoric to reason.* Upper Saddle River, NJ: Prentice Hall.

POLYAMORY AND POLYGAMY

Various forms of intimate relationships and families are practiced in the Unites States today, following several transitions such as the rise in single parenthood, stepfamilies, cohabitation, the retreat from marriage, and visibility of lesbian and gay partnerships. *Polyamory* is a relationship and familial form, practice, and identity that translates literally as "many loves." Polyamorous ("poly") relationships are those in which people engage in meaningful, ongoing, loving, and/or sexual relationships with multiple partners simultaneously. *Polygamy* is a form of polyamory in which one person maintains several spousal relationships simultaneously. However, the two practices differ substantially, particularly in terms of marriage, motivation, and values. This entry introduces polyamory and polygamy as practiced in North America, discusses related contemporary social debate, and examines how these practices challenge dominant social norms.

Polyamory

Polyamory is one of several types of nonmonogamy, which is any relationship form that involves multiple partners simultaneously. Specifically, polyamory involves consensual nonmonogamy, a relationship practice in which people actively negotiate and agree to relationships with multiple partners.

Polyamorous relationships differ from other types of open relationships or marriages because the latter are those in which partners may seek external sexual and/or romantic relationships outside of a primary partnership(s) without mutual negotiation and agreement. For example, someone who engages in open relationships may engage in external casual sex without his or her partners' knowledge. In contrast, poly partners are open and honest regarding additional relationships and often feel "compersion" (happiness or excitement) for their partners' other intimate relationships.

Likewise, polyamory differs from swinging because swinging generally involves short-term acts of casual sex with couples or individuals by couples who engage in primary dyadic relationships. Although some poly relationships are sexual in nature, the emphasis on meaningful relationships differentiates polyamory from swinging. In addition, group marriage is a form of polyamory commonly known as polyfidelity (closed-group relationships); however, group marriage differs from other forms of polyamory because partners do not maintain any additional relationships outside of the group marriage.

Historical Perspective

Several communities and movements that promoted forms of nonmonogamy influenced the evolution of polyamory, including the practice of polygamy by members of the Church of Jesus Christ of Latter-day Saints in the early to mid-19th century. Over the past two centuries, several additional communities have practiced multipartner relationships, such as complex marriage in the Oneida Community, in which all members of the community were married and had (hetero)sexual access to each other. Additionally, the first wave of the sexual revolution in the early 20th century encouraged freedom from relational and familial hegemonic patriarchy, while the second sexual revolution of the 1960s and the feminist movement promoted sexual liberation and various forms of nonmonogamies.

In addition to political support, polyamory received attention in popular media and literature. Robert Heinlein's 1960s *Stranger in a Strange Land* and other literature that followed encouraged alternative forms of intimate relating that promotes various ideals of polyamorous living and challenges conventional ideals of monogamy. As the poly movement grew, publications continued that promoted the advantages of polyamory, further increasing its visibility. For example, *Loving More* magazine was founded to organize and support the poly community, and authors such as Deborah Anapol and Ryam Nearing have released several books that describe polyamorous values. In addition, several recent films portray poly struggles and realities, and a few were publicized on popular television channels such as the MTV documentaries *Sex in the 90's: It's a Group Thing* and *True Life* and TLC's *Strange Sex*.

Polyamory in Practice

Polyamorous relationships and familial forms are heterogeneous. Primary partnerships are long-term, committed relationships in which partners are romantically or sexually involved in meaningful relationships with other individuals. Primary dyadic poly partnerships reflect conventional monogamous relationships because of the emphasis on dyadic intimate relating; however, poly individuals in these relationships value nonpossessiveness and multipartner relating, and may be open to group relationships should the opportunity arise. Secondary partnerships involve meaningful sexual or romantic relationships that may have less commitment than primary partnerships. Some people form mono/poly relationships, which refer to partnerships in which one person is monogamous and the other has external relationships.

The "wedge in a V" refers to individuals who are dating two people separately and simultaneously. In contrast, triads comprise three individuals who are each involved in a primary relationship or who cohabit together as a triadic family. Quads refer to partnerships in which four people are each romantically involved or two couples are romantically involved. Intimate friendships and intimate networks involve relationships with or webs of close friends, current partners, partners' other partners (metamours), and ex-partners. These relationships may be sexually or romantically based but often focus on upholding strong meaningful friendships. Furthermore, poly partners often cohabit as families or tribes (multifamily cohabitation or intimate networks). Polyamorous practices are highly complex, diverse, and individualized. In contrast, polygamy is more homogeneous in practice.

Polygamy

Polygamy is a form of polyamory; however, polygamy differs in several substantial ways. First, polygamists practice multiple dyadic marriage, in that one person maintains several marriages simultaneously, but that person's spouses are not married to each other. Specifically, *polygyny* involves multiple marriage between one man and several wives, where the wives only engage in familial but not marital relations. Likewise, *polyandry* involves the marriage of one woman to several husbands, where the husbands are not married to each other. In contrast, polyamory is inclusive of groups in which all partners maintain relationships (as in triads or polyfidelity) and does not inherently involve multiple marriage.

Additionally, polygamous families are often patriarchal, and members adhere to more gendered marital roles that are governed by cultural norms, while polyamory is more flexible, open to individual interpretation, and generally values egalitarianism and balanced power relations. Furthermore, polyamorists generally practice mutual consent, wherein new partners are negotiated and agreed on by all existing partners; however, new spouses can be at the discretion of the family head in polygamous families. Moreover, polygamy is commonly practiced in response to religious doctrine, while polyamory may be practiced for spiritual or secular purposes. Finally, polygamy generally operates in the realm of heterosexuality, while polyamorous sexual identities are fluid and transcend heteronormativity.

Historical Perspective

Historically, polygamy has been an organizing agent for several communities across North America. Various Native Indian tribes practiced forms of polygamy, and several ethnic groups of early European settlers practiced polygamy within their communities. Polygamy existed on the basis of cultural, religious, and economic motives. For example, some native tribes utilized this practice so that widowed women were cared for after their husbands' deaths, while the Mormon community practiced polygamy in response to Joseph Smith's doctrine of plural marriage. Consequently, American polygamy surfaced as a social issue in the mid-19th century after polygamist practices of members in the Church of Jesus Christ of Latter-day Saints were made public. Governmental pressure eventually resulted in church president Wilford Woodruff's release of the 1890 Manifesto that prohibited polygamous practices in the Mormon community.

Contemporary Polygamy

Polygamy continues to be practiced today by thousands of American families. Many polygamous families continue to follow the doctrine of plural marriage. The Church of Jesus Christ of Latter-day Saints officially condemns this practice and members risk expulsion if they engage in plural marriage; however, individual sects of the church reject the prohibition and continue to practice polygamy. For example, the Fundamentalist Church of Jesus Christ of Latter-day Saints condemns Woodruff's Manifesto on the basis of false teachings, and several members of this sect actively practice plural marriage.

Polygamy recently gained public visibility due to popular television series, such as HBO's *Big Love* and TLC's *Sister Wives*. As public debate on Mormon polygamy surged in response to these shows and related media, other polygamist groups in America enjoy protections of invisibility from the public realm, such as some Islamic and Black Muslim families. In addition, several families and communities practice a contemporary secularized form of polygamy.

Social Controversy and the Law

Polygamy and U.S. law have been in tension for more than a century. Antipolygamy laws were established in the 1860s, and the practice is currently illegal in each of the 50 states. Polygamous Mormons challenged the constitutionality of the laws on the basis of freedom of religion; however, the government responded by distinguishing religious opinion and practice, claiming the law is constitutional in forbidding the practice of multiple marriage. Federal and state laws affect polyamorists and polygamists in several additional ways. Specifically, laws prohibit nonbiological parents from having access to children at hospitals or schools. For example, a parent of a poly triad who shares full child-rearing responsibilities may not have visitation or decision-making rights to a hospitalized child if he or she cannot prove biological relatedness. In addition, some bigamy laws extend to additional cohabiting relationships among persons engaged in legal dyadic marriage, and adultery laws prohibit married persons from engaging in sexual activity with anyone other than a legal spouse.

Children in polygamous and polyamorous families have been the focus of social controversy. Polygamists have been criminalized for sexual abuse and marriage of minority children, and both polygamous and polyamorous parents have lost rights to their children. Some contemporary polygamist communities marry daughters at exceedingly young ages, which raises concerns regarding sexual agency and consent. Traditionalist organizations argue against polyamorous and polygamous families, citing the decay of the moral fabric of American families. Opposition to alternative family arrangements often comes at the hand of religious organizations that argue the immorality of multipartner intimate relating and family construction, reflecting arguments made against same-sex partnerships.

Furthermore, the common misconception that polyamorous and polygamist practices result from infidelities damages social perceptions, and public misunderstandings such as this contribute to the marginalized state of these individuals and families. Several families practice polygamy and polyamory secretly, for fear of discrimination, public humiliation, or legal separation. In contrast, others celebrate alternative family arrangements, arguing that polyamory and/or polygamy justifiably encourage diversity of families and relationships.

Social phenomena that transcend cultural norms are often considered radical and at the forefront of social change. However, polyamory and polygamy have different locations within this perspective. Polyamory has gained momentum as a relationship practice that challenges dominant social expectations of intimate relationships; however, polygamy is often connected to religion in social thought and has not necessarily been utilized as a mechanism for social change. In addition, a competing perspective argues that polyamory and polygamy should be privatized instead of treated as social concerns. Yet both practices fundamentally challenge the social norms of intimate relationships.

Challenges to Normative Intimate Relating

Polyamory and polygamy contest dominant forms of intimate relating, particularly monogamy and dyadic marriage. The prevailing culture of coupledom designates monogamy as the only appropriate relationship practice, and marriage continues to be the most highly revered form of relationship in American society. However, in the emergent culture of individualized intimacy, people have greater choices of partners and rights to define their own happiness and to negotiate personalized relationships. Polyamorists and polygamists have constructed new boundaries of relationships that challenge dominant modes of intimate relating; however, these practices often uphold social norms regarding dyadic intimate relating. For example, many polyamorous individuals

maintain primary dyadic partnerships, and polygamists engage in simultaneous dyadic relationships.

Nevertheless, both polygamy and polyamory highlight that relationships are socially constructed and challenge mononormative relationship norms and the culturally valued family structure that consists of two married, heterosexual, biological parents and their children. Furthermore, polyamory presents challenges to compulsory heterosexuality, patriarchal hegemony, and imbalanced relational power dynamics. The institution of heterosexuality is the basis of social organization of sexuality. Individuals are compelled to adhere to this governing agent and continuously reproduce heterosexual expectations through this cyclical process. Polyamory's fluidity and diversity of sexual practices and identities directly oppose compulsory heterosexuality and the dominant sexual dichotomy (heterosexual/homosexual). Additionally, values associated with polyamorous living combat hegemonic relationships and familial practices by encouraging gender egalitarianism and equal power dynamics among partners.

In addition, polyamory and polygamy address some contradictions of conventional contemporary relationships. Specifically, having multiple partners may appease the conflict between the desire for individualized identities and meaningful partnerships. Likewise, because people partially define their identities by their partner(s), being attached to more than one person means that any one particular person cannot monopolize how people define themselves, allowing room for greater individualization. Furthermore, these practices address the conflict between commitment and sexual excitement by allowing individuals to acquire new sexual partners while maintaining commitments to long-term partners. However, polygamy and polyamory continue to be stigmatized and marginalized in American culture.

Emily Pain

See also Hegemony; Identity; Individualism; Infidelity; Moral Panics; Self, The; Social Change and Deviance; Subculture; Swinging

Further Readings

Altman, I., & Ginat, J. (1996). *Polygamous families in contemporary society.* Cambridge, NY: Cambridge University Press.

Anapol, D. M. (2010). *Polyamory in the twenty-first century: Love and intimacy with multiple partners.* Lanham, MD: Rowman & Littlefield.

Barker, M., & Langdridge, D. (2010). *Understanding non-monogamies*. New York, NY: Routledge.

Cardell, J. K., & Burton, L. (Eds.). (2011). *Modern polygamy in the United States*. New York, NY: Oxford University Press.

Klesse, C., Haritaworn, J., & Lin, C. (Eds.). (2006). Special issue on polyamory. *Sexualities, 9*, 515–650.

Nearing, R. (1992). *Loving more: The polyfidelity primer*. Captain Cook, HI: PEP Publishing.

Sheff, E. (2011). Polyamorous families, same-sex marriage, and the slippery slope. *Journal of Contemporary Ethnography, 40*, 487–520.

PONZI SCHEMES

A Ponzi scheme is a financial fraud perpetrated with the intent of separating an investor from his or her investment, using false and misleading statements. Over the past several years, Ponzi schemes have bilked investors out of billions of dollars, while ruining thousands of lives in the process. Names like Marc Drier and Bernie Madoff have now joined a growing list of popularly known white-collar criminals (e.g., Ken Lay, Andrew Fastow, Bernie Ebbers, and Raj Rajaratnam, to name just a few). Yet Drier and Madoff reached ignominy by operating large-scale, multibillion dollar Ponzi schemes. While most Ponzi schemes never reach the multibillion dollar mark, many do reach into the millions and tens of millions of dollars. Collectively, these schemes present a significant risk to the financial viability of both investors and the economic system. By diverting capital that would otherwise have found its way into legitimate investment products, Ponzi schemes reduce investor wealth and reduce the overall amount of capital within financial markets. Additionally, they create fear and panic within the marketplace, reducing investor confidence and robbing individuals of their hard-earned funds. This entry details how Ponzi schemes typically operate and briefly discusses the inherent instability of these frauds. It concludes with a brief discussion of the social and financial impact of these frauds on individual investors and the market as a whole.

A Brief History

The Ponzi scheme has existed in varied forms for many centuries and takes its name from Charles Ponzi who in 1920 committed a multimillion dollar investment fraud involving the sale of foreign postal coupons. Ponzi was able to solicit funds from investors by promising a 50% return on their investment within 90 days. In total, Ponzi took more than $10 million from thousands of individuals who were hoping to see a significant return on their invested funds. However, instead of investing the funds as promised, Ponzi pocketed a large portion of the funds, while using the remaining to pay "returns" to investors. Ultimately, his scheme collapsed, and Ponzi was convicted of fraud and sentenced to jail. The investors never saw their money again. While this crime has existed for many years, the basic operation of the fraud, as well as the means used to obtain new investors, are the same today. What have changed over the years are the techniques used to perpetrate this offence; these have adapted to technological advancements and prevention efforts.

How Ponzi Schemes Work

Ponzi schemes are typically perpetrated by either a single individual or a small group (two to three) of individuals working collaboratively. Contrary to popular opinion, all Ponzi schemes do not develop as outright frauds. In many cases, Ponzi schemes are initiated by well-intentioned individuals seeking to secure funding for a business or other legitimate financial opportunity. However, these individuals may quickly find that their initial financing plans were either inadequate or severely anorexic. As a result, these initially well-intentioned individuals have found themselves within the realm of pure fraudsters and criminal opportunists.

Regardless of whether the Ponzi scheme initiator has legitimate or deviant intentions, all Ponzi schemes begin at the same point: the offering of a high-value investment opportunity. Potential investors are enticed to make a stake in the scheme because of the promise of high net returns on their investment and the understanding that the investment itself is a solid opportunity. Up to this point, Ponzi schemes operate like any other type of investment where individuals seek to make financial gains on the funds they have invested. In legitimate investment opportunities, investors receive some stated rate of return on their investment, which typically is proportionate to the risk associated with the investment. However, in a Ponzi scheme, investors are not paid returns based on the performance of some financial instrument. Instead, investors continue to receive funds from their investment so long as the scheme initiator is able to secure new investors.

In a Ponzi scheme, revenue to pay investors is not generated through investment activities. Instead, early investors are paid based on the funds invested by later investors. The difference between what new investors pay into the scheme and what is paid out to earlier investors is pocketed by the scheme initiator. Accordingly, the success of the scheme depends on the ability of the initiator to continue creating interest in the opportunity, which should lead to new investors. However, this presents a significant quandary to the scheme initiator: To pay off early investors, new investors need to be brought into the scheme, all of whom will need to be paid through the continued infusion of funds from new investors. This cycle of shifting funds from later groups of investors to earlier investors makes Ponzi schemes inherently unstable for two distinct reasons: (1) the longer they are in operation, the more people the initiator(s) need to involve in the fraudulent activity, and (2) they are reliant on a lack of investor attrition.

An Example of a Ponzi Scheme

Because Ponzi schemes pay early investors with the funds of later investors, as the scheme grows there is an exponential growth in the demand for funds. The following example highlights this problem. A group of 10 investors is asked by a friend (the schemer) to invest in his or her new company at an initial investment level of $5,000 each. The investors are brought in with the promise of receiving a 40% annualized return on their investment. Since all 10 of the schemer's friends agreed to contribute funds, the schemer has collected a total of $50,000 from his or her friends. However, he or she has also guaranteed them each a yearly return of approximately $2,410. Since there is no legitimate financial return on the investors' funds, at the end of the year the schemer must find some way to come up with the $24,100. The failure to produce returns for his or her initial investors would likely lead to their desire to withdraw from the investment opportunity. Furthermore, the original investors would not be likely to assist the schemer in finding new clients when they themselves have realized no financial benefit. Because the schemer requires a consistent infusion of capital, the $50,000 obtained from the initial investors is not enough to satisfy his or her ongoing financial needs. To meet these needs, the schemer must obtain new investors. However, he or she must now find enough investors to be able to pocket another $50,000 as well as pay the initial investors their stated returns of $24,100.

Essentially, the schemer needs to come up with about $75,000 in new capital. This he or she does through the recruitment of 15 new investors, each of whom contributes $5,000 for a total of $75,000 in new investments. Yet this situation creates a significant problem for the following year: The schemer will have to provide returns on investment obligations to the tune of $60,250. If he or she wishes to maintain his or her pocketed income of $50,000, he or she must now come up with more than $110,000 of new investments, or an additional 22 investors. The following year, this cycle is repeated, and the schemer now needs to come up with more than $113,000 simply to cover the returns promised to investors. At some point, this cycle becomes unstable, and the scheme collapses as a result of the schemer's inability to pay the annual returns.

Identifying Ponzi Schemes

Ponzi schemes typically share a similar collection of elements. Potential investors can look for these elements/characteristics when attempting to determine if the opportunity in front of them has the possibility of being a Ponzi scheme.

Promise of an unusually high rate of return: The returns found in Ponzi schemes are not based on the market, but rather, they reflect a significantly higher rate than can be assumed under normal market conditions. As with many other things, if it sounds too good to be true, it probably is.

Absence of a decline in performance or a lack of loss: Every investment carries a risk of loss, yet Ponzi schemes are known for showing consistently high performance and rarely, if ever, showing a loss. Losses are bad for business, and Ponzi schemes begin to fall apart when investors ask to pull out of the investment opportunity because they have begun to take losses.

Investments are not listed or registered with federal or state agencies: Government regulators require that, for certain investment vehicles, information pertaining to the investment be made available to potential investors. Because Ponzi schemes offer no legitimate investment product, the absence of governmental registration is to be expected.

Complex paperwork or a lack of official documentation: Some Ponzi schemes, like Bernard Madoff's, have very convincing documentation; most do not. The operators of Ponzi schemes will often utilize overly complex language in an attempt to dissuade investors from making inquiries into the investment. Some do not distribute any information at all, but rather, they rely on controlling any verbal or electronic communication used to disseminate information.

Conclusion

Ponzi schemes appear to offer the promise of stable, high-return investments at a time when little is certain in the financial marketplace. Yet the lure of these schemes is overshadowed by the fact that investors may never see their funds returned to them. Many Ponzi schemes remain out of the public eye because the investors bilked out of their money are too embarrassed to report the crime to authorities. If an investor does receive a full, or partial, return on investment in a Ponzi scheme, the federal government may later "clawback" these funds when looking to redress defrauded parties. As a result, the ultimate losers in Ponzi schemes are the individual investors, who oftentimes lose many times over—at least once at the hands of the fraudster and again, potentially, at the hands of authorities.

Ponzi schemes also take a toll on the overall financial marketplace. The funds investors sink into Ponzi schemes typically do not make their way into the open market. As such, there is less money available for investment in legitimate vehicles such as stocks, bonds, and venture capital offerings. While it can be argued that, because of the relatively small nature of most Ponzi schemes, the impact on the financial markets as a whole is minimal, several recent large-scale Ponzi schemes support the idea that these frauds remove a significant amount of wealth from the market. Finally, it can never be forgotten that irrespective of the potential losses within the market as a whole, individual investors lose a considerable amount of their own net worth as a result of these schemes. While the long history of the Ponzi scheme suggests that it may never be prevented or disappear from the financial and criminal landscape, the ability of fraudsters to ruin an investor financially can be mitigated if potential investors are cognizant of the typical warning signs of Ponzi schemes.

Jay P. Kennedy

See also Fraud; White-Collar Crime

Further Readings

Barasch, S. C., & Chesnut, S. J. (2009). Controversial uses of the "clawback" remedy in the current financial crisis. *Texas Law Journal, 72*(11), 922–928.

Drew, J. M., & Drew, M. E. (2010). The identification of Ponzi schemes: Can a picture tell a thousand frauds? (Griffith University Business School Discussion Papers No. 2010–08). Brisbane, Queensland, Australia: Griffith University Business School.

Greenspan, S. (2009, June). Fooled by Madoff: The psychology of Ponzi scheme [Online]. *Madconomist .com*. Retrieved from http://madconomist.com/fooled-by-madoff-the-psychology-of-ponzi-scheme

Jacobs, P., & Schain, L. (2011). The never ending attraction of the Ponzi scheme. *Journal of Comprehensive Research, 9*, 40–46.

Larsen, J., & Hinton, P. (2009). *SEC settlements in Ponzi scheme cases: Putting Madoff and Stanford in context.* New York, NY: NERA Economic Consulting.

Trahan, A., Marquart, J. W., & Mullins, J. (2005). Fraud and the American dream: Toward an understanding of fraud victimization. *Deviant Behavior, 26*, 601–620.

Wilkins, A. M., Scuff, W. W., & Hermanson, D. R. (2012). Understanding a Ponzi scheme: Victims' perspectives. *Journal of Forensic and Investigative Accounting, 4*, 1–19.

PORNOGRAPHY

Definitions of pornography vary from time to time and place to place: Something defined as pornographic 50 years ago may now be considered erotic, or even literature. Drawings, paintings, and sculpture depicting sexual behavior have always been part of human history and have even been used in religious rituals. The term and concept of *pornography* is relatively recent. The French *pornographie* was used in the 1800s, and it found its way into the English language via New Orleans, Louisiana, in 1842, becoming part of the vernacular in 1857. The term itself is derived from the Greek words *pornographia*, meaning "prostitute," and *graphien*, meaning "written or an illustration." Pornography began as drawings of prostitutes. In the past 150 or so years, many books, movies, and works of art have been defined as pornographic simply because they portray nudism and sexual activity. Medical textbooks, anthropological works, and even *National Geographic* have been banned in some areas as obscene. The Miller test, created and applied by the Supreme Court in *Miller v. California* (1973), developed a definition of obscenity (which may or may not include pornography). According to the Miller test, material can be judged obscene if it appeals to a prurient interest in sex and lacks literary, artistic, political, or scientific value. Since *Miller*, however, there has been considerable debate as to what constitutes literary, artistic, political, and scientific value. Pornography can be described as an explicit description or image intended to stimulate sexual feelings. Thus, pornography may or may not be obscene; as long as the pornographer can successfully argue that his or her work has literary, artistic, political, or scientific value, it is not obscene. Literature such as the *Joy of Sex* and the art of Robert Mapplethorpe (or even "feature porn" utilizing parodies of titles from legitimate movies and loosely following the plot) can be considered scientific, artistic, or literary. Pornography is not necessarily obscene, and some pornographic films (*Last Tango in Paris*), books (*Fifty Shades of Grey*), and artwork can be argued to have significant artistic merit. Before further examining the constitutionality and criminality of pornography, this entry discusses pornography's history and its effects on society.

History

Erotic art has been a part of human history since the Paleolithic era. Carvings of voluptuous pregnant women, carved out of wood or stone, have been found by archeologists and are believed to be fertility symbols or religious icons. Ancient Greeks and Romans created paintings and sculpture featuring a wide variety of sexual behavior, including gay sex, three-way sex, and oral sex. Art at the site of Pompeii was so explicit that the Victorians who unearthed Pompeii went to great lengths to hide the ancient brothels and bedrooms featuring the artwork. The *Kama Sutra* was published in India during the 2nd century. Featuring explicit drawings of a variety of sexual practices and positions, it was meant to enhance the sexual and spiritual facets of human relationships. In Western nations what would now be considered pornographic was most often political in nature, with politicians and royal families being portrayed as sexual deviants or in other unsavory situations. The Marquise de Sade, part philosopher and part pornographer, skewered the Catholic Church and European governments with his libertine novels about violence, sadomasochism, and pedophilia.

The first true pornographic novel (appearing in 1748) was *Memoirs of a Woman of Pleasure*, also known as *Fanny Hill*. Not surprisingly, technological advances spurred the creation of pornography, and the first "porn" picture is dated 1846—just seven years after the invention of the daguerreotype. Not just erotic, this daguerreotype featured an explicit depiction of intercourse. The first soft-core porn video, *Le Coucher de la Marie* (Bed With Marie) was produced in 1896 and featured a striptease. Hard-core porn, featuring real (rather than simulated) sex, followed in the very early 1900s. Until the 1970s, porn was mainly for men and did not change much in content or style for some 70 years. However, in the 1970s and 1980s, the porn industry, spurred on by changing sexual mores, blossomed, becoming what is known as the Golden Age of Porn. Videos introduced plot and sets, and many movies were marketed not just to men but to couples too. Some of the most famous adult films of this era include *Deep Throat, The Devil in Miss Jones, Behind the Green Door, Emmanuelle, The Story of O,* and *Debbie Does Dallas*. Many of the stars of these films, such as Linda Lovelace, Marilyn Chambers, and John Holmes, became household names. Mainstream movies also flirted with pornography; films like *Last Tango in Paris* and *Midnight Cowboy* received an X rating from the Motion Picture Association of America. The Golden Age of Porn was dramatized in the 1997 movie *Boogie Nights*.

In the past 40 years, pornography has continued to evolve. Contemporary pornography is not a homogeneous subgenre of the entertainment industry. Pornography can typically be classified as either soft core (no genitalia visible, no penetration) or hard core (visible genitalia and penetration). Subgenres of pornography are classified on the basis of characteristics of the participants (e.g., gay, ethnic, teen, chubby) and/or on the basis of the type of sexual activity (e.g., oral, anal, gangbang). A fairly recent phenomenon, amateur pornography has become very popular on the Internet, with free sites such as youporn.com and others featuring videos made, without pay, by nonprofessionals. Inspired by amateur pornography, Gonzo pornography is a pornographic film shot by one or more participants, rather than by a third (outside) person. A recent addition to the soft-core or erotica subgenre is mommy porn—raunchy romance novels and videos catering to 30-something and 40-something women, described as X-rated Cinderella stories. One of the most popular products in this line is the novel *Fifty Shades of Grey*.

Effects

The effect of pornography on society has been widely debated, and with no clear consensus in the

United States. Academic research has suggested that exposure to pornography, particularly as an adolescent, leads to increased sexual violence by adults. A Swedish study suggests that young men who are frequent users of pornography are more likely to sell sex themselves. Others have linked exposure to pornography with adolescent sex abuse of a sibling. Apart from apparently leading to increased violent sexual behavior and sex abuse, use of pornography has been described as not only addictive but also an escalating addiction, with the porn addict requiring increasingly extreme depictions of sexual acts and subsequent decreased ability to interact with others and/or maintain a normal sexual relationship. The rise of cyberporn has escalated this trend, leaving the user with all the characteristics of an addiction—even though the *Diagnostic and Statistical Manual for Mental Disorders* as yet does not define pornography as an addiction.

In recent years, pornography has become less marginalized and is less likely to be considered a deviant behavior. Researchers have begun to study pornography from the point of view of its consumers, rather than just its supporters and opponents. Nearly 20 years ago, Harold Leitenberg and Kris Henning stated that fantasy (presumably facilitated by pornography) allows one to imagine whatever one wanted, without the fear of embarrassment, rejection, or legal restrictions. Others have found that viewing pornography expanded consumers' sexual scripts, and at least in the case of female viewers, it did not lead them to seek partners outside their relationship, but it did expand their sexual horizons. Their review of the literature also found that pornography made both men and women more willing to experiment, although a causal link could not be proven. Pornography has even become part of the pop culture mainstream, from music (indie rock band The New Pornographers and quasi-pornographic and true pornographic music videos such as "Pussy" by German Metal Band Rammstein) to fashion (T-shirts with *Porn Star* emblazoned across the front) to personal hygiene (Brazilian waxes and "manscaping").

Criminalization and Constitutionality

Pornography, while not necessarily considered normative (although many ancient societies did consider pornography normal and in fact beneficial), was not criminalized in England until the Obscene Publications Act in 1857. In the United States, the Hayes Code (January 1, 1930) was the first attempt to regulate the movie industry, restricting contact that may have been considered sexual in nature. *Jacobellis v. Ohio* (1964) was an early "free speech" case involving a theater's right to show an "obscene" film: The state of Ohio fined a theater owner for showing an erotic French film; the U.S. Supreme Court reversed the decision. While the court did not explicitly state that the First Amendment right of free speech protected pornography, it did reject the labeling of a film under the Hayes Code, paving the way for later court cases that would attempt to define both pornography (or obscenity) and the application of the First Amendment to the public display of erotica. In 1969, the U.S. Supreme Court ruled, in the case of *Stanley v. Georgia*, that the First and Fourteenth Amendments prohibit making mere private possession of obscene material a crime.

Miller v. California (1973) was the first case to test the applicability of the First Amendment to pornography. Marvin Miller operated an "adult" mail order business, and was convicted of a misdemeanor for distributing obscene materials. The U.S. Supreme Court upheld the conviction, arguing that pornography was not protected by the Constitution. The Miller case also helped define pornography, stating that material can be judged obscene if it appeals to a prurient interest in sex and lacks literary, artistic, political, or scientific value (the Miller test). With the exception of child pornography, the rise of Internet pornography has added another layer of complexity to the legal issues surrounding the production, distribution, and consumption of pornography. The laws of an individual's home nation apply to the creation and distribution of pornography: A distributor may be well within his or her rights to produce and distribute porn; however, if a consumer lives in a country that prohibits the use of that particular type of pornography (e.g., age of consent variations), the consumer can be prosecuted.

So is pornography protected by the Constitution or not? Material that is considered obscene is not protected by the First Amendment. Pornography, assuming it fails the Miller test, is not protected by the First Amendment. Hence, pornography may or may not be obscene. It may or may not be protected by the Constitution. Given the vagueness inherent in the definition of obscenity under *Miller*, many in the business of pornography could easily argue the case that what they do is art, not obscenity; however, one's private possession of obscene material does not constitute a crime.

Pamela Black

See also Erotica Versus Pornography; Fetishes; Masturbation; Sexual Addiction

Further Readings

Bloem, F. (2006). Pornography and obscene material. In E. W. Hickey (Ed.), *Sex crimes and paraphilia* (pp. 45–54). Upper Saddle River, NJ: Prentice Hall.

Hall, A. C., & Bishop, M. J. (2007). *Pop-porn: Pornography in America's culture.* Westport, CT: Praeger.

Jacobellis v. Ohio, 378 U.S. 184 (1964).

Latzman, N. E., Viljoen, J. L., Scalora, M. J., & Ullman, D. (2011). Sexual offending in adolescence: A comparison of sibling offenders and nonsibling offenders across domains of risk and treatment need. *Journal of Child Sexual Abuse, 20*(3), 245–263. doi:10.1080/10538712.2011.571233

Leitenberg, H., & Henning, K. (1995). Sexual fantasy. *Psychological Bulletin, 17,* 469–496.

Mancini, C., Reckdenwald, A., & Beauregard, E. (2012). Pornographic exposure over the life course and the severity of sexual offenses: Imitation and cathartic effects. *Journal of Criminal Justice, 40*(41), 21–30. doi:10.1016/j.jcrimjus.2011.11.004

Miller v. California, 413 U.S. 15 (1973).

Stanley v. Georgia, 394 U.S. 557 (1969).

Svedin, C. G., Aakerman, I., & Priebe, G. (2011). Frequent users of pornography. A population based epidemiological study of Swedish male adolescents. *Journal of Adolescence, 34*(4), 779–788.

Weinberg, M. S., Williams, C. J., Kleiner, S., & Irizarry, Y. (2010). Pornography, normalization, and empowerment. *Archives of Sexual Behavior, 39*(6), 1389–1401.

POSITIVE DEVIANCE

The word *deviance* and acts of deviant behavior are overwhelmingly associated with negativity. Although most sociologists would argue that deviance is socially constructed and that a deviant behavior is one that is misaligned with a society, culture, or other group's norms, the word conjures up delinquency, weirdness, or other undesirable or unconventional behavior. However, nontraditional behavior is not always negative. In fact, some nonnormative behaviors are quite positive. For example, although safety is a public norm, some individuals run into burning buildings to save lives. Therefore, even though this goes against all rules of safety enforced by parents, peers, and public safety officials, these individuals deviate from the safety norm in a positive way. There has been a debate among sociologists as to whether the term *positive deviance* is useful. Nonetheless, to understand the full spectrum of human behavior, studying this type of deviation from the norm is necessary.

All categories of deviance are some combination of the interaction between norms and the reaction to the violation of these norms. That is, the concept of deviance is not only characterized by a violation of normative expectations but also by the reaction of audiences, specifically the people's evaluation of the behavior. That is, an individual may conform, overconform, underconform, or not conform at all (nonconformity) to the norms of a group or society. In addition, the level of conformity a person adheres to can be met with positive or negative social evaluations.

When individuals conform, they change an action or belief due to real or imagined group pressure. This does not necessarily involve private acceptance of the norm. That is, individuals can conform behaviorally (often without consciously recognizing the change in themselves), yet they may not internalize the change in their attitudes. An example of this is the behavior of teenagers in high school. Boys and girls often change their behaviors to fit into a particular clique, but the individual may privately reject the change. Conformity levels vary greatly from person to person and among different situations, actions, and beliefs.

Most underconformists or nonconformists, such as the thief or the illicit drug user, are judged negatively in our culture. However, there are some underconformists or nonconformists who, depending on the audience, might be viewed positively. A gang member in a particular community, who breaks the law to provide for his or her community, is an example of this type of deviant.

Most sociological research on deviance has been conducted on underconformists or nonconformists. There are relatively fewer studies conducted on overconformity. Overconformity involves going beyond societal normative expectations. An example of negatively valued overconformity in American society is the school overachiever, sometimes referred to as a dork or geek. This student is an incessantly studious person and is often ridiculed by his or her peers. Alternatively, some individuals overconform to the delight of an audience. Positive deviance is overconformity that is positively evaluated. When an individual's behavior exceeds the expectations of others in ways that people admire, it fits the definition of positive deviance. Out of the ordinary acts, particularly those that are self-sacrificing, fit this category. Therefore, religious figures are often placed in the positive deviance category due to their unwavering gifts to humanity. Other examples of positive deviants include the following: virginity pledgers, Olympic athletes, and war heroes.

Although opponents argue that the term *positive deviance* is an oxymoron, scholars who use the concept to investigate overconformity say that normative deviation does indeed go both ways and that we must examine all forms of it. Stressing that the word *deviance* itself is stigmatized by almost anyone who hears it, opponents reason that the term should be avoided. After all, if practically any behavior could be labeled deviant, then the concept "deviance" itself becomes irrelevant. Furthermore, opponents argue that although positive deviance scholars recognize both the norm violation component as well as the reactive component in their categorization of deviance, the reactions, especially by authority figures, to overconformity and nonconformity are very different. The implication is that overconformity will not produce the negative reactions and consequences as will underconformity or nonconformity, and therefore, these are clearly two very different types of behavior that should be distinctly titled.

Pam Hunt

See also Defining Deviance; Normal Deviance; Norms and Societal Expectations

Further Readings

Goode, E. (1991). Positive deviance: A viable concept? *Deviant Behavior, 12,* 289–309.

Heckert, A., & Heckert, D. M. (2002). A new typology of deviance: Integrating normative and reactivist definitions of deviance. *Deviant Behavior, 23,* 449–479.

Heckert, D. M. (2003). Positive deviance: A classificatory model. In D. H. Kelly & E. J. Clarke (Eds.), *Deviant behavior: A text reader in the sociology of deviance* (6th ed., pp. 20–32). New York, NY: Worth.

Sorokin, P. A. (1950). *Altruistic love.* Boston, MA: Beacon Press.

POSITIVIST DEFINITIONS OF DEVIANCE

Scholars have not yet reached consensus on a common definition of deviance. This is partly due to changing perception and understanding of deviance among various social groups and in different times. Hence, deviance can be conceptualized in many forms. Contributions to the definition of deviance have been made through two competing approaches: (1) positivism and (2) constructionism. Positivist understanding of the concept originates from classical sociological thought, which uses positivist methodology to investigate the empirical causes of social facts. On the other hand, the constructionist approach emerged as a reaction to the dominance of the positivist approach. This approach negates the absolutist understanding of deviance. This entry focuses on the positivist approach and discusses theories that use this approach to explain deviance.

Positivist Approach

The positivist approach explains deviance using the three principles of absolutism, determinism, and objectivism. Positivists see deviance as real, measurable, and observable and as the product of certain causes. The idea of absolutism suggests that deviance is caused by psychological or physiological traits of the deviant actors. These traits are intrinsic to individuals and are thought to make deviants different from other nondeviant actors. Early criminologists adopted this aspect of the positivist approach and made analyses on the basis of the physical appearance of the individuals. For example, some facial features were accepted as determinants that an individual would engage in deviant behavior. More recently, some scholars, such as Michael Gottfredson and Travis Hirschi, contend that deviance and crime are caused by people's underlying level of self-control. This trait of self-control is associated with impulsiveness, egocentricity, and lack of empathy, each of which increases the likelihood that an individual will engage in deviance.

Similar to absolutism, the idea of determinism is that the cause of deviant behavior is outside an individual's choice. Following this dictate, positivists often see the social environment or other external factors as the root causes of deviance. Assumptions of anomie, social disorganization, and social control theories are based on this aspect of the positivist approach. Finally, objectivism is the idea that deviant acts and actors are observable and measurable objects in the outside world and can be studied objectively by neutral researchers.

The positivist point of view disregards subjective or phenomenological traits of the deviant act or actor, such as the meaning of deviance to the actor and the experience of deviance. Instead, positivists focus on general observable characteristics of the act and their causes. The positivist approach focuses on norm violations and the etiology of deviant acts and behaviors.

Theories Explaining Deviance With a Positivist Approach

Various theoretical approaches use positivist methodology when studying deviance. In fact, the majority of theories designed to explain deviance are positivist. The main premise shared by these approaches is that deviance emerges under the influence of external forces that constrain individual behaviors and that researchers can study deviance in the same way they study the hard sciences. Positivist theories explain deviance at various levels of analysis and stem from a variety of disciplines (e.g., sociology, psychology, and economics). Major theories focusing on deviance include anomie and related structural theories, control theory, social disorganization theory, and various psychological theories.

Anomie and other structural theories explain deviance as a given response to strain that is experienced by individuals due to the failure of social structure or to social change. Strain theorists argue that crime results when individuals are unable to achieve positively valued goals through legitimate channels. In such cases, individuals become frustrated, and they may try to satisfy their wants through illegitimate channels, or they may strike out at others in anger. Classic strain theory, as described by Robert Merton, suggests that individuals are socialized to desire culturally valued goals (e.g., financial success) by engaging in legitimate behaviors (e.g., hard work). However, not everyone is provided equal access to accomplishing their goals through legitimate means. As a consequence, some individuals adapt to this frustration by engaging in crime and deviance.

Control theories argue that crime and deviance are the result of weak social control or self-control. They argue that deviance occurs due to failure of individual's attachment to society and conventional norms. Lack or inadequate level of positive social ties and attachment to family, school, and larger society or belief in social norms increases the chances of being a deviant individual. In short, a weakened social bond is thought to free individuals to engage in crime and deviance.

Social disorganization theorists also assume that deviance is caused by external factors shaping the social structure. Socioeconomic changes in social structure have certain negative effects on social institutions, norms, and values of the community. Unexpected consequences of urbanization, continuous population mobility, and norm conflict caused by ethnic heterogeneity, family disruption, and poor economic conditions decrease the influence of social control mechanisms, and this may create the conditions leading to deviance. Within this theoretical framework, deviance is a result of long-term social processes.

In short, positivist definitions of deviance are based on the idea that behavior is determined by its biological, psychological, and social traits. Those using a positivist definition of deviance seek scientific proof that deviance is caused by features within or around the individual.

Fatih Irmak

See also Changing Deviance Designations; Defining Deviance; Quantitative Methods in Studying Deviance

Further Readings

Franzese, R. J. (2009). *The sociology of deviance: Differences, tradition, and stigma.* Springfield, IL: Charles C Thomas.

Sampson, R. J., & Groves, W. B. (1989). Community structure and crime: Testing social-disorganization theory. *American Journal of Sociology, 94*(4), 774–802.

PREMARITAL SEX

Premarital sex has traditionally referred to sexual intercourse within a heterosexual romantic relationship that eventually led to marriage. This definition emphasized both the timing of the first sexual intercourse (i.e., before marriage) and with whom one engages in sex (i.e., a future spouse). Recent trends toward delayed marriage and increased nonmarital cohabitation, as well as broadening sexual scripts among young people, however, have altered the concept's contemporary meaning. Today, premarital sex generally refers to vaginal intercourse in which an individual engages—often within a series of monogamous relationships—before he or she eventually marries. Current estimates based on large-scale surveys suggest that 82% to 95% of Americans have had premarital intercourse. While once considered deviant behavior, premarital sex has become statistically normative. This entry explores the changing attitudes toward premarital sex as well as changes in premarital sexual behavior and discusses other issues associated with these changes.

Attitudes Toward Premarital Sex

The Christian tradition that colonists brought from Europe heavily influenced ideas about premarital sex in colonial America. Social norms restricted sexual relations to the confines of marriage. These norms applied to both men and women. Historical records, however, indicate that approximately 30% of women's firstborn children were conceived out of wedlock. Clearly, premarital sex occurred within colonial America; yet marriage easily remedied this breach of social norms. Well into the 20th century, sexual interactions between individuals with no plans to marry continued to be unacceptable. Historical evidence, once again, suggests that premarital sex was common among the urban working class well before the sexual revolutions of the 1920s and 1960s. However, by the 1950s, the stigma associated with premarital sex began to wane due to numerous social and cultural changes. First, the expansion of secondary education and the recognition of adolescence as a stage of development delayed young people's transition into adulthood. Second, technological advances such as telephones and automobiles promoted a shift from courtship to dating, thereby reducing parental supervision. Third, the availability of birth control reduced the risks associated with sex. In short, American cultural standards regarding premarital sex have often reflected a middle-class ideal more so than actual practice. The dominant discourse continues to associate premarital sex primarily with people of color and the poor. Policing sexual practice by these standards continue to provide white, middle-class Americans a way to distance themselves from groups that they considered to be dangerous classes.

Americans' disapproval of premarital sex has waned in recent years. While a substantial majority (75%) of Americans disapproved of premarital sex in 1969, a minority (37%) disapproved by the 1980s. By 2006, only a quarter of Americans reported that sex is "always wrong" outside of marriage. Americans' attitudes toward premarital sex often hinge on the age of the individuals involved. The 2002 National Study of Family Growth found

that only 15% of men and women thought that consensual sex between 16-year-olds was acceptable. However, 55% of Americans thought it was acceptable for 18-year-olds. Attitudes among the elderly, typically the most conservative group, provide a social barometer for this issue. While Americans between the ages of 65 and 89 years tend to be less approving of sex for both 16- and 18-year-olds, longitudinal data from the General Social Survey indicate that their attitudes are softening. In 1970, 57% of respondents in this group reported that premarital sex was "always wrong"; however, only 18% of this age-group held such a position in 2002.

Comparative studies suggest that American attitudes toward premarital sex tend to be more conservative than those held in many other Western countries. For example, 54% of Hungarians and 89% of Swedes report that premarital sexual intercourse is "not wrong at all," compared with approximately 42% of Americans. In general, attitudes toward premarital sex are becoming more permissive throughout North America, Eastern Europe, Western Europe, Australia, and New Zealand.

Premarital Sexual Behavior

Changes in attitudes toward premarital sex have been accompanied by changes in behavior. Today, more American teens are sexually active than was the case in previous generations. Among Americans born before 1900, only 37% of men and 3% of women reported engaging in premarital sex by 18 years of age. The percentage of sexually active teens has increased linearly for each successive cohort. Recent surveys report that approximately 60% of 18-year-olds have engaged in sexual intercourse. According to 2007 data from the U.S. Centers for Disease Control and Prevention, nearly half (47.8%) of high school students—49.8% of males and 45.9% of females—have had sex. Approximately two thirds (68%) of African American high school students have had sex compared with 51% of Latino and 43% of white students. Males across each racial group are consistently more likely than similar females to have had sex. Moreover, American teens are becoming sexually active at younger ages. The age at first sex was 18 years for men and 19 years for women in the 1970s, but it is now 15 years for both men and women. Today, approximately 57% of 17-year-olds and 33% of 15-year-olds have engaged in vaginal intercourse. Thus, a majority of today's teenagers are sexually active by age 18, and the age at which they are becoming sexually active is decreasing. These patterns are similar to those in most Western countries.

Scholars attribute the rise in premarital sex to increases in the age at first marriage and increases in rates of nonmarital cohabitation. Americans are delaying marriage. In 1970, the average age at first marriage was 23 years for men and 21 years for women. Currently, age at first marriage has reached an all-time high at 28 years for men and 26 years for women. Individuals report numerous reasons for choosing to postpone marriage. They include the inability to afford marriage, belief that it is too soon for individuals to have children, the desire to be one's "own" person, and even a weakened confidence in the institution of marriage. Scholars point to delayed marriage as evidence that the transition to adulthood is now marked by a period of "emerging adulthood," or extended adolescence. In 2000, only one in four Americans had met all five traditional benchmarks for adulthood (e.g., economic independence, residence outside of parents' home, completed education, marriage, and having children) by age 30, providing empirical support for this claim.

Recent increases in premarital sex are also associated with a trend toward nonmarital cohabitation. Approximately two thirds of recently married couples cohabited before marriage. Cohabitation is most common among individuals with lower levels of educational attainment and lower social class standing. African Americans are more likely to cohabit than are whites or Latinos. Researchers continue to explore whether cohabitation is a precursor to marriage or an alternative to marriage. Marriage and cohabitation patterns suggest that the meaning that marriage holds for Americans may be changing: Marriage is for settling down rather than a prerequisite for sex. Moreover, the fact that the poor and people of color are less likely to marry suggests that marriage is associated with other forms of privilege. Taken together, trends toward delayed marriage and increased cohabitation raise questions about the nature and functioning of marriage in contemporary America.

An extended adolescence paired with the failure to delay first sex has contributed to the development of two new sexual scripts for young people: (1) "friends with benefits" and (2) "hooking up." Whereas friends with benefits involves associational sex (i.e., repeated sexual encounters with a friend or acquaintance), hooking up generally refers to a one-night stand. Young people often use "hook up" to describe a wide range of intimate behaviors, ranging from kissing and petting to oral sex and sexual intercourse. According to Add Health data, a quarter of relationships among 18- to 23-year-olds are sexual but not romantic. Paula England's 2005–2008 College Social Life Study, an online survey of 10,000 college students, indicates that about half of female students and 62% of male students would engage in sexual activities with a partner they did not love.

Despite these trends, some individuals choose to remain a virgin until marriage. According to Add Health data, 16% of young adults between the ages of 18 and 23 years have not had vaginal intercourse. On average, those individuals who abstain from premarital sex tend to be religious, risk averse, and hold high expectations for self and their romantic partners.

Associated Issues

What Americans think about premarital sex and how they behave are each marked by a sexual double standard that is more permissive toward male sexuality than toward female sexuality. Moreover, standards for hegemonic masculinity and emphasized femininity legitimize—if not require—early sexual experiences in boys but stigmatize them among girls. Not surprisingly, American males, on average, hold more accepting attitudes toward premarital sex than do women, although men and women's attitudes continue to converge. Men also tend to report more sexual partners than women and having engaged in first sex at younger ages. The sexual double standard is seen in common metaphors young people use to make meaning of virginity loss. While young women often remain virgins out of fear that losing it will be a source of stigma, young men often feel that virginity itself is a source of stigma. Scholars suggest that this double standard and the social pressures it exerts may affect official estimates about sexual behavior. Statistics may overreport men's behavior but underreport women's behavior.

Since the 1980s, American attitudes toward premarital sex have fueled the debate on whether public schools should provide comprehensive or abstinence-only sexual education. The discourse reflects concerns that premarital sex is a precursor to other social problems, such as sexually transmitted disease, teen pregnancy, and even abortion. In the late 1990s, Evangelic Christian proponents of premarital chastity introduced purity rings and purity balls, rituals through which teenagers—primarily young women—publicly pledge to maintain their virginity until marriage. Motivated in part to assess the claims espoused by both sides of this debate, social scientists have explored possible associations between premarital sex and increased feelings of guilt, relationship dissolution, and poor psychological well-being. Evidence that premarital sex is associated with these negative outcomes remains mixed and largely inconclusive. It is interesting to note that little attention has been given to possible positive outcomes associated with the first sexual experience.

How social scientists conceptualize and study premarital sex is likely to continue to evolve. Eleven countries, nine U.S. states, and the District of Columbia have legalized same-sex marriage. Numerous other states recognize same-sex marriages performed elsewhere. As who can marry who changes, our current definition of premarital sex and our understanding of it are also likely to expand.

Daniel Renfrow and Dylan Bruce

See also Teen Pregnancy

Further Readings

Bogle, K. (2008). *Hooking up: Sex, dating, and relationships on campus.* New York: New York University Press.

Harding, D. J., & Jencks, C. (2003). Changing attitudes toward premarital sex. *Public Opinion Quarterly, 67,* 211–226.

Regnerus, M., & Uecker, J. (2011). *Premarital sex in America: How young Americans meet, mate, and think about marrying.* New York, NY: Oxford University Press.

Vespa, J., & Painter, M. A., II. (2011). Cohabitation history, marriage, and wealth accumulation. *Demography, 48,* 983–1004.

Wellings, K., Collumbien, M., Slaymaker, E., Singh, S., Hodges, Z., Patel, D., & Bajos, N. (2006). Sexual behavior in context: A global perspective. *Lancet, 368,* 1706–1728.

Wells, B. E., & Twenge, J. M. (2005). Changes in young people's sexual behavior and attitudes, 1943–1999: A cross-temporal meta-analysis. *Review of General Psychology, 3,* 249–261.

Widmer, E. D., Treas, J., & Newcomb, R. (1998). Attitudes toward nonmarital sex in 24 countries. *Journal of Sex Research, 35,* 349–358.

PRESCRIPTION DRUG MISUSE

Most people first encounter prescription drugs at a young age, given for legal purposes to treat common medical issues such as colds and headaches. In 2011, the White House, through the Office of National Drug Control Policy, issued an executive plan of action titled *Epidemic: Responding to America's Prescription Drug Abuse Crisis*, citing prescription drug misuse as the fastest growing drug problem in the United States. Recent scholarly articles agree that opioids are the most abused category of prescription drugs. *Diversion* is the U.S. Department of Justice Drug Enforcement Administration's term for any prescription drugs that are misused or diverted from their original purpose. This entry describes patterns and techniques of prescription drug misuse, a form of deviant behavior, and presents possible solutions to the problem.

Patterns of Drug Misuse

While many prescription drugs are misused or diverted, opioids (often referred to by their brand names Oxycontin, Oxycodone, Roxicodone, Hydrocodone, and Percocet) are of the greatest concern with a per person per milligram increase in use of more than 400% between the years 1997 and 2007. Opioids are highly addictive, and they are often referred to as synthetic heroin. Opioids are used to treat legitimate, medically diagnosed pain associated with spinal, orthopedic, and oncological issues. Misused opioids are most commonly obtained first through a doctor, friend, or relative, but those who become addicted may resort to "doctor shopping," street purchases, obtaining prescriptions by fraud, or through visiting "pill mills."

Doctor shopping refers to the practice of scheduling visits with more than one doctor and failing to disclose the multiple visits while attempting to obtain large quantities of prescription medication for use or sale. Prescriptions are obtained by fraud through the use of altered prescriptions, fictitious prescriptions presented to a pharmacy, or by theft of a prescription pad. The term *pill mill* is used to refer to a doctor, clinic, or pharmacy that prescribes or dispenses narcotics inappropriately or for nonmedical reasons.

Techniques

Opioids, when prescribed and used legally, are in the form of a small manufactured pill taken orally.

As addiction sets in, users may begin to build a tolerance, requiring more opioids to obtain a recreational high. In an effort to reduce the amount of pills required and the time delay (which is an extra ingredient sometimes manufactured into the drug), abusers may turn to injecting the drug. To do so, the user places one or more pills into a metal spoon. The spoon is then heated to the point of liquefying the pill. A cotton ball is then placed in the liquid and a syringe is inserted into the mixture. The cotton ball removes all of the impurities (and the time release ingredients), and the pure opioid is then injected intravenously. Abusers often have telltale signs of abuse, known as tract or track marks, which are areas where repeated intravenous drug use has deteriorated the skin. Tract or track marks are most often found on the arms and feet of users, as these are the choice areas for injection sites.

Alternative abuse techniques include heating the pill in a spoon with very high heat, causing the pill to melt into a vapor, which is then inhaled through a straw. Using this method, addicts can include other pills or illicit drugs, such as cocaine, in the spoon and obtain an alternative high. *Skittle parties* is a term used by teenagers and middle school–age children to describe a particularly deviant type of prescription drug misuse. Without their parent's knowledge, the teenagers or children obtain various prescription medications from their parents' or grandparents' medicine cabinets and bring them to the party. At the party, all of the prescription drugs are mixed into a bowl, and each child or teenager grabs a handful of prescription drugs and takes them orally to see what kind of high can be obtained.

Suggested Solutions

In an effort to curb prescription drug misuse, programs such as the Prescription Drug Monitoring Program began appearing in the early 2000s. PDMP allows doctors and pharmacists to input prescription information into a centralized computer database to neutralize doctor shopping and prescription fraud. As of 2011, only 37 states have an operational PDMP.

Law enforcement agencies have also attempted to curtail prescription drug misuse through educational programs, arrests of those trafficking and selling prescription drugs, and by closing pill mills. Legislation in many states has attempted to address this epidemic with little success. Scholars have suggested that prescription drug abuse is not new and

that techniques developed in the 1970s aimed at educating doctors on the dangers of overprescribing and the importance of patient care are the best avenues to reversing this epidemic.

The U.S. Drug Enforcement Administration has also expanded its efforts to take back old, unwanted, or unused prescription narcotics that clutter many household medicine cabinets. The U.S. Drug Enforcement Administration established a program whereby on two days each year agents assemble in various locations throughout the United States and accept all prescription drugs without question. The drugs are then incinerated to properly dispose of them. This is done not only to prevent prescription drugs from ending up in the hands of children or teenagers but also to prevent citizens from flushing old, unwanted, and unused prescription drugs down the toilet or drains and polluting the water system.

Eric S. Flowers

See also Club Drugs; Cocaine; Heroin; Legal Highs

Further Readings

Maxwell, J. C. (2011). The prescription drug epidemic in the United States: A perfect storm. *Drug and Alcohol Review, 30,* 264–270.

Office of National Drug Control Policy, White House. (2011). *Epidemic: Responding to America's prescription drug abuse crisis.* Retrieved from http://www.whitehouse .gov/sites/default/files/ondcp/policy-and-research/ rx_abuse_plan.pdf

Smith, D. E. (2012). Prescribing practices and the prescription drug epidemic: Physician intervention strategies. *Journal of Psychoactive Drugs, 44,* 68–71.

PRIMARY AND SECONDARY DEVIANCE

Primary and secondary deviance are processes in the development of deviant roles and careers. Primary deviance occurs when an individual first violates conventional expectations for behavior, while secondary deviance involves the problems created by the reactions of family, friends, authorities, or institutions.

Primary and secondary deviance were first discussed by Edwin Lemert in his 1951 book *Social Pathology.* The concepts became important to the larger movement in sociology to de-emphasize individual qualities and behaviors and to concentrate attention on social responses. Rather than a quest to identify the causes of individual deviance, Lemert argued for the study of social actions and responses important to the production of deviance. He proposed that a sequence of interactions would lead from primary to secondary deviance. This process can be signified in eight steps: (1) primary deviation; (2) social penalties; (3) further primary deviation; (4) stronger penalties and rejections; (5) further deviation, perhaps with hostilities and resentment beginning to focus on those doing the penalizing; (6) crisis reached in the tolerance quotient, expressed in formal action by the community stigmatizing of the deviant; (7) strengthening of the deviant conduct as a reaction to the stigmatizing and penalties; and (8) ultimate acceptance of deviant social status and efforts at adjustment on the basis of the associate role.

Many primary deviations are insignificant instances of rule breaking and go unnoticed or unobserved. They may be repeated infrequently or not at all. Initial acts of rule breaking are therefore not considered sociologically important unless there are social reactions that create problems for a deviant individual. Nor are the origins of deviance especially relevant to sociology. Instead, the meanings assigned to acts and individuals and societal responses to these meanings are sociologically important. Or as Lemert (1951) observed, "Deviations are not significant until they are organized subjectively and transformed into active roles and become the social criteria for assigning status" (p. 75).

In the process of an individual adjusting to social reactions, deviance becomes more or less entrenched in identity. Social reactions to an individual deviant guide expectations for behavior and narrow the range of roles available for an individual to play. Secondary deviance thus occurs when an individual feels constrained by a deviant role, sees some rewards in playing out a deviant role, applies a deviant definition to the self, or engages in other deviant behaviors in support of a deviant role. A common illustration of the process of secondary deviance is the evolution of a drug user into a drug addict. A drug user experiences the pleasures of intoxication and camaraderie with other drug users, may commit crimes in support of an expensive drug habit, and perhaps participates in rehabilitation programs that require an acceptance and admission of one's addiction.

This kind of example reveals the centrality of the concept of secondary deviance to the labeling theory. As elaborated by Howard Becker in his 1963 book, *Outsiders: Studies in the Sociology of Deviance*, deviance depends on public reactions. An individual who sustains "a pattern of deviance over a long period of time" and whose identity is organized around deviant behavior is one who has been caught, labeled, and subjected to the enforcement of rules for behavior. Social reactions to deviance contribute to difficulties in conforming to rules for behavior that might not otherwise be broken. In Becker's well-known example, the deceit and crime in which a drug addict engages are consequences of the public reaction to drug use.

The concept of secondary deviance crept into public debate in the late 20th century with regard to anticipated or imagined benefits of drug legalization. Controversies centered on the possibilities for reducing street crimes by making drugs readily available and less expensive and so eliminating the need for addicts to deal in drugs or commit robberies. These arguments went largely unresolved. Narrower sociological contentions that developed over the influence of labeling in the prognosis of mental illnesses resulted in some consensus that mentally ill people are treated differently after diagnosis, but disputes remained over the importance of public reaction to the subjective experience of mental illness. Throughout the 1970s, 1980s, and 1990s, the concepts of primary and secondary deviance helped orient studies in a diverse array of research sites, including crime and delinquency, recidivism, physical disability, alcoholism, sexual variation, high-risk sexual behavior, obesity, and tattooing and body piercing. Much sociological research into global phenomena such as moral panics and culture wars is also indebted to early formulations of primary and secondary deviance concepts.

The use of primary deviance and secondary deviance as terms declined somewhat in the late 20th and early 21st centuries. However, the concepts are staples in introductory college courses, and the idea that societal reactions are the key phenomena in sociological understandings of deviance is an enduring legacy.

Joel Powell and Zachary Tolliver

See also Labeling Approach; Reintegrative Shaming; Solitary Deviance; Symbolic Interactionism

Further Readings

Becker, H. S. (1963). *Outsiders: Studies in the sociology of deviance*. New York, NY: Free Press.

Gove, W. (1982). Labelling theory's explanation of mental illness: An update of recent evidence. *Deviant Behavior: An Interdisciplinary Journal, 3*, 307–327.

Lemert, E. M. (1951). *Social pathology: Systematic approaches to the study of sociopathic behavior*. New York, NY: McGraw-Hill.

Lemert, E. M. (1967). *Human deviance, social problems, and social control*. Englewood Cliffs, NJ: Prentice Hall.

PRISON CULTURE/INMATE CODE

Academic interest in the study of prisons and the inmate ethos has been largely attributed to the emergence of the "Big House" model of incarceration. Proliferating in the early 20th century, the Big House was more a hybrid of the penitentiary and industrial prison than one unique type of structure. These maximum-security facilities housed several thousand prisoners at any given time; to accommodate such large populations, Big Houses were typically characterized by cavernous cell houses containing as many as five to six levels, or tiers. Although Big House prisoners were permitted to congregate and socialize, order, monotony, boredom, and regimentation punctuated their lives. Coupled with the likelihood of serving sentences spanning decades versus months or years, the oppressive culture of the total institution created what Joseph Fishman first deemed an inmate subculture. While correctional architecture, goals, and policies have transformed the institution of prison, the inmate subculture remains an immutable and enigmatic feature of contemporary U.S. correctional facilities.

By its very nature, the culture of prison creates an immediate and overwhelming degree of deprivation in the newly admitted inmate (or "fish," as they are oftentimes referred to by both prisoners and staff). This deprivation takes many forms, namely, the loss of one's freedom and liberty, material goods and services, heterosexual contact or physical interaction with loved ones, privacy, security and safety, and individualism or autonomy. The sociologist and criminologist Gresham Sykes referred to these forms of deprivation as the pains of imprisonment and noted that in many cases, they are far more difficult to navigate than the corporal and physical punishments associated with early prison life. In his essays *Asylums*, the sociologist Erving Goffman further conceptualized the deprivations incurred on incarceration, but on a more individualistic plane. The new inmate, Goffman noted, is stripped of any prior "homeworld" value. This process, deemed the mortification of the self, involves the conspicuous removal of any personal property or identifying unique apparel. The prisoner is then issued standard, institutional clothing identical to that of his or her fellow convicts. He or she is subjected to additional rites of passage, or degradation ceremonies—delousing, haircuts, measurements, and body cavity searches in full view of others. He or she is treated more as a child than as an adult and is immediately stigmatized and stereotyped as a marginal being. It follows, then, that the formation and proliferation of unique inmate subcultures is a group-generated defense mechanism—a manner of coping with the austere, mundane, and controlling atmosphere of the penitentiary. As in conventional society, subcultures emerge when persons sharing similar status, conditions, or situations form social enclaves for support and solidarity. For inmates, then, subcultural formation is the equivalent of creating and reestablishing some semblance of identity, power, and control where none previously existed. This entry focuses on two aspects of inmate subculture: (1) the convict code, or normative standard of prisoner conduct, and (2) the convict argot, or the language of prison.

The Convict Code

The penitentiary is a bastion of rules, codes, and expectations of conduct. Given that the average inmate prison sentence spans roughly two years, these informal convict norms are foisted on new arrivals almost immediately on admission to the prison. The process of immersing oneself into this subculture, as well as adopting and internalizing these distinct convict codes, is a phenomenon termed *prisonization*. How successfully an inmate adapts to the process of prisonization is correlated with how the inmate manages the environment of deprivation. Yet some research has found that a prisoner's ability to acclimate is directly related to the social experiences, personality characteristics, and criminogenic variables the prisoner brings in, or "imports," from the outside world. The Importation and Deprivation models of prison subcultural formation have proven invaluable in this area, and more contemporary research has suggested applying a hybrid or integrated approach using both perspectives.

New inmates are provided the facility's official conduct handbook on intake; however, new admissions are simultaneously "schooled" in the unofficial rules of incarceration that are enforced by respected inmates in positions of power, or by "shot callers." Should the new arrival share a cell with another inmate, this cellmate, or "cellie," is typically the first tutor to provide a crash course relating to ideal prisoner conduct. While prisons vary in degrees of population, offender typologies, programs, and administrative styles, the convict code does share several fundamental tenets across prison systems. The universal umbrella under which all other convict rules fall is that of the 3 Rs—reputation, respect, and retaliation.

Reputation

On entering prison, inmates are initially forced to perceive themselves as powerless, weak, and subservient to a formal bureaucratic organization. All of these qualities are psychologically emasculating, and the convict code favors the inmate whose masculinity is unquestioned and undeniable. Perhaps the most significant concern an inmate has on admission to prison is how he or she appears to other prisoners. During the classification process, intake counselors and administrators will take the necessary precautions to ensure the safety of inmates; yet these efforts are not fail proof. New inmates may posture, perform, and interact with other prisoners so as to convey an image of toughness. While a diminutive, slightly built, or young male inmate may feel little need in hyperilluminating his masculinity in conventional society, he may present himself in the opposite manner while incarcerated merely to establish the illusion that he is a formidable and fearless opponent. Solidifying one's reputation in prison often requires engaging in an act of violence, typically, at the directive of other inmates. An inmate who accepts the challenge to assault another inmate or staff almost instantaneously increases his stock as "reputable" among the population. Even if a prisoner loses in combat, his willingness alone to fight earns him initial respect.

Respect

In conventional society, the concept of respect generally entails gestures of basic courtesies, feelings of admiration, or the ability to empathize with, or understand, the positions of others. As a major tenet of the convict code, however, failure to impart respect toward fellow inmates becomes a matter of personal safety and even survival. Inmates grant or withhold respect for any number of reasons, but typically, respect is directly correlated with hierarchical status, group affiliation, longevity in the prison system, or an inmate's criminal history and reputation. For example, the criminal hierarchy is oftentimes used as a barometer by which to measure the degree of respect afforded to prisoners. Those incarcerated for violent crimes against adult male victims garner a greater level of respect than those whose crimes were perpetrated against women, children, the elderly, and in some cases, animals. Inmates whose crimes involved the murder or assault of a police officer are generally viewed with admiration, while sex offenders, child molesters, rapists, and those who have killed or harmed a parent are oftentimes admonished and viewed with disdain and contempt. Respect may also involve the understanding that in the end, prisoners are all in the same institutional predicament. As such, the convict code dictates that a prisoner mind his own business, exercise basic courtesies regarding the cleanliness of shared cells, refrain from discussing prison politics with outsiders or competing groups, and pay all debts incurred through gambling or services.

Traditional imagery of prisoners and hardened convicts has typically depicted men as being heavily tattooed from head to toe. Prison "ink," or inmate-generated tattoos, has played an important role within the inmate subculture and the convict code as well. A convict's tattoos are conspicuous symbols of his life behind bars, and are indicative of his status within the prison culture. These permanent images range from memorials to his homeworld family, to gang affiliations, to his criminal life and battles with substance abuse, and to the amount of time he has served in the system. Prison tattoos also function as visible warning beacons, which are intentionally placed on obvious areas of the body to remind other convicts of the owner's gang affiliation and racial loyalty. In these cases, the tattoo is referred to as a brand or patch, and frequently replicates a gang's official symbol. Inmates affiliated with the Mexican Mafia, for example, proudly display tattoos of a black hand, the letter *M*, or the phrase *La Eme* (The M). Inmates affiliated with white supremacist factions or security threat groups commonly acquire tattoos of swastikas, SS bolts, the Totenkopfverbände (or Nazi Death Head Squads), or abbreviations of their respective gangs. Inmates claiming membership in the Aryan Brotherhood often tattoo the gang's patch on their chests, backs, and stomachs. These patches contain three-leaf clovers, the letters "AB," Celtic symbols, or Nordic imagery such as Thor's hammer or bearded Vikings. The very nature of the tattoo, then, simultaneously declares an inmate's identity, as well as the inmate's loyalty to both race and gang.

Retaliation

Inmate-on-inmate, inmate-on-staff, or staff-on-inmate retaliation typically takes the form of a violent or assaultive encounter. Yet, within the prison subculture, even the use of violence is a carefully scrutinized and monitored rule within the informal convict code. Sociologically, the eruption of violence is symbolic of the manifestation of power imbalances (whether perceived or actual) between or among individuals or groups. While violence is not the sole manner by which interpersonal conflicts are resolved in society, it is not an uncommon occurrence when the nature of the penitentiary is taken into account. The incidence of violence in U.S. correctional facilities is both expressive and instrumental; inmates may become assaultive or confrontational to simply garner attention from staff, or may engage in combat to maintain and establish a reputation, avenge perceived disrespect, defend a fellow gang member or member of one's race, or sanction another inmate whose conduct violated the prison code. Should an inmate refuse to retaliate under the expectations of the convict code, he draws the integrity of his masculinity into specific relief. Moreover, an inmate who exhibits hesitation or an unwillingness to engage in violence risks becoming a future target of retaliation himself, usually in the form of sexual assault or exploitation.

Although participating in violence is integral in formulating an identity or impression as tough, it can also function as a detriment to the inmates' ultimate goal of timely parole or release. As with all components of the convict code, then, when and where to fight is also an informal, negotiated process. New inmates are versed in the repercussions associated with obligatory combat, and *veteraños* ("veteran convicts") or OGs (original gangsters) are typically those who dictate the most ideal times and places to engage in violent conduct. Thus, physical retaliation is a subcultural instrument that prisoners rely on to maintain order in their social world while carefully balancing the degree of unwanted attention it brings to their group.

Although the supporting pillars of the convict code are reputation, respect, and retaliation, there is an ever-changing litany of norms and rules to be absorbed and followed by a new inmate. Depending on the security level, region, racial composition, and overall environmental attributes of prison units, the convict codes and prison politics can vary to some degree from facility to facility. While not exhaustive, the following are several of the more widely acknowledged rules of the inmate subculture:

- Do your own time (don't meddle in the business of others).
- Pay your debts.
- Be trustworthy, honorable, and loyal.
- Don't disrespect others.
- Don't snitch, associate with staff, or talk about inmate business.
- Be tough, and don't retreat from a challenge.
- Don't steal from, lie to, or exploit other inmates.
- Never reveal gang activity, information, or secrets.
- Be a man.
- Defend, and only associate with, those of your own race.

Race

A brief glance onto any prison recreation yard or communal gathering area will readily illuminate a critical aspect of the convict code—self-segregation by race. Although deemed judicially unconstitutional nearly 45 years ago, the subculture of the prison remains one of the last vestiges of U.S. segregation in which the practice is considered largely beneficial for all involved. On entering prison for the first time, inmates are informed both of the formal and informal codes of conduct that will guide their behavior during incarceration. During the informal initiation, new prisoners are quickly reminded of the racial politics that will govern their lives while serving time.

Concepts at play in the free world—racial harmony, tolerance, colorblindness, and unity—would be essentially impossible to take root and flourish in the total institution of a penitentiary, at least in the minds of many correctional staff and the inmates under their charge. Voluntary racial segregation is a socially negotiated process between and among inmate leaders. These inmate negotiations further solidify the convict code, dictating when interracial social exchanges may or may not take place, under what conditions interracial transactions are condoned, and under what circumstances an inmate must engage in acts of violence where the inmate's racial group is concerned. Should an inmate of one race attack or assault a member of another race, all available inmates of both races involved in the initial fight are expected to come to the aid of their "homie" or "bro." A prisoner who runs from such an altercation or who fails to fight for his race can later be seriously assaulted himself, or worse. Interracial socialization does occur, however—while on the recreation yard, while playing cards or games in communal spaces, and during more clandestine interactions such as trading drugs or contraband. Yet again, these racial exceptions are negotiated beforehand, and carefully monitored by gang and inmate leaders of their respective racial groups.

The philosophies undergirding racial politics in prison are power and control and involve impression management, posturing, and a coalescing racist ideology (whether believed or merely verbalized as a front). To provide one example, inmates of different races will not share a cell, or "cell up" together—indeed an unwritten, informal convict policy but respected by staff nonetheless. Bathroom facilities in cell blocks fall within the racial geography as well, as banks of urinals, sinks, and shower stalls are all claimed by different races of inmates. In open or dormitory-style cell houses, regions of bunks are designated as white, black, or Hispanic sections; to overwhelm a new arrival even more so, the various race groups have predetermined pathways or walkways by which inmates must navigate through another race's bunk area. The exercise yard, or "yard," is historically the most dangerous and volatile location within the perimeter of the prison. At a time when inmates may outnumber correctional officers 400 to 1, inmates participate in reducing racially based conflicts and other serious issues by designating each part of the yard race specific. No feature is overlooked, from outdoor toilet areas to basketball courts, to handball slabs, to picnic tables, to weightlifting stations, and to even the maze of sidewalks crisscrossing the expanse of fenced space. Groups in consistent states of turmoil, or "war," are typically those placed at the furthest opposing ends of the area. *Sureños* and *Norteños*, or Southern and Northern Mexican inmates, are generally sequestered separately both on the yard and in the cell houses or tiers. While both groups are Hispanic, gang affiliations and hostilities outside the institution warrant such action. Historically, black rival street gang members, such as the Crips and Bloods,

are generally affiliated with the Black Guerilla Family once they enter the prison system. Strictly white prison gangs, which emerged in the late 1960s and into the 1970s, did so as a strategy for protection, safety, and power. As the racial complexion of prison populations shifted heavily toward black, Hispanic, and other racial groups, white inmates began to view themselves in terms of an out-group on incarceration and used violence and intimidation to bolster their numbers inside a disproportionately minority prison system. Today, these racial politics thrive in prisons and correctional institutions across the United States, due in large part to mutual understandings between staff and inmates that this racialized system decreases tension and de-escalates violence and conflict.

The Convict Argot

Although Sykes brilliantly illuminated the lives and subculture of imprisoned men more than 50 years ago, social dialogues between convicts today are still peppered with unique, mysterious, and sometimes even humorous or nonsensical vernacular that Sykes termed the inmate argot, or the language of prison. This argot expands to inmates' names, to items within one's cell, to the correctional staff, to sexual conduct, and even to the roles and statuses assumed by these incarcerated men.

Cultures, whether conventional, deviant, or criminal, all revolve around a set of beliefs, norms, values, symbols, artifacts, and languages; these components are what set apart each culture as unique, and the inmate subculture is no different in this regard. For example, law enforcement is (traditionally) a masculine subculture, rife with regulations, codes, abstract language, gestures and signals, styles of dress, and expectations of social comportment. The language of the police is designed and spoken in such a manner as to confuse potential criminals, deter the public from hearing or deciphering sensitive information, and bond together those who share a similar dangerous existence as "brothers in arms" or as "us against them." There are types of crimes to respond to, each with a corresponding numerical code—even the manner of response (emergency equipment, silent) is coded as well. In similar fashion, then, the inmate subculture employs this argot more as a tool by which to differentiate themselves from the sterile, impersonal authoritarian language used by the staff on a daily basis. In prison, the inmate is depersonalized and is no longer a conventional cultural being to which unique and colorful descriptors apply. Furthermore, the inmate argot is ever evolving and changing—should corrections staff decipher written convict codes or terms, prisoners will merely change them, sometimes daily, to once again claim a modicum of control and power over a tedious existence overtaken by what the prison sociologist and the convict criminologist John Irwin deemed an almost catatonic state of stupefaction.

Conclusion

This entry has provided a survey of the U.S. prison subculture and the attendant convict code that exists and operates within it. The penitentiary is a total social institution that serves as a functional entity for both conforming society and the criminal element housed there. More than 50% of all male inmates serving time today are doing so for violent crimes; with such a volatile and unique population of individuals confined in these totalistic environments, organization, order, and power dynamics are all socially negotiated between staff and prisoners and among the inmates themselves.

The convict code, or normative standard of prisoner conduct, comprises intricate interpersonal dynamics taking their cues from status, race, language, the presentation of self, impression management and performances, and ideas of ideal masculinity. Hierarchies are established along racial, criminal, and gang affiliations, and the entire convict code falls under the vital concepts of reputation, respect, and retaliation. While not necessary for survival in outside society, these basic tenets can mean the difference between doing "good time" or "hard time," and at times, they have life or death implications for those failing to acknowledge their significance in a culture of convicts.

Trina Seitz

See also Argot; Code of the Street; Criminal Lifestyles

Further Readings

Carroll, L. (1974). *Hacks, blacks, and cons: Race relations in a maximum security prison.* Lexington, MA: Lexington Books.

Goffman, E. (1961). *Asylums: Essays on the social situation of mental patients and other inmates.* Garden City, NY: Anchor Books.

Irwin, J., & Cressey, D. (1962). Thieves, convicts, and the inmate culture. *Social Problems 10*(2), 142–155.

Sykes, G. M. (1958). *The society of captives: A study of a maximum security prison.* Princeton, NJ: Princeton University Press.

Trammell, R. (2012). *Enforcing the convict code: Violence and prison culture.* Boulder, CO: Lynne Rienner.

PRISON RAPE

Prison rape is a serious, not especially well-understood, form of deviance that runs across U.S. prisons. In response to a growing recognition of the scope and severity of the problem, there are national efforts in place to try to address the problem. At present, however, there remains much research that needs to be done to fully understand—and combat—prison rape. This entry reviews the research that has been performed, describes the characteristics of both victims and perpetrators, and identifies the physical environments that facilitate prison rape.

Research

There is limited research focused on the occurrence and prevalence of sexual violence in correctional settings. Most research addressing prison rape has been conducted in the United States over the past 40 years. The first valid and reliable incidence rate comes from a 1968 study of more than 3,300 inmates. This study estimated that the true number of incidents for the more than 60,000 inmates to pass through the system during the 26-month study period was close to 2,000.

More recent research has shown a range of victimization rates. A 1982 study reported that 14% of inmates in one California prison had been sexually victimized, with many forced into long-term sexual victimization patterns, including protective pairings (e.g., partnering with another inmate in a sex-for-protection exchange). Similar rates of victimization were reported at about the same time for a stratified sample of inmates in 17 facilities of the Federal Bureau of Prisons.

Cindy and David Struckman-Johnson conducted a series of studies that provide the next significant work to address prison sexual violence and produced very different results. This line of research reports that between 20% and 22% of inmates in midwestern prisons are victimized. More recent research continues to report a wide range of rates of victimization. Others have reported that only 1% of a sample of men incarcerated in Oklahoma were sexual violence victims (although 14% reported being threatened or attempted to be coerced). Elsewhere, reports suggest that 8.5% of inmates have been sexually victimized while incarcerated.

Public concern about high rates of prison rape victimization was one reason behind the passage of the federal Prison Rape Elimination Act (PREA) of 2003. In addition to creating a mechanism to develop national standards for institutional operations and providing funds for facilities to partially implement such standards, PREA also created a rush of research on prison rape.

One obvious point here is that there are wide discrepancies in the estimates of the rate of prison rape in the United States. Until recently, prison rape was not uniformly defined, and many researchers relied on small and nonrandom samples with poor methods of data collection. Today there are standard definitions, as established by PREA, and used by the PREA-mandated national study of prison rape conducted by the U.S. Department of Justice, Bureau of Justice Statistics in the National Inmate Survey. The series of surveys, begun in 2007, of a random sample of 10% of all prisons (as well as jails) in the United States collects data directly from inmates using an audio computer-assisted self-interview that is anonymous and confidential. Widely recognized as the most methodologically sophisticated study of prison rape victimization in the United States, this series of reports consistently shows 4.4% of prison inmates (and 3.1% of jail inmates) report some form of sexual victimization while incarcerated in the prior years. However, more than one half of the instances of sexual victimization reported by inmates were perpetrated by a correctional staff member. Also, female inmates are twice as likely (4.7% vs. 1.9%) to report a sexual victimization while incarcerated.

Research focused on documenting and identifying rates of sexual violence among incarcerated women is extremely rare. It was not until the 1990s that serious scholarly attention was devoted to this issue, with the initial studies reporting a 7% rate of victimization for female inmates (compared with a rate of 22% for males across six facilities) in one small study. Later, a subsequent study drew on data from 263 inmates in three women's prisons and showed victimization rates ranging from 6% to 19%. A survey of 245 women in one southern prison reported a 5% victimization rate. Most recently, the National Inmate Survey reported that women are more than twice as likely as men (4.7% versus 1.9%) to be sexually victimized by another inmate.

Characteristics of Victims

A number of factors have been identified by both researchers and advocacy groups as correlated with increased risk of sexual victimization during incarceration. For the most part, these findings are consistent across studies and advocates.

Most attention to the issue of what places an inmate at increased risk for sexual victimization centers on demographics. Two of the strongest associations are age and race. Almost all research identifies that younger inmates are at greater risk for victimization. Nearly all studies show that white inmates are more likely to be victimized than African Americans or Hispanics. In fact, white inmates constitute a larger proportion of all known (through both official reports and confidential reporting) victims of prison rape than the proportion of inmates that they represent.

An additional set of demographic factors that are strongly associated with victimization risk are gender and sexuality. Gay/bisexual inmates are typically twice more likely than other inmates to be victimized. Transgender inmates have also been shown to be frequently targeted for prison rape. Neither of these trends should be surprising, as those inmates who are known (or even just perceived) to be sexually attracted to men and/or identifying as female are more likely than other inmates to be seen as vulnerable and perhaps even interested and desiring of sexual activities while incarcerated. This is usually not the case, and just because an inmate identifies as gay/bisexual or transgender does not mean that he or she wants to be raped.

An additional strong association is seen between victimization risks and mental state. Mentally ill or intellectually impaired inmates are significantly more likely than other inmates to be victims of prison rape. However, it is not just that inmates who have diminished mental capabilities are at increased risk, for some researchers report that 40% of male and 51% of female victims have at least some college education.

Victims of prison rape are most likely to be serving a sentence for a serious offense. Also, inmates convicted of sexual offenses have higher rates of victimization than other inmates. Popular assumptions hold that inmates who are raped in prison tend to be so soon after arrival. However, at least some research questions this belief, showing that victimization rates are higher for inmates who have been incarcerated for longer periods of time. The National Inmates Survey reports that only 13% of males and 4% of females are victimized in their first 24 hours of incarceration.

As summarized by the advocacy group Stop Prisoner Rape in its 2006 report *In the Shadows: Sexual Violence in U.S. Detention Facilities,*

While anyone can become a victim of sexual assault while in detention, certain groups of inmates are especially vulnerable. Among the chief targets of sexual violence are: non-violent, first-time offenders who are inexperienced in the ways of prison life; youth held in juvenile and adult facilities; gay and transgendered detainees, or those who are perceived to be gay or gender variant; and, finally, those held in immigration detention centers. (pp. 1–2)

Characteristics of Perpetrators

While research has identified a consistent set of factors associated with increased likelihood of victimization, less is known about common characteristics of inmates who perpetrate sexual violence. As with victims, perpetrators can be identified through demographics. Age and race have been the two most consistently identified factors related to likelihood of perpetration of prison sexual violence. Whereas victimization likelihood is related to younger age and being white, perpetration likelihood is related to being older than victims and being African American or Hispanic. Across all substantiated cases of sexual violence in U.S. prisons in 2005, 51% of known inmate perpetrators were 35 years or older (compared with only 23.7% of victims being 35 years or older). With regard to race, research results have supported both the idea that perpetrators are more likely to be minorities and that they are more likely to not be minorities. This appears to be largely the consequence of geography, with different jurisdictions showing different patterns in racial identities of known prison rape perpetrators.

In terms of criminal background and institutional behavior, known perpetrators are more likely to have violent offense convictions than other types of conviction offenses. Also inmates who have been in prison for longer periods of time are more likely to be perpetrators of prison rape. Overall, it appears that perpetrators of prison rape are more likely to be older, sentenced for violent offenses, have higher custody levels, and have served longer sentences than their victims.

Physical Environments of Incidents

Identifying specific physical environments that facilitate prison rape means focusing on physical locations, temporal issues, and social contexts of institutional housing and program areas. Generally, the most likely place in prison for prison rape to occur is in an inmate's cell or dormitory, followed by showers or bathrooms, and common areas (e.g., dayrooms, workplaces, and cafeterias). Cells that have solid front doors (that do not permit ease of viewing inside) are especially likely to be locations of sexual assaults.

On the institutional level, facilities with larger populations, higher than minimum custody level, and facilities with conjugal visitation are more likely to have at least one officially reported sexual assault. Contrary to popular belief, research has not shown overcrowding to be related to increased rates of prison rape.

Contrary evidence exists surrounding when prison rapes are most likely to occur. Across the nation, the National Inmate Survey report that nearly one half of reported incidents occurred between 6:00 p.m. and midnight, but in Texas, others found that the majority of sexual assaults known to correctional authorities occurred between 6 a.m. and 6 p.m.

Richard Tewksbury

See also Prison Culture/Inmate Code; Rape

Further Readings

Austin, J., Fabelo, T., Gunter, A., & McGinnis, K. (2006). *Sexual violence in the Texas prison system.* Washington, DC: JFA Institute.

Beck, A. J., Harrison, P. M., Berzofsky, M., Caspar, R., & Krebs, C. (2010). *Sexual victimization in prisons and jails reported by inmates, 2008–09.* Washington, DC: Bureau of Justice Statistics.

Jenness, V., Maxson, C. L., Matsuda, K. N., & Sumner, J. M. (2007). *Violence in California correctional facilities: An empirical examination of sexual assault.* Irvine, CA: Center for Evidence Based Corrections.

Stop Prisoner Rape. (2006). *In the shadows: Sexual violence in U.S. detention facilities.* Los Angeles, CA: Author.

Wooden, W. S., & Parker, J. (1982). *Men behind bars: Sexual exploitation in prison.* New York, NY: Plenum Press.

PROFESSIONAL WRESTLING

Professional wrestling, a substantial force in popular culture, has often been criticized and seen as a fringe entertainment enjoyed by deviant groups, so much so that being a fan of professional wrestling may carry a social stigma. This entry discusses the origins of professional wrestling, the ebb and flow of wrestling's popularity, standouts in both wrestling organizations and performers, and what makes wrestling fans such a unique, if possibly deviant, group.

Professional wrestling has a long and varied history throughout the world, having proven to be particularly popular and prominent in Japan, Central America, and North America, with various professional wrestling organizations operating from a regional level to a global level. While the sport of wrestling dates back as far as 3000 BCE, the roots of what is now considered professional wrestling originated in the 1880s, and for a time, it was operated and considered to be on par with "legitimate" sports. As opposed to the historic Greco-Roman style of wrestling, this "catch as catch can" style of wrestling differed by incorporating fewer rules for grappling and holds. This tradition continued through the 1920s, when the more common type of professional wrestling, a pseudo-sport consisting of theatric, scripted elements (the act of maintaining the illusion of wrestling as a true sport referred to as "kayfabe"), including predetermined winners to wrestling matches, began to increase in prevalence.

While professional wrestling originated in the United States as a carnival and sideshow attraction, it expanded in scope and popularity in a system of territories, each run by a separate promoter. The National Wrestling Alliance, founded in 1948, acted as a governing body of the territory system, often negotiating talent sharing between territories. This continued until the 1980s, when professional wrestling changed dramatically due to the advent of cable television, the rise of the World Wrestling Federation (WWF), and the success of its flagship pay-per-view event *Wrestlemania*. The WWF and its chairman and CEO, Vince McMahon Jr., eventually bought out most of the professional wrestling territories in the United States and made professional wrestling a prominent piece of popular culture. As the remaining territory organizations closed their doors, the WWF became the preferred organization for both fans and for professional wrestlers themselves.

Professional wrestling experienced another boom in the mid-1990s, with other wrestling companies such as World Championship Wrestling and Extreme Championship Wrestling (ECW) also becoming popular, though both organizations have since gone out of business after the popularity of wrestling began to decline once again in the late 1990s. ECW in particular operated a cult phenomenon within wrestling, characterized by an "underground" feel, hyperviolent, "hard-core" wrestling matches, profanity, and sexuality. ECW went to great lengths to differentiate itself from other more mainstream organizations, popularizing the hardcore style of wrestling.

Although professional wrestling has diminished in popularity since the boom periods of the 1980s and 1990s, the WWF (now rebranded as World Wrestling Entertainment, or the WWE) continues with a near monopoly on professional wrestling in the United States, with a loyal fan base supporting it through pay-per-view orders, live event attendance, and merchandise sales.

Historically, professional organizations have employed a head writer, called a "booker," who created the wrestlers' characters, determined what matches would take place during a particular event, and crafted long-term storylines. However, this practice has diminished as the WWE now instead employs a team of writers, similar to the method of more traditional television shows.

While professional wrestlers were originally carnival workers or nondescript athletes, after the popularity of "Gorgeous" George Wagner (known for his "glamorous," effeminate behavior) in the 1940s, it became commonplace for wrestlers to develop a character, either as a hero ("babyface" or "face") or villain ("heel"), with many wrestlers switching from face to heel several times over the course of their career, or changing types when moving to a new territory.

Fans of professional wrestling were notable in previous decades for engaging in a practice known as tape trading. This habit was popularized prior to the advent of the Internet, and while it has significantly diminished since, it still exists among small segments of the wrestling fandom. To pass along specific matches, particularly those difficult to view over local or cable television, such as matches from Japan, Lucha Libre style–wrestling matches from Mexico, or smaller organizations within the United States, professional wrestling fans in the United States would acquire and trade tapes of wrestling matches with one another, either at live events or through fan-written professional wrestling magazines.

Professional wrestling fans were responsible for the creation and publication of numerous magazines covering the sport, particularly through the late 1970s and into the wrestling boom period of the 1980s. Many of these magazines were notable for their maintenance of kayfabe, or the illusion that professional wrestling was a legitimate sport, without scripting or predetermined winners. Perhaps the most popular of these is *Pro Wrestling Illustrated* (*PWI*), which began publication in 1979 and continues today. *PWI* is especially known among fans of professional wrestling for its annual *PWI* awards, a series of awards including Wrestler of the Year, and Rookie of the Year, which are determined entirely by fan input.

Wrestling fans are unique in their use of certain terminology to differentiate among different groups among the fandom. Fans who continue to believe that wrestling is "true," or not predetermined, are commonly referred to as "marks," a term that likely dates back to wrestling's origins in the United States as a carnival attraction. To differentiate themselves from these types of fans, individuals who readily accept the theatrics of wrestling refer to themselves as "smart-marks," or wrestling fans who consider themselves to be smart to the inside rules and nature of the wrestling business. Because of this distinction, the label of "mark" is also commonly used as an insult among wrestling fans.

Wrestling fans are also notable for the creation of "backyard" wrestling organizations. This practice is considered to be controversial, as it consists typically of young, untrained wrestling fans performing matches in backyards or other various low-budget environments. These wrestling matches and events are characterized within the media as incorporating violent aspects of hardcore wrestling, such as weapons and blood-letting. Backyard wrestling is regarded negatively within the media because of its violent and dangerous nature. Previously within the limited domain of individuals engaging in videotape trading, it has become more widely popularized largely due to the advent of Internet video sharing.

Scott A. Richmond

See also Female Bodybuilding; Roller Derby

Further Readings

Beekman, S. (2006). *Ringside: A history of professional wrestling in America*. Westport, CT: Praeger.

Greenberg, K. E. (2000). *Pro wrestling: From carnivals to cable TV*. Minneapolis, MN: Lerner.

Mazer, S. (1998). *Professional wrestling: Sport and spectacle*. Jackson: University Press of Mississippi.

PROHIBITION

Prohibition, the legal ban on the manufacture, sale, and trafficking of alcohol from 1920 to 1933, has been referred to as both the Great Experiment and a great failure. For some, Prohibition was an effort to try to solve social and economic problems through the elimination of alcoholic beverages, while others viewed Prohibition as an effort to legally mandate a narrow version of morality. From a deviance perspective, the case of Prohibition is helpful for understanding how battles over the regulation of behavior often mask much larger social issues. Prohibition can be viewed as a landscape for battles over what it meant to be American in the wake of industrialization. The discussion that follows will show how a movement among white rural women to encourage men to temper their own alcohol consumption eventually became a national movement to amend the Constitution only to be overturned 13 years later. These changes are mapped onto larger changes in the U.S. population through immigration and urbanization.

Temperance Movements

Americans drank alcohol routinely in the first half of the 19th century. Beer and whiskey offered a cheap and widely available alternative to unsafe water, and men, women, and children drank alcohol with their breakfast, lunch, and dinner. Laborers and farmworkers took regular breaks to drink a bit during the day. And alcohol flowed freely at celebrations and gatherings. Alcohol was plentiful, but social norms prohibited people from appearing drunk in public, so the extent of drinking problems is unknown.

During the religious revival of the mid-19th century known as the Great Awakening, the first temperance movements in the United States focused on convincing people to moderate their own drinking. Temperance societies spread across the United States and the goal of these societies shifted from moderation to complete abstinence. In 1840, six men met to form the first Washingtonian Society, an organization in which men gathered to tell their own stories of drunkenness, to find support from others, and to sign a pledge promising total abstinence. Women formed auxiliary societies and engaged in some of the earliest women's political activism. Leaders like Susan B. Anthony and Elizabeth Cady Stanton linked temperance with women's suffrage and anti-slavery movements. And by 1851, the teetotalers achieved a clear win in the declaration of Maine as a dry state. However, the start of the Civil War in 1861 took attention away from the temperance cause, and the movement went dormant for several decades.

Following the close of the Civil War, new immigrant groups from southern and central Europe began moving to U.S. cities, bringing with them new drinking habits. Similarly, working-class men began moving to cities to work in factories. As city populations swelled, the saloon emerged as an important social and political space for immigrant and working-class men. In the saloon, men could escape the workday and a crowded home. They could meet with veterans, unions, and immigrant societies. They could network to find jobs, learn English, and even cast a ballot for elections. Also, saloons often offered opportunities for vice, such as prostitution and gambling.

For middle-class Americans, the saloon became a site of anxiety. The saloon made immigrant and working-class men's drinking visible and the belief that these men were organizing politically fueled fears about how American society could change as cities grew in the shadow of industrialization. In addition, German American brewers, who represented the threat of immigrant success, owned most of the saloons.

Temperance societies grew up once again to address the alcohol problem, and once again, women played a prominent role. Temperance societies were most active in rural areas as rural white women had the most concern about the activities of city men. Rural white women viewed public drinking and the vice associated with saloons as serious threats to morality, thereby making cities unsafe for women and children. Eliza Jane Thompson led one of the earliest protests of wives and mothers in Hillsboro, Ohio, in 1873. These women marched through the streets, prayed before druggists and saloons, and eventually convinced 1,300 liquor sellers to stop selling alcohol. Their strategy was one of moral suasion, and they sought to convince men to voluntarily abstain.

Gradually, these local efforts built to a national movement, and in 1879, Francis Willard founded the Women's Christian Temperance Union. Strategically, Willard linked the temperance association with calls for women's suffrage. To persuade more conservative women to join the suffrage cause, Willard connected temperance and suffrage under the banner of "home protection," in which women would be able to vote on issues important to women and children. Willard's movement also supported causes such as free kindergarten, raising the age of consent for girls, advocating labor rights and custody rights for women, and improving women's mental hospitals and prisons. Perhaps their most notable achievement was the national incorporation of a temperance curriculum into public schools.

While rural white women felt strongly about the temperance cause, the time and labor of organizing proved unsustainable for women who were simultaneously responsible for the household. Moreover, the efforts to convince men to choose abstinence were not compelling to the men of the saloon. Temperance women marching and praying in front of saloons could convince owners to stop selling alcohol for a short period, but often saloon keepers eventually returned to their alcohol businesses.

The Anti-Saloon League and Prohibition

White, middle-class men followed the lead of their wives and mothers and turned to the anti-alcohol cause. However, they believed that moral suasion and voluntary abstinence was too modest a goal. Instead, men who joined the temperance decided that the cause would be better served by legal change. Male antialcohol advocates founded the Anti-Saloon League in Oberlin, Ohio, in 1893 as a nonpartisan, single-issue organization that used alcohol as a wedge issue to divide local electorates. Under the guidance of Wayne Wheeler, the Anti-Saloon League called for dry laws at the local, county, and state levels. The organization supported dry candidates against wet candidates for office. Prior to the establishment of the Anti-Saloon League, both Republicans and Democrats had been reluctant to take a stance on Prohibition. However, as the Anti-Saloon League capitalized on Prohibition as a wedge issue, both parties began to feel the pressure to side with the prohibitionists. In addition, the Anti-Saloon League's success was buoyed by its focus on breweries and saloons rather than personal use of alcohol.

In contrast, the wets had more difficulty organizing around the cause to support alcohol.

Adolphus Bush, the founder of the Bush brewery, and his son-in-law Eberhard Anheuser founded the German-American Alliance as an antiprohibitionist organization. Initially, Bush was successful at gaining a stronghold against Prohibition, but several missteps undermined the cause. For example, the beer industry tried to distance itself from liquor distillers by claiming that liquor was the real problem, while beer was a health beverage. This quarrel prevented the two industries from pooling their financial and political resources to fight against dry laws.

However, beyond the cleverness of the Anti-Saloon League and the missteps of the German-American Alliance, several social trends and historical events served to expand political support to the prohibitionist cause. First, Progressive Era politics of the early 20th century viewed law as a viable path for improving society over relying on moral suasion. Second, the anti-immigration sentiments of rural whites in the northeast and Midwest combined easily with the antiblack sentiments of white southerners around the antialcohol cause. Third, the passage of the Sixteenth Amendment for a national income tax undermined the federal government's reliance on alcohol taxes for financial support. Finally, the entry of the United States into World War I in 1917 helped establish a national identity that was virulently anti-German and focused on self-restraint and resource conservation. German beer producers were constructed as anti-American. A series of laws prevented the use of grain in the production of beer and liquor, eventually shutting down all breweries and distilleries by the end of 1918. Thus, the United States was dry through federal law before a constitutional amendment was ratified in 1919.

The Anti-Saloon League viewed a constitutional amendment as necessary because variations in local, county, and state law meant that alcohol was legally available in some parts of the nation. In addition, the federal government was limited in its ability to regulate alcohol without a change to the constitution granting the federal government authority over the states on the alcohol issue. The initial amendment proposed by the Anti-Saloon League focused on the manufacture and sale of alcohol. Later additions to ban personal use and interstate trafficking caused the Anti-Saloon League to drop its support for the amendment. In spite of the Anti-Saloon League's dissatisfaction with the amendment, the Senate and House passed the Eighteenth Amendment prohibiting "the manufacture, sale, and transportation of intoxicating liquors" by the end of 1917. The Eighteenth Amendment was ratified by the states in only 13 months and went into effect on January 17, 1920.

Many had high hopes that national Prohibition would serve as a panacea to solve social problems. As the preacher Billy Sunday declared in a sermon on the day before Prohibition went into effect.

> The reign of tears is over. The slums will soon be a memory. We will turn our prisons into factories and our jails into storehouses and corncribs. Men will walk upright now, women will smile and children will laugh. Hell will be forever rent. (Okrent, 2011, p. 2)

The Limits of Prohibition

Enforcement of Prohibition turned out to be a crucial problem, as the Eighteenth Amendment did not define what qualified as intoxicating nor did it lay out a plan for enforcement. The Volstead Act of 1919 addressed these problems by strictly setting the alcohol standard at 0.5% and placing the Internal Revenue Service in charge of enforcement. The Volstead Act offered several exceptions to Prohibition for medicinal liquor, sacramental wine, and industrial alcohol. The Volstead Act also allowed individuals to possess alcohol for personal use and permitted home brewing of cider and fruit juices. Thus, the Volstead Act was simultaneously strict and lenient, adding to confusion over enforcement.

The federal government depended on states to pass similar prohibition laws and to take responsibility for enforcement. To that end, the Bureau of Prohibition was formed, but only 1,500 agents were hired and very little training was provided. The agents were poorly paid and morale was low; eventually 1 out of every 12 agents was fired for corruption. Meanwhile, the states had hoped that the federal government would take responsibility for enforcement. Most states passed legislation mirroring the Volstead Act, but many of those states offered no additional funding for enforcement. Enforcement in cities was particularly lax as city leaders were often opposed to close scrutiny and implementation. In 1920, a group of police officers in San Francisco, California, were reprimanded for enforcing Prohibition. Eventually, New York, Massachusetts, Montana, and Wisconsin went so far as to repeal their enforcement laws.

Politicians also tended to favor the light enforcement approach. They viewed the passage of the Eighteenth Amendment as a symbolic support for the dry cause, but they were not deeply invested in resolving the challenges of enforcement. Moreover, after the Eighteenth Amendment passed, support for the Anti-Saloon League dried up as people stopped giving money or writing letters to their representatives. Thus, the Anti-Saloon League lost its ability to use alcohol to intimidate less sympathetic politicians.

In the wake of lax enforcement, alcohol continued to be available for those who were able to pay. Speakeasies offered an alternative social space to the saloon, but women were welcome and could drink publicly for the first time. Demand for sacramental wine increased 800,000 gallons in a two-year period. And the membership in synagogues swelled as Jewish families were allowed to purchase 10 gallons of wine per adult every year. Prescriptions for medicinal alcohol were easily purchased from willing doctors and in its concentrated form could easily be transformed into larger volumes of alcohol. And grape growers began to sell grape concentrate with labels warning buyers not to let the juice ferment or it would turn to wine. Former beer producers began to sell malt extract once home stills became cheap and widely available.

One of the most well-known outcomes of Prohibition was the bolstering of the illegal trafficking of alcohol through organized crime. Alcohol was brought into the United States from Canada and the Bahamas. Moonshiners and bootleggers made and trafficked liquor in the United States. Enterprising men claiming to be druggists gained access to the liquor that was stored before Prohibition went into effect. Industrial alcohol was diverted for sale for consumption. Violence around alcohol trafficking increased dramatically as organized crime groups sought to protect their interests from law enforcement and rival organizations. And poison-related deaths through adulterated alcohol also spread since the substance could no longer be regulated.

Over all, alcohol consumption did decrease during Prohibition, particularly among the working class who could no longer afford the inflated price of liquors. However, those who continued to drink alcohol consumed more. Drinking culture shifted as saloons closed down and nightclubs and cafes began serving alcohol. Organized crime became a new problem for cities to deal with while rural areas changed little. Moreover, the social ills that were supposed to be solved by the elimination of alcohol persisted, making clear that Prohibition alone could not solve these problems.

Repealing Prohibition

By the late 1920s, support for Prohibition eroded. The failures of Prohibition were clear. Moreover, the Anti-Saloon League became embroiled in battles over segregation as the Ku Klux Klan became associated with the dry cause. Wheeler tried to keep the Anti-Saloon League separate from the white supremacist movement, but the Klan was one of the only remaining supporters of complete Prohibition and crossover between the two organizations was unavoidable. The Klan's prominence at the 1928 Democratic convention forced the party to reconsider its dry stance as Al Smith, the governor of New York and a pronounced wet, won the nomination. The Republican candidate, Herbert Hoover, won the election, but Smith's criticism of Prohibition laid roots for a growing protest.

On February 14, 1929, in Chicago, Illinois, a conflict between two organized crime gangs that trafficked alcohol escalated into violence in which seven mob members were killed. The St. Valentine's Day Massacre, as it is commonly called, came to symbolize the worst of mob violence. Although no one was arrested for the crime, it propelled mob leader Al Capone to cultural prominence. The image of gangsters in control and police futility highlighted the fundamental problems of passing a highly restrictive law like Prohibition, with little funds for enforcement. President Hoover attempted to overcome this problem by revising the Volstead Act to increase sanctions and build more prisons.

After the stock market crashed in October 1929, support for Prohibition waned further. Critics began arguing that legalizing of the alcohol market could create jobs and increase tax revenue. A variety of organizations began publicly supporting the overturn of the Eighteenth Amendment. Two of the most prominent organizations were the Women's Organization for National Prohibition Reform and the Association Against the Prohibition Amendment. These organizations quickly became the leaders in the call to repeal the Eighteenth Amendment.

President Hoover had been critical of Prohibition, but he also believed firmly in upholding the law. Hoover's stance on Prohibition became linked with his conservative economic policies during the early years of the Great Depression, and critics, particularly Democrats, claimed that both were outdated.

Furthermore, in 1931, Hoover's own investigation of Prohibition, the Wickersham Commission, outlined serious failures of efforts to eliminate alcohol. Of the 11 members of the committee, only 1 member favored the current law. Nevertheless, Hoover maintained his support for Prohibition.

During the 1932 presidential race, Franklin Roosevelt, the Democratic candidate, opposed Prohibition and eventually won the election. In March 1933, Roosevelt signed the Cullen–Harrison Act, modifying the Volstead Act to authorize the sale of light beer and wine. But the modification was not enough to satisfy the populace, and by the end of 1933, the states ratified the Twenty-First Amendment to repeal Prohibition. The Association Against the Prohibition Amendment had emphasized states' rights in its call for repeal. Although states supported the repeal of Prohibition at the national level, several states kept their dry laws on the books. Mississippi was the last state to repeal its alcohol ban in 1966. States continue to strictly monitor the sale of alcohol through license systems, and several states still monopolize the sale of hard liquor. Hundreds of counties and communities in the United States currently have dry laws on their books.

Prohibition's Legacy

The organized crime groups who had trafficked alcohol throughout Prohibition turned to trafficking other illegal substances in the wake of repeal. Lucky Luciano is one of the most prominent examples of this transition. He rose to prominence and wealth during Prohibition, but eventually became a linchpin in the heroin trade. Once the networks were in place, any illegal activity could be passed through the same channels.

Alcohol prohibition has been called the Great Experiment, but the enactment and repeal of the Eighteenth Amendment in only 13 years suggests the failure of this experiment. National prohibition was not considered again until the passage of the Controlled Substances Act in 1970. This law categorizes substances into a series of five schedules, and all substances that fall into Schedule I are ruled completely illegal. This category includes psychedelics, heroin, and marijuana. As states begin passing laws to legalize marijuana under certain circumstances that conflict with federal law, the question about how far the federal government can extend its power when citizens resist is raised.

Kimberly M. Baker

See also Agents of Social Control; Decriminalization and Legalization; Drug Policy; Drug War (War on Drugs); Moral Entrepreneurs

Further Readings

Burns, K., & Novick, L (2011). *Prohibition.* Retrieved from http://www.pbs.org/kenburns/prohibition/

Murdock, C. G. (2001). *Domesticating drink: Women, men, and alcohol in America, 1870–1940.* Baltimore, MD: Johns Hopkins University Press.

Okrent, D. (2011). *Last call: The rise and fall of prohibition.* New York, NY: Scribner.

Pegram, T. R. (1998). *Battling demon rum: The struggle for a dry America, 1800–1933.* New York, NY: Ivan R. Dee.

PROPERTY CRIME

Property crime can be defined as the unlawful damage or taking of the property of another without the use of force or threat. The Federal Bureau of Investigation identifies four types of property crime as part of their Uniform Crime Reporting program, which are as follows:

1. *Burglary (breaking or entering)* is the unlawful entering of a structure to commit a felony or a theft. Attempted forcible entry is included.

2. *Larceny/theft (except motor vehicle theft)* relates to the unlawful taking, carrying, leading, or riding away of property from the possession or constructive possession of another. Examples are thefts of bicycles, motor vehicle parts and accessories, shoplifting, pocket picking, or the stealing of any property or article that is not taken by force and violence or by fraud. Attempted larcenies are included. Embezzlement, confidence games, forgery, and check fraud are excluded.

3. *Motor vehicle theft* is the theft or attempted theft of a motor vehicle. A motor vehicle is self-propelled and runs on land surface and not on rails. Motorboats, construction equipment, airplanes, and farming equipment are specifically excluded from this category.

4. *Arson* refers to any willful or malicious burning or attempt to burn, with or without intent to defraud, a dwelling house, public building, motor vehicle or aircraft, or personal property of another.

This entry focuses on those who perpetrate property crime, discussing relevant patterns and providing explanations of this form of social deviance.

Property Crime Patterns

Overall, property crime rates have fluctuated significantly over time in the United States. From the early 1960s until the early 1980s, the United States experienced a steady and dramatic increase in property crime rates. After some fluctuation in the 1980s, a downward trend in property crime has occurred and has been sustained for approximately two decades. Trends for disaggregated property crime rates illustrate two key facts. First, larceny/theft is by far the most prevalent type of property crime and motor vehicle theft is the least. Second, the massive increases and decreases in total property crime rates observed over the 50-year period are primarily driven by changing rates of larceny/theft and burglary. There is comparatively little variation in motor vehicle theft rates.

In addition to variation over time in property crime rates, there are pronounced patterns by offender age and gender as well. It is notable that property crime is primarily a young adult phenomenon. Longitudinal studies of arrests show that the age range of most offenders is late 20s to early 30s. After this age, participation in property crime falls off notably. In terms of the distribution by sex, both burglary and motor vehicle theft are largely dominated by males, who account for more than 80% of arrestees. Larceny/theft, on the other hand, is more evenly distributed by gender.

Explanations

A number of criminological theories have been advanced over the years that provide reasonable explanations for these observed variations. In terms of temporal trends, routine activity theory, also called opportunity theory, can explain the massive increases in property crime during the 1960s and 1970s as a function of the increasing availability of suitable and attractive targets of theft, coupled with decreases in guardianship over this property, given a constant level of motivated offenders. During this period, a proliferation of easily portable but valuable and durable consumer goods fostered by continuing American prosperity resulted in an aggregate increase in desirable targets of theft. At the same time, significant changes in the structure of the labor force and the nature of work life, including people traveling longer to work thus leaving their homes unoccupied for longer periods of time, probably contributed to increases in burglary, for example. During the second half of the trend, any number of societal level changes could help explain the decrease, including an explosion in the home and retail security and surveillance industries and a reduction in motivated offenders due to historical changes in sentencing policies and other factors.

Sex differences in property crime are less pronounced than typically observed for violent crime but remain substantial nonetheless. Gendered theories of criminal behavior frequently attribute the differential to long-term socialization processes that channel males into more aggressive and risk-taking behaviors, while females are socialized to be more nurturing, caring, less risk taking, and generally more maternal. Criminal behavior, generally speaking, is not consistent with female social roles and patterns. In addition, the socialization process leads to sex segregation in the criminal underworld where women typically take subordinate roles to men when conducting criminal enterprises anyway. For burglary and motor vehicle theft, this explanation makes sense. The much smaller discrepancy between men and women for larceny/theft is also partly explainable. Unlike burglary (or robbery), for example, larceny/theft involves comparatively little risk of confrontation in the sense that by definition offenders do not have to confront a victim, nor do they directly enter a victim's home. It is therefore less inconsistent with female social roles. In addition, anticipated punishments for larceny/theft are substantially less than they are for burglary or motor vehicle theft, and so the discrepancy in an offender's cost-benefit analysis of the potential rewards of the crime versus the risk of committing it and getting caught are smaller.

Matthew R. Lee and Dari Green

See also Arson; Burglary; Larceny; Motor Vehicle Theft; Shoplifting; Violent Crime

Further Readings

Cohen, L. E., & Felson, M. (1979). Social change and crime rate trends: A routine activity approach. *American Sociological Review, 44*, 588–608.

Gottfredson, D. C., & Soule, D. A. (2005). The timing of property crime, violent crime, and substance use among juveniles. *Journal of Research in Crime and Delinquency, 42*, 110–120.

Gould, L. C. (1969). The changing structure of property crime in an affluent society. *Social Forces, 48,* 50–59.

PUBLIC SEX

Public sex is a product of specific social, cultural, and historical processes and is considered a deviant activity because participants are involved in sexual interactions that are generally considered to be private activities, and sex becomes a casual, recreational, impersonal activity potentially with multiple and unknown partners. Consequently, participants in public sex focus on the social management of their identity and their reputation to avoid stigmatization. Public sex in itself could also be regarded as an oxymoron since sex pertains to the private realm and the public dimension is not suitable for intimate interactions such as sexual activities: private usually refers to the individual and the personal, to secrecy and everything that has to be set apart from the "public." The "public" is firmly connected to what it is possible to see and can be seen, to visibility, and, also, to what is taken for granted. Analysis of this deviant activity must pay attention to the social performance of bodies and identities; to the characteristics of their sexual interaction; to the specificity of space and locales within which sexual interactions take place; to the pattern of communication and the different strategies and signaling practices participants enact to hide their practice, to recruit sexual partners, and to avoid stigmatization; and to the general social contexts and environments (different groups involved and interacting in those sites, architectural design of places where public sex is common, and social structural characteristics that contribute to the prevalence of it).

Public Versus Private

Space is not neutral but has to be considered as a product of complex economic, social, cultural, and power relations. To occupy a space is directly connected *to possessing a space* and *to being seen.* It is a question of visibility and of social recognition: If someone is recognized, he or she is given a place in a visibility regime. Otherwise, one is neither seen nor recognized, and sometimes misrecognized: Soon one is forced to be *out of sight* and *out of place.* Social identities are performed in a spatial recognition and are considered as *natural* inhabitants of that social space—some are stigmatized, others are tolerated, and some others are celebrated. Public sex, like any other social interaction in public space, is to be interpreted considering also the public sphere and the tacit mechanisms that contribute to the creation of specific actions embodied by standard citizens. Modern societies have contributed to the construction of a specific public space whose inhabitants are mainly universalized as males who have occupied and colonized public space and civil society, privatizing sex, (hetero)sexualizing, and gendering public space.

Those idealized citizens who are legitimately positioned within public settings are expected to have specific roles and identities, whose intimate and private aspects are classified according to the model of a public and rational individual. All the public aspects of civil society are perceived to contradict all of what can be defined as private interests. Public identity, thus defined, makes it difficult to consider all of the instances related to private matters such as gender, sex, and sexualities. The ideal liberal citizen still remains a male, middle class, white individual who controls all the questions that could arise or be claimed by subordinated or alternative individuals when dealing with private and intimate matters. Liberal theories have contributed to the removal of some aspects of social life (e.g., private, intimate relations and sexual interactions) from the formal definition of civil society and the construction of an abstracted, disembodied, and asexual public sphere. The public sphere remains a gendered and sexualized locale that offers symbolic and material resources especially to males. All intruders far from these standardized conditions are put in the process of becoming deviants. By making sex a personal or private matter, the male public sphere controls (females' and nonnormative males') sexuality, avoiding the development of public sexual cultures.

These assumptions explain why intimacy and sex are not that private, since they are mediated through spatial arrangements (e.g., separation of female toilets from male ones), mass media, advertising representation, and urban zoning. Public space is a context deeply marked by social divisions (e.g., gender, sexual practice, disabilities, and race) and participation in a public setting is firmly connected to the ways in which individuals interact with each other in recognizable and legitimate sexual interactions, manners, and gestures. It is a question of management of reputation and identity, gestures, and codes of communication repertoires, whose openness and unambiguousness are direct consequences of the perceived security of the site. The social definition of public sex and its social reactions heavily depend on social sexual arrangements, on situational events, on the characteristics of urban environment, and on its design and management. So, for example, bathrooms could be considered at the same time both public and private settings: Potential patrons share the space, those spaces are consequently available, but at the same time it is possible to get possession of portions of those locales. This example illustrates that the borders of public and private spaces are blurring, they strongly depend on social timing, on the quality of use of that space, on the risk of being seen by others, on private and public manifest, and on specific structural and power arrangements. When dealing with sexual interactions, the concepts of public and private are relative, produced by symbolic representations of what is legitimate and moral and what is not, and thus, those concepts are relational and closely interdependent.

Social Organization of Public Sex

Research on public sex has usually considered the coexistence and interaction (and potentially conflicts) of several differentiated social groups (e.g., general participants, marginal individuals, motorists, truck drivers, and police). Specific locations lead to a different coexistence of social worlds according to different social groups and social use of space and spatial interactions. Regarding what has been variously defined as "anonymous," "impersonal," or "instant" sex, deviance and criminological interpretations have mainly focused on the profiles of participants and especially on the repertory of techniques, verbal and nonverbal communication, used to recruit a potential sexual partner. A central activity in the spatialization of impersonal sexual intercourse is what is defined in homosexual argot as the process of "cruising," the active search for a potential sexual anonymous partner in different public settings. Through this activity, spatial users learn different communication techniques, which differ greatly according to the spatialization of sexual interaction (techniques and cruising activities of participants differ greatly if they participate in noncommercial sex in outdoor or semipublic places, e.g., adult cinemas' toilets). These techniques imply various communication repertoires whose analysis is quite compelling for deviance studies because they take into account classic interactionist research

areas such as face-to-face human interaction, game playing, face work, loss of face, and the consequent management of stigma. Researchers have mainly highlighted the characteristic of the silence of the interactions and the use of body signaling and cues, enacted by participants to construct privacy in public, to preserve the anonymity and impersonality of sexual interaction and to avoid social and criminal stigmatization because of social exposure, arrest by police, or simply aggression.

According to various qualitative research, public sex depends heavily on the nature and characteristics of the location; it is related to the time of conduct of sexual activities and to the different typologies of sexual activities, making any easy and simplistic generalization impossible, so it could vary greatly from dispersed to more structured patterns of interaction. In general terms, it is possible to state that the more spatially concentrated public sex is, the less ambiguous the interaction, and the more it is dispersed, the more complex the communication dynamics and interactional patterns. The primary aim of social actors is to distinguish potential participants from nonparticipants (e.g., intruders or potential aggressors) so that participation in public sex is firmly connected to the ways through which individuals interact with each other and social space in recognizable sexual interactions, manners, and gestures. It is mainly a question of management of reputation and signaling identity.

The openness and unambiguousness of cultural and communication repertoires are direct consequences of the perceived security of the site. These characteristics lead to the construction of public sex cultures (mainly men's public sex cultures) with their codes, communication practices, locations, and sexual practices, while women's public sex is a less researched and interpreted phenomenon.

According to the specificities of spatial arrangements, researchers usually distinguish between indoor locations (e.g., bathrooms of clubs or pubs) and outdoor locations (e.g., streets, parks, public toilets, alleys, beaches, parking lots, woods, docks, streets, tram/bus stations, and rest areas). In these locales, especially in outdoor settings, sexual activities and practices can be casual or more organized, and actors can choose specific and/or not specific locations. These flexible features can give rise to highly standardized or flexible sets of roles, so it is possible to consider regular, casual, and regulated public sex. In the case of gay men's public sexual encounters, activities are usually structured in specific and organized subcultures, as in the case of sex working and cruising. Social actors choose public sex for several reasons—as a means of sexual experimentation, for desire and pleasure, for fun, or to challenge moral and normative codes. So motivations for the activities vary from physical and emotional reasons to social and political concerns, and consequently, the nature of the participation in public sex can be impulsive or rational.

Attention must also be paid to the quality of the experience in locations intended for public sex: According to the results of the most significant research, the experiences of the individuals involved vary from depersonalization, bounding encounters, and connection to more open-ended meetings. Obviously, this depends on the characteristics of individuals' participation in public sex practices (there are regular and nonregular participants) and also on the level of involvement. In this case too, participants are more or less regular, varying from furtive to lasting involvement.

Public sex has been associated with deviance because of the overlapping of some stigmatized social groups (e.g., gay men or sex workers) with deviant sexual activities interpreted as promiscuous and considered causes of pandemics, such as AIDS (acquired immune deficiency syndrome), and with casual sex as a self-obsessed, irrational, and pathological conduct. Attention is to be paid to the adaptation and rationalization of this "deviant activity," since, as noted earlier, when social space is considered to be public, actors must be aware that the presence of uninvolved people in the sexual activity who could witness the sexual interactions can have consequences. For this reason, actors voluntarily involved in public sex pay attention to reputation management, especially in blatant cruising, to avoid stigmatization and association with discreditable characteristics.

Recently, new sociological perspectives such as queer theory have taken into account the topic of the risk of normalization relating to public sex, starting to consider this practice as a "space" of resistance against heterosexist culture: Queer politics strongly react against the privatization and heterosexualization of intimacy. A political and radical interpretation of public sex stresses the way through which identities are constructed and constituted in specific settings (e.g., public bathrooms) where the sexual interactions are enacted to counteract heterosexist production and consumption of space and to create new forms of public sex narratives and practices.

According to these new interpretations, public sex highlights the political meaning of radical and transgressive sexual activity as a space of identity construction and resistance by sexual minorities.

Cirus Rinaldi

See also Deviant Places; Male Prostitution; Street Hustling; Tearooms

Further Readings

Bell, D., & Binnie, J. (Eds.). (1995). *Mapping desire: Geographies of sexualities.* London, England: Routledge.

Califia, P. (1994). *Public sex: The culture of radical sex.* San Francisco, CA: Cleis Press.

Delph, E. W. (1978). *The silent community: Public homosexual encounters.* Beverly Hills, CA: Sage.

Humphreys, L. (1970). *Tearoom trade: Impersonal sex in public places.* Chicago, IL: Aldine.

Leap, W. L. (Ed.). (1999). *Public sex/gay space.* New York, NY: Columbia University Press.

PUNISHMENT AND RULE ENFORCEMENT

Societies develop rules to preserve peace and order. The source of these rules can be religious texts or traditions, customs, common values, societal judgments, or written laws. These norms are transferred to individuals during the socialization process and can be divided into two groups: formal and informal norms. Sources of informal norms are primarily social values, and the sanctions against violating these norms are defined based on their value to a specific society, culture, subculture, or family or social class. Formal norms are those that have been transformed into rule of laws or rules of an organization. Sanctions against the violation of a society's formal norms are enforced using the public authority. People who violate informal norms are punished with various levels of sanctions.

There are three levels of norms. In ascending order of importance, they are folkways, mores, and taboos. Each has implications for punishment and rule enforcement. Norms that are most important in achieving the goals of the group or are most central to the values of the group are the most regulated and the most stringently enforced. *Folkways* include the customary normal habitual ways a group does things. Examples of folkways are shaking hands, eating with certain utensils, and wearing a suit and tie on certain occasions. *Mores* are those ideas of right and wrong, which require certain acts and forbid others. Examples of mores are using foul language in the wrong social circumstance and issues of modesty. *Taboos* are forbidden mores. Examples include incest and the eating of certain meats.

The enforcement of these norms and the punishment associated with their violation are all culturally and social-structurally specific. Punishments can be enforced within the context of the criminal justice system or by the family, school, religion, and other social institutions. Sanctions may be applied when a player violates a rule in a football game, a taxpayer avoids paying taxes, a student fights in a classroom, a kid does not obey the rules at home, or a burglar tries to break into a home. This entry focuses on the goals and qualities of punishment and discusses punishment and rule enforcement by family, schools, and the criminal justice system.

Goals and Qualities of Punishment

Punishment is a phenomenon aimed at controlling, rehabilitating, and deterring the individuals who deviate from the societal norms, values, and laws. Punishment is the consequence that can be seen anywhere there is a rule. Areas such as family, school, business, and legal systems all transmit their rules to the individuals, and various sanctions are stipulated for the individuals who act in violation of these rules. These sanctions play an important role in preserving the order of society and cultural expectations.

Four principal aims underlie punishment: (1) retribution, (2) deterrence, (3) incapacitation, and (4) rehabilitation. *Retribution* is a reflection of the anger and revenge of the society against the offender and a sign of disapproval for the violation of the rule. The existing belief in most members of the society that wrongdoings should be punished points to this aim. Retribution provides the rationale for the modern punishment and sentencing approach known as "just deserts." Just deserts is part of the classical model that dictates the punishment should fit the crime. *Deterrence* reflects the necessity of the punishment, such that humans as rational beings can calculate the consequences of their actions and refrain from conducting any misdeeds. When members of the society know of the punishment of crimes, they will likely avoid violating rules or committing crimes. *Incapacitation* uses punishment methods,

such as imprisonment or exile, and is intended to prevent the deviant from repeating the offending act. *Rehabilitation* is the process of reclaiming the deviant as a beneficial member of society by treatment, education, and/or guidance.

The form and quality of the punishment has an important impact on the effective application of rules. To cultivate the belief that rules are implemented effectively, punishments must have some qualities, such as being swift, severe, just, and certain. The existence of the belief that no crime will go unpunished is highly effective in preventing individuals from engaging in criminal activities. Another important aspect of deterrence is the analogy between the nature and the results of the crime and the corresponding punishment. Many problems arise if punishments are disproportional to the offense. If punishments are lighter when compared with the gains of a committed act, an individual may make a profit-and-loss calculation and resort to offending. Also other members of the society may perceive the situation as a rewarding mechanism for crime and may become encouraged to commit crimes. On the other hand, if punishments are heavier when compared with the gains of the crime, individuals may see them as unjust and lose faith with the system, which reduces the deterrent effect of the punishment. If deterrence is to be effective, punishments should come soon after the deviant acts. A short interval between the crime and punishment is important for the process of deterrence.

Punishment and Rule Enforcement in the Family and Schools

The family is the major agent of socialization and location of punishment. Typically, the first place an individual experiences punishment is the family. Parents usually set rules and require their children to obey these rules. The family also has the ability to control the other areas of socialization, although resources play a part in determining this ability. The school is considered the second most important agent of socialization. Punishment in the schools is an accepted tool for enforcing discipline, creating order, and ensuring implementation of the rules. Various responsibilities related to proper dressing, attending lectures, and behaving in accordance with a predefined behavior set are assigned to the students in schools. The content and implementation methods of these rules vary among societies. Teachers actively participate in the application of rules in the schools.

Effective supervision, adequacy, and respectability of the teachers and the school administration, and their proper communication with the students are important in defining the students' behaviors in obeying or disobeying the rules.

Until recently, physical punishment of children who violate the rules was accepted as normal in many societies. However, physical punishment in school today is forbidden in many places. Creating a democratic environment and allowing participation of the students in the process of defining the rules and supporting these rules with various rewards and sanctions are socialization techniques that transferred the culture of a society to its members; although the significance of the role of schools in the transfer of culture has changed historically.

Punishment and Rule Enforcement in the Criminal Justice System

The criminal justice system implements necessary sanctions and punishments to prevent members of society from violating the rules of law. Even though punishment has many alternatives within the process of law enforcement, it is still indispensable. Previously, it was assumed that more severe punishments would deter criminals from committing crimes.

Within the context of criminal justice system reforms, various adjustments have been made to sentencing practices in recent decades, which has led to more humane forms of punishment based on concepts of restorative justice. Efforts continue to be made toward rehabilitating those convicted of criminal behavior with alternative methods including education, occupational training, and psychological counseling. Another recently expanding practice within the punishment process is the reparation of damages and compensation to the victim. The aim of this practice is to restore the victim and/or the victim's property to the state it was in before the damage, if possible, and if not, paying compensation for reparation of the damages.

Nurullah Altun

See also Delinquency; Norms and Societal Expectations; Social Control

Further Readings

Beccaria, C. (2003). An essay on crimes and punishments. In F. T. Cullen & R. Agnew (Eds.), *Criminological theory: Past to present essential readings* (pp. 20–22). Los Angeles, CA: Roxbury.

Dupper, D. R. (2010). *A new model of school discipline: Engaging students and preventing behavior problems.* Oxford, England: Oxford University Press.

Foucault, M. (1979). *Discipline and punish: The birth of the prison* (A. Sheridan, Trans.). New York, NY: Vintage Books.

Zimring, F. E., & Hawkings, G. J. (1973). *Deterrence: The legal threat in crime control.* Chicago, IL: University of Chicago Press.

PUNK SUBCULTURE

Even though the punk subculture has existed since the early 1970s and has been extensively researched, there is still no encompassing definition of what punk is, neither by researchers nor by participants. Instead, the saying goes that there is a definition of punk for every punk in the world. Although the events surrounding the band Sex Pistols and punk in London in the mid-1970s, as well as the punk style of mohawks and studded leather jackets that emerged in the early 1980s in England, are what most people associate with the subculture, punk today is a global phenomenon, present on every continent and in several different styles. There are punks who drink and do drugs, and there are punks who refuse both alcohol and drugs. There are political punks and there are those who are apolitical, punks who refute religion and others who include religion in their subcultural style (e.g., Hare Krishna punks, Taqwacore, and Christian punks). Some punks signal their adherence through conspicuous style, whereas others denote such a style to be spectacular and ignorant.

Still the research on punk points to consistency within these variations in terms of the defining traits. First, punk, it is argued, is a distinction in contrast to a perceived mainstream—differing from pop music, the general public, the capitalist society, parents, authorities, and other punks. Second, punk is said to be a freedom from the restrictions imposed by this mainstream, be they collective or individual. Third is a focus on do-it-yourself (DIY)—that is, creating one's own music and infrastructure both as a means to resist this mainstream and maintain control over the subculture.

Although the origins of punk have been and are still being discussed, researchers and participants agree on punk being developed in the United States in the late 1960s and early 1970s in New York City and Detroit. Proto-punk bands, such as the

New York Dolls, MC5, and the Stooges, refused the image of the contemporary rock musician as a musically virtuous and posturing super star. Instead the lack of musical talent was stressed and songs were kept fast and short. The burgeoning subculture got its name "punk" from a fanzine with the same name that documented the proto-punk scene in the early 1970s around the club CBGBs on the Lower East Side of Manhattan in New York City. They were "punks"; the lowest of the low, those who had been rejected by society. Nevertheless, they defined their deviance as something positive; they were outsiders yet worked collectively to create their own music and their own rules. The first punk bands such as the Ramones and Television stressed their own lack of musical talent and dressed and acted as if they had just taken the step from the audience to the stage. This blurring of the border between the performer and the audience, that anyone can, and should, grab a guitar and start a band, influenced members of the audience and the subculture caught on.

In its early days, however, punk was limited to a few hundred people on the East Coast of the United States. But one of the patrons at the CBGBs, and also the former manager of New York Dolls, was Malcolm McLaren, who brought home photos and recordings to London to influence a forming English band. The band named itself Sex Pistols and did its first show in late 1975. Similar to its American counterpart, English punk focused on a DIY-spirit that urged members of the audience to become performers themselves—either by starting bands, organizing shows, or putting out fanzines. A major difference between English and American punk was the force by which the former attacked the general public. Early American punk had been rather anonymous and local; participants considered themselves to be different from the rest of society, but this distinction had mainly been against contemporary rock music. The London punks also defined themselves as rejected by society, but at the same time, they rejected that very society through their provocative and confrontational style: Clothes were ripped apart and put together with safety pins and multiple zippers, hair was spiked and dyed, and foul language was used both verbally and written on clothes. The subculture was not confined to a small club anymore but was played on a public stage set in the streets and in the spotlight of the media. Punk's public rejection of authorities and the general public made it the prime example of subcultural studies that in the late 1970s and early 1980s defined

subcultures as a stylistic resistance against the dominant culture. Punk, these researchers argued, was a symbolic means for working class youth to address the problems that they encountered in school, on the job market, and through media. Punks' allegedly working class background has since then been questioned by later research arguing that English punk emerged from the art schools rather than the streets, pointing to several key actors' art school background. More recent studies on contemporary punk show a diversity of participants, ranging from the working class to the upper middle class.

As this first wave of punk research focused on resistance and style, punk was said to have died when it attracted the very same mainstream it had resisted. When subcultural objects were picked up by fashion designers and the mass media ran stories explaining it, punk had lost its authenticity and had become just another commodity. This was supported by the development within the subculture to move away from what punk had become. Some bands chose the more neutral label "new wave," while others, such as the anarchist collective Crass and the second wave of English punk, stressed an even more political and radical stance. With the media coverage that had surrounded bands like Sex Pistols, punk spread over the European continent and back to North America. The music became harder, the style even more confrontational with spiked, dyed hair; studded leather jackets; and combat boots. This new style was referred to as "hardcore punk" to distance it from earlier, less committed versions of punk. In line with this emphasis of commitment, researchers began to address punks' style and appearances as signs of subcultural status. Relying on fieldwork and interviews, they investigated the meanings that punks attached to stylistic objects, claiming that the more radical and distanced from the mainstream society a participant was, the more committed he or she was. Still there is no consensus among researchers as to what punk signifies or what attracts participants in the first place. While some withhold that punk is a *working class resistance* to the dominant culture, others argue that punk provides an *alternative community* for those who seek change. A third explanation is the more postmodern approach that punk is an *individual distinction* that sets participants apart from what they conceive as the bland and boring mainstream.

Hardcore punk in turn led to the definition of different punk styles. Anarcho-punk developed across Europe in the early 1980s with a clear political and activist take on both freedom and DIY, while style was downplayed. Straight edge punk arose on the U.S. East Coast in the mid-1980s, and its adherents claimed to have an "edge" on other punks by not drinking, smoking, or using drugs. Although dissimilar in many ways, both straight edge and anarcho-punk share an emphasis on downplaying conspicuous style in favor of action as well as the focus on vegetarianism. Anarcho-punk had expanded punk's focus on freedom to include those mistreated by society but who nevertheless were outside of punk in its stress on vegetarianism, anticapitalism, antihomophobia, and antisexism. Many straight edge punks took up the cause of animal rights to include antispeciesism and veganism. Together, anarcho-punk and straight edge punk have had a huge impact on what is today referred to as DIY-punk. Furthering the call for action over style, DIY-punks connect the DIY-spirit to anticapitalism, linking punk to political action.

Hardcore punk also brought changes in terms of style and appearances. The American and English punks of the 1970s sported a heterogeneous style that often included mixing masculine and feminine elements. The 1980s punk, on the other hand, introduced the punk uniform with mohawks, studded leather jackets, chains, and boots. Punk style took on a more masculine emphasis. This coincided with a change in audience behavior. The pogo dancing of the 1970s—in which the audience jumped up and down to the music—was replaced by new styles of dancing as the music became faster. Slam dancing and thrashing became popular. Here members of the audience violently push each other around in front of the stage. Feminist researchers have pointed out that the consequence of this was that female participants were pushed out from actively participating in the subculture. From the beginning, female participants have had a huge impact on the punk subculture, as both performers and consumers. Hardcore punk changed this and the hardcore punk bands and fans of the 1980s were almost entirely male.

Although some parts of the punk subculture, such as DIY-punk, do include a fair share of women today, punk remains a male-dominated subculture. To be sure, punk has included an antisexist stance since the late 1970s, but this has been largely directed against a sexist mainstream society and not within punk. The rise of Riot Grrrl punk in the early 1990s meant a critique against male domination within punk combining feminism and gender equality with an anticapitalist stance. As part of the political and ideological fractions of the subculture, Riot Grrrl and the DIY-punks have raised the issue of female participants within the subculture.

Similarly, even though North American and European punks have had an antiracist focus since the beginning, the punk subculture remains largely white in the West. The London punks of the late 1970s did have clear ties with the reggae subculture resulting in Bob Marley's 1976 song "Punky Reggae Party" and punk bands, such as the Clash, mixing punk and reggae and participating in the Rock Against Racism campaign. Similarly, the American hardcore punk had ties to both reggae and hip-hop in the 1980s, with one of the most defining hardcore bands being the all black reggae/hardcore band Bad Brains in Washington, D.C. The hip-hop group Beastie Boys, for example, started out as a hardcore punk band in New York City. Nevertheless, these are exceptions to Western punk's whiteness. The rise of racist punks and skinheads in the vicinity of and within the subculture has also reinforced the image of punk as being white.

Globally, however, the punk subculture is present in every continent and has been since the Sex Pistols and the Clash helped establish the subculture in countries such as Japan, Iran, Brazil, Australia, and Israel. The international success of melodic hardcore punk in the mid-1990s with bands such as Bad Religion, Rancid, and Offspring reinforced punk's global character, especially in South America, Northern Africa, and Asia. Malaysia, Turkey, Mexico, and Japan are examples of countries in which punk has existed since the 1980s and that have had an impact on the punk subculture as a whole. The punk subculture today is kept together by bands touring the world playing in both large music festivals and smaller punk squats, global fanzines, punk record labels, online forums, and distribution of records and merchandise through the Internet.

Erik Hannerz

See also Moral Panics; Skinheads; Straight Edge; Subculture; Vegetarianism and Veganism

Further Readings

Duncombe, S., & Tremblay, M. (2011). *White riot: Punk rock and the politics of race.* London, England: Verso.

Hebdige, D. (1979). *Subculture: The meaning of style.* London, England: Routledge.

Leblanc, L. (1999). *Pretty in punk: Girls' gender resistance in a boys subculture.* New Brunswick, NJ: Rutgers University Press.

O'Connor, A. (2008). *Punk record labels and the struggle for autonomy: The emergence of DIY.* Plymouth, MA: Lexington Books.

Thompson, S. (2004). *Punk productions: Unfinished business.* Albany: State University of New York Press.

Williams, P. J. (2011). *Subcultural theory: Traditions and concepts.* Cambridge, England: Polity Press.

QUALITATIVE METHODS IN STUDYING DEVIANCE

Any research study in the social sciences seeks to provide understandings about a particular phenomenon, including describing the situation under study, explaining how and why the phenomenon operates as it does, what other activities and conditions are related to the occurrence of this issue, and how those who are involved in or aware of the issue being studied are experiencing and responding to it. This means that social science attempts to explain what something is, where it fits into a setting and group of people, and what its consequences are for those involved and others. These are ambitious goals. When the focus of study is something deviant, extra challenges may be introduced, such as people trying to hide their involvement, limited public awareness of the deviant activity, and communities trying to deny the existence of this "unwanted" or "bad" behavior in their midst.

All of this means that researchers need to be dedicated, resourceful, and perhaps a bit creative when trying to gain a thorough understanding of the deviance under study. All of this also means that qualitative research methods are likely to be the most beneficial approach to getting information, especially "inside" information about how, why, where, by whom, when, and with what consequences the particular form of deviance operates.

To understand what it is like to be involved in any activity, deviant activities included, it is important to get the views and experiences of people who are involved. Simply gathering statistical information about deviant persons' demographics, or how often they engage in some particular activity or whether they also engage in various other (deviant and nondeviant) activities, is only a small part of understanding. To understand the experience of a deviant activity, it is necessary to either talk with such persons or get to know them and spend time with them, including the time when they are engaging in whatever deviant activity the researcher is interested in. Qualitative methods allow researchers to get "inside" the deviant activity or group and see and experience the topic of study from the perspective of someone who is a regular member of the deviant community. Quantitative methods typically do not allow for such insights.

Three primary qualitative method approaches are especially valuable for studying deviance: (1) interviews, (2) participant observation, and (3) reviews of social artifacts (e.g., records and documents produced and/or used by the purveyors of the form of deviance being studied). Each of these approaches and the unique contributions they provide to the study of deviance will be discussed next.

Interviews

Interviews, perhaps the most commonly used qualitative research method, require talking with people about their experiences, views, and expectations and understanding a particular topic. Interviews can take any of a number of forms, including the highly structured interview in which very specific questions are asked of all persons interviewed, with all questions asked the same way, in the same order, essentially a questionnaire that the interviewee answers verbally. Such highly structured interviews are best used when the researcher already knows a fair amount about the topic being studied and can know what the important and relevant questions are prior to doing the first interview. Although significantly different, the highly structured interview is the most similar of all qualitative methods to quantitative research approaches.

In contrast to the highly structured interview is the unstructured interview. An unstructured interview is typically used when a researcher does not know very much about the type of deviance being studied. This approach to interviewing would appear to an observer as a free-flowing conversation between the researcher and the interviewee where the researcher asks very general questions and allows the conversation to go where the interviewee takes it. The researcher knows, going into this type of interview, that he or she wants to know about a particular set of "big issues" (e.g., what type of people are involved, why do you do these activities, and what makes this enjoyable for you), and the researcher simply needs to be sure that at some point during the conversation, the interviewee discusses these issues. Think of the unstructured interview as an exploration by the researchers in which they ask a few questions but mostly listen to the interviewee, so that they can start to understand the big issues involved and move toward an understanding of what the particular type of deviance being studied is all about.

In practice, most qualitative interviews about deviance have characteristics of both structured and unstructured interviews. It is important to recognize that qualitative interviews come in myriad forms and could be placed along a continuum from structured to unstructured. The particular approach that a researcher employs depends on his or her existing degree of knowledge about the form of deviance being studied, his or her relationship with the persons being interviewed, and the situations in which interviews are conducted. Typically, unstructured interviews are longer and more in-depth than structured interviews, and the more familiar a researcher is with the persons being interviewed, the more advantageous is the unstructured approach.

Regardless of the specific type of interview that a researcher conducts with persons involved in a form of deviance, it is imperative that the researcher treats his or her interviewees with respect and courtesy. While the interviews are being done to further our understanding of some form of socially unacceptable and probably stigmatized behavior, persons who are involved in such deviance likely do not see or think of their actions as "bad," "wrong," or "deviant." These are simply activities they enjoy doing. If researchers fail to show respect for those they interview, they will likely get few interviews and very little information from those who do participate.

Participant observation is the qualitative approach of both participating in (to some degree) the deviant behaviors and settings being studied and observing such people, places, and activities. Similar to interviews, participant observation can take any of a number of forms. Some approaches of participant observation emphasize the participant role, other approaches emphasize the observer role. In the former, researchers immerse themselves in the world they are studying and become active members of the community and group under study. For some, this means engaging in the deviant behavior being studied; for others, it means being in the setting and present when deviant acts occur, allowing the researcher an "up close" view from the inside. Other participant observers take the role of being in and around the deviant setting and activities but staying on the sidelines and observing.

Participant observation in the study of deviance can also occur with or without the people who are being observed/studied knowing that the researcher is a researcher. When a researcher is "open," he or she is honest and shares with those being studied that he or she is in fact observing and conducting research. A "closed" approach is covert, meaning that the researcher enters the setting and activities of those being studied but presents himself or herself just as anyone else would who is new to the setting. Although an open approach may be considered more ethical and honest, it also carries the potential problems of those who are told, "Hi, I'm here to watch you and study you," either refusing to allow the researcher access or behaving differently (because they know they are being watched and studied). Covert approaches are typically considered to provide researchers with a more "real" view of the deviant behavior and settings, but it also means that researchers may find themselves in positions where they would be expected to participate in activities they may find distasteful or unacceptable. After all, if they are present in the setting and pretending to be just another one of the people involved, they will probably be expected to take part.

Quantitative Methods in Studying Deviance   567

Gaining access to a group or setting involved in a particular form of deviance can be a challenge. Most deviant settings and groups do not advertise for new members, do not publicize their activities, and do not always welcome newcomers with open arms. After all, these are people who have been marginalized and in at least some ways stigmatized by others; it only makes sense that they might be leery of newcomers. This all means that the qualitative participant observation researcher needs to think creatively of ways to become involved, and especially if engaging in covert approaches to observation, he or she has to have a believable reason and espoused motivation for being involved.

An alternative way, commonly used to supplement rather than replace interviews and/or participant observation, is to examine the "things" that are used by and produced by members of the deviant community being studied. Here, the researcher needs to recognize that things such as records of a deviant group's activities (any official minutes, newsletters, Internet pages, and blogs from individuals who engage in the deviant activity being studied) and actual items used in the conduct of the deviant activities (paraphernalia of drug users, "toys," and apparatus of people involved in particular sexual activities) can tell a researcher much about a particular form of deviance. Some information may be easily available (e.g., records of chat room conversations or newsletters of "clubs") and others accessible only when provided by practitioners of the deviance (e.g., displays of restraints, clothing, and sex toys from an S&M club or photographs of group activities). Gaining access to such artifacts and documents may require some creativity on the part of the qualitative researcher.

One of the unique challenges of employing qualitative methods in the study of deviance is the need to get one's research approach reviewed and approved by an institutional review board prior to beginning any research activities. Although all research, including quantitative research, that involves gathering data from people must be reviewed and approved by an institutional review board, the fact that qualitative methods necessitate "getting your hands dirty" by meeting, knowing the identities of those involved, and perhaps becoming a part of a setting where the deviant behavior being studied is occurring requires extra precautions to make sure no one being studied is harmed by the acts of the researcher.

Richard Tewksbury

See also Autoethnography; Edge Ethnography; Ethnography and Deviance; Interviews; Participant Observation

Further Readings

Miller, J. M. (1995). Covert participant observation: Reconsidering the least used method. *Journal of Contemporary Criminal Justice, 11*(2), 97–105.
Miller, J. M., & Tewksbury, R. (2001). *Extreme methods: Innovative approaches to social science research.* Boston, MA: Allyn & Bacon.
Tewksbury, R. (2009). Qualitative versus quantitative methods: Understanding why qualitative methods are superior for criminology and criminal justice. *Journal of Theoretical and Philosophical Criminology, 1*(1), 38–58.

QUANTITATIVE METHODS IN STUDYING DEVIANCE

Quantitative methods involve the gathering, analysis, and presentation of numerical data. Welfare agencies, legislators, policymakers, and other groups concerned with alleviating or containing social problems rely heavily on numerical data on deviants (e.g., criminal offenders, drug users, the poor, and the homeless) to better understand these social problems and to evaluate social and legal programs. Social scientists use quantitative methods to determine the extent of deviance and to investigate the causes and consequences of deviant attitudes, behaviors, and conditions. This entry provides an overview of quantitative methods, the primary sources of numerical data on deviance and ways of analyzing and presenting it, and the differences between quantitative and qualitative methods in studying deviance.

Sources of Numerical Data on Deviance

There are two primary sources of numerical data on deviance: (1) official statistics and (2) unofficial statistics. Official statistics refer to numerical data that are gathered, analyzed, and presented by national government agencies and are often compiled by international entities such as the United Nations Interregional Crime and Justice Research Institute. The Federal Bureau of Investigation collects perhaps the most well-known official statistics on deviance in the United States: the Uniform Crime Reports (UCR). Published annually, the

UCR record crimes reported to local law enforcement agencies and the number of arrests made. Other official statistics on deviance include data on suicides from the National Center for Injury Prevention and Control, data on drug abuse from the Drug Abuse Warning Network, and census data on poverty and homelessness. Official statistics are invaluable for those interested in deviance, not the least because the aim of official statistics is to include the entire population of interest (e.g., all suicides in a given country). For researchers, official data are also relatively inexpensive to obtain and quick to access since they have already been collected and published. Furthermore, official statistics are available as far back as they have been kept. Nonetheless, despite rapid advances in record keeping, certain validity and reliability problems plague official statistics.

Many have falsely assumed that official statistics accurately reflect the prevalence of deviance in society. Now, however, most accept that official statistics must be interpreted with care. For instance, on the whole, the UCR underreport crime, although the situation for different crimes and law enforcement agencies varies depending on a range of political and bureaucratic factors. Surveys of those engaged in criminal activities and of crime victims suggest that less than half of all crimes get reported to the police, which calls into question the validity of the UCR data. There are various reasons for this: Victims might consider some crimes too trivial to report, they might fear revenge, or they do not want to involve the police authorities because they themselves are involved in illegal behavior. The case of underreporting of crime reflects the fact that much deviance is hidden from view due to its stigmatized and often illegitimate status.

Social scientists interested in deviance often collect their own, unofficial statistics (i.e., numerical data not verified or confirmed by a national government agency). This approach allows researchers more room to maneuver, without being hampered by the constraints inherent to official sources and official definitions. The most popular method of gathering unofficial statistics is with the use of questionnaires. This type of research involves surveying a representative sample of the larger population to inquire about their attitudes, values, characteristics, and experiences. If the sampling is done properly, the responses should accurately represent the larger population from where the sample was drawn.

Surveys carried out regularly over long periods yield important insights into various forms of deviance. An example of a large-scale survey used for gathering unofficial statistics on deviance is the ongoing "Monitoring the Future" (MTF) study, conducted by the Institute for Social Research at the University of Michigan. The MTF study surveys the behaviors, attitudes, and values of American secondary school students, college students, and young adults and tracks trends in legal and illicit drug use, among other things. Surveys are a major source of information on deviance and are preferred by influential groups, such as legislators and policymakers, because they are usually more objective and generalizable than other, more qualitative methods. However, conducting survey research, as with collecting unofficial statistics in general, is more expensive and time-consuming than using official statistics. Other methods of gathering unofficial statistics range from laboratory and field experiments to sampling the earnings records of drug-selling gangs.

Analyzing and Presenting Numerical Data on Deviance

There are two ways of analyzing and presenting numerical data: (1) descriptive statistics and (2) inferential statistics. Descriptive statistics are used to describe the basic properties of the data and measurements used in a given study. The goal of descriptive statistics is to summarize and present large quantities of data in a reasonable manner. Examples of common descriptive statistics include averages, percentages, rates, and distributions. As an example, the MTF study reports percentages on the prevalence of cigarette smoking among 8th, 10th, and 12th graders in its sample. It should be noted that reducing a large number of observations to one measure, such as an average, risks distorting the data or losing sight of important information. Nevertheless, despite these limitations, descriptive statistics are tools that offer valuable insights and are fundamental to much quantitative research.

Descriptive statistics are distinguished from inferential statistics. Whereas descriptive statistics are only used to describe your sample, inferential statistics are used to draw conclusions (infer) about the larger population from which the sample data were drawn. Examples of inferential statistics relating to deviance are quite common in our daily lives. Media outlets, for example, regularly run news reports on what percentage of the American adult population supports the legalization of marijuana or same-sex marriage. In these cases, not every single adult has been surveyed about their attitudes toward the legalization of marijuana or same-sex marriage. Instead, a representative sample of the population has been surveyed with the goal of drawing conclusions about the population and its various subgroups, based on race, class, gender, and education.

Other examples of inferential statistics include making predictions and testing whether observed differences between subgroups are significant or might have happened by chance. Inferential statistics can, for instance, be used to determine the probability of whether observed differences between groups are real and should, therefore, emerge with regularity in other studies using comparable data sources. For instance, a famous survey of the sexual behavior of Americans tested for whether the observed difference in the same-sex sexual activity of men and women was statistically significant. Inferential statistics are the cornerstone of quantitative methods because they allow researchers to generalize about the larger population and because it is nearly impossible, given the time and financial constraints, to survey the whole population of interest.

Quantitative Versus Qualitative Methods in Studying Deviance

Quantitative methods are distinguished from qualitative methods (i.e., methods that do not produce data expressed in numerical form). Instead of numbers presented as statistics, tables, or charts, researchers using qualitative methods use quotes, observations, or descriptions of deviant attitudes, behaviors, or conditions to support their claims. Examples of qualitative methods include unstructured interviews and participant observation. The latter method, for instance, studies behavior in its natural setting: where a researcher might, for example, study a white supremacist group up close and personal. Quantitative methods, especially surveys, remain the methodology of choice for most social scientists. However, a disproportionate number of scholars specializing in deviance opt for qualitative methods, particularly participant observation.

Neither quantitative methods nor qualitative methods are superior to the other. Instead, the two approaches are complementary. Each approach has its advantages and disadvantages and choosing between them, or opting for a mix of the two,

depends to a large extent on the questions the researcher is interested in. Whereas quantitative methods in studying deviance are generally used to answer questions of "what" deviant beliefs people have, "what" deviant acts they are engaged in, or "what" social factors strongly correlate with certain deviant behaviors, qualitative methods are generally used to address questions of "why" people hold said beliefs or "how" people go about committing certain deviant acts. For instance, a survey can identify what factors predict continued marijuana use; however, participant observation or in-depth interviews would be better to learn about how people learn to smoke marijuana for pleasure.

Comparing and contrasting surveys and participant observation highlights some of the key differences between quantitative methods and qualitative methods. Surveys are standardized, and researchers rarely, if ever, meet their many respondents eye to eye. Respondents in objective and carefully administered surveys are selected using a randomized and representative sample, which means that its results can be generalized to the larger population from which it was drawn. This also means that surveys can establish correlations between specific social factors and deviance.

In contrast, participant observation allows one to study many fewer people than a typical survey. However, because researchers engaged in participant observation interact closely with their subjects, often over long periods, it yields deeper information about the people being studied. Also, in contrast with the more objective approach of survey research, researchers using participant observation rely heavily on their own and their subjects' subjectivity and their personal relationship. This way, researchers are often able to get at information that is often hidden from view when using survey data. Nevertheless, participant observation is more time-consuming than survey research and lacks the same generalizability and explanatory power due to the low number of subjects, which also tend to be solicited, using referrals from other deviants.

Conclusion

Quantitative methods refer to the gathering, analysis, and presentation of numerical data. Social scientists use quantitative methods to measure the extent of deviance and to study the causes and consequences of deviant attitudes, behaviors, and conditions. The two primary sources of numerical data on deviance are official statistics and unofficial statistics. Descriptive statistics are used to describe the specific data we have at our disposal, whereas inferential statistics are used to draw conclusions about general conditions. Quantitative methods are generally distinguished from qualitative methods, but neither method is superior to the other. Instead, the two approaches are complementary, and a mixed-methods approach can give a researcher in the field of deviance the best of both worlds: the in-depth and contextualized insights of qualitative methods, coupled with the objective results and compelling explanatory power of quantitative methods.

Guðmundur Oddsson

See also Crime Statistics; Ethics and Deviance Research; Institutional Review Boards and Studying Deviance; Qualitative Methods in Studying Deviance; Triangulation

Further Readings

Bachman, J. G., O'Malley, P. M., Schulenberg, J. E., Johnston, L. D., Freedman-Doan, P., & Messersmith, E. E. (2007). *The education–drug use connection: How successes and failures in school relate to adolescent smoking, drinking, drug use, and delinquency*. New York, NY: Taylor & Francis.

Bailey, S. L., Flewelling, R. L., & Valley, J. (1992). Predicting continued use of marijuana among adolescents: The relative influence of drug-specific and social context factors. *Journal of Health and Social Behavior, 33*(1), 51–65.

Kovandzic, T. V., Vieraitis, L. M., & Boots, D. P. (2009). Does the death penalty save lives? New evidence from state panel data, 1977 to 2006. *Criminology & Public Policy, 8*(4), 803–843.

Laumann, E. O., Gagnon, J. H., Michael, R. T., & Michaels, S. (1994). *The social organization of sexuality: Sexual practices in the United States*. Chicago, IL: University of Chicago Press.

Levitt, S. D., & Venkatesh, S. A. (2000). An economic analysis of a drug-selling gang's finances. *Quarterly Journal of Economics, 115*(3), 755–789.

Lieberson, S., & Bell, E. O. (1992). Children's first names: An empirical study of social taste. *American Journal of Sociology, 98*(3), 511–554.

Milgram, S. (1974). *Obedience to authority: An experimental view*. New York, NY: Harper & Row.

Neuman, W. L. (2009). *Social research methods: Qualitative and quantitative approaches* (7th ed.). Upper Saddle River, NJ: Pearson.

Sharpe, E. B. (2002). Culture, institutions, and urban officials' responses to morality issues. *Political Research Quarterly, 55*(4), 861–883.

QUEER NATION

Queer Nation was a radical queer activist organization formed in 1990 by members of ACT UP who believed that ACT UP (an organization dedicated to political action on behalf of people with AIDS/HIV [acquired immune deficiency syndrome/human immunodeficiency virus]) did not represent their concerns. The group burst onto the scene at New York's Gay Pride celebration in 1990 where it passed out its Queer Manifesto, which boldly proclaimed, "I Hate Straights!" and "Queers Read This!" Queer Nation's antiassimilationist stance and controversial activism practices, including publicly outing celebrities and staging kiss-ins, made it a deviant group in the eyes of many gay and lesbian people and heterosexual people alike. Queer Nation was also different from other organizations in that it never became a formally organized group. It did not have a charter or a budget, but rather, it wished simply to remain an organization of individuals with the freedom to take whatever actions it deemed necessary.

Despite its name, Queer Nation was not a separatist movement. Indeed, as Lauren Berlant and Elizabeth Freeman assert, disidentification with U.S. nationality was not even an option for queers due to the need for state support for people with HIV/AIDS and the continued policing of nonnormative sexual expressions. Rather, Queer Nation was an attempt to show that queers make up the nation just as heterosexuals do. It sought to make queers visible within the nation while fighting homophobia and heterosexism. As Henry Abelove states, "What Queer Nation really means is America."

Defining a Queer Nation

The label "deviant" would likely be rejected by members of Queer Nation for the same reason that labels such as "gay" and "lesbian" were—they represent limited, exclusionary categories imposed on marginalized groups by those in power. Conversely, some queer nationals may also view a "deviant" label as a point of pride, for Queer Nation actively sought to be inclusive of the most marginalized and excluded segments of the lesbian and gay population, such as queers of color, lower- and working-class queers, bisexuals, and other sexual groups not well represented by more mainstream gay organizations (e.g., sadomasochists). This seemingly contradictory stance is characteristic of Queer Nation, whose very name offers its first contradiction: *Queer* signals difference, while *nation* suggests sameness. As Allan Bérubé and Jeffrey Escoffier suggest, Queer Nation was replete with these contradictions. On the one hand, members rejected identity labels, and on the other hand, they affirmed their queer identity. They rejected mainstream assimilation yet demanded the mainstream's attention with their radical tactics. They sought to include those who felt marginalized by society but threatened to marginalize those whose difference did not conform to the new Queer Nation. These internal contradictions may have been the cause of Queer Nation's rapid dissolution; by the mid-1990s, most chapters of Queer Nation were defunct.

However, these very contradictions are what made Queer Nation so queer. In embracing the term *queer*, Queer Nation was, in fact, trying to highlight difference and emphasize nonnormativity in stark contrast to more mainstream approaches to gay rights, which asserted that lesbians and gay people were just like heterosexuals and should be included in mainstream, heterosexual society. Queer Nation argued that queers *were* different from heterosexuals but that difference did not justify oppression. Moreover, queer nationalists took issue with the perceived white, middle-class identity of mainstream gay and lesbian organizations. To mobilize a large gay and lesbian movement, mainstream gay and lesbian organizations emphasized similarity on the basis of sexuality, which often elided differences of race, gender, class, and even sexuality within the movement. Queer Nation tried to remedy this marginalization by rejecting the labels associated with traditional gay and lesbian politics and instead forming a movement based on the affirmation of difference. Thus, "queer" was less an identity label than an announcement that one celebrated difference and rejected assimilationist politics. In many respects, then, Queer Nation was consonant with the new queer theory taking root in the academy at the same time. Queer theory was a poststructuralist critique of identity that sought to deconstruct the homo/hetero binary in Western culture and place sexuality at the center of cultural analysis. Like Queer Nation, queer theory actively opposed labels such as "gay" and "lesbian" because of its exclusionary connotations related to

gay liberation. But also like Queer Nation, queer theory's refusal to name a subject or define what "queer" meant earned it much criticism. In the context of Queer Nation, the lack of clarity surrounding the word *queer* meant that some simply used it as a synonym for "gay and lesbian," while others used it to signify a radical inclusion of all marginalized sexualities, and still others believed that "queer" was the basis for creating a more fluid concept of sexuality. This same lack of clarity found its way into Queer Nation's actions, as well, and sometimes resulted in messages that were not readily recognizable to the public.

Queer Tactics

Unlike many activist groups, Queer Nation was extremely decentralized and had no governing body that set the goals and agenda of the organization. Each chapter was autonomous, and within each chapter, there existed several subgroups that focused on particular issues. Some of these subgroups included LABIA (Lesbians and Bisexuals in Action), SHOP (Suburban Homosexual Outreach Program), ASLUT (Artists Slaving Under Tyranny), HI MOM (Homosexual Ideological Mobilization against the Military), and many others. Subgroups would often organize actions independently of the rest of the chapter that focused on the subgroup's particular priorities, which likely contributed to the perceived lack of coherent messaging from Queer Nation as a whole.

One of the actions that Queer Nation became most well-known for was the kiss-in. During a kiss-in, large groups of same-sex couples would meet in a designated area and begin kissing on cue. Kiss-ins would generally occur in a highly visible area and were meant to promote queer visibility—a primary goal of Queer Nation. Akin to the kiss-ins were Queer Nights Out, in which a group of queers would "invade" a straight bar and stage a kiss-in or play games such as spin the bottle to mimic mundane heterosexual acts. Similar in its goals were the actions of SHOP, wherein a group of queers would descend on a suburban shopping mall dressed in ostentatiously queer attire, march through the mall, mingle with shoppers, and pass out safe-sex information. These actions served to highlight the tacit heterosexuality of the public space and the invisibility and vulnerability of queer people within it.

Queer Nation also pursued a media strategy of queering mainstream advertisements to contest the invisibility of queer culture within mainstream culture and the corporate practice of covertly targeting the "gay market" by using gay subcultural semiotics that heterosexuals would not readily recognize. For example, a Queer Nation New York campaign changed the "P" in Gap to a "Y" so that it read "Gay." As Berlant and Freeman point out, this had a double meaning. First, Queer Nation was outing the queer models often used in Gap advertisements. Second, it was "outing" the corporation for using gay style without acknowledging its queer origins. Other Queer Nation media campaigns parodied the "gay business" approach favored by gay liberationists, which advocated assimilation and equated queer citizenship with capitalist legitimation.

Queer Nation also formed a group called the Pink Panthers, whose goal was to patrol the borders of gay neighborhoods to deter would-be gay bashers. The group's motto, "Queers Bash Back," was meant to counter the image of the effeminate gay man who could not defend himself, and the group would sometimes graffiti its logo across billboards after a gay bashing.

With so many action groups and a polymorphous definition of "queer," it is understandable that many people saw only contradictions and incoherencies in Queer Nation. Berlant and Freeman suggest that Queer Nation, in fact, did not seek theoretical coherence in its actions, but rather, it allowed its tactics to be "imagined in the streets." Mary Gray concedes that Queer Nation never found a way to effectively communicate its critique of identity, but she argues that the media played a large role in this by constantly reducing the group to "gays and lesbians" in its portrayals. For instance, a kiss-in meant to draw attention to the arraignment of a man accused of gay bashing was interpreted by the media as merely an act of "gay and lesbian visibility." These portrayals, Gray argues, solidified Queer Nation's image as only a gay and lesbian visibility group, discounting its radical critique of identity politics.

Queer Nation's Legacy

Queer Nation is perhaps best known for being the first major public organization to attempt to reclaim the word *queer* from its formerly pejorative connotations as demonstrated by its now well-known slogan "We're here. We're queer. Get used to it." Its success in this regard can be seen in popular television shows such as *Queer Eye for the Straight Guy* and *Queer as Folk*. Queer Nation has also been credited with other now commonplace phrases among queer activists, such as "Out of the closet and into the streets" and "Two, four, six, eight, how do you know your kids are straight?" Queer Nation's radical tactics and its critique of identity and the exclusionary tendencies of the gay liberation model have also had a lasting impact on today's LGBT (lesbian, gay, bisexual, and transgender) movement. Current notions of a race, class, and gender inclusive LGBT movement must be credited in part to Queer Nation's efforts.

Stefan Vogler

See also Feminist Theory; Gay Bashing; Homophobia; Homosexuality; Queer Theory

Further Readings

Abelove, H. (1993). From Thoreau to queer politics. *Yale Journal of Criticism, 6,* 17–28.

Berlant, L., & Freeman, E. (1992). Queer nationality. *boundary 2, 19*(1), 149–180.

Bérubé, A., & Escoffier, J. (1991). Queer/nation. *Out/Look: National Lesbian and Gay Quarterly, 11,* 13–14.

Chee, A. (1991). A queer nationalism. *Out/Look: National Lesbian and Gay Quarterly, 11,* 15–19.

Gray, M. (2009). Queer nation is dead/long live queer nation: The politics and poetics of social movement and media representation. *Critical Studies in Media Communication, 26,* 212–236.

Jagose, A. (1996). *Queer theory: An introduction.* New York: New York University Press.

Warner, M. (Ed.). (1993). *Fear of a queer planet.* Minneapolis: University of Minnesota Press.

QUEER THEORY

Queer theory can be seen as an extension of the critique of objective knowledge leveled by critical feminist theorists, gay and lesbian theorists, social constructionists, and postmodernists. Queer theory draws on multiple disciplines, including biology, anthropology, sociology, philosophy, psychology, and literary and cultural studies. Queer theorists most prominently critique essentialism, or the belief that categories (sexuality, gender, or other aspects of supposed reality) are fixed such that each member of a category possesses a set of identical characteristics that differentiate the member from other categories. Typically, although not exclusively, essentialism relies on binary dichotomies (male/female, woman/

man, or heterosexual/homosexual) and follows the conviction that categories reflect the essence of the properties of the objects in those categories. In contrast, queer theorists argue that categories tell more about the social and cultural context of those who do the categorizing than they do about reality. Queer theory, while most often applied to the study of sexualities, is also applicable to the study of people with disabilities, mental illnesses, or any other phenomenon that relies on normative standards to create an abstract ideal. In this way, queer theory questions the very existence of deviance and the legitimacy of social control. This entry introduces some of the main concepts used, gives examples of applications, and summarizes the contributions and critiques of queer theory.

Using the concept of performativity, queer theorists examine gender and sexuality as a locally (culturally and historically) specific "performance" rather than a universal category that exists outside of people making and doing gender. Proponents examine how different societies at different times create cultural beliefs and institutional practices that justify and legitimate the gender/sexual social order. Because there are a variety of beliefs and practices, there will necessarily be a variety of performances. Indeed, there are no behaviors or traits that have been associated with the category *woman* or *man* across all time and space. The very idea that there are only two genders and/or sexualities is not universal as evidenced by the Navajo "middle gender" and the Indian *Hijra*. The variety of gender performances cross-culturally and historically (and even across one individual's lifetime) shows that normative categories generally and gender and sexuality specifically are shifting and fluid. Therefore, rather than categories (gender/sexuality/ability) being natural, universal, essential, and static, they depend on performativity, the continued repetition of stylized bodily acts for coherence.

Queer theorists deconstruct "texts" to show that sexuality is not simply an individual's choice of performance but is deeply embedded in the social structure. Texts include not just the printed or spoken word (e.g., newspapers or song lyrics) but anything produced by social groups (e.g., laws, religious doctrine, political platforms, educational curriculum and policy, medical and psychiatric definitions, etc.). These texts define legitimate categories and impose sanctions on those who do not follow the normative order. Deconstructing involves examining the overt meanings as well as what is hinted at (the subtext).

For example, queer theorists argue that deconstructing texts promulgated by major institutions reveal a social order based on *compulsory heterosexuality*. That is, normative constraints privileging heterosexuality as the only appropriate sexual expression are embedded in social institutions/ structure, and heterosexuality is the only form of sexual expression that is legitimated by the major institutions in society. For example, laws ban homosexuals from marriage, religious texts are used to promote homosexuality as evil, and schools are banned from discussing alternative sexualities. The assumption (subtext) is that heterosexuality is normal and universal and men and women are naturally attracted to each other.

Queer theorists argue that these supposed normative categories appear natural not because they are natural but because of the power of discourses promulgated by institutions such as medicine, the state, and education. These institutions are seen as disciplinary regimes in that normative definitions themselves discipline individuals by limiting the kinds of acts/actors that are considered appropriate and justifying sanctions for transgressions (e.g., arrest, humiliation, loss of job, self-respect, and family and friends). In this way, discourses limit the kinds of gender and/or sexuality performances and serve to coerce individuals into performances that reproduce the given order of things.

Therefore, binary social categories are not apolitical descriptions of reality but rather political proscriptions for appropriate behavior that carry with them rewards/privilege and punishments/oppression.

In addition, queer theorists argue that texts reproduce rigid binaries and dichotomized opposites (man/woman, male/female, heterosexual/homosexual, and able-bodied/disabled) by overstating the differences and ignoring the similarities between the perceived opposites. The oversimplification of complex reality is evident in the critique that the "pure" heterosexual, homosexual man or woman only exists as an abstract ideal. However, rather than adjust the categories to fit reality, those that do not fit neatly into one category or another are deemed "deviant" and the subject of social control. Perhaps the best example of the rigidity of social categories is that of those born "intersexed"— those not clearly male or female. Queer theorists point out that rather than change social categories to include multiple sexes, these individuals are physically changed with surgeries to fit the social categories. That sex is embedded in the social order becomes clear by noting that to not be "sexed" (to be neither male nor female) means not to exist in that there is no word for people who are not either "he" or "she."

Queer theory has been used to argue that not only are heterosexuality and sex compulsory but so is gender, ability, and any other socially created and discursively supported normative standard. For example, queer theory has been extended to the dichotomized and hierarchically positioned social categories of able-bodied versus disabled. Using insights from queer theory, the critical disability theory deconstructs and critiques the disciplinary and coercive power of societal texts and practices in creating the definition "able-bodied." Building on the idea that perfect heterosexuality is a normative illusion, critical disability theorists argue that the perfectly able-bodied individual does not exist except as a normative ideal. In addition, similar to compulsory heterosexuality, compulsory able-bodiedness is also embedded in all of our social institutions. Finally, similar to queer theory, critical disability theorists do not seek to garner acceptance for the less valued status of "disabled" but rather to reject both the division of bodies into able/disabled as well as the goal of "fixing" those that normative standards deem lacking.

Contributions

Queer theory is useful in revealing the commonalities of the seemingly opposite perspectives of social constructionism and essentialism. Social constructionists typically see reality, in this case gender or sexuality, as created in interaction. In contrast, essentialists view gender and sexuality as a fixed property of the individual. Queer theory moves past the debate over where sexuality originates from (society or nature) and sees binaries as a product of social relations rather than as exclusive (either natural or social) categories of inherently oppositional characteristics. Queer theorists argue that examining sexuality as either natural or a social construction depends on a dichotomized and stable view of sexuality that queer theory challenges. Thus, it is the dichotomized views evident in binary categories that leave in place social and psychological boundaries, which in turn give rise to hierarchal ranking of inferior and superior sexual identities. In this way, proponents challenge a social order that perpetuates a fixed division of heterosexual and homosexual or able-bodied and disabled.

Queer theory has also informed the goals of social activists. Proponents argue that it is the artificial binary division that is at the root of inequality and oppression. Specifically, these divisions are the first step to the hierarchal placement of one normative category over another. Rather than political activism aimed at naturalizing homosexuality as a sexual minority and thereby keeping in place the preestablished dichotomized view of sexuality, Queer theorists challenge the coherence of *any* identity/category. They argue that discourses limit the kinds of gender and/or sexuality performances and serve to coerce individuals into performances that reproduce the given order of things. Therefore, the goal of queer theory is not to explain the repression or expression of a homosexual minority but to analyze how power and knowledge influence and order desires, behaviors, social relations, and social institutions. The aim of the proponents of queer theory is to destabilize and disrupt foundational cultural categories. In this way, the implications of queer theory are a profound critique of the politics of knowledge rather than just an attempt to include "sexual minorities" in the production of knowledge.

Queer theory is also useful in revealing the links between micro (identity), meso (interaction), and macro (social structure). Individuals, to form their gender/sexuality identities internalize (micro) and display in interaction (meso) normative definitions of sexuality/gender promulgated by the major institutions (macro). Those who uphold normative expressions receive positive sanctions, and those who transgress are subject to negative sanctions (from self, in interaction, and in institutional settings). In this way, gender/sexuality is not a simple choice of the individual or a result of socialization, or tradition. Rather gender/sexuality is a fundamental way of organizing social life that is deeply embedded in the core social practices of modern societies and sustained at multiple levels of analysis, in identity formation, in interaction, and in institutional practices.

Finally, seeing heterosexuality as both compulsory and embedded in institutional practices helps explain not only why most people adhere to the normative categories but also why those who do not display normatively appropriate gender, sexuality, and so on are subject to social controls. Those who transgress by their actions are questioning not only the very basis of individual identity (gender and/or sexuality) but also the deeply embedded culturally and institutionally legitimated belief systems that are necessary for hierarchical social order (the given order of things). First, arguing that the gender/sexuality dichotomy and hierarchy does not flow naturally from an internal state but rather is a set of ritually performed acts means that the very notion of our identity as men and women is called into question. Second, if there is no gender/sexuality dichotomy and hierarchy, the very basis of social order (e.g., the division of labor) as well as gender/sexuality privilege is illegitimate. Such challenges have the ability to disrupt the division of the social into privileged and subordinate categories. If gender/sexuality does not exist, or there are as many genders/sexualities as there are people, there is no way to discriminate by gender/sexuality.

Critiques

Critics have argued that there are notable contradictions in queer theory. First, Queer theory resists definition. Indeed, because of the radical critique of categorization, the very act of attempting to define it is antithetical to the spirit of queer theory. If a theory cannot be defined, then it is not a theory. Proponents of queer theory argue that the lack of definition is its strength because it maintains the dynamism of the perspective. Rather than limiting what the theory is with definition, proponents argue that the strength of the perspective lies in its refusal to exclude. Other critics argue that if the perspective resists definition, it would not be possible to limit the application or any definition. Therefore, the theory becomes

meaningless. Indeed, the goal of the theory is to show how rigid categories are incapable of encompassing the diversity of expressions. In this way, there is so much variation that everyone can be considered at least a bit "queer." If potentially everything is queer, then queer means nothing at all. The irony is revealed in that if queer theory attains its goal of breaking down social categories, the category of queer theory itself will not exist. Therefore, the "success" of the theory is to be found in its dissolution.

Tina Hebert Deshotels

See also Constructionist Theories; Death of Sociology of Deviance; Intersexuality; Queer Nation; Transsexuals

Further Readings

Butler, J. (1990). *Gender trouble: Feminism and the subversion of identity.* New York, NY: Routledge.

Flax, J. (1987). Postmodernism and gender relations in feminist theory. *Signs, 12,* 626–627, 641–643.

Foucault, M. (1978). *The history of sexuality.* New York, NY: Random House.

McRuer, R., & Bérubé, M. F. (2006). *Crip theory: Cultural signs of queerness and disability.* New York: New York University Press.

Seidman, S. (1997). *Differences troubles: Queering social theory and sexual politics.* New York, NY: Cambridge University Press.

Sullivan, N. (2003). *A critical introduction to queer theory.* New York: New York University Press.

RACE/ETHNICITY AND DRUG USE

The relationships among race/ethnicity and drug use, disparity in arrests, and sentencing have long been controversial issues, especially in the United States. Current research addressing these relationships shows that race and ethnicity have significant effects on drug use habits, likelihood of being arrested, and sentencing outcomes. According to statistics from the 2010 National Survey on Drug Use and Health, prevalence of drug use is highest among American Indians (12.5%), African Americans (10.7%), Whites (9.1%), Hispanics (8.1%), and Asians (3.5%). Such patterns of drug use by race have been consistent since 2002. However, a significant increase in drug use among Hispanics and Whites has been recorded after 2008. In that year, prevalence of drug use increased from 6.2% to 8.1% for Hispanics and from 8.2% to 9.1% for Whites.

It has also long been asserted that there is a disparity in sentencing based on race. According to statistics from the Uniform Crime Reporting, between 1980 and 2007 African Americans were arrested for drug offenses more than Whites and other races (American Indians, Alaskan Natives, Asians, and Pacific Islanders are regarded as other races by the Uniform Crime Report). In different years during this period, rates of arrest for African Americans were 2.8 to 5.5 times higher than for Whites. The arrest rate of African Americans has increased dramatically over the past several decades. For example, arrests of Whites tripled from 1980 to 2007 but increased fivefold for African Americans during this same period. Although African Americans represented approximately 13% of the total population in the United States, they accounted for almost 35% of all drug arrests. More than 70% of the African Americans convicted for drug-related offenses were eventually incarcerated, while only 63% of Whites were incarcerated. Regardless of race, 64% of all arrests made in the United States between 1980 and 2007 were for drug possession. This rate was 80% for the period of 1999 and 2007. The majority of possession arrests were for marijuana possession, which is approximately 40% of all drug arrests.

Statistics clearly show that African Americans were arrested more often than Whites and other races. The reasons for this difference have been debated. Some argue that Whites constitute the majority of drug users, but African Americans are the principal targets of law enforcement agencies' war on drugs. As a result, there is a disproportionate rate of arrests between races. According to official statistics, it appears that African Americans engage more in drug-related offenses. Advocates of the above-mentioned view say that the statistics are likely accurate, but they do not reflect the real situation. They argue that Whites, Hispanics, and American Indians use drugs at rates comparable with those of African Americans, but African Americans are more often arrested and sentenced. They claim that this disparity in arrest rates stems from politics, biases in law enforcement, and social and economic dynamics, all of which are affected by racial concerns and issues.

Others argue that although African Americans are arrested more often than members of other races, this is not a result of bias. Instead, it is a reflection of drug use patterns. For example, sentencing disparities are mostly seen in crack cocaine and powder cocaine arrests. American law enforcement agencies have been criticized for focusing on crack cocaine users and employing strict techniques to capture them, while ignoring powder cocaine users. Crack cocaine is an inexpensive drug to produce and to buy. As a result, it is widely used in inner cities where poor people, who are mostly African Americans, live. When combined with law enforcement agencies' focus on crack cocaine capture, African American people are arrested and sentenced more than other races. In addition to these factors, education and employment opportunities, availability of drugs of choice, cultural differences, and attitudes toward rehabilitation programs all affect the rate of drug use, arrests, and sentences.

In contrast to law enforcement agencies' focus on cocaine, UNODC World Drug Report statistics show that the most used drug in the United States is marijuana. In North America, 10.7% of the citizens between the ages of 15 and 64 have consumed marijuana. Nearly 2% of this age-group has used cocaine, which makes it the second most consumed drug. Cocaine users in the United States constitute almost 37% of total worldwide users.

Globally, marijuana is the most commonly used drug. Marijuana consumption is highest in Central and South America. Marijuana consumers in these regions represent nearly 5% of all users in the world. Consumption of other drugs in the region is below the world average. In Europe, where Whites are the dominant inhabitants, marijuana and cocaine are the most commonly used drugs. In all, 30% of all cocaine users live in Europe, mainly in West and Central Europe. In Africa, having the largest Black population in the world, marijuana consumption constitutes 64% of all drug consumption. Opioids and cocaine are the other most consumed drugs in Africa. In Asia, opiate users are almost equal to half of the world usage. Marijuana is the most commonly used drug, while cocaine is the least. Last, in Oceania, marijuana, ecstasy, amphetamines, and cocaine are the most consumed drugs.

Whether in the United States or in the rest of the world, there appears to be a relationship between races and their drug use habits, arrest rates, and sentencing outcomes. The factors affecting these relationships are diverse and continue to be debated.

Serdar Yildiz

See also Age and Drug Use; Club Drugs; Cocaine; Drug Dependence Treatment; Drug Policy; Drug War (War on Drugs); Socioeconomic Status and Drug Use

Further Readings

Greene, H. T., & Gabbidon, S. L. (2009). *Encyclopedia of race and crime*. Thousand Oaks, CA: Sage.

Human Rights Watch. (2009). *Decades of disparity: Drug arrests and race in the United States*. New York, NY: Author.

The National Survey on Drug Use and Health. *Results from the 2010 National Survey on Drug Use and Health: Summary of national findings*. Retrieved from https://nsduhweb.rti.org

United Nations Office on Drugs and Crime. (2011). *World drug report, 2011*. New York, NY: Author.

RACISM

Racism is the belief that members of a particular race are superior to members of other races. This belief results in the practice of preferential treatment toward the "superior" races and discriminatory practices toward the "inferior" races. Racism generally leads to the advancement of the majority group while contributing to the decline of the minority groups. In recent decades, the pseudoscientific basis of racism has been discredited; mainstream scholarship now recognizes the notion of race itself to be a social construct.

Overt and Discrete Practices

Practices of racism can range from overt to discrete. Overt practices of racism include public denunciation of particular races, membership in race supremacy groups, and using certain races as scapegoats for social problems. Discrete practices of racism include assuming characteristic traits based on race and barring equal access to resources to nondominant races. Members of different ethnicities or religions who are perceived to be of "inferior" races are also subject to racism.

History of Racism

The conceptualization of racism has evolved considerably. Prior to the 20th century, displays of racism were the social norm; today, racism is generally considered socially deviant. Historically, racism has taken many forms. In Europe prior to the Middle Ages, there are no clear instances of racism as we define it today. In the 13th and 14th centuries, Christians' association of Jews with the devil and witchcraft are indicative of what might be called preracism, since even Jews who converted to Christianity continued to be discriminated against for centuries, and Jews who maintained their traditional faith were subject to outbreaks of persecution.

The Renaissance and Reformation periods brought Europeans into contact with darker-skinned people from outside Europe. This in turn caused a stir in assumptions about the culture and characteristic traits of the non-Europeans. In the 17th and 18th centuries, the slave trade in America deepened the belief in racism. Native Americans were too few and too susceptible to diseases to work as laborers for the original 13 British colonies, and the need for cheap labor was high. As a result, Africans were brought to America as slaves. Traders and owners rationalized slavery through the biblical story of Ham who, in the book of Genesis, was cursed to be a slave for having disobeyed his father. Because Ham settled in Africa, his presumably black descendants purportedly inherited his curse. In 1667, Virginia decided to keep slaves in bondage on the basis of their race rather than on account of the biblical rationale; this solidified the justification of black servitude. Laws passed in the late 17th century made cross-racial (white and black) marriage illegal and discrimination against biracial children was prevalent. The underlying implication of the laws was that dark-skinned individuals were of lower stature than light-skinned individuals.

The Enlightenment period witnessed an increasing rejection of the biblical rationale as an argument for the singularity of the human race. Ethnologists in the 18th century, who considered the human race as part of the natural world, categorized it into three to five races. In the late 18th and early 19th centuries, those in favor of slavery wrote that races were composed of distinct species.

Racism was not solely bound to Africans. Spaniards during the colonial period developed a complicated caste system using race as a basis for social control and determining an individual's place in society. In the Spanish colonial social hierarchy, Peninsulares (whites born in Spain) followed by Criollos (whites born in the Americas) formed the ruling elite. *Mestizos*, those who were of mixed American Indian and European ancestry, had a structural advantage over the peasant and working class (indigenous people).

The 19th century brought about events—emancipation, nationalism, and imperialism—that supplied the escalation of ideological racism in both Europe and in the United States. These reforms also intensified the racism toward minorities, particularly in the case of blacks and Jews. The instability of industrial capitalism caused insecurity and anxiety around issues of employment and job security: As a result, race relations became more troubled. Charles Darwin's idea of natural selection and Herbert Spencer's notion of "survival of the fittest" contributed to the advancement of a scientifically credited racism during a period where race relations were volatile and unstable.

The rise of nationalism in turn gave rise to themes based on racist ideology. Since the medieval period, Jews throughout Europe had routinely been denied the privileges of citizenship accorded to Christians—were required to live apart in ghettoes and to pay special taxes; were forbidden to own land, to enter the professions and most trades, or to join guilds; and were required to wear special clothing identifying them as Jews. For centuries, the Jews were subjected to indignities and treated as scapegoats, and their emancipation occurred only in the 19th century in those countries governed by the Napoleonic Code. The term *antisemitism* became endemic in the late 1870s and early 1880s, especially in Germany and Austria, and was based on the notion that Jews by definition were not only the adherents of a religious group but also an inferior race. The ideology of antisemitism held the Jews to be "racially impure," as contrasted with the purportedly superior bloodlines of the Germanic people (the "Aryan" race). In addition, Western imperialism's peak in the late 19th century led to struggles between nations in obtaining control of parts of Africa, Asia, and the Pacific islands and exemplified the competitive ethnic nationalism nascent in the European countries. Also implicit in such empire building was the belief that Europeans were destined by virtue of natural superiority to rule over Africans and Asians.

In the same period, many non-Protestant European immigrant groups, particularly Irish, Jews, Italians, and Poles, suffered discrimination in the American society. This was partly due to anti-Catholic sentiment (as in the case of Irish Americans) and to Nordicism, the idea that all groups were inferior to immigrants of Scandinavian and British descent.

The pinnacle of racism came with the rise and fall of blatantly racist regimes during the 20th century. Racist propaganda aimed at portraying black men as animals lusting after white women rationalized lynching in the southern United States. The irrational fear of the mixing of races through rape or intermarriage was key to the maintenance of the racist regime supported by state law; this resulted in all efforts to prevent the joining of whites with any known or hidden African blood. The southern United States passed racial segregation laws and restrictions of black voting rights to diminish the status of African Americans as citizens.

Racist ideology fully took form in Nazi Germany. The calculated effort to exterminate the entire Jewish people highlights the extremes to which the Nazis took racist ideology. Approximately 6 million Jewish civilians died as a result of the Holocaust; its non-Jewish victims include homosexuals, physically and mentally handicapped people, political and religious rebels, Jehovah's witnesses, Romani, ethnic Poles, Slovenes, and Slavs. Following the end of World War II, when the full magnitude of the Nazis' systematic genocidal crime was revealed, worldwide public horror and revulsion fueled an increasingly negative attitude toward racism itself. At the same time, scientific racism, the use of science to provide evidence in support of racism, came under scrutiny, and the respectability it had won in the United States and Europe before the war was largely discredited.

The United States took to heart the moral lesson from Germany. The 1960s Civil Rights Movement in the United States successfully outlawed legalized racial segregation and discrimination—this garnered immense support from the understanding that national interests were in jeopardy if discrimination against blacks was not abolished.

Similar to the decline of racism in Western countries, overt racism was also condemned in the new nations forming from the decolonization of Africa and Asia. The South African regime was the only racist regime that endured after 1948. The obsession with "race purity" was evident in the laws banning the marriage and sexual relations between whites and blacks. State-imposed residential segregation explicitly preventing the intermixing of racial households further aggravated the racial overtones. After the Holocaust, international pressure to prevent breeding grounds for extreme racist ideology caused apologists for South Africa to claim that its policy of apartheid was based on cultural rather than on racial differences.

Racial Discrimination

Racial discrimination can manifest through legal routes or informal routes. Individuals may discriminate on the basis of skin color (as in the case of lighter-skinned blacks discriminating against darker-skinned blacks) or other physical characteristics. Living in poorer neighborhoods, having a minority-sounding name, or coming from a working-class background can also stir discrimination. Alternatively, institutions of work or education may discriminate against the white majority to promote diversity. Minority members can be hired so that claims of discrimination are countered, even if other white job candidates are equally qualified.

Economics of Racism

Those who suffer racism experience real economic disadvantages. This can include limitations in job opportunities, wages, goods and resources, and capital investment available for new businesses. It can also include discrimination against minority workers and consumers in addition to minority-owned businesses. The "cycle of poverty" has been associated with racism.

In the United States, life outcomes are consistently tied to race. Minority groups such as blacks and Latinos consistently have less income, less employment, less education, and higher rates of incarceration compared with whites. Although improving, the incarceration rates of black people in the United States are extremely disproportionate. The decline in incarceration rates for black Americans is seen in large part to revisions in federal drug sentencing laws.

Racial Segregation

Residential segregation advanced through the passage of discriminatory American policies in the 19th century. Prior to 1900, African Americans lived around white neighborhoods as servants and laborers—with the advent of World War I, the "urban ghetto" became an instrument of residential segregation. Jobs were placed far from the city, and industries moved from cities to suburbs to create all-white towns. Exclusionary zoning practices and federal and local government housing discrimination and private discrimination also served as fuel for the overt racism toward disenfranchised minority members.

Institutional Racism

A term coined by the Black Power activist Stokely Carmichaels in the 1960s, *institutional racism* (also referred to as state racism, structural racism, or systemic racism), is racial discrimination practiced by governments, religions, educational institutions, corporations, and other large organizations that have authority over many individuals. Institutional racism spurs inequality through unequal access to resources, goods, and opportunities based on racial differences. Chief among its effects is the deterioration of the quality of life of the nondominant group. The development of the urban ghetto and the role of the government in creating housing segregation are examples of institutional racism. Maulana Karenga argues that the practices of racism have led to the erosion of culture, religion, language, and human possibility and that racism practiced in the past continues to pervade the lives of Africans today. The Southern Poverty Law Center lists the Nation of Islam and the New Black Panther Party as active national antiwhite hate groups.

Contemporary Analysis of Racism

The fall of Nazi Germany, racial segregation in the American South, and apartheid in South Africa suggest that regimes running on racist ideology no longer enjoy popular support and approval. The public in democratic nations does not generally support politicians who run on a race-based ideology. To many, the election of Barack Obama to the presidency of the United States in 2008 was a sign that the era of overt racism had ended. In general, U.S. society has moved past laws that explicitly stem from racist ideology. For example, Employers Title VII of the 1964 Civil Rights Act prevents discrimination in employment matters on the basis of race, color, religion, sex, or national origin.

Despite significant improvements in recent decades, racism remains in American society through urban segregation, disparities between educational attainment and income, and the lack of equal minority representation in Congress and the criminal justice system. Despite the decline of overtly racist laws, racism continues to affect the life outcomes of minorities and majorities.

Daniela Pila

See also Ku Klux Klan; Lynching; Police Profiling; Race/Ethnicity and Drug Use; Symbolic Crusade; White Supremacist Groups

Further Readings

Aptheker, H. (1993). *Anti-racism in U.S. history: The first two hundred years.* Westport, CT: Praeger.

Bonilla-Silva, E. (2010). *Racism without racists: Color-blind racism and the persistence of racial inequality in the United States.* Lanham, MD: Rowman & Littlefield.

Frederickson, G. M. (2002). *Racism: A short history.* Princeton, NJ: Princeton University Press.

McWhorter, L. (2009). *Racism and sexual oppression in Anglo-America: A genealogy.* Bloomington: Indiana University Press.

Mosse, G. L. (1997). *Toward the final solution: A history of European racism.* New York, NY: Howard Fertig.

O'Brien, E. (2008). *The racial middle: Latinos and Asian Americans living beyond the racial divide.* New York: New York University Press.

Trepagnier, B. (2010). *Silent racism: How well-meaning white people perpetuate the racial divide* (Expanded ed.). Boulder, CO: Paradigm.

RAPE

In the context of women's rights movements and a heightened awareness of the pervasiveness of gender-based violence, rape has become increasingly researched by sociologists. Rape is defined as unwanted sexual intercourse via physical or psychological coercion with no consent given. Rape can be committed with the use of a foreign object. A challenge to individuals reporting is that often they do not characterize coerced sexual intercourse as rape, although, by legal definition it does constitute rape. Victims who are otherwise willing to report rape are often intimidated by the legal system that requires them to describe the incident in detail and, in so doing, to relive the trauma. As a result, rape is an underreported crime.

On the basis of changing legal definitions, rape has been characterized as a crime that targets women who do not give consent to sexual intercourse. Rape has been viewed by some scholars, such as Diana Russell and Rachel Whaley, as a social control mechanism of women, based on a variety of circumstances that stem from gender inequalities, in which socially, politically, and economically, women lack the same rights as men. On this view, high rates of rape are linked to patriarchal-based societies, media sexual objectification of women, men's inherent power in the family and other institutions, and sex role stereotypes according to which women seduce men but limit men's access to sexual intercourse.

This entry provides an overview of key issues, particularly types of rape and settings in which rape risk is high. Importantly, although sexual assault by definition can include a variety of unwanted sexual contact ranging from sexual harassment to rape, the entry uses the terms *sexual assault* and *rape* interchangeably to mean forced sexual intercourse without consent.

Types of Rape

A discrepancy exists between commonly held rape myths and what scholarly research suggests about sexual assault. Public advocates of precautionary behaviors aimed at reducing the risk of rape tend to focus on stranger rape. For instance, the stranger rape scenario is based on a male perpetrator initiating a blitz attack on an unknowing female victim at night. Precautionary behaviors that develop around the stranger rape script reinforce beliefs about the typical perpetrator, victim, and context in which rape occurs: Specifically, the perpetrator is a scary, overpowering male who targets a defenseless, isolated female. Research has shown that in fact acquaintance rapes tend to be more common than stranger rapes. In fact, four of five rapes are acquaintance based. The focus on stranger rapes leads, however, to difficulties for understanding risk in familiar settings and problematizes acquaintance rape victims, because their actions do not conform to notions of the stranger rape victim. Even if women do recognize that acquaintance rape is more common than stranger rape, their actions do not support this awareness. Although many women have stated that they believe they can prevent acquaintance rape, advocates have associated this belief with a sense of false security that contributes to women's vulnerability to acquaintance rape. Based on assumptions made about determining what type of male is risky, many women believe that they are capable of identifying risky males and avoiding risk by changing their behaviors, such as avoiding certain locations or traveling in groups. Advocates have raised concerns that precautionary behaviors may not be as effective for acquaintance rape risk and that the trustworthy assumptions made of male peers can contribute to greater sexual assault risk.

Blaming the Victim

In cases of stranger and acquaintance rape, many people, including law enforcement officers, emphasize the victim's accountability for her actions to explain the event. Thus, research has found that victims are commonly blamed for certain behaviors, such as what attire they wore, their alcohol and/or drug intake, being alone, or even for exhibiting flirtatious behavior. Many activists have criticized this focus on the victim, claiming that a victim never asks to be raped. Such focus on the victim's behavior unjustly downplays the perpetrator's role and accountability for the use of violence.

Since rape falls under the category of gendered violence, victims encounter difficulties in reporting and seeking justice. Rape is stigmatizing for victims because they not only experience shame but are often criticized by law enforcement, courts, and lay individuals with regard to their assumed role. Additionally, stereotypes circulate to undermine the victims' testimony and legitimacy of their claims by suggesting that the rape claim is used to protect a reputation after casual sex or a way to seek revenge on a male. Prior to greater advocacy for victims, testifying in court typically focused on victims' actions, making it difficult for victims to find the courage to report and follow through with prosecution.

Rapists' Beliefs

Rapists often normalize their sexually violent behavior by invoking traditional gender roles to portray women as seductresses and their own actions as justified, or perhaps excused because of the consumption of alcohol. In the context of a patriarchal society, male rapists may explain away responsibility for rape by relying on one of the following three explanations: (1) sexual intercourse could not be stopped, (2) there was miscommunication with the victim, or (3) they have a right as men to be sexually aggressive and dominant. First, the reasoning associated with the inability to not commit rape is often based on biological stereotypes according to which men are unable to stop a sexual encounter because physiologically they are aroused and desire to reach orgasm. However, this explanation has been deemed a social stereotype, and awareness efforts have reported that men can in fact stop sexual encounters at any stage. Second, often in acquaintance-based situations in which rape occurs, the perpetrator commonly claims that he believed the victim was a willing sexual partner or did not think she really meant no. Acquaintance rapists may receive support for these interpretations because lay audiences tend to believe the rapist's claim that the female in question seemed to be a willing sexual partner, but she changed her mind at the last moment. The last example is based on gender inequalities whereby some men believe they are sexually entitled to women, and through socialization messages, men may exaggerate ideas that women are available for sexual accessibility.

Risk Factors

Research on sexual assault has been characterized by three overarching themes. Initially, researchers focused on identifying and predicting perpetrator and victim characteristics. This micro theme advanced into a more macro focus by an analysis of the structural settings in which rapes are more prevalent. The term *rape-prone atmospheres* emerged to categorize contexts in which rape rates were high. For example, sexual assaults on college campuses, in fraternity and sport team settings, in the military, and during war revealed that risk derived from traditional gender roles, sex-role stereotypes, male hypermasculinity and camaraderie, and the perception of women as sexualized objects. These environments are linked to higher amounts of risk; however, many individuals minimize the structurally induced risk by falsely assuming that a particular occurrence of rape was an isolated event. Current research addresses the impact of bystanders' involvement in perpetuating risk rather than disrupting it. Media reports have highlighted individual and group rape crimes and focused concern on what is perceived as bystanders failing to intervene or report a rape situation. Although these media reports call on psychologists to explain mind-set and behavior, sociologists in particular examine the interaction setting, role values, and rules that may hinder the ability of bystanders to identify a situation as rape and then take action to stop it. For instance, bystanders' rationales for failing to report the incident are typically based on waiting for other individuals to do so or feeling intimidated to report for fear of being held responsible.

College Rape

Specific attention has addressed sexual assault as manifesting in college social environments. Statistics reveal that one in four women will be victimized by attempted or completed rape during their college career. College parties on or off campus, including those at bars and clubs, seem to be especially risky locations for women. College parties generate a greater potential risk of sexual assault for women because typically these parties lack supervisors, and other variables, such as the use of drugs and alcohol, add to the possible occurrence of sexual assault. Furthermore, research on fraternity party environments characterizes these social scenes as male dominant and risky for women. Male camaraderie exaggerated in fraternity atmospheres and frequently at college parties makes it increasingly difficult for women to avoid being objectified. These social settings typically include elements of alcohol, a motive to drink alcohol to become intoxicated, and an undercurrent of sexual arousal and female sexual objectification. Research findings reveal that a proportion of college men self-reported sexual acts that met the legal standard for rape. However, their perceptions of the act were not self-identified as rape.

Despite a pattern of college parties, fraternity parties, and even male sports events correlating positively with rape risks, studies have also shown that this vast generalization is problematic. College parties and various males' membership categories are not homogeneous, and thus, risk can be placed on a continuum in which some affiliations of men generate atmospheres of low risk, while others could be considerably higher. A major factor to address in the prevalence of rape on college campuses is alcohol. Studies have shown that the majority of sexual assaults occur when the perpetrator and/or victim are intoxicated, or in an atmosphere of binge drinking.

Military and War Rape

Rape in military contexts, including war, has been theorized to mean that the pervasiveness of risk stems from a lack of full participation by women because of institutionalized male dominance. Rapes of military women, as well as of gay men, have been linked to a hostile effort to minimize women's participation and to punish deviations from normative masculine gender roles in a dominant male setting. Women's participation is seen as compromising the masculine role of men and their willingness to be considered equal among women, who by patriarchal definition are designated the weaker sex. Similarly, rape in war has been used as a strategy to break down the adversary's community, devalue women and exile them from their communities, forcibly impregnate them with the enemy's offspring, and indirectly imply male adversaries' impotence and inability to protect women, thus symbolically rejecting their masculinity.

Rape during wartime has historically been construed as a by-product of war, rather than a specific form of violence. In war and armed conflict, women's rights are largely ignored on the grounds that they occupy a subordinate position to men's rights. It is likely that rape was seen as a spoil of war because it is perceived as an individual, deviant sexual act and not a motivated form of violence. On this basis, rape understood as a spoil of war functions to disguise it as either strategic or a form of violence that preys on women's gendered vulnerability. This historical lack of understanding of rape as a *weapon* of war is sustained by masculine privilege that devalues women as a traditional practice based on social gender norms. For example, Susan Brownmiller confirms the strict practice of gender roles that subordinate women as a method to accomplish military war objectives.

International laws developed in response to the implementation of mass rape as a means of oppressing vulnerable social groups. In 1945, rape became tacitly associated with the potential to be incorporated as a crime against humanity fitted under the clause of inhumane acts against any civilian population. Particularly, the International Court Tribunals of the Former Yugoslavia and Rwanda explicitly prosecuted perpetrators of mass rape based on their efforts to achieve genocide and eliminate a subethnic group. The recognition of rape as a weapon of war emerged from its connection to episodes of ethnic cleansing or genocidal conflict in which the widespread and systematic practice of rape argued for its being considered a crime against humanity. Rape became reconceptualized because it became associated with a visible effort to commit the destruction of particular social groups.

Rape in association with ethnic cleansing serves not only to dehumanize women but also drastically alters the ethnic relations of a particular group in efforts of forced impregnation. Thus, the targeting of women effectively makes vulnerable an entire social community, including male members. The implication of the specific targeting of an entire community through the use of sexual violence is to displace the gendered vulnerability of the rape and associate rape with the undermining of the social organization of the community. The use of rape as a form of ethnic cleansing is premised on targeting women as linked to their representation of the community, and as a result, the self/cultural identity of men belonging to that community is at risk.

Male Victims

Although rape is a gendered crime, the idea that men are only perpetrators and women only victims is false. Men have been victimized by rape by other men and women. Lay audiences tend not to fully acknowledge the ability of women to rape men; however, consent is verbal and women are capable of oral, anal, and vaginal–penile rape of men. In similarity to the difficulties for women victims to report rape, male victims also encounter many barriers in reporting. Advocacy centers for rape victims tend to focus on the standard of a female victim. Male victims may also face criticism by others with regard to their masculinity. There are also expectations that a "real" man could physically resist a male or female perpetrator, so the inability to do so is typically blamed on the male victim, who is then vulnerable to ridicule. Male victims in general face scrutiny in being legitimated as victims of rape. Thus, statistics for both male and female victims tend to be interpreted as conservative estimates.

Erin Rider

See also Feminist Theory; Military Deviance; Prison Rape; Sex Discrimination

Further Readings

Abbey, A. (2011). Alcohol's role in sexual violence perpetration: Theoretical explanations, existing evidence and future directions. *Drug and Alcohol Review, 30,* 481–489.

Armstrong, E., Hamilton, L., & Sweeney, B. (2006). Sexual assault on campus: A multilevel, integrative approach to party rape. *Social Problems, 53,* 483–499.

Basow, S., & Minieri, A. (2011). "You owe me": Effects of date cost, who pays, participant gender, rape myth beliefs on perceptions of rape. *Journal of Interpersonal Violence, 26,* 479–497.

Ellis, M. (2006). Breaking the silence: Rape as an international crime. *Case Western Reserve Journal of International Law, 38,* 225–247.

Koss, M. (2011). Hidden, unacknowledged, acquaintance, and date rape: Looking back, looking forward. *Psychology of Women Quarterly, 35,* 348–354.

Milillo, D. (2006). Rape as a tactic of war: Social and psychological perspectives. *Affilia: Journal of Women and Social Work, 21,* 196–205.

Potter, S., & Stapleton, J. (2012). Translating sexual assault prevention from a college campus to a United States military installation: Piloting the know-your-power bystander social marketing campaign. *Journal of Interpersonal Violence, 27,* 1593–1621.

Rusinko, H., Bradley, A., & Miller, J. (2011). Assertiveness and attributions of blame toward victims of sexual assault. *Journal of Aggression, Maltreatment & Trauma, 19*, 357–371.

Russell, D. E. H. (1975). *The politics of rape.* New York, NY: Stein & Day.

Sleath, E., & Bull, R. (2011). Male rape victim and perpetrator blaming. *Journal of Interpersonal Violence, 25*, 969–988.

Whaley, R. B. (2001). The paradoxical relationship between gender inequality and rape. *Gender & Society, 15*, 531–555.

RATIONAL CHOICE THEORY

Rational choice theory of human behavior is valued for its purported ability to explain and predict behavior with relative guilelessness. The theory postulates human behavior to be rational since humans, with the faculty to reason, tend to choose what is best in terms of their self-interest. Humans employ reasoning and reflection prior to acting, and their actions routinely indicate a preference in a particular direction. Such a preference is predicated on the determination that a specific course of action is the best for the purpose of maximizing pleasure and minimizing pain. The choice is made subsequent to considering the prevailing circumstances, since choosing the best option with the promise of most rewards is conditional to it. The type of behavior opted for and the manner in which that behavior gets enacted depends on a host of factors, including social, psychological, and even biological ones.

According to the rational choice model, the secret to understanding human behavior is in knowing the elements that make up the perpetrator's decision-making process. Exposing the relevant decision-making process in the commission of an act will help unravel the mystery of human behavior. Once exposed, behavior will come to be understood as intelligible, explainable, and predictable. Normally, the context for human behavior is occurrence of a need demanding to be satisfied. The individual contemplates different courses of action by contrasting the rewards and costs involved. Generally, the one that appears to cost less and reward the most wins.

The canons of rational choice theory are reflective of the hedonistic theories of the past, dating as far back as the first millennium BCE. Epicurus (341–270 BCE), founder of Epicureanism, considered avoidance of pain and maximizing pleasure to be one of the fundamental goals in life. For Epicureans, pleasure constituted the good, and pain, the evil. Avoidance of pain was to be the mission in life—an end that humans constantly strived for by carefully weighing their options. Later echoes of the Epicurean philosophy can be found in the likes of Jeremy Bentham (1748–1832) and Cesare Beccaria (1738–1794), jurists and philosophers, who applied them to the concept of deviance.

Rational choice theory first became popular in economist circles before being embraced by others in behavioral sciences such as sociology, psychology, political science, and criminology. In sociology, there are a variety of theories including differential association, labeling, social strain, control, and conflict theories that subscribe to rational choice–based explanation of human behavior. By describing deviant behavior as a case of exerting rational choice, an effort is made to transform the approach to deviance in a more humane direction. The following sections of this entry present an elucidation of the theory as applied to the concepts of deviance and deviant behavior by exploring its main tenets, strengths, and vulnerabilities.

Rational Choice Theory of Deviance: Main Tenets

The notion of deviance and deviant behavior as purposeful human conduct, as implied in the rational choice model of deviance, has been extant persistently but with occasional reformulations. As with any behavior, deviant behavior is also human behavior. The only difference between deviant behavior and its counterpart is that the former happens to be in a deviant direction. Deviant behavior is understood to be freely chosen by its perpetrators and the basis for the choice is that it presented the optimal means to achieve certain intended goals. The guiding principle in the selection process is the desire to maximize rewards and avoid punishment.

The corollary to the contentions of the rational choice model is that there is nothing intrinsically deviant about deviance, deviant behavior, or the deviant person. Deviants choose to think and behave in a certain way and prefer to live a certain kind of lifestyle. Deviant acts involve behavior that deviates from the norm, while conforming behavior entails deeds in accordance with the norms. Regardless of the type, all behavior is human behavior and, therefore, purposeful and rational. Behavior, including deviant behavior, is mediated by the hedonistic principle that seeks to capitalize on pleasure and thwart pain. Thus, deviance is to be understood on par with nondeviance, and both are outcomes of a deliberative process involving pertinent variables in a specific milieu; deviants simply favor a course of action that happens to deviate from the norm.

Rational choice theory seems to apply well to deviant behavior and display a respectable level of explanatory power. First, the rationality tenet—in committing deviant behavior, deviants are trying to reach desired goals through meaningful measures—leads to an inference that deviance can never be attributed to irrationality or some cognitive deficiency. Second, the choice tenet—deviants prefer to act in a particular way usually within certain parameters as dictated by circumstances (e.g., rob instead of beg for money, rob a store vs. a person, use force as opposed to nonuse of force, etc.)—endorses that deviant behavior is substantively the same as other behavior types. The quality of deviantness in deviant behavior has to be, thus, extrinsic to the behavior itself.

The extrinsic ingredient that can help in comprehending deviance is none other than norms. Understanding deviance is predicated on knowing the nature of norms, as deviance implies deviation from them. Norms refer to standards of behavior citizens are expected to follow; they inform the public as to what is good and desirable and what is bad and undesirable; they are the source for information on appropriate behavior.

Norms are relative as they tend to vary depending on locality, region, nationality, and culture. In addition, they may differ according to the level of acceptance among people, how they are enforced by society, how society transmits them, and the degree of conformity people require. Thus, what is considered normal in one context may be the opposite in another. The content of deviance also varies correspondingly since the concept of deviance is always seen in juxtaposition to prevailing norms. What is deviant to some could be nondeviant to others, as in the case of prostitution or similar deviance.

One upshot of the norm–deviance association is the affirmation that the linkage between the concept of deviance and deviant behavior is not automatic, and the best explanation of deviance is vis-à-vis norms, not deviant acts. Deviance becomes meaningful only in comparison with a norm and requires certain judgment in reference to it. For instance, societies with legalized prostitution statutes, unlike their counterparts, subscribe to a distinctive set of norms pertaining to sexual behavior and interpret and understand those norms differently as well. Prostitution as an act or behavior has only an ephemeral reference to the concept of deviance.

The common belief is that there is strong social consensus behind all normative standards prevalent in society; however, this may not be true regarding some norms as their foundation had to do with controversial processes, both arbitrary and coercive. Norms commonly have a social origin and are supported with varying degrees of consensus among members of society; those norms with greater accord command firmer commitment and wider adherence; deviation from them would elicit a different kind of response versus deviation from norms with little agreement.

Given the complex and relative nature of norms and its relation to deviance, the role of rationality attributed to human behavior under rational choice theory beseech closer scrutiny. Two successful entrepreneurs dealing in legal versus illegal merchandise, respectively, could be making equally rational decisions about their career choices. Both share in the goal of becoming financially successful just like any other person; both are resorting to socially approved means—selling goods—to realize their goal; however, one of them, unlike the other, decides to sell products that are judged illegal. This decision may be based on any number of factors, including a high demand for the merchandise in question despite its being deemed illegal, generally low level of enforcement of statutes and laws, or a lack of access to legal merchandise and potential customers. Additionally, the individual may be cognizant of the reality of ever-changing laws, regarding the production, distribution, and consumption of goods and services (e.g., alcohol and tobacco). In short, the entrepreneurs have made their decisions based on reality as they perceived it; their assessment of reality was, no doubt, guided by facts, beliefs, and desires circumscribed by the prevailing social context. They acted rationally to serve their self-interest in the most propitious way, regardless of the nature of their decisions.

Likewise, a decision to deal in drugs, steal, or commit fraud or even suicide may be the culmination of a reflection process that weighs the pros and cons of the behavior in question and resorts to the most beneficial and rewarding course of action. Whether a particular course of action is pleasurable will remain subjective to the actor; in some instances, the pleasure aspect may not be apparent at all to observers; regardless, the behavior continues to be pleasurable as far as the actor is concerned.

Any type of human behavior would pass the muster of rationality as proposed in the rational choice model as they are perpetrated with a goal to promote their authors' self-interests. Deviance, as the outcome of rational decision making, is the culmination of a process that contrasts the risks and rewards associated with each alternative course of action and choosing of one that delivers the best performance. The rational and instrumental nature of deviant behavior is, thus, self-evident. Even seemingly nonrational and impulsive behavior may be rational in the sense that its authors are pursuing a strategy to maximize rewards though under vague circumstances. What is rational for one individual may not be so to another; nonetheless, it is rational as far as the actor is concerned.

While seeking out behavior that generates pleasure and avoids pain, the individual is bound to go through a learning sequence. Behavior that engenders pleasure is likely to be repeated or favored in the future, and painful acts, shunned. This explains why people, deviants and nondeviants alike, tend to make a career out of their favorite behavior patterns. Deviant choices, just as nondeviant preferences may have positive or negative outcomes, some of which may be immediate and others, remote. The type of outcome influences future decisions on opting for deviant choices.

There appears to be an individualistic thrust in the rational choice model of deviance, which may not be completely accurate. Even though the individual, on the basis of free will, chooses to act in a deviant way to serve his or her best interest, the fact that this preference does not happen in a vacuum is evidence for the presence of exterior factors. Often, the determination to engage or not engage in deviant behavior is made in a context constricted by incomplete information and the existing social, economic, and political milieu. Factors such as socialization, self-concept, role status, or identity may also be relevant in terms of the dimensions these choices may assume. Some crimes are committed because the perpetrators believe they would not be caught or prosecuted; others take place in the context of overwhelming strains including severe poverty; yet other instances of deviance may stem from a lack of clarity on the prevailing norms. Deviance, thus, is hardly a purely individualistic act; it occurs in conjunction with the prevailing social context.

What does rational choice theory propose as interdiction strategies to reduce deviance? The ideal way to ensure conformity to norms and prevention of deviance is to apprehend and punish perpetrators, making sure that the pain from the pursuit of deviant preferences is overwhelmingly greater than any possible reward. Deviants should be punished promptly and swiftly, with sufficient severity. Such an interdiction strategy should be coupled with lessening the opportunities available for individuals to make deviant choices. For instance, appropriate and sufficient level of surveillance can certainly serve as deterrence to deviance.

Rational Choice Theory of Deviance: Strengths and Weaknesses

Rational choice theory proffers a useful tool in advancing novel ways to understand deviance. It points to the processual nature of deviant activity in a utilitarian framework; it tries to address the motivational and behavioral components of the deviance enterprise.

Deviance is the end product of a gradual process with different stages consisting of preparation, target selection, behavior selection, commission of the act, and dealing with the aftermath. Attending to these stages can provide insights on additional analytical tools and interdiction strategies, which, in turn, would invariably mean better understanding deviance and deviant behavior.

By holding deviant behavior as rational behavior, rational choice theory encourages a paradigmatic shift in dealing with deviance—from a confrontational orientation to a dialectical one. The latter would imply more civility and understanding with a call to engagement and interaction in resolving deviance. The new viewpoint can help speed up situational deviance prevention strategies.

In spite of the seeming clarity of argument, the theory has its share of problems. First of all, does the theory really explain deviance? It definitely speaks to the opportunistic and motivational aspects of deviant behavior. The reason behind the behavior rests with availability of opportunity and the existence of a motivated perpetrator looking to achieve certain objectives, albeit self-serving. However, these aspects are not primary in rendering something deviant. The fundamental feature of deviance is that it violates a norm, and the rational choice theory does little to explain why. Moreover, the rationality-based explanation of deviance it provides could be termed tautological.

Research on the rational choice model has demonstrated that individuals have a propensity not only to choose deviance but also to abandon it voluntarily as well; there is also evidence that, at times, certain types of deviance may be favored more than others. Thus, there may be some nonrandomness in the behavioral outcome from the application of rational choice. This nonrandomness in people's preference to deviate or not, in terms of one type of deviance versus another, may add credence to the alleged role of rational choice in deviance but does not seem to be a sufficient explanation for deviance.

Rational choice theory assumes that people choose optimally on a routine basis because theirs is a rational choice. However, there is preponderance for nonoptimal choices that deviants make, causing one to wonder about their rationality. Preferences may not be formed optimally for a variety of reasons such as nonoptimal beliefs and affect, problems with available information, lack of adequate reflection and deliberation, and the ritualistic manner in which decisions are reached and enacted. Thus, it may be unfair to label all human behavior as uniformly rational and attribute culpability on that basis. The realistic outlook may be that people are rational in a graded fashion and they think they are acting rationally most of the time. Rationality in deviance is a matter of degree rather than something categorical. Some individuals may have more and better options to choose from, making their choices more optimal than others'. Any attempt to explain deviance as purposeful behavior may inadvertently create victims out of every person.

Another assumption of the theory that has been called into question relates to the idea of "free" choice. No doubt, instances abound where deviant behavior appears to be impulsive and resulting from a possible emotional outburst. Known factors impeding free choice of behavior include constraints of time, available information, and mental capacities. Human actions are generally circumscribed by forces beyond their control, including biological, social, and psychological ones. They are far from being autonomous agents of actions, and it is imperative that the factors behind "free choice" of a particular course of action be exposed if one is to understand the nature of choice and behavior comprehensively.

In spite of lingering problems with its formulations, rational choice theory serves as yet another tool to tame the perennially elusive phenomena of deviance and deviant behavior. Its potential in assisting with situational remedies that can interdict the deviance process here and now has to be continually admired.

George Parangimalil

See also Biosocial Perspectives on Deviance; Integrated Theories; Routine Activity Theory

Further Readings

Abell, P. (Ed.). (1991). *Rational choice theory.* Aldershot, England: Elgar.

Becker, G. S. (1968). Crime and punishment: An economic approach. *Journal of Political Economy, 76,* 169–217.

Clarke, R. L., & Felson, M. (Eds.). (1993). *Routine activities and rational choice.* New Brunswick, NJ: Transaction Books.

Coleman, J. S., & Fararo, T. J. (1992). *Rational choice theory: Advocacy and critique.* Newbury Park, CA: Sage.

Cornish, D. B., & Clarke, R. V. (Eds.). (1986). *The reasoning criminal: Rational choice perspective on offending.* New York, NY: Springer-Verlag.

Herrnstein, R. J. (1990). Rational choice theory: Necessary but not sufficient. *American Psychologist, 45*(3), 356–367.

Holzman, H. R. (1982). The rationalistic opportunity perspective on human behavior: Toward a reformulation of the theoretical basis for the notion of property crime as work. *Crime & Delinquency, 28*(2), 233–246.

Wilson, J. Q., & Herrnstein, R. J. (1985). *Crime and human nature.* New York, NY: Simon & Schuster.

RAVE CULTURE

Raves are parties (ranging from a few hundred to thousands of people) that typically feature a number of different electronic music genres, DJs (disc jockeys), light shows, and, in some cases, live performances. To enter a rave is to be admitted into a world of electronic music, lights, and dancing that usually starts late in the evening and continues until early the following morning. Although rave culture shares many qualities of other "party" cultures throughout the globe, there is a specific tone or type of partying that occurs among those who attend raves and/or live a lifestyle associated with raves. Although rave culture and the practices associated with a rave have certainly shifted and changed since the late 1980s, rave culture has always been considered deviant or in contrast to mainstream nightlife cultures and practices; that is, rave culture has always been in dialogue with the alternative, thus offering new ways to experience nightlife, dancing, music, community, and one's body. Beginning with a brief history of the rave and an explanation of its place in society today, this entry covers a global perspective of rave culture, drug use among partygoers, dancing styles and practices, different types of electronic music and how it relates to the culture, rave events, and other details regarding those both fully and marginally involved in the rave culture.

Origins and Development

The contemporary rave culture emerged from acid house parties that typically featured electronic music and various kinds of light shows. Much like these acid house parties, raves into the 1990s and, in some cases, even today are places in which people can listen to a full range of electronic music such as house, trance, techno, dubstep, jungle, drum and bass, and much more, while dancing and socializing. It should be noted, however, that raves today are very different from the raves of the 1990s. Thus, while raves are discussed here as a current phenomenon, many of the features of the 1980s and 1990s raves have been lost or have faded with a drop in popularity, numerous law enforcement crackdowns on the culture and related practices, and changes in the first generation of ravers and their interests.

Furthermore, and very much connected to the culture, raves have typically featured both local and "global" DJs. Over and above the venue, light shows, and even the crowd, the DJ lineup is central to the popularity of any particular rave; if the lineup or featured DJ is very well-known and respected for the type of genre he or she performs, this will raise the value of the rave, thus resulting in more expensive tickets, a larger crowd, and/or the increased popularity of particular rave producers or clubs. For instance, while not a rave per se, a current club in San Francisco called Mighty frequently features well-known, respected, and longtime electronic DJs such as Mark Farina, Jeno, and Garth, thus drawing large crowds and acknowledgment among those involved in and interested in the culture.

While the word *rave* has emerged in and through alternative cultures since the late 1950s, raves and the rave culture that we understand today and, to a certain extent, experience now was born during the wave of psychedelic and other electronic dance music found at acid house and techno parties in the late 1980s. These parties mushroomed throughout

clubs, warehouses, and small venues in London and Manchester, eventually making their way into similar venues throughout the world and particularly in developed countries, such as the United Kingdom, the United States, Australia, and Canada. By the 1990s, for example, rave culture had certainly made a mark in the United States, with raves, or "parties," as described by those immersed in the culture, taking place in both large and small cities throughout the country.

The early raves of London, Manchester, and other cities in the United Kingdom as a whole were different from raves in the United States, for example. Raves essentially started in the United Kingdom, so much of what was seen and experienced elsewhere began in London. Furthermore, unlike the United States in the early 1990s, by 1991, U.K.-based organizations such as Fantazia, Universe, Raindance, and Amnesia House were organizing massive legal raves in fields and warehouses throughout the country. These parties were large, all-night events that attracted upward of 30,000 to 40,000 people, much larger than anything that was available during the same period in the United States. Whereas in the United States, the rave scene changed with the advent of commercialization and growing popularity, the United Kingdom experienced changes due to shifts in the electronic music genres featured at the huge events and government action against the event as a whole. Beginning in 1994, for example, the government used the Criminal Justice and Public Order Act 1994 to shut down raves with music that emitted a succession of repetitive beats. While raves still take place in the United Kingdom and throughout Europe, government action against both legal and illegal gatherings of people for raves certainly had an impact on the so-called golden age of 1990s raves. Reflecting on this time, contemporary musician M.I.A. wrote a song about the early 1990s London rave scene called "XR2" in which she sings: "Where were you in 92? . . . DJs, MCs, private raves, keep it secret, light it, mate," reflecting on the time before U.K. raves lost their intimate and private nature and before the government used various tactics to close them down.

Particularly in U.S. cities in the early 1990s, rave culture and the raves that took place were infamous for their mysterious nature. Raves, for example, were not easy to find; much like a scavenger hunt, partygoers would find out about a particular rave and then have to start with a phone number, then a recorded phone message, and then additional messages to arrive at the final destination. This also prompted a certain quality of the "underground" venue or rave, wherein those who attended expected the majority of people present to know how to behave at the rave, perhaps how to dance well, and it also included a place where the vibe was exciting yet mellow enough to experience the party as a whole and the high that one might have on a chosen set of drugs such as MDMA (3,4-methylenedioxymethamphetamine) or ecstasy, methamphetamines, acid, or any other available choice in a safe and welcoming place. In other words, these early raves set up an expectation for the rave that often included an ethos of peace and love, much drug taking, and dancing with little or no patience for large crowds, bad behavior, and those who could not handle any number of practices associated with the culture. Completing ethnographic work on rave culture, the sociologist Tammy L. Anderson refers to some of these "imposters" or outsiders as pretenders and spillovers; that is, rave culture "insiders" often refer to pretenders and spillovers as partygoers who do not essentially belong in the scene. While most ravers were not entirely aware of the particular acronym PLUR, or peace, love, unity and respect, its underlying philosophy implied an often unspoken understanding. In line with this philosophy, drugs such as ecstasy certainly supported the theme of love and respect. For example, those who take ecstasy ("E") report feelings of being open to love, share, and communicate and being generous with their time and attention to others; thus, taking E encouraged that kind of behavior as a template for how to do rave culture. More recently, however, and due to numerous cases of irresponsible drug use, many people still involved in the culture have advocated for harm reduction approaches that promoted attending raves and dance parties without feeling obligated to take drugs. Some of the groups that have addressed drug use at raves are the Electronic Music Defense and Education Fund, the Toronto Raver Info Project, and DanceSafe.

In the United States, in particular, the "golden age" of raves, or "parties," was certainly the early to mid-1990s as raves had not yet become so enormous and commercialized. By the mid-1990s, however, the age of the megarave had arrived. While still relatively small in comparison with the highly commercialized and radio-advertised raves of the late 1990s, a large warehouse at Hegenberger Road in Oakland, California, signaled the beginning of the end of California's "underground" rave scene.

Though these raves were epic in size and scope, featured multiple rooms and music genres, had a weekly and impressive lineup of DJs, and had enough room for thousands of ravers, their size and popularity also diminished the ability for the rave culture to remain as it was in the early 1990s. For example, soon after Hegenberger Road parties emerged and grew in popularity, promoters started throwing enormous "raves" that were advertised on the radio, held in enormous venues, and always drew crowds who were not intimately connected to the current rave culture and were unfamiliar with the unspoken expectations of those attending a rave.

In addition to the growing commercialization of raves and the subsequent shifting dynamics of the rave culture, local government and law enforcement began forcefully cracking down on any illegal gatherings of people, particularly parties that featured electronic music. Thus, while the large, commercialized parties were largely frowned on by ravers because of how they were promoted and the subsequent crowds that they attracted, they were also easier for promoters to organize because they were done legally (and, to a certain extent, without police interference). Furthermore, they also shifted the types of people who attended because the tickets were typically much more expensive than an average $10 or $20 rave. Like the United Kingdom, many of the government crackdowns on raves stemmed from widespread and often sensational media attention paid to the use of drugs at raves and the presumed disturbance caused by the loud music. In response to the massive and widespread crackdowns on raves, the U.S.-based Global Underworld created a political movement called RTD or RIGHT TO DANCE that held nonviolent protests in San Diego and Los Angeles, insisting that the rave culture was about community, peace, and love rather than a dirty word or something to be feared.

Contemporary Rave Culture

Currently, rave culture continues much as it did before its heyday. That is, "old school" DJs are featured at ravelike events in nightclubs and large dance clubs rather than warehouses and small underground venues. Rave culture is also making somewhat of a comeback during the summer months as parties such as Soul Camp feature an impressive lineup of DJs over several days of camping, dancing, and listening to "old school" house and other electronic music.

Although clothing and accessories in the rave culture have changed since the 1990s, during that time, there were a few defining features of the raver look that included large, loose-fitting pants for all genders; tight and short halter tops for women; oversized, loose-fitting T-shirts; white gloves and white belts; fluorescent yellow jackets; shoes and boots with very large soles; fairy wings and fairy tattoos; any clothing (particularly T-shirts) that glowed in the dark; nasal decongestant vapor inhalers and rub (used while taking E); suckers or pacifiers to suck on while taking E; glow sticks to dance with and entertain other drug users and friends; Adidas jackets, T-shirts, and matching pants; and glitter, to name a few. Notably, this look set those attending a rave on the margins of mainstream society, thus further augmenting one's deviant status. Ravers usually and certainly looked like they were going somewhere other than work or school. Finally, given these particular features of adornment, some ravers who looked especially "cute" and sucked on pacifiers earned themselves names such as candy ravers or candy kids.

Dancing and moving one's body to an intense beat are central to rave culture. While break dancing occurred long before rave culture emerged as a defining feature of youth culture, it most certainly made its mark at raves throughout the 1990s. Though it was not entirely central, as almost everyone danced at raves, there were many occasions in which break dancers formed circles and informally competed or danced off of one another at parties. Also, however, in contrast to break dancing competitions in which large circles form around two break dancers competing against one another, break dancing occurred both with and without dance circles at a rave; that is, other dancers who simply house-danced or free-danced (danced specifically and fluidly with the music rather than perform break dancing) danced alongside break dancers throughout a rave. Furthermore, candy ravers often had a particular style of dancing that included pumping their arms to the beat with glow sticks, swaying their hips fluidly with the melody, and switching their feet to yet another beat. The sites in which raves occurred, particularly in the early days, also promoted dancing; in warehouses with multiple rooms, for example, ravers had a number of areas in which they could dance, thus offering them more options for dancing with or without a large crowd.

Almost all electronic genres of music that emerged in and through the early rave culture have had an impact on contemporary pop and other music. As DJs and other electronic groups experienced widespread popularity during those early years, many of them made their way into popular culture, such as Moby, Prodigy, Daft Punk, Chemical Brothers, DJ Keoki, and Crystal Method. In many respects, these artists have continued performing today. Daft Punk, an extremely popular electronic music duo throughout the 1990s, was commissioned to perform the entire soundtrack for the recent movie *Tron*. Chemical Brothers, Moby, and Crystal Method continued releasing soundtracks throughout the 2000s, and in the early days, both Moby and Prodigy released music videos on MTV (Music Television) and performed in a number of music award shows. Also, Chemical Brothers recently released a live album and live concert film called "Don't Think." Furthermore, there are a number of DJs such as Paul Oakenfold, DJ Tiesto, and the groups listed above who tour the world on a regular basis. Thus, while rave culture found itself on the margins of society and many of the practices associated with this culture were considered deviant, mainstream culture has co-opted many of the music genres and dance styles of rave culture.

Just as house music is making its way into the mainstream, electronic music is often heard in mainstream nightclubs worldwide, even if the club event is not considered a rave per se. Bangkok, Thailand, and other Asian cities often feature famous "global" DJs at clubs or simply offer house music played by local DJs. In 2008, for example, a central club called Flix in Bangkok played house music every weekend night, drawing large crowds of clubbers who did not consider themselves ravers and had little affiliation with rave culture.

Finally, raves continue in some of the founding areas of rave culture such as Ibiza, Spain, continuing to draw huge crowds. Both local Ibiza and global DJs frequent its numerous clubs and events, thus signaling a culture that, although different and less popular among a younger generation, certainly still shares a place in deviant nightlife partying and dancing. The late 1980s and 1990s generation of ravers have moved into their 30s, 40s, and 50s, again shifting the rave culture landscape, though certainly still reviving rave practices at random events and clubs throughout the world.

Danielle Antoinette Hidalgo

See also Club Drugs; Methamphetamine

Further Readings

Anderson, T. L. (2009). *Rave culture: The alteration and decline of a Philadelphia music scene*. Philadelphia, PA: Temple University Press.

Brown, E. R., Jarvie, D. R., & Simpson, D. (1995). Use of drugs at "raves." *Scottish Journal, 40*, 437–451.

Brownmiller, S. (1975). *Against our will: Men, women, and rape*. New York: Simon and Schuster.

Collin, M. (1997). *Altered state: The story of ecstasy culture and acid house*. London, England: Serpents Tail.

Critcher, C. (2000). "Still raving": Social reaction to ecstasy. *Leisure Studies, 19*, 145–162.

Dundes, L. (2003). Dancesafe and ecstasy: Protection or promotion? *Journal of Health and Social Policy, 17*, 19–37.

Erenberg, L. A. (1984). *Steppin' out: New York nightlife and the transformation of American culture, 1890–1930*. Chicago, IL: University of Chicago Press.

Forsyth, A. J. M. (1996). Are raves drug supermarkets? *International Journal of Drug Policy, 7*, 105–110.

Grazian, D. (2008). *On the make: The hustle of urban nightlife*. Chicago, IL: University of Chicago Press.

Thornton, S. (1996). *Club cultures: Music, media and subcultural capital*. Middletown, CT: Wesleyan University Press.

Williams, R. (2008). Night spaces: Darkness, deterritorialization, and social control. *Space and Culture, 11*(4), 514–532.

REINTEGRATIVE SHAMING

In 1989, John Braithwaite outlined the theory of reintegrative shaming in his book *Crime, Shame, and Reintegration*. Establishing a foundation on which research could seek empirical evidence of its applicability, this book served as a springboard for Braithwaite and others to explore varied aspects of the theory. Reintegrative shaming is a manner of managing social deviance through a process of social control that involves treating the offender with respect and empathy. Through reintegrative processes, an individual who engages in criminal activity is separated from his or her crime so that the community can express disapproval of the act without stigmatizing the person. Instead of being seen as a bad person, the individual is seen as an inherently good person who has committed a bad act. The process reaffirms both the offender's and the community's commitment to the law and the collective ideas regarding what is "right." The offender is expected to take responsibility for his or her crime,

show remorse for the negative effects of the act, and make efforts to repair the harm. Once the offender has made amends through such acts as apology, repentance, restitution, or other reparations, he or she is reintegrated into the community. Key concepts within the theory are detailed below, as is the current state of empirical research.

Restorative Justice

The theory of reintegrative shaming is an integrative theory guided by principles of restorative justice, in which practices are designed to heal at both the individual and societal levels. Unlike retributive justice systems, which focus on punishment of the offender by the state, restorative justice programs focus on bringing victims, offenders, and the community together to repair the harm that resulted from the crime. Restorative justice acknowledges the wide range of people who are negatively affected by a crime, including the offender and society at large. As the name implies, rather than reducing the status of the offender through punishment, restorative justice aims to restore justice and balance by elevating the status of the victim and healing the wrongs brought about by the crime. Offenders are encouraged to acknowledge responsibility for their crimes, express remorse, and make reparations. Aspects of restorative justice that are most relevant to the theory of reintegrative shaming include respect for the offender, acknowledgment of the criminal act and its resulting social harm, and ritualized reintegration of the offender back into society as a valued member of the group.

Shaming

Shaming is an important aspect of social control. As Thomas Scheff points out, a feeling of shame signifies that one's bond with society is at risk or has been broken. If one feels shame after committing a crime, he or she will be less likely to recidivate, or reoffend. There are two types of shaming, that which stigmatizes the offender (stigmatizing shaming) and that which accompanies reintegration of the offender back into society as a valued member of the community (reintegrative shaming).

Shaming scales have been established to better operationalize the concept of shaming. In 1994, Toni Makkai and John Braithwaite created one such scale that included continuums designed to measure participants' attitudes toward the use of reintegrative shaming. This scale ranged from humiliation (disrespectful disapproval) to avoidance of humiliation (respectful disapproval), establishing the utility of a continuum with each type of shaming at opposite poles. As these researchers pointed out, such scales are acceptable measurement tools but are in need of further testing and refinement to offer consistency and reliability across studies. In *Shame Management and Regulation*, John Braithwaite and Valerie Braithwaite note that rather than scaling shame on a continuum, stigmatic and reintegrative shaming are more usefully conceptualized as separate dimensions that may have independent or interactive effects. For example, in situations where there is a high level of shame, both types of shaming have independent effects but do not interact, while in contexts of low shame, these two forms of shame are likely to interact.

Stigmatizing Shame

Shaming that is stigmatizing results when the individual is degraded, outcast, and labeled as a bad person. Research has shown that stigmatizing shaming is likely to lead to further criminal activity. This is due to the effects of the label on one's identity. This type of shame is internalized as self-hatred or rejection of the self, becoming a master status. At the same time, this form of shame is externalized, resulting in anger toward others. This anger weakens the individual's bonds to society and promotes further criminal activity. As large numbers of offenders are stigmatized in this way and ostracized from the larger community, there is increased risk that they will join together to form subcultures within which criminal behavior can be reinforced, opportunities for criminal activity become plentiful, and criminal techniques can be honed.

Reintegrative Shame

Shaming is most effective as a form of social control when it is directed at the act rather than at the actor or at his or her character. While stigmatizing shame brings feelings of humiliation and exposure while inciting anger toward those doing the shaming, reintegrative shaming brings about guilt, anger at one's self and one's actions, remorse regarding the negative impact one's act brought on others, and a feeling that the act was wrong. Here, the goal is for the individuals to feel shame regarding their wrongdoing but not feel ashamed of themselves as individuals. Ideally, even after committing an offense and bringing about harm to others, the offender would recognize that he or she is inherently a good person but may need to alter ways of thinking, relating, or behaving to live in a manner that is consistent with this goodness. Some believe a more accurate use of terms would involve discussing reintegrative processes as "guilt-inducing" rather than using the term *shame*. One can feel guilty about poor choices or destructive acts, seek to make amends, and commit to more ethical actions in the future without identifying as a bad person and negatively affecting one's sense of self.

An important part of reintegrative shaming is acknowledging the shame itself. Shame left unacknowledged can be destructive to one's sense of self. By expressing one's remorse and seeking forgiveness for one's act, an individual can discharge shame, acknowledging the shame rather than externalizing or internalizing it.

When reintegrative shaming is used in a society, research shows that crime rates are lowered. This form of shaming results in low levels of criminal activity because the criminal act is dissuaded through disapproval, but the individual who engaged in the act is not rejected from the group and therefore remains susceptible to future shaming. Through this process, the attachments to conventional society are not lost. Furthermore, the individual is not permanently labeled or outcast and, therefore, is not enticed into criminal subcultures.

Interdependence

Interdependence is a key concept within the theory of reintegrative shaming. Interdependence is born of relationships in which people are mutually dependent on one another. When people are interdependent, each relies on the other and is responsible for the other in some way. Dependence can come in many forms, including financial, emotional, spiritual, educational, or moral dependence. Different levels of interdependency exist both at the individual and the societal levels. Reintegrative shaming is most effective when interdependency exists between those being shamed and those shaming.

At the individual level, people are more or less interdependent based on factors such as age, marital status, gender, employment status, and aspirations for education and employment. Those who are less interdependent have fewer bonds to conventional society (e.g., the young, unmarried, or unemployed). At the societal level, communities can be more or less bonded by feelings of interdependency. Societies with high levels of interdependencies (known as communitarian societies) also tend to have low levels of residential mobility and are less likely to be urbanized. Communitarian societies are more likely to utilize reintegrative shaming, and such shaming is most effective within this type of community.

Moral Education

Most members of society do not engage in criminal activity, owing to a personal revulsion toward the thought of doing so. This feeling emerges through moral education from within family and community relationships. Through cultural processes like childhood stories, gossip, and media coverage of criminal acts and the shame the offenders feel afterward, moral education is coupled with reintegration. Each time a crime and the resulting shame are discussed, those witnessing the discussion have their convictions as to what is "right" strengthened. The internal effects of breaking the law then carry an immediate punishment of sorts, as the act is followed by guilt and internal shame. This immediacy and certainty are powerful deterrents of illegal behavior. In this way, fear of shame is deterrent rather than fear of formal punishment. Self-regulation or internal control is born from external control.

Tests of the Theory

Tests and elaboration of the theory of reintegrative shaming have been conducted using survey, historical, ethnographic, observational, and experimental research. This research has been conducted in several countries, including the United States, New Zealand, and Australia. Research has shown mixed results in regard to the validity and applicability of reintegrative shaming.

Makkai and John Braithwaite were the first to use direct, quantitative measures of reintegration and shaming by studying Australian nursing home inspections in 1994. Researchers sought to determine if compliance was affected by inspectors' attitudes regarding disapproval and reintegration. Findings supported the theory of reintegrative shaming, and the authors conclude that reintegrative shaming is most effective when there is interdependency between those being shamed and those who are shaming.

The general validity of the theory has been shown in a number of case study analyses carried out by John Braithwaite in the years following the publication of *Crime, Shame, and Reintegration*. Nonetheless, the realm of research in this area remains inconclusive, as many studies have reported supportive (or partially supportive) evidence, while several others have reported what appear to be contradictory results. These contradictory findings do not invalidate the theory, however, because many are based on weak or incorrect assumptions. There is also disagreement as to how many of the relevant variables are best conceptualized and measured, including *interdependency*, *guilt*, and *shame*. Clarification is also warranted in regard to the terms *stigma* and *reintegration*. These concepts are sometimes discussed in terms of long-range effects like outcasting, while in other discussions, the difference between the two forms of shaming is based on tone and style of disapproval expression. Such ambiguity can make comparisons across studies less meaningful. Research has also been inconclusive in its aim to determine if the central aspects of the theory are best conceptualized as independent main effects or as interactional effects depending on contextual variables.

Specifically designed to systematically investigate the effectiveness of reintegrative shaming processes, the Re-Integrative Shaming Experiment, carried out in Canberra, Australia, between 1995 and 1999 by Lawrence Sherman, Heather Strang, and Daniel Woods, also yielded mixed results. Comparing recidivism rates of offenders taking part in standard court processes with those involved in more restorative processes, researchers found within the more reintegrative cases a reduction in recidivism for violent offenders but an increase in reoffending for property offenders.

Several empirical studies have also been carried out to test various aspects of the theory's assumptions and hypotheses. In 2001, Carter Hay uncovered a strong relationship between interdependency and reintegration. In this research, shaming was also found to be significantly and negatively related to delinquency when controlling for demographic variables and prior antisocial behavior. However, the relationship between reintegration and delinquency was found to be the result of a spurious relationship to interdependency.

Conclusion

The theory of reintegrative shaming is still in its infancy. To date, it has endured a modest amount of empirical scrutiny as compared with other theories of social control, indicating little need for revision. Overall, it seems this theory is well positioned to offer many insights into both causes and consequences of wrongdoing not only relative to offenders but also to victims and to society at large.

Kristen L. Hourigan

See also Informal Social Control; Integrated Theories; Labeling Approach; Peacemaking Criminology; Primary and Secondary Deviance; Social Disapproval; Stigma and Stigma Management

Further Readings

Ahmad, N. H., Braithwaite, J., & Braithwaite, V. (Eds.). (2001). *Shame management through reintegration.* Cambridge, England: Cambridge University Press.

Braithwaite, J. (1989). *Crime, shame, and reintegration.* Cambridge, England: Cambridge University Press.

Hay, C. (2001). An exploratory test of Braithwaite's reintegrative shaming theory. *Journal of Research in Crime & Delinquency, 38*(2), 132–153.

Makkai, T., & Braithwaite, J. (1994). Reintegrative shaming and compliance with regulatory standards. *Criminology, 32,* 361–383.

Rebellon, C. J., Piquero, N. L., Piquero, A. R., & Tibbetts, S. G. (2010). Anticipated shaming and criminal offending. *Journal of Criminal Justice, 38*(5), 988–997.

Scheff, T. J., & Retzinger, S. (1991). *Emotions and violence: Shame and rage in destructive conflicts.* Lexington, MA: Lexington Books.

Sherman, L. W., Strang, H., & Woods. D. (2000). *Recidivism patterns in the Canberra Reintegrative Shaming Experiments (RISE).* Canberra, ACT, Australia: Centre for Restorative Justice, Australian National University.

RELIGIOSITY AND DEVIANCE

Researchers have long sought to understand the relationship between religiosity and deviant or criminal behaviors. Religiosity can be defined as a cognitive and behavioral commitment to organized religion. The pioneering French sociologist Émile Durkheim believed that religion operated as a social force in that greater levels of religious commitment would lead to fewer deviant behaviors. Empirical research since the 1960s has produced widely varying results. Whereas many studies have found that religion significantly reduces many deviant and criminal behaviors, others have found no relationship. This entry is divided into two sections. First, research on the relationship between religiosity and

deviance/crime in the general public is reviewed. Second, research on religiosity and deviance/crime in the prison context is reviewed.

Religiosity and Deviance/Crime in Free Society

The first major empirical study of religion and deviance/crime was published by Travis Hirschi and Rodney Stark in 1969. These researchers used survey data on youths from California to test what they called the Hellfire Hypothesis, which predicted that religion could deter crime through the fear of supernatural punishment and at the same time could encourage prosocial behaviors through the hope of supernatural rewards. The authors investigated whether individuals who attended church were less likely to engage in a variety of deviant behaviors than individuals who did not attend church. They also investigated whether belief in supernatural sanctions for bad behaviors could deter those bad behaviors. Hirschi and Stark found no relationship between religious attendance or belief in supernatural sanctions and self-reported deviant acts. The researchers concluded that the youths' decisions to commit deviant acts were linked with perceptions of pleasure and pain on earth rather than on purported heavenly rewards for good behavior or hellfire for sinful acts.

In a subsequent study, however, Stark and colleagues reconsidered their original findings. They argued that their previous findings were due largely to the moral makeup of the area in which it was conducted (Richmond, California). In what has become known as the *moral communities hypothesis*, Stark contends that religion is most likely to reduce deviance/crime in more religious areas of the country (e.g., southeast and Midwest) than in less religious areas (e.g., northeast and Pacific Northwest). Stark characterized Richmond, California, as a "secular community" rather than as a "moral community." The moral makeup of the community thus helped explain why religiosity did not reduce deviance/crime in the original study.

Steven Burkett and Mervin White offered a competing explanation for Hirschi and Stark's findings. They suggested that the effects of religion on crime will vary depending on the type of crime. Using survey data on high school students in Pennsylvania, they found that religion is most likely to reduce behaviors that have a strong moral or ascetic connotation in religious circles but are not universally condemned in society (e.g., alcohol/drug use, premarital sex, and gambling). The authors reported that higher levels of religious participation led to significant decreases in students' use of alcohol and marijuana but did not affect involvement in property or violent offenses. Burkett and White's work has been called the *antiasceticism hypothesis*.

Using data on middle and high school students in three midwestern states, John Cochran and Ronald Akers found support for the antiasceticism hypothesis. Specifically, they reported that the more religious students in the sample reported significantly lower levels of alcohol and marijuana use than less or nonreligious students, but there was no significant effect of religion on other types of crimes.

Lee Ellis and others have suggested that the relationship between religiosity and deviance/crime is spurious. This means that the relationship is contingent on other factors such as arousal level and self-control of individuals. According to Ellis's *arousal theory*, criminals are naturally prone to boredom, and criminal actions are a means of finding arousal through risk-seeking behavior. Not all stimulation sought by risk seekers will be criminal, but risk-seeking behaviors may often be deviant and, in some cases, criminal. Ellis predicted that individuals who have low arousal levels will have low levels of church attendance because religious services tend to be routine and solemn events. From his analysis, Ellis concluded that religious participation was associated with lower levels of deviance/crime. However, he found that the relationship between religion and deviance/crime was no longer strong once the level of arousal was taken into account.

Michael Welch, Charles Tittle, and Harold Grasmick examined the relationships among religiosity, self-control, and crime. The authors analyzed survey data on adults in Oklahoma to determine the predictors of five types of crimes. The authors found that religiosity and self-control operate on significant and independent tracks for deterring crime; that is, higher levels of religious commitment directly reduced the likelihood of criminal activities even after accounting for individuals' level of self-control.

Of particular importance are three systematic reviews of the empirical literature on religiosity and deleterious outcomes such as deviance, crime, and delinquency. Colin Baier and Bradley Wright reviewed 60 studies of religion and deviance/crime conducted between 1969 and 1998. They concluded that religion had a "moderate effect." Byron Johnson and colleagues reviewed 40 studies of the relationship between religion and delinquency

conducted between 1985 and 1997. They found that in 30 of the studies, religion led to significant reductions. The most recent and comprehensive review of the empirical literature appears in Johnson's book, *More God, Less Crime*. Johnson reviewed 272 studies conducted between 1944 and 2010. He found that in 90% of the studies, the authors reported that religion significantly reduced deviance, crime, or delinquency.

Religiosity and Deviance/Crime in Prison

In addition to studying the relationship between religiosity and deviance/crime in free society, researchers have also begun to study this relationship in the prison context. Religion has been a method of correctional treatment since the genesis of the penal system in the United States. In fact, the first penitentiaries were developed by Quakers for offenders to study the Bible as part of their rehabilitation. Currently, most states employ full-time chaplains and allow members of local religious congregations to promote faith to the incarcerated. Researchers studying religion in prison have focused on two issues: (1) whether inmates' level of religiosity affects prison behavior and (2) whether religiosity reduces the likelihood of postrelease arrest (i.e., recidivism).

The first major study of religion in the prison context was conducted by Johnson and colleagues. They conducted an evaluation of a faith-based program sponsored by Prison Fellowship Ministries (PFM) in four New York state prisons. A total of 201 male prisoners were chosen based on their similarities to a control group. Inmates were categorized based on how often they participated in religious programs. The researchers found that participation in PFM activities was not related to prison infractions, and inmates involved in PFM activities did not have a significantly reduced likelihood of recidivism compared with the control group. However, Johnson and colleagues found that inmates who were most heavily involved in PFM activities were less likely to have been arrested within one year after their release than those in the control group. In 2004, Johnson conducted a follow-up study in which he changed the definition of active participation (from ten or more to only five or more) and increased the amount of time evaluated after the inmates were released (from one to eight years). He found little difference between the median arrest times and reincarceration rates between PFM and non-PFM inmates. The rate at which the inmates were arrested after release was slightly lower for the PFM group at eight years, but the only significant difference appeared when the most active inmates were compared with the least active inmates.

Todd Clear and colleagues collected survey data and an ethnography of inmates involved in Christian and Muslim religious activities over the course of 10 months. They looked at the intrinsic value of being outwardly religious for prisoners, which they defined as the part that religion plays in helping them deal with the bad feelings they experienced due to their incarceration. The results indicated that faith allowed inmates to receive forgiveness and to make restitution for their offenses and gave them hope that they could turn their lives around once released. The authors also examined the extrinsic value of religious participation in terms of how faith affects inmates' relationships with others. Involvement in religious activities benefited inmates by providing them with a safe context, by keeping them out of trouble and in safe places such as the chapel, and by allowing them to create relationships with individuals in free society.

Kent Kerley and colleagues studied whether religiosity could reduce deviant prison behaviors such as arguments and fights. A random sample of inmates at a large southeastern prison facility completed a survey relating to personal background, religious background, involvement in religious activities, and fighting or arguing with other inmates. The authors found that inmates who reported belief in a higher power and regularly attended prison religious services had a significantly lower likelihood of arguing once or more per month than those who did not. Religiosity did not directly reduce inmate fighting but did so indirectly by reducing the frequency of arguments. In a follow-up study, Kerley and colleagues found that religiosity did not lead to a significant reduction in the experience of a range of negative emotions among inmates. They concluded that prison life is emotionally debilitating to the point that religion does not reduce the experience of negative emotions.

Kerley and colleagues recently used data on Iowa parolees to conduct the first investigation of religiosity, self-control, and deviant behavior in the prison context. Their results indicated declining statistical significance as they tracked the impact of religiosity on prison deviance. By themselves, all measures of religiosity were significant predictors of prison deviance, but when measures of criminal history and demographic background were added, only two measures were significant. Once the authors accounted for the level of self-control, only one measure of religiosity (frequency of attending religious services) was significant. This led the authors to conclude that both religiosity and self-control were important theoretical constructs in explaining prison deviance.

Scott Camp and colleagues collected survey data from 407 inmates participating in the faith-based Life Connections Program (LCP) at five treatment prisons and 592 comparison subjects at five other prisons. They found that inmates who had a religious identity prior to incarceration were less likely to volunteer for religious programs offered in prison. They concluded that religious programs are effective in reducing prison deviance only for those inmates who are highly involved and not for inmates who have only limited involvement. In a follow-up study that included survey data and official prison records, Camp and colleagues found that LCP participation decreased the probability of inmates engaging in serious forms of prison deviance. However, there was no effect of LCP participation on less serious forms of prison deviance.

Kent R. Kerley

See also Agents of Social Control; Informal Social Control; Social Control

Further Readings

Baier, C., & Wright, B. R. E. (2001). If you love me, keep my commandments: A meta-analysis of the effect of religion on crime. *Journal of Research in Crime & Delinquency, 38,* 3–21.

Hirschi, T., & Stark, R. (1969). Hellfire and delinquency. *Social Problems, 17,* 202–213.

Johnson, B. R. (2011). *More god, less crime: Why faith matters and how it could matter more.* West Conshohocken, PA: Templeton Press.

Johnson, B. R., De Li, S., Larson, D. B., & McCullough, M. (2000). A systematic review of the religiosity and delinquency literature. *Journal of Contemporary Criminal Justice, 16,* 32–52.

Kerley, K. R., Copes, H., Tewksbury, R., & Dabney, D. A. (2011). Examining the relationship between religiosity and self-control as predictors of prison deviance. *International Journal of Offender Therapy and Comparative Criminology, 55,* 1251–1271.

Kerley, K. R., Matthews, T. L., & Blanchard, T. C. (2005). Religiosity, religious participation, and negative prison behaviors. *Journal for the Scientific Study of Religion, 44,* 443–457.

Stark, R., Kent, L., & Doyle, D. P. (1982). Religion and delinquency: The ecology of a "lost" relationship. *Journal of Research in Crime & Delinquency, 19*, 4–24.

ROAD WHORES

Street-level prostitution as a form of social deviance has been empirically examined for decades; nevertheless, there remains a subculture within this occupational class that has not received as much attention. The literature on road whores in particular is limited at best, providing readers with an introduction to this deviant population but not the extent of what they do and how it affects crime control policies and the overall health of the population they service. *Road whore* is a dated term that is used to encompass the prostitution base that services the commercial trucking industry. These sex workers advertise their services via the Citizens' Band radio (CB), which is the main communication device used by truckers to connect and converse with one another.

This area of research and inquiry is important to criminologists and law enforcement alike for several reasons. Criminologists can empirically examine the phenomenon further to determine the causes and consequences of this level of prostitution on trucking industries and law enforcement policies. Extended research can thereby aid in the evaluation and implementation of new evidence-based policies geared toward this socially deviant subculture. With the limited attention given to this problem, many policies and law enforcement strategies could potentially be underdeveloped and unequipped when combating risky sexual practices along U.S. highways. Understanding the underlying nature and full extent of the phenomenon would provide law enforcement agencies the tools necessary to proactively control this form of deviance and assess the impending health risks associated with it.

The Truck Stop Milieu

Road whore is a term rarely encountered in any contemporary body of literature. This term was once used to describe a sex worker who traveled interstate highways frequenting truck stops, rest areas, and weigh stations in hopes of soliciting sex for money and/or illegal substances. A road whore, or what contemporary literature refers to as a "CB prostitute" or "lot lizard," is a subculture of street-level prostitution. Unlike any other prostitute, these workers connect with truckers by implicitly advertising their services using the CB radio. Furthermore, these prostitutes intentionally target commercial truckers due to the nature and characteristics associated with long-haul trucking. Transporting loads cross-country leaves truckers vulnerable to feelings of social isolation and loneliness, being separated from family and friends for extended periods of time. Road whores take advantage of these characteristics, promising female companionship and sexual services over CB airwaves in exchange for financial compensation. Sexual services are performed in empty lots and rest areas out of view of the public and the police, making this form of prostitution easy to conceal.

The reasons pertaining to entry into this occupation are similar to those relating to the dominant street-level culture of prostitution. In their recent work on truck stop prostitution, Yorghos Apostolopoulos and colleagues explored the phenomenon by interviewing 39 female sex workers servicing truckers along U.S. highways. Through qualitative interviews, the authors were able to gain insight into this segment of sex work, discovering that a majority of women entered the profession to support a drug habit that was commonly worsened by the experience of social isolation and estrangement from family and friends. Discussions of sex work as both coping and survival mechanisms disclosed that many of these women had experienced physical and sexual abuse, which ultimately contributed to the escapist mentality many of them shared as reasons for entering the profession.

Implications for New Directions in Research and Policy

Because current statistics on the prevalence of form of prostitution are not available, gauging the prevalence of this phenomenon is difficult. Given the limited research surrounding the culture of truck stop prostitution, the low visibility of the issues associated with this form of deviance impose limits on our knowledge of how best to address it. There is brief mention of crime control tactics in the literature that aim to combat truck stop prostitution and the specific health risks surrounding it. Increased surveillance and security of truck stops and rest areas as well as sting operations to target and contain prostitutes have been implemented. Nevertheless, the resulting crime control effects on CB prostitution remain unknown. Issues involving human sex trafficking also arise within this body of literature, with truck stops serving as an outlet for sex traffickers to use in the exploitation of sex workers.

Risks associated with the contraction and spread of HIV (human immunodeficiency virus) and other sexually transmitted diseases are significant because of the high incidence of drug use and unprotected sexual encounters. There has been some discussion of implementing sex education programs for truckers to inform them of the risks associated with unprotected sexual practices along U.S. highways. Existing literature emphasizing the prevalence of HIV/AIDS (acquired immune deficiency syndrome) in trucking industries in other nations underscores the need to fully examine this phenomenon within the United States. Future research should be directed toward a better understanding of the nature and extent of this form of prostitution and how it relates to health risks and crime control practices that surround it.

Arynn Alexandria Infante

See also Deviant Places; Female Prostitution; Public Sex

Further Readings

Apostolopoulos, Y., Sonmez, S., Kronenfeld, J., & Smith, D. (2007). Sexual networks of truckers, truckchasers, and disease risk. In G. Herdt & C. Howe (Eds.), *21st century sexualities: Contemporary issues in health, education, and rights* (pp. 112–114). London, England: Routledge.

Apostolopoulos, Y., Sonmez, S., Shattell, M., & Kronenfeld, J. (2012). Sex work in trucking milieux: "Lot lizards," truckers, and risk. *Nursing Forum, 47,* 140–152.

Lichtenstein, B., Hook, E. W., Grimley, D. M., St. Lawrence, J. S., & Bachmann, L. H. (2008). HIV risk among long-haul truckers in the USA. *Culture, Health & Sexuality, 10,* 43–56.

Luxenburg, J., & Klein, L. (1984). CB radio prostitution: Technology and the displacement of deviance. *Journal of Offender Counseling Services Rehabilitation, 9,* 71–87.

ROBBERY

The Federal Bureau of Investigation's Uniform Crime Reporting Program defines robbery as the taking or attempting to take anything of value from the care, custody, or control of a person or persons by force or threat of force or violence and/or by putting the victim in fear. Larceny is differentiated from robbery by not requiring a force element, whereas burglary does not require victim presence. Therefore, while larceny and burglary are similar to robbery, they are not interchangeable. The taking of one's property is a deviant act due to its illegality and potential for harm. This entry provides an overview of the types and prevalence of robbery, along with descriptions of the typical victims and offenders, followed by information on how offenders select their targets and type of techniques used in the crimes.

Types of Robbery

To understand robbery, it is first necessary to know that there are many forms in which it can take place. The different types can be classified by the location and what is taken by the offender. The most common, street robbery, occurs when the act takes place outdoors, between one or more individuals. If the act occurs within the victim's home, it is identified as a residential robbery, also known as a home invasion. Drug robbery can occur inside or outside but is characterized by a drug dealer victim who is being targeted due to the likelihood of drugs and money being available. Commercial robbery is the taking of property by force within a place of business, such as a gas station or a convenience store. Bank robberies are considered as a separate category due to the differences that characterize the event. Bank robberies involve money being demanded by force within a bank or from a user of an automated teller machine. Last, there is carjacking, which involves the taking of a vehicle by force. The object being stolen sets carjacking apart, but it still fits the definition of robbery since it is property being taken by force. Because carjacking is often treated under a separate statute in the law, however, it will not be discussed in this entry.

Patterns of Robbery

Prevalence

Depending on whether official statistics or victimization data are used, there were between 354,396 and 556,760 robberies that occurred in 2011. These numbers amount to a decrease of about 4% from the 2010 statistics. Comparing the 2011 and 2007 data, there was about a 21% decrease in robberies overall over those four years. The costs of robbery are significant, with losses totaling $409 million in value of property stolen, during 2011 alone. The banks are the hardest hit with an average of $4,704 lost per offense, compared with $1,153 per average robbery. Though bank robberies are relatively uncommon (about 2% of robberies overall), the losses accrued are significant. Unlike the overall rate, the rate of bank robberies has been increasing, partly due to the availability of more banks offering longer hours along with a greater potential for a payout.

The most prevalent form of robbery is street robbery (44%) followed by residential robbery (17%). Convenience stores (5%) and gas stations (2.4%) are among the remaining locations identified. With regard to weapons use, strong-arm (42.3%), defined as force without the use of a weapon, and firearms (41.3%) are occurring most frequently. Knives (7.8%) follow as the next most commonly used weapon.

Time/Location

Depending on the specific type of robbery, the most likely time and location of the event varies. In the rest of this entry, we will focus on bank, commercial, and street robbery to facilitate a discussion of the differences between categories of robbery. Residential and street robberies occur in similar types of places and times. Namely, the locations of most robberies are urban areas and places near an offender's home and the majority take place after dark.

Bars, convenience stores, pawnshops, and gas stations are the most likely targets for a commercial robbery. Street robberies occur in more open and less predictable areas. Parking lots and garages are examples of these more open areas and are where street robberies are most frequent. Regarding time, bank robberies occur mostly between morning and midday, with Friday being the most likely. This is likely due to the misconception that banks have more money on Fridays due to paydays. Unlike bank robberies, commercial and street robberies tend to take place at night and on the weekends.

Victims

The victims of street robbery are most often young males. Overall, the victims tend to be white. However, for acquaintance robberies, the victims are more likely to be young, black, poor, and unmarried. Acquaintance robberies are scenarios in which the victim and the offender know each other and cannot be considered strangers.

Offenders

There is similarity between the characteristics of the victim and the offender. When looking at overall robberies, the offenders are young and male. However, there is no racial differentiation. Separating robbers out by their style of preparedness (i.e., professional or opportunistic), there is a shift in the characteristics of the average offender. Professional robbers tend to be more experienced and are more careful in the planning of the offense, whereas opportunistic robbers tend to be more desperate and search for opportunities with less planning. Professional robbers are older and typically white. Opportunistic robbers are younger and generally nonwhite.

Separating offenders out by the type of robbery they commit, bank robbers tend to be older, while commercial and street robbers tend to have the same characteristics as the overall robbers, young and male. However, according to the Uniform Crime Report, the majority of people arrested for robbery are black.

Motivation

Obviously, there are many types of individuals who commit robberies, but their motivations tend to be similar. The primary motivation for robbers (regardless of race or gender) is to obtain money and material goods. Robbers view robbery as being the quickest and easiest way they know to get those items. While money and goods motivate all offenders, the reasoning for wanting them may vary. The basic three reasons money and material goods are motivations are for personal expenses such as paying off debts and producing an income for a family, supporting a drug habit, and supporting the criminal lifestyle, which typically involves drugs, alcohol, and a need to always have the best clothing, shoes, and jewelry. Often, robbers have a secondary motivation for their crimes. There is an excitement or thrill inherent in being violent and controlling another individual; this works as a secondary motivator. A third motivation is that of revenge or retaliation, but this is still considered secondary to the desire for money and goods.

Younger offenders tend to put more emphasis on the excitement they derive from the robbery, whereas older offenders emphasize almost exclusively the financial rewards and desire for high living. In the case of robbers who frequently and repeatedly offend for many years, a lifestyle pattern emerges, with situational demands such as high living expenses to support the criminal lifestyle, plus their affinity for violence, keeping them motivated to continue the behavior.

Target Selection

Bank Robbery

For a motivated offender to commit a robbery, he or she must select a suitable target. Target selection varies by type of robbery as well as by the number of individuals involved. Pinpointing which bank to target is shaped by two factors, type of transportation and ease and number of escape routes. Individuals who are attempting to rob a bank alone typically look for a place that is accessible to foot traffic. Solo bank robbers often do not use a car because they do not have a driver for a quick getaway; thus, the location is often relatively close to their residence. Being on foot encourages them to look for banks with escape routes that make it difficult for someone to follow them. This entails locations that are open directly to foot traffic or are near dense residential areas where they can blend in to the surroundings. In addition, locations that have obstructions to the view of their potential escape route from the bank are ideal.

Those who commit robbery in a group tend to escape in a car, with a driver waiting and ready for immediate departure. Thus, an ideal location for the group would include easy access for a vehicle—for example, a bank near a multiple lane road with two-way traffic. The best location would be busy but not so busy that the traffic is not moving at all. The key is to blend in easily with the other cars on the road.

Commercial Robbery

When searching for a target for a commercial robbery, offenders tend to look in areas that they are familiar with and choose businesses that are readily accessible. The types of businesses often selected are liquor stores, taverns, pawnshops, gas stations, and other small local enterprises. Those with large parking lots that distance prying eyes or with poorly lit outside areas and stores with interiors that cannot be clearly seen from the street are the favored locations to scout. All of the previous elements reduce the likelihood of being detected. Another factor is the limitation that the store places on the amount of cash kept in the register, knowledge of which can help the offender achieve the biggest payoff available.

Street Robbery

Street robbery involves two elements, finding a location to scout and looking for a potential victim. First, robbers determine a location where they can find a potential victim. Characteristics of the best locations are where the offender can blend into the surroundings and not draw unnecessary attention. These locations are often comfortable and familiar to the offender and typically near their home. Being familiar with the location helps the offender plan the approach and escape routes and predict the behavior and potential profit of the individuals. In addition, the close, familiar location enables them to unload goods quickly if necessary.

Victim selection follows the decision of the best location. A person who appears to have money and valuables, such as someone who flashes money around or wears expensive jewelry, is considered an attractive target. A potential victim appears vulnerable (easily intimidated, subdued, or overpowered), seems unaware of his or her immediate surroundings, or is distracted, making for easier access, and is less likely to resist.

Techniques of Enactment

The actual commission of the robbery follows target selection. The techniques used for different types of robberies vary, and multiple techniques are possible for use in a given type.

Bank Robbery

Contrary to popular belief, many bank robberies are spontaneous and opportunistic, with most of them being committed alone (about 80%). Most offenders do not bother disguising themselves even though there are security cameras (about 60%). Even though bank robberies are often spontaneous, they involve more planning than other forms of robbery. In general, wielding a weapon is a typical means of communicating that a robbery is underway.

Individuals operating alone typically commit the robbery around midday when it is expected that the bank will be full of customers. Groups committing bank robberies, however, tend to enter shortly after opening when there is an expectation of more money from the morning deliveries and the night drop. Also, groups tend to prefer a time when there are fewer customers to make the robbery occur faster and run more smoothly.

Commercial Robbery

Unlike a bank robbery, weapons in a commercial robbery are not generally drawn immediately on entering the business. The presence of an accomplice increases the chances a hostage will be taken to communicate demands and makes it less likely that the weapon will actually be used against someone rather than just brandished. If there is resistance by the employee, injury often follows to avoid delay and interference.

Three types of techniques are commonly used in commercial robberies: straight, customer, and merchandise. The most common type is customer robbery, where the actual robbery typically occurs a while after entering the building. This technique involves the offender pretending to be a customer and waiting to express demands until at the register, behaving as though a purchase is going to be made. A straight robbery is more straightforward; the offender demands the money immediately after entering the business. Merchandise robbery is the forcible taking of material goods from a business. Interestingly, this type of commercial robbery is associated with a higher frequency of injuries than the others because employees are more likely to show resistance.

Street Robbery

With regard to street violence, there are four techniques that are commonly used by male offenders. Some offenders will only use one technique, whereas others will change according to the situation. The technique chosen often depends on the personality of the offender and the characteristics of the environment and victim. In addition, men and women tend to rely on different techniques in the commission of street robbery.

Male robbers typically use physical violence, which often escalates if they experience resistance. Oftentimes, their victims are other men who are in some way connected to the criminal lifestyle, such as a drug dealer. It is common for a man to commit robbery with a partner.

Four techniques used by males are blitz, confrontation, con, and snatch. In the *blitz* technique, the offender approaches the victim with violence first, and when the victim is immobilized, the robbery ensues. The *confrontation* technique involves the offender's approaching the victim and immediately demanding the property through verbal commands, resorting to violence only in case of noncompliance.

Using a *con* to achieve success involves approaching a potential victim through false pretenses as a distraction to catch the victim off guard and to allow contact without suspicion. An example of the con technique is asking someone for the time to get close before making robbery demands. Last, the *snatch* technique is the grabbing of visible property and escaping, with the victim aware of what is happening. This is not universally considered a technique of robbery in that it lacks a straightforward element of force, but it does involve a forceful grabbing and causes fear.

Women tend to rob in one of three ways: (1) targeting females with physical confrontation, (2) targeting male victims by appearing sexually available, and (3) participating in robbery with a male. Targeting females with physical confrontation is the most common form of robbery used by women. This form involves physical force against the victim, but typically not the use of a weapon. However, when a weapon is present, it is typically a knife. In addition, when targeting females, the robber typically does not have a male accomplice. The second technique is targeting males through sexual interest. In this scenario, the women almost always use a gun and do not use direct physical contact. Perceived sexual availability is similar to the con technique used by males. The women pretend to want the man sexually to catch the victim off guard and make the robbery safer. This technique may involve an accomplice, but it is not necessary. However, it is useful for the woman to have a male backup since the male victim often believes females will not go through with the robbery and may try to resist. The third technique a female uses is to participate together with males. These robberies have the same characteristics as a typical male robbery, with the female playing either an equal or a more secondary role.

Mindy Bernhardt

See also Burglary; Larceny; Property Crime; Violent Crime

Further Readings

Altizio, A., & York, D. (2007). *Robbery of convenience stores: Problem-oriented guides for police* (Problem-Specific Guide Series, Guide No. 49). Washington, DC: U.S. Department of Justice, Office of Community Oriented Policing Services.

Bernasco, W., & Block, R. (2009). Where offenders choose to attack: A discrete choice model of robberies in Chicago. *Criminology, 47,* 93–130.

Felson, R. B., Baumer, E. P., & Messner, S. F. (2000). Acquaintance robbery. *Journal of Research in Crime & Delinquency, 37,* 284–305.

Katz, J. (1991). The motivation of the persistent robber. *Crime and Justice, 14,* 277–306.

Miller, J. (1998). Up it up: Gender and the accomplishment of street robbery. *Criminology, 36,* 37–66.

Monk, K. M., Heinonen, J. A., & Eck, J. E. (2010). *Street robbery: Problem-oriented guides for police* (Problem-Specific Guide Series, Guide No. 59). Washington, DC: U.S. Department of Justice, Office of Community Oriented Policing Services.

Smith, J. (2003). *The nature of personal property* (Home Office Research Study No. 254). London, England: Home Office.

Weisel, D. L. (2007). *Bank robbery: Problem-oriented guides for police* (Problem-Specific Guide Series, Guide No. 48). Washington, DC: U.S. Department of Justice, Office of Community Oriented Policing Services.

Wright, R., & Decker, S. H. (1997). *Armed robbers in action: Stick-ups and street culture.* Boston, MA: Northeastern University Press.

ROLLER DERBY

Roller derby is an amateur, competitive, contact sport that has experienced a revival within the past 10 years in the United States and abroad. The Women's Flat Track Derby Association notes that there are currently 156 full-member leagues and 58 apprentice leagues worldwide. The sport is heavily dominated by women, although leagues for men and youth exist as well.

Derby skaters utilize quad roller skates, specially formulated wheels, helmets, mouth guards, and elbow-, wrist-, and kneepads. Today, the vast majority of roller derby is played on oval-shaped flat tracks. During a bout (game), two teams compete for points, and the team with the most points at the end of the game wins. Each bout consists of two 30-minute periods; each period is made up of an indeterminate number of jams (as jams can last anywhere from a few seconds to 2 minutes). At the beginning of a new jam, each team sends out a lineup consisting of one "jammer," three "blockers," and a "pivot." Blockers and pivots from both teams constitute "the pack." To score points, jammers make an initial pass through the pack and then collect one point for every opposing skater they pass legally during subsequent passes. Blockers hip check and booty block opposing skaters while providing assists in the form of whips and pushes to their own jammer. After two minutes of play or after the lead jammer (the first jammer to break through the pack legally) calls off the jam, a new lineup of skaters are sent onto the track.

Until recently, the sport was most notably associated with over-the-top theatrics and premeditated scripts reminiscent of professional wrestling; such antics were commonly used as marketing ploys for televised roller derbies of the 1960s and 1970s. Today, participants challenge the misconception that bouts are staged or faked by emphasizing derby's legitimacy as a "real" sport, and their own legitimacy as "real" athletes. Skaters highlight how derby incorporates aggressive physical contact, fierce competition, offensive and defensive strategies, strength, and speed. Skaters also talk of the countless hours spent training and conditioning, describe injuries they have both dealt and endured, and trade insider knowledge regarding the merits of various wheels, skate setups, and track surfaces.

Most research on roller derby focuses on the do-it-yourself nature of the sport, the potential for women's gender transgression within the sport, and players' violations of traditional appearance norms. Similar to music subcultures, roller derby leagues are do-it-yourself grassroots organizations run "by the skaters, for the skaters." League members do more than just skate; they donate their time as board members, captains, trainers, accountants, and committee heads. This collective labor ensures that skaters retain control over their leagues, their organizations, their bodies, and the sport of roller derby itself. In this way, skaters actively create and maintain derby as a female-dominated, nonconventional sport subculture, thereby challenging the exclusion of women from most subcultural spaces.

This commitment to independence has prompted the emergence of underground economies within roller derby communities. Skaters, volunteers, and fans support these underground economies by purchasing skates, gear, clothing, accessories, art, and services (e.g., photography and web design) from "skater owned and operated" businesses. Derby leagues are not managed by large sport corporations, thereby making it easier to resist commercialization. The revenue generated from fund-raisers, the sale of bout tickets, and skaters' monthly dues goes directly toward paying training facility rental fees, advertising and marketing costs, travel stipends for away games, and bout production overheads. Additionally, most leagues are nonprofit and donate portions of their proceeds to local, charitable organizations.

Derby skaters' gender transgression has also been of recent academic interest. Research on women's athletic participation suggests that female athletes have been channeled into sports that reinforce and uphold conventional beliefs about femininity. Sports such as yoga, synchronized swimming, and aerobics comply with gender norms that require women to be slender, graceful, toned (not ripped), stylish, and attractive. Typically, sports that involve bodily contact, aggression, competition, risk of injury and pain, building muscle mass, and profuse sweating, smelliness, or dirtiness have been considered off-limits for women. Roller derby poses a clear challenge to these gendered behavioral expectations as women skate fast, hit hard, perform challenging skating maneuvers, fall down and recover quickly, get sweaty, sustain injuries, and endure elbow- and kneepad "stink."

Additional research suggests that derby skaters challenge hegemonic gender norms through the adoption of witty, raunchy, provocative, and intimidating pseudonyms ("derby names"), such as Pussy Venom, Zsa Zsa LaGore, Sarah Impalin, Heavy Flo, Ivana Dreihump, Slutnik, and Tuff Tits. Here, overt references to violence, sexuality, and the body allow skaters to parody and mock traditional notions of femininity. Furthermore, skaters engage in "gender maneuvering," or the disruption of seemingly complementary relations between femininity and masculinity, through the pairing of hypersexualized clothing items with masculinized sporting and fashion accoutrements. At bouts, spectators are confronted by skaters of all sizes outfitted in revealing booty shorts, fishnet stockings, bulky protective padding, and football-style "eye black." Such pairings may disrupt the sexual objectification that typically occurs when women wear hyperfeminized clothing alone.

Researchers have also been interested in derby skaters' violations of physical appearance norms, namely, those regarding body size and adornment. As an institution, sport has the potential to normalize certain bodies while marginalizing others. Today, the norms that govern sporting bodies privilege young, white, lean, muscular, male bodies. When women do participate in sport, they are subject to a beauty-related exercise culture, which stresses slimness and weight-loss as primary goals. Roller derby destabilizes this normalizing regime by embracing skaters of all shapes, sizes, and weights and by teaching them how to effectively use their bodies (regardless of size and shape) as "weapons" on the track. This emphasis on the utility of skaters' bodies provides women with an alternative exercise discourse, and encourages them to rethink their own embodiment and corporeal potential.

Skaters' adornment practices also pose challenges to hegemonic appearance norms. Some skaters sport offbeat hairstyles and colors, multiple piercings, and large, visible tattoos. Others don clothing and accessories (e.g., vintage cardigans, skinny jeans, and nerd glasses) linked to various music subcultures. In this way, derby is a subcultural niche that attracts modified and alternatively styled women. As with any sporting subculture, new members learn and adopt the attitudes, styles, and practices common among older members. On joining, some previously unmodified skaters begin engaging in counterhegemonic adornment practices. Roller derby creates space for women to be transgressively embodied in sport.

Natalie M. Peluso

See also Female Bodybuilding; Feminist Theory; Professional Wrestling; Punk Subculture; Sport and Deviance

Further Readings

Beaver, T. D. (2012). "By the skaters, for the skaters" the DIY ethos of the roller derby revival. *Journal of Sport and Social Issues, 36,* 25–49.

Carlson, J. (2010). The female significant in all-women's amateur roller derby. *Sociology of Sport Journal, 27,* 428–440.

Finley, N. J. (2010). Skating femininity: Gender maneuvering in women's roller derby. *Journal of Contemporary Ethnography, 39,* 359–387.

Peluso, N. M. (2011). "Cruisin' for a bruisin'": Women's flat track roller derby. In C. Bobel & S. Kwan (Eds.), *Embodied resistance: Challenging the norms, breaking the rules* (pp. 37–47). Nashville, TN: Vanderbilt University Press.

ROUTINE ACTIVITY THEORY

Similar to the mantra of real estate agents, the recent focus of criminologists has become location. Increasingly, sociological research has found that the setting of crime is just as important in understanding deviance as is why people violate norms. One early theory that started this shift in perspective is routine activity theory developed by Lawrence Cohen and Marcus Felson in 1979. Routine activity theory provides the basis for criminal examinations that highlight place, risk, and opportunity rather than culture, motivation, and socialization.

At the core of routine activity theory are three necessary locational elements that must be present for crime to occur: (1) presence of potential offenders (individuals seeking/able/willing to commit offenses), (2) suitable targets (individuals or property that are vulnerable, desirable, and available), and (3) an absence of capable and willing guardians (a lack of protection/supervision or individuals/devices able to ward off offenders). With the postulation that these three elements are present in a setting, the theory is based on two central propositions. First, lifestyles or routine activities create criminal opportunity structures by increasing the frequency and intensity of contacts between potential offenders and suitable targets. Second, these criminal opportunity structures, or criminogenic locations, are enhanced by the absence of capable and willing guardians. To illustrate, if we use the assumption that potential offenders are all around, criminal opportunities are increased when suitable targets are in locations where they are less able to protect themselves, or social control is harder to maintain, thereby making the suitable targets even more vulnerable and available. In this way, routine activity theory differs from other criminological theories in that it does not identify or specify reasons for crime commission but instead focuses on differential risks for victimization that individuals and locations possess.

Additionally, routine activity theory not only provides insights regarding when, where, and against whom criminal events are more likely to be perpetrated but also explains how various aspects of individuals' daily routines are correlated with these differential patterns of victimization. Research using this perspective, then, identifies which typical behaviors of persons and which characteristics of situations/locations are associated with increased or decreased risks for criminal victimization.

Theoretically, even though persons may be willing to commit crime given sufficient opportunities, if those opportunities never arise, their crimes will not occur. Routine activity theory offers multiple reasons that opportunities may not arise. It may be that potential offenders cannot find persons sufficiently vulnerable or who possess property sufficiently valuable to merit interest. And, even if valuable or

vulnerable targets are present, it may happen that these persons or items are accompanied by guardians who are capable and willing to intervene. As such, both structural aspects of specific locational contexts (e.g., where one lives and works and the conditions and structures that are present in those locations that may increase the number of potential offenders who are present and/or the types of guardianship that is available in the general area) and individual choices (e.g., where one goes for leisure, what one does, with whom one is, and any self-protective measures one takes to increase or decrease their vulnerability/suitability as a target) are important for understanding where, when, and to whom criminal events happen.

Furthermore, by identifying characteristics of persons, their behaviors, and the locations in which these activities take place, those individuals interested in policy can use routine activity theory research to expand our understanding of the interactions and locations of criminal events so as to develop and implement effective crime prevention programs. Once the actions, places, and types of people who are more likely to be victimized are known, it may be possible to develop concrete strategies to enhance the number and quality of capable guardians in particular types of settings to reduce the number of potential offenders who are present, to reduce the suitability of targets that are present, or to educate people about actions and locations that are more dangerous for them so they may make smarter decisions about their routine activities. Furthermore, routine activity theory can suggest ways in which communities and individuals can prevent crime through the reduction of criminal opportunities, how they can utilize law enforcement most efficiently to increase the guardianship present, and how residents can guide the continued social development of their communities to provide greater crime awareness and prevention.

Lifestyle Factors/Routines That Correlate With Victimization

Five important components of lifestyle have been identified by research as contributing to the likelihood of criminal victimization. While each of these categories of factors has important influences on crime, it is the combination of these factors, as indications of individuals' daily routines that may best explain criminal victimization. The factors that are important in explanations of criminal victimization are demographics, social activity, alcohol and drug use, economic status, and structural elements of communities.

Demographics

The earliest focus and today the best established type of risk factor for criminal victimization concerns demographic aspects of individuals. Research has consistently shown that victimization rates are highest for men, adolescents and young adults, African Americans, those who have never been married, and persons who live in central cities.

Within a routine activity theory approach to explaining crime, demographic factors are not taken on their own but instead are interpreted to be indicators (or "proxy measures") of lifestyle activity. For example, research usually finds that married individuals are less likely to be victimized than are single people. The explanation for this is that single persons usually live lifestyles that take them out of the home, especially at night, to places that attract potential offenders, such as bars or nightclubs. The links between demographic factors and their presumed lifestyle factors are theorized, not proven, and as such should be viewed with some degree of skepticism. Presuming what people do and where they do these things based on demographic characteristics provides, at best, weak links to policy and practice. While knowing the personal characteristics of criminal victims is useful, it may not be as useful as understanding their actual lifestyle activity, particularly, if one considers possible crime prevention efforts. Therefore, demographic variables should be included in research but should not be relied on exclusively.

Social Activity

Whereas demographics are used by researchers as indirect/proxy measures of activity, it is also possible to use variables in research that directly measure what social activity people engage in, as well as when, where, with whom, and in what types of contexts/settings. Uses of these types of measures have been shown to be the most salient predictors of criminal victimization, and as such social activity measures are significant influences on victimization risks. Maintaining the focus on the routines of people's lives, some research suggests that some relatively common and mundane social aspects of life (e.g., going to shopping malls, eating out frequently, participating in school-related clubs and

organizations, and going to a gym or playing team sports) are related to some types of criminal victimization. The types of social activity in which an individual engages, and where and with whom they do these actions are clearly related to victimization risks.

Alcohol and Drug Use

One type of social activity that garners special attention in routine activity theory is the use of alcohol and illicit drugs. This should not be surprising in that alcohol/drug use is perhaps the most well-established correlate of both criminal offending and victimization. Regardless of the specifics of place and time, use of alcohol and other drugs is strongly related to violence. When the alcohol/drug use is placed in the context of young adults, there is an overwhelmingly strong association between alcohol/drug use and (most often violent) criminality. From the perspective of routine activity theory, this relationship can be explained in several ways. First, since alcohol is so closely associated with criminal behavior, engaging in activity, or frequenting places where alcohol is present would increase one's exposure to potential offenders, or, said differently, in places where people are imbibing in substances that seem to trigger crime, simply being in that setting is risky. Furthermore, drinking alcohol may reduce people's ability to protect themselves and their belongings; in this way, guardianship is reduced and perceived vulnerability of targets is enhanced. Here, it is the effect of alcohol on routines of activity that is important, not merely the social act of being around alcohol and drug use. Research has also found that the type of people one is with when in these substance-enriched settings is important (e.g., people who drink alcohol with others who are younger are more likely to be victims of crime than people who drink with older others). Also, the type of setting in which one imbibes is relevant, as drinking out in public is more dangerous than drinking at a party at a friend's house.

Economic Status

Although crime affects all segments of society, and no persons or parts of society are immune to crime, it remains that crime is disproportionately found among lower socioeconomic segments of communities. While at first this may seem counterintuitive to routine activity theory (How desirable are poor people and their things to a criminal?), it fits very well with routine activity theory. In lower-income neighborhoods and among lower-income persons, it is less common to see as heavy a saturation of guardians or instruments of guardianship (e.g., burglar alarms, sturdy locks and doors, and personal awareness of dangerous situations), and this can make potential targets seem more attractive to potential offenders. Also, since potential offenders (for at least some types of offenses) are more prominently found among the lower-income classes, being in the presence of such less advantaged persons or places (e.g., in the same physical locations) makes one more exposed and therefore more vulnerable.

Going along with this, although employed persons are more likely to be crime victims, this may be due to increased exposure to potential offenders because they must leave the home every weekday. However, unemployed persons are more likely to be victimized than individuals who remain in their homes. Routine activity theory suggests that unemployed persons are more likely to be victimized because they have characteristics (or at least one characteristic) in common with many motivated offenders. Simply stated, both unemployed persons and many motivated offenders lack sufficient activity to occupy their time and also lack a ready pool of financial and material resources, and these facts are likely to lead them to encounter one another throughout the course of each other's daily routines of activity.

Community Structural Variables

In general, once someone leaves the home, his or her risks of being a victim of crime increase. Being out and about, moving in and among a variety of (typically unknown) other persons on a daily basis exposes an individual to more potential offenders. However, when leaving the home, individuals typically move in and out of a number of different types of physical locations/domains and will interact with a wide range of others and social events. Therefore, it is not simply leaving home that exposes one to greater victimization risks; it is *where* one goes after leaving home that provides the most useful understanding of one's increased or decreased risks. Here, research has shown that community aspects such as a neglected physical appearance or incivility among neighbors tend to increase crime rates in those neighborhoods. Also, locations with businesses that attract potential offenders have higher rates of crime. For example, the presence of bars/taverns in a community and gas stations with convenience stores located near highways

has been related to increased rates of crime, as is the presence of high schools, fast-food restaurants, public parks, transportation hubs, and liquor stores. These are places where potential offenders are more likely to gather and where guardianship is likely to be low (or absent). Therefore, individuals whose routines take them to these sorts of locations are at greater risks for criminal victimization.

Practical Uses of Routine Activity Theory

Routine activity theory has several important practical implications, primarily focused on the development of crime prevention programs. Routine activity theory is most useful and makes important contributions to social policy by predicting conditions under which victimization risks are enhanced and identifying patterns of social events associated with criminal incidents. Specifically, the first general implication of the theory is on programming efforts targeting potential victims' vulnerability (e.g., "attractiveness" as possible victims), which can be devised easily from understanding when and where particular types of persons may be more likely to fall victims to crime. If we understand that in a particular domain, persons who engage in behaviors X, Y, and Z are more likely to be victims, it becomes possible to educate persons into being more careful of having guardianship present when they are engaging in those dangerous behaviors or to structure settings so as to minimize these persons' exposure to potential offenders.

Prevention efforts may also focus on increasing guardianship efforts. This can take the form of increasing law enforcement presence in certain places at certain times and also altering the structural aspects of environments. Called crime prevention through environmental design, these types of crime prevention programs may include simple measures such as increasing lighting (to make offenses more easily observed), removing hidden "blind" spots in settings, or simply using more and more effective means of protecting one's person and property (carrying a weapon for protection or installing new and stronger locks on doors).

Regardless of the specific actions that are taken to better separate motivated offenders and vulnerable targets, or reducing the perceived vulnerability of particular persons or places, routine activity theory is behind many efforts to reduce criminal victimization risks. However, where crime prevention efforts spawned by routine activity theory differ significantly from the efforts borne of other criminological theories is that the focus is not on eliminating or removing motivated offenders but instead on reducing such persons' opportunities and attractions to criminal events. Simply put, routine activity theory gives a theoretical foundation to crime prevention. This can only enhance societal efforts in this area.

Conclusion

Routine activity theory is one of the newer theoretical perspectives in criminology and is unique among theories in that it seeks to explain varying victimization risks among individuals and the role of criminal location in the incidence of criminal events. At the core of routine activity theory is the idea that crimes can and will occur but only when three elements of a situation are present: (1) potential offenders, (2) suitable targets, and (3) incapable, unwilling, or absent guardians. When these three situational elements come together in place and time, the likelihood of a criminal event taking place is greatly increased.

Since its inception, routine activity theory researchers have tested many elements of the criminal incident to fully identify which lifestyles and lifestyle components have higher risks for victimization than others. Researchers have identified five general categories of factors that increase risk, demographics, social activity, alcohol and drug use, economic status, and community structures.

Additionally, by identifying when, where, and under what conditions crime is more likely to occur, we can develop greater understandings of how crime occurs in patterned ways in society. In this respect, routine activity theory allows for more informed efforts to prevent and intervene in crime. As such, perhaps the strongest application for routine activity theory is in the area of crime prevention. Using the

concepts, principles, and findings of routine activity theory research, we can begin to identify how individuals in various settings can take steps to protect themselves and their belongings from criminal victimization.

Elizabeth Ehrhardt Mustaine

See also Broken Windows Thesis; Deviant Places; Rational Choice Theory; Social Disorganization Theory

Further Readings

Cohen, L., & Felson, M. (1979). Social change and crime rate trends: A routine activity approach. *American Sociological Review, 44*, 588–608.

Felson, M. (2002). *Crime and everyday life: Insight and implications for society* (3rd ed.). Thousand Oaks, CA: Sage.

Kennedy, L. W., & Forde, D. R. (1999). *When push comes to shove: A routine conflict approach to violence.* Albany: State University of New York Press.

Meithe, T. D., & Meier, R. F. (1990). Opportunity, choice, and criminal victimization: A test of a theoretical model. *Journal of Research in Crime & Delinquency, 27*, 243–266.

Miethe, T. D., & Meier, R. F. (1994). *Crime and its social context: Toward an integrated theory of offenders, victims, and situations.* Albany: State University of New York Press.

Mustaine, E. E., & Tewksbury, R. (1997). Obstacles in the assessment of routine activity theory. *Social Pathology, 3*, 177–194.

Sacco, V. F., & Kennedy, L. W. (1996). *The criminal event.* Belmont, CA: Wadsworth.

Schwartz, M. D., & Pitts, V. L. (1995). Exploring a feminist routine activity approach to explaining sexual assault. *Justice Quarterly, 12*, 9–31.

S

SADISM AND MASOCHISM

Sadism and masochism, more commonly referred to as S&M, have permeated the larger culture so much that most people have some idea of what these behaviors involve. Sex shops now sell handcuffs, whips, and bondage gear. Fashion designers have incorporated leather, vinyl, chains, and other S&M-associated accoutrements. S&M is rampant in popular culture, including literature, art, music, and television. Despite this presence, S&M is still considered by some to be pathological—an abnormal desire to inflict or to receive pain, humiliation, or some physical or emotional sensation that pushes the limits of experience to the edge.

S&M behaviors run the gamut of the imagination. Some examples are flogging, whipping, binding, torture, knife play, needle play, blood play, mummification, genital torture, mutilation, breath play, rope play, rape play, electrical play, mind play, branding, burning, boot licking, foot worship, medical play, role play, verbal humiliation, and leather worship. Although early examinations of S&M focused on the element of pain, it is important to note that pain is not necessarily involved in S&M, and many practitioners report that they are not necessarily excited by pain and do not engage in painful activities.

Individuals' involvement in S&M varies greatly—some may practice with romantic partners, and some may practice with strangers or acquaintances. Some individuals are open about their involvement, and some believe that they need to keep these activities private. The level of involvement also varies greatly—some people engage in these behaviors as experimentation, occasionally, and for some, it is a "24/7" lifestyle. *Kinks* refer to what a person enjoys or what excites him or her. S&M activity is termed *play*, and this play is usually done in the context of a "scene" or a frame of activity that is heavily negotiated and agreed on by all parties beforehand. "Safe, sane, and consensual" is a frequently used expression that demonstrates the need to take precautions before play and to make sure that the experience is pleasurable for all involved. More recently, practitioners have developed the phrase "risk-aware consensual kink," which recognizes the fact that things can go wrong despite the best intentions and negotiations but emphasizes the need to take all precautions. Many individuals use "safe words" during play, which are code words devised to slow down or stop a scene without completely breaking the scene. The most commonly used system is the traffic light or red, yellow, and green system, with red meaning "stop," yellow meaning "slow down," and green meaning "continue."

Individuals can engage in these behaviors in the privacy of their home, or they can join like-minded individuals to play in public dungeons. These dungeons usually charge a fee and have rules such as no nudity, no sexual intercourse, and no photography or video recording. These clubs or public play parties are not illegal; however, there is usually community backlash against these types of establishments. Another way to engage in S&M is to use the services of professional dominatrices. These professionals advertise in magazines and online, and services can be rendered via phone, webcam, or in person. The outlets for S&M play have grown significantly with the advent of the Internet. What was once considered to be an underground and closeted subculture has become an experience more readily available to individuals seeking S&M play.

Origins of S&M

Although these behaviors have been practiced for centuries, they were not systematically studied or conceptualized until the 19th century. The term *sadism* was coined by a German psychiatrist, Richard von Krafft-Ebing, who was studying sexual pathology. This term was based on the writings of the Marquis de Sade (1740–1814) and described an individual for whom inflicting pain and suffering on others brought excitement or thrills. De Sade's work, formerly widely banned, has often been cited as a basis for extreme individualism, sexual exploration, and personal freedom.

The term *masochism* was also coined by Krafft-Ebing to describe an individual who enjoyed pain and suffering being inflicted on himself or herself. This was based on the book *Venus in Furs* (1870), by Leopold von Sacher-Masoch, in which the protagonist enters into a relationship with a dominant woman and actively courts his own destruction of self through submission to her. Sacher-Masoch detailed the emotional and physical journey of giving oneself completely to another and surrendering power—essentially complete submission to another human being.

Both Sade and Masoch's work shared the central theme of pain and power as pleasure: in Sade's case having both in totality, while in Masoch's case surrendering them to someone else. This power exchange is the central component of S&M. The sadist thrives on having complete control and mastery over another, while the masochist relishes complete powerlessness and submission to another individual.

The terms *sadism* and *masochism*, as Krafft-Ebing used them, were considered to be mutually exclusive. Subsequent research by Sigmund Freud and, later, by the psychologist Albert Ellis argued that the two constructs could be found in the same individual, and the term *sadomasochism* was used to capture these dynamic relationships. This term dominated the academic and popular literature for some time, but among practitioners, the term *BDSM* became more commonly used. BDSM stands for

bondage/discipline/sadism/masochism and is now the preferred nomenclature as it captures the wide range of relationships and activities in which individuals engage. Based on this literature, participants in S&M use specific terminology to refer to the roles they adopt and the activities in which they engage. A sadist, dominant, top, mistress, or master prefers to be in control or the one providing the stimulation. Masochists, submissives, slaves, or bottoms prefer to receive the stimulation. Last, a switch is someone who is interested in both roles.

Research has demonstrated that individuals who engage in sadism and masochism represent a diverse group, with ranges in demographic characteristics such as age, sexual preference, education, and employment. One commonality is that individuals who report that they enjoy these behaviors also tend to be more sexually adventurous than individuals who do not. They tend to report having more sexual partners and trying more varied sexual activities.

S&M as Pathology

Sadism and masochism have traditionally been viewed as pathological, although there have been strides made in understanding and in the awareness of alternative sexualities in the past few decades. Both terms are included as disorders in the American Psychiatric Association's *Diagnostic and Statistical Manual of Mental Disorders* (*DSM-IV-TR*) and the psychological literature has attempted to frame these activities as stemming from traumatic events, such as sexual or physical abuse. The act of inflicting pain or humiliation is seen as an attempt to gain control that previous victimization robbed them of, and masochistic acts are assumed to be reenactments of victimization. Although some practitioners of S&M report past histories of abuse, it is clear that not all have experienced such trauma. Additionally, these individuals show no more mental illness or psychiatric diagnoses than the general population. Still, S&M is considered to be an abnormal appetite, although there is now a dearth of "kink-friendly" therapists who recognize alternative sexualities as natural. Individuals can frequent these therapists without worry that they will attempt to "treat" their S&M. Recently, several countries have removed sadism and masochism from the list of diagnosable disorders, recognizing that these behaviors may not necessarily be harmful to those who engage in them.

Social Explanations

Social explanations of sadism and masochism posit that these behaviors are embedded in culture, as all relationships operate on the principles of dominance and submission, and society values aggression. Cultural explanations assert that in complex societies S&M is most likely to develop as a result of a commingling of pain and pleasure. Levels of sadism and masochism, it is argued, can be found in all relationships. Some feminist theorists assert that sadism and masochism are the result of a patriarchal society, while others argue that it is empowering as women freely choose to be dominant or submissive. This continues to be a contentious debate.

The sociological literature discusses sadism and masochism as being learned behaviors that are a result of interactions with other individuals. From this view, one does not necessarily have any predilection toward S&M until one is introduced to it. Individuals then seek out others who are involved and learn values, norms, and techniques. Thus, S&M is not considered a result of some pathology but instead a set of skills and techniques learned through initiation into a subculture.

S&M as Edgework

Additionally, sadism and masochism have been described as forms of deviant leisure activities or what has been termed as *edgework*. These behaviors push the limits and allow individuals to transcend boundaries (examples of other types of edgework are sky diving, drag racing, etc.). For all participants, S&M involves some sort of physical or emotional sensation that is meant to arouse excitement, thrill, and strong reactions. Some view S&M as just another form of risk-taking behavior that allows the individual to escape reality and lose himself or herself in fantasy and sensation. Alternatively, others view it as an opportunity to see how much sensation they can handle. This desire to push boundaries, challenge sexual norms, and explore all aspects of power relationships makes S&M activities an exciting and transgressive experience.

S&M and the Law

S&M in itself is not illegal; however, many legal issues have arisen. High-profile cases involving sadomasochistic elements have increased the stigma of these activities. The work of Federal Bureau of Investigation profilers in the 1980s and 1990s on serial rape and sexual murder highlighted the sadistic elements found in these types of crimes, and this has inextricably linked S&M with the idea of harm.

The main legal issues that surround sadism and masochism are the rights to privacy and sexual freedom and issues of consent. The courts have had to grapple with the public versus private issues regarding sexuality. When S&M has come to the notice of law enforcement officials, most courts have a difficult time believing that rational individuals would consent to S&M activities, and these actions have reinforced the idea that S&M is pathological. Individuals have been charged with assault and other crimes as a result of what they claimed to be consensual activity. The court generally has ruled that protecting the citizens of the state, in these cases from themselves and their sexual desires, outweighs the right to sexual freedom.

Additionally, there are also concerns when it comes to child custody, domestic violence, and employment discrimination. An S&M lifestyle can make an individual seem less fit as a parent, a guardian, or a potential employee. Since many "vanilla" (conventional) individuals who do not participate in S&M do not understand the behaviors or the motivations for the behaviors, it can raise questions regarding safety and responsibility.

Conclusion

While there is no agreed-on cause for the interest in S&M behaviors, it is apparent that there is great variety in the types of individuals who engage in them and their reasons for participation. Although there are some predatory individuals for whom S&M is a nonconsensual, harmful activity to be inflicted on an unwilling participant, this seems to be the minority of cases. Most S&M appears to occur between consenting partners who are interested in exploring the boundaries of human experience. Whether or not these behaviors will gain more acceptance among the general public remains to be seen.

Karen Holt

See also Bondage and Discipline; Erotica Versus Pornography; Fetishes

Further Readings

Chancer, L. (1992). *Sadomasochism and everyday life: The dynamics of power and powerlessness*. New Brunswick, NJ: Rutgers University Press.

Krafft-Ebing, R. (1998). *Psychopathia sexualis*. New York, NY: Arcade. (Original work published 1903)

Reage, P. (1954). *The story of O*. Paris, France: Jean-Jacques Pauvert.

Sacher-Masoch, L. von. (2000). *Venus in furs*. London, England: Penguin Books. (Original work published 1870)

Sade, M. de. (1990). *Justine, philosophy in the bedroom and other writings*. New York, NY: Grove Press.

Weinburg, T. S. (1995). *S & M: Studies in dominance and submission*. Amherst, NY: Prometheus Books.

Same-Sex Marriages

Marriage in the United States is a contractual agreement between two people that creates legal kinship. Entering into the agreement allows for certain rights and obligations between the two individuals. For instance, the two share responsibilities for one another's debts and the burden of providing financial support for children born in the marriage, among many others. The rights and benefits are also numerous and include sharing property, health insurance, social security benefits, and tax and survivor benefits and obtaining permanent residence for his or her spouse if the spouse is a noncitizen. Even if a marriage is dissolved, the once-married individuals often receive future benefits as a result of the marriage. In addition to the practical benefits of marriage, there are social and symbolic meanings that make it desirable to couples in love. Marriage is highly coveted and respected as the union that tells the world that the couple are in love, devoted, and committed to one another. These benefits are sought after not only by different-sex couples but by same-sex couples as well. According to the Williams Institute, as of November 2011, there were 646,464 same-sex couples in the United States, and nearly 50,000 same-sex couples have married.

Laws governing the demographics of marriage have changed over time but especially over the past 10 years. Specifically, there is an increasing acceptance by states to allow individuals of the same sex to marry. Although some states allow marriage of same-sex couples, federal law does not recognize these marriages. States are also protected, by federal law, from being required to recognize a same-sex marriage from another state. There are several variations on the formal commitment ceremony and contractual agreement that some states accept for same-sex couples. Civil unions, domestic partnerships, and reciprocal beneficiaries are a few of these nonmarriage unions. In the United States, the federal government does not recognize civil unions, and states are not required to recognize them either. The rights and responsibilities associated with each type of union depend on each state's law. More than 20% of same-sex couples living in the United States today have committed to one another in a nonmarital ceremony. Same-sex couples overwhelmingly prefer, however, to marry. In fact, the economic and social reasons to marry are much the same for same-sex couples as they are for different-sex couples.

National polls demonstrate an increased acceptance of lesbian and gay people and same-sex couples. As a testament to this, more politicians are stating their acceptance. On May 9, 2012, President Barack Obama became the first president in U.S. history to publicly support gay marriage. This endorsement followed his earlier disavowal of a federal law defining marriage as between a man and a woman (The Defense of Marriage Act, or DOMA, signed into law by the former president Bill Clinton in 1996), as well as his repeal of the law that prohibited openly gay people in the military (a result of the Don't Ask Don't Tell policy also implemented by Clinton in 1993). As a result of DOMA, the federal government does not recognize marriage between individuals of the same sex. In recent years, however, several states now grant marriage licenses to such couples. In addition to the states, several cities, Native American tribal jurisdictions, and municipal districts now recognize same-sex marriage, including Washington, D.C., Oregon's Coquille Tribe, and Washington State's Suquamish Tribe. And while DOMA was passed in part to ensure that states would not be required to recognize a same-sex marriage performed in another state, California, Maryland, and Rhode Island do recognize these marriages. For a brief period (approximately two months in 2008), California allowed the performance of same-sex marriage ceremonies until voters passed Proposition 8, prohibiting the unions. Thirty states now have bans on gay marriage, with North Carolina becoming the latest, passing a law in May 2012.

Another testament to the increasing tolerance of gay couples can be found in the way data are collected by the federal government. In the past, the Census included in the counts only same-sex couples where one partner was identified as the unmarried partner of the other. However, for the first time in history, the 2010 U.S. Census counted both unmarried same-sex partners and legally married same-sex spouses.

Several organizations have been outspoken in their support for same-sex marriage. For example, since 1973, Lambda Legal, a national legal organization, has been working to protect and enhance the rights of lesbian and gay people. The Williams Institute, an organization at the University of California, Los Angeles School of Law, conducts research and provides testimonies about gender identity and gay and lesbian discrimination. There are also nationwide campaigns like Freedom to Marry, which are developed for the purpose of raising awareness and social change about the issue of same-sex marriage.

About 20% of same-sex couples are raising children. The rates of child rearing are higher for ethnic and racial minority same-sex couples—at 38% for African American couples and 27% for Latina couples. Denying these families the right to marry carries systemic social, psychological, health, and economic consequences for the couple and the children. For example, family medical leave and benefits for spouses are unavailable for many same-sex couples. When health benefits are given to partners of same-sex employees, the benefits are taxed. In addition, benefits such as those available to married couples under the Family Medical Leave Act and under several "spousal impoverishment protections" are unavailable to same-sex couples. However, denying marriage does not simply deny same-sex couples the tangible rewards and resources listed above. Federal legislation of this sort also reinforces social stigma against homosexual, bisexual, and transgendered individuals. Specifically, individuals who are allowed the right to marry feel more socially included and, therefore, more happy and healthy than those who are not. Furthermore, researchers have found that married same-sex couples are able to get social support from their families once their commitment is formalized by marriage. The positive effects of this level of social inclusion, acceptance, and support should not be understated.

Pam Hunt

See also Discrimination; Gays as Parents; Homophobia; Homosexuality

Further Readings

Hull, K. E. (2006). *Same-sex marriage: The cultural politics of love and law.* Cambridge, England: Cambridge University Press.

Lee Badgett, M. V. (2009). *When gay people get married: What happens when societies legalize same-sex marriage.* New York: New York University Press.

Pinello, D. R. (2006). *America's struggle for same-sex marriage.* Cambridge, England: Cambridge University Press.

Weston, K. (1991). *Families we choose: Lesbians, gays, and kinship.* New York, NY: Columbia University Press.

SATANISM

The term *Satanism* refers to Devil worship, or the cult of the Devil, and often to the Church of Satan. Satanism is described as a structured system of satanic religion and consists of both philosophical and ideological views. It focuses on the respect or veneration of Satan and related characters, phenomena, symbols, and figures. Satan is commonly depicted as the chief of devils. The activities of Satanism include worship of Satan, satanic violence or destructiveness, and black magic. Certain rituals and symbols are specifically related to Satanism; however, activities such as palm reading, tarot cards, Wicca or witchcraft groups, and the practice of various forms of mysticism are not considered an integral part of Satanism.

Satanism has developed as an alternative to conventional religion in general and particularly to the Abrahamic religions, especially Christianity. Some see it as a protest religion. Satanism's aim is to influence all aspects of social and personal life. Christianity and Islam consider Satan (*Shaitan* in Arabic) as the adversary of their belief systems. According to these beliefs, Satan exploits the weaknesses and desires of human beings based on their goals. They argue that Satan has been attempting to cause human beings to stray from the approved paths. Thus, some believers of Abrahamic religions, particularly in Christianity, see Satan as an enemy of their faith. Within liberal Christianity, Satan is often understood figuratively or metaphorically.

The emergence of Satanism dates to the beginnings of the Common Era (CE) and the emergence of Christianity. During this time, the practices of Satanism appeared as witchcraft, the supernatural, and fortune-telling. Satanism was mainly related to supernatural beings, as Auguste Comte (1798–1857) explained in what he referred to as the theological stage in his theory of the law of three stages—(1) the theological, (2) the metaphysical, and (3) the positive—as they pertain to social development. Comte determined that at this stage, humans explained natural and social phenomena as the will of supernatural beings, who are visualized mythically. Today, however, Satanism is viewed as a new religio-philosophical stream representing an adversarial stance to all high human paradigms and values.

Early Christians commonly considered the pagan gods to be devils. The image of a horned demon, which emerged in the medieval period, is probably based on a number of pagan horned gods; there is no physical depiction of Satan in biblical texts. Although in pagan or religious traditions, both good and bad qualities and attributes are often found in combination in a particular god or goddess, the Judeo-Christian and Islamic traditions represent God as entirely good, while Satan, a creation of God, is a bad, or fallen, angel and the enemy of goodness. Satan and the activities of Satanism are seen as a threat to divine authority, and in turn, they have the potential to weaken the beliefs of the faithful.

In the late 20th century, Satanism, or at least its symbolism, underwent a revival in popularity and emerged as a new countercultural trend or fashion in Western countries. This phenomenon has been called "pop culture Satanism" or "adolescent Satanism." Its followers cultivated an image, as popularized by some rock musicians (especially of heavy metal and its offshoots), of wearing black garments along with Satanic symbols and tattoos, as a means to express a rejection not only of Judeo-Christian and Islamic values but also the common values of mainstream secular society.

Anton Szandor LaVey, an American author, musician, and occultist, founded the Church of Satan in 1966 and published the Satanic Bible in 1969. Some scholars accept that the early 20th-century British occultist Aleister Crowley (1875–1947) was the founding father of modern Satanism because his doctrines and ideas are followed by contemporary Satanists. Under the organization of the Church of Satan, many Satanist groups have been openly conducting their activities throughout the world.

Most scholars agree on the categorization of practitioners of Satanism as dabblers (generally teenagers), self-styled Satanists (commonly loners), religious Satanists (groups versed in the teachings of the Church of Satan), and satanic cults (some such groups have become involved in criminal activities). There is no clear distinction between these groups; some of them can share many of the same characteristics.

There are several fundamental dogmas important to Satanism. The first is the God of Self. This dogma refers to the final aim of Satanism. According to the Satanic Bible, the practitioner of Satanism represents indulgence, undefiled wisdom, vital existence, vengeance, and all of the so-called sins and satisfaction. The second dogma is moral relativism, according to which there is no clear-cut distinction between bad and good or right and wrong. Such distinctions are based on individual approaches. The third dogma is the rejection of Christianity, as expressed in all rituals and beliefs of Satanism. Ritualism is the fourth dogma of Satanism. Rituals may vary from group to group and can be relatively harmless or dangerous. For instance, according to the Satanic Ritual Calendar, January 7 is St. Winebald Day, during which adherents perform blood rituals. The fifth dogma is spells. They are as follows: spells of love create desire within someone, spells of compassion help someone, and hexes bring harm to someone. The last dogma of Satanism is sacrifices, covering the self, pain, body parts, and living things. According to Anton LaVey, the satanist can destroy a victim symbolically.

Idris Guclu

See also Cults; Fortune-Telling

Further Readings

Clark, C. M. (1994). Clinical assessment of adolescents involved in Satanism. *Adolescence, 29,* 461–468.

Emerson, S., & Syron, Y. (1995). Adolescent Satanism: Rebellion masquerading as religion. *Counsel Values, 39,* 149–159.

Johnston, J. (1989). *The edge of evil: The rise of Satanism in North America.* Dallas, TX: Word.

LaVey, A. S. (1969). *The Satanic Bible.* New York, NY: Avon Books.

Russell, J. B. (1977). *The Devil: Perceptions of evil from antiquity to primitive Christianity.* Ithaca. NY: Cornell University Press.

SECRET DEVIANCE

The study of deviant behavior has focused primarily on types of behaviors that are controversial with respect to their causes, extent of harm, and concerns for what, if anything, should be done about them. Such behaviors generally fall outside the realm of traditionally criminally deviant behaviors such as those represented in the Uniform Crime Reports: murder, aggravated assault, rape, robbery, burglary, larceny, automobile theft, arson, and kidnapping. Some deviant behaviors may be illegal, but unlike more serious criminal behaviors, they do not generate strong public consensus about whether, or even how, to control them.

In many cases, deviance is a matter of degree and cannot be easily labeled. Edwin Schur identifies behavior as deviant to the extent that it is viewed as involving an individual whose departure from social norms or laws is deemed discreditable, eliciting either interpersonal or collective reactions that isolate, treat, punish, or correct. Any given act can be more or less deviant, depending on numerous factors, such as whether or not that act is noticed—and if so, whether the act is taken seriously as a violation of norms, whether it is attributable to the individual committing the deviant act, and whether sanctions, informal or formal (police or courts), are assigned.

Occasionally, a behavior is definitely against the rules but is so well hidden that no one sees it, or, if seen, no one does anything about it. Howard Becker refers to these behaviors as *secret deviance*. Such behaviors occur frequently but usually are conducted in private and without the attention of nonparticipants. Although the behavior is considered deviant, because nonparticipants are unaware of it, there are no outside sanctions and no deviant labels are applied. Some behaviors considered to be secretly deviant include certain sexual activities, such as swinging, fetishism, sodomy, online pornography, and autoerotic asphyxiation.

Maintaining secrecy about deviant behavior depends largely on the ability of the individual to hide the transgression. Therefore, secret deviance is often committed and controlled by persons with power and the means and ability to hide. Examples include the physician who is cited for driving while intoxicated and is able to have it "fixed" or the high-level corporate executive who defrauds clients but is not convicted of corporate crime. Such individuals are unlikely to experience the full impact of the legal system, as they have the financial means to avoid full prosecution or public humiliation. Such power, associated with high social status, allows the doctor and the business executive to transcend the stigmatizing label of deviant.

Closely related to secret deviance are "victimless crimes." This term, coined by Edwin Schur, refers to the willing exchange of strongly demanded, but legally prohibited, goods and services between consenting adults. In a victimless crime, a transaction occurs between two parties who desire to enter into an exchange relationship that violates laws. However, as with secret deviance, the laws are relatively unenforceable because neither party complains to the authorities—in this case, usually the vice squad. Thus, most of these behaviors continue unabated. Examples of victimless crimes are prostitution, illegal gambling, and drug addiction.

Margot Hasha and DeAnn Kalich

See also Arson; Autoerotic Asphyxiation; Fetishes; Male Prostitution; Voyeurism

Further Readings

Becker, H. S. (1963). *Outsiders: Studies in the sociology of deviance.* New York, NY: Free Press.

Little, C. B. (1983). *Understanding deviance and control: Theory, research, and social policy.* Itasca, IL: F. E. Peacock.

Schur, E. M. (1965). *Crimes without victims.* Englewood Cliffs, NJ: Prentice Hall.

Schur, E. M. (1979). *Interpreting deviance: A sociological introduction.* New York, NY: Harper & Row.

SELF, THE

From a philosophical standpoint, the self represents all distinctive qualities that separate him or her from others and is considered responsible for the thoughts and actions of a person as the source of awareness. The self is understood as having substance, and therefore, one's thoughts and actions can be attributed to himself or herself. Thus, to have a self, one needs to be aware that he or she is a separate entity and that he or she is an object or substance.

In psychology, the self is considered the cognitive delineation of a person's identity. Modern psychology has identified two kinds of self, namely, the self as "I" and the self as "me." While the "I" refers to the subject that knows, the "me" refers to the object that is known. Psychologists view the self as an essential part of one's cognitive state and social identity. Sigmund Freud's psychoanalytic definition of the self makes a distinction between the unconscious and conscious aspects of personality (the *id* and the *ego*, respectively). While the *id* seeks immediate gratification of personal needs and wants regardless of its possibility and social acceptability, the *ego* acts based on reality, weighing the cost and benefits of possible options.

In addition to the above philosophical, psychological, and psychoanalytical accounts, D. W. Winnicott offered a pragmatic description of the self by identifying two kinds of self: the true self and false self. The *true self* refers to the core and original behaviors of someone, which have not been shaped by social factors. The *false self*, on the other hand, refers to the behaviors adapted and altered to better fit societal expectations.

Formation of the Self

The psychologist Michael Lewis suggests two distinct phases for the formation of the self. In the first phase, referred to as the *existential self*, one is aware that he or she has a separate body different from others. The existential self is realized in infancy, as early as at two or three months of age. In the second phase, known as the *categorical self*, the child realizes that he or she is an object with some properties that can be experienced (e.g., height, hair, foot, and leg). He or she can then put himself or herself into some categories in reference to these properties, like "I am tall" and "my hair color is brown." One can then enhance the extent of these properties to his or her psychological traits, like "I am nervous" or "I am patient." Whereas self-description is more concrete in early childhood, it becomes more abstract as one grows older.

According to Carl Rogers, the self-concept has three elements: (1) self-image, (2) self-esteem, and (3) ideal self. *Self-image* is what one sees in himself or herself, even though it may not reflect reality. For example, if one sees oneself as physically fit, one's self-image is that of a fit person, even though one may not in fact be physically fit. Self-image is influenced by a variety of factors, including family, friends, and the media. In his Twenty Statements Test, Manfred Kuhn found that one's responses to the question of self-image can be categorized into one of two groups: (1) social roles and (2) personality traits. One's social role reflects his or her external and objective aspects such as father, mother, son, daughter, student, or teacher. Personality traits, on the other hand, reflect one's internal and subjective aspects (nervous, patient, smart, etc.).

Self-esteem refers to the extent to which someone values himself or herself. The degree of evaluation of oneself varies between low and high. Low self-esteem is one's negative view of himself or herself, and it may result in lack of self-confidence, over-reliance on others, or pessimism. High self-esteem, on the other hand, is one's positive view of himself or herself. A person with high self-esteem has confidence in his or her own abilities, has a high self-acceptance, and is optimistic. The evaluation of self may fluctuate depending on the reactions of others, comparison of the self with reference to others, social roles, and personal identity.

The *ideal self* represents the ideal that one would like to reach. The degree to which one values oneself, or self-esteem, is affected by the degree of difference between the self-image and the ideal self. The higher the difference, the higher the probability of incongruence and the lower the probability of self-actualization or vice versa.

Ismail Yilmaz and Ilkay Akyay

See also Identity; Individualism

Further Readings

Argyle, M. (2008). *Social encounters: Contributions to social interaction*. Piscataway, NJ: Aldine Transaction.

Kuhn, M. H. (1960). Self-attitudes by age, sex and professional training. *Sociological Quarterly, 1*, 39–56.

Lewis, M. (1990). Self-knowledge and social development in early life. In L. A. Pervin (Ed.), *Handbook of personality* (pp. 277–300). New York, NY: Guilford Press.

Winnicott, D. W. (1960). Ego distortion in terms of true and false self. In *The maturational process and the facilitating environment: Studies in the theory of emotional development* (pp. 140–152). New York, NY: International Universities Press.

SELF-CONTROL THEORY

Michael Gottfredson and Travis Hirschi's book *A General Theory of Crime* has received much attention from criminologists since its publication in 1990. As the title implies, the theory covers all forms of crime committed by perpetrators of any age, race, and ethnicity; of either sex; and across international borders. Also known as self-control theory, its main proposition is that crime is the result of the interaction between low self-control and the opportunity for crime to occur. Because much of the research does not emphasize crime opportunity, a main focus of this entry is on the theory's key proposition about self-control. According to Gottfredson and Hirschi, low self-control is the cause of crime at the individual level.

The propositions of Gottfredson and Hirschi to explain criminal behavior run counter to most criminological theories, and in fact, they dismiss many explanations of crime. Gottfredson and Hirschi are evidently convinced that other theories of crime propose casual links between social and behavioral domains that can be accounted for by low self-control. For example, they argue that associating with delinquent peers will not lead to involvement in crime because low self-control explains why individuals decide to affiliate with delinquent peers and also why they commit criminal acts. Thus, both criminal behavior and the relationship between peers can be accounted for by an individual's level of self-control. Such claims make Gottfredson and Hirschi's theory controversial among researchers and theorists. Criminologists, however, have remained attentive to Gottfredson and Hirschi's theory. This attentiveness is likely due to the theory's simple explanation of criminal behavior, its potential explanatory power, and its offerings for understanding differences in criminal behavior across various demographics groups and the life course.

Overview of Self-Control Theory

According to Gottfredson and Hirschi, crime is defined as an act of "force or fraud under the pursuit of self-interest," which does not limit crime to acts that are defined as illegal under federal and state jurisdictions. This definition allows the application of their theory to span across societies and different points in time. The theory also purports to explain behaviors that are in certain respects analogous to crime, including drinking, smoking, and gambling, among others. These behaviors are performed in the pursuit of perceived self-interest, and they provide immediate gratification for an individual with low self-control.

Gottfredson and Hirschi suggest that there are six components of low self-control: (1) the inability to delay gratification, (2) preference for engaging in risky behavior, (3) preference for simple tasks, (4) more self-centered/do not consider the long term, (5), short tempered, and (6) preference for physical activity. The theorists claim that low self-control is the cause of an individual's tendency to commit crime, and once the variable "self-control" is controlled for, no other variable should be important

for explaining crime. While research paints a slightly different picture, this is the main theoretical idea.

Although a central theoretical proposition of self-control theory is that crime and analogous behaviors are a result of low self-control, Gottfredson and Hirschi identify factors that will influence the development of low-self control. They claim that self-control is malleable in the first decade of life and then becomes relatively stable from this point forward. Gottfredson and Hirschi identify parenting as a major source for the development of self-control during childhood. For parenting to affect a child's self-control, three minimum conditions must occur. First, the behavior of the child must be monitored. Second, if/when deviant behavior occurs, it must be recognized. Third, the behavior must be punished when it is recognized. These are all more likely to occur if parents have strong attachments to their children.

Gottfredson and Hirschi also provide a discussion on how self-control theory can account for gender and racial differences in crime and deviance. For instance, they argue that males are more likely to be involved in crime and analogous behaviors, compared with females, because of differences in how they are treated and cared for by their parents. They argue that differences exist in how parents monitor or supervise male and female children's behaviors. That is, the behavior of male children may be monitored and reacted to very differently than that of female children who engage in similar types of behaviors. These differences result in differences in self-control across gender. Gottfredson and Hirschi argue that these differences in self-control lead males to become more involved in criminal behavior over the life course than females. Likewise, Gottfredson and Hirschi propose that racial differences can be largely explained through inadequate child rearing, which leads to differences in self-control across racial groups. In sum, they argue that differences in self-control, not parenting practices, will prevail in understanding differences in crime and delinquency across gender, race, and ethnicity.

The controversy surrounding Gottfredson and Hirschi's theory has resulted in criticisms by criminologists. Some have criticized the theory for being too general by trying to explain so many types of criminal and analogous behaviors. Others argue that the theory does not acknowledge that different risk factors may be responsible for the prevalence and frequency of criminal involvement or the different dimensions of a criminal career and that Gottfredson and Hirschi misinterpret the age–crime curve. Finally, one of the largest criticisms of their theory is that it is tautological. To this end, explaining crime as a function of low self-control is problematic because they are both, by definition, one and the same.

Old and New Research on Self-Control Theory

Many criminologists were eager to test the controversial core propositions put forward by Gottfredson and Hirschi. In one of the first studies, Harold Grasmick and colleagues tested self-control theory using a large community sample of adults. They concluded that the theory has some validity; low self-control was shown to have a moderate association with crime. This study also developed a reliable measure of self-control, which is now widely known as the Grasmick et al. Self-Control Scale and is used often by criminologists when testing self-control theory. With almost a decade of self-control research since the Grasmick and colleagues study, a meta-analysis was undertaken by Travis Pratt and Francis Cullen to summarize the influence that low self-control had on delinquency and crime across. The results of the meta-analysis supported the validity of self-control theory, and low self-control's influence on crime and deviance continued to be robust when delinquent peers and other variables were accounted for.

While much of the research on self-control theory has addressed the relationship between self-control and crime and delinquency, the link between low self-control and other lifestyle characteristics and behaviors has also been examined. Research by Gibson, Moffitt, Schreck, Piquero, and others has shown that low self-control is related to binge drinking, intimate partner violence, victimization, academic dishonesty, driving without a seat belt, gambling, substance use, the number of nights/evenings out, hanging out with delinquent peers, marriage quality, school achievement, financial accomplishments, and health in adulthood. In sum, research concludes that individuals possessing lower self-control are not only at a higher risk for involvement in crime and delinquency, but they are also more likely to experience numerous short-term and long-term social consequences stemming from their inability to delay gratification.

Some empirical support has been garnered for the proposition that parenting practices predict differences in self-control among children and adolescents. For instance, Carter Hay discovered that a lack of primary caregiver monitoring and disciplining partially explained why some kids have lower self-control. Employing various samples, several other studies have been published that support his conclusions.

Recent research focuses on other factors that may help explain the development of self-control and why children are different from one another in their levels of this trait. While some research, as mentioned, does support that parenting practices partially explain differences in children and adolescent's self-control, recent research has considered how genetic differences may have implications for self-control development. For instance, John Wright and Kevin Beaver analyzed a sample of twins to determine that genetics may account for why some children differ from others in their levels of self-control. Importantly, they discovered that the influence of parenting on self-control was substantially reduced once genetic differences were accounted for and that genetics had nontrivial influences on self-control. Research by Jay Belsky and Kevin Beaver also shows that particular genetic polymorphisms interact with parenting practices to explain differences in children's levels of self-control.

Other researchers have explored socialization practices outside the family unit such as neighborhood influences. Beyond parenting, studies have investigated how neighborhood dynamics may influence children's self-control. The few studies that have investigated this source of self-control have found that differences do exist across neighborhoods and that neighborhood factors such as cohesion may be important for explaining self-control differences among children.

The malleability of self-control over one's life course has also been a recent research interest among criminologists. Some studies have been conducted to test this hypothesis and have found some support for it. Most studies assessing the relative stability of self-control, or whether people maintain their high or low self-control rankings compared with others over time, show that this trait has moderate short-term stability. However, newer studies have investigated trajectories of self-control over time to determine whether a person changes or remains more stable compared with his or her prior level on the trait. These studies show some evidence for both change and stability in self-control over time. It will be important for future research to determine factors that cause changes and stability in self-control over the life course. These factors may not be limited to childhood; events and experiences during adolescence and adulthood may be instrumental for understanding how self-control continues to change across developmental stages.

Since the 1990s, a handful of criminological studies have been published that focus explicitly on the measurement properties of Gottfredson and Hirschi's concept of self-control. As noted earlier, many studies have not only used the Grasmick et al. Self-Control Scale to test Gottfredson and Hirschi's main theoretical propositions, but most studies on the reliability and validity of self-control measurement have centered on Grasmick and colleagues' 24-Item Self-Report Attitudinal Measure of Self-Control. This particular measure was designed to tap into each of the six dimensions of self-control hypothesized by Gottfredson and Hirschi. Research on the measurement of self-control should be open to new ideas that can hold promise for understanding the validity of the self-control theory.

Some researchers have begun to use different methods for measuring self-control. These consist of parent or primary caregiver reports of children's behavior and self-reported behavioral indicators of self-control by children and adolescents that stretch across developmental stages and behavioral domains to gauge stability of the trait over time. However, several new ideas can help advance our understanding of self-control measurement. First, compiling a list of all self-control measures used in past criminological research would be beneficial for researchers interested in exploring self-control theory. In this way, criminologists would be able to assess the positive and negative attributes of each measure and make research decisions about which ones best fit their purpose. Criminologists should also pursue various definitions of self-control, especially given Gottfredson and Hirschi's disapproval of attitudinal measures and Travis Hirschi's more recent reconceptualization of the self-control concept that suggests self-control and social control are the same.

Given Gottfredson and Hirschi's preference for the use of behavioral self-control measures, an important line of future research on self-control is to create behavioral measures and compare them with Grasmick et al.'s Self-Control Scale. For instance, Bernd Marcus has created a self-control measure that consists of 67 behavioral items that are designed to assess the frequency of prior conduct that can have long-term consequences across developmental

stages. Future research should not only investigate how Marcus's scale correlates with Grasmick et al.'s measure but should also assess the predictive validity of his measure and compare it with the predictive validity of Grasmick et al.'s measure.

Researchers should also investigate the accuracy of self-control measures for different groups of people, especially given the possibility that one's own self-control can affect survey responses. Responses may be less valid for individuals who have committed more serious offenses, are repeat offenders, and those possessing lower self-control. Hirschi and Gottfredson have argued that a potential solution would be to collect behavioral indicators of self-control that are measured independent of respondents—for instance, having parents or teachers report on a child's behavior.

Policy and Intervention

Gottfredson and Hirschi offered limited implications for policy in their initial publication on self-control theory, although an entire chapter was dedicated to it. Nevertheless, some recommendations were made. First, support was given for an offense-based model of prevention. They suggested that focusing efforts on reducing one specific type of crime would not cause displacement into other types of offending if crime is the result of immediate gratification. Offenders will be deterred if the certainty of getting caught is increased, and making a crime harder to commit will be the most effective means of crime control.

Since the original publication of their self-control theory, Gottfredson and Hirschi have listed eight policy implications that focus on crime control. These are as follows:

1. Do not attempt to control crime by incapacitating adults.

2. Do not attempt to control the crime rate by rehabilitating adults.

3. Do not attempt to control crime by altering the penalties available to the criminal justice system.

4. Restrict the unsupervised activities of teenagers.

5. Limit proactive policing, including police sweeps, police stings, intensive arrest programs, and aggressive drug policies.

6. Question the characterization of crime offered by agents of the criminal justice system and uncritically repeated by the media.

7. Support programs designed to provide early education and effective child care.

8. Support policies that promote and facilitate two-parent families and that increase the number of caregivers relative to the number of children. (Hirschi & Gottfredson, 2001, pp. 81–96)

The policy recommendations from this list would not fare well with many politicians and criminal justice policymakers. Gottfredson and Hirschi see minimal use for the criminal justice system and correctional interventions on the grounds that deterrence does not work with offenders because they are unlikely to consider the future consequences of their actions and are more interested in behaviors that produce immediate gratification or pleasure. They do suggest that limiting unsupervised activities will be beneficial because this restricts opportunity for crime. They also suggest that interventions need to be early and focused on parenting practices such as early education and effective child care. Gottfredson and Hirschi are clear that prevention strategies targeting early socialization and parenting practices should improve self-control.

Unfortunately, criminologists have done little to develop and evaluate programs that can assist in increasing healthy levels of self-control for children. But they have investigated correlates of low self-control that provide insights into factors that should be targeted for intervention purposes. As noted earlier, these include parental monitoring, disciplining, and parental recognition of misbehavior in childhood. Some researchers have identified socialization efforts beyond the family, such as neighborhood and school influences, on children's self-control, and others have identified that self-control may be influenced by an interaction between genetic and socialization efforts. Criminologists know less about how these factors can be manipulated and how targeted interventions can lead to improvements in self-control for children and adolescents in the short and long term.

Some research investment from other disciplines has been made to determine what programmatic efforts can improve children's self-control. In a study published in 2010, Alex Piquero and colleagues conducted a meta-analysis of 34 studies that systematically investigated the effectiveness of programs designed to improve self-control before the age of 10, the age at which Gottfredson and Hirschi theorize self-control levels are fixed. Studies were selected for inclusion if they used randomized controlled designs and measured self-control (and delinquency or problems behaviors) during a posttest examination. Piquero and colleagues concluded that self-control improvement programs are effective interventions for improving self-control, which then reduce delinquency. The improvement programs reviewed by Piquero and colleagues differed with respect to the types of interventions and training delivered. Some centered on the improvement of social skills by focusing on communication, skills related to friendship and self-control, and problem-solving techniques. Others involved treatment through role-playing interventions, immediate/delayed reward interventions, and relaxation.

It is yet to be determined whether intervention efforts are effective in changing self-control beyond the childhood years. Although early prevention is important, promising research does suggest that self-control is malleable and is susceptible to change in later life stages. As such, the development of prevention and intervention efforts are needed to target sensitive periods to teach individuals to make informed decisions before acting, to seriously consider how their actions affect others, and to teach individuals to think about the personal consequences and collateral damages caused by their own behavior. Long-term developmental studies that offer self-control enhancement programming would provide researchers, intervention specialists, and policymakers with a better idea of when the effectiveness of intervention and prevention efforts is optimal.

Chris L. Gibson and Elise T. Costa

See also Biosocial Perspectives on Deviance; Control Theory; Integrated Theories; Positivist Definitions of Deviance

Further Readings

Gottfredson, M. R., & Hirschi, T. (1990). *A general theory of crime.* Stanford, CA: Stanford University Press.

Grasmick, H. G., Tittle, C. R., Bursik, R. J., Jr., & Arneklev, B. J. (1993). Testing the core empirical implications of Gottfredson and Hirschi's *General Theory of Crime. Journal of Research in Crime and Delinquency, 30*(5), 5–29.

Hirschi, T., & Gottfredson, M. R. (2001). Self-control theory. In R. Paternoster & R. Bachman (Eds.), *Explaining criminals and crime: Essays in contemporary criminological theory* (pp. 81–96). New York, NY: Oxford University Press.

Moffitt, T. E., Arseneault, L., Belsky, D., Dickson, N., Hancox, R. J., Harrington, H., . . . Caspi, A. (2011). A gradient of childhood self-control predicts health, wealth, and public safety. *Proceedings of the National Academy of Sciences, 108*(7), 2693–2698.

Piquero, A. R. (2010). A general theory of crime and public policy. In H. D. Barlow & S. H. Decker (Eds.), *Criminology and public policy: Putting theory to work* (pp. 66–83). Philadelphia, PA: Temple University Press.

Piquero, A. R., Jennings, W. G., & Farrington, D. P. (2010). Self-control interventions for children under age 10 for improving self-control and delinquency and problem behaviors. *Campbell Systematic Reviews, 6*(2), 1–117.

Pratt, T. C., & Cullen, F. T. (2000). The empirical status of Gottfredson and Hirschi's *General Theory of Crime*: A meta-analysis. *Criminology, 38*(3), 931–964.

Wright, J. P., & Beaver, K. B. (2005). Do parents matter in creating self-control in their children? A genetically informed test of Gottfredson and Hirschi's theory of low self-control. *Criminology, 43*(4), 1169–1202.

SELF-ESTEEM AND DEVIANCE

Broadly defined as a sense of well-being and self-worth, self-esteem reflects one's opinions about oneself. The relationship between self-esteem and deviance is one that is often investigated by researchers and provides a framework for evaluating both the causes and effects of engaging in deviant behavior.

A common perspective in the discussion of self-esteem and deviance is that low self-esteem predisposes an individual to reject positive social norms and to commit deviant acts. Many theoretical explanations, such as social bonding, social learning, or strain, predict that a lack of positive views about the self can increase the lure of participating in nonnormative activities such as deviance. Numerous studies have shown that people of different ages, genders, and racial backgrounds who have low self-esteem are more likely to commit an act of deviance than people who have high self-esteem. From this perspective, committing deviance is thought to be a mechanism for increasing self-esteem. However, it is important to acknowledge that the specific causal factors that lead those with low self-esteem to engage in deviance are still unclear.

Just as it is plausible that low self-esteem may lead to deviance, theoretical arguments can also be made that deviance may lead to low self-esteem. The participation in deviant behavior may result in stigma or shame; if the result is that the individual feels ostracized or overly criticized, his or her self-esteem may suffer. Additionally, some research shows that victimization may lead to offending and that victimization may lead to low self-esteem. Despite the potential for low self-esteem to be either a cause or effect of deviance, there is much greater emphasis in the literature on low self-esteem as a cause of deviance.

Although most research that examines the relationship between self-esteem and deviance addresses how low self-esteem can predict levels of deviance, many researchers have also examined the role of high self-esteem in contributing to deviant behaviors. Although high self-esteem is often viewed as a protective factor that encourages participation in normative behaviors, proponents of the position suggest that high self-esteem is often wrongly judged as low self-esteem. For example, it may be viewed a characteristic of low self-esteem when an individual isolates himself or herself from others, but this could also be due to high self-esteem that leads the individual to devalue the need to associate with others.

High self-esteem predicting deviance is reflective of the concepts of egotism and narcissism, which occur when people have extremely high evaluations of themselves regardless of outside feedback. Outside threats to these high self-perceptions can result in deviant, including aggressive, responses. Critics of this position defend the low–self-esteem position by arguing that there is multidisciplinary support showing how high self-esteem not only is predictive of normative behaviors but also is considered a protective factor against deviance because people with high self-esteem have been shown to be more mature and have diverse coping mechanisms.

The development of self-esteem continues throughout one's life course as people are continually exposed to new experiences and environments, but it is considered to be less subject to fluctuation during adulthood than in childhood. The literature on deviant behavior across the life course provides additional insight on the role that self-esteem plays in understanding deviance. Instead of focusing on group difference, life course criminology provides insights on changes within the individual over time.

Longitudinal research on deviance focuses on adolescence as a vital time in development, but it also allows for specific comparison with other points in adulthood. Such research shows that self-esteem is developing and still fragile during adolescence and becomes more stable during adulthood. Neuroscientists have conducted longitudinal research showing that brain function changes at this point in time. This indicates that when a youth has low self-esteem, he or she may have fewer tools developed to handle issues than do adults. An inability to properly handle conflicting situations with normative behaviors may lead to erratic behaviors in adolescents. When frustrating situations are coupled with ineffective coping mechanisms, youth may suffer formal or informal consequences. If they become ostracized for their behavior, they may develop a sense of blocked legitimate opportunities that could result in deviance. For instance, low self-esteem is linked to several negative consequences during this phase of life—risk-taking/sensation-seeking behavior and relationships may develop with peers who encourage deviant behaviors. From this perspective, low self-esteem is seen as maladaptive in childhood.

The relationship between self-esteem and deviance spans a variety of fields. Throughout adolescence and into adulthood, it is expected that individuals are still experiencing biological and neurological changes and are highly influenced by their surroundings. Biological explanations focus on the role of internal factors in developing self-esteem. For example, body chemistry can affect hormone levels, which can in turn affect how people view themselves and the world. Social–psychological explanations focus on how one's social environment contributes to self-esteem acquisition. For example, love and acceptance from family and peers are thought to promote the development of self-esteem. Sociological factors—race, socioeconomic status, gender identity—can also be critical to self-esteem. Both internal and external factors operate within different contexts to provide unique developmental experiences for people. As people experience change, through the life course and in their environment, self-esteem can act as either a protective factor or a risk factor in their decision whether or not to engage in deviant behaviors.

Danielle A. Tolson

See also Focal Concerns Theory; Identity; Neutralization Theory

Further Readings

Andrews, D. A., & Bonta, J. (2010). *The psychology of criminal conduct*. Philadelphia, PA: Elsevier Science.

Baumeister, R. F., Smart, L., & Boden, J. M. (1996). Relation of threatened egotism to violence and aggression: The dark side of high self-esteem. *Psychological Review, 103*(1), 5–33.

Ferris, D. L., Brown, D. J., Lian, H., & Keeping, L. M. (2009). When does self-esteem relate to deviant behavior? The role of contingencies of self-worth. *Journal of Applied Psychology, 94*(5), 1345–1353.

McCarthy, J. D., & Hoge, D. R. (1984). The dynamics of self-esteem and delinquency. *American Journal of Sociology, 90*(2), 396–410.

Mruk, C. (2006). *Self-esteem research, theory, and practice: Toward a positive psychology of self-esteem* (3rd ed.). Berlin, Germany: Springer.

Rosenberg, F. R., Rosenberg, M., & McCord, J. (1978). Self-esteem and delinquency. *Journal of Youth and Adolescence, 7*(3), 279–294.

SELF-INJURY

Self-injury, the deliberate, nonsuicidal destruction of one's own body tissue, emerged from obscurity in the 1990s and spread dramatically among adolescents. Self-injury has gone by several names including self-harm, deliberate self-harm syndrome, self-mutilation, self-cutting, self-injurious behavior, and self-wounding. Although a range of behaviors may be considered self-injurious, the psychiatric community has defined this syndrome as including self-cutting, burning, branding, scratching, picking at skin or reopening wounds, biting, headbanging, hair pulling (trichotillomania), hitting (with a hammer or other object), and bone breaking.

Self-injury, long considered a suicidal gesture, is recognized today as offering a short-term release from anxiety, depersonalization, and rapidly fluctuating emotions leading to the lessening of tension, grounding, euphoria, reduced anger, satisfaction of self-punishment urges, and relief from feelings of depression, loneliness, loss, and alienation. It represents an emotion regulation strategy providing a sense of control, reconfirming the presence of one's body, dull feelings, and converting unbearable emotional pain into manageable physical pain.

The psychomedical community considers self-injury an impulse disorder, often starting in early adolescence, with most practitioners still adolescent. Girls are regarded as more frequent practitioners than boys, although some assert that there are more, or nearly equal, male practitioners. Like eating disorders, self-injury has been thought to originate and remain located primarily among a disproportionately Caucasian, intelligent, middle- or upper-class population.

Historical Background

Three significant historical periods can be discerned that affect the population, prevalence, meaning, and practice of self-injury. Self-injury has clearly existed for a long time, although throughout most of history there has been little public awareness of the phenomenon. During this first era, practitioners acted mostly alone and in a social vacuum. Early mentions of self-injury from the time of Herodotus in the 5th century BCE through the Middle Ages depict self-injurers as religious fanatics, social outcasts, and the severely disturbed or mentally ill. People who injured themselves often referred to their acts by simply saying that they "hurt" themselves without realizing that there were others doing it as well.

During the mid-1990s, public knowledge of self-injury began to rise and a second era dawned, with depictions of the behavior appearing in books, films, television shows, magazines, newspapers, and other media. Several celebrities came out in public and admitted to having committed self-injury, and discussions of it flourished in many high schools. This burgeoning awareness, although still limited in scope, spread rapidly through segments of the population that were most likely to come into contact with self-injurers: adolescents, young adults, educators, doctors, and psychologists. It affected the way self-injurers thought about themselves and were regarded by others, but they still mainly kept to themselves, operating as loner deviants.

A third period began around 2001–2002, when websites began to appear on the Internet that focused on self-injury (self-mutilation, self-harm) complete with public chat rooms where people could interact with fellow and former self-injurers, those who wished to discourage the practice, and other visitors. Internet self-injury sites and groups have enabled the development of cyber subcultures and cyber relationships where communities of self-injurers flourish and grow. At the same time, the practice of self-injury became widespread among a broader range of people. Disaffected, alternative populations seized on it as a way to rebel and express their rejection of mainstream values. Structurally disadvantaged populations, such as homeless youth, minorities, the poor, and people in prisons and juvenile detention centers, turned to it out of frustration. Ordinary teenagers adopted it as a way to relieve the travails of typical adolescent development. Older people started revealing their self-injury to establish themselves as a group and differentiate from the "young and trendy" cutters. Young men channeled their anger and rage into injuring their bodies. A growing group of older hard-core users, who begin the practice to seek relief, settled into a lifetime pattern of chronic self-injury.

Once the media discovered self-injury, it spread like wildfire. People who heard about it, and learned that others had gotten relief from their emotional troubles by doing it, tried it on themselves. Wannabes and copycatters did it just to fit in. The stigma of mental illness abated, so that people were regarded as being merely unhappy and, possibly, too needy. Instead of scaring the populace, self-injury increasingly became known, especially among youth, as "that thing that people do." As this happened, self-injury left the realm of the purely psychological and became a social phenomenon, spread through social contagion.

Apart from the expanded demographics of the population, self-injury displays distinctly sociological characteristics in two other areas. First, in contrast to the psychological model that views self-injury as arising from internal disorders, we are frequently witnessing the social learning of the behavior. Once it began to emerge in the mid-1990s, people heard about it via the media, in health classes, and from their peers. Watching its depiction on television, films, and magazines and hearing about it from individuals they knew taught them that this was something that relieved emotional distress. Despite the messages to avoid it, this represented a strong draw. Second, although the psychological model suggests that self-injury occurs when people experience strong self-harming impulses that cannot be controlled, many self-injurers actually plan their acts in advance. They may defer their injuring until it is more convenient or enjoyable. They may rationally weigh the pros and cons of injuring, quitting or resuming the behavior when the balance shifts. Some make bargains with themselves, promising to do it at a later time to avoid strong urges. It has become, for many, an instrumental behavior.

Effects of the Internet and Other Social Media

Many wonder about the effect of the Internet on self-injury. Does it encourage the behavior or promote recovery? Do Internet support groups and relationships prepare individuals for better functioning in the "real world," or do they draw people away from it, further into the cyberworld? Although many view the Internet as the reason for the dramatic rise in self-injury between the mid-1990s and 2000s, this is not the case. People primarily learn about injuring via the media and through face-to-face communication and generally turn to the Internet only once they have become involved with it. There they find a wide range of options. The first of these is passive participation. Many go online to gather information about this practice for themselves or loved ones. Often, people post blogs, diaries, or websites filled with medical or pseudomedical advice, give long accounts of their own experiences, or offer referrals to other sources of information. Those wanting a more interactive experience turn to message boards, cyber support groups, or listservs. These offer communication with others all around the world and let individuals compose their thoughts before they posted them, opting out from replying to those they found triggering. A third group finds the delay in response from cyber groups unsatisfying and seeks out venues where they can interact with others immediately. Self-injury chat rooms are much less common, but many boards and groups offer chat rooms on the side where members can log in and hang out online.

These cyber venues range in their size, level of activity, demographics, and orientation. Some house younger members while others create havens for older participants. Some are exclusive in their focus, while others welcome people with a range of issues. Most important, some are highly regulated and mandate a strictly recovery-oriented focus, while others are less regulated and more open about members' attitudes toward their self-injury. When people find a community that fits them, they tend to stick with it (although this might change over time). The strictest groups feature a host of moderators in addition to the site owner who screens postings and mediates disputes. Words such as "cutting" or "burning" are banned. Using initials or acronyms instead of real words is mandated, such as SA for sexual assault, ED for eating disorders, and SI for self-injury. Violators are subject to prompt expulsion. Past injurious behavior cannot be mentioned, nor can implements for injuring. Moderators and members of such highly regulated groups accept people's slips into self-injury as long as they only discuss their feelings about it and not their injurious acts and as long as they remain staunchly committed to quitting.

At the other end are communities that avow and embrace their self-injury in much the same way as the pro-Ana (anorexia) and pro-Mia (bulimia) sites. These pro-SI groups represent those who are longer-term or more seriously committed self-injurers, often some who had lasted through the "new frontier" period, and represented a smaller, more hard-core group. They often espouse a loosely pro-SI orientation that begins by accepting it as a lifestyle choice. They compare self-injuring with other coping mechanisms, such as alcohol or drugs, but consider it preferable because they believe it lacks the addictive and medically damaging consequences. Their bodies are their own, they reasoned, and their injuring only hurt themselves, not others. The behavior is deviant, but not illegal. Since they need it and it helps them, they take a positive attitude toward it. Especially for those who are trapped in family, living, or socioeconomic difficulties, self-injury represents a way to escape or to assert a measure of self-control. People adopting this view do not necessarily favor it as a lifetime adaptation, but one that works for them in the moment. Regarding it as a lifestyle choice rather than a disability, they view it as a positive coping mechanism that helps them self-soothe, often transferring blame for the stigma from themselves to others who judge them. For those trapped in bad situations, it can be a way to make it through until their lives improve.

In the middle of the spectrum are groups and boards that are more moderate in their orientation and control. The mid-2000s saw most sites falling into this category, offering a broader orientation toward self-injury and supervision. They serve to mediate interaction but not stifle communication. These range from sites that are generally recovery oriented to those that are somewhat but not too venting. Such sites involve myriad groups, from people who love cutting, to those who are ambivalent about their self-injury, to those who have quit. If people want to stop, there are those who support them. If people want to continue, others accept them.

Patterns of Self-Injury

Like other deviants, self-injurers follow predictable patterns in progressing through their deviant careers. Many pick it up during their early teens, when the stresses of life are high and people's coping skills are undeveloped. The largest population of self-injurers still falls within the adolescent years. Well-known within middle and high school populations, self-injury has become more accepted as a means of dealing with stress and emotional pain from the deeply scarring to the situational. Some young people escalate their injuring rapidly once they begin, moving to more frequent and serious acts as they seek greater relief. Individuals who are driven to self-injury due to less deeply troubling life circumstances often ramp up and spin out quickly, moving through the phases of onset, escalation, intense involvement, and cessation. Some get help in this passage from friends, others from parents, therapists, medication, significant others, or Internet support groups.

Those who stick with the behavior for longer tend to drop out of the population at predictable stages in the life course. Some quit when they move from high school to college or out of their parents' homes, freeing themselves from dysfunctional living situations and difficult friends and family relations. Those who continue into college may quit when their lives get better, when friends or significant others plead with them, or when they are ready to move on to other things. The end of school offers another drop-off point, as individuals face the prospect of applying for employment and fear the stigma of their scars. Marriage represents another point of transition out of self-injury as does childbearing, as they do not want to role model this behavior to their kids. Those who continue into adulthood and later adulthood sometimes give it up through a process of oscillating in and out of the behavior, never quite knowing which quit will be the last one. Many of these find support in Internet communities. These sites offer not only help but also an alternate to the psychomedical community's model of self-injury as pathological. They aid people in realizing that this behavior does not mean that they are crazy, weak willed, sick, or bad. In fact, our longitudinal data show that many people who struggle with self-injury during their formative years, like those who try drugs, eating disorders, or delinquency, grow out of it to live fully functioning productive lives as professionals, parents, spouses, without further problems.

Peter Adler and Patricia A. Adler

See also Eating Disorders

Further Readings

Adler, P. A., & Adler, P. (2011). *The tender cut: Inside the hidden world of self-injury.* New York: New York University Press.

Belknap, J., Holsinger, K., & Little, J. (2012). Sexual minority status, abuse, and self-harming behaviors among delinquent girls. *Journal of Child & Adolescent Trauma, 5*(2), 173–185.

Conterio, K., & Lader, W. (1998). *Bodily harm: The breakthrough healing program for self-injurers.* New York, NY: Hyperion.

Favazza, A. R. (1998). The coming of age of self-mutilation. *Journal of Nervous and Mental Disease, 186,* 259–268.

Hodgson, S. (2004). Cutting through the silence: A sociological construction of self-injury. *Sociological Inquiry, 74,* 162–179.

Nock, M. K. (2010). Self-injury. *Annual Review of Clinical Psychology, 6,* 339–363.

Plante, L. G. (2007). *Bleeding to ease the pain: Cutting, self-injury, and the adolescent search for self.* Westport, CT: Praeger.

Rodham, K., Gavin, J., & Miles, M. (2007). I hear, I listen and I care: A qualitative investigation into the function of a self-harm message board. *Suicide and Life-Threatening Behavior, 37,* 422–430.

SELF-REPORT SURVEYS

Measurement has been an important issue in the social sciences in general and in the study of deviance in particular. Scholars, policymakers, the media, and the public have paid a great deal of attention to levels of deviance, especially crime. Following a criminal act, it is possible to get information about a crime from three different sources: (1) the police, (2) the victim, and (3) (if apprehended) the offender. Official crime statistics, victimization surveys, and self-report surveys are developed to get information about crimes from these three different data sources, respectively. In the United States, the most commonly used data come from the Uniform Crime Reports (UCR), National Crime Victimization Survey, and Self-Report Surveys. While official reports and victimization surveys are valuable sources of data, scholars have voiced concerns about these types of data sources. That is, the UCR and the National Crime Victimization Survey might provide a biased picture of the extent of crime, since these data are produced by government agencies. These concerns led to the development of the self-report method of data collection about criminal and delinquent acts in 1940s and 1950s.

The idea of the self-report method of data collection is to ask people about the crimes that they have committed. One of the important strengths of this method is that information collected by self-report surveys is not filtered by the formal processes within the criminal justice system. On the other hand, information provided by individuals about their criminal behavior may not be accurate due to the unreliability of memory and the tendency of individuals to lie and exaggerate about their past behavior. The focus on the behavior of adolescents rather than adults and wording of questions is also an important limitation of the self-report method. Another major problem with self-report studies is their tendency to focus on less serious crimes because individuals may not be willing to report their past involvement in serious crimes, especially undetected and unsolved ones. As a result, self-report studies usually focus on behaviors, such as truancy, simple assault, drug and alcohol use, violation of hunting or fishing laws, and similar activities. Despite these limitations concerning the validity and reliability of self-report studies, some scholars nevertheless consider the self-report method an asset to criminological research. For instance, Terence P. Thornberry and Marvin D. Krohn hold that the introduction and use of the self-report method for measuring crime represent one of the most important improvements in criminology.

Early self-report studies include the works of James F. Short and Ivan Nye in the late 1950s. These studies revealed that an important aspect of delinquency and crime was not officially recorded, thus providing a strong justification for using the self-report method of data collection.

The three major self-report studies are National Youth Survey (NYS), Monitoring the Future Survey (MTF), and the National Household Survey on Drug Abuse (NHSDA). NYS, a longitudinal survey, has been conducted since 1977 using a national sample of young people aged 11 to 17 years. The NYS includes questions about offenses that are listed in the Federal Bureau of Investigation's UCR, excluding homicide. Participants are interviewed in their homes in the NYS study.

MTF is also a longitudinal study that provides information about illicit drug, alcohol, and tobacco use by young people since 1975. Besides exploring the prevalence and incidence of substance abuse, MTF also provides data about the regular (e.g., daily and weekly) use of certain substances. Nearly 20,000 students in 8th, 10th, and 12th grades in public and private high schools complete a questionnaire every year. In addition, college students and young adults (i.e., 19–28 years old) also complete

MTF questionnaires. MTF is administered to the same sample each year.

The NHSDA provides data about illicit drug, alcohol, and tobacco use by young people since 1971. It is administered to noninstitutionalized people who are ages 12 years or older and involves face-to-face interviews in the United States. The NHSDA is administered to a different sample each year.

In the past six decades, self-report studies have revealed results that are not in agreement with results indicated by official crime data. According to self-report studies, for example, females reported being as criminal as males, youth from middle and upper classes reported similar levels of involvement in crime as youth from lower class, and whites and blacks reported similar levels of involvement in crime and delinquency. Thus, self-report studies have sparked a debate about the relationship between gender, social class, and race in criminology.

Some scholars hold, however, that official crime statistics and self-report data do not measure the same phenomenon. That is, self-report studies reflect data from a different sample than do the official crime statistics. Despite their limitations, self-report data are still being used widely in criminology.

Ibrahim Mese

See also Collecting Data Online; Interviews; Quantitative Methods in Studying Deviance; Triangulation

Further Readings

Cantor, D., & James, P. L. (2000). Self-report surveys as measures of crime and criminal victimization. In D. Duffee (Ed.), *Measurement and analysis of crime and justice* (pp. 85–138). Washington, DC: U.S. Department of Justice.

Nye, F. I., & Short, J. (1957). Scaling delinquent behavior. *American Sociological Review, 22*, 326–331.

Nye, F. I., Short, J., & Olson, V. J. (1958). Socioeconomic status and delinquent behavior. *American Journal of Sociology, 63*, 381–389.

Thornberry, T. P., & Marvin, D. K. (2000). The self-report method for measuring delinquency and crime. In D. Duffee (Ed.), *Measurement and analysis of crime and justice* (pp. 33–83). Washington, DC: U.S. Department of Justice.

Serial Murder

Serial murder is one of the most deviant and taboo acts imaginable. Most researchers concur that an individual must kill a minimum of two people over an extended period to be considered a serial murderer. The killings must also be separate events that occur on different occasions. For example, Seung-Hui Cho, who shot and killed 32 people during the Virginia Tech massacre in April 2007, would be considered a mass murderer, rather than a serial murderer. Mass murderers, such as the Virginia Tech shooter, kill groups of people at one time, while serial killers prefer to individualize each murder. It is estimated that only 2% to 4% of serial murderers are legally insane. Research indicates that the overwhelming majority of serial murderers have the ability to distinguish between right and wrong. Many of these individuals are sexual sociopaths who choose not to control their violent behavior. This entry discusses various aspects of serial murder, including information on serial murderers' motivations, targets, cultural differences, admirers, as well as the media's interest in serial murder.

Paraphilias

Researchers agree that serial murders tend to be sexually motivated and often exhibit paraphilias. According to the American Psychiatric Association's *Diagnostic and Statistical Manual of Mental Disorders*, fourth edition (*DSM-IV*), paraphilias occur in individuals who obtain sexual arousal and gratification from sex acts that are considered to be atypical or extreme with respect to cultural norms. Paraphilic behaviors are much more prevalent among males than females and may be a manifestation of unresolved conflicts during a person's psychosexual development. While paraphilias may vary from person to person in their intensity, frequency, and duration, the behavior must last at least 6 months for there to be a clinical diagnosis.

The literature on serial killers is replete with examples of lust murderers who were fueled by deviant and abnormal fantasies. Albert DeSalvo, also known as the Boston Strangler, is a prime example of an individual plagued with gerontophilia. During the 1960s, DeSalvo raped and strangled elderly females to death for sexual purposes. While it is true that DeSalvo also murdered young women, 8 of his 13 victims (62%) were above 55 years of age. The serial killer Jerry Brudos found sexual gratification by sometimes substituting shoes for a sexual partner. At an early age, Brudos developed a fetish for women's shoes, especially those which were black and spike heeled. It is also not uncommon for serial killers to

engage in necrophilia, which entails having sexual relations with corpses. Jeffrey Dahmer, who murdered 17 men, is particularly known for engaging in this act. In fact, Dahmer even went so far as to drill holes into his victims' skulls in an attempt to make zombies out of them. Dahmer had extreme abandonment issues and fantasized about having sex slaves who would never leave him. Other serial murderers have engaged in anthropophagy where they eat their victim's flesh. Edmund Kemper, a sexual sadist who shot, stabbed, and strangled female hitchhikers on one occasion sliced off body parts of his victims and cooked them in a macaroni casserole. Researchers contend that the element of fantasy plays an important role in facilitating the above type of behaviors.

Victims of Serial Murder

Female sex workers tend to disproportionately be the victims of misogynist serial killers, who may perceive they are doing society a favor by ridding the world of drug addicts and prostitutes. In fact, as many as 78% of all victims of serial murder in the United States are female prostitutes. It has been estimated that female sex workers are 18 times more likely to be the victims of murder than women who do not engage in prostitution. Some scholars have characterized female sex workers as belonging to the "less dead," a term indicating that prostitutes are devalued, stigmatized, and marginalized by society prior to becoming homicide victims.

Gary Ridgeway, also known as the Green River Killer, was convicted of murdering 49 female victims and claimed that he specifically targeted prostitutes due to the fact that he perceived that police officers simply refused to investigate these acts. Because prostitution is an illegal act throughout most of the United States, it is possible that the general public may not empathize with sex workers who become homicide victims. In fact, these murders may even be viewed by many as an occupational hazard. According to Tomas Guillen's (2007) book titled *Serial Killers: Issues Explored Through the Green River Murders*, Ridgeway told investigators,

> I was doing you guys a favor, killing prostitutes, here you guys can't control them, but I can. I mean if it's illegal aliens, you can take 'em to the border and fly 'em back out 'a there. But, if it's a prostitute, you'd arrest 'em, they were back on the street as soon as they get bail and change their uh, name, and you guys, you guys had the problem . . . I had the answer. (p. 25)

Serial Murder Across the Globe

While serial murder has been viewed as being primarily a Western phenomenon, this type of deviant behavior occurs throughout the world. Nevertheless, serial murderer profiles constructed by law enforcement officials in the United States can seldom be applied globally. This may be due, in a large part, to the fact that cultural differences heavily influence the motives and methods of serial murder. For example, sex work in Germany is currently not illegal; therefore, prostitutes are not forced to secretly advertise their services under the guise of escorting or exotic body massages, as they do in the United States. Perhaps, more important, sex workers who operate in Germany are not at odds with law enforcement officers. Given this, it may come as little surprise that female prostitutes in Germany are considerably less likely to be the victims of violent sexual predators or serial murderers. In Germany, prostitutes are not forced to work covertly and are more likely to be missed. Ridgeway, the Green River Killer, preyed on prostitutes primarily due to the fact that prostitution was criminalized. Eric Hickey in the latest edition of his book, *Serial Murderers and Their Victims*, documents Ridgeway's hatred of sex workers. After his apprehension, Ridgeway told investigators,

> I picked prostitutes as my victims because I hate most prostitutes and did not want to pay them for sex. I also picked prostitutes as victims because they were easy to pick up without being noticed. I knew they would not be reported missing right away and might never be reported missing. I picked prostitutes because I thought I could kill as many of them as I wanted without getting caught. (p. 25)

The above quotation provides insights as to why sex workers in the United States are considered to be attractive targets for many serial murderers. Due to the fact that prostitution is illegal throughout the vast majority of the United States, sex workers are considered to be criminals under the eyes of the law. In most cases, the illegal nature of sex work permits serial murderers to dehumanize their victims and even neutralize or justify the killing of prostitutes. Serial murderers may rationalize their crimes by telling themselves that they are actually doing society a favor by ridding the world of sexual deviants. In the eyes of Ridgeway, a Pentecostal who brought his Bible to work and even tried to convert a few of his coworkers to Christianity, prostitutes were violating God's law

and deserved to be punished. Had prostitution been regulated and legalized, as it is in Germany, it is highly unlikely that Ridgeway would have been able to kill as many sex workers as he did. Although it is true that there are a handful of cases where German serial killers have preyed on prostitutes, the motivations behind these killings are completely different. For example, Gerard Schroeder from Bremen murdered three sex workers during the 1980s for economic reasons. Unlike Ridgeway, who was sexually motivated, Schroeder selected prostitutes as his victims simply because he believed they would have a substantial amount of money on their person.

While serial murderers across the globe tend to have different motivations and modus operandi, this is not to say that the United States is the only country that has produced sexually motivated lust murderers. Andrei Chikatilo, who is known as the Russian Ripper, brutally killed 53 people, mainly young children. Chikatilo was sexually inadequate and would often ejaculate on his victims' corpses. The Russian Ripper also suffered from a massive inferiority complex and would not allow his victims to look at him during the attacks. He soon began stabbing the victims in their eyes. While Chikatilo resembles sexually motivated serial killers in the United States, his crimes were still unique in many respects. For example, the Russian Ripper did not kill his first victim until he was 42 years old. Most serial murderers, on the other hand, kill their first victim when they are in their mid- to late 20s. Also, Chikatilo killed his victims between 1978 and 1990, which is a killing career substantially longer than that of most serial murderers. Additionally, unlike most serial killers, Chikatilo had a highly skilled occupation. He was a senior engineer whose job required constant travel. Chikatilo used this as an opportunity to murder victims who resided throughout the region. Eventually, the Russian Ripper was captured, and he ultimately confessed to all of the murders. Chikatilo was executed in 1994 by a single bullet fired into the back of his head.

Serial Killer Admirers

Once serial murderers are apprehended and convicted of their crimes, it is not at all uncommon for them to establish romantic relationships with individuals who reside outside of prison. Serial killers, such as John Wayne Gacy (the Clown Killer), Richard Ramirez (the Night Stalker), Kenneth

Bianchi and Angelo Buono (the Hillside Stranglers), and Ted Bundy have managed to find admirers and even get married while incarcerated. In fact, even after he was convicted of committing multiple murders, Bundy managed to father a child while incarcerated in a death row prison facility in Florida. While most people would certainly not involve themselves romantically with a vicious criminal, there are nevertheless some individuals who are attracted to high-profile prisoners, such as serial murderers. This phenomenon, known as hybristophilia, tends to be found more in females than in males. It is likely that many hybristophiles have been victims of domestic abuse and may harbor tremendous feelings of guilt and inadequacy. Research indicates that hybristophiles are also socially isolated and decide to become romantically involved with incarcerated serial killers in order to achieve a sense of belongingness. In 1996, Doreen Lioy, a freelance magazine editor, married serial killer Richard Ramirez in a California prison, despite the fact that he had been convicted of multiple murders and sentenced to death by a jury. Lioy, a virgin, wore a white dress during the ceremony and proclaimed that she would commit suicide if Ramirez were ever executed for his crimes. Ramirez died, of unknown causes, in prison on June 7, 2013. Doreen Lioy refused to be interviewed at the time of his death.

While some sex researchers have argued that women who marry serial murderers usually have sexual paraphilias or suffer from mental illnesses, it is also possible that incarcerated serial killers are very adept at identifying vulnerable individuals and luring them into inside-outside relationships. Kenneth Bianchi, one of the infamous Hillside Stranglers, was able to persuade an outside woman to attempt murder in order to help him establish an alibi. Bianchi and his cousin Angelo Buono terrorized the city of Los Angeles when they raped and murdered at least 10 women over a span of five months between 1977 and 1978. Although most of their victims were prostitutes, they also killed two young school girls. This deadly duo was soon dubbed by the media as the "Hillside Strangler," although there were two killers. Bianchi and Buono were especially vicious toward many of their victims. In one particularly brutal case, the cousins injected a woman with cleaning fluid before placing a bag over her head that was attached to a stove. After the cousins were apprehended, both proved to be manipulative as inmates. Bianchi, the younger of the two killers, proved to be especially conniving. He had become pen pals with

several eligible bachelorettes and even convinced one woman, Veronica Compton, to attempt murder. Compton later became an inmate herself as a result of her association with Bianchi.

As a young woman, Compton appeared to have everything going for her. She was a model and an aspiring screenwriter, but her world changed when she began corresponding with Bianchi. Bianchi eventually persuaded the 24-year-old actress to visit him in jail where he was being held for the strangulation deaths of two female students. Soon, Compton professed her love to this vicious serial killer. Bianchi seized on the opportunity and convinced Compton to commit murder to establish an alibi that would convince authorities that he was not the real killer.

The above example is significant because it illustrates the dangers posed by notorious serial killers even after they are incarcerated. In extreme cases, serial killers may have the capability to persuade vulnerable individuals to commit atrocious crimes, despite the fact that they are behind bars. In 1981, Compton attempted to strangle a cocktail waitress as a favor to Bianchi. Fortunately, the victim managed to escape, and Compton was given a life sentence for attempted murder. Compton later alleged that she was heavily addicted to cocaine during her courtship with Bianchi and that this made her susceptible to his inappropriate suggestions. In a bizarre twist of fate, Compton began exchanging romantic letters with a college professor who was 27 years her senior. As an inmate, she convinced the professor to visit her, and this led to a unique marriage ceremony that took place within the confines of the prison. Compton was granted conjugal visits, and the couple even had a child. It is noteworthy that Compton, who was lured into an alliance with a notorious inmate, also managed to establish an inside-outside relationship following her incarceration.

Serial Murder and the Media

The media have always been fascinated with grisly accounts of serial murder. During the late 19th century, Jack the Ripper, who killed at least five victims within the Whitechapel district of London, was the subject of intense media coverage. There is strong evidence that Jack the Ripper even taunted the police by sending letters to news organizations. The media eventually adopted a nickname for the killer, which has become a common practice even to this day. The media frenzy surrounding serial murder continues to be prevalent, and there is an enormous amount of public interest in this very deviant form of behavior. Serial murder has been depicted in popular films, such as *Silence of the Lambs*, *The Texas Chainsaw Massacre*, the Saw series, and *Hostel* among others. Television shows including *Criminal Minds*, *CSI*, and *Dexter* have also portrayed serial murderers. Some scholars have noted that fictional works, such as these, give many offenders an elevated status while completely disregarding the victims of actual murders. There is strong evidence that U.S. society has a tendency to glamorize acts of serial murderer. For example, there is typically a strong demand among some consumers for "murderabilia," which refers to merchandise that is associated with serial killers. Presently, one can find comic books, art work, music, and even trading cards that depict violent serial murderers. There is also a demand for any item that is directly tied to serial murderers themselves. For example, during his incarceration, John Wayne Gacy sold his painting for thousands of dollars and even had gallery exhibitions. The serial murderer David Berkowitz, also known as the Son of Sam Killer, has recently led a crusade from prison to prevent websites from profiting from the sale of serial murder–related paraphernalia. While serial murder is one of the most taboo acts imaginable, the continued focus of both news outlets and popular media have made the actors, in this very deviant form of behavior, cultural icons. As a result of the sensational nature of this crime, the aura surrounding serial murder has assumed a life of its own and is now itself a subject of academic inquiry by many scholars.

Robert M. Worley

See also Female Prostitution; Homicide; Necrophilia

Further Readings

Earley, P. (2012). *The serial killer whisperer: How one man's tragedy helped unlock the deadliest secrets of the world's most terrifying killers.* New York, NY: Touchstone.

Federal Bureau of Investigation. (2008). *Serial murder: Multi-disciplinary perspectives for investigators: Behavioral Analysis Unit, National Center for the Analysis of Violent Crime.* Washington, DC: U.S. Department of Justice.

Fox, J. A., & Levin, J. (2011). *Extreme killing: Understanding serial and mass murder.* Thousand Oaks, CA: Sage.

Guillen, T. (2007). *Serial killers: Issues explored through the green river murders.* Upper Saddle River, NJ: Prentice Hall.

Hickey, E. (2006). *Sex crimes and paraphilia.* Upper Saddle River, NJ: Pearson.

Hickey, E. (2010). *Serial murderers and their victims* (5th ed.). Belmont, CA: Wadsworth Cengage Learning.

Holmes, R. M., & Holmes, S. T. (2008). *Profiling violent crimes: An investigative tool* (4th ed.). Thousand Oaks, CA: Sage.

Holmes, R. M., & Holmes, S. T. (2009). *Serial murder* (3rd ed.). Thousand Oaks, CA: Sage.

Keppel, R. D., & Birnes, W. J. (2008). *Serial violence: Analysis of modus operandi and signature characteristics of killers.* Boca Raton, FL: CRC Press.

Rule, A. (2008). *The stranger beside me.* New York, NY: Pocket Books.

SEX DISCRIMINATION

Institutionalized discrimination based specifically on sexism is termed sex discrimination or gender discrimination. Sex discrimination is based on either preference for one sex over the other or disadvantage based on sex. There seems to be a common expectation for victims to report and mitigate sex discrimination; however, due to power inequalities between the perpetrator and the victim, as well as normalized sexism, victims may find it difficult to find support for reporting discrimination. Literature on sex discrimination tends to address workplace forms of discrimination (occupational sex discrimination) in which men are typically preferred in recruitment, hiring, and promotion compared with their female counterparts. In female-dominated fields (e.g., gender typing), there is evidence to suggest that men are valued and promoted above women, referred to as a glass escalator effect.

As certain fields and occupations become gender typed, general characteristics emerge to determine the ideal male or female candidate, which serves to hinder gender crossover. For example, gender segregation is observed in males as doctors and females as nurses and is sustained due to the masculine and feminine characteristics that are normalized for each occupation. Many scholars have explained sex discrimination by suggesting that patriarchal ideologies tend to favor or overvalue masculine-based traits particularly in the workforce, while feminine traits receive less attention and value. For instance, the glass ceiling effect represents a prominent form of institutionalized sex discrimination in which women face invisible promotion barriers despite qualifications and experience. Similarly, in traditionally male-dominated fields and industries, women are presumed to be less capable of performing job tasks when compared with male applicants and workers. Historically and contemporarily, sex discrimination is a normalized workplace factor that tends to treat men and women unequally, by underrepresenting women in hiring, promotions, and pay grades in comparison with men. This entry addresses key forms of sex discrimination in settings such as in the workforce and in sports, as well as discrimination related to sexual minority groups.

Occupational Sex Segregation

Females tend to be disadvantaged in the workforce based on occupational sex segregation. Historically, women's career entry in the formal paid labor force has been socially hindered due to societal expectations that women become stay-at-home mothers. In terms of race and ethnic minority, women and low-income women in general tend to fill lower paid jobs, such as domestic workers or secretarial assistant positions. Female-dominated jobs typically receive less prestige and incur lower salary and pay grades compared with male counterparts. In both white- and blue-collar jobs, male domination and work roles linked to masculine-based tasks tend to limit women's equal entry as applicants and workers. Masculine and feminine traits underlie interpretations made of job applicants. Particularly masculine traits tend to be valued by employers, while female job applicants may experience prejudice based on feminine skills linked to less appreciation in the workplace. Patterns consistently show that male employers prefer male rather than female applicants.

Research also demonstrates that women's career pathways are bimodal and less linear than men's career trajectories. Women tend to enter the labor force for a period of time, then leave to raise a family, before eventually returning once their children have reached a certain age. In terms of sex discrimination, men's career paths are less interrupted, giving them greater opportunity to advance their careers. Women employees, therefore, are socially obligated to negotiate and balance family caretaking responsibilities with work, meaning that they may be expected to take time off in the case of sick children, for example. Furthermore, their salary contributions are perceived as supplementary to their male counterparts.

Workplace

The Equal Employer Opportunity Commission (EEOC) has remained at the forefront for addressing, monitoring, and mitigating sex discrimination in the workforce. The EEOC serves to prevent favoring or denying employees on the basis of their gender and, particularly, disputes sexual harassment. Protection from sex discrimination is upheld by Title VII of the Civil Rights Act of 1964. Prevention efforts put forth by the EEOC advocate that employers and employees consult policy information and participate in educational seminars to identify sexual harassment and proactively strive to reduce and resolve cases. A key form of sex discrimination is the favoritism of an employee on the basis of sex. Preferential treatment on the basis of sex is considered discriminatory due to the coercion between the perpetrator and victim as a result of uneven power relations. Individuals' job skills may be undermined when advancements or positive sanctions are based on sexual favoritism. Furthermore, employees may find that their job security, safety, and ability to refuse sexual favoritism may be compromised. Additionally, sex discrimination creates an atmosphere of unfair advantages and disadvantages for workers and employers, contributing to a general hostility.

Sexual Harassment

Sexual harassment has been a pervasive social problem linked to workplaces. Sexual harassment is not only an independent social problem but also a predictor of other social problems within the workforce, such as disruption in worker productivity. Thus, the EEOC has developed policies and procedures devised for preventing and reporting. Two types of sexual harassment for which the EEOC has designed policies to address are quid pro quo and hostile workplaces. According to the EEOC, the former defines that coerced sexual advances influence employment decisions, while the latter states that sexual advances negatively affect job performances and generates a hostile atmosphere. The hostility creates both physical and psychological health consequences for the victim. Workplace sexual harassment functions to undermine the rights of women by reducing their role to sexual objectification. Because of men's greater likelihood to hold managerial and supervisory positions, the uneven balance of power between male and female workers undermines sexual harassment opportunities. Considering racial differences among perpetrators and victims, research shows that African American women are more likely to identify sexual harassment when the perpetrator is white compared with white women. Hence, race and sex discrimination merge to place many African American female employees in potentially hostile workplaces.

Title IX and Education

Sex discrimination has been largely mitigated by the 1972 passing of Title IX, which sought to prevent sex discrimination in educational settings with regard to academic programs and sports. Education has largely encountered sex selection in major fields offered. Traditionally, women have been encouraged into female-dominated areas, deterred from male fields due to presumed lack of capability, and even internalized social messages to follow traditional education and career pathways that correspond to sex. Although women have been disadvantaged based on deterrence from male-dominated areas, similar arguments can be made for men who have been pushed into male-dominated areas rather than female-dominated fields, despite their interests and abilities. Many of the societal supports for male- and female-dominated fields of study and professions have been upheld due to preferences for masculine and feminine traits and traditional gender roles. As a result, men have been socialized to be leaders and secure corporate, prestigious, or labor-intensive jobs, while women have been urged to pursue assistant, teaching, or caretaking roles, both of which coincide with gender role expectations.

Title IX and Female Sports

Sex discrimination has also received attention and criticism in higher education, particularly with regard to women's sports. Emphasis on male sports as revenue generators and widespread media popularity have disserviced female sports' legitimacy. Title IX sought to remedy the inequality between male and female sports with mixed outcomes. In general, male sports—football, basketball, and baseball—have generated significant recruitment, larger teams, greater fund-raising, and consistent fan presence. In comparison, women's sports have attempted to achieve similar results, but with less success. Female athletes tend to be devalued for their skills and abilities, and thus, attention is placed on sexualizing them to coincide with feminine ideals. Certain female sports, such as softball, are vulnerable to outside stigma that characterizes women athletes as lesbians, thus undermining their athleticism. Even with efforts to minimize sex discrimination under Title IX, a lack of support has emerged when these efforts have been perceived as adding a female team at the expense of eliminating a popular male sports team. Advocates and participants of male sports have claimed that reducing or eliminating funding and teams are forms of sex discrimination as well.

Sexual Minorities

Sex discrimination is not limited to ascribed differences associated with gender but also pertains to sexual minority groups that are not defined as the dominant heterosexual group. Patriarchal societies tend to support divisive traditional gender roles in which men have greater power over women. This tendency is further sustained by a predominant valuing of heterosexuality. A climate of heterosexism undermines the tolerance and validation for sexualities alternative to heterosexuality, because the latter is determined to be normal (even natural to some arguments) and institutionalized as the standard. For example, cultural customs tend to sustain heterosexuality, such as the media's overrepresentation of heterosexual relations and the institution of marriage and correlating benefits. Individuals and social groups identifying as gay, lesbian, transgender/sexual, or bisexual face varying degrees of individual and societal discrimination, such as stigma, homophobia, lack of civil rights, and even violence.

Additionally, alternative sexualities tend to be socially interpreted by the dominant heterosexual group as jeopardizing complementary, albeit unequal gender and sexual roles. For example, men who identify and/or engage in an alternative sexuality to heterosexuality are subjected to ridicule, discrimination, and violence because society perceives them as not only failing to uphold male gender scripts but also weakening the construction of masculinity. Women who identify as lesbians or bisexuals, for instance, also face similar ridicule and societal rejection for failing to subscribe to feminine expectations and failing to sexually attract and attain a male sexual partner. Ironically, due to a heterosexist environment in which the predominance of heterosexuality aligns with gender inequality, women sometimes face mixed messages in which bisexual behavior or any sexual involvement between two or more women is sensationalized. Social messages have been made to suggest that bisexuality and lesbianism could be tolerated by heterosexist environments if they support male sexual scripts of sexual involvement with multiple women. In comparison, gay and bisexual men may be more severely victimized by heterosexism compared with lesbian and bisexual women due to traditional gender roles. The categories of what makes an ideal man or woman tend to be more restrictive of men than of women. Socialization in part influenced by changes in women's access to rights has been more permissive of girls and women engaging in masculine characteristics and tasks, but less supportive of boys and men who take on feminine roles. Thus, homosexuality among males may directly threaten the power afforded to masculinity and linked to men to a greater extent than homosexuality among women. Overall, sex discrimination correlates to the normalization of traditional gender roles in which men and heterosexuality are considered socially dominant compared with their counterparts.

Erin Rider

See also Feminist Theory; Sexual Harassment; Workplace Violence

Further Readings

Dermer, S., Smith, S., & Barto, K. (2010). Identifying and correctly labeling sexual prejudice, discrimination, and oppression. *Journal of Counseling & Development, 88,* 325–331.

Gorman, E. (2009). Hierarchical rank and women's organizational mobility: Glass ceilings in corporate law firms. *American Journal of Sociology, 114,* 1428–1474.

Jewell, E. (2010). Athletics and Title IX of the 1972 education amendments. *Georgetown Journal of Gender and the Law, 11,* 245–271.

Levine, J. (2009). It's a man's job, or so they say: The maintenance of sex segregation in a manufacturing plant. *Sociological Quarterly, 50,* 257–282.

Sheridan, M. (2007). Just because it's sex doesn't mean it's because of sex: The need for new legislation to target sexual favoritism. *Columbia Journal of Law and Social Problems, 40,* 379–423.

Woods, K. (2009). Sexual harassment across the color line: Experiences and outcomes of cross- versus intraracial sexual harassment among black women. *Cultural Diversity and Ethnic Minority Psychology, 15,* 67–76.

SEX TOURISM

Sex tourism occurs when a person or group of persons travels domestically or internationally to engage in sexual relations, particularly commercial sexual relations, with persons in prostitution. However, there is no consistent definition, as sex in tourism falls under the scope of sex tourism, yet the two are distinct; that is, sex in tourism, is when travelers may not be specifically motivated to engage in sexual relations but may travel to locations with greater or different commercial or noncommercial sexual opportunities than they have locally. Despite these differences, sex tourism involves monetary, emotional, or romantic payment. This entry provides an overview of what is known about sex tourism. Toward that end, this entry discusses the history of sex tourism, the characteristics of sex tourists and sex providers, and the mechanisms by which sex tourism occurs.

Historical Context of Sex Tourism

The development of sex tourism hinged on two things: (1) colonization and (2) military involvement. Initially, sexual relations between colonizer men and colonized women were forbidden on the grounds of racial and class differences, but over time, colonizers and military men were in effect rewarded for colonial domination by being given sexual access without responsibility to colonized women. Degrading the colonized women and viewing them as promiscuous and immoral while protecting the colonizer women created a dichotomous image of good woman/bad woman and reinforced a racial boundary. This dynamic continues to nourish contemporary sex tourism's demand for buying the "Other" women, that is, women viewed as exotic and erotic.

Second, sex tourism developed due to involvement of foreign military. Military men had sex with women outside their race while abroad as a way to help create the military's national identity, satisfy the male urge, build group cohesion, provide reward, guard against loneliness, and defuse homoerotic tensions. Despite these claims, sex tourism has rapidly developed during the past century at destinations without this history of military presence and colonization, yet research suggests that sex tourism destinations depend on racial differences between buyer and seller.

Similarly, female sex tourism dates back several decades to women traveling to the Caribbean to engage in sex with Caribbean men. Today, female sex tourists travel to the Caribbean, Kenya, and Bali with the similar motivation of male sex tourists to travel to destinations based on racial differences between the buyer and the seller. Finally, the development of gay sex tourism dates back a century when homosexual men from northern Europe explored their sexuality in the Mediterranean away from the constraints of societal disapproval of homosexuality. Research suggests that gay sex tourism today is often for this reason as males living heterosexual identities travel abroad to have sex with males.

Contemporary sex tourism in the United States has hot spots in 10 of Nevada's rural counties in addition to recent research citing hot spots in Detroit, Michigan, and New York City, New York. International hot spots for sex tourism are Thailand and the Philippines; Brazil, Israel, and Mexico for homosexual sex tourism; southern Europe, the Caribbean, Southeast Asia, and Kenya for female sex tourism; and Thailand, Cambodia, India, Brazil, and Mexico for child sex tourism. These destinations for sex tourism share characteristics of female poverty and inexpensive travel opportunities for sex tourists to engage in sexual relations with marginalized people.

Nature of Sex Tourism

It is difficult to provide accurate estimates of the size and the impact of the sex tourism industry because of the informal and illegal nature of sex tourism, the stigma associated with persons in prostitution, the reluctance to study it, and the unwillingness from governments and politicians to acknowledge the industry. There is a significant discrepancy in government estimates and academic estimates of sex tourism; nonetheless, academic estimates agree that there are millions of sex workers, including approximately 2 million children in a multibillion dollar sex industry that may contribute to health concerns, exploitation, oppression, human trafficking, and/or sex slavery. Surveys suggest that 25% of young people engage in sex in tourism with another traveler in addition to 51% of heterosexual males, 36% of homosexual males, and 20% of females engaging in sex with locals abroad as sex tourists. It is estimated that more than 600,000 women have been involved in sex tourism within the past 25 years.

It is also difficult to paint a portrait of the typical sex tourist due to the lack of reliable data, stigma attached to prostitution, and definitional issues for individuals who participate in sex tourism. It appears that the largest group of sex tourists is Western, heterosexual, married, white men. They predominantly originate from Western Europe, North America, Australia, and Japan. There is some evidence that sex tourists have higher incomes than the rest of the population, which helps facilitate their sex tourism. Sex tourists who visit red-light districts and window advertisement areas are less affluent than those visiting clubs or escort services. In addition, female sex tourists and homosexual sex tourists are predominantly affluent Westerners.

Child sex tourists fall into three categories and often have seasonal or traveling jobs that facilitate their sex tourism. First, they may be pedophiles with a specific sexual interest in prepubertal children. Second, they may be preferential child sex abusers with a preferred sexual interest in children who have reached puberty. Third, they may be situational child sex abusers who are not consistently or consciously seeking children for sex but do have sex with children. Overall, sex tourists are diverse in their racial, social, and economic backgrounds in addition to age and gender identity. Despite their diversity, however, they are similar in their motivations for participating in sex tourism.

Most research on sex tourism comes from clients; thus, it is also difficult to describe the persons providing sexual services. What is known about persons who provide services in sex tourism is that they are predominantly exploited boys and girls generally under the age of 12 years or young adult women in their late teens or early 20s. Male sex workers of female sex tourism are usually between the ages of 15 and 36 years with an average age of 24 years. However, sex tourism destinations vary in their makeup, as child prostitution in Thailand is almost exclusively female, while child prostitution in Sri Lanka is almost exclusively male, and in the Philippines the makeup is half male and half female.

Most sex workers in Europe and North America cite their reasons for participating in sex tourism as trying to achieve greater financial security, flexible working hours, a step to marriage, or the ability to meet their own needs for sex or experience within a gendered society of structural constraints. Often, those providing sexual services are impoverished women, men, and children of color, adhering to the Western male fantasy of buying the Other. Female sex workers speak fewer languages than male sex workers, and often, male sex workers have other jobs, while female sex workers do not. Red-light and window advertisement workers and male sex workers may be independent and have a lack of anonymity, while club or escort workers have anonymity and a controlled transaction by the owner.

Mechanisms of Sex Tourism

The advertisement and commission of sex tourism occurs in a variety of ways as suggested by information collected by researchers, law enforcement agencies, and clients. First, sex tourists may be attracted to sex tourism due to the reduced costs of sexual services, easier access to children for sexual purposes, access to legal prostitution, or more relaxed enforcement of prostitution in foreign countries. Sex tourists may plan their trip through a tourist agency or outside a tourist agency. Sex tourism is advertised through brochures, hotels, travel agencies, newspaper advertisements, street promotions, and Internet advertisements and guidebooks.

The growing trend in planning a sex tourism trip is through the Internet. Many destinations, such as Thailand, advertise descriptions of the kinds of sexual services available and the costs. Internet websites provide sex tourists with a community in which to exchange information and recommendations with other sex tourists about sex tourism destinations, "products," and costs. Since their registrations, the 20 most popular Internet websites for sex tourism reviews have been visited more than 2 million times, with the most popular Internet page visited nearly 100 million times.

Once the sex tourist arrives in the chosen destination, he or she may be approached directly by a pimp or a person in prostitution on the street or other venue or may be contacted indirectly through bars, massage parlors, restaurants, and other venues. Sex tourists may also travel to or call brothels or escort agencies. Often, it is the male sex worker who initiates contact with a female sex tourist on a beach or a disco where he offers nonsexual services. This method, such as suggesting places to visit, is unlike that for contacting male clients, which focuses on sex for money soon after contact.

The commission of sex tourism on the street or in red-light areas or window displays provides blatant marketing and immediate transactions in a controlled, contained, and tolerated environment that is under health surveillance. The sex tourist and the pimp or the provider agree on a service and a price, and the transaction is completed in another location from the direct contact. This kind of sex tourism can be opportunistic. The commission of sex tourism from an agency has minimal controls and the owner has control of the transaction. The sex tourist can call and go to the location, or the agency can arrange a hotel call and send the provider to the hotel of the client. Sex providers may also take the client to their house. Sex tourists may also visit sex shows or topless bars with lap dancing and give money for the shows or negotiate sexual services with the providers outside of the show. The commission of sex tourism may also occur by the person in prostitution doing the traveling to a foreign area where the sexual encounters take place.

There are four categories of sex tourism. First, voluntary and commercial sex tourism is when the sex worker provides sexual services for money of free will, such as prostitution, production of videos, or exotic dancing. However, some prostitution is sex slavery and is nonvoluntary and commercial when the sex worker is coerced or kidnapped and forced to work. Third, sex tourism can be noncommercial and voluntary, often cited by female sex tourists as romantic or situational encounters with a nonsex worker or a sex worker. This can include one-time access, nonsexual or sexual services across the duration of the sex tourist's trip, or recurring visits and ongoing relationships. Finally, sex tourism can be noncommercial and nonvoluntary, such as mail-order brides.

Whitney A. Flesher

See also Child Sexual Abuse; Female Prostitution; Human Sex Trafficking; Human Trafficking; Male Prostitution

Further Readings

Brents, B. G., Jackson, C. A., & Hausbeck, K. (2010). *The state of sex: Tourism, sex, and sin in the New American heartland*. London, England: Routledge.

Clift, S., & Carter, S. (Eds.). (2000). *Tourism and sex: Culture, commerce, and coercion*. London, England: Pinter.

Evans, R. D., Forsyth, C. J., & Wooddell, G. (2000). Macro and micro view of erotic tourism. *Deviant Behavior, 21*(6), 537–550.

Kempadoo, K., & Doezema, J. (Eds.). (1998). *Global sex workers: Rights, resistance, and redefinition*. London, England: Routledge.

Pettman, J. J. (1999). Sex tourism. In T. Skelton & T. Allen (Eds.), *Culture and global change* (pp. 109–116). London, England: Routledge.

Ryan, C., & Hall, C. M. (2001). *Sex tourism: Marginal people and liminalities*. London, England: Routledge.

Truong, T. (1996). Serving the tourist market: Female labour in international tourism. In S. Jackson & S. Scott (Eds.), *Feminism and sexuality: A reader* (pp. 373–378). New York, NY: Columbia University Press.

SEXTING

Sexting occurs when sexually explicit images are sent by cell phones or the Internet to another person. Sexting becomes an offense when sexually explicit images of minors, which constitute child pornography, are produced, distributed, or possessed. Sexting is a strange offense because sexted images are usually created, disseminated, and or possessed by minors, who view it as an outlet for sexual expression. This method of sexual expression does not come as a surprise, considering the fact that youth today have grown up with cell phones. Antonio Haynes, in an article on sexting, wrote that teenagers are responsible for sending out about 75 billion text messages every month. There is no doubt that quite a few of these are sext messages.

The federal age at which an individual ceases to be a minor is 18 years. This leads to a tricky situation where persons 18 years or older, being no longer children, can sext messages to each other, while those not quite 18 could be charged with child pornography in some states and registered as sex offenders. While several states are enacting sexting statutes, states with no sexting laws are continuing to prosecute sexting minors under child pornography laws. If registered as sex offenders, these minors may be labeled for life. Some believe that this penalty is highly disproportionate to the crime committed and should be considered a cruel and unusual punishment under the Eighth Amendment.

Sexting usually occurs in any of three social contexts: (1) between two persons who are in a romantic relationship, (2) from one person to a prospective boyfriend or girlfriend to initiate a relationship, and (3) from those outside of the relationship where sexting had initially occurred. While the expectation of privacy can be considered in the first social context, these minors are taking a risk in the two latter contexts. Even the first situation may not be foolproof as relationships among minors are usually quite transitory, and once a relationship is broken, the minor in possession of a sexted image may distribute it out of spite. The second circumstance can be quite hazardous as well. While it is hoped by the person sending the sext message that a romantic relationship will be ignited, it is possible that the recipient will distribute the images. The third context usually draws on the first two social situations to obtain the sexually explicit pictures, which are then possessed and distributed. Minors in this case could be charged with invasion of privacy, if the pictures are not in public domain. It is important for legislators to keep in mind that children are not mature enough to appreciate the long-term consequences of their actions. Accordingly, sexting may be more a result of immaturity and irresponsible behavior rather than calculated attempts to destroy the reputation of other children.

Nonetheless, sexting can cause much harm to those children who are the subjects of these images, especially in the latter two contexts. These images could lead to bullying at school. This is a serious problem, and because of this harm, sexting among minors should not be treated lightly. Cyberbullying has led to several suicides among teens, as in the highly publicized cases of Megan Meier and Ryan Halligan. Moreover, once the images are available on the Internet, they come into public domain and anyone can access them. This can lead to further victimization and mortification to those who are subjects of these images, leading to thoughts of suicide and, in some cases, suicide. Effective educational sessions should be put in place in middle schools and high schools because of the vulnerable population, so that teenagers can be taught about the long-term effects of sexting and cyberbullying.

Besides the danger of cyberbullying, sexted images on the Internet can be accessed by sexual predators. Without greater awareness among these teens, pedophiles may coerce minors to pose for sexually explicit images and later claim that the images were created by the minors on their own volition. This becomes a double-edged sword. While the states without sexting laws can prosecute such pedophiles as long as child pornography is involved, sex predators might succeed in taking cover under the pretext of voluntary creation of these images by minors in states that do have sexting laws, whereby sexting is classified not as a felony but as a misdemeanor. On the other hand, registering sexting minors as sex offenders will be quite confusing, as it will be hard to distinguish sex predators from sextors. Moreover, putting minors in the same population as sex offenders will afford them little protection. The purpose of prohibiting child pornography is to prevent the exploitation and abuse of children. Yet the very children who are to be protected are found guilty of offending against themselves, even though it is a result of immaturity and lack of judgment on the part of the children, unlike sex offenders, who victimize children.

Another interesting point that has surfaced in the literature on sexting is the age of consent. In most states, the age of consent when children are legally allowed to have sexual intercourse is below 18 years. However, the federal law continues to regard 18 as the age for adulthood. This brings about the dilemma: How can the act of sexual intercourse be legal, yet the sexually explicit pictures exchanged by two consenting minors who have attained the age of consent be illegal? This is a gray area that has not been addressed by the new sexting laws. Sexting laws are reducing the offense of sexting from felony to misdemeanor and advocating education rather than penalty for sexting minors, especially in the case of first-time offenders. Some observers have pointed out that along with education and increasing awareness, the age of consent should be taken into consideration.

Vidisha Barua Worley

See also Bullying; Cyberbullying; Cybercrime; Cybersex; Pornography

Further Readings

Briggs, M. M. (2012). Send me a picture baby, you know I'd never leak it: The role of *Miller v. Mitchell* in the ongoing debate concerning the prosecution of sexting. *Villanova Sports and Entertainment Law Journal, 19,* 169–202.

Chang, C. (2010). Internet safety survey: Who will protect the children? *Berkeley Technology Law Journal, 25,* 501–527.

Haynes, A. M. (2012). The age of consent: When is sexting no longer "speech integral to criminal conduct"? *Cornell Law Review, 97,* 369–404.

Meredith, J. P. (2010). Combating cyberbullying: Emphasizing education over criminalization. *Federal Communications Law Journal, 63,* 311–340.

Nunziato, D. C. (2012). Romeo and Juliet online and in trouble: Criminalizing depictions of teen sexuality (C U L8R: G2G 2 Jail). *Northwestern Journal of Technology & Intellectual Property, 10,* 57–78.

Szymialis, J. J. (2010). Sexting: A response to prosecuting those growing up with a growing trend. *Indiana Law Review, 44,* 301–339.

SEXUAL ADDICTION

Over the past several decades, sex addiction has become widely recognized as a social problem. This is mainly because of the many celebrities who have been recognized as having this addiction—actor Charlie Sheen, professional golfer Tiger Woods, and reality show host Jesse James, to name a few. Aviel Goodman (1992), a physician at the Minnesota Institute of Psychiatry, explained sexual addiction as

a disorder in which a behavior that can function both to produce pleasure and to provide escape from internal discomfort is employed in a pattern characterized by (1) recurrent failure to control the behavior, and (2) continuation of the behavior despite significant harmful consequences. (p. 303)

The medical community has long struggled with the idea of "sexual addiction" and whether it meets the scientific criteria for it to be referred to as an addiction. The word *addiction* is usually used to describe psychological and/or physiological or metabolic dependency on a drug. Using the diagnosis of addiction also implies the addict will experience tolerance over time and withdrawal if the behavior is terminated. As such, some researchers suggest that labels such as *compulsive sexual behavior, hypersexuality,* or *sexuality impulsivity disorder* would better explain the behavior rather than "sexual addiction" because tolerance and withdrawal do not seem to be present with sex addiction. Similarly, a diagnosis of obsessive-compulsive disorder or impulsivity, according to some, may better explain the behavior often associated with sex addiction.

Diagnosis

In the late 1970s and early 1980s, Patrick Carnes was the first to use the diagnosis of sexual addiction. He explained that sex addicts often rely on sex to provide comfort from pain or relief from stress, much in the same way that alcoholics rely on alcohol. He added that sex addicts transform sex into the primary relationship. In doing so, they may sacrifice family, friends, values, health, safety, and work. Carnes suggested that there was an addiction cycle present in people addicted to sex. This cycle repeats and becomes stronger with every repetition. The four stages of this cycle are the following. (1) Preoccupation: The trance or mood wherein the addicts' minds are completely engrossed with thoughts of sex. This mental state creates an obsessive search for sexual stimulation. (2) Ritualization: The addicts' own special routines that lead up to the sexual behavior. The ritual intensifies the preoccupation, adding arousal and excitement. (3) Compulsive sexual behavior: The actual sex act, which is the end goal of the preoccupation and ritualization. Sexual addicts are unable to control or stop this behavior. (4) Despair: The feeling of utter hopelessness addicts have about their behavior and their powerlessness. It was from Carnes's studies that sexual addiction became recognized as a legitimate addiction in the medical community.

In 1987, the American Psychiatric Association's *Diagnostic and Statistical Manual of Mental Disorders*, third edition, revised (*DSM-III-R*) referred to sexual addiction as "distress about a pattern of repeated sexual conquests or other forms of nonparaphilic sexual addiction, involving a succession of people who exist only as things to be used." There was debate in the medical community over this definition, and many thought the term *impulse control disorder* better encapsulated these sorts of sexual behaviors. A more recent edition of the manual (*DSM-IV-TR*) no longer recognized sexual addiction as a disorder but did include an entry called Sexual Disorder Not Otherwise Specified, which is included for coding sexual disturbances that do not meet the criteria for any specific sexual disorder. Examples of a Sexual Disorder Not Otherwise Specified include (a) marked feelings of inadequacy concerning sexual performance or other traits related to self-imposed standards of masculinity or femininity, (b) distress about a pattern of repeated sexual relationships involving a succession of lovers who are experienced by the individual only as things to be used, and (c) persistent and marked distress about sexual orientation.

Sex addiction has been rejected from the newest *DSM*, published in 2013. The *DSM-5* is using "hypersexuality" instead of "sex addiction" to explain sexual compulsivity. To be diagnosed as hypersexual, one must meet the following requirements.

(a) Over a period of at least six months, recurrent and intense sexual fantasies, sexual urges, and sexual behavior in association with four or more of the following five criteria:
  (1) Excessive time is consumed by sexual fantasies and urges, and by planning for and engaging in sexual behavior;
  (2) repetitively engaging in these sexual fantasies, urges, and behavior in response to dysphoric mood states (e.g., anxiety, depression, boredom, irritability);
  (3) repetitively engaging in sexual fantasies, urges, and behavior in response to stressful life events;
  (4) repetitive but unsuccessful efforts to control or significantly reduce these sexual fantasies, urges, and behavior; and
  (5) repetitively engaging in sexual behavior while disregarding the risk for physical or emotional harm to self or others.
(b) There is clinically significant distress or impairment in social, occupational, or other important areas of functioning associated with the frequency and intensity of these sexual fantasies, urges, and behavior.
(c) These sexual fantasies, urges, and behavior are not due to direct physiological effects of exogenous substances (e.g., drugs of abuse or medications), a co-occurring general medical condition, or to manic episodes.
(d) The individual is at least 18 years of age.

The World Health Organization's International Classification of Diseases (ICD) recognizes "Excessive Sexual Drive" and "Excessive Masturbation" as legitimate disorders. The ICD classification of excessive sexual drive is broken into two groups: nymphomania (for females) and satyriasis (for males). Many countries recognize and adopt the ICD—the United States being one of them. However, the medical community in the United States tends to place more emphasis on the *DSM* than on the ICD. Still, many believe that the ICD is more generalizable than the *DSM* because of its approval by the World Health Assembly, which is composed of health ministries of the 193 World Health Organization member countries. There have been recent attempts to minimize the discrepancies of the disorder definitions in the *DSM* and ICD. The 11th revision of the ICD is scheduled for publication in 2015 and should be more similar to the *DSM* because of recent collaborations between the American Psychological Association and the World Health Organization. For instance, one of the suggestions for both the *DSM-5* and ICD-11 is the introduction of excessive (hyperactive) sexual desire.

Because of the problems associated with diagnosis and identification, there are no accurate statistics on how many people could be diagnosed as hypersexual. However, it is estimated that perhaps 3% to 6% of the U.S. population have characteristics that would warrant a diagnosis of hypersexuality. Similarly, there is no scientific evidence as to what causes sex addiction (or hypersexuality). Some researchers argue that hypersexuality is a result of biochemical factors, while some believe that psychological factors such as low self-esteem are far more influential in contributing to compulsive sexual behaviors or hypersexuality. Still other researchers assert that societal factors, such as our beliefs about appropriate sexual behaviors, are to blame for the widespread belief that sex addiction is a legitimate disorder.

There are many researchers who do not believe in the validity of sexual addiction. Many believe that our views of sexual addiction are very much influenced by societal standards of "appropriate" sexuality and sexual behavior. Our society puts an emphasis on restrained sexual behavior and monogamy within relationships. For this reason, behaviors that deviate from these standards are considered disorders or diseases.

There is also a divide in the medical community about whether addictions can be nonchemical. As was mentioned before, most addictions are based on a metabolic dependency on a drug, such as alcohol or cocaine. This dependency leads to tolerance over time or withdrawal if the drug is no longer introduced into the body. Because sex addiction does not lead to tolerance or withdrawal, classifying it as an addiction seems inappropriate to many in the medical community. Other researchers believe that addictions are simply repetitive, high-emotion, and high-frequency experiences. As a result, many addiction specialists believe that sexual addiction has much in common with other addictions in that it relies on a system of rewards, dependence, craving, and repetitive behaviors. Numerous studies have also found that the brain function of sex addicts resembles the brain activity of those addicted to cocaine.

Treatment

Today, there are many ways in which a sex addict (or someone who is diagnosed as "hypersexual") may seek help. Many sex addicts seek therapy for their behavior. Therapy is aimed at helping the addicts find healthy ways to deal with their emotions. Cognitive–behavioral therapy is most often used when treating those diagnosed as hypersexual. Cognitive–behavioral therapy focuses on the thoughts people have that lead up to their behaviors. Cognitive–behavioral therapists would help the addict recognize situations and thoughts that lead up

to their behavior (the actual sex act). The therapists would work with the addict to change these thoughts and avoid these situations so that they would be better able to control their behavior. Often, cognitive–behavioral therapists help the addict replace their compulsive thoughts about sex with something more socially acceptable, such as exercise.

There are also treatment programs sexual addicts may attend for more in-depth and intensive therapy. For instance, Tiger Woods attended Gentle Path, a sex addiction treatment program at a private treatment center in Mississippi called Pine Grove. The best known treatment programs include Sierra Tucson in Arizona, Tulane University's program in New Orleans, and the Menninger Clinic's program in Topeka, Kansas. Unlike other addiction treatment programs, the goal of sex addiction therapy is not lifelong abstinence but the termination of the compulsive sexual behavior. Most programs do, however, suggest a 60- to 90-day period where the addict should abstain from sex. Similarly, there are a few 12-step programs that stress abstaining from the addict's compulsive sexual behaviors. Such programs include groups such as Sex Addicts Anonymous, Sexaholics Anonymous, Sex and Love Addicts Anonymous, and Sexual Compulsives Anonymous.

Conclusion

Many in the medical community believe that psychological issues other than addiction may be at work when one is unable to stop or slow one's sexual compulsivity and, as a result, is diagnosed as hypersexual. For example, past studies have noted that individuals who self-identify as sex addicts generally have some sort of psychological disorder that better accounts for their sexual behaviors, such as substance abuse, anxiety, or mood disorders. As such, many sex addicts are prescribed medication to help handle the psychological discomfort they experience. Antidepressants or stabilizing drugs are often used for this reason. Carnes explained that sex addicts tend to have four core beliefs. (1) *Self image:* I am basically a bad, unworthy person. (2) *Relationships:* No one would love me as I am. (3) *Needs:* My needs are never going to be met if I have to depend on others. (4) *Sexuality:* Sex is my most important need. Medication, along with therapy, is often used to help the addict dispel of these core beliefs.

In summary, there is debate within the medical community over whether sex addiction is, in fact, still present and will continue to affect the way in which people are diagnosed and treated for hypersexuality. Most people agree that there is a spectrum associated with sexual desire and that some individuals desire more sex than others. The labels we assign to those who are hypersexual not only affect the individual diagnosed but societal notions about sexuality in general.

Katie Schubert

See also Alcoholism; Gambling Addiction; Pornography

Further Readings

Becker, P. (2012). *Recovery from sexual addiction: A man's guide.* Bloomington, IN: AuthorHouse.

Canning, M. (2008). *Lust, anger, love: Understanding sexual addiction and the road to healthy intimacy.* Naperville, IL: Sourcebooks.

Carnes, P. (2001). *Out of the shadows: Understanding sexual addiction* (2nd ed.). Center City, MN: Hazelden.

Cheever, S. (2008). *Desire: Where sex meets addiction.* New York, NY: Simon & Schuster.

Coleman, E., & Edwards, B. (1986). Sexual compulsion vs. sexual addiction: The debate continues. *SIECUS Report, 14,* 7–10.

Goodman, A. (1992). Sexual addiction: Designation and treatment. *Sex & Marital Therapy, 18*(4), 303–314.

Holden, C. (2001). "Behavioral" addictions: Do they exist? *Science, 294*(5544), 980–982.

Ley, D. J. (2012). *The myth of sex addiction.* Lanham, MD: Rowman & Littlefield.

Sexual Harassment

According to the U.S. Equal Employment Opportunity Commission (EEOC), sexual harassment is a type of unlawful discrimination addressed by Title VII of the Civil Rights Act of 1964 (Pub. L. 88–352). Sexual harassment is also covered by discrimination prohibitions in Title IX regulations that are focused on academic settings. Behaviors categorized as sexual harassment include requests for sexual favors, sexually suggestive remarks, or unsolicited verbal or physical advances of a sexual nature. Sexual harassment can also occur when an individual feels threatened or offended by sexually suggestive visual items, such as posters, calendars, drawings, or screen savers. Sexual harassment can occur between persons of the opposite sex or

between persons of the same sex. It can occur in workplace or educational or online settings and can be experienced by or perpetrated by minors, adults, or senior citizens. Allegations of sexual harassment can lead to serious legal repercussions. Federal law mandates that employers and academic institutions must actively prevent, investigate, and correct sexual harassment. This encyclopedia entry provides an overview of sexual harassment, covering the history, trends, effects, and prevention efforts related to this type of discrimination.

History of Sexual Harassment

Unsolicited advances such as sexually suggestive remarks, coerced sexual activity, and sexually derogative comments have historically been a component of all social life, but it was not until fairly recently that the term *sexual harassment* became recognized as a type of discrimination and that this classification of behaviors became illegal according to federal law. With the Civil Rights Act prohibiting workplaces and educational settings from discriminating against gender, females began entering the workforce with males, and sexual harassment became defined as a legal issue. Although sexual harassment has become subject to legislation only recently, a wide variety of behaviors that have been unsolicited, unwanted, and of a sexually harassing nature have been embedded in power structures throughout time.

African American female slaves frequently endured sexual coercion from their white male owners, while working-class women also experienced sexual advances from their supervisors in both factory settings and in domestic service positions. The early legal system of the United States offered no recourse to unsolicited behaviors of a sexual nature except for the act of rape, and even then, the protection of rape laws did not extend to slaves. In the late 1800s and the early 1900s, the demands of female workers to be protected from unwanted sexual advances were vocalized through women's rights organizations (though these groups were primarily composed of white, middle-class women concerned with moral purity and middle-class sexual standards).

Title VII of the Civil Rights Act of 1964 prohibited discrimination by race, religion, and sex, among other things, and lent itself to protecting sexually related discrimination. The 1974 lawsuit *Barnes v. Train* is widely considered the first test of sexual harassment in the courts. In this case, a female employee claimed discrimination when she refused the sexual advances of a superior and subsequently lost her position.

In 1986, the Supreme Court heard *Meritor Savings Bank v. Vinson* and determined that a hostile work environment was another component of sexual harassment. A hostile work environment can be anything from nude calendars posted on a cubicle wall to using sexually derogative terms when talking to coworkers to telling dirty jokes.

The issue of sexual harassment captured the public's attention in 1991 when attorney Anita Hill testified against Clarence Thomas during hearings related to his Supreme Court nomination. Viewers were glued to their television for three days in October as Hill detailed the sexual harassment she experienced while working for Thomas from 1981 through 1983. While Thomas did go on to be confirmed, the incident sparked a wave of awareness about sexual harassment.

In the past few years, sexual harassment allegations have been lodged against many high-profile celebrities, including political commentator Bill O'Reilly, 2012 presidential candidate hopeful Herman Cain, professional football quarterback Brett Favre, late night host David Letterman, and singer Britney Spears. Other noteworthy sexual harassment cases occurred within the arenas of the military, automobile manufacturers, and university football programs.

While sexual harassment tends to be conceptualized as a workplace problem, it is also an issue in academic settings. The first school setting sexual harassment case to reach the Supreme Court was *Franklin v. Gwinnett County Public Schools* in 1992, when a high school student filed charges against her teacher and coach for constant harassment and abuse. The Court ruled that an individual could sue a school under Title IX for damages.

A lawsuit, *Jennings v. University of North Carolina*, was brought against a soccer coach who allegedly made highly sexualized comments about the soccer girls' bodies and sex lives on a constant basis. The player who brought suit thought she was subject to humiliating and degrading comments as part of the team environment. The case, which took 10 years to resolve, finally settled in favor of the player in 2008 (CA-99–400–1 No. 04–2447).

Title IX and Title VII are legally equipped to address incidents of sexual harassments in a wide variety of settings. The examples of sexual harassment cases above illustrate two kinds of sexual harassment, quid pro quo and hostile environment.

Types of Sexual Harassment

The law recognizes two distinct types of sexual harassment. The first is quid pro quo. It involves the loss of a job, a promotion, or continuation of an employee's position based on the employee's rejection or acceptance of a sexual advance or sexually related suggestion from a supervisor. In a school-based context, quid pro quo occurs when a certain grade or a letter of recommendation is offered in exchange for a sexual favor. According to Title IX legislation, quid pro quo sexual harassment includes any kind of unsolicited behavior that may interfere with or affect a student's grade or some other kind of benefit.

When the outcome of an unsolicited sexual advance will not affect the employee's job, but the employee is nonetheless subjected to unwelcome advances or comments from other workers or supervisors, the type of sexual harassment is known as a hostile work environment. A hostile environment can also apply in an educational context, with approximately 30% of undergraduate women having been exposed to some type of sexual harassment in an academic setting during their undergraduate years, including inappropriate touching, comments, and suggestions from professors or other students. When coworkers, supervisors, or instructors use suggestive language, display sexually suggestive artwork, or stare at a person's anatomy, these incidents can contribute to a hostile work environment. The perpetrator or instigator of a hostile environment can be subject to legal recourse. In addition, general statements or jokes that insult a gender group as a whole are considered part of a hostile environment and subject to sexual harassment legal recourse.

Patterns and Trends in Sexual Harassment

The EEOC's latest figures show a total of 7,571 charges of sexual harassment received for the fiscal year 2012. Although workplaces and higher education settings are familiar settings for sexual harassment cases, minors in primary schools are not immune to the experience of this type of harassment. The American Association of University Women (AAUW) conducted a study of students in Grades 7 through 12 in 2011 and found that 44% of respondents had experienced sexual harassment at school. Although females are typically the object of unwanted and unsolicited sexual advances, Title IX research shows that more males today are sexually harassed than were males 20 years ago.

A new trend in sexual harassment has evolved alongside new technologies, such as blogs and social media sites. Female and LGBTQ (lesbian, gay, bisexual, transgender, and questioning) bloggers have reported that, even when writing on non-gender-related topics, many abusive comments are gender-specific and involve sexually abusive and inappropriate language, while male, heterosexual bloggers rarely found their comment sections inundated with sexual comments.

Social media sites such as Facebook have opened up new avenues for delivering suggestive messages or threats. Coworkers, employers, other students, or faculty members may post sexually inappropriate comments, innuendos, or photos to a member's page. As a form of harassment, some harassers may send their victims links to websites that turn out to have pornographic content. In effect, no gender or age is immune to the experience of sexual harassment. This type of harassment can occur online, in person, or simultaneously.

Effects of Sexual Harassment

The emotional and psychological effects of sexual harassment vary widely from victim to victim. Similar to other types of abuse, the effects experienced by any individual depend on the severity and the duration of the harassment. The symptoms experienced may also vary based on the outcome of the harassment allegation. For example, the loss of a job or backlash from the accusation may lead to significantly more damaging emotional and psychological effects than a more positive outcome.

Some emotional and psychological effects may include loss of self-esteem, posttraumatic stress disorder, sleeping issues, sexual dysfunction, depression, eating disorders, feelings of betrayal, high blood pressure, or suicidal thoughts. Effects may also be professional (e.g., loss of reputation or label of "troublemaker" in the corporate world), or economic (e.g., loss of income because of inability to work in a hostile work environment). Effects in an academic environment may include the student dropping out of college or changing school districts, in addition to emotional and psychological effects.

Prevention and Investigation of Sexual Harassment

The EEOC suggests that employers take steps to prevent sexual harassment before it has the chance to occur. Many states have special agencies that oversee the implementation of antiharassment policies, and some states require that employers post notices that define sexual harassment and hostile workplace environments for employees. Because employers can be liable for sexual harassment incidents, employers must show that they have both taken steps to prevent and thoroughly investigate occurrences in order to limit liability. Title IX legislation requires that every school receiving federal funding must have a Title IX coordinator responsible for overseeing sexual harassment training, preventive efforts, reporting methods, and investigation processes.

Prevention measures that can be implemented by employers and schools include providing sexual harassment training to all employees on an annual basis, ensuring that a process is in place to handle allegations of sexual harassment, and acting promptly and efficiently to any complaints. Employees, faculty, and students should be made aware that no amount of sexual harassment in the workplace or the school is to be tolerated.

Workplace administrators and the Title IX coordinator on each campus are responsible to investigate allegations of sexual harassment in workplaces and on school campuses. At the very least, the accused must be asked if the allegations are true or false. Further investigation, if necessary, must be implemented immediately and should be coordinated by a neutral third party (in other words, an individual who is not directly supervised by the harasser). The investigation process includes ensuring the safety of the accuser by advising all parties that retaliation, in any form, will not be tolerated.

If a harassment claim against an individual is substantiated, the employer or school must then take appropriate action to conclude the investigation and resolve the matter. Actions include firing the perpetrator or suspending him or her without pay. Other options include a permanent record of the finding in the perpetrator's file, with the acknowledgment that further offenses will lead to termination. The harasser could also be transferred to an alternative division or department, away from the victim.

Ami E. Stearns

See also Sex Discrimination; Sexual Harassment; Workplace Violence

Further Readings

Barnes v. Train, 13 FEP Cases 123 (D.C. 1974).

Franklin v. Gwinnett County Public Schools, 503 U.S. 60 (1992).

Jennings v. University of North Carolina, CA-99–400–1 No. 04–2447 (2006).

Landrine, H., & Klonoff, E. A. (1997). *Discrimination against women: Prevalence, consequences, and remedies.* Thousand Oaks, CA: Sage.

Lundy-Wagner, V., & Winkle-Wagner, R. (2013). A harassing climate? Sexual harassment and campus racial climate research. *Journal of Diversity in Higher Education, 6*(1), 51–68.

MacKinnon, C. (1979). *Sexual harassment of working women: A case of sex discrimination.* New Haven, CT: Yale University Press.

McLaughlin, H., Uggen, C., & Blackstone, A. (2012). Sexual harassment, workplace authority, and the paradox of power. *American Sociological Review, 77*(4), 625–647.

Meritor Savings Bank v. Vinson, 477 U.S. 57 (1986).

Wiener, R. L., Watts, B. A., Goldkamp, K. H., & Gasper, C. (1995). Social analytic investigation of hostile work environments: A test of the reasonable woman standard. *Law and Human Behavior, 19*(3), 263–281.

Shoplifting

Shoplifting is defined as the theft of merchandise from retailers that are open for business to customers at the time of theft. Shoplifters usually attempt to blend in as law-abiding customers of stores to avoid detection and apprehension. Shoplifting is a common crime that is committed by people from all walks of life. Roughly 1 in 11 people regularly shoplift from stores. Although shoplifting is generally regarded as a minor crime, it consistently ranks as one of the most costly property crimes. In 2011 alone, shoplifting accounted for an estimated $51 billion in worldwide retail losses. It is also estimated that the cost of shoplifting to businesses inflates the price of consumer products by 10% to 15%; stores must raise prices of items that are shoplifted more often to offset losses. Despite sustained investments in retail security (e.g., uniformed guards, closed-circuit television [CCTV] cameras), shoplifting remains a substantial problem for most retailers. In addition to the enormous negative financial impacts of shoplifting on both employees and consumers, there are tangible and intangible costs. These costs include reduced staff morale, loss of work because of physical and psychological damage, and even loss of life.

There are several methods used by offenders to remove unpaid products from stores. These include (a) the "traditional" concealment in pocket or carried bag; (b) simply carrying (or pushing in a cart) the product out, with no attempt to conceal; and (c) ticket switching—replacing a price tag with a less expensive tag to pay less for a product.

Traditionally, shoplifting was thought to be a crime committed mainly by juveniles, women, opportunistic criminals, drug addicts, and the mentally ill. This is now widely regarded as a fallacy; in fact, shoplifting has become popular and profitable for career criminals. For example, some burglars have indicated that they shoplift to supplement their incomes when burglary may be too risky to attempt. Shoplifting is usually a nonviolent form of theft, but some prolific shoplifters are known to take more risks than amateurs and have been known to rob, attack, or abuse store staff when detected and their apprehension is attempted. The motivations for shoplifting vary, as do the types of shoplifters. Most shoplifters can be grouped into two categories: professionals and amateurs. Mary Cameron's *The Booster and the Snitch* provides a basic typology of shoplifters. She found that shoplifters tended to be professional or amateur thieves, which she referred to as "boosters" and "snitches," respectively. In all, 10% were professional thieves who shoplifted products to sell them, which was their main form of income. These thieves are skilled and difficult to detect in a store, even for seasoned store security workers. Professionals accounted for only 10% of the shoplifters in Cameron's study, although they clearly caused significantly more losses than amateurs. The remaining 90% of shoplifters in Cameron's model were amateurs. These amateurs ("snitches") were less unpredictable in their method and reason for shoplifting. Cameron noted that they would seem like ordinary, "respectable" citizens if their thievery had not been detected. They tended not to resell the products that they stole, nor were they desperately poor people, stealing out of necessity. For the most part, the amateurs were not observed to have compulsive, neurotic personalities.

Measuring the Effects of Shoplifting

To determine the nature and extent of shoplifting, data can be examined from several sources, including official government arrest reports, store shrinkage reports (see below), and counts of items (i.e., inventories of store merchandise). The sources that provide the official U.S. crime statistics are generally inadequate measures of shoplifting for several reasons. The National Crime Victimization Survey only records larceny-thefts against persons and not businesses. The Federal Bureau of Investigation's Uniform Crime Reports only records shoplifting incidents when a suspect has been formally charged. Apprehension data from store security can be even more problematic because only a small fraction of shoplifters are turned over to the police, and even smaller percentages are formally charged. The detection and apprehension of suspected shoplifters are the responsibility of the retail store's security personnel, because police officers generally do not have the jurisdiction to patrol private property. Police will usually only get involved to make an arrest if a retail store reports the theft and apprehension. Therefore, the true numbers of shoplifting apprehensions and arrests are somewhat difficult to measure and subsequently difficult to analyze for statistical purposes.

Counting individual items held by stores is one of the oldest and perhaps the most reliable techniques to measure shoplifting. However, physically counting items by hand is time-consuming and costly. Due to relatively large inventories, shoplifting losses tend to be bundled with other types of losses when stores calculate their "shrinkage" rates. It is difficult to disaggregate the true amount of shoplifting from the overall shrinkage. Approximately two thirds of shrinkage occurs at the end of the retail supply chain (i.e., in-store) in stores, perhaps because customers and thieves can handle merchandise firsthand in stores. Surveys of retail executives reveal that they are unable to accurately determine the proportion of missing shrinkage that is directly attributed to shoplifting; the best estimate is that it accounts for approximately 40% of the total shrinkage.

Many stores—namely, larger, chain stores—employ security guards or off-duty police officers to serve as "store detectives" to detect and apprehend shoplifters caught in the act. Once apprehended, the decision to prosecute apprehended shoplifters varies by store. Research has indicated that roughly a quarter of apprehended shoplifters will be referred to police for official sanctions. In many of these stores, the in-store detectives must conform to certain benchmarks when making the decision to prosecute or release a shoplifter. Many stores will notify the police if the suspect does not have proper identification, refused to cooperate, or fought with the store's security personnel during the apprehension process. The decision to notify the police can seem somewhat arbitrary at times.

Both the laws and penalties related to shoplifting vary. First-time shoplifters may receive sanctions, such as jail time, community service, or a fine. Some local jurisdictions have ordinances in place to downgrade shoplifting to a noncriminal petty offense. This fact has led some researchers to suggest that policymakers and police departments should elevate the importance of the crime of shoplifting. However, similar to police executives, policymakers sometimes believe that retailers are responsible for being vigilant for crimes in their own place of business. When responding to complaints from concerned retailers, some police departments have indicated that retailers have not sufficiently involved the police. In fact, because corporate retailers have performed little to engage law enforcement, the police seem to be content with letting businesses deal with their own crime problems.

Why Do People Shoplift?

There are many possible explanations as to why people engage in shoplifting. It is likely that many people are influenced by economic factors, peer pressure, moral attitudes, and perceptions of low apprehension risks. Only a minority of shoplifters are likely to suffer from psychological or psychiatric disorders. Some of the psychological classifications of motives for shoplifting include (a) mental health problems—such as anxiety, depression, bipolar disorder, and so on, (b) substance abuse—many shoplifters might think that they are only stealing to get their next "fix" of an addictive drug, and (c) kleptomania—a psychiatric disorder in which people compulsively steal for no apparent reason. However, actual documented cases of kleptomania are rare, leading courts to disregard it as a defense under most circumstances.

Those advocating a rational choice perspective suggest that potential offenders weigh the risk versus the reward of the crime. Although research conducted from this perspective has provided invaluable data about retail security, more information is needed about the shoplifter. Effective crime prevention depends on understanding why people offend, and little attention has been focused on how the antishoplifting strategies employed by retailers interact with the attitudes, beliefs, and perceptions of potential offenders to influence their shoplifting decision, or on systematically evaluating the factors that inhibit or encourage customer theft. Another middle-range theory that can explain shoplifting is *routine activity theory*. Routine activity theory requires an absence of a capable guardian, a motivated offender, and a suitable target for a crime to occur. This sequence of events is applicable to shoplifting. The target and guardian can be manipulated into a hardened target (e.g., electronic article surveillance tags on clothing items) and a capable guardian (whether CCTV or security officers).

Shoplifting is a crime that is perhaps best understood through an environmental criminology approach. Shoplifters make decisions based on the environment at hand when committing shoplifting through the following sequence: (a) choosing the store, (b) entering the store, (c) locating the product, (d) concealing the product, (e) leaving the store, and (f) disposing (i.e., selling) of the products, when necessary. Environmental criminologists have identified some key attributes of products that make them more likely targets of theft by shoplifters. For example, items are more likely to be stolen if they have high Value, low Inertia (how easily moved), high Visibility (how easily observed), and easy Access. "Hot products" such as alcohol, cigarettes, beauty products, and contraceptives are shoplifted from stores in much higher quantities than other products, largely because of having many of the "VIVA" attributes.

Conclusion

Using a situational crime prevention approach, Ronald Clarke has proposed several specific responses to reduce shoplifting depending on its causes. These include (a) improving retail practice by improving store layout and displays, tightening stock controls, upgrading retail security and posting warning signs on high-risk merchandise; (b) increasing store staffing by hiring more and better-trained sales staff, hiring store detectives, and hiring security guards; (c) updating shoplifting policies by using civil recovery, using informal police sanctions, establishing early warning systems, banning known shoplifters, launching public information campaigns; and (d) upgrading technology through the installation and monitoring of CCTV, using electronic article surveillance, and attaching ink tags to merchandise. As products evolve and become more innovative, shoplifting and how it is carried out will also change. It is important that manufacturers and stores keep crime in mind when designing products to be displayed for sale in stores.

Brian T. Smith

See also Burglary; Larceny; Property Crime; Stolen Goods Network

Further Readings

Cameron, M. O. (1964). *The booster and the snitch: Department store shoplifting.* New York, NY: Free Press of Glencoe.

Clarke, R. V. (2002). Shoplifting: Problem-oriented guides for police series, problem-specific (Guide No. 11). Washington, DC: U.S. Department of Justice, Office of Community Oriented Policing Services.

Cohen, L. E., & Stark, R. (1974). Discriminatory labeling and the five-finger discount: An empirical analysis of differential shoplifting dispositions. *Journal of Research in Crime & Delinquency, 11*(1), 25–39.

Dabney, D., Hollinger, R., & Dugan, L. (2004). Who actually steals? A study of covertly observed shoplifters. *Justice Quarterly, 21*(4), 693–728.

Klemke, L. (1992). *The sociology of shoplifting: Boosters and snitches today.* Westport, CT: Praeger.

Krasnovsky, T., & Lane, R. (1998). Shoplifting: A review of the literature. *Aggression and Violent Behavior, 3,* 219–235.

Schneider, J. (2005). The link between shoplifting and burglary: The booster burglar. *British Journal of Criminology, 45*(3), 395–401.

SKINHEADS

Despite lay perceptions of a uniform and homogeneous group, skinheads are a fractured subculture. Mainstream media coverage focuses primarily on white supremacists who are a conspicuous skinhead faction. According to conservative estimates, there are more than 100 racist skinhead groups operating in the United States. Not only are these groups part of a violent street culture, but they are also active promoters of a racist ideology used to rationalize violence against racial and ethnic minorities and other marginalized groups, such as homosexuals. Beyond the conspicuous markers of skinhead identity such as shaved heads, lace-up boots, and suspenders, the subculture is also defined by competing ideologies that intersect class, race, and politics. Mindful of the material and ideational aspects of skinhead culture, and their departure from the mainstream, analysts identify the group as both deviant and a subculture. The following will address the history of the skinheads, the factional divides, and the coverage of the subculture in the literature.

Origins

The origins of the subculture call into question popular perceptions and further make clear the contentious ground that is skinhead identity. Skinhead groups trace their lineage to working-class youth in post–World War II England. In the early 1960s, West Indian immigrant enclaves surfaced in Britain's working-class neighborhoods. Their presence soon influenced youth culture and contributed to a precursor subculture, the mods. Skinhead lineage can be traced to the mods, and before them the teddy boys, whose roots are also tied to England's working-class neighborhoods. Like the teddy boys, the mods emphasized style. Mod groups created and projected their vision of affluence through elegance and a sophisticated image. They attempted through appearance to overcome the economic circumstances of their neighborhoods.

Although mods were influenced by the Edwardian, aristocratic style of teddy boys, their working-class backgrounds were not completely subsumed. Additionally, observant of their surroundings, they also drew on their West Indian neighbors who introduced them to the musical genres of ska, rocksteady, and reggae. By the late 1960s, the mod subculture had fractured into "hard mods" and "fashion mods." Hard mods remained loyal to the groups' original musical genres and began to reconnect with their working-class backgrounds. In contrast, fashion mods were drawn into London's acid rock and fashion conscious cultures. While working-class elements were diffused in the hard mod subculture, they did not fully accept the working-class background and image.

The "original" skinheads first emerged in 1967 and borrowed elements from the mod style that included a shared connection with Jamaican ska along with parts of dress such as the button-down polo shirts and boots. During this period, skinheads helped propel the musical genre and were further influenced by the rude boy subculture imported by an influx of Jamaican immigrants in the 1960s. Of significance, and a point of distinction with their mod predecessors, skinheads fully embraced their working-class backgrounds. Unlike the mods, skinheads were far from flamboyant and developed a style that expressed their vision of the everyday working-class

man. Many of the cultural objects adopted by the group are utilitarian and, coupled with the clean-cut look of the rude boy and mod subcultures, make for skinhead style: work boots, suspenders, jeans, and plain or striped button-down shirts were to be used for work and recreation. The adoption of specific cultural elements, such as clothing, music, and language, is important within the subculture. Although a layperson may at first note the similarities in appearance between skinheads, there are cultural markers that serve to delineate factions.

Factions

By the late 1970s, the moniker "traditional" surfaced within the subculture. Traditional skinheads can be considered purists for their adherence to original skinhead culture that includes style and music. Original skinhead clothing can still be found, and musical bands such as Mobtown and the Scofflaws, part of a third wave of ska music, revived traditional elements. Cultural markers such as music, language, and fashion are used by traditional skinheads to emphasize their connections with the roots of the subculture as well as to distance themselves from racist elements. Traditional skinheads believe racism to be inconsistent with the history of a skinhead movement influenced by West Indian blacks. To date, as there was in the past, there are skinheads of non-European ancestry who are active members of the subculture. Although some traditional skinheads may consider themselves apolitical and simply followers of the style and music, there is an ideology that surfaces within this faction that emphasizes working-class pride and racial unity.

While noting the fissures that exist within the subculture, it is clear that group identity within skinhead groups is shaped by ideological differences. Political debates among skinheads include considerations on the importance of both class and race. To the latter, some traditional skinheads have joined organizations such as Skinheads Against Racial Prejudice, Anti-Racist Action, and United Front. These organizations seek, as part of their mission, to educate both the mainstream public and racist skinheads on the nonracist history of the subculture. According to antiracist and traditional skinheads, "boneheads," the derogatory term used for racist skinheads, have hijacked the movement. Antiracists engage in a variety of activities to promote racial unity while attempting to weed out or to create distance between themselves and a racist element. In some instances, claiming skinhead subcultural territory has meant violent clashes between racist and nonracist skinheads that have resulted in deaths.

During a time characterized by job scarcity in the 1970s Britain, a racist skinhead faction emerged. For young men faced with economic uncertainty, the explanations provided by England's newly formed National Front Political party resonated. The party's message focused attention on Britain's nonwhite immigrant population who served as a convenient scapegoat for political leaders who attempted to free themselves of responsibility from Britain's economic woes and those interested in courting angry, frustrated youth. In a historical period where competing political explanations abound and where youth attempt to make sense of declining economic circumstances, anarchist and socialist skinheads also emerged. In this period, skinhead politics not only played out in the political arena, but diverse messages also surfaced in music. Racism in Britain was diffused by "white power" rock bands such as Skrewdriver, whose lead singer was an organizer for the National Front. Unlike traditional skinheads who follow Jamaican ska, racist skinheads gravitated toward rock and Oi music; the latter is a subgenre of punk rock music. Although not all Oi music carries racist themes and, in fact, many traditional skinheads follow bands that focus on nonracist or class issues, it is a popular subgenre within the subculture.

A historical overview of the subculture reveals that there are multiple factions with conflicting positions on race. Traditional skinheads lay claim to the subculture by noting the inconsistencies between the progenitors of the movement and those who adopt white power beliefs. Consistent with subcultural history, and the emphasis on linkages between past and present groups, they continue to support the musical genres of ska, rocksteady, and reggae. In contrast, racist skinheads distanced themselves from the multiracial bands associated with "skinhead reggae," the label given to ska for its skinhead following, and adopted the music of "white power" rock bands. Racist and nationalist factions, some nonwhite, actively propagate racial conflict and hatred. Despite their drastic ideological differences, it can again be difficult to distinguish between various skinhead factions because of the shared appearance and dress that characterize the subculture—more specifically, the shaved heads, buttoned-down shirts and suspenders.

Beyond considering differences in musical tastes, there are other important aspects of culture that serve to delineate between skinhead factions. Tangible boundaries surface in the style and dress of subcultural factions. For example, skinhead factions will adopt different color laces in their boots to identify and express to others their political orientation. Although the color coding of laces can vary from one region or group, several understood meanings surface among groups: white laces symbolize white power, red laces are symbolic of anarchy and communism, and a combination of yellow, black, and blue laces are often used to identify antiracist Skinheads Against Racial Prejudice. Political orientation can also be advertised through the donning of pins and patches worn on jackets. Tattoos are also used to express affiliation to a particular faction or express a particular subcultural message. For example, some traditional skinheads will tattoo the number 69, or the phrase "Spirit of 69." The tattooed number or phrase is in part meant to reassert ownership claims made by traditional skinheads. The year 1969 is considered to be the peak of the original skinhead movement.

Historically, women have been, and continue to be, important contributors to the subculture. The label "chelsea" has been used broadly to refer to female skinheads. The term is also used to describe a hairstyle embraced by skinhead women. The top of the head is either shaved or cut very short with long fringes of hair falling along the sides. Skinhead women don dress similar to men that can include boots, polo or buttoned-down shirts, suspenders, and flight jackets. Like their male counterparts, women populate the ranks of both racist and nonracist factions.

Research

Research on skinheads is primarily grounded in the subculture literature, with the majority of investigations focusing on racist elements. Traditionally, research on subcultures has placed considerable emphasis on deviance. For example, Albert Cohen's (1955) seminal work on youth subculture emphasizes deviance as a central feature among members. This early literature in the area argued that factors such as political disenfranchisement, economic inequality, and dissatisfaction with mainstream society motivate individuals to join subcultures. Analysts later began to argue that youth subcultures are, in many respects, aligned more closely with mainstream society. Far from the periphery of the larger society's value system, they embrace ideational aspects of culture present in the parent culture.

Against a backdrop of mainstream perceptions and competing definitions between factions, studies on skinheads have also focused on the discursive practices and narratives used by subcultural members. To the former, physical and virtual environments facilitate the diffusion of group identity and reinforce shared in-group perceptions. Definitions adopted are also diffused by the symbolic meanings attached to the material culture of the social world inhabited by skinheads. Clearly, there is a heterogeneity that aptly describes the subculture. Skinhead factions do not all adopt one conceptualization of identity. Contradictions surface between groups as they lay claim to the subculture. To a layperson, a group populated by anti- or nonracists, along with gay racialists, may make no sense. However, within the social worlds of the subculture are members who draw on both material and ideational culture to rationalize their membership.

Daniel Sarabia

See also Subculture

Further Readings

Brake, M. (1985). *Comparative youth culture: The sociology of youth culture and youth subcultures in America, Britain and Canada.* New York, NY: Routledge.

Brown, T. S. (2004). Subcultures, pop music and politics: Skinheads and "Nazi rock" in England and Germany. *Journal of Social History, 38,* 157–178.

Cohen, A. K. (1955). *Delinquent boys: The culture of the gang.* New York, NY: Free Press.

Cooter, A. B. (2006). Neo-Nazi normalization: The skinhead movement and integration into normative structures. *Sociological Inquiry, 76,* 145–165.

Marshall, G. (1991). *The Spirit of '69: A skinhead Bible.* Dunoon, Scotland: S. T. Publishing.

Suall, I., & Halpern, T. (1993). *Young Nazi killers and the rising skinhead danger.* New York, NY: Anti-Defamation League.

Waldner, L. K., Martin, H., & Capeder, L. (2006). Ideology of gay racialist skinheads and stigma management techniques. *Journal of Political & Military Sociology, 34,* 165–184.

Wood, R. T. (1999). The indigenous, nonracist origins of the American skinhead subculture. *Youth & Society, 31,* 131–151.

SOCIAL BONDS

According to Travis Hirschi, one of the leading contemporary control theory scholars, social bonds refer to any given individual's connections and relations to his or her immediate community and play a major role in influencing behavior. The concept of social bonds owes its intellectual origins to Hirschi's social bond theory, a contemporary and prominent variation of the classic control perspective in sociological explanations of crime and deviance. Social bond theory is among the most frequently assessed and cited criminological theory and has enjoyed considerable empirical validity. This entry discusses assumptions underlying control theories and details the principal elements of social bonds.

Assumptions

Although there are many contemporary extensions of the classic control perspective, all versions of the theory (both early and contemporary) share a common underlying assumption. That is, control theories all assume to some extent that people are alike in the sense that they will always prioritize and, at the same time, seek self-interests by perpetually trying to increase pleasure, while minimizing pain and effort. It has been argued that because most criminal and deviant behavior can address such basic human desires, the motivation to offend is assumed to be evenly distributed among the population. More important, all versions of the theory also assume that people will commit crime or deviance if social controls are absent or weak. According to this line of reasoning then, variations in crime and deviance are the outcome of failure of different social controls acting to restrain individuals from engaging in socially undesired behavior. What makes the control perspective unique from other criminological theories is that it seeks to address the reasons people do not commit crime and not as much to emphasize the reasons that make individuals engage in crime.

The Principal Elements of Social Bonds

Even in light of numerous predecessors, Hirschi's social bond theory is widely considered to be the most efficacious to the prominence of the control perspective. The concept of social bonds features a particularly sociological dimension due to its specific emphasis on a given person's ties and relations to others in society and how these connections, in turn, may affect that individual's criminal and deviant behavior. Consistent with early versions of control theory, social bonds theory posits that crime and deviance are the outcome when a person's ties to his or her community are weakened or absent. As a result, the crux of social bonds theory can be summarized by its proposed inverse relationship to crime as well as its four principal elements of attachment, commitment, involvement, and beliefs. What drives the theory is a thorough exploration of the extent to which these different social bonds exert control over individuals and their behaviors. This section elaborates on each of the stated elements.

The first element, *attachment*, is primarily concerned with the quality of relationships that a person has with his or her immediate social environment. For instance, relationships with parents are often cited as being of high importance with respect to this element of social bonds. According to Hirschi, these intimate connections are important to a person's behavior due to the fact that they are a measure of how much a person cares about others' expectations of him or her. More specifically, this element of social bond theory suggests that the less a person cares about others' expectations, the less he or she may be restrained by the norms that they all share, and as a result, the more likely he or she may disregard said norms. For example, when the opportunity to commit crime or deviance is presented, a person who is more worried about disappointing others, such as family and friends, is more likely to refrain than a person who is not concerned about disappointing those around him or her.

Although parental influence is often considered an important source of attachment, connections to peers are argued to have the potential to produce similar outcomes as said familial ties. As such, irrespective of the source of attachment, social bonds theory posits an inverse relationship between a person's attachment and his or her crime and delinquency involvement.

The second element, *commitment*, is primarily concerned with how much of a vested interest a given person has in being a part of conventional society. Social bond theory argues that the higher the level of this investment that a person has, the more he or she will stand to lose. In other words, and akin to the previous element, commitment is posited to be inversely related to criminal and deviant behavior. Social bond theory often refers to those who have high levels of commitment as ones who have a high stake in conformity. It is noteworthy to emphasize that Hirschi believed there exists a rational component to conformist behavior. For instance, those who are more committed to their education and careers are less likely to be involved in behaviors that may jeopardize their futures, while those who are less committed to their education and careers

have far less to lose and are therefore more likely to violate norms and laws.

A time dimension is taken into consideration in Hirschi's formulation of the next principal elements of social bonds. This third element, *involvement*, refers to the time in which a given person spends on conventional activities and wholesome events. The theory argues for another inverse relationship between crime and social bonds: The more time that a person devotes to activities such as sports, school work, time with family, and so on, the less time that person will have to engage in criminal and deviant behavior. In other words, a given person is therefore restrained from crime or deviance because he or she is too preoccupied with conforming or with recreational pursuits.

Finally, Hirschi posited that persons who believe that they should defer to the norms and rules of their communities are the ones who are less likely to breach them. The fourth element of social bonds theory, belief, refers to the extent to which a given person may buy a set of conventional values, or social norms. This endorsement is considered a direct measure of the level of morality or lack thereof that one may be able to perceive in such norms and values. Similar to the other elements, the theory argues that when a person's take on the moral validity of norms and laws has been weakened or broken, the less that he or she is subjected to those rules, the more he or she is likely to break them.

Conclusion

Hirschi's social bond theory argues that a given individual is more likely to live by society's rules, norms, and laws if he or she has higher levels of the four principal elements with sources such as peers, adults, teachers, and above all, parents. In instances where such bonds are threatened, or taken away, the individual will be more likely to violate the norms and laws. Last, the theory strongly emphasize considering the four principal elements as highly intercorrelated. In other words, the weakening of one element is expected to contribute to the weakening of others.

Hirschi has since taken a noticeable departure from his social bond theory and has collaborated with Michael Gottfredson to formulate a separate control theory that emphasizes only one form of control: self-control theory.

Allen W. Wong

See also Self-Control Theory; Social Control

Further Readings

Gottfredson, M. R., & Hirschi, T. (1990). *A general theory of crime.* Stanford, CA: Stanford University Press.

Hirschi, T. (1969). *Causes of delinquency.* Berkeley: University of California Press.

Hirschi, T., & Gottfredson, M. R. (1995). Control theory and the life-course perspective. *Studies on Crime and Crime Prevention, 4,* 131–142.

Nye, F. I. (1958). *Family relationships and delinquent behavior.* New York, NY: Wiley.

Reckless, W. C. (1961). *The crime problem* (3rd ed.). New York, NY: Appleton-Century-Crofts.

Reiss, A. J., Jr. (1951). Delinquency as the failure of personal and social controls. *American Sociological Review, 16,* 196–207.

Social Change and Deviance

Social change, which sociologists see as the destiny of societies, is one of the basic issues of sociology. Within this framework, sociologists emphasize that social change is natural, constant, and inevitable. Although the speed of social change varies from one society to another, there are similarities between societies' social change processes. In addition, deviant behaviors manifest structural or regional differences within the framework of social change theories.

Social structure is shaped by the interaction of individuals, and change in individuals' attitudes, values, and behaviors and in individuals' interactions can bring about a change in social structure, a process known as social change. Changes in social structure are of two types. The first type is gradual general change in social structure. The second type is characterized by change in relations between institutions within the social structure. Yet these two change types are so much intertwined that it is almost impossible to consider one apart from the other.

Social changes can establish new social institutions; they can also raise existing social institutions to a higher position or make them unimportant. For instance, the Industrial Revolution brought about a change in relations between the ruler and the ruled as well as created new social institutions such as the proletariat class or syndicates.

Although opinions about social change differ from one writer to another, there is a consensus on certain aspects. These agreed-on aspects can be summarized as follows: change is a natural, inevitable, constant, and necessary phenomenon, and it

shares several similarities among societies. As can be inferred from this, social change is not a concept emphasizing a negative or positive impact. That is to say, social change expresses any kind of positive or negative impact in micro- and macrolevels on social structure and social institutions. Therefore, social change should not be confused with concepts such as improvement, development, growth, or modernization, which tend to emphasize the impact.

Because source, direction, impact, speed, or results of change cannot determine whether the process is social change, social change does not depend on any one principle or rule. Because these aspects of change can affect different societies in different ways and at different speeds, outcomes and results of change also vary from one society to another. For instance, while technological innovations in the information sector can quickly and radically influence the industrial environment, the business world, or the science community, they do not generally influence the agricultural sector as radically or as quickly. Yet innovations in gene technology, for example, can have a profound effect on the agricultural sector.

Types of Social Change

Social changes can be examined in two categories: (1) free social change and (2) forced social change. Free social changes are changes that occur without force and that often arise randomly. It is widely accepted that these kinds of social changes cannot organize and develop society. The geneticist Richard Lewontin's example of playing cards is illustrative of free social changes: When a deck of playing cards is randomly shuffled and rebundled, it is possible to talk about kind of a change because the playing cards are no longer in their original order. However, it cannot be said that the deck has been reorganized in a desired way (progress/maturity) as the change is executed without any thinking and formed randomly. That is to say, a positive change cannot be seen in this process.

According to another perspective, free change emerges as a result of the interaction of one society or group with another one without pressure or force. In such changes, groups or societies accept some impacts of the change while refusing other ones rather than accepting or refusing all effects of the change. For example, individuals who live in a city receiving large numbers of immigrants establish contact with these newcomers to their city and experience some changes within this framework. Because it is not based on any pressure or force, this change is seen as a free social change, and the society accepts many such renewals or reforms in cultural, social, and economic levels.

Conversely, forced social change is the process of actors accepting renewals or reforms as a result of compulsion. Forced social change in democratic societies is achieved through legal statutes and sanctions, while in antidemocratic societies, it is often achieved through the power of force and violence. Revolutions in history are the most explicit examples of forced social change. In other words, forced social changes can be described as one society or social group oppressing the other so that the oppressed group accepts the conditions determined by the other group. Groups or societies can force social changes by using various tools, such as coups (coups d'état), colonialism, and invasions.

Social Change Theories

Social changes vary from one society to another, one social structure to another, and from time to time, as explained above. While some societies are affected little by the changes, others may be affected greatly; some societies may be affected quickly, whereas others may be affected quite slowly. A similar situation exists within a society as well. While some social structures or social institutions may be affected little or not at all by the changes, others may be fully affected by the same changes. While analyzing social change, sociologists have pointed out the differences among social change examples and have put forward different theories and perspectives. Several of these theories are discussed in this section.

Evolutionary Social Change

Evolutionary social change theory is based on the assumption that social change emerges in certain phases. The ideas of Auguste Comte, Karl Marx, Max Weber, Émile Durkheim, and Herbert Spencer have an important place in evolutionary social change theory. A presupposition of humanity's moving on a linear course lies at the heart of evolutionary social change theory. In this respect, societies can only change by going through certain phases along this development line.

Comte, by emphasizing the static and dynamic aspects of society, prefers to discuss both changing/improving and unchanging sides of societies. Comte asserts that the knowledge levels of individuals within societies increase or improve day by day, and societies also gradually improve in parallel to that.

Spencer, in contrast, asserts that societies evolve from simple structures to complex structures. He explains the change of social structures, emergence of new social institutions, population growth, and relations between social structures becoming more complex within the framework of evolutionary social change approach. Durkheim views social change as a result of social division of labor and explains the transformation of social division of labor from simple to complex in parallel with evolutionary social change. Weber, for whom ideas and thoughts are the engines of societal change, relates social change to the improvement and evolution of beliefs and ideas. Marx sees social change in relation to production and emphasizes that social change emerges with the struggle between social classes. What is more, he sees economic relations and material factors that establish the infrastructure as the main variables of social change.

Structural Functional Theory

Supporters of the structural functional theory see society as a web of interrelated relations. According to this approach, each relation and each tool has a function. In this regard, social change functions to reestablish the balance in a society that has deteriorated.

Structural functional theory centers on relations between social structure and functions, and it asserts that the components of social structure and functions create the social system. Each social structure develops as it has a function. That is to say, functions emerge before the structures and the structures necessary for the function are formed later. This approach sees society as a functioning whole and sees change in the differentiation and renewal of the components of the social structure.

Talcott Parsons, Robert Merton, William Ogburn, Alfred Radcliffe-Brown, and Bronisław Malinowski are some of the prominent sociologists of structural functional theory. Parsons starts out from the concept of a social system constituted of related parts. According to this perspective, all parts perform the inevitable main functions necessary for the existence of the whole. The assumption of the parts' coming together in harmony and balance and creating the group or society lies at the heart of the constitutional functional theory. Parsons also defends that social order rests on consensus of values among group members. This approach explains institutional changes specifically as a result of modernization in society more than explaining social change in general.

According to Merton, each part constituting the system may not be in harmony with the system, and aberrant behaviors in the society are as much legitimate products of the society as are appropriate and harmonized behaviors. Regarding Merton's approach, positive contributions to the establishment of a new social structure should be expected from such aberrant behaviors, and examination of the influence of each part of the social system should be made more carefully.

Cyclical Social Change Theory

According to cyclical social change theory, changes and improvements within society emerge in a constant cyclical process. Vilfredo Pareto's "rise and fall of elites" approach is an example of this model. According to this approach, the elites, who hold the ability and power to rule a system, will eventually pass this power on to another elite group. Elites, then, can maintain their hold of power by constantly shifting power from one elite group to another elite group. Pareto developed this theory (roaming of elites theory) by examining historical events in the Roman Empire. The theory is based on the assumption that as old cells are replaced by new ones, renewal and recovery takes place in society, such as with constant shifts of population from lower classes to upper classes.

According to Pitirim Sorokin's social change theory, nothing can proceed endlessly in one direction. The powers pushing a component toward a certain direction replete and weaken themselves in time, and the opposite powers strengthen. Therefore, the social life is always in a constant change and movement.

Conflictual Social Change Theory

Conflictual social change theory assumes that society is composed of conflicting components. The conflictual relation web among the components within society resembles the functional relation web in structural functional theory. According to Marx, as one of the leading theorists of this theory, if there is no conflict, there is no development. He states that conflicting interests in society creates the social change. Marx asserts that social and cultural forms of societies are determined by the economic structure

of societies (mode of production). Sociologists supporting the conflictual social change theory see conflict as a normal process rather than a destructive and abnormal process.

Ralf Dahrendorf, another theorist specializing in conflict, states that there is conflict in any place or area where there is social life, and the level of conflict can vary widely from civil war to parliamentarian conflicts. Conflict cannot be abolished or removed but temporarily suppressed, controlled, or canalized to other directions. Coercion of society brings about conflict, and conflict brings along social change. This theory explains society with the conflictual relations among its constituent components and assumes that social change can happen through conflictual relations.

Social Change and Deviance

The concept of deviance, which is used to define behaviors that are described as abnormal within a framework of social expectations and culturally unapproved by the group, cannot be universally defined and changes or varies in line with the society structure, time, and social group. In other words, deviant behaviors can change as a result of social change. That is to say, a behavior that is seen as deviant in Turkey might not be accepted as deviant in South Africa. Or a behavior that is seen as having been deviant in 1970s Turkey may not be seen as deviant behavior in today's Turkey.

Fatih Beren

See also Changing Deviance Designations; Defining Deviance; Labeling Approach

Further Readings

Bernburg, J. G. (2002). Anomie, social change and crime. *British Journal of Criminology, 42,* 729–742.

Jones, T. A. (1981). Durkheim, deviance and development: Opportunities lost and regained. *Social Forces, 59*(4), 1009–1024.

Rubington, E., & Weinberg, M. S. (1969). *Deviance: The interactionist perspective.* London, England: Macmillan.

SOCIAL CONTROL

Social control is a central concept in the sociology of deviance. A broad term with a variety of sociological definitions, it typically refers to how people are held in check by various social arrangements such as the family, the state, the economic system, or the norms and rules of their culture. Social control is often used synonymously with social order when referring to the ongoing maintenance of coordination and harmony across society. In the sociology of deviance, social control specifically refers to all the mechanisms and resources by which members of society try to ensure the norm-conforming behavior of those around them.

Edward A. Ross introduced social control into the sociological lexicon in 1896. In that year, Ross published an article in the *American Journal of Sociology* titled "Social Control." Ross distinguished between social coordination, or the rules and arrangements that efficiently order societal activity, and social control, which regulates the incompatible or disruptive actions in society. Although this distinction between social control and social coordination is no longer prevalent in sociology, since that time, social control has been used as an expansive concept for explaining methods involved in the regulation, integration, coordination, or modification of individual or group behavior to some normative standard of conduct.

In the sociology of deviance, social controls are generally responses to deviant attitudes, conditions, or behaviors. This traditional view of controlling deviance is reactive; for example, a person commits a deviant act (e.g., burglary), and the police are called; a person expresses an offensive attitude (e.g., sexism), and he or she is given the silent treatment by friends; or a person is born with an abnormal condition (e.g., stuttering), and he or she is not called on by the teacher to speak in class. Although the involvement of police is an example of formal social control, in deviance the informal and often subtle responses to certain attitudes, behaviors, or conditions are considered methods of ordering and coordinating society and interaction. Formal social control is generally a response to a violation of the law or institutional regulations, or behavior that would be considered criminal, while informal controls occur through sanctions that are not codified into law or subject to the legal system.

In the sociology of deviance, social controls have traditionally been termed *sanctions*, which are responses to a violation of norms. Sanctions can be either positive or negative, as they are socially constructed expressions of approval or disapproval. Positive sanctions develop conformity and control by rewarding people for following norms. Positive sanctions can be formal, such as an official

admittance to graduate school for hard work and high grades, or informal, which could include kind words or gestures. Negative sanctions encourage conforming behavior by reprimanding people for violating normative behavior. Like positive sanctions, negative sanctions can also be formal, such as a speeding ticket or a prison sentence, or informal, such as an angry friend or dirty looks from fellow citizens. Sanctions are important in the field of deviance when examining social control, as they offer people incentives or punishments for certain forms of behavior.

As discussed, negative sanctions are elicited when a person violates a norm, while positive sanctions result from conforming behavior. Norms are behavioral codes or guidelines that direct people into the behaviors, attitudes, or self-presentations that conform to societal acceptability. Although every member of society rarely agrees on all norms, there is typically a general consensus regarding the normative guideline. The social control responses elicited for violating a norm vary depending on what types of norms are violated. There are three types of norms: folkways, mores, and laws. *Folkways* are basic everyday norms regarding custom, tradition, or politeness. Violations of folkway norms do not produce serious consequences, but people might consider the violator as weird, rude, or naive. *Mores* are norms based on general social consensus, and violators can experience serious social criticism because abiding by these norms is viewed as critical to social harmony and cohesion. The violation of mores is seen to threaten the social order, and people who violate them may be considered immoral or dangerous to society. *Laws* are norms that are supported by codified social sanctions. People who violate laws are subject to fines, arrest, imprisonment, and sometimes death. Laws are official policy, and violators are subject to formal sanctions. Thus, people are controlled or pressured to conform by different sanctions that depend on the types of norms that they have violated. In the sociology of deviance, there are four forms of social control that warrant further discussion: formal, informal, medical, and self.

Formal Social Control

Formal social control is generally a response to a violation of the law, or behavior, that would be considered criminal. Formal controls are also found in established institutions and agencies of society (e.g., universities, the Food and Drug Administration, the Environmental Protection Agency, and corporations). The overlap between crime and deviance is extensive. There are forms of deviance that are not crimes (e.g., homosexuality), and there are crimes that are rarely considered deviant (e.g., speeding). Actually, much of what is considered deviant or nonconforming (e.g., obesity, stuttering, pink hair, and tattoos) is not considered or defined as criminal. However, much of what is considered criminal behavior is also defined as deviant because codified norms (i.e., laws) are being violated.

Legal control is the type of formal social control that garners media attention and, thus, the attention of the public. Handled principally by governmental agencies that include the criminal justice system, formal control is expansive and comprises the police, the courts, and the prisons, although formal controls have increasingly become privatized (i.e., private prisons, surveillance cameras, and private security) and may be handled by companies and businesses. In the sociology of deviance, formal control has come under scrutiny for disproportionately affecting the poor and the minorities in society, or those people with less social power to defend themselves from formal control apparatuses.

The fundamental rationale behind formal control mechanisms is deterrence. Deterrence theory posits that swift and certain punishment will deter people from deviant and criminal behavior and disregards evidence that crime and deviance do not readily respond to severe sentences or new police powers. Formal control relies primarily on deterrence and aims to control through arrest and incarceration. A central problem with this perspective is that it assumes that people rationally calculate the costs and benefits of criminal or deviant behavior and act accordingly. In reality, people rarely have knowledge of the long- or even short-term sanctions they may face as a result of their actions. In contrast to a rational actor, who looks into the future for gains and losses associated with certain actions, social control is primarily derived from past experiences as people determine what sanctions might apply to their behavior. People generally rely on their past learning experiences, or socialization, when determining lines of action and the potential sanctions.

Informal Social Control

The socialization process described above socializes people to the norms and sanctions associated with formal and informal controls. In contrast to formal control, informal controls occur through sanctions that are not codified into law or subject to the legal system. In the sociology of deviance, informal controls operate through the ongoing processes of social interaction as people learn what behaviors are normative and what activities will elicit sanctions. Informal controls occur in everyday, ordinary life and document the ways in which people of a particular culture or society regulate, modify, and influence the behavior of their fellow citizens. As discussed previously, informal controls are grounded in the process of socialization and would be ineffective without the learning people experience through family, community, peers, school, work, religion, and even the mass media.

Medical Social Control

Throughout the 20th century, numerous behaviors and conditions considered deviant have come to be controlled through medical institutions. This process is referred to as the medicalization of deviance. Medicalization occurs when a problem is described in medical terms, defined using medical language, and treated with medical intervention. From shoplifting to mental illness to gambling to drug abuse to sexual dysfunction, the increasing medicalization of certain behaviors allegedly destigmatizes a variety of human and social problems. As treatments rather than punishment become preferred sanctions for deviance, medical practitioners increasingly function as agents of social control, constructing and enforcing medical norms and disseminating new forms of medical counsel and intervention. By framing deviant behavior as biological, medical social control in essence is the use of medicine as a means to minimize, eliminate, or normalize deviant behavior in an effort to secure adherence to norms.

On the most abstract level, medical social control is the acceptance of a medical perspective as the dominant definition of certain phenomena. When medical perspectives of problems and their solutions become dominant, they diminish competing definitions. At a more concrete level, medical social control is professional medical intervention via medical treatment (although it may include some types of self-treatment). This intervention aims at returning "sick" or deviant individuals to a state of health and to their conventional social roles, adjusting them to new roles, or making individuals more comfortable with their condition. Medical social control of deviant behavior is usually a variation of medical intervention that tries to eliminate, modify, isolate, or regulate behavior, socially defined as deviant, with medical means and in the name of health.

Thus, deviant behaviors once controlled informally may come to be controlled either legally or medically as an issue of public safety or justice. The interesting aspect of medical control and legal control in the sociology of deviance is that the ideologies behind these forms of control are intertwined and may conflict or cooperate with one another. For example, in the criminal justice system, defendants charged with a criminal offense are protected by due process and are safe from illegitimate government or state power being used against them. In contrast, medical control, often mandated as a public safety issue, requires expedient and swift actions on the part of the government or other agencies to protect the public from health and safety concerns. Thus, people with mental health issues or other deviant conditions may not receive the same procedural safeguards offered by the criminal justice system.

Labeling and Social Control

The major focus in deviance and social control concentrates on the societal responses to deviant activities and the social factors that lead to or produce social control. In contrast, sociologists have also focused on the outcomes or processes that result from certain forms of social control. A classic example is labeling theory. The sociologists Edwin Lemert, Howard Becker, and Erving Goffman developed this labeling approach. They noted that historically it was held that deviance leads to social control, but they stated that social control also leads to deviance. According to labeling theorists, behaviors labeled as deviant are not inherently deviant. They examined how certain acts and behaviors come to be defined as deviant, especially by those with the social power to do so. They contend that it makes little sense to distinguish social control or deviance from the definitions applied to certain behaviors by agents of control. This is because the activities of agents of social control, such as those of the police, the courts, mental hospitals, and doctors, not only respond to deviance but also actually play a large role in defining what behaviors and conditions are deviant and warrant social control. Furthermore, others in society may disagree with the definitions and labels created by these agents of control, but the agents' social power allows them to create the

definitions and labels. This relativity of deviance can be seen across cultures, time, and place, as certain behaviors warranting social control in one society may be viewed as normal in another society. Hence, labeling theorists have argued that behaviors such as drug use come to be seen as activities warranting social control because of the labeling power of elite members of society rather than of a collapse in social order.

Overall, sanctioning people for deviant behavior reminds them of the normative expectations of their social groups. Social control responses also socialize people to the consequences of not conforming to culturally agreed-on norms and guidelines. Whether these control mechanisms are formal, informal, or medical, they constitute the forms of social control that maintain order and coordination in society.

Socialization and Self-Control

In the tradition of symbolic interactionism, the socialization of self has been used to conceptualize a potent method for the social control of deviance. This perspective, pioneered by George Herbert Mead and Charles Horton Cooley and supported by scholars such as Erving Goffman and Herbert Blumer, states that the socialization of the self to the norms of the community, social groups, and significant others serves to preserve the social order as people come to see themselves in relation to the norms and sanctions of society. Furthermore, the perspective of symbolic interactionism presupposes that social order is the product of an ongoing process of social interaction and communication. Thus, the social control of deviance is created and sustained through interaction, as people take the role of others and work to find the socially acceptable response to their situation. People learn the normative and expected responses of social life and generally behave in a manner to preserve the interaction order and to avoid formal and informal sanctions.

From this theoretical standpoint, the maintenance of social order is a dynamic social process between a human being and society that provides the socialization necessary for self-control and social control. The critical locus of social control is the process of role taking and viewing and interpreting the self through the eyes of others. This process transforms the biological being into a social being, and from this distinctly human reflexive process, there emerges a sense or conception of the self as an object. Early in this reflexive socialization, individuals take on the role of significant others present in the interaction. As this socialization process evolves, individuals begin to take on the role of larger groups, the community, and different facets of society. This stage of the process refers to taking on the role of the "generalized other," which includes the norms, rules, and expectations governing various positions and roles of a group, community, or society. Thus, the individual is continually socialized to take on the role of more abstract and institutionalized facets of society, and this notion of the generalized other constitutes a powerful form of self-control and social control as the individual internalizes and behaves according to institutionalized norms and beliefs. Thus, self-control is social control, and the normative socialization process guides people into conforming behavior.

Patrick K. O'Brien

See also Agents of Social Control; Control Theory; Informal Social Control; Medicalization of Deviance

Further Readings

Adler, P. A., & Adler, P. (2003). *Constructions of deviance: Social power, context, and interaction.* Belmont, CA: Wadsworth.

Becker, H. S. (1963). *Outsiders: Studies in the sociology of deviance.* New York, NY: Free Press.

Blumer, H. (1969). *Symbolic interactionism: Perspective and method.* Englewood Cliffs, NJ: Prentice Hall.

Criss, J. J. (2007). *Social control: An introduction.* Malden, MA: Polity Press.

Goffman, E. (1961). *Asylums: Essays on the social situation of mental patients and other patients.* New York, NY: Anchor Books.

Mead, G. H. (1934). *Mind, self, and society.* Chicago, IL: University of Chicago Press.

Ross, E. A. (1896). Social control. *American Journal of Sociology, 1,* 513–535.

SOCIAL DISAPPROVAL

Social disapproval is an informal type of social control thought to curtail deviant behaviors. Exact definitions of social disapproval vary, but they draw from the basic assumption that the reactions of a peer group can influence an individual's behavior. In one sense, fear of rejection or criticism from significant others is enough of a deterrent to stop the majority of individuals from committing deviant acts. An individual's deviant instinct is essentially held

in check by the thought of negative feedback from friends and family. If deviant behavior does occur, disapproval from others reflects the group's collective sense of right and wrong in the hopes that the individual now understands what lines should not be crossed. In this entry, the mechanisms and forms of social disapproval are presented, and research findings are discussed.

Mechanisms of Social Disapproval

In the absence of, or in concert with, more formal and institutional methods of behavior control (e.g., policing, neighborhood watch programs, after-school activities, detention centers, corporal punishment, and community service sentences), social disapproval acts as a barrier to deviant behaviors. Some suggest that social disapproval, when robust enough, can function efficiently as the sole form of behavior control in a society. The effectiveness of social control depends on the strength of ties between the individual and the peer group. An individual, when weighing the pros and cons of committing some type of deviant behavior, considers how those close to him or her will react. It is the certainty of friends' and family's disapproval that thwarts the intended deviant act. Social disapproval fails to efficiently curb deviant behavior when the individual has little care for what others think, or when the individual maintains no close ties with anyone.

Effective social disapproval is internalized, so that actors are constantly reminded of the threat of disapproval at all times. For example, a middle school student considers throwing a rock through one of the school's windows after hours, but the thought of his favorite teacher's disappointment checks his behavior. A young girl wants to steal a small item of clothing but thinks about how embarrassed she would be if her peer group found out. In both of these examples, the actor is able to see himself or herself as others might and wishes to escape certain disapproval from meaningful groups.

Social disapproval also works to notify an individual of the boundaries of acceptable behavior. For example, if an individual belches loudly in the middle of a religious service, he or she may receive a multitude of angry looks. This informal social display informs the actor that the behavior was considered inappropriate. A high school student might commit a minor act of deviance such as wearing an unpopular brand of jeans and be ridiculed by his or her peers the remainder of the day. The peer group has signaled to the individual the inappropriateness of the brand he or she has worn. Even deviant body types can garner social disapproval, as larger people who squeeze into airplane seats often receive dirty looks or audible sighs of exasperation by their seatmates.

Social disapproval operates within the context of group-specific norms. If a book club participant monopolizes the conversation, he may receive a dirty look or a catty remark from another member. If a drug cartel member is suspected of being an informant, the other members may ostracize her. Social disapproval serves to keep a member of the group in line with the accepted behavior of the majority, even if the group itself is considered deviant by society.

Forms of Social Disapproval

Some forms of social disapproval were discussed in the previous section: ridicule, dirty looks, ostracism, and annoyed sighs. Assuming that humans seek to maximize pleasure and minimize pain, we desire acceptance from significant others and avoid putting ourselves in a position to be rejected. Social disapproval informs us of behaviors that put us at risk of rejection, and the fear of this possible rejection keeps us from committing deviant acts. Groups demonstrate rejection through ignoring the offender, withholding affection, directing stern glances, criticizing, and rejecting, to name a few.

Some forms of social disapproval, such as an annoyed sigh, are relatively harmless, while other forms of social disapproval, such as shunning, can be psychologically damaging. In Jean Auel's prehistoric novel *Clan of the Cave Bear*, the protagonist is shunned for her behavior, a display of social disapproval so unbearable that she leaves the group forever. Communal groups, such as the Amish, employ shunning or the threat of being shunned as an effective deterrent to deviant acts.

Social disapproval is an important element in the socialization process as well, whereby new members of a culture (i.e., children) are taught the unwritten rules and norms. A parent might ridicule a young boy for putting on his sister's dress to convey the inappropriateness of boys wearing female clothing. A teacher may ignore a first grader who constantly asks questions until the child raises her hand to be called on, letting the student know that talking before hand raising is inappropriate in a classroom setting. The teacher's silence is a form of social control.

Research Studies

Social disapproval is a powerful form of deviance control, with the ability to shape thoughts, behaviors, and emotions. Criminologists have shown that the threat of social disapproval, along with internalizing norms and perceiving a risk of legal punishment, has an effect on the likelihood of committing an illegal act. Social psychologists have found that marginalized romantic relationships (e.g., same-sex or interracial couples) experiencing high amounts of social disapproval tend to invest less in each other than do partners in relationships not suffering from social disapproval. Psychologists have concluded that women dieters who perceive increased social disapproval because of their weight suffer from more depression and dissatisfaction with their body type.

Ami E. Stearns

See also Agents of Social Control; Informal Social Control; Social Control

Further Readings

Gottfredson, M. R., & Hirschi, T. (1990). *A general theory of crime.* Stanford, CA: Stanford University Press.

Grasmick, H. G., & Green, D. E. (1980). Legal punishment, social disapproval and internalization as inhibitors of illegal behavior. *Journal of Criminal Law and Criminology, 71,* 325–335.

Lehmiller, J. J., & Agnew, C. R. (2006). Marginalized relationships: The impact of social disapproval on romantic relationship commitment. *Personality and Social Psychology Bulletin, 32,* 40–51.

Oates-Johnson, T., & Clark, D. A. (2004). Sociotropy, body dissatisfaction and perceived social disapproval in dieting women: A prospective diathesis-stress study of dysphoria. *Cognitive Therapy and Research, 28,* 715–731.

Parsons, T. (1951). *The social system.* Glencoe, IL: Free Press.

Pogarsky, G. (2002). Identifying "deterrable" offenders: Implications for research on deterrence. *Justice Quarterly, 19,* 431–452.

SOCIAL DISORGANIZATION THEORY

Most theorists and researchers alike trace the emergence of social disorganization theory to the Chicago school of sociology, particularly to the work by Clifford Shaw and Henry McKay. Beginning during the late 1920s, Shaw and McKay studied juvenile delinquency in Chicago, Illinois, by obtaining the addresses of court-identified delinquents and mapping the results by community or zone. Expanding on earlier works, Shaw and McKay explained varying rates of delinquency using Robert Park and Ernest Burgess's ecological perspective on urban life. In brief, they argued that neighborhood or community areas where delinquency rates were higher than average existed because of the detrimental effects of city life, a point of view quite common among early sociologists. Like Park and Burgess, Shaw and McKay asserted that juvenile delinquency, measured by youth misbehavior serious enough to gain the attention of the juvenile court system, was directly related to the physical and social structure of a city. Specifically, they hypothesized that physically deteriorated and socially disorganized communities would have significantly higher rates of delinquency. Their research supported that hypothesis: The highest rates of delinquency were most likely to occur in the central business and industrial districts and generally decreased proportionate to the distance from the center of the city. Other factors they associated with high rates of juvenile delinquency included rapid population change, above-average percentages of the population comprising foreign-born and Black persons, and symptoms of poverty such as greater proportions of the population on relief (now called welfare), living in substandard housing, more adult crime, truancy, infant mortality, tuberculosis, and mental disorders. Today, social disorganization theory is a dominant perspective for explaining the spatial distribution of crime and delinquency within cities and urban areas and is occasionally used in studies of rural jurisdictions.

Early Research in Chicago and Other Cities

As Shaw and McKay recorded Chicago juvenile delinquency data over time, they found that no matter what ethnic groups inhabited the physically and socially deteriorated sections of Chicago, delinquency rates were high. Once people could afford to move to more desirable neighborhoods, however, the delinquency rates for their ethnic group subsided.

Thus, Shaw and McKay asserted that it was, in fact, the extreme conditions that existed in poorer areas of the city, rather than the traits of a particular immigrant group, that caused higher rates of juvenile delinquency in those districts. Briefly stated, there is a direct relationship between community conditions and juvenile delinquency rates. Specifically, they

argued that the urban world with its greater impersonal character and anonymity provided a setting in which children could more easily develop deviations from the moral norms and behaviors than in smaller rural communities. Thus, working with individuals would not successfully reduce delinquency rates in a city. Instead, Shaw and McKay suggested employing broad programs to improve the overall economic and social conditions for children living in socially disorganized sections of cities.

Following the research done in Chicago, social disorganization theory was employed to explain rates of juvenile delinquency in a number of cities across the United States. Included among these studies are those done in Philadelphia, Pennsylvania; Cincinnati, Ohio; Cleveland, Ohio; Omaha, Nebraska; Baltimore, Maryland; Minneapolis, Minnesota; Columbus, Ohio; Birmingham, Alabama; Little Rock, Arkansas; Denver, Colorado; Seattle, Washington; Portland, Oregon; Spokane, Washington; and Tacoma, Washington. In nearly every city, the highest rates of official delinquency were found in the central business and industrial districts, where the rates of poverty and other indicators of neighborhood disorganization were highest. Exceptions to the social disorganization theory explanation were exhibited in cities, such as Seattle, where "Orientals [*sic*]" made up higher percentages of the population in the low-income, generally more disorganized sections of the city. The best justification offered for this finding was that "Orientals [*sic*]," as a group, desired to maintain a good reputation. To this day, however, no one has presented a reasonable explanation for this aberration. The idea that compared with immigrants from Germany, Italy, and other nations, people relocating to the United States from China, Japan, and other Asian countries had a significantly greater desire to maintain a good reputation is not satisfactory. Even if this group aspired to be held in high esteem, what factors played into their ability to maintain social control over their youth? Being able to answer this question would foster our understanding of how to reduce delinquency among the poorest, most socially disorganized city neighborhoods. By the time Shaw and McKay's revised edition of their book *Juvenile Delinquency and Urban Areas* was published in 1969, findings from Seattle and other cities in the northwest were absent. Thus, the challenge to find a reasonable explanation for these early results stands. Perhaps, the timing of their immigration, the area of the country they immigrated to, the type of work they did, or even the fact that their appearance was significantly different from others living in the same socially disorganized city neighborhoods served to reduce their delinquency rates.

A Broader Theory of Social Disorganization

As applied by the early Chicago school and their followers, social disorganization theory was mostly limited to the study of juvenile delinquency. Writing at approximately the same time, however, Mabel Elliott and Francis Merrill published a detailed book on social disorganization in 1934, applying the theory to a broad range of topics. According to their book, college courses on social problems and social pathology, which were among the most popular offerings at the time, did not normally focus on the social processes that lead to higher rates of problems and pathologies. Social disorganization theory grew out of the need to understand these social processes. However, to identify social disorganization, they argued that the scholar must also know what it means to be socially organized. In brief, for Elliott and Merrill, social organization was made up of a combination of all characteristics making up individuals' personalities, including all of their attitudes and values, as well as all of the social institutions in which they acted and that interacted in complex interrelationships to make up the framework of human existence. For these authors, social organization was the antithesis of social disorganization; thus, social disorganization theory was based directly within the conflict perspective. According to their view, as soon as complete social organization was in sight, the differences among people's personalities, attitudes, and ideas within a particular social institution would come into conflict, and some degree of social disorganization would result. They also asserted that social disorganization was a continuous process: It is just more obvious when it grows out of or causes crisis situations.

Like Shaw and McKay, Elliott and Merrill assert that people often get blamed for problems that are due to disjunctures in the social structure. Unlike Shaw and McKay, however, Elliott and Merrill broaden the use of social disorganization theory to include situations at the individual, family, and community levels of social structure rather than focusing strictly on the community. Topics in their work, primarily designed as texts for courses on social disorganization, included delinquency, criminality, prostitution, mobility, alcoholism, suicide, unemployment, divorce, romantic fallacy, the small town, leisure, and political corruption, to name a few.

For a number of reasons, Elliott and Merrill's views on social disorganization received little attention among research scholars of the time. One reason noted by those writing about Elliott is that she was a woman—a feminist and pacifist—during a time when women were not well accepted in academe and when the United States had recently won "The World War." Another reason that their work may not have entered the mainstream is that Elliott was at the University of Kansas and Merrill taught at Dartmouth College when the focus in sociology was on the Chicago school. A third reason, and perhaps one of the most important for their views remaining virtually dormant in sociological research, is that much of their writing was done as textbooks for courses in sociology. Their work reached students in more than 900 courses across the United States for which their books were adopted, but like Shaw and McKay, most researchers publishing in academic journals do not quote textbooks. Unfortunately, this fact also meant that scholars employing social disorganization theory to guide their research dropped its application to individual and small group settings and limited it to studies of juvenile delinquency and adult crime where it was employed by leading criminologists.

A Revival of Social Disorganization Theory

Researchers, following the Chicago school, continued to employ social disorganization theory's explanation for crime and delinquency, but after Shaw and McKay's 1969 publication applying it to updated information about juvenile delinquency in Chicago, for two decades social disorganization was rarely used by researchers.

A revival of the Chicago school style of social disorganization theory was fostered by Robert Bursik's 1988 article "Social Disorganization and Theories of Crime and Delinquency: Problems and Prospects," which appeared in the journal *Criminology*. At the most basic level, neighborhood social disorganization points to the inability of people living in certain communities to regulate the behavior of residents and outsiders to achieve commonly held goals, including safety from crime. It is assumed that neighborhood residents agree that acts of crime and juvenile delinquency committed by persons living in the community are undesirable. Therefore, if a particular neighborhood has a high percentage of juveniles who are delinquent, the common goals are not being met.

In a later book, *Neighborhoods and Crime*, with Harold Grasmick, Bursik outlined three levels of control for neighborhoods: (1) personal control, (2) parochial control, and (3) public control. *Personal control* is based on interpersonal ties between neighbors, family, and friends. *Parochial control* is based on ties between neighborhood residents and formal institutions, including churches and schools. *Public control* is grounded in relationships between neighborhoods and formal social control institutions, notably the police. These ideas are grounded in the work of the urban sociologist Albert Hunter.

Bursik's reformulation of classical social disorganization theory led to a strong resurgence of empirical research focused on neighborhood characteristics and crime. Although there have been some inconsistencies, most investigators have found that traditional measures of disorganization, population heterogeneity, poverty, and population mobility, as well as new measures such as family disruption, are robust predictors of crime and delinquency in the urban context. Overall, neighborhoods and communities with high levels of social disorganization have high rates of both violent and property crimes.

Recent Theoretical and Empirical Advances

As greater numbers of researchers began using social disorganization theory to guide their investigations, conceptual development, methodological advances, and expansion of the perspective's scope have enhanced our understanding of crime and delinquency.

Most, if not all, recent research has dropped from consideration several indicators used in early studies, including community-level rates of tuberculosis, truancy, infant mortality, and mental disorders. However, a number of new variables have been examined, including the potential influences from population density, family disruption, social cohesion, social support, trust among neighbors, social capital, informal and formal surveillance, and collective efficacy. Developed by Robert Sampson and colleagues, the concept of "collective efficacy" has become of central importance. It refers to social cohesion among neighbors and their willingness to intervene in situations when it is for the common good of the community. In a sense, collective efficacy follows the idea that "it takes a village to raise a child." Whether the person noticing a child's misbehavior is related to the youngster or not, it is important that he or she intervenes for the common good of the community.

Several studies have investigated the importance of the interaction between social ties and social control. Generally, research finds that people who live close to relatives and who trust others living in their neighborhood have more social ties and exert more social control over the youth. Social cohesion has even been found to mediate the negative effects of socioeconomic disadvantage. Thus, compared with poverty, social organization is likely to have a stronger influence on youth.

The level of family disruption may also affect the amount of attention an adult gives to neighborhood children who are misbehaving. Family disruption, which has been measured using the proportion of divorced and separated persons among those who have ever married plus the percentage of households with single parents, has been shown to influence social disorganization, which, in turn, significantly increases crime and delinquency.

Of course, the influence of, and attitudes toward, official social control agencies should not be overlooked in research exploring crime and juvenile delinquency. In this respect, studies have shown that crime and delinquency rates are lower in neighborhoods where the population generally has confidence in the local police. If the adult population is skeptical about police reactions to their calls, they will be less likely to notify them about problems.

Other researchers have focused on updating the statistical methodology used in their studies. The rapid population changes taking place during the early part of the 20th century allowed observers to see how the movement of an ethnic group from poverty-level conditions to relative prosperity meant that their delinquency rates would decrease. Given larger city populations and slower rates of population change, the need for longitudinal studies has become more essential. For these studies, some have called for the use of hierarchical linear models so that both the neighborhood and individual variables can be examined in the same study.

Another methodological issue that has been suggested is the use of spatial models to investigate the influences of nearby neighborhoods. Finding that geographically adjacent areas significantly influence one another leads to questions about how neighborhoods can insulate their population from the negative effects of nearby areas where delinquency rates are exceptionally high.

Some researchers have pointed out that the focus on urban areas means that rural delinquency has been overlooked. We know very little about juvenile delinquency in the rural areas of the United States, in part because the social disorganization perspective has kept researchers' attention centered on the effects of urban life. Thus, one of the challenges is for social disorganization theorists to spend more time examining delinquency in rural areas.

Along with the influences of living in socially disorganized urban neighborhoods on delinquency and crime, several studies have emerged that examine victimization rates in these areas. Combined with insights from routine activities theory, aspects of social disorganization have been found to significantly increase the chances of being a crime victim. Studies have generally found that first- and second-generation immigrants are less likely to be perpetrators of crime, but little attention has been given to influences of being an immigrant, especially an illegal immigrant, on victimization rates.

The Future of Social Disorganization Theory

Future studies employing social disorganization should follow the lead of works producing significant findings, such as those noted above. However, there is also a periodic need to reexamine definitions and the operationalization of concepts. The concept of single-parent homes, for example, is more inclusive than the frequently used concept of female-headed households. What researchers are often trying to measure is the level of oversight of youth, and having one parent rather than two decreases that adult surveillance by half. What is overlooked by using single-parent homes is the presence or absence of other adults in the household. If a grandparent is present, for example, the level of oversight of juveniles may be equal to or even cover more hours of the day than that provided by two parents. Future studies need to examine this issue.

Much more research needs to focus on the broader formulation of social disorganization as outlined by Elliott and Merrill. Doing so would encourage a much broader use of social disorganization theory within sociology. In addition to studies of crime and delinquency focused on community influences, their work suggests examining social disorganization within groups, such as the family, as well as within individuals. According to Elliott and Merrill, social organization and disorganization are at the opposite ends of the same spectrum. When social disorganization outweighs social organization, there is a breakdown in the equilibrium, the social structure begins to decay, and social control no longer functions effectively. For them, the individual and the group are not two distinct phenomena. Instead, the same phenomenon is simply being viewed from different angles. Individual disorganization is merely a particular aspect of social disorganization.

Although individual, family, and community levels of organization cannot be totally separated, at the individual level, a sociologist may not only focus on statistics related to delinquency and crime but also investigate issues such as insanity, drug use, suicide, unemployment, and any other influence on individual-level behaviors. Thus, in addition to criminologists, sociologists who study mental health, work, and any other sociological topic could employ the social disorganization perspective.

At the family group level, rates of divorce, domestic violence, and child abuse may be of particular interest to a social disorganization theorist. A researcher might also be interested in how the family is changing over time and the effects of increasing unemployment rates on the family. Finally, at the community level, issues related to poverty, vice, and crime may be a researcher's focus, but political corruption, war, terrorism, and even the use of leisure time may also be examined using the social disorganization perspective.

Summary

Although social disorganization theory has enjoyed a major revitalization and has been successfully employed for the study of crime and delinquency, its use for the investigation of other social issues is largely unexplored. Future studies guided by this perspective, therefore, should expand on the narrow application of this theory to date.

Lin Huff-Corzine and Jay Corzine

See also Agents of Social Control; Broken Windows Thesis; Chicago School; Informal Social Control; Social Control

Further Readings

Bursik, R. J., Jr. (1988). Social disorganization and theories of crime and delinquency: Problems and prospects. *Criminology, 26,* 519–551.

Bursik, R. J., Jr., & Grasmick, H. G. (1993). *Neighborhoods and crime: The dimensions of effective community control.* Lanham, MD: Lexington Books.

Elliott, M. A., & Merrill, F. E. (1941). *Social disorganization* (Rev. ed.). New York, NY: Harper. (Original work published 1934)

Sampson, R. J., Raudenbush, S. W., & Earls, F. (1997). Neighborhoods and violent crime: A multidimensional study of collective efficacy. *Science, 277,* 918–924.

Shaw, C. R., & McKay, H. D. (1969). *Juvenile delinquency and urban areas.* Chicago, IL: University of Chicago Press. (Original work published 1942)

SOCIAL LEARNING THEORY

Social learning theory posits that human behavior results from learning that occurs during socialization. Individuals observe the behavior of others, learn, and replicate. While the content of what is learned may differ, the learning process is the same for all types of behavior, deviant or conforming. By allusion, appropriate intervention in the learning process can be an effective strategy to channel behavior toward desired directions. Although originally developed within the framework of psychology, the theory has witnessed several modifications and adaptations by psychologists and nonpsychologists alike. Drawing from psychology and sociology, the ensuing treatise provides an elucidation of the theory in terms of the main themes pertaining to deviance, which is followed by an appraisal of its contemporary relevance in explaining deviant behavior.

Main Concepts

Social learning theory belongs to the cluster of psychological theories that attempt to explain human behavior in terms of social psychological processes. In contrast to biological and social structural theories, psychological theories consider human behavior as resulting from psychological processes within the individual in conjunction with socialization. Psychological theories are generally thought to include psychoanalytic theory, personality theory, and social learning theory, each with its own focus. Social learning theory differs from its counterparts, given that it focuses on socialization, especially interaction among humans in a social context, to explain human behavior.

Social learning theory was proposed as an alternative to contemporaneous theories that stressed psychoanalysis and personality and sought to acknowledge the influence of the social context along with individual characteristics in shaping human behavior. The theory has evolved, but its basic premise that the cognitive, emotional, and behavioral aspects of human behavior stem from experiences involving reinforcement, modeling, and imitation during the formative years remains the same. The development of personality characteristics along with skills related to academics, sports, or arts emerge from learning experiences in the context of culture and social structure. When proposed, the theory was enthusiastically received, and it has continued to influence a variety of behavior analysts in spite of some later misgivings.

Social learning theory was eventually modified and applied to deviant behavior, begetting social learning theory of deviance. Deviant behavior is any behavior that deviates from the norm, the standard as to how humans should think and act in given circumstances. Behavior that conforms to the norms would constitute nondeviant behavior. The chief precepts of social learning theory of deviance are the following: Deviant behavior is learned during the course of socialization, the process by which humans acquire the skills to live in society; as a product of learning, deviance precludes being influenced by anything innate; the learning process is essentially the same for deviant and conforming behavior; the major difference between the two has to do with the direction and content of what is being learned.

Deviance is always seen in reference to norms as it depends on the latter. Norms vary considerably from society to society, group to group, and person to person. Norms present in a religious monastery or a nudist colony are likely to be different in terms of content, acceptance, enforcement, and adherence. Likewise, what is considered deviant would differ along similar lines. Any theory attempting to explain deviance would have to account for this relative nature of norms and deviance, and social learning theory of deviance, with its focus on socialization, is poised to do just that.

Albert Bandura's pioneering research in behavior modeling paved the way for a clearer articulation of the learning process, especially learning of deviance and aggression. Behavior modeling is the type of learning that takes place as a result of observing someone's behavior. Bandura proposed that human learning involved observation, modeling, and imitation, and a reciprocal relationship existed among behavior, person, and the environment. Behavior modeling occurs when the observer pays attention to the behavior model and is able to retain the details of the behavior; in addition, the observer has to be endowed with the necessary motor skills to reproduce the behavior and ought to be motivated enough to actually imitate it. People are born essentially with a blank slate with the potential to learn; they are introduced to both deviant and nondeviant ways during the socialization process. Some choose to associate with deviant ways as against nondeviant ways and develop deviant self-concepts. Individuals are seldom predisposed to deviance at birth; rather, they learn to respond to situations in deviant ways based on what they perceive to be occurring around them.

In his celebrated series of experiments involving Bobo dolls, Bandura demonstrated the likely patterns of imitation associated with aggression among young children, three to six years of age. Three groups of children watched a Bobo doll being treated with aggression; the doll was being hit, kicked, and yelled at by a perpetrator for no apparent reason. One group of children saw the perpetrator being rewarded by being praised for the aggressive behavior; the second group saw him being punished by means of time-out; and the third group saw the person being neither rewarded nor punished as he simply walked out after the bout of aggression. When the children themselves were allowed into the room, their behavior toward the doll resonated with what they had observed earlier, demonstrating that children learn by observing others' behavior, and they imitate what they observed. Bandura found that the children exposed to the aggressive model were more likely to engage in physical aggression than those who were not exposed to the aggressive model, effectively supporting social learning theory's contention.

Human learning process is mediated by demands of the immediate cultural and structural contexts, including family, peers, and the media. Behavior modeling varies accordingly. Children observe the behavior of adults around them in close family settings and imitate. If children grow up watching their adult models resorting to violence as a means to resolving issues, chances are greater for them to develop a deviant self-concept and display related behavior patterns. Children growing up in residential areas replete with deviancy are more likely to engage in deviant behavior than their counterparts. If media products such as television, film, and video games depict violence in a positive way as being cathartic or rewarding, it is likely that values favorable to violence will be internalized by the consumers. The scenario

would be reversed if the context is inverted: Behavior modeling would be along a nondeviant trajectory.

People are generally exposed to deviant and nondeviant behavior on a regular basis through a variety of sources, including family, community, and the media. However, their response to what is observed and learned may differ. For instance, some growing up in exemplary families may choose to deviate and vice versa. What accounts for such counterintuitive outcomes? The answer lies in the dynamics of the learning process. Observational learning is a complex process, as merely observing and learning a behavior does not necessarily lead to that behavior being imitated. In terms of deviant behavior, along with learning to commit deviance, people need to acquire the cognitive mind-set needed to employ those techniques, namely, the specific associated motives, drives, attitudes, and rationalizations. They must decide on the attitude to be formed about what was learned taking into account the existing social context including prevailing social norms. One's willingness to violate social norms or conform to them, imitate or not imitate a type of behavior, thus, would depend on the social cognition acquired by the person in interacting with the environment. The content of what is learned can vary depending on the specific learning processes involved and the particular social context that exists. Thus, a person socialized into a law-abiding social group may decide to deviate if convinced that the laws are utterly unjust.

A related factor that may persuade someone to the path of deviance or conformity is anticipated consequences. To embrace deviance, the learner would need to internalize the idea that deviance can be rewarding materially or emotionally. Anticipated consequences of the behavior form a major element in reinforcing a particular behavior. They can be in the form of external reinforcement in which an individual receives either punishments such as reprimand or rewards like promotion that discourage or encourage engaging in a particular type of behavior; vicarious reinforcement is another form of anticipated consequences, and these involve instances where an individual observes others being rewarded or punished for their behavior; a third type of anticipated consequences have to do with the would-be actors' sense of self-fulfillment or self-disappointment associated with engaging in an act. Some may engage in deviance for the "thrill factor" involved.

Echoing similar views, Hans J. Eysenck observes that people get conditioned to behave in a certain way due to the presence of rewards or punishments.

People are presented with models of appropriate behavior while being rewarded for behaving properly and punished for behaving improperly. Over time, they develop a conscience, incorporating what they have learned, which constitutes the moral preferences they formed according to the models with which they were presented. This conscience further ensures that individuals will behave according to expectations, as failure to do so will be accompanied by feelings of shame and guilt.

Differential association theory, proposed by Edwin Sutherland, is one of the most prominent renditions of the social learning theory of deviance in sociology and criminology. In addition to its explanatory appeal, the theory is known for its insights on the etiology (causation) and epidemiology (distribution) of deviance and, hence, has been recognized as one of the foremost theoretical formulations on crime and deviance. In the process, the individualist thrust of its version in psychology is supplanted with a greater social focus.

Differential association refers to the process whereby an individual forms an association with other individuals or "definitions" in a unique and different way. Definitions refer to attitudes or meaning attached to behavior, which may take the form of orientations, rationalizations, or evaluative points of reference that render commission of an act as right or wrong, desirable or undesirable, good or bad, or justified or unjustified. A preponderance of deviant definitions will likely make people commit deviant acts and a predominance of conforming definitions will likely lead to conformity.

Differential association theory, similar to social learning theory, subscribes to the idea that deviant behavior is learned and not inherited. It is learned by way of interaction or association with others. Intimate, personal, and close-knit groups, such as the family and peers, form the primary learning context, while sources like the media constitute the secondary setting. The learning of deviance includes, first, learning the techniques of committing deviance and, second, acquisition of a definition—a mind-set with a specific direction or definition in terms of rationale, motives, attitudes, rationalizations, and drives—that favors commission of the deviant act. For someone to engage in deviance, he or she has to have learned how to commit the act; in addition, one has to have acquired an orientation in favor of going the deviant way. A person becomes deviant when definitions favorable to acting in a deviant way exceed those that are unfavorable. Deviance

results when deviant norms outnumber conventional norms or exceed them in importance. The act of stealing, for example, usually follows a learning process in which the thief masters the techniques of stealing and acquires the confidence on the appropriateness of stealing.

The specific direction or definition inferred by the individual about the appropriateness of the act is predicated on existing standards of behavior or norms as perceived by that person. One may define a particular norm as favorable or unfavorable and, therefore, desirable or undesirable, depending on how that norm fares in the real world, in the eyes of the learner. Norms against stealing may assume varying dimensions in the presence of persistent inequality and alter-induced deprivation, and the resulting negative attitude toward them may prompt one to choose deviance and rationalize that choice.

Certain factors related to differential association can influence the individual in choosing deviant behavior, namely, the frequency, duration, priority, and intensity of the association. Frequency and duration refer to the number and length of time one is exposed to deviant definitions, while priority and intensity have to do with how early in life one starts getting exposed to definitions favorable to committing deviance and how close the source of deviant association is. The higher the frequency, the longer the duration, the earlier the exposure, and the closer the source of association with deviant definitions, the greater the chance someone will choose deviant behavior. Thus, general needs and values such as poverty and greed alone cannot explain deviant choices adequately, since the same is true of nondeviant preferences as well. Sometimes, deviance is committed by individuals living in abundance or seemingly exemplary.

Differential association theory seeks to explain why the rates of deviance vary among groups and individuals. The rate fluctuations result from differential association generating an excess of definitions favorable to violating the norms over those that are unfavorable to violating the same. The ratio between the two holds the key to understanding whether deviance will be embraced by a person.

There have been efforts at perfecting the differential association theory by addressing its alleged deficiencies. Robert Burgess and Ronald Akers's differential association–reinforcement theory is noteworthy in this regard. It states that excess definitions, on their own, do not propel someone to commit deviant behavior. It is the promise of rewards that serves as ultimate element that propels individuals to act in a deviant way. In the presence of promised rewards, excess definitions in favor of violating norms get reinforced. Whether deviant behavior is committed or repeated depends on the balance of anticipated or actual rewards and punishment for the behavior, a phenomenon referred to as differential reinforcement. Commission of deviance at a particular point depends on the balance of the past, present, or future anticipated consequences. It is differential reinforcement coupled with differential association that results in deviance.

Appraisal

Social learning theory offers an insightful means to understand deviant behavior so it can be dealt with more effectively. If deviance is the result of problems in the underlying social psychological sphere, resolving those problems would have a direct impact on the propensity for people to engage in deviance. Social learning theory would seek those solutions within the framework of the socialization process, the contour of human behavior.

Developed as an alternative to psychoanalytical and personality-based theories in psychology, social learning theory sought to acknowledge the importance of the social context in explaining human behavior. Differential association theory considered socialization process as the primary variable in understanding human behavior. Differential association is capable of addressing the glaring variations in patterns of behavior, deviant and conforming, and it is better equipped to account for relativity of norms and deviance. The theory is celebrated as one with the most explanatory power in addressing deviance.

The theory has received strong support from research involving deviant, delinquent, and criminal behavior. For instance, children have been found to be influenced by their deviant parents and siblings. Differential association with deviant peers has been shown to be the foremost predictor of the onset and continuance of juvenile delinquency. Influence of the media and other secondary sources on deviance has been amply demonstrated using the differential association model.

Also demonstrated is the usefulness of interdiction strategies that involved nondeviant associations in combating deviance including substance abuse. Presenting children with positive, nondeviant role models from an early age can help bring down the rate of deviance and delinquency. Even though sheltering them from deviant images and associations may be difficult, it is possible to surround them with positive images and impressions to a level where excess definitions in favor of conforming behavior would surpass those in favor of deviant ones.

Despite its seeming clarity and candor, social learning theory is not without its critics. Methodological and theoretical deficiencies have been pointed out as vexing issues by the detractors. The theory has been accused of being vague in that its variables cannot be fully empirically tested. The exact mechanism by which one forms definitions about the social context is still to be uncovered and verified. Similarly, the implied causal relationship between differential association and deviance has been characterized as spurious and tautological by some. For them, it is a case of simple correlation that does not indicate causality—differential association and deviance just happen to coexist. Deviance may be what leads its perpetrators to form differential association in the first place, not the other way around. In spite of some attempts, the objections are yet to be refuted effectively.

George Parangimalil

See also Accounts, Sociology of; Differential Association Theory; Neutralization Theory

Further Readings

Akers, R. L. (1998). *Social learning and social structure: A general theory of crime and deviance.* Boston, MA: Northeastern University Press.

Bandura, A. (1962). *Social learning through imitation.* Lincoln: University of Nebraska Press.

Bandura, A. (1977). *Social learning theory.* Englewood Cliffs, NJ: Prentice Hall.

Becker, H. S. (1963). *Outsiders: Studies in the sociology of deviance.* New York, NY: Free Press.

Burgess, R. L., & Akers, R. L. (1966). A differential association-reinforcement theory of criminal behavior. *Social Problems, 14,* 128–147.

Rotter, J. B. (1954). *Social learning and clinical psychology.* Englewood Cliffs, NJ: Prentice Hall.

Sutherland, E. H. (1947). *Principles of criminology* (4th ed.). Philadelphia, PA: Lippincott.

Sutherland, E. H., Cressey, D. R., & Luckenbill, D. F. (1992). *Principles of criminology* (11th ed.). Chicago, IL: General Hall.

SOCIAL REALITY THEORY

Social reality theory falls under the conflict approach, which was developed in the late 1960s and early 1970s. Conflict theory emerged from the labeling school and focuses on the following three interrelated processes: (1) How and why certain acts are defined as deviant or criminal, (2) official responses to deviance and crime, and (3) the effects of constructed definitions and official reaction on people who are labeled as deviant or criminal.

According to conflict theory, different groups in a given society have vested interests in public policy making, and the formulation of criminal law and criminal justice policies is no exception. Each group of society has its own norms, values, and ideological stance, and these groups will try to incorporate their own interests in formulation of criminal law and conceptions. As a result, conflict theory argues that societies are characterized by conflict rather than consensus. The power to affect policy-making decisions will depend on the available resources (i.e., money, political power) a particular segment of the society possesses.

One of the prominent analyses of crime and criminal behavior in the conflict tradition is Richard Quinney's approach to the social reality of crime. This approach is built on four concepts: process, conflict, power, and social action. *Process* is a continuous complex network of social relations taking place in society. These social relations have duration and tend to change over time. *Conflict* is inevitable between people in any society that is characterized by diversity, and such conflict leads to continuous change. *Power* is the major element used as a means for application and enforcement of certain values in society. Powerful groups in society have the ability to influence public policy decisions to ensure that their own interests are represented. The final concept, *social action*, refers to people's ability to engage in intentional behavior. Although people are influenced by social and cultural experiences, they also have the potential capability to rationally choose the best course of action independent of forces beyond their control.

Quinney's concept of the social reality of crime consists of six components: (1) the official definition of crime, (2) formulation of criminal definitions, (3) application of criminal definitions, (4) how behavior patterns develop in relation to definitions of crime, (5) construction of criminal definitions, and (6) constructing the social reality of crime.

First, the definition of crime and deviance has long been an issue of concern for scholars, politicians, the media, and the general public. People with diverse interests have tried to get their own definitions of crime accepted. Social reality theory holds that there is nothing inherently deviant or criminal in behavior itself, but that social definitions, constructed on the basis of power relations, define some acts deviant or criminal and other as nondeviant. Thus, agents of the dominant class *create* crime as a legal definition of human conduct.

Second, definitions of crime include behaviors of the groups that conflict with the interests of the dominant class, which has the power to shape legal policies. In other words, definitions of crime are shaped by those who hold the political and economic power in society; therefore, the dominant class protects their interests by shaping criminal definitions.

Third, since formulating criminal law is not enough to effectively protect the interests of powerful groups, enforcement of the law is required as well. The powerful members of society do not directly apply and enforce criminal law; rather, they delegate this task to authorized legal agents (i.e., police, prosecutors, the courts). In other words, definitions of crime are applied by those who have power to shape the enforcement and administration of criminal law. These legal agents, in turn, represent the interests of the powerful groups in society.

Fourth, since there is nothing inherently wrong in behavior, but rather, it is the reaction to the behavior that makes it criminal, powerless groups in society are more likely to act in ways that will be considered as criminal than are those who have the political power to shape criminal law. Those who are labeled as criminals will adjust to the definitions of crime that are created for them by the dominant class in society.

Fifth, the definitions and conceptions of crime are socially constructed and disseminated through mass communication. In this way, the powerful groups in society maintain particular norms and values by creating and communicating criminal conceptions. As a result, people do not recognize that criminal definitions have been socially constructed for them by powerful segments of society. Simultaneously, socially desirable or acceptable behaviors are also socially constructed through the exercise of political power and the use of mass communications.

Thus, according to Quinney, the social reality of crime is created by the formulation and application of criminal definitions, development of specific behaviors in accordance with criminal definitions, and the construction of an ideology of crime.

Bearing in mind the propositions of the social reality of crime, it becomes evident that actions of the offenders are not of primary importance for criminologists in this tradition. That is, the focus is shifted from actions of the offender to the power structure in society. As a result, crime is seen as a product of the action of powerful groups through formulation and application of criminal definitions. Consequently, acts by members of powerless groups are more likely to be labeled as criminal than the acts of those who hold economic and political power.

Ibrahim Mese

See also Conflict Theory; Feminist Theory; Marxist Theory; Queer Theory

Further Readings

Becker, H. S. (1963). *Outsiders: Studies in the sociology of deviance.* New York, NY: Free Press.

Quinney, R. (1970). *The social reality of crime.* Boston, MA: Little, Brown.

Quinney, R. (1974). *Critique of legal order: Crime control in capitalist society.* Boston, MA: Little, Brown.

Vold, G. B., Thomas, J. B., & Jeffrey, B. S. (2002). *Theoretical criminology* (5th ed.). New York, NY: Oxford University Press.

Williams, F. P., III, & McShane, M. D. (2004). *Criminological theory* (4th ed.). Upper Saddle River, NJ: Prentice Hall.

Socioeconomic Status and Drug Use

Socioeconomic status describes individuals' position in society relative to others in terms of material resources, including income, assets, and wealth. The more resources that individuals have, the higher their socioeconomic status, and presumably, the more power or control they have within society in terms of political decisions, laws, and the like. High socioeconomic status is also closely related to prestige, or being viewed with more respect for occupying an advantaged position in the social order. For reasons of practicality, researchers typically measure socioeconomic status by education, occupation, or income rather than by an assessment of wealth in large samples of the general population.

Drug use is defined as the act of ingesting a mood-altering substance. Mood-altering substances include widely used legal substances like caffeine, nicotine, and alcohol; illegal substances such as cocaine and heroin; and substances whose legal status varies depending on specific factors, for instance, marijuana and prescription drugs in the United States. Particular drugs may be illicit or legal in any given society, but social acceptance versus punishment for use varies with geography, history, and other dimensions of the social context.

Based on public records of who is arrested and incarcerated for drug abuse violations in the United States, the data overwhelmingly imply that poorer segments of society, or individuals of low socioeconomic status, are disproportionately larger users of illicit drugs. However, arrest and incarceration rates are a function of broader structural factors such as the nature of drug laws, enforcement patterns, and the like, rather than who is actually using illicit drugs. In fact, arrest and incarceration patterns are closely tied to individual socioeconomic status but mostly in the sense that low social class rank is associated with the likelihood of receiving law enforcement attention as well as criminal justice sanctions for drug use.

According to Monitoring the Future, a long-term, statistically rigorous data collection effort focused on adolescent and young-adult legal and illicit substance use, differences in drug use rates in general by socioeconomic status are small, and use trends over the past three decades in the United States are actually quite similar. These findings are consistent with a considerable body of research on substance users. Despite similar trends of overall drug use, however, there are distinct patterns by socioeconomic status and type of drug use in the United States. Individuals of higher socioeconomic status are more likely to use certain substances, while those of lower socioeconomic status are more likely to use other substances. Research indicates that this is a function of availability and other structural factors associated with certain drugs rather than inherent differences between users of different social classes.

Marijuana

Marijuana is the most widely used illicit substance in the United States across all social classes. However, there is an association between higher social class and marijuana use, both in the United States and abroad. Marijuana is the drug of choice among college students and youth in general in wealthy, industrialized nations. Researchers theorize that this may be due to marijuana's use in social settings since those of higher incomes presumably have more time for leisurely activities than do poorer individuals struggling to make ends meet. In much of Europe, marijuana use is decriminalized, unlike in most regions of the United States, where violations constitute the largest proportion of drug abuse arrests each year. Despite the association between high socioeconomic status and marijuana use, most of those arrested for marijuana use are from poorer segments of society. As of 2013, 19 states have legalized medical marijuana use, which suggests that stigma toward this substance is declining and that perhaps the United States will follow the pattern of other nations with regard to decriminalizing illicit use. However, all marijuana use is prohibited and subject to criminal sanctions by the federal government, so only time will tell what future patterns will emerge for the nation as a whole.

Opiates

The association between opiate use and socioeconomic status has evolved over time in the United States. Opiates are derived from the poppy plant and have been used to make a wide array of mood-altering substances throughout history, the most currently popular of which are opium, morphine, and codeine. Opium was brought into the United States by the Chinese who immigrated to work on the railroads in the late 1800s, and the first antidrug law in the United States was enacted in California to eradicate use and, presumably, to reduce the perceived threat to native-born workers sanctioning Chinese laborers who were competing for their jobs. Although opium was illegal in California, use of opiate derivatives was legal under federal law until the Harrison Act of 1914. Up until this point, higher social classes were just as likely, and maybe even more likely, to use morphine and other opiate derivatives, a common ingredient used in medicine for a broad range of physical ailments. During this period, opiate use was especially associated with the middle and upper classes, women in particular. When opiates became illegal, the typical user shifted. Opiate use became more popular in urban areas where it was distributed via black markets. Once this happened, opiates became more popular among the lower classes, and this trend holds to this day regarding illicit opiate use.

After marijuana, heroin, a drug that is not directly derived from the poppy plant but has a similar chemical structure, is the illicit substance of choice among the poor in inner-city neighborhoods. Higher social classes tended to avoid this substance until recently, even throughout the 1960s, a period known for widespread drug experimentation among the middle- and upper-income youth. Since the 1990s, there has been an upsurge in heroin use among more affluent individuals, much of which is credited to developments in the administration of the drug. Because heroin has increased in potency, it has become possible to snort or smoke the drug rather than inject it. Given the negative stigma and perceived dangerousness of being an intravenous drug user, researchers postulate that heroin use among the higher social classes increased when it became possible to snort or smoke heroin.

Synthetic opiates, or drugs created entirely in a laboratory to mimic the effects of natural opiates, are used to make legal pain medications such as Percocet (endocet), oxycodone, and methadone. These drugs tend to be more popular among higher social classes and in particular college students. Despite the reduced negative stigma when a drug is used legally, synthetic opiates are associated with adverse consequences that rival illicit opiate use. Recreational use of synthetic opiates is on the rise in general due to its wide availability and is getting more popular among lower socioeconomic classes. Still, heroin remains the opiate drug of choice for the poor because synthetic opiates are much more expensive on the black market. Also, if obtained legally, these drugs require a doctor visit and presumably medical insurance to be affordable, which makes it more difficult for poorer segments of the population to acquire them legally for legitimate pain management or recreational use.

Cocaine

Much like opiate use, the association between cocaine use and socioeconomic status has evolved over time in the United States and is strongly tied to the route of administration. Derivatives of the coca plant have long been used in medicine in the United States and continue to be used today—for instance, the use of Novocain as an anesthetic at the dentist's office. Prior to the Harrison Act of 1914, use of cocaine derivatives was widespread among all social classes. With regard to illicit use, cocaine was primarily used by the higher social classes in the mid- to late 20th century given the high price of cocaine and hence its inaccessibility to the less affluent. However, all this changed in the 1980s, when crack, a derivative of cocaine that is essentially a cooked-down version of the drug that users smoke, was introduced to society. Crack is cheap because so much less of the drug is needed to induce a high when inhaled into the lungs, so its use exploded in poor inner-city neighborhoods when it became widely available.

Social class distinction by cocaine and crack use is stronger than for any other illicit substance. Cocaine continues to be associated with the affluent and crack with the poorer segments of society. Interestingly, despite the fact that cocaine and crack are essentially the same drug, law enforcement efforts have targeted crack use, resulting in disproportionately long sentences for poor crack users and dealers. Only recently have legal developments ensued to reduce some of the disparity between higher- and lower-class users of the drug in the criminal courts by leveling sentences for crack and cocaine offenses, to some degree.

Methamphetamine

Methamphetamine, much like cocaine in its effects on the user, is a synthetic drug created out of common household items. Methamphetamine, or meth for short, came into wider use in the 1980s as a cheap alternative to cocaine and even crack. At first, meth was most popular among working-class rural men who initially manufactured the substance. However, as methamphetamine use spread along with the knowledge that virtually anyone could theoretically produce the drug at home (albeit with considerable risk as the wrong combination of chemicals could result in an explosion), it became more popular among a wider segment of society. Today, meth is still most popular among the lower social classes, but it has replaced cocaine as the Number 1 illicit drug of choice in the United States in general after marijuana. Meth is increasingly used by the affluent as a club or "party drug."

Prescription Stimulants

Many drugs prescribed to treat attention-deficit/hyperactivity disorder in children and adults are stimulants and affect the brain in much the same way that cocaine and methamphetamine do, with similar effects on the recreational user. Legal use of these stimulants is much more popular among the higher social classes, who have regular access to doctors and are more likely to have medical insurance. Illicit use of prescription stimulants among college students to cram for exams or to get by on little sleep in social settings is widespread, and it appears to be getting more popular among a broader spectrum of society as availability increases.

Club Drugs

Club drugs are illicit substances such as ecstasy, flunitrazepam, ketamine, and gamma-hydroxybutyric acid. Club drugs are typically used sporadically in social settings and are less likely to be used chronically on a daily basis than drugs such as marijuana, heroin, cocaine, or amphetamines. Ecstasy, which was initially used legally by psychologists in the 1980s in the clinical setting to treat patients with posttraumatic stress disorder, became increasingly popular among middle-class and affluent youth, college students, and young professionals involved in the rave culture of the 1990s and early 2000s as a party drug. Flunitraxepam (Rohypnol) is a depressant, similar to alcohol in effect, that was initially used predominantly by the working class. However, its use has become increasingly popular among the more affluent as a party drug and also on college campuses. It is commonly referred to as the "date rape drug," along with ketamine, a tranquilizer typically used by veterinarians on animals during surgery, and gamma-hydroxybutyric acid, a synthetic sedative. These substances are also considered party drugs, and they tend to be used predominantly by the middle and upper classes.

Tobacco

Tobacco use rates did not differ much by socioeconomic status until the past few decades, when public awareness about physical problems and diseases associated with tobacco increased due to widespread public campaign efforts. Currently, education and employment status are the strongest social class measures associated with tobacco use. Individuals who are unemployed or have 12 years of education or less are most likely to use tobacco. Youth of all social classes are likely to experiment with using tobacco, but adult smokers are significantly more likely to be of low socioeconomic status. One widely accepted explanation for this is the economic deprivation theory, the notion that people who experience significant financial stressors and deprivation are less inclined to avoid harmful behaviors or even engage in them as coping mechanisms despite the consequences. Lack of education about the extent of harm associated with tobacco despite aggressive public marketing campaigns is another possible explanation for increased use in the poorest of inner-city neighborhoods, segregated from mainstream society. The relationship between tobacco use and low socioeconomic status holds in cross-national comparison as well, whereby tobacco use in wealthy countries has decreased over the past three decades, while tobacco use in poor, less developed countries remains high.

Alcohol

Alcohol use by socioeconomic status is uniquely patterned relative to the use of other substances. In general, individuals from higher social classes are more likely to use alcohol, while individuals from lower social classes are more likely to abstain completely from alcohol. However, when lower social class individuals do use alcohol, research indicates that they are more likely to have problems related to its use, such as legal troubles and addiction. As with tobacco use, this may be attributed to the economic deprivation theory, whereby the poor are using alcohol as a maladaptive strategy to cope with significant financial stressors. On the other hand, people from the higher social classes may simply be better equipped to hide their alcohol-related problems by avoiding legal troubles altogether or going to private rehabilitation centers rather than being processed through the criminal justice system or court-ordered treatment. Much research on alcohol use analyzes data from offender populations given the high proportion of substance users and abusers processed through the system, a convenient source for data collection efforts given an available pool of individuals and financial resources invested in the criminal justice system that can potentially be used for studying offenders. Unfortunately, while relevant to understanding alcohol use among the predominantly lower-class individuals, this research does not provide the complete picture of what is actually going on in terms of alcohol abuse prevalence in the United States across social classes.

Substance Use Versus Abuse

Much as with alcohol abuse, individuals from lower social classes are more likely to have illicit drug abuse problems than individuals from higher social classes. Again, this may be related to the economic deprivation theory and the additional stressors faced by poor people struggling to survive and meet the most basic necessities. This trend does not appear to be changing, or even leveling off in the United States. As wealth inequality has increased in the past three decades in particular, the structural constraints preventing the reduction of substance-related problems are perpetuated. Those in poor inner-city neighborhoods with few job opportunities are still turning to the drug trade to survive; thus, the drug market is a considerable source of illicit income, and hence survival, for a large population of desperate individuals struggling to make it through another day. Among the higher social classes where substance abuse is still a problem but often with fewer detrimental effects such as the mark of a criminal record, individuals will continue to use it for leisure, for social interaction, and to cope with other types of life stressors.

Conclusion

Throughout human history and across all cultures, human beings have always used and abused substances. The types of drugs used and the social responses and sanctions toward them shift and evolve, but substance use is a universal phenomenon. In the United States, the type of substance used and the likelihood of negative consequences, such as abuse and criminal justice involvement, are closely tied to individual socioeconomic status. Furthermore, given the considerable overlap between race/ethnicity/immigrant status and social class rank, it is important to understand that it appears that non-Whites are more likely to be drug users in the United States based on arrest and incarceration data, and that this has more to do with individual socioeconomic position than the tendency to use mood-altering substances. Even though the "typical" drug user in the United States is not the reality when structural factors are considered, it is important to acknowledge substance use patterns by socioeconomic status to reduce the harms associated with substance abuse in terms of crime and public health outcomes.

Rachael Anne Gossett

See also Age and Drug Use; Alcoholism; Cocaine; Drug War (War on Drugs); Heroin

Further Readings

Goode, E. (2012). *Drugs in American society* (8th ed.). New York, NY: McGraw-Hill.

Johnston, L. D., O'Malley, P. M., Bachman, J. G., & Schulenberg, J. E. (2013). *Monitoring the Future national results on drug use: 2012 Overview, key findings on adolescent drug use.* Ann Arbor: University of Michigan, Institute for Social Research.

Keventhal, C. F. (2011). *Drugs, behavior and modern society* (7th ed.). Upper Saddle River, NJ: Prentice Hall.

Maisto, S. A., Galizio, M., & Connors, G. J. (2011). *Drug use and abuse* (6th ed.). Belmont, CA: Wadsworth.

Reiman, J. (2010). *The rich get richer and the poor get prison: Ideology, class, and criminal justice* (9th ed.). Boston, MA: Allyn & Bacon.

Reinarman, C. (1994). The social construction of drug scares. In P. A. Adler & P. Adler (Eds.), *Constructions of deviance: Social power, context, and interaction* (pp. 137–146). Belmont, CA: Wadsworth.

Stevens, A. (2010). *Drugs, crime, and public health: The political economy of public policy.* New York, NY: Routledge.

SOCIOLINGUISTIC THEORIES

When addressing the role of theory in sociolinguistics, it is appropriate to describe this entry in the plural since there is no single all-embracing sociolinguistic theory. This is not because sociolinguistics is atheoretical. Rather, due to the fact that sociolinguists investigate a great diversity of phenomena, multiple theoretical orientations are employed across several major areas of investigation.

When considering sociolinguistic theories in light of the study of deviance, there are a number of connections that can and have been made. First, the field methods developed within sociolinguistics have paved the way for naturalistic data collection across the social sciences when addressing the role of language and communication, and the analytic procedures developed within social network theory and speech accommodation theory have led to a better understanding of numerous social-interactional variables. This is noted, for example, in the work done on the role of slang and interactional patterns in defining identity for outlier groups. Similarly, the work done in language prescription and standardization discusses and demonstrates the influence of one's language style on how one is perceived by others. Finally, many of the sociolinguistic orientations have been effective in revealing more about a number of topics of interest to deviance studies. Specific examples include the study of verbal aggression, status and power relationships, descriptions of social processes such as social stereotyping and prejudice, and how language is employed by subcultural groups like teenagers to set themselves apart.

The Scope of Sociolinguistics

Sociolinguistics is a subdiscipline of linguistics, and its primary intent is to study both language in its social contexts and social life through the prism of language. Since it is concerned with describing language use as a social phenomenon, a primary focus of sociolinguistics is the investigation of the correlations between language use and social structures, and at times, there is an attempt to establish causal links between language and society. This means that the pursuit of questions revolving around how language contributes to the establishment and maintenance of community, as well as how a community shapes language usage through beliefs and social characteristics, are often the foci of investigation. While the questions asked in sociolinguistics are predominantly social questions and although linguistics and sociology are the foundational fields employed within this interdisciplinary hybrid, other fields such as anthropology, social psychology, human communication, education, cultural maintenance and change, and literacy criticism also function as areas of interest for sociolinguistics.

The subdiscipline of sociolinguistics can be organized into two major divisions—micro sociolinguistics and macro sociolinguistics. As the name suggests, the "micro" division is oriented to investigation in the narrow sense; the foci are on how social structure influences how people talk and interact; how language patterns, varieties, and codes are influenced by social variables; and which social variables (e.g., sex, socioeconomic class, or age) most specifically correlate with language usage patterns. These questions are typically investigated by dialectologists, linguists, and others in language-oriented fields.

Macro sociolinguistics deals with broader societal issues that are more often the purview of sociologists and social psychologists. The primary questions in macro sociolinguistics revolve around language as an institutional mechanism in society, how attitudes and attachments help account for the functional distribution of speech forms in society, the role of language in extending and/or limiting mobility and opportunity in communities, how language maintenance and change occur within societies, and how these issues affect language users. For this reason, some aspects of macro sociolinguistics are also referred to as the sociology of language. The overall result of such widespread queries into the relationship between language and society is that sociolinguistics crosses many other fields interested in language usage and societal mobility and has established distinct theoretical orientations to address these diverse phenomena.

Theoretical Considerations

Sociolinguistics has been developed according to the needs of each of the interdisciplinary foci, and this has been done without a broad overarching theoretical perspective from its two primary disciplines—linguistics and sociology. The lack of an overarching perspective is because unlike the more formal aspects of linguistics and sociology, which are oriented to theory formulation and testing, sociolinguistics is a field that is oriented to descriptive rather than explanatory research. Its primary intent is to study actual data in the field and then describe the relationship between language and social variables. Only after these descriptions are created are there attempts to create some understanding of the operational mechanisms, and it is the focus on these operational mechanisms—when they are studied—that eventually leads to various theoretical orientations in sociolinguistics.

Directing these efforts is the idea that language as an abstraction depends on the actions and activities of the users of that language. Summarizing Robert LePage, languages do not act, people do. Languages are merely abstractions from what people do. This fact, as a basic assumption of socially oriented language investigators, has led sociolinguists to focus on language usage from the perspective of the actual users and their societal patterns and beliefs. This has enabled sociolinguistics to create explanatory mechanisms that operate in various major areas of investigation. Several of the primary theories employed in sociolinguistics are briefly described below. These theories have been employed to address phenomena in the micro- and macro-sociolinguistic areas.

Variational Theory

As discussed by J. K. Chambers, at the heart of sociolinguistics is the correlation of dependent linguistic variables with independent social variables. Breaking from the axiom of categoricity that treated linguistic data as nonvariant, language researchers started investigating differences in the speech styles of various speakers in the late 1950s. John Fischer studied stylistic changes in Boston schoolchildren, and by focusing on alternations between -ing and -in' in participles (as in running versus runnin'), he demonstrated that there were correlations between this variable usage and the formality of setting as well as other variables. Following Fischer, other investigators started focusing on speech variations and their correlations with other variables. The most influential, William Labov, focused on sound change on Martha's Vineyard by examining the distribution of raised or centralized variants in (ay) and (aw) diphthongs, and then he conducted a survey in New York City investigating social stratification of English by focusing on five phonemes known to vary in the city. In these studies, he was interested in when linguistic features varied systematically and what social factors might influence this systematic variation. As a result of these and other studies, the axiom of categoricity has been replaced with the understanding that many linguistic/speech features do vary in a systematic fashion and that this variation depends on one or more social variables.

Within this variationist research, there has been strong documentation of how social class and other social factors covary with dialect standardness and linguistic variation in urban communities. The data reveal that there appear to be three social characteristics that serve as primary determinants of social roles and are the primary independent variables that influence speech variation—socioeconomic class, sex, and age—and while the correlations of these independent variables with the identified dependent variables of speech are complex, they make up the bulk of work in variational theory. This theoretical orientation addresses the fact that individual linguistic behaviors can be stratified according to various social factors, such as age, education level, social class, and so on, and that there are both language-internal factors and language-external factors that operate to determine linguistic variations. Furthermore, the theory suggests that language is inherently varied and that such variation is both the normal result of the progress of linguistic innovations and the mechanism by which linguistic change takes place.

Social Network Theory

Linked to variational theory, social network theory suggests that one of the primary language-external factors that influence language performance and change is how people organize their lives socially via social networking. For example, ties between people can be stronger or weaker, and strong ties working within dense networks can explain how speech forms may remain stable over long periods of time. Correspondingly, weak ties may provide a crucial means by which change—either linguistic or cultural—infiltrates social networks. This approach is modeled on sociological studies of interpersonal relations within communities and allows the researcher to distinguish between communities that are resistant to innovation, including linguistic innovation, and those that are more open to such modification.

Speech Accommodation Theory

Speech accommodation theory (SAT) has been advanced by Howard Giles and colleagues as an explanatory model for prediction of interindividual sociolinguistic behaviors and their effects. According to SAT, psychological characteristics, previous experiences, and contextual/social demands placed on individual speakers operate to establish in the speaker various sociopsychological orientations vis-à-vis their interlocutors, and these orientations help determine how the individual will react to and interact with others during communication and social action. For example, an individual may adopt either a convergent or a divergent orientation toward others in their sociolinguistic context, and this will result in particular motivations for talk and interaction. If they are convergent in orientation, the individual will likely seek others' social approval to help establish themselves within that social group. If divergent, so that they want to hold their own social group as distinct from the interlocutors' and/or their social groups, they will select strategies that will establish and sustain that separation. From the sociolinguistic perspective, these actions will be manifested by variation according to a range of linguistic and social strategies that are based on attending to or anticipating their recipient's productive performance. SAT predicts that convergence strategies will be positively evaluated by receivers, provided they are perceived to be implementing psychological convergence, to be at an optimal sociolinguistic distance from the receiver's own speech patterns, and to adhere to prevailing sociolinguistic norms for the situation. Speech maintenance and divergence will trigger generally negative evaluations and responses, again given various contextual constraints. SAT has been employed in both individual-speaker settings to explain speech variation and assimilation issues in multilingualism, as well as addressing issues in cross-cultural contact, various kinds of negotiation behaviors, and the dynamics of international communications (diplomacy).

Language and Status

Theoretical models have also been employed in sociolinguistics to address how the functions of status and solidarity as manifested in language choice are managed by the individual speaker and the context within which that individual socially interacts. Discussed earlier in the field as issues of power and solidarity, these two competing social variables have explanatory power in predicting whether asymmetric or symmetric social relationships are established, modified, or maintained by variational language usage. The classic studies involved the use of pronouns and various kinds of politeness forms, but the linguistic forms that help formulate status-power-solidarity dimensions cross gender lines, business relationships, how stereotypes are established and sustained, and nearly all vestiges of prestige (or lack thereof) in our society. Investigating these relationship dimensions through language manifestation has effectively reorganized the ways in which status-power-solidarity issues are addressed. Additionally, these notions can also be employed to understand the choices made between larger linguistic systems, be they social or regional dialects or separate languages in bilingual situations.

Dialect Contact Theory

This is an extremely productive area of sociolinguistic theorizing when attempting to predict and explain situations of contact between speakers of different dialects (or even languages), typically, in newly formed communities. Within these contact situations, dialect contact theory provides a mechanism for achieving greater clarity involving how compromises and innovations occur when two dialects or languages come into contact. An aspect of this orientation, koineization theory, seeks to explain the creation of entirely new dialects under conditions of new-town development and under other conditions in which speakers of different varieties are drawn into new settlements, including colonial settlements. Within this theoretical orientation, new dialects and the circumstances of their development and use are explained—including why simpler or even the simplest linguistic features expressed across the competing dialects/languages will be placed in circulation.

There are, of course, other theoretical orientations that may be discussed within sociolinguistics, and as the discipline continues to develop, more and better theories will be formulated. The theories and references discussed here, however, provide some of the best utilized explanatory mechanisms within the first five decades of this developing field of investigation.

Holly L. Damico and Karen E. Lynch

See also Accounts, Sociology of; Constructionist
    Theories; Dramaturgy; Integrated Theories

Further Readings

Chambers, J. K. (2008). *Sociolinguistic theory* (Rev. ed.).
    Oxford, England: Wiley-Blackwell.

Chambers, J. K., Trudgill, P., & Schilling-Estes, N. (Eds.).
    (2002). *The handbook of language variation and
    change*. Oxford, England: Blackwell.

Coulmas, F. (Ed.). (1998). *The handbook of
    sociolinguistics*. Oxford, England: Blackwell.

Fasold, R. (1990). *The sociolinguistics of language*. Oxford,
    England: Blackwell.

Giles, H. (1984). The dynamics of speech accommodation.
    International Journal of the Sociology of language, 46,
    1–155.

Giles, H., & Coupland, J. (Eds.). (1991). *The contexts of
    accommodation: Dimensions of applied sociolinguistics*.
    Cambridge, England: Cambridge University Press.

Labov, W. (1963). The social motivation of a sound change.
    Word, 19, 273–309.

Labov, W. (1972). *Sociolinguistic patterns*. Philadelphia:
    University of Pennsylvania Press.

Milroy, L., & Milroy, J. (1992). Social network and social
    class: Toward an integrated sociolinguistic model.
    Language in Society, 21, 1–26.

Trudgill, P. (1986). *Dialects in contact*. Oxford, England:
    Blackwell.

SOLITARY DEVIANCE

Even when a person is alone, he or she is alone in the
world of the other. In fact, a person can work very
hard at finding private spaces, excluding others, and
striking out on one's own for the purpose of engaging in activities that the person and/or others define
as objectionable, offensive, or deviant in some way.
Solitary deviance, therefore, refers to deviant behavior that individuals undertake in a community context, yet, at the same time, on a more individual basis.

Solitary deviance stands relative to subcultural deviance. Whereas subcultural deviance is a group-based
activity, at times associated with complex boundaries of membership, territories, practices, activities,
and a shared and available history, solitary deviance
is undertaken on a more isolated basis but may be
much more related to subcultural activities than initially thought. For example, those who are members
of drug use subcultures may find themselves isolated
from other members on a voluntarily or involuntarily
basis. Under such circumstances, deviant activities

that were originally subculturally based may be continued on a more individualistic basis. This entry discusses the types and processes of solitary deviance as
well as the vicarious deviant experiences.

Types of Solitary Deviance

Joel Best and David Luckenbill have suggested distinguishing between two types of solitary actors:
loners and individual deviants. The distinction here
is helpful for understanding the range of solitary
deviant behavior.

Loners are those who have no regular association with others who engage in similar deviant
activities and have no membership in related deviant subcultures. Therefore, even though a related
deviant subculture may exist, the loner does not
seek membership within the group. This does not
speak to self-identity, however. Loners may develop
rather complex self-identities that are organized
around solitary deviant activities. Loners participate in deviant behaviors in relative isolation from
other participants, but they do so in a larger community context. For example, someone engaged in
embezzlement often does so in an organizational
context and may develop a concept of self that is
rather centrally organized around accomplishments
as a successful thief. Embezzlers, as loners, also may
come to identify themselves as occupying a position
of superiority over the others who are the targets of
their actions. Therefore, the success of some forms
of deviance by loners depends on maintaining the
secrecy of the deviant behavior.

Whereas the embezzler needs someone to embezzle, the individual deviant is the initiator of the deviant behavior as well as the target of the behavior.
Individual deviants are those who can undertake
deviant acts by themselves and direct the action to
themselves. Deviant acts by individual deviants are
victimless in the sense that no one other than the
individual deviant himself or herself is involved.
While one may argue that in cases of self-harm, the
deviant and the victim are one and the same, the
very idea of the individual deviant resists any
traditional distinction between perpetrator and
victim. Examples of individual deviants include self-
mutilators, anorexics, bulimics, the homeless, the
mentally ill, the depressed, and those who hold deviant worldviews (e.g., religious or political perspectives). While the deviance is individual, individual
deviants can and do come together on the basis of
their deviant involvements.

Solitary Operators and Careers of Involvement

Like subcultural participants, solitary deviants may experience a variety of sequential involvements with deviant activities. Solitary operators may develop certain fascinations or intrigues with particular activities that may be abandoned in the face of new associations with others, an appreciation of the salience of previously discounted risks, or a redefinition of one's activities as less desirable over time. Therefore, when one thinks of solitary operators' involvements with deviant behavior, it may be advantageous to distinguish between the processes of initial involvement, continuing involvement, disinvolvement, and reinvolvement.

For example, the adult hard-core pornography industry in the United States is a multibillion dollar industry. Its primary formats—adult video, Internet sites, magazines, pay-per-view, and smartphone/tablet applications—are designed to facilitate solitary consumption. However, involvements of solitary operators with pornography may vary considerably over time, reflecting initial fascinations or intrigues, continuancy commitments, subsequent redefinitions of their activities, disinvolvement, and potential reinvolvement.

Like other forms of deviance, involvements with solitary deviance may also be relatively singular with little intent or interest in maintaining involvements. Examples may include self-induced abortion, self-amputation, suicide, and cutting. Even here, it is helpful to recognize that solitary operators may come to, for example, define the near-death experience of autoasphyxiation as pleasurable, thrill seeking, or otherwise engaging and may develop unanticipated continuing involvements.

The Vicarious Experience of Deviance

Solitary deviance may also allow for the vicarious experience of deviant behavior. While the activity that an individual actor is engaged in may in and of itself be defined as deviant by some audience, it may serve as a stand in or proxy for the real thing. Websites that promote adulterous sexual relations may also offer a cybercheating option, online poker may be played with virtual dollars, and novels may be sought out that allow for the mediated experiences of imagined deviant activities. While the vicarious experiences afforded by solitary deviance are clearly stand-ins or substitutes for another form of deviant behavior, participants may in fact view the vicarious experience as advantageous in many respects over living out the experience in everyday life. Various mediated settings allow for the vicarious experience of the assassin, rapist, or voyeur without the accompanying risks to the person himself or herself and the other who accompany the completion of the act.

Scott Grills

See also Autoerotic Asphyxiation; Body Modification; Cybersex; Deviant Career; Embezzlement; Secret Deviance; Self-Injury

Further Readings

Adler, P., & Adler, P. (2005). Self-injurers as loners: The social organization of solitary deviance. *Deviant Behavior, 26*(4), 345–378.

Best, J., & Luckenbill, D. F. (1982). *Organizing deviance.* Englewood Cliffs, NJ: Prentice Hall.

Goode, E., & Vail, D. A. (2008). *Extreme deviance.* Thousand Oaks, CA: Pine Forge Press.

Karp, D. A. (1996). *Speaking of sadness: Depression, disconnection, and the meanings of illness.* New York, NY: Oxford University Press.

McLorg, P. A., & Taub, D. E. (1987). Anorexia and bulimia: The development of deviant identities. *Deviant Behavior, 8,* 177–189.

Petrunik, M., & Shearing, C. (1983). Fragile facades: Stuttering and the strategic manipulation of awareness. *Social Problems, 31,* 125–138.

Prus, R., & Grills, S. (2003). *The deviant mystique: Involvements, realities and regulation.* Westport, CT: Praeger.

SOMATOTYPES: SHELDON, WILLIAM

William Sheldon developed somatotypes to explain the relationship between body shape and delinquency. He concluded that males with broad shoulders and a narrow waist have aggressive personalities and subsequently engage in criminal behavior at higher rates. Sheldon's work is controversial, but it continues to provide scholars with data related to deviant populations. This entry focuses on Sheldon's research, including subsequent research and criticisms.

Biographical Information

William Herbert Sheldon was born on November 19, 1898, in Warwick, Rhode Island. His parents were William Herbert Sheldon Sr. and Mary Abby Greene.

He developed an interest in the outdoors from his father. He was an exceptional shooter and coin collector. He attended Brown University in 1915, earned a master's degree at the University of Colorado in 1923, and earned a PhD in psychology from the University of Chicago in 1925. He graduated from medical school at the University of Wisconsin in 1933, but he never obtained a medical license. From 1947 to 1959, he was director of the Constitutional Laboratory at the Columbia University College of Physicians and Surgeons. He died in Cambridge, Massachusetts, on September 17, 1977.

The Physique-Criminality Link

In the late 1800s, Cesare Lombroso argued that some people are biologically predisposed to criminal behavior. These people, referred to as "atavists," have physical characteristics implying that they are genetic throwbacks. Subsequently, other scholars made viable attempts to study physique and crime based on characteristics such as height and weight. For example, Earnest Hooten studied 17,000 inmates from 10 state prisons and found that criminals tend to be smaller in weight and height. Regardless of other research, the physique–criminality link is mostly associated with Sheldon.

In 1940, Sheldon published *The Varieties of Human Physique*. It involves a discussion of somatotypes—a score related to the genetically inborn body type of a person based on measures of physical characteristics. Sheldon took the work of Ernst Kretschmer, a psychiatrist who previously argued that personal character relates to body type, and applied it to criminogenic predisposition. Sheldon used several characteristics to calculate a somatotype. This included, but was not limited to, bone structure, head size, and muscle tone. According to Sheldon, three body types exist: (1) endomorphic, (2) mesomorphic, and (3) ectomorphic.

Endomorphs are overweight, have a large bone structure, and a wide waist. Their personalities reflect a relaxed, comfortable, and extroverted demeanor. *Mesomorphs* are muscular, have medium bone structure, wide shoulders, and a narrow waist. Their personalities reflect an assertive, aggressive demeanor. *Ectomorphs* are thin, frail, and weak. Their personalities produce a sensitive, introverted, and shy demeanor. His categories were not mutually exclusive, but merely ideal types. A person might be predominately ectomorphic but still have some mesomorphic or endomorphic characteristics.

Sheldon initially studied his somatotype theory with an analysis of 400 male undergraduates at the University of Chicago. He photographed nude subjects from three angles: the front, the back, and the side. With a total of 4,000 pictures, Sheldon created 17 different precise measurements on each body and subsequently created a three-number scale with a range of 1 to 7. The first score reflected levels of endomorphy, the second mesomorphy, and the third ectomorphy. For example, an extreme endomorph would rate 7–1–1, an extreme mesomorph 1–7–1, and an extreme ectomorph 1–1–7. This led to the possibility of 343 different somatotypes.

In 1949, Sheldon published *Varieties of Delinquent Youth*. Sheldon finally systematically implemented his theory of somatotypes on a criminal sample. The research was on 200 young males from Hayden Goodwill Inn in Boston, Massachusetts, a facility operated by a social service agency for antisocial and delinquent boys. Using body measures based on photographs, he concluded that the mean somatotype for the delinquent sample was mesomorphic.

Subsequent Research

Sheldon and Eleanor Glueck examined the relationship between body type and delinquency in 500 institutionalized delinquents in the 1950s. They used a control sample of 500 nondelinquents. They also measured body types by analyzing photographs and found that more than 60% of the delinquents in their study were mesomorphic, while only 31% of the nondelinquents were so. Only 14% were ectomorphic, while nearly 40% of the nondelinquents were so. Their research also found mesomorphs have high levels of emotional instability. Juan Cortes and Florence Gatti conducted a study in 1972 using skin folds, muscle tone, bone structure, and body weight and height on a sample of high school students. They did not use photographs believing that actual measurements of body characteristics were more valid and reliable. Results showed that 57% of the 100 delinquents examined had a mesomorphic body type, compared with 19% of the 100 nondelinquents. They found that only 14% of the delinquents were endomorphic, while 37% of the nondelinquents were so.

A follow-up study on Sheldon's research on the Hayden Goodwill Inn boys took place in the 1980s. The biographies of the 200 antisocial and delinquent boys in the original study provided researchers with information to compare against adult criminal records. Some of the research showed that the boys who ended up being adult criminals were the ones with mesomorphic builds. However, when running a multiple regression analysis on a variety of data associated with the sample, there was no statistically significant relationship between body type and criminality.

Criticisms

Critics argue that Sheldon's body measurements based on photographs do not accurately reflect scientific measures of body characteristics. Critics also argue that body type is not consistent throughout life. Feminist scholars point out that Sheldon only used males for samples. Others consider Sheldon's work as subjective interpretations characterized by racist tendencies. However, his work continues to provide scholars with data related to deviant populations. Recent research on a sample of prison inmates found that body mass index is a viable alternative to traditional somatotyping. The research showed that regardless of the type of offense, criminals are more likely to have mesomorphic builds.

Kristen Ulsperger

See also Abominations of the Body; Biosocial Perspectives on Deviance; Delinquency; Physical Characteristics as Deviance; Positivist Definitions of Deviance

Further Readings

Carter, J. E. L., & Heath, B. H. (1990). *Somatotyping: Development and applications.* Cambridge, England: Cambridge University Press.

Cortes, J. B., & Gatti, F. M. (1972). *Delinquency and crime, a biopsychosocial approach: Empirical, theoretical, and practical aspects of criminal behavior.* New York, NY: Seminar Press.

Glueck, S., & Glueck, E. (1950). *Unraveling juvenile delinquency.* New York, NY: Commonwealth Fund.

Hartl, E. M., Monnelly, E. P., Elderkin, R. D., & Sheldon, W. H. (1982). *Physique and delinquent behavior: A thirty-year follow-up of William H. Sheldon's varieties of delinquent youth.* New York, NY: Academic Press.

Maddan, S., Walker, J., & Miller, J. M. (2008). Does size really matter? A reexamination of Sheldon's somatotypes and criminal behavior. *Social Science Journal, 45,* 330–344.

Sheldon, W. H. (1940). *The varieties of human physique.* New York, NY: Harper.

Sheldon, W. H. (1949). *Varieties of delinquent youth.* New York, NY: Harper.

SOUTHERN SUBCULTURE OF VIOLENCE

The "southern subculture of violence" (SSV) concept is based on data showing that the American South is more violent than the rest of the United States and that the reasons for this are, at least, partly cultural. This is not a new idea. Writers predating the American Revolution noted the frequency of fighting among all classes of southerners, often commenting on the particular ferocity of lower-class assaults. Surveying the topic recently, a historian noted,

> The violent south confronts [us] . . . at every turn: dueling gentlemen and masters whipping slaves, flatboatmen indulging in rough-and-tumble fights, lynching mobs . . . brutal police . . . slave revolts, robed night riders engaging in systematic terrorism. (Hackney, 1969, p. 906)

Attempts to explain southern violence over the years have ranged from the analytical and quantitative to the improbable and impressionistic, including the view that "perhaps there are just more folks in the South than need killin." While each of these theories explains some part or aspect of southern violence, none are entirely supported by or consistent with the evidence. Thus, there is no consensus on the causes, origins, or even extent of an SSV. However, most researchers do conclude that the South has elevated levels of particular kinds of violence relative to the rest of the United States and that some of this violence may be related to cultural factors. Data supporting the SSV and the major arguments advanced to explain it are presented below, along with the problems that have prevented a consensus of opinion.

Data

Historically, the South has had distinctively high rates of homicide and aggravated assault compared with the rest of the United States, even while the United States as a whole has rates of homicide much higher than the other industrialized democracies. Based on newspaper accounts in 1880, it was estimated that 10 times as much murder was taking place in the South as in the North. Another researcher in the 1930s found that murders in the South occurred at more than twice the rate per 100,000 as they did in nonsouthern states. In particular times and places, this ratio was even more extreme. Nisbett and Cohen cite a study of the Cumberland Mountain Region between 1865 and 1915, where the homicide rate was 10 times greater than today's national rate. This violence was concentrated in the former Confederate states, where even the least violent state (Louisiana) had a murder rate 74% greater than the national average. The violence then was thought to be linked to white men and possibly women in rural areas. Research today continues along this same track, attempting to show that the South's reputation for violence may be traced to the activities of this same group. While current research reveals exaggerated levels of homicide and assault in the South, explanations for this phenomenon and the importance of culture for these explanations vary widely.

Explanation

The active debate currently swirling around the SSV thesis was reignited in 1969 by Sheldon Hackney, a Princeton researcher who published an article titled "Southern Violence." Hackney's study noted the distinctively high murder and low suicide rates of the southern region of the United States and sketched out a number of explanations in response. One principal distinction Hackney made was between "cultural" and "structural" factors. While there are many well-supported studies connecting higher levels of violence with factors that might be called "structural," like poverty, poor education, and residential segregation, this entry focuses on those factors that are primarily "cultural" in nature.

The crux of the cultural argument for an SSV is that southerners (or at least some southerners) possess a set of beliefs and a code of action that condones and justifies violence in certain circumstances. Southerners are socialized into this culture in the family. This culture is then reinforced by the wider community. In operation, culture shapes action by indicating the appropriate response to a particular set of circumstances. As inheritors of the SSV culture, southerners are more likely than Americans in other regions to respond violently to precipitating events like an insult or a slur. However, the SSV

thesis does not hold that all southerners are more violent; typically, researchers focus on specific groups of southerners who are thought to be particularly inclined to violence.

Lack of Civil Authority: The Frontier Thesis

One explanation of southern violence points to the lack of civil authority in the frontier South, which led to the development of a philosophy of "self-help" in settling protection and disputes. Spread across the South in settlements and farms, southerners solved problems by themselves without government involvement. This included administering "justice" or punishment for transgressions both personal (a killing) and communal (a lynching). In Wilbur J. Cash's influential book *The Mind of the South*, the lack of law enforcement was compounded and reinforced by the other challenges to order in southern society, such as antigovernment fervor, rugged individualism, runaway slaves, the Civil War, Reconstruction and occupation by Union forces, and carpetbaggers. The disorder occasioned by these events was met violently by southerners who believed in solving their problems themselves. The continued existence of unsettled areas in the South well into the 20th century provided room for this violent subculture to persist, even as law enforcement improved elsewhere.

Critics of the frontier explanation for southern violence point out that the western states were unsettled even longer than the South, yet they have lower rates of violence and assault. However, this challenge to the frontier theory has been undercut by recent studies, indicating a convergence between violence rates in the South and the West. Today, both regions are more violent than the rest of the United States, although no one has proposed a "Western" subculture of violence as a result.

Scots-Irish, Herding, and Culture of Honor

A related explanation for southern violence has focused on the cultural characteristics of the Scots-Irish immigrants who settled in the southern backcountry between 1715 and 1775. In this view, these early settlers arrived in America hardened by centuries of struggle with the English crown and each other in the English borderlands, the Scottish Highlands, and the Ulster Plantation in Ireland. They brought with them a distrust of government and a history of herding cattle because the poor soil of their homeland was unsuited for productive agriculture. One important difference between live-stock herders and farmers is that herders are constantly threatened with the theft of their livelihood. Over centuries of invasion and struggle, the border herders learned to respond quickly and violently to any threat to their livelihood. In addition, the herders cultivated what was an equally effective deterrent, a reputation for violence. Gradually, vigilance against threat and willingness to use violence if necessary hardened into a "code of honor." This code compelled the herder to react to any insult or slight, no matter how small, with violence to protect his standing in the tight-knit communities of the border country and later in the American backcountry.

A culture of honor is based on face-to-face relationships in close-knit communities. This view relies on what sociologists call a *Gemeinschaft* or folk culture view of the South, in contrast to the more impersonal and bureaucratic society *Gesellschaft* in the North. In a community in which everyone knows everyone else, a man's character is a matter of public record. A reputation as a coward in such a face-to-face community would be a crushing burden and would result in an immediate loss of standing and, potentially, ostracism. Thus, a culture of honor demands a violent response to any provocation or slight to protect reputation and maintain standing.

Understanding the implications of a personal insult or injury has led southern juries to refuse to find defendants guilty of assault or homicide, feeling that the violence was just, when measured by the provocation. As one juror put it in a case in which the violent defendant went free, "He wouldn't have been much of a man" to ignore such an insult.

Southern Exceptionalism

Building on the frontier, herding, and culture-of-honor theses, some argue that an SSV may be explained by looking at the totality of southern history, which has diverged from American history in a number of important respects. In this view, the historical origins of southern violence may be found in a history of slavery, racial domination, economic stratification, and patriarchy. Routinized violence and domination are implicit in a slave society with a stratified economic structure. This routinization of violence desensitized the southerners to violence generally, which led to an acceptance of levels of violence far greater than would have been tolerated in New England, for example, or any other region of the United States.

This view has been challenged by those who point out that most homicides and assaults in the South are within rather than across racial lines. Outside of lynchings and other mob violence, whites kill and assault whites, while blacks kill and assault blacks. Less often does violence cross the color line. While this may support the use of violence to maintain standing within a rank, it does less to support the idea that race relations and the routinized exclusion of blacks from southern society led to an increased incidence of violence elsewhere in southern society. Second, levels of black violence in the South are not exceptional compared with other regions of the country, while levels of white violence are. If racial stratification led to violence, one would expect southern black violence to be atypical as well.

Gun Ownership

Some students of the SSV suggest that the number and availability of guns in the South may be linked to high rates of homicide and assault. Estimates have shown that there are 200 to 400 million privately owned firearms in the United States. Currently, 52% of southern whites own guns compared with 27% of nonsouthern whites. The motivation for possessing these weapons may vary as well. Indeed, although hunters exist in every region, southern white men are twice as likely to possess a gun for "protection" as are white men in the rural Midwest. Thus, widespread gun ownership and easier requirements for purchasing firearms in the southern states provide the opportunity for more violence, especially when combined with attitudes that justify violence to protect honor, home, family, and property.

This gun-based explanation for SSV has been embellished and modified in two ways. Some argue that what was once a culture preoccupied with honor and place has evolved into a culture that considers weapon ownership for protection a fundamental right. Higher rates of homicide and assault are thus related to the greater number and availability of arms. Another view suggests that hunting animals, particularly deer, may have a desensitizing effect on those who hunt. In this view, it is not a great leap from shooting a deer to shooting a human. This argument is strengthened by data showing that whites, who are most often the subject of SSV research, are five times as likely as blacks to hunt deer. But this argument is undermined by data showing that deer hunting is as prevalent in other regions of the country as it is in the South, while violence is not.

The gun ownership–violence connection is further weakened by data showing that defensive violence is only marginally linked with handgun ownership and not at all with firearm (long-gun) ownership in general. The same problem plagues the hunting thesis; the thread connecting those who hunt with those who commit violence in the South has yet to be established, if it exists at all.

Evangelical Protestantism

Another explanation for an SSV focuses on the evangelical Protestant religion practiced by most whites in the American South. This area of America, known informally as the "Bible Belt," contains the largest group of evangelical Christians anywhere in the world. The Scots-Irish immigrants who settled in the South before and after the Revolutionary War were largely Presbyterian Calvinists. Once in America, they became Baptists and Methodists, converted by the "plain style" of worship and a doctrine that placed the burden of salvation on the individual believer. Numerous studies have shown that conservative and evangelical Christian beliefs are correlated with greater support for violence in self-defense or in situations in which individuals are shown to have transgressed.

Support for corporal punishment, the death penalty, and violence in defense of property or self is markedly higher among evangelical Protestants than it is in the general public. The underlying religious argument is that the ability to judge and punish is given to each man by God. A strongly individualistic and judgmental mode of belief and worship inclines its believers to handle challenges individually and violently, eschewing government or law enforcement. Thus, the righteous believer dispenses justice or correction when called to do so in much the same way that God does.

Problems and Issues

All iterations of the SSV theory struggle with the difficulties inherent in measuring "culture" and specifying its effect. Perhaps the largest difficulty is showing how culture "caused" any particular person to do anything, violent or otherwise. This is known as the "ecological fallacy," which is a universal problem for studies of the SSV. The principal defect in a cultural explanation of an individual act is that it is not possible to assert with any certainty that the person

committing the act is, in fact, a person possessing or ascribing to the culture or that the culture was the underlying motive for the act. Statistics on homicide and assault, which are the raw material used in most studies, are generally gathered by state, county, or region, and are broken down statistically by race, gender, ethnicity, and other demographic factors. Statistical data make it possible to state with some certainty that a white man from a rural county in the South is more likely to commit a homicide or assault than a white man in an urban county in the northeast; but there is no way of using the data to show that the man's beliefs or culture is, was, or would be important in that violence. Any assertion of such connection must remain in the realm of conjecture only.

Based on the argument above, it is logical to ask if all southerners contribute to the SSV or just some. Or, to put it another way, are all southerners equally southern? As noted above, a distinction between the violent proclivities of whites and blacks has been made in a number of studies. Other studies have argued for differences in the cultural attitudes of people living in agricultural and nonagricultural areas. However, regions, farms, hills, and fields do not have a culture; people who live in those regions do. Therefore, using region as a proxy for culture as some studies do is, ipso facto, inaccurate. Other studies attempt to isolate the SSV in particular subcultures, as in the white descendents of the Scots-Irish immigrants. In this view, other groups in the southern region, including blacks, Jews, northern transplants, elites, urban dwellers, and Catholics (to name a few), would be less likely to be bearers of the SSV.

Given these difficulties, one promising line of research would be to conduct attitudinal studies of southern perpetrators of violent acts, measuring the extent to which they possess the markers of the SSV. If a significant number of violent individuals were connected to the SSV in this way, then a researcher could point to the attitudinal factors constituting SSV as a contributing factor in the homicides studied. In the absence of such studies, researchers parse statistical data ever more closely for concrete evidence of such.

Structure Versus Culture

An additional problem facing proponents of the SSV theory is separating the structural factors commonly associated with violence from cultural factors. Structural factors are nonattitudinal characteristics correlated with increased levels of violence. These factors include poverty, broken families, lack of education, income inequality, drug use, residential segregation, unequal access to jobs, and several others. Separating the structural factors underlying increased levels of violence in the South from the cultural ones is an ongoing problem for research in this area, particularly given that the South historically has been high in many of these measures. While structural factors are no more likely to avoid the ecological fallacy than are cultural ones, they complicate the ability of the researcher to say with certainty that they have demonstrated the existence of the SSV and that it was instrumental in the South's high rates of homicide and assault.

Conclusion

Although a scholarly consensus on the existence, extent, and effect of an SSV is uncertain, a flurry of recent studies has created a mountain of evidence and arguments to suggest that the question is both viable and engaging. This research comes at a time when, by nearly every measure, the southern region is becoming more like the rest of the United States. Perhaps what is still exceptional about the South may be found in a residual culture that validates violence as an appropriate response to provocation.

G. Pearson Cross

See also Code of the Street

Further Readings

Andreescu, V., Shutt, J. E., & Vito, G. F. (2011). The violent South: Culture of honor, social disorganization, and murder in Appalachia. *Criminal Justice Review, 36,* 76–103.

Cash, W. J. (1941). *The mind of the South.* New York, NY: Vintage Books.

Ellison, C. G. (1991). An eye for an eye? A note on the southern subculture of violence thesis. *Social Forces, 69,* 1223–1239.

Gorn, E. J. (1985). Gouge and bite, pull hair and scratch: The social significance of fighting in the southern backcountry. *American Historical Review, 90,* 18–43.

Hackney, S. (1969). Southern violence. *American Historical Review, 74,* 906–925.

Lee, M. R., Bankston, W., Hayes, T. C., & Thomas, S. A. (2007). Revisiting the southern culture of honor. *Sociological Quarterly, 48,* 253–275.

Lee, M. R., Thomas, S., & Ousey, G. C. (2010). Southern culture and homicide: Examining the cracker culture/black rednecks thesis. *Deviant Behavior, 31,* 60–96.

Nisbett, R. E., & Cohen, D. (1996). *Culture of honor: The psychology of violence in the South.* Boulder, CO: Westview Press.

Webb, J. (2004). *Born fighting: How the Scots-Irish shaped America.* New York, NY: Broadway Books.

Wyatt-Brown, B. (1982). *Southern honor: Ethics and behavior in the Old South.* New York, NY: Oxford University Press.

Spamming

Internet spamming is a term used to describe the high-volume sending of unsolicited electronic messages. The content of spam can range from harmless unwanted advertisements to potential scams and computer viruses. While spam is most commonly distributed via e-mail messages, it can be sent through all electronic channels that can receive messages, such as short message service (SMS) text messaging and social networks.

The word *spam* is in reference to the popular, processed canned-meat product with the same name. Internet spam got its nickname from a Monty Python skit in which a group of Vikings chanted "SPAM, SPAM, SPAM" loudly to drown out other conversations. The name was adopted to describe unsolicited Internet junk mail, perceived as overwhelming legitimate messages.

The ubiquity of the Internet coupled with the development of spam software in the mid-1990s allowed spammers to send high-volume messages cheaply and easily. Early spammers exploited mail relay servers using inexpensive software that automatically harvests e-mail addresses from America Online (AOL) member directories and other sources and sends bulk messages. Today, the Internet security company Symantec estimates that approximately 70% of all global e-mail is spam.

The volume and persistence of spam is very costly. Researchers at Microsoft and Google estimate that spam costs Americans $20 billion annually. Other researchers put the worldwide figure closer to $50 billion if one takes into account the cost in time workers spend sorting through and deleting spam. Other costs include storage on network servers, security software, and related expenses.

The nature and motivations for spamming often go beyond its common perception as an inexpensive, albeit annoying, form of mass advertising. Spam can serve as a mechanism for malicious activities that result in significant harm against victims. The varieties of spam, including its malicious forms and methods of defending against it, are discussed in the following section.

Types of Spam

The most common form of spam is unsolicited e-mail messages from advertisers. Many companies and organizations store e-mail addresses in a database that are commonly sold or distributed to other advertisers. Customer e-mail addresses are often matched with other personal information to create a direct marketing profile. Targeted advertising can include all types of electronic communication.

Companies are increasingly sending SMS text messaging spam to mobile devices. However, SMS spam is much less prevalent compared with e-mail spam. U.S. regulatory bodies, such as the Federal Communications Commission and the Federal Trade Commission, consider SMS spam illegal under the Controlling the Assault of Non-Solicited Pornography and Marketing Act of 2003 (CAN-SPAM 15 U.S.C. § 7701). In addition, telephone service providers often flag and block large volumes of SMS messages sent through their networks.

More recently, social networks, blogs, and instant messenger services have been plagued by spam. For example, Facebook users who accept a fake friend request expose their entire friend network to unsolicited advertisements and fraudulent messages. Despite aggressive spam filtering, spammers continue to thrive on social networking sites. Facebook has reduced the number of spammers to only 0.9% of all users in 2013, but that still equates to 9.5 million spammers still on the site.

Phishing and Identity Theft

More harmful Internet crime, such as phishing scams and identity theft, can come in the form of innocuous spam. Spam is often associated with phishing scams, in which a prospective victim is presented with bogus business proposals, requests for help, and other ruses. The most infamous phishing scam, known as advance fee Nigerian 419 scams, was named after the Nigerian penal code for fraud. Advance-fee scammers solicit financial help from victims to resolve a financial dilemma with the promise of a large return.

Spam is often used in identity theft. A potential victim lured by an irresistible sale may click on a link that redirects him or her to a legitimate-looking commercial site that is designed to steal personal information. Criminals use the stolen personal information to assume the victim's identity for financial gain.

Spam is also an intermediary for computer malware or harmful software that can damage or compromise computer systems and networks. Victims can be lured to open attached files presented as coupons or documents. Once open, these files can install a variety of malware, ranging from self-replicating viruses and spyware that capture user information to pop-up ads that can drastically degrade a computer's performance.

One type of malware installed by recipients of spam infects their computers and turns them into "web robots," or bots. These bots can allow an attacker to gain access to the contents of a computer and network. Thousands of networked computers can be infected, creating a network of "zombie" bots, or botnets, which can be used to distribute spam, viruses, spyware. Moreover, botnets can be used to attack websites and servers.

Defending Against Spam

Spam is dealt with primarily by network administrators and computer software companies. Eliminating spam is an elusive game of cat and mouse with companies and spammers. Increasingly, sophisticated antispam technologies have been met with creative circumventions. For example, early antispam technologies that filtered out common words associated with spam, such as "Viagra" and "Rolex," were circumvented by spammers who misspelled filtered words.

Many Internet spam watchdog groups offer help to spam victims. Victims and recipients of spam can report spam to a variety of watchdog sites. Using this information, these advocacy groups offer resources and helpful tips to avoid being victims of spam, as well as tools for tracking spam.

Police have cracked down on a number of high-volume spammers in the past few years. In 2007, police arrested 27-year-old Robert Alan Soloway, known as the "Spam King," and charged him with 40 felony counts, including mail fraud, money laundering, and identity theft. Police were praised for their action for taking down an individual responsible for millions of spam messages, but security experts did not see any lasting impact on spam traffic. Moreover, Soloway served less than 36 months of his 47-month sentence.

Spam remains a constant problem for all Internet users despite antispam technologies, watchdog groups, and law enforcement efforts. Spammers remain undeterred given its lucrative nature and unlikelihood of apprehension.

Johnny Nhan

See also Cybercrime; Hacking; Phishing

Further Readings

Holt, T. J., & Graves, D. C. (2007). A qualitative analysis of advance fee fraud e-mail schemes. *International Journal of Cyber Criminology, 1*(1), 137–154.

Kigrel, A. C. (2009). CAN SPAM Act: An empirical analysis. *International Journal of Cyber Criminology, 3*(2), 566–589.

Nahorney, B. (2013). Symantec intelligence report: January 2013. *Symantec Intelligence.* Retrieved from http://www.symantec.com/content/en/us/enterprise/other_resources/b-intelligence_report_01-2013.en-us.pdf

Nhan, J., Kinkade, P., & Burns, R. (2009). Finding the pot of gold at the end of an Internet rainbow: Further examination of fraudulent email solicitation. *International Journal of Cyber Criminology, 3*(1), 452–475.

Rao, J. M., & Reiley, D. H. (2012). The economics of spam. *Journal of Economic Perspectives, 26*(3), 87–110.

Yu, S. (2011). Email spam and the CAN-SPAM Act: A qualitative analysis. *International Journal of Cyber Criminology, 5*(1), 715–735.

Sport and Deviance

Neither deviancy nor criminological theory has ever really attained widespread popularity or usage in the sociology of sport. Yet many research ventures into sports worlds illustrate how there are both formal and informal rules of order in these worlds that are policed, tested, sanctioned, and altered. People breaking such rules face private and public sanctions from time to time, and these sanctions carry concrete consequences for those labeled as offenders. What is especially interesting is how sports institutions and cultures themselves actively promote and then punish rule violations, player misconduct, and general "bad behavior" in a range of ways. Simply put, sport and exercise cultures are rife with the performance of *wanted deviance*. Wanted deviance is a behavior, perspective, or symbol that violates accepted social or cultural rules, norms or standards within an institutional/cultural setting, but does not raise the alarm as something requiring either outright condemnation or strict control. Stated differently, while the behavior might violate ostensible rules of a culture, and audiences regard it as socially "problematic" in one manner or another, it may be permitted as it serves as social function in one capacity or another. For example, these forms of deviance may even be exciting for both participants and spectators at times. When wanted rule violations are relatively controlled, they are not seen as being symptomatic of pathological circumstances.

Considerable evidence suggests that rule violations in sports are indeed wanted by players, coaches, leagues, audiences, and other stakeholders. Watching physical manifestations of deviance, such as a fistfight in ice hockey, for example, can be physiologically pleasurable and, thus, emotionally meaningful for audiences. Learning that an athlete used performance-enhancing drugs ("doping") to win may be interesting because it leads to record-breaking times, and discovering that the athlete cheated brings an added element of excitement as it adds further drama to the sport spectacle itself. The violation may thrill, intrigue, or reinforce meaningful social allegiances between participants and audiences. However, rule violators are not always excused of their wrongdoing or granted an unchecked license to thrill with their particular behavior—as evidenced by the increasing intervention of sports authorities into high hits or headshots in ice hockey and in American football regarding concussions and other head injuries.

What sport insiders and their audiences define as acceptable and unacceptable behavior is, at best, inconsistent. As such, studying and theorizing (wanted and unwanted) sport deviance, misconduct, or inappropriate behavior is challenging. In contact sports such as rugby, ice hockey, soccer, and American football, there is considerable tension regarding the tactical use of wanted deviance by coaches and athletes in the throes of competition and its mass mediation by sport promoters. Marketers of North American ice hockey might find permissible on-ice violence hard to sell if both wanted (e.g., body checks or fistfighting) and unwanted (e.g., stick swinging leading to injury) forms of physical violence in the game did not create excitement and tension for audiences. To make sense of such accommodations and contradictions, the emotional-tension balances of safety and risk underpinning competitive sports are a defining feature of their appeal. Quite simply, establishing something that clearly "crosses the line" in the world of sport can be tricky. This entry explores the social control and criminality of deviance in sport.

The Social Control of Deviance in Sport

"Deviance" is everywhere in the world of sport. Consider, just to begin, some of the following substantive areas in which news stories of corruption, abuse, cheating, and violations of rules or laws take place on an almost daily basis: the rise and proliferation of so-called alternative sport cultures designed to contest social normalcy in mainstream sports (snowboarding, skate and street boarding, Parkour, X Games, extreme fighting cultures, mixed martial arts, animal blood sports); health, drug, and doping cultures in sport (steroid use and abuse, gene manipulation, corruption in drug-testing policies, obesity, anorexia nervosa and body pathologies, the use of supplements and so-called fitness products); and participant misconduct (cheating, abusing opponents and officials, player–fan conflicts, initiation traditions, cultures of sexual aggressiveness and rape, overtraining, injury, self-abuse, gambling). This list is far from exhaustive, but little empirical research exists on most of the behaviors mentioned, and mainstream sociologists of sports, crime, and deviance have tended to ignore the situational, cultural, and political–institutional aspects of these behaviors. With the above said, the concept of deviance continues to appear in existing strands of sociological research on sports bodies and their performances in a range of ways. For the sake of comparison, these are bracketed into four strands: (1) violence and aggression theories, (2) subculture theories, (3) identity politics theories, and (4) victimology theories.

Violence and Aggression Theories

Deviance in sport is often understood to be synonymous with violence and aggression in sport. Whether showcased as eye-catching behavior during a "Highlight of the Night" feature on sports television or critiqued in the popular press as reprehensible, on-field and off-field violence involving athletes, fans, and officials is the subject of widespread public attention and debate. Numerous sociologists of sport have theorized the causes of violence and aggression and related sociocultural experiences in a variety of games.

Many attempts to understand violence and aggression in sport focus on how specific situations of emotionally intense competition trigger aggressive cues within individuals. These are biopsychological theories that root human behavior and expression within genes and/or minds. One of the earliest examples explains all forms of aggression and violence as a product of frustration arising from blocked goals. From this perspective, a wide range of violent acts on the playing field, from beanballs in baseball to fistfights in ice hockey to reckless tackles in soccer, can be explained as reactionary and relatively unreflexive emotional responses to conditions of frustration occurring between contestants. Violent outbursts between athletes are explained as natural, genetically expressive, and predictable phenomena that occur in social spaces defined by intense competition for an object or a prize. Frustration may also manifest itself in response to officiating that is perceived to be inept or biased or as a result of taunting by other players or fans.

A second subcategory of violence and aggression theories commonly employed in the sociology of sport literature is social-psychological in orientation and cites deprivation as the dominant motivation for deviance on the field. In this case, a player's perceived deprivation within the game (i.e., being treated unfairly compared with others) leads to frustration and aggression and is not based on wants or needs alone but on wants and needs that the player thinks he or she deserves. Therefore, an athlete who thinks that his or her performance warrants victory also feels a sense of entitlement to accolade. When an entire group such as a sports team holds a similar skill–outcome mind-set, a collective sense of entitlement toward winning, recognition, and success develops. If an individual or team feels deprived by the outcome, violence toward the source of the perceived deprivation may result.

Subculture Theories

Sociologists have studied groups of sports and athletes as distinct collectivities replete with their own value systems. A sport subculture might be a youth team that shares perspectives on its characteristics and goals. Children in youth baseball or ice hockey leagues, for instance, are approached as special populations, distinct in their shared ideologies, statuses, identities, and collective rituals. Studies in this vein highlight the uniqueness of sports subcultures by explaining what it means to be a member of such a group, and how different their values might be from the social mainstream. For example, groups including elite rowers, skateboarders, sports physicians, coaches, sports media producers, bodybuilders, and many others have been studied as unique social enclaves whose respective values and practices (e.g., painkiller consumption, involvement in street crime, resistance to corporate sport culture, willingness to send unhealthy athletes back to play, abuse and bullying as teaching, lying to get a good story, and steroid consumption) might seem bizarre from the outside but normative and ethical from the inside.

Identity Politics Theories

Identity politics is the process of aligning oneself with others who share feelings of marginality and oppression. Eschewing conventionally ascribed characteristics revered by dominant social hierarchies such as White or heterosexual, individuals engage in an identity struggle to redefine personal (and collective) identity in the process of winning (cultural) space. In this process, violating dominant norms, values, and beliefs that provide the ideological support for cultural practices is critical. A consistent thread in this research is the reproduction and contestation of dominant gender codes or bodies. Gender researchers examine how opportunities for participation and leadership in sport (e.g., access to sport for men and women, coaching and administration opportunities, economic power positions in sport) are structured rigidly by traditional ideologies that place masculinity (i.e., strong, powerful, aggressive, authoritarian) as the gender norm and femininity (i.e., weak, docile, dominated, domestic) as the deviant gender. Racial and ethnic discrimination is also an important dimension of gender politics in sports. For more than 50 years, racialized athletes have been portrayed as deviant and as biologically gifted or as part of a criminal or bestial athlete underclass characterized by hubris and aggression. Similar research has been conducted on the systematic exclusion of Latinos and Native Canadians from mainstream White, middle-class sports cultures in North America and elsewhere.

Victimology Theories

A radical departure from existing thinking about deviance in sport, victimological perspectives encourage us to focus on people who are affected firsthand by rule violation. Victimology is rooted in the idea that people who participate in sport hold inherent rights to freedom, safety, and personal welfare. Moreover, athletes who are paid to participate in sport and are members of complex economic organizations should be viewed as workers who deserve institutional and legal protections.

To date, however, few sociologists of sport have pursued victimological perspectives; far more emphasize the subcultural kudos athletes receive for competing while under physical, emotional, or psychological duress. For example, the sexual and physical abuse of children in sport (including child trafficking through sports) is still a theoretical black hole. The abuse of children in local or global sports cultures is relatively ignored, and the sports insiders in highly competitive athletic circles rarely question whether intensive training, ideological indoctrination into winning at all costs, isolation from nonathletes, emotional manipulation, dietary control, sexualization, and corporeal punishment for performance failure are appropriate for children and youth.

The expanding globalization literature attends to how the mass commercialization and market development of Western sport creates victim communities in economically developing nations. The labor practices of corporations such as Nike, the spread of professional sports cultures into new regions, and even Olympic movements are linked to the economic exploitation of indigenous labor (through product development, facility construction, and gentrification) in countries such as Mexico, Argentina, Brazil, South Africa, Indonesia, China, and Pakistan. Other work addresses the nonhuman victims of global sport through investigations of the environmental effects of organized sports such as golf.

Can Sport Deviance Be Criminal?

With minor exceptions, sport organizations have successfully maintained their autonomy over episodes of violence occurring within their jurisdictions and kept the courts from prosecuting athletes, even when such conduct violates formal and informal rules prohibiting the use of violence or violates local, state, or national laws. In many cases of flamboyant on-field sport violence, some may find it difficult to comprehend why the perpetrators were not criminally prosecuted in a court of law. However, even flagrant forms of violence in professional or amateur—and especially contact—sports tend to be treated as something socially special or unthreatening and controlled principally by sports organizations.

First, from a social problems perspective, when communities face pressing social and physical challenges such as health and disease crises, unemployment, environmental degradation, and discrimination, issues that may be perceived as only mildly criminal or culturally allowable tend to receive minimal public or official attention. Social problems involving statistically few members of a population also tend to be placed at the bottom of the agenda for social control. Underscoring how a hierarchy of social problems argument might resonate for sport is the fact that scholars have uncovered troubling cultures of body distortion and self-starvation among female athletes in sports such as gymnastics, figure skating, and track. By investigating girls' eating pathologies (e.g., bulimia and anorexia nervosa) as types of body dysmorphic disorder, researchers have found that certain athlete personalities are more predisposed to eating problems than are others. The extent of eating disorders in young female sport, or in sport more generally, is not known, but it seems unlikely that anorexia nervosa in female sport is a more pressing problem than obesity in adolescent populations in North America and elsewhere. From this perspective, it might be argued that time and money are better directed toward addressing more common eating, body, and weight problems in the broader population than in the relatively smaller athlete populations.

Second, in 2003, Wade Exum, the former director of the drug control administration for the U.S. Olympic Committee (USOC), spoke to a global television audience about the extent of drug cheating in U.S. track-and-field events. As a longtime insider to U.S. track-and-field events, he controversially released private files indicating that 19 U.S. medalists were allowed to compete at various Olympic Games from 1988 to 2000 despite having failed drug tests leading up to the respective competitions. Exum alleged that more than 100 U.S. athletes in several different sports tested positive for banned substances between 1988 and 2000. The athletes were cleared by internal appeals processes within respective sport federations such as the USOC, the International Olympic Committee, the International Association of Athletics Federations, and the World Anti-Doping Agency. The long-standing argument, promulgated by the USOC and International Association of Athletics Federations following Exum's claims, is that only sports federations themselves understand how to police their own forms of deviance. Critics, encouraged by Exum's files, may

ask how the extensive network of drug consumption and distribution within sports such as track-and-field events has avoided legal scrutiny: Given that steroid possession and distribution violates criminal law in the United States and other countries, why do sports federations continue to receive discretionary power to enforce, or ignore, antidrug rules? The sports world is filled with teams, leagues, and administrative structures that justify their internal policing by pointing to individual cases, while other cases involving precisely the same behaviors escape close scrutiny.

Third, if the sport world is seen as a social theater in which spectators are deliberately aroused by the tension balances created through athletic contests, sport may be described as *mimetic* because it deliberately resembles warlike competition. Sport is socially and emotionally significant to individuals because it elicits excitement through controlled violence in a battle that is not as perilous to the participants as an actual war. Spectators may be excited by the often rough and rule-violating competitive exchange between the participants, yet they may feel neither guilt nor repugnance in watching the action because the struggles are not real acts of war. For example, during a race in American NASCAR (National Association for Stock Car Auto Racing) racing, drivers may illegally push, nudge, or crash into each other's vehicles as a maneuvering and jockeying strategy. High-speed crashes, rollovers, and multiple-car pileups occasionally result from the bumping. In a 2003, NASCAR race in Miami, Florida, Juan Pablo Montoya clashed cars with Ryan Newman. Newman bumped Montoya at high speed and sent his car head-on into the track's inner wall. Montoya, a former Formula One (F1) racecar driver, received only minor injuries from the incident, even though flames engulfed his car shortly after the crash. Newman received no reprimand from NASCAR officials for the accident.

Fourth, the subcultural perspective that views athletes as a special population with a license to participate in rule-violating behavior is crucial. From this perspective, athletes, especially young males participating in power and performance sports, are socialized into believing that they are privileged people whose social transgressions in and around the playing field will be excused by parents, coaches, teachers, and even police. Athletes who participate in highly visible and culturally revered sports, even at young ages and amateur levels, may become celebrities in their communities. The public fall and punishment of an athlete-celebrity because of rule-violating behavior not only challenges cultural constructions of the athlete's moral character but also challenges cultural ideals about sport itself as a virtue-producing social institution. Cultures of hubris often germinate within athlete groups or teams who feel as if their actions are beyond reproach. Studies of U.S. high school football, amateur ice hockey in Canada, and others underline the degree to which communities remain willing to overlook the deviance and crimes of athletes who are protected as special populations.

Fifth, sport apologists tend to perceive the indiscretions of athletes, however common and statistically typical, as unusual and unrepresentative of sport culture. Pete Rose's (baseball) or Michael Jordan's (basketball) gambling is defined as atypical, Michael Irvin's (American football) or Theoren Fleury's (ice hockey) use of recreational drugs is interpreted as individually problematic but not widely victimizing, and the spousal abuse perpetrated by star athletes such as O. J. Simpson (American football), Sugar Ray Leonard (boxing), and Stan Collymore (soccer) is interpreted using "rotten apple" rather than "spoiled barrel" logic, meaning that these instances are not indicative of a more widespread problem, that is, one rotten apple does not spoil the whole barrel. By pathologizing individuals and not the cultures that help produce their psychologies, characteristics, and patterns of action, sports advocates deflect attention away from sports as a system of values that allows certain behaviors and personalities to emerge, endure, and remain relatively immune from sanction.

Sixth, sport is likely one of the few remaining social institutions that consistently escapes the modern reflex toward settling order and controlling problems litigiously. Among the most cited reasons as to why police and criminal prosecutors avoid cases of violence and aggression in sports is the perceived lack of criminal intent in a player's actions, the inherent risks and dangers in competitive sport, and the apparent consent players give to being hurt during play. Some amount of sports violence is summarily dismissed by agents of social control due to a belief in the impossibility of convincing athletes, the public, and the courts that sports deviance constitutes criminal behavior. More than a century's worth of case examples of failed police intervention into North American athletics supports this claim. Consider the example of the beanball in baseball, and imagine if the police were asked to intervene into every case wherein a pitcher deliberately threw a fastball at an opposing batter's head as a tactic of competition or revenge.

Finally, the media often hyperbolize cases of rule violation and crime, thus distorting the public's understanding of social problems in the community. Vincent Sacco notes that with such media overexposure, grand claims about the sheer presence of deviance, and sensationalization of deviance, people become accustomed to seeing deviance in everyday life and, thus, are less shocked by its occurrence. For example, the Nike corporation experienced intense media scrutiny in the mid-1990s from reports detailing worker victimization in several of the company's manufacturing facilities located in developing countries. Accounts of corporal punishment, sexual abuse, slave wages, dangerous and unhealthy working conditions, and forced labor surfaced out of countries such as Thailand, Pakistan, China, and Vietnam. A subsequent global "Anti-Nike," "Boycott Nike," and "Just Don't Do It" social movement and a massive media blitz into Nike's corporate practices demanded that the company and certain nations, including the United States, initiate immediate industry reform. Nike acknowledged problematic behavior in a few regions but maintained that several alleged and isolated cases of (especially female) worker abuse were exaggerated by the global media. Apparently, consumers of Nike products agreed, as the company set profit records during the second half of the 1990s, a trend that continues.

Conclusion

Theorizing sport deviance or crime is difficult, at least in part because so much of it has been and continues to be comfortably rationalized by audiences using special arguments that render it tolerable, even preferred. When sociologists have studied its manifestations, behavior considered as sport deviance often falls under one of the explanatory umbrellas reviewed in this entry: violence and aggression, subcultural identity, political and ideological identity, and the realm of abuse and victimization. It seems likely that as students of crime and deviance continue to examine sport deviance, the applicability of the concept of "wanted deviance" will become even more obvious.

Michael Atkinson

See also Defining Deviance; Female Bodybuilding; Hooliganism; Normalization; Performance-Enhancing Drugs; Roller Derby; Total Institutions

Further Readings

Atkinson, M., & Young, K. (2008). *Deviance and social control in sport.* Champaign, IL: Human Kinetics.

Blackshaw, T., & Crabbe, T. (2004). *New perspectives on sport and deviance.* London, England: Routledge.

Dunning, E. (1999). *Sport matters: Sociological studies of sport, violence, and civilization.* London, England: Routledge.

Hughes, R., & Coakley, J. (1991). Positive deviance among athletes: The implications of over-conformity to the sport ethic. *Sociology of Sport Journal, 8,* 307–325.

Kerr, J. (2004). *Rethinking violence and aggression in sport.* London, England: Routledge.

Stebbins, R. (1996). *Tolerable differences: Living with deviance.* Whitby, ON: McGraw-Hill.

Young, K. (2012). *Sport, violence and society.* London, England: Routledge.

STALKING

Stalking occurs when an individual is pursued through physical means, threats, or surveillance to the point where the individual fears for her or his safety. An individual is most likely to be stalked by someone the individual knows, and a woman is more likely to be stalked than a man. In recent years, stalking has evolved from a stalker physically pursuing and watching a victim to include cyberstalking, whereby a stalker may observe and harass a victim relentlessly without ever coming into direct physical contact. Unfortunately, stalking is often dismissed by onlookers, authorities, and even victims as "a bad breakup" or a mere annoyance instead of being taken seriously. When ignored, stalkers may escalate the intensity and aggressive tenor of the harassment to provoke a reaction (e.g., fear, desperation, anger) from their victims. Stalkers practice deviance by willfully ignoring the social ethic of reciprocity; that people will respond to others in similar ways and consent to force a relationship, even one that is structured negatively on the victim. Stalking is based on the perpetrator attempting to exert control over the victim through fear.

Stalking was brought to public attention with a number of high-profile cases of celebrities experiencing persistent unwanted contact in the 1980s. These cases drew national attention to the issue, and since 1990, each of the U.S. states and the District of Colombia has enacted stalking legislation. After stalking became a criminal offense, it began to be studied by criminal justice authorities, psychologists, and mental health professionals. This entry examines several aspects of stalking—its prevalence, associated behaviors, and patterns; describes legal ramifications and other consequences; and discusses methods for alleviating stalking.

Prevalence

Stalking is a growing behavior. The U.S. Department of Justice reported in 2009 that 3.4 million people reported stalking in a single year. According to the National Violence Against Women survey, almost 10% of women and 2% of men report being stalked during their lifetimes. One survey indicates that stalking victimization is reported at a much higher rate in the college population, from 25% to 31%. Studies suggest that it may be one of the most underreported crimes. According to the National Crime Victimization Survey (NCVS), only 37% of male victims and 41% of female victims reported stalking to the police, and approximately half of all victims never seek any type of help. The most common reasons victims give for not seeking help are that they did not think the stalking behavior was serious; they wanted to handle the situation themselves; or because they believed the situation was "too private." In addition to these reasons, victims indicated that they did not contact the police because they feared revenge from the stalker or worried that the police would not believe them.

Stalking Behaviors

It is important to consider the context of stalking victimization beyond individual incidents. The behaviors that constitute stalking may seem benign at first to both the victims and the law enforcement. An offender may make repeated phone calls, send e-mails or gifts, follow or watch the victim, and wait for or appear in public places the victim frequents. A threat may be explicit or implied. For example, a stalker who sends his victim a present from her Amazon "wish list" may be demonstrating that he now knows where she lives and her password on the site. While data from the NCVS reports that 1 in 5 stalking victims fear bodily harm to themselves, about 4 in 10 have also received threats to their families, friends, coworkers, or family pet.

Increasingly, men and women report being stalked through technology, including cell phones, the Internet, GPS (Global Positioning System) equipment, and wireless video cameras. E-mail, instant messaging, use of social networking, and text messages are the primary methods stalkers access to send threatening or intimidating messages. A stalker may post information about the victim publicly on the Internet or spread rumors about the victim. With many people now using smartphones, victims may unknowingly leak their whereabouts through GPS location pinpointing or pick up via radio scanner. On the computer, spyware installations and keystroke loggers are capable of revealing a victim's Internet activity to the stalker. Stalkers may also impersonate their victims on the Internet to gain information about their activities and/or further instill fear.

Patterns of Stalking

The most prevalent form of stalking is by a rejected intimate partner following the end of a relationship. The ex-intimate partner may believe that he or she is entitled to access to the former partner and resentment builds, leading to stalking behaviors. When asked about their behavior, stalkers regularly express their frustration at unmet expectations from someone who has not treated them as they feel they deserved. Even those who know that what they are doing is illegal often justify their behaviors as attempts at seeking justice for themselves. Despite sensitivity to their own rights, stalkers do not show respect for their victims' rights. Research is consistent that a prior relationship between stalker and victim results in an increased severity of stalking victimization. Intimate partner stalkers are more likely to approach their victims in person, to threaten them with a weapon, and to reoffend.

While some stalkers are mentally ill, there is no evidence that most are. Risk of being stalked decreases with age, with persons aged 18 to 24 years being at the highest risk. Individuals who have been divorced or separated are more likely than those with other marital statuses to report stalking. Victims more often report being stalked by offenders the same age and race as themselves.

Laws Against Stalking

Since 1990, every state and territory in the United States has passed antistalking laws. Many states have stalking/harassment protection orders, and the laws against stalking vary from state to state. States often require that a "course of conduct" be established, proving that one or more intentional acts have occurred that display a continuity of purpose. State stalking statutes require either "general intent"

or "specific intent" to establish stalking as a crime. In those states with general intent requirements, it must be established that the suspect intended his or her actions, even if the suspect did not intend the outcomes. Specific intent requires that a stalking suspect also intended the outcomes of his or her actions, such as a victim's fear, mental health issues, or losing a job. Thus, specific intent may be more difficult to prove in the states that require it. Some states require that a reasonable person would feel fear as a result of the stalking behaviors, while others require that the victim demonstrate the fear experienced and its outcomes. A level of fear may also be stipulated; in some states, the victim must fear for her or his life and/or fear bodily harm, while in others, the victim may simply suffer from emotional distress or concern for her or his safety. Whether proof of an explicit threat is required or not depends on the state. Thirty-five states consider stalking a felony on the second offense or if there are aggravating factors (e.g., a weapon or violation of a court order) on the first offense, while 14 states consider the first offense a felony and 1 state (Maryland) classifies stalking as a misdemeanor regardless.

On a national level in the United States, the Violence Against Women Act was passed in 1994 and reaffirmed in 2000, 2005, 2006, and 2013. The Violence Against Women Act now allocates $3.9 billion to state and federal programs that assist survivors of rape, intimate partner violence, and stalking. Interstate stalking is defined by federal law 18 U.S.C. § 2261A.

Vulnerable Populations

Some of the populations that experience higher rates of stalking are also targets of other types of oppression or disadvantage: homosexuals, Native Americans, disabled persons, those living in rural communities, the poor, and immigrants. Those who have less access to resources or fear discrimination by these resources tend to be less likely to seek help, which may embolden the offenders. Those who experience oppression from multiple identity markers may internalize the stalker's language and believe that they deserve the harassment and that no one would believe them if they reported it.

Consequences

Often, stalking is a precursor to physical or sexual assault. Stalking is often concurrent with a domestic violence situation, as a means of control that the abusive partner exercises over the victim. Whether the relationship is intact at the time or has been dissolved, the abuser may employ stalking techniques to remind the victim that he or she owns the victim and is entitled to watch the victim's every move. In the context of an abusive relationship, stalking acts to increase the victim's terror of the abuser and makes the victim less likely to believe that she or he can leave the relationship for good. The abusive partner is likely to harass the victim at work, follow the victim's daily activities, and/or cyberstalk the victim. Thus, even when out of physical reach, the victim is taught to fear and anticipate the abuser at every turn, which often restricts the victim's movements and inhibits recovery.

Negative outcomes experienced by stalking victims include loss of time from work, the need to relocate, anxiety, insomnia, and severe depression. Victims report a range of fears, such as not knowing the stalker's next move, fear that it will never stop, and worry for their own and/or a loved one's safety. The debilitating nature of these fears often makes it difficult for a victim to function normally in society, keep employment, and interact regularly with friends and family. As a result, the victim may become isolated. If stalking occurs over a long period of time (according to the NCVS, 11% of victims report being stalked for 5 years or more), personality adaptations and/or posttraumatic stress disorder may result.

Misogyny, the hatred of women, plays a role in the deviant behavior of men stalking women. Stalking is a salient risk factor for intimate partner femicide, or the killing of women because they are women. One study reports that 89% of femicide victims were stalked in the 12 months prior to their murders, and most had been abused by their stalkers. A little more than half of this population reported stalking to police before their stalkers murdered them.

Alleviating Stalking

The most common methods victims use to seek help are to tell family or friends, ask people not to release information about them, and change their usual activities to avoid the stalker. Victims should report stalking to community leaders and authorities whenever possible. Beyond seeking assistance from law enforcement, a victim may choose to work with a shelter or stalking resource center. Victims are advised to work with these resources to construct a safety plan, which includes a plan for avoiding

contact as well as a back-up strategy for the possibility of encountering the stalker. Stalking does not usually "just go away" if left alone, but any attempt to confront the stalker should be handled using a third party to protect the victim (e.g., law enforcement officer, lawyer, commanding officer). The National Center for Victims of Crime also suggests creating a stalking log to record incidences of unwanted contact or harassment, which may be useful if the victim decides to prosecute or if the behavior increases in frequency or severity. Support groups have also been known to provide victims with the relief of knowing that they are not alone in their experience. Thirty-two states have launched address confidentiality programs to protect the address of the victim using a P.O. box (post office box) in place of the address required in public records that a stalker may access. Collaboration between law enforcement and system or community-based advocates (coordinated community responses) has been shown to be highly effective at protecting victims and holding stalkers accountable.

Molly Ferguson

See also Feminist Theory; Rape; Sexual Harassment

Further Readings

Baum, K., Catalano, S., Rand, M., & Rose, K. (2009). *National Crime Victimization Survey: Stalking victimization in the United States.* Bureau of Justice Statistics Special Report [Online]. Retrieved from http://www.ovw.usdoj.gov/docs/stalking-victimization.pdf

Buhi, E. R., Clayton, H., & Surrency, H. H. (2008). Stalking victimization among college women and subsequent help-seeking behaviors. *Journal of American College Health, 57*(4), 419–425.

McFarlane, J., Campbell, J., Wilt, S., Sachs, C., Ulrich, Y., & Xu, X. (1999). Stalking and intimate partner femicide. *Homicide Studies, 3,* 300–316.

Mohandie, K., Meloy J. R., McGowan, M. G., & Williams, J. (2006). The RECON typology of stalking: Reliability and validity based upon a large sample of North American stalkers. *Journal of Forensic Sciences, 51*(1), 147–155.

National Center for Victims of Crime. (2011). *Stalking resource center* [Online]. Retrieved from http://www.ncvc.org/src

Pinals, D. (2007). *Stalking: Psychiatric perspectives and practical approaches.* New York, NY: Oxford University Press.

Sheridan, L. P., & Grant, T. (2007). Is cyber-stalking different? *Psychology, Crime & Law, 13*(6), 627–640.

Sheridan, L. P., & Roberts, K. (2011). Key questions to consider in stalking cases. *Behavioral Sciences and the Law, 29*(2), 255–270.

Stigma and Stigma Management

Stigma is a mark of disgrace that is ascribed to individuals of specific social groups. It is an attribute that is highly discrediting to one's social reputation, and it effectively diminishes and discounts the character of individuals. According to the sociologist Erving Goffman, stigmatized individuals are no longer whole and usual people but instead find themselves as tainted and discounted. Those who are socially stigmatized are often perceived as deviant, devalued, and undesirable. Stigmas are also powerful influences on both social opportunities and one's place in socially structured groups and communities. As a result, stigmatized individuals often adopt various strategies to protect and maintain a positive social identity.

Background and Characteristics of Stigma and Stigmatization

In ancient Greece, the word *stigma* referred to the branding of slaves. However, in English, it refers to the rejection of an individual, or even entire groups of people, for various reasons. For example, for two millennia, Jewish individuals residing in Europe, who were the minority among a majority population of Christians, were stigmatized as outsiders. In a similar fashion, individuals in the United States today, such as the mentally ill, the physically disfigured, and criminal offenders, are commonly labeled as deviant, as are others who deviate from the mainstream norms and expectations of a cultural or societal group.

Stigmatization of individuals deviating from the social norms of a group, according to the sociologist Émile Durkheim, functions to facilitate group solidarity. Those individuals who successfully comply with the expected behavior of the group form stronger bonds with each other while rejecting those who fail to follow the social code. This phenomenon can be illustrated by the "witch-hunt" in Massachusetts in the 17th century. Individuals labeled as practitioners of witchcraft looked or acted in ways that did not adhere to mainstream social conventions. Once an individual was considered to be a witch, as a result of his or her peculiar appearance or unusual behavior, others associated with or supportive of such an individual were commonly viewed with similar suspicion and subsequently accused of witchcraft. Those individuals who did not participate in the labeling of others as witches risked becoming targets of accusations themselves, further encouraging individuals to unite against alleged witches. Individuals who appear or behave differently are often labeled as outsiders or deviants or discredited in society. In this way, deviance can be created by societal expectations.

Stigma may be situational or temporal in nature. Stigma may also be attached to certain behaviors under some circumstances and not others. For example, there is often a stigma attached to expressing one's anguish and distress at the workplace; however, it is widely acceptable to show such emotion at a funeral. Stigmas of a temporal nature are those that change over time. For example, in 1950, women occupied a much different position in society. A stigma was commonly attached to women who worked outside the home. This stigma, though, has largely diminished in recent times.

An individual who is stigmatized is labeled as deviant and undesirable. According to Goffman, a stigma fundamentally illustrates a discrepancy between how an individual identifies himself or herself and how society perceives and reacts to that individual. While an individual may be perceived as deviant, dangerous, or undesirable by others, that individual likely has a very different, most likely more positive, perception of himself or herself. For those stigmatized individuals, then, there is a divergence between how they are actually seen externally and how one believes they are seen. For example, physically disfigured individuals are often stigmatized by mainstream society, but these individuals likely do not share similar negative views of themselves.

Commonly Stigmatized Social Groups

Sociological research has examined a wide variety of stigmatized social groups. These groups include sex workers, teenage mothers, the elderly, women who are voluntarily unmarried or childless, individuals with HIV/AIDS (human immunodeficiency virus/acquired immune deficiency syndrome), and even those with red hair. Most commonly, however, this literature has focused on individuals suffering from mental illness, developmental disabilities, and obesity. In addition, the stigmatization of gay and lesbian individuals, those who are homeless, and criminal offenders has been widely discussed.

Individuals Suffering From Mental Illness

Individuals with mental illness are often stigmatized in modern societies. Because certain mental illnesses may lead to unusual behavior, such individuals are often characterized as dangerous or undesirable. Beginning in the 1970s in the United States, the guidelines regarding the commitment of mentally ill individuals began to change, and as a result, individuals with mental illness were no longer hidden in psychiatric hospitals away from the public.

Today, many homeless individuals experience mental illness. This is partially a result of the closing of many psychiatric hospitals and the lack of available resources dedicated to treating these individuals. Those with mental illness are often labeled as incompetent and dangerous, without regard to their ability to function in society. As a result, these individuals are perceived by society as nothing more than their illness.

The Developmentally Disabled

Individuals with developmental disabilities are often characterized as being identical to those with mental illness, but there are distinct differences between these social groups. Because some individuals with developmental disabilities display physical or behavioral signs of their condition, these individuals are more easily identified as outsiders. The labeling of these individuals then leads to their stigmatization within, and subsequent rejection by, society.

The eugenics movement in the United States in the early 20th century was a reflection of the popular belief that developmental disabilities and mental illnesses were genetic in nature. It was thought that procreation among individuals with developmental disabilities, mental illnesses, or physical disabilities would result in the "contamination" of American society. Consequently, there was widespread support for the sterilization of individuals exhibiting "symptoms" of such conditions, to ensure that future generations would be free from such disabilities.

Obese Individuals

In addition to negative treatment, including emotional and physical violence, individuals who are obese are restricted in their daily lives by the limited choices available in clothing, travel, and other products and services that are not designed with obese customers in mind.

However, cultural differences exist in the acceptance of obesity between different groups in the United States. For example, while individuals residing in urban areas are more likely to perceive obesity as undesirable or deviant, individuals living in rural areas often display less hostility for overweight individuals. In addition, the stigmatization of overweight or obese individuals often results in psychological repercussions.

Gays and Lesbians

As an example of decreasing stigmatization over time, gay and lesbian individuals once faced a powerful, negative label resulting from their sexual orientation. Until 1974, homosexuality was considered a mental illness, according to the American Psychological Association's *Diagnostic and Statistical Manual of Mental Disorders* (*DSM*). This has since changed, as the American Psychological Association now asserts that individuals do not choose their sexual identity. As such, the stigmatization of gay and lesbian individuals is now commonly regarded by many as inappropriate. In the 1980s, however, many associated the HIV/AIDS epidemic with the gay and lesbian population, further stigmatizing these individuals.

Homeless Individuals

Approximately 2 million Americans will be homeless for at least one night every year, while 700,000 individuals are homeless for extended periods of time. Homeless individuals are stigmatized by society because they lack legitimate social ties to groups and organizations, such as neighborhoods, the workforce, and families. Because homeless individuals have no residential address, they are unable to receive mail and are often unable to vote or maintain employment due to their vagrancy. The stigma is also the result of common assumptions about homeless individuals. Because of their homeless status, individuals are often viewed as incompetent, criminal, deranged, and dirty. For these reasons, among others, the homeless are stigmatized by the general public.

Criminal Offenders

For many ex-inmates, the stigma associated with imprisonment is perhaps the most obstructive barrier to successfully reentering society from prison.

In many cases, stigmatization—setting a mark of disgrace on a social group—that goes with a prison record is nearly insurmountable. There is considerable evidence that social stigma significantly hinders necessary aspects of societal reintegration, especially housing and employment opportunities, for those previously incarcerated. Background checks and personal inquiries, for instance, have become customary for all applicants looking to rent an apartment or work in most entry-level jobs. The stigma of incarceration and criminal conviction makes ex-inmates unattractive candidates for even the most undesirable living spaces or jobs. As there are more people than jobs or available housing opportunities, it is not surprising that employers and landlords are likely to prefer the noncriminal to the individual just coming out of prison. Making matters worse, with a drop in the success of the U.S. economy, finding employment may be especially difficult for newly released offenders, as the number of other (more desirable) candidates increases.

Stigma Management

Stigmas are often conceptual in nature and affect societal activities and exchanges as a moral issue. Stigmas play a powerful role in a stigmatized individual's place in society and subsequently affect interaction opportunities between individuals. Labeling those who are different as deviant results in cognitive separations and reactions focused on stigmatized individuals. Therefore, stigmatized individuals suffer negative consequences with regard to social relationships and emotional well-being, as well as limited opportunities to participate in societal activities. In particular, negative consequences of stigmatization include public identification as undesirable or deviant, discrimination by social groups and organizations, and social isolation, as well as loneliness, depression, and other emotional and mental illnesses.

Stigmas are powerfully influential on an individual's ability to participate in societal groups and organizations. They often limit the social opportunities available to the stigmatized individual. However, stigmatized individuals are often able to manage their place within society by protecting and maintaining positive social identities, despite the negative connotations of the labels attributed to them. Stigmatized individuals have a variety of options available to manage the negative effects of their label and position in society. For example, individuals can attempt to transfer their own stigmatized status by identifying the abundance of others who possess the same stigma or simply reject the stigma. Conversely, some individuals choose to acknowledge and accept—or even celebrate—their status as stigmatized individuals. In fact, some individuals use their personal stigmatization to empower individuals in similar situations and foster social change with regard to their stigmatized status. For example, teenage mothers may actively seek out individuals in similar situations to garner support and understanding. In this way, individuals who have been stigmatized are able to identify with and accept the label attributed to them and seek support from individuals in similar situations to manage the negative effects of their stigmatization.

While the acceptance of one's stigma and subsequent alignment with similarly stigmatized individuals may prove beneficial to those within the group, Goffman asserts that this management strategy has serious limitations. Individuals who define themselves by their stigmatized status, according to Goffman, are essentially sacrificing part of their personal identities to take on the status as stigmatized. This is because within a stigmatized group, the most important (and perhaps only) commonality among members is that which differentiates them from nongroup members. As such, the stigma attached to these group members becomes a rallying point, a feature to be encouraged, as the stigmatizing condition is seen as essential to an individual's identity. Because of this, any active attempt among members to disregard or distance themselves from the stigma may be ostracized within their group. Thus, stigmatized individuals face a quandary; they must attempt to maintain a delicate balance between acceptance of their stigma and acquiescence to normative pressures. As such, Goffman asserts that this means of stigma management is largely ineffective and contradictory.

According to Goffman, the most successful stigma management strategy involves the disidentification with individuals who share the same stigma. This strategy involves actively distancing oneself from similarly stigmatized individuals to encourage a more favorable perception from those that are not stigmatized. However, because this management strategy perpetuates the stigmatization of individuals unwilling or unable to minimize their differences from the mainstream, it has received criticism from those who strive to enact change regarding the status of such stigmas. Regardless of this criticism, reducing the import of a stigma on one's identity, to gain acceptance by the nonstigmatized, can be an effective stigma management strategy.

David Patrick Connor

See also Discrimination; Outsiders; Tribal Stigma

Further Readings

Corrigan, P. W., Roe, D., & Tsang, H. W. H. (2011). *Challenging the stigma of mental illness: Lessons for therapists and advocates.* Malden, MA: Wiley-Blackwell.

Crocker, J., & Major, B. (1989). Social stigma and self-esteem: The self-protective properties of stigma. *Psychological Review, 96*(4), 608–630.

Goffman, E. (1963). *Stigma: Notes on the management of spoiled identity.* Englewood Cliffs, NJ: Prentice Hall.

Harding, D. J. (2003). Jean Valjean's dilemma: The management of ex-convict identity in the search for employment. *Deviant Behavior, 24*(6), 571–596.

Heatherton, T. F., Kleck, R. E., Hebl, M. R., & Hull, J. G. (Eds.). (2003). *The social psychology of stigma.* New York, NY: Guilford Press.

Jones, E. E. (1984). *Social stigma: The psychology of marked relationships.* New York, NY: W. H. Freeman.

Jones, R. S. (2003). Excon: Managing a spoiled identity. In J. I. Ross & S. C. Richards (Eds.), *Convict criminology* (pp. 191–208). Belmont, CA: Wadsworth.

Levin, S., & van Laar, C. (Eds.). (2006). *Stigma and group inequality: Social psychological perspectives.* Mahwah, NJ: Lawrence Erlbaum.

Link, B. G., & Phelan, J. C. (2001). Conceptualizing stigma. *Annual Review of Sociology, 27,* 363–385.

Stolen Goods Network

Some stolen goods dealers operate completely outside the law, while others flourish under the cover of the appearance of legitimate businesses, albeit businesses that are sustained by the provision of stolen stock. Compared with other areas of offending, such as burglary and robbery, there has been little research into stolen goods. Relatively little is known about who buys stolen goods, how offenders sell them, and how dealers in stolen goods operate. Not surprisingly, therefore, property thieves—particularly prolific ones—are generally perceived by criminologists and the wider public to be "bent" offenders whose predation on "straight society" can be explained in large part as a motivated response to their poverty, subculture, cultural influences, substance addiction, or individual pathology. Contrastingly, research into the markets where thieves sell stolen goods reveals that many so-called legitimate businesses, run by those widely perceived to be respectably "straight" citizens, indirectly motivate and directly encourage people to steal property.

One thing that research into stolen goods networks reveals is that most stolen goods are sold rather than retained by thieves for their own enjoyment. Therefore, stolen goods markets motivate thieves. Most goods stolen from houses and cars, or from businesses such as shops, are sold within half an hour of the theft and are then openly enjoyed by other people. Because of this crucial role that stolen goods markets play in the property theft system, they and their associated local, national, and international networks warrant close attention from criminologists, policymakers, police, and the courts.

Compared with those who do the stealing, business owners and other members of the public who buy and deal in stolen goods seldom serve time in young offender institutions or adult prisons. Social hypocrisy is at work here, which has clear implications for civic society. Apparent stalwarts of the community who encourage and facilitate theft are at large in communities and operating profitable businesses or otherwise enjoying the proceeds of crime. Meanwhile, those who do the stealing for them are regularly targeted by the police and taken out of circulation. This observation is important because, at the time of writing, many youth offender programs stress the importance of being socially included within a broadly perceived notion of straight society. But many in high-crime areas observe that society is not straight, because every day they see that trade in stolen goods markets is going on.

Crimes and their organization develop according to access to, and ability to foster, mutual cooperation. Their expansion is limited in large part by a mixture of distrust, domination, and the inability to legitimately warehouse and transport stock or delegate illegal tasks to all but the most trusted of employees. Some types of stolen goods markets, like the so-called black markets that thrived in various nation-states suffering shortages of food and goods during World War II, depend on almost universal public tolerance to operate. One of the most frequent justifications for both buying or trading in the black markets of World War II was that violations of laws that prohibit illegal trading were not considered by offenders to be "real" crimes, and so they believed that they should not be punished.

Stolen Goods Markets

Mike Sutton has identified six stolen goods market types. All are distinctive in the ways that thieves, dealers, and consumers operate. However, no one market type is more serious or important than another in terms of the role it plays in promoting theft. Thieves may operate in more than one type. The six market types are as follows:

1. *Commercial fence supplies:* Stolen goods are sold by thieves to commercial fences operating out of shops, such as jewelers, pawnbrokers, and secondhand dealers.

2. *Commercial sales:* Commercial fences usually pose as legitimate business owners while secretly selling stolen goods for a profit, either directly to the (innocent) consumer or more rarely to another distributor who thinks the goods can be sold again for additional profit.

3. *Commercially facilitated sales:* This market type involves either the thief or a residential or commercial fence knowingly selling stolen goods through a "respectable" third-party trading medium such as classified advertisements in traditional newspapers and magazines, through traditional auctions or websites such as craigslist. They may also sell stolen goods on online auctions such as eBay.

4. *Residential fence supplies:* Stolen goods (particularly electrical goods) are sold by thieves to fences, usually at the fence's home. The fence may be a drug dealer, may be a prolific dealer in stolen goods, or may deal only occasionally.

5. *Network sales:* Stolen goods are passed on and each participant adds a little to the price until a consumer is found. This may involve a residential fence or commercial fence selling to other fences. Alternatively, the buyer may be the final consumer or may sell the goods on again through friendship networks.

6. *Hawking:* Thieves, or their friends, sell stolen goods directly to consumers on the street or in places such as bars and pubs or door to door in residential areas (e.g., shoplifters selling cigarettes, toiletries, clothes, or food).

Common knowledge that some things are more desirable to thieves and the buying public than others is supported by research that explains what types of things thieves are most likely to steal. Products at the top of thieves' shopping lists will vary among offenders and change from time to time. As past and current crime waves reveal, such products might include base, alloys or precious metals, cigarettes, computer chips, catalytic converters, high-tech entertainment equipment, cell phones, smartphones, laptops, electronic communications tablets, or the next must-have high-tech device.

Most crimes require the convergence in space and time of capable and motivated offenders, suitably attractive and relatively vulnerable targets, and the absence of capable guardianship against crime. Although it is widely acknowledged that this applies to situations where theft occurs, a relatively neglected finding is that the same convergence of offenders, targets, and lack of guardianship provides a necessary set of intersecting market conditions for stolen goods to be sold to those who create the demand for their theft. Furthermore, a sizable proportion of the general public is not particularly capable as guardians of law and order when it comes to the opportunity to resist an illegitimate bargain. The extent of national deviance in this area was provided by analysis of the 1994 British Crime Survey stolen goods segment, which revealed that 11% of the population admitted buying stolen goods in the past five years, and 70% thought that their neighbors had stolen goods, such as televisions, in their homes.

The Role of Shortages and Demand on Crime Waves

While some thieves *steal to order* and others *steal to offer*, general market willingness to pay for particular items, products, materials, and resources plays an essential role in their theft. Demand and prices in legitimate markets play a causal role in influencing what things are "hot" in stolen goods markets, and this means that perception of value is an essential component of the potential offender's perception of what represents a rational theft opportunity. For example, demand is fuelled by market prices, which helps explains why lethal electric current ceased to be a capable guardian of live copper cable in the new millennium, as thieves were willing to risk death in order to profit. Every theft crime wave is caused in large part by the intersecting influences of shortages, market prices, ready stolen goods markets and their motivating influence on offender perceptions, and actual relative vulnerability of targets. In sum, the impact of markets on theft is important in terms of influencing thieves' perceptions of worthwhile crime opportunities.

Tackling Stolen Goods Trading

Traditional responses to stolen goods markets and the networks that operate both across and within these markets include official regulation of particular trades such as pawnbrokers and antiques and secondhand dealers. In such cases, official inspections of premises and business accounts may be underpinned by both legislation and local ordinances designed to regulate the stolen goods trade.

Police traditionally tend to set up sting operations by posing as fencing operations to identify burglars selling stolen goods. However, evidence that this leads to an increase in theft in the location of such stings has led police to prefer to conduct reverse sting operations. This method involves undercover officers posing as thieves and offering stolen goods for sale to unsuspecting business owners to see if they are operating illegitimately. Another method of attempting to reduce stolen goods dealing involves publicity campaigns highlighting the link between stolen goods consumption and theft. Other similar campaigns encourage members of the public to report dealers via anonymous police telephone hotlines, websites, and, more recently, via Twitter.

In terms of systematic attempts at theft reduction and the evaluation of their effectiveness, market reduction approach (MRA) is currently a popular method for seeking to reduce theft by tackling the markets that facilitate it. The MRA is a strategic toolkit for working out how to seek to identify, prioritize, and then reduce the number of stolen goods dealers at the local area level. This is done by seeking to reduce the number of offers made to potential buyers and to increase resistance to offers when they do occur. The main premise behind the approach is that it will work by increasing both the perceived and objective risks of both stealing and dealing at the point of illicit trading. Although it has been recommended as a good crime reduction practice by government departments in the United Kingdom, the United States, Australia, and New Zealand, the MRA has not been proven to work. Here, then, is one area where more research is required.

Michael Sutton

See also Burglary; Deviant Places; Larceny; Normal Deviance; Occupational Criminality; Pawnbrokers; Property Crime; Routine Activity Theory

Further Readings

Harris, C., Hale, C., & Uglow, S (2003). Theory into practice: Implementing a market reduction approach to property crime. In K. Bullock & N. Tilley (Eds.), *Crime reduction and problem-oriented policing* (pp. 154–182). Cullompton, England: Willian Press.

Klockars, C. (1974). *The professional fence*. New York, NY: Free Press.

Levi, M. (2007). Organized crime and terrorism. In M. Maguire, R. Morgan, & R. Reiner (Eds.), The Oxford handbook of criminology (4th ed., pp. 771–802). Oxford, England: Oxford University Press.

Quennell, R. (1996). *London's underworld*. London, England: Spring Books.

Steffensmeier, D. J. (1986). *The fence: In the shadow of two worlds*. Totowa, NJ: Rowman & Littlefield.

Sutton, M. (1993). *From receiving to thieving: The market for stolen goods and the incidence of theft* (Home Office Research Bulletin No 34). London, England: Home Office.

Sutton, M. (1998). *Handling stolen goods and theft: A market reduction approach* (Home Office Research Study No. 178). London, England. Home Office.

Sutton, M. (2010). *Stolen goods markets* (Problem Oriented Policing Guide No. 57). Washington, DC: Department of Justice COPS Program.

STRAIGHT EDGE

Straight edge (sXe) is a clean-living youth culture that emerged from the punk rock subculture in the early 1980s. Originating in Washington, D.C., it appealed to kids drawn to punk's subversive style, music, do-it-yourself ethos, and "question everything" mentality but turned off by the alcohol and drug abuse common in the scene. Minor Threat's 1981 song "Straight Edge" provided the movement its name, and the chorus of its 1983 song "Out of Step" furnished its credo. Straight edgers abstain, completely, from alcohol, drug, and tobacco use, and many also abstain from promiscuous sex, reserving intimacy for ongoing relationships. They frame their abstinence as a lifelong commitment, with most insisting that even a single drink forfeits any claim to the identity. Straight edge quickly spread across the United States and then the world. By the early 1980s, straight edgers were visible in New York, Boston, Los Angeles, Reno, and very quickly in nearly every city in between. Although many straight edgers still maintain a connection to the hard-core scene, others identify with emo, punk, goth, hip-hop, indie rock, and other youth cultures, and some maintain little connection to music scenes at all. Straight edge has thousands of adherents in countries as diverse as Brazil, Australia, South Africa, Israel, Mexico, Norway, Japan, and Italy. Straight edgers make for an interesting case of deviance, simultaneously resisting and reinforcing dominant social patterns. Their abstinent ideology sets them apart from many other youth while reinforcing more mainstream notions of temperance and self-control. While some are indistinguishable from their more conventional peers, many adopt subcultural fashions, including being heavily tattooed and pierced, marking them as deviant.

Straight edgers often display the movement's symbol, an X, on their clothing, in their tattoos, or marked on their hands with black marking pen. The symbol emerged in the early 1980s when club owners in Washington, D.C., barred underage kids from attending shows (the legal drinking age then was 18 years). Because venues made substantial profits from alcohol sales, they typically catered to an adult clientele. Underage drinkers also posed a risk of fines or even revocation of a liquor license. To accommodate young fans, venues marked underage kids' hands with large Xs as a clear signal that club workers should deny the youths alcohol. Youth quickly transformed the X from a social stigma to a symbol of pride and defiance, a way to say, "not only *can't* we drink, we don't *want* to drink." Straight edgers, even those of legal drinking age, began marking their own hands prior to shows and wearing shirts with slogans such as "It's OK Not to Drink."

Some straight edgers consider themselves part of a diffuse lifestyle movement challenging the cultural pressures to drink alcohol, do drugs, and smoke cigarettes. Believing alcohol and tobacco companies intentionally market to youth and profit by others' suffering, they seek to both carve out a space for young people to feel valued for *not* drinking and also to set an example for other youth. Other straight edgers claim that straight edge is purely their own individual choice for their own health or well-being. Many believe that abstinence allows them to have a "clear mind," helping them to resist peer pressure and the pressures to conform to the larger culture. Vegetarianism and veganism have been associated with straight edge since the mid-1980s, with many adherents seeing animal rights and environmentalism as logical outgrowths of their self-styled

"positive" lifestyle. A significant minority of straight edgers participates in causes such as feminism, antifascist, antiracist, peace, and other progressive movements, and a few blend their straight-edge identity to religious traditions, primarily Christianity but also Islam and Krishna Consciousness.

Straight-edge kids come from many different backgrounds, though young white men dominate the scene in the United States, giving rise to the belief that straight edge is a white suburban scene. Like many youth cultures, men occupy most positions of influence, primarily as members of bands. However, many women and people of color claim the identity and make substantial contributions to the scene. Women claim that straight edge offers opportunities to challenge dominant femininities (e.g., appearance norms), while abstinence offers a sense of bodily safety and control. Furthermore, while many straight edgers eventually abandon the identity and begin (or return to) using alcohol or drugs, a substantial number of adults maintain their abstinence into their 30s and 40s, even as their participation in a straight-edge scene often declines.

In the 1990s, straight edge gained a reputation as a violent subculture, with news media reporting attacks on smokers and alcohol users. Even within the scene, straight-edge "crews"—invite-only subgroups with their own codes and symbols—became an intimidating presence at many shows, sometimes picking fights with newcomers or outsiders. Some jurisdictions, particularly in Utah and Nevada, labeled straight edge a street gang, and a few schools banned clothing with straight-edge messages or symbols. While few straight edgers actively seek out confrontations, the vast majority do not, with most condemning violence and what they call "tough guy" attitudes. Because the subculture has little mainstream presence, and due to some straight edgers' "spectacular" appearance, so-called militant straight edgers stand out, erroneously coming to represent the subculture as a whole. Rarely, straight edge has also been linked to eco-terrorism due to a few adherents' connections to radical animal rights organizations. For most participants, however, straight edge simply offers a meaningful countercultural identity.

Ross Haenfler

See also Positive Deviance; Punk Subculture; Social
    Change and Deviance; Subculture; Vegetarianism and
    Veganism

Further Readings

Haenfler, R. (2006). *Straight edge: Clean living youth, hardcore punk, and social change.* New Brunswick, NJ: Rutgers University Press.

Kuhn, G. (2010). *Sober living for the revolution: Hardcore punk, straight edge, and radical politics.* Oakland, CA: PM Press.

Wood, R. T. (2006). *Straightedge youth: Complexity and contradictions of a subculture.* Syracuse, NY: Syracuse University Press.

STRANGER

Most, if not all, societies have some concept of the stranger, many of which appear to be quite straightforward. The word comes to us through the Latin word *extraneus* meaning foreign or external, and while this meaning is retained in English, the uses of the concept of the stranger are more complex. In Ancient Greece, non-Greek speakers (*barbaros*) were considered to be strangers or barbarians, while the term *xenos* (as in *xenophobia*) was used to mean both foreigner, in the sense of somebody to be feared, and guest, in the sense of someone to be welcomed. The Latin term *hospes* (as in *hospitality*) means both stranger and host. The stranger, then, is a curiously contradictory figure on whom opposing forces seem to coalesce: A stranger who receives hospitality may later be viewed as hostile or vice versa. While popular usage implies a shared understanding of what the term means, a precise definition of the stranger is difficult to formulate. The German sociologist Georg Simmel describes the stranger as one who is both near and far, one who is physically proximate but socially distant. That is, a stranger is someone who is located close to us in space but about whom we know little; the stranger is both inside and outside. At base, a stranger is someone unknown to us.

This entry begins with a discussion of the stranger as a socially defined category, followed by an examination of the stranger's inside/outside status, and a brief exploration of the stranger as an object of fear and hostility.

While the term gathers a number of seemingly contradictory ideas, the category "stranger" is socially defined. That is, no person has an innate quality that makes him or her into a stranger; rather, persons or groups are defined (or may define themselves) as strangers in particular social contexts. Few of us could claim to be strangers in every social context, but most of us have firsthand experience of being a stranger. As a socially defined category, it is of particular interest to scholars of deviance. Indeed, being a stranger in a particular social situation might make us feel as if we are in some way deviant. As with deviance more generally, this quality of being stranger is always in relation to the social situations in which we find ourselves. For example, immigrants have traditionally been described as strangers, not only because they may be unknown but more specifically because they are often unfamiliar with the norms and expectations that members of the host society take for granted.

The social position of the stranger is of special value in knowledge production and dispute resolution. Social scientists have long used this particular social position as a valuable methodological tool. Ethnographers, for example, immerse themselves in groups and societies to which they are alien to develop a better understanding of social processes. In a similar vein, students of sociology are taught to "make the familiar strange," that is, to look at their own experiences and society as if through the eyes of a stranger. In situations where we are strangers, we have a tendency to poke holes in taken-for-granted knowledge and question background assumptions. This is because strangers are unshackled by social conventions and preconceptions: They may have a clearer vision of how a society operates because of their lack of connection and social obligation or because the underlying structures that organize a given context become visible to them. Employing the duality of the stranger's insider/outsider position, black feminists, for example, have offered insightful critiques of the workings of predominantly male and white institutions. The stranger's ability to see differently is especially useful in adjudication and dispute resolution. For example, in most Canadian jurisdictions, law enforcement officers cannot be posted to communities where they are from in the belief that they are more likely to be biased in their home communities. Similarly, a couple having difficulties is unlikely to seek help from a relationship counselor who is a close friend of one partner but not of the other. The stranger's lack of familiarity can facilitate objective judgment and unbiased intervention. Put simply, a stranger has a capacity for objectivity that group members might lack.

The stranger is not always treated with respect or seen in a positive light. He or she may sometimes be feared and treated with hostility, often for the very reasons outlined above. In many societies, the stranger is feared merely because he or she is different and/or because his or her presence signals a threat to social order. This leads to some curious paradoxes. For example, fear of violent crime tends to be oriented toward strangers, whereas research shows that one is much more likely to be a victim of a violent crime committed by someone already known to the victim. Similarly, children in the United States are taught about "stranger danger" from a young age, where strangers are spoken about as predatory and potential abductors. This is despite the fact that most child abductions are carried out by people who the abductee knows personally, with most child abductions in the United States, for example, carried out by family members, not by strangers.

In the contemporary context of increased global mobility, many scholars say that we now live in a "society of strangers," and some have begun to use the term *strangership* to describe today's dominant form of social relations. In summary, the stranger is a figure who gathers a range of contradictory orientations and evokes widely varying responses: from fear to hospitality, and sometimes, indifference.

Mervyn Horgan

See also Ethnography and Deviance; Homecomer; Marginality; Moral Panics; Norms and Societal Expectations; Outsiders

Further Readings

Hill Collins, P. (1986). Learning from the outsider within. *Social Problems, 33*(6), 14–32.

Horgan, M. (2012). Strangers and strangership. *Journal of Intercultural Studies, 33*(6), 607–622.

Miethe, T. (1995). Fear and withdrawal from urban life. *ANNALS of the American Academy of Political and Social Science, 539*(1), 14–27.

Simmel, G. (1971). *On individuality and social forms.* Chicago, IL: University of Chicago Press.

STREET HUSTLING

A street hustler is a male prostitute who participates in discrediting behavior (i.e., male street prostitution). A brief overview of the various forms of male prostitution and their differences is needed to separate the street hustler. There are four primary types of male prostitutes: (1) the escort prostitute, (2) the bar hustler, (3) the kept boy, and (4) the street hustler. The escort typically works through an escort service or modeling agency. This helps protect the escort's and customer's identities. Bar hustlers frequently visit gay bars and clubs to meet potential customers. This approach can be risky due to the attention law enforcement may give bars. The kept boy is arguably the least identifiable due to the nature of the relationship—the male prostitute is financially dependent on one customer, who keeps the prostitute off the streets and out of bars from detection of law enforcement. The street hustler is the most visible type of male prostitute because he operates in public places such as street corners, bus terminals, and hotel lobbies. The street hustler's behavior is the male equivalent to female street prostitution, and this entry provides a general overview of male street hustlers and their interactions.

Male Street Hustling Overview

The number of males involved in male street hustling is unknown. Some start hustling as young as age 13 years and continue as adults. Male street hustlers are different from child prostitutes, also commonly referenced as commercially sexually exploited children. Street hustlers choose to practice this behavior, while many commercially sexually exploited children are typically forced or coerced to participate in the street-level sex market.

Male street hustlers are difficult to identify. First, they do not have visible markings that link them to male prostitution. Second, they may only hustle during times of personal financial troubles, which makes their behavior sporadic. Third, they are commonly around areas with much of the public present into the late hours of night (e.g., bars, streets, movie theaters), which does not automatically link someone to prostitution.

Overall, street hustlers engage in illegal and discrediting behavior. The label of a "homosexual prostitute" may have severe consequences for how they view themselves and their social reputation; they violate multiple cultural norms. They are engaging in an activity that is illegal (i.e., prostitution) and still not socially accepted in many settings (i.e., homosexuality).

Economic need has been identified as the primary motivating factor for street hustlers. Some use this as their primary source of income, while others use it to supplement their legitimate income. Other motivations are usually connected to sexual recreation, experimentation, or both. This activity provides opportunities for individuals to discretely engage in stigmatizing homosexual behavior while living more "traditional" lives.

Street Hustler Transactions

There is a typical order in which sexual interaction occurs; however, not all interactions pass through each stage. The stages are initial contact, confirmation, negotiation of the sexual act and fees, and negotiation of location.

During initial contact, male prostitutes utilize strategies to identify a potential client. One method of identifying a potential client is "cruising." Cruising occurs when a potential client cruises around the same area multiple times while looking at the hustler each time around. Once a potential customer has been identified, the hustler may nod his head or wave and the potential customer may do the same. The exchanges do not guarantee the two will share sexual activities. Structured interaction is then used to decide if the hustler would want to do business with the potential client. This structured interaction can help rule out if this is law enforcement or someone else who may stigmatize the hustler.

Next, the hustler attempts to confirm that this potential client is not a law enforcement officer. If the hustler is satisfied with his assessment of the potential customer, he will generally ask if the potential customer is an officer. Asking serves two purposes. First, hustlers believe if the potential customer does not answer the question truthfully, then any subsequent court case will be dismissed should the hustler be arrested for prostitution. Second, if the law enforcement officer informs the hustler of his identity, the hustler can terminate the conversation without telling the officer he is a prostitute. The hustlers' understanding of the law is not accurate because if an individual is predisposed to engage in any criminal behavior, the police are not obligated to inform the person that they are a law enforcement officer, but overall, hustlers do their best to avoid interaction with the criminal justice system.

Negotiation of the sexual act and fee occurs if the hustler finds the potential client acceptable. At this stage, the potential customer can inform the hustler of the sexual activity he desires. They may go back and forth in negotiating which sexual services will be provided. If they cannot agree, the interaction stops. Many factors influence the cost: the nature of the act being requested, the perception of the customer, and other situational factors, such as the amount of time needed for the requested sexual services.

The final decision to be made is the negotiation of the location. The most common places for the sexual activity to occur are in apartments or houses, cars in parking lots, and motels or hotels. The major concern of the hustler is how to best protect his privacy. The sexual act can also influence the location. For example, anal intercourse is not easily accomplished in a car. Once again, privacy is a major concern for both the hustler and customer.

Once the act is complete, the customer is expected to return the prostitute to the initial meeting area or take him to another location. Most hustlers are dropped off at another location to avoid detection. A successful male street hustler will be able to continue his practice without being identified and publicly labeled.

Cyber Hustling

The Internet has affected the dynamics of street hustling. There are more than 100 websites that advertise male prostitutes. The cyberworld provides an outlet for prostitutes and customers to effectively locate each other while remaining anonymous behind a computer, computer tablet, or smartphone. Exploratory studies have revealed that the Internet allows individuals to pick and choose male prostitutes based on physical appearance, prices, payment options, preferred sexual activities, and overall ratings. "Cyber hustlers" have blurred the clear line that once existed between male escorts, bar hustlers, kept boys, and street hustlers because they can all be viewed as cyber hustlers if advertising via the Internet. Through the Internet, experienced and novice hustlers can all go to similar sites and advertise their sex work. Traditional street hustling is still common, but the overall impact of the Internet on this deviant activity has yet to be determined.

Conclusion

Male prostitution continues to be an overlooked phenomenon. Male street hustlers are not forced or coerced into this activity. Each hustler might rationally decide whether the perceived benefits outweigh the potential negative consequences, such as the negative stigma associated with both homosexuality and prostitution and the likelihood of arrest, violence, and sexually transmitted diseases.

Thomas Calhoun and Addrain Conyers

See also Cybersex; Female Prostitution; Homosexuality; Male Prostitution

Further Readings

Calhoun, T. C. (1992). Male street hustling: Introduction processes and stigma containment. *Sociological Spectrum, 12,* 35–52.

Calhoun, T. C., & Weaver, G. (1996). Rational decision-making among male street prostitutes. *Deviant Behavior, 17,* 209–227.

Lee-Gonyea, J. A., Castle, T., & Lee-Gonyea, N. E. (2009). Laid to order: Male escorts advertising on the Internet. *Deviant Behavior, 30,* 321–348.

Pruitt, M., & Krull, A. (2011). Escort advertisements and male patronage of prostitutes. *Deviant Behavior, 32,* 38–63.

STRIPPERS, FEMALE

Female strippers may be referred to as adult entertainers, exotic dancers, topless dancers, nude dancers, "tittie" dancers, or simply as strippers. Whatever the moniker, the phenomenon is the same: A woman begins either partially or fully clothed, and while dancing to music, eventually becomes either partially or fully nude. Although some women may strip for fun or pleasure, generally some type of monetary compensation is involved in the form of wages, tips, or both. Although legal in all 50 states and throughout much of the world, stripping for a living is generally considered to be a deviant occupation or career. As such, like many other forms of specific deviance, those involved may become viewed as general deviants. As a result, the deviant status accorded female strippers may be associated with negative stereotypes that insinuate sexual promiscuity, prostitution, alcoholism, drug abuse, and other forms of deviant or criminal behavior. Consequently, female strippers must deal with a certain amount of stigma associated with stripping in both their personal and professional lives.

Historical Background

Although the act of women removing clothing to sexually arouse men is probably as old as wearing clothing itself, historically, female stripping in the United States can most readily be traced to its western European background in burlesque. By the late 19th century, the *Moulin Rouge* and *Folies Bergere* in Paris routinely featured scantily clad dancers and women removing their clothes to music to entertain mostly male audiences. Their popularity and profitability spawned many imitators in other European cities, and shortly after the return of U.S. soldiers who had visited those cities during World War I, similar shows gained popularity in the United States. Although female stripping in the United States predates the First World War primarily as sideshows at traveling carnivals, it gained popularity in the mid-1920s with the advent of Minsky's Burlesque theater on New York City's famed 42nd Street. The fan dancer Sally Rand and the burlesque queen Gypsy Rose Lee were among the first female entertainers to gain national fame by removing their clothes, and although considered risqué, they helped introduce striptease to mainstream America. Although their acts involved more illusion, peekaboo, and tease than nudity, almost immediately, states and municipalities began passing laws to regulate and, in some cases, ban striptease shows and other forms of nudity in both public areas and private clubs. As American vaudeville became more popular, it prominently featured singing, comedy, and burlesque as entertainment staples, somewhat "legitimizing" female stripping.

During the post–World War II era, female stripping became less popular as the United States became more politically as well as socially conservative. Television, replete with a host of censors, became the dominant form of public entertainment, and anything related to nudity, sexuality, and/or the sex industry became increasingly viewed as deviant behavior.

The 1960s witnessed renewed interest in striptease and the emphasis shifted from the "tease" to the "strip." San Francisco's topless and fully nude clubs gained widespread media attention, and other cities followed suit. Although the more liberal areas of the West Coast, New York City, and New Orleans seemed natural venues for stripping and nude dancing, the so-called Bible Belt with some of the strictest and most repressive informal and formal norms against nudity and sexuality soon joined them as popular and profitable areas for topless and fully nude clubs. Female stripping also became somewhat more athletic with many dancers using poles and other props to demonstrate balance, physical strength, and agility in addition to dancing and removing clothing. Municipalities passed numerous ordinances and zoning restrictions in attempts to control, regulate, and even ban topless dancing and nude entertainment, but female stripping was far too lucrative and profitable to go away. As social and cultural changes contributed to the proliferation of female stripping, clubs around the country began to feature male stripping catering to female and gay male audiences. Although it is virtually impossible to know the exact numbers, today there are thousands of private and public clubs that feature female strippers and a lesser number that highlight male strippers in the United States as part of a multibillion dollar industry.

Sociologically, female stripping is of interest because it combines at least four aspects of life highly valued by most Americans: (1) work, (2) entertainment, (3) money, and (4) sex. In a postindustrial society like that of the United States, where people's jobs are an important part of both their personal and social identities, a person's occupation often becomes a master status. In other words, what you do is who you are. Workers in the sex industry are often viewed negatively by members of the larger society and are routinely confronted with stigma and disenfranchisement from those who disapprove of how they make their living. Consequently, female strippers are considered to be engaged in a deviant occupation/career, and therefore, they have developed a variety of ways to neutralize the stigma directed at them as a result of their job.

Dealing With the Stigma

One of the mechanisms used by many female strippers to minimize the stigma associated with their occupation is to divide their social world into two distinct camps: a small number of family members, friends, and colleagues who know what they do for a living, and the rest of the world who does not. This can be accomplished in several ways. Perhaps the most obvious is by simply avoiding conversations about work. When pressed, female strippers often give vague answers to questions about what they do for a living, alluding to waitressing, working in a club, dancing, or being in the entertainment industry. Some may even claim to be between jobs, as unemployment often elicits a more positive response than revealing their true occupation. Those "in the know" may help them with this deception whenever possible.

Deviant identities have been shown to negatively affect self-esteem. As a result, another common technique of stigma avoidance among female strippers is to emotionally detach themselves from their work. While it is common for doctors, lawyers, teachers, and other professionals to become absorbed in their work and to merge their occupational identities with their personal and social identities, female strippers often do exactly the opposite, totally separating their occupational selves from their personal selves. Many female strippers use pseudonyms while on the job, and several even adopt an entirely different persona. Shy and introverted women may become gregarious and flirtatious, extroverts may act shy and coy, lesbians may act heterosexual, married women may feign availability, and feminists may take on the role of sex objects. This cognitive dissonance allows female strippers to emotionally detach from their jobs, retaining their nondeviant self-image and avoiding the role engulfment often associated with deviance.

In the late 1950s, Gresham Sykes and David Matza theorized that juvenile delinquents realize that they are challenging widely accepted values and are violating established norms, but they have an uncanny ability to rationalize their deviant behavior by using various techniques to neutralize its potentially negative consequences. Research on female strippers indicates that they often use several of these same neutralization techniques to reduce the emotional stress and stigma associated with their occupation, especially denial of injury, condemnation of the condemners, and appeal to higher loyalties.

Female strippers maintain that although their occupation may be viewed as deviant because it violates some people's moral codes and occasionally may even involve law violation, nobody is actually harmed by it. Strip clubs often post a sign on the door indicating that minors are not allowed and that anybody who is offended by nudity should not enter. Consequently, those who enter the premises know very well what to expect. When confronted with the acknowledgment that although nobody is physically, or arguably even emotionally, harmed, but perhaps the overall morality of a community is threatened, female strippers are quick to point out the hypocrisy of those who condemn their occupation yet participate in a host of other activities that are potentially far more harmful to individuals and the community, such as drinking and driving, cheating on their spouses, or other deviant and/or criminal behaviors. Female strippers also often point to altruistic reasons for their participation in a deviant occupation, citing the need to support a child or children, parents or grandparents, working to pay for higher education, or preventing more serious forms of deviant behavior such as child molestation or rape by fulfilling fantasies of those who otherwise might participate in those criminal acts.

Another variable that may help assuage some of the negativity associated with stripping is the money that women can make doing it. It is difficult to know how much strippers make, but while some are apparently struggling to make ends meet, others seem to be doing quite well financially. Despite its lack of prestige, for an occupation that requires no academic preparation, no formal education, and no experience, stripping can be quite lucrative. In many venues, strippers are not considered employees of the club where they perform. Instead, they are considered self-employed independent contractors. In fact, in many cases, the strippers may be required to pay a fee to reserve stage time. Thus, they do not earn wages, but rely almost solely on tips for their income. There are no hourly wages, no salary scales, no paychecks or paycheck stubs, no Social Security withholding, no W-2 or 1099 forms, and essentially no other documentations of income. As a result, strippers are on somewhat of an "honor system" when it comes to reporting income and paying taxes. Correspondingly, the benefits associated with "tax-free" income may be offset by the lack of unemployment benefits, medical or disability insurance, and no retirement plan for what is most likely a relatively short career expectancy.

As cultural values, social mores, and gender norms have changed over time, female stripping and other forms of adult entertainment have been viewed differently by various segments of society. Whether viewed as art, comedy, entertainment, eroticism, harmless fun, or moral depravity, female stripping remains a source of curiosity. As with many so-called deviant occupations, few female strippers are invited to "Career Day" at the local schools, even fewer are likely to participate in "Take Your Daughters to Work Day," and almost none dream of the day when their children will grow up to follow in their mother's career footsteps.

William E. Thompson

See also Deviant Career; Neutralization Theory; Self-Esteem and Deviance; Stigma and Stigma Management

Further Readings

Boles, J., & Garbin, A. P. (1974). Stripping for a living: An occupational study of the nightclub stripper. In C. D. Bryant (Ed.), *Deviant behavior* (pp. 319–328). Chicago, IL: Rand McNally.

Cody, D. (2006). *Candy girl: A year in the life of an unlikely stripper.* New York, NY: Gotham Books.

Forsyth, C. J., & Deshotels, T. H. (1997). The occupational milieu of the nude dancer. *Deviant Behavior, 18,* 125–142.

Goffman, E. (1963). *Stigma: Notes on the management of a spoiled identity.* Englewood Cliffs, NJ: Prentice Hall.

Skipper, J. K., & McCaghy, C. H. (1970). Stripteasers: The anatomy and career contingencies of a deviant occupation. *Social Problems, 17,* 664–670.

Thompson, W. E., & Harred, J. L. (1992). Topless dancers: Managing stigma in a deviant occupation. *Deviant Behavior, 13,* 291–311.

Thompson, W. E., Harred, J. L., & Burks, B. E. (2003). Managing the stigma of topless dancing: A decade later. *Deviant Behavior, 24,* 551–570.

STRIPPERS, MALE

When most people think about strippers, they think of women who remove their clothing while dancing for purposes of earning money from men who watch them in nightclubs that are centered on such activities. However, it is important to note that men are also a part of the stripping world, although they are not as quickly or commonly thought of as their female counterparts. As part of the sex industry, male strippers represent social deviance to many.

When discussing male strippers, it is important to recognize that there are several important distinctions that are not present in the world of female strippers. First, the primary audience for which a male stripper dances is either other men or women. Second, whereas the vast majority of female strippers work at one nightclub (at a time) pretty much exclusively, male strippers may either work out of a primary nightclub (like women) or be a member of a travelling troupe of dancers who work at different bars or nightclubs and in different cities, rarely working in one location for more than one or two dates in a row.

When many people do think about male strippers, they think about high-profile, well-known groups of travelling performers, such as Chippendales, who work out of particular nightclubs in entertainment destinations such as Las Vegas, Nevada. These types of male strippers usually work exclusively for female audiences (often with males prohibited from entering the venue). In such shows, there are usually both men who are dancers (and often do not remove clothing or remove only a shirt) and men who primarily remove their clothing but do not do much dancing (sometimes referred to pejoratively as "stand and model" men).

Studies of male strippers are relatively few. When these men and their activities are studied, it is most often with a focus on audience reactions and interactions at and during shows. As such, this research primarily draws on participant observation with researchers attending shows and documenting how audiences receive and interpret such performances. These studies suggest that male strippers (like their female counterparts) are focused on establishing both an erotic image and counterfeit intimacy with audience members.

Others have studied male strippers directly, drawing on participant observation inside groups of dancers and interviews. This line of research suggests that men enter stripping for purposes of both access to easy financial gain and for recreational purposes. As with female strippers, the "easy money" that entices individuals into stripping is seen as the primary reason to begin stripping. However, for some men, especially those who strip only or primarily for female audiences, stripping is seen as fun, exciting, and an opportunity to establish desired social contacts. Among men who strip for men, the limited research suggests that while strippers may be regularly solicited for sex (sometimes with offers of payment), they rarely date or engage in sex with patrons. The male strippers who do it decide to do so largely because they find the potential financial benefits too great to resist.

Interestingly, several studies of male strippers have shown that male strippers often actively construct a sexual image not only for performance but also for public identity, reflecting a sexual orientation that is not commensurate with their authentic off-stage self. Although some early studies of female strippers suggested that many were lesbian, little attention has been devoted to the issue of sexual orientation of male strippers. The literature that is available regarding male strippers introduces the idea that some dancers truly are constructing a performance that is largely removed from their real identities. In other words, not all male strippers who perform for women are heterosexual, and not all who perform for men are gay or bisexual.

As a site of deviance, strip clubs are often thought of as marginal environments, where sex and drugs proliferate. While strip clubs are clearly financially successful, there are also moral restrictions associated with them, such as a belief that stripping is sinful, alcohol and drug use is wrong and to be avoided, and only persons with low personal values and morals would strip, which are frequently cited as foundations for the stigmatization of such locales. However, strip clubs, especially those presenting

men performing for men, are often viewed, even by "liberal" and open-minded persons, as among the most deviant sexual environments in society. When one considers sexual performances, homosexuality, and the general stigma of strip clubs, it is not uncommon to develop a view of such places and persons as exceptionally deviant.

In short, male strippers are clearly a part of the sex industry, represent social deviance to many, and yet they remain one of the segments of contemporary society that is least studied and about which little is known. This leaves numerous research opportunities open to present and future scholars interested in the world of male stripping. New lines of inquiry should provide more extensive descriptions and revelations concerning the phenomenon of male strippers and stripping.

Richard Tewksbury

See also Pornography; Sex Tourism; Strippers, Female

Further Readings

Boden, D. M. (2007). Alienation of sexuality in male erotic dancing. *Journal of Homosexuality, 53,* 129–152.

DeMarco, J. R. G. (2007). Power and control in gay strip clubs. *Journal of Homosexuality, 53,* 111–127.

Tewksbury, R. (1994). A dramaturgical analysis of male strippers. *Journal of Men's Studies, 2,* 325–342.

STRUCTURAL FUNCTIONALISM

Structural functionalism derives from functionalist theories that view society as an integrated whole based on the functioning properties of social institutions and members. Émile Durkheim's theory of society's stability derives from correlations to medical models of organisms' interdependent organs functioning to support the organism's existence, and the process in which external social norms that are given become internalized by social members. In the same way as Durkheim, Talcott Parsons concurs that societies generate a degree of cooperation based on the interdependent social organization between actors and social systems, but he is more interested in offering explanation of how individuals and the structure secure their needs in equilibrium. This entry theorizes structural functionalism primarily from Parsons's standpoint, concluding with Robert Merton's contribution.

Parsons's Theory

Parsonian structural–functional theory extends functionalism by addressing the functional requisites of social systems. Parsons borrows Durkheim's concepts of social facts as given and externally imposed on individuals to sustain moral order and become internalized as the voluntary adherence to duty. Parsons's theoretical development emphasizes the social organization of complementary, independent roles that are arrayed over a variety of social institutions. His three-part subsystem refers to the personality, social, and cultural system. This interrelated system achieves social functioning among diverse needs-dispositions, social roles, and cultural values. These three systems are conceptualized as boundary-maintaining systems that Parsons claims represent their analytical distinction from each other, albeit their interpenetrating structure. As such, individuals' needs-dispositions are expected to be complementary to social roles mediated by cultural values as well.

Structural functionalism is further theorized by Parsons in his concepts of pattern variables, which are based on components individuals must consider in order to orient their actions to a specific situation. The five variables include the dichotomies between (1) the self and collective, (2) ascription and achievement, (3) particular and universal, (4) specific and diffuse, and (5) affective and affective-neutral. Pattern variables correlate to each of the three subsystems. The personality system comprises the needs-dispositions of particular actors, such as whether their orientation to action is based on subjective gratification or not; the social system is composed of roles, which include orientations toward self or collective, affective or affective neutrality, or ascriptive or achievement. These pattern variables seek to orient individuals' actions either toward their own needs-dispositions or social roles. The final subsystem is the cultural system, which is composed of social norms that attempt to regulate and integrate the personality needs-dispositions of various actors with the general social roles central to the social system. In addition, the pattern variable, universal or particular, can apply to social roles and social norms based on the situation and individual at hand. Here, an individual must evaluate his or her role based on cathectic and cognitive needs and meaning making to proceed and act appropriately in an interaction setting. For example, Parsons characterizes that a doctor must engage in an affective-neutral role when providing medical services to a patient; however, this neutral role may change in another setting, such as his or her interactions with a family member. Individual and societal relations demonstrate action as incorporating a wide range of possible role performances that correspond to certain social institutions.

Underlying the development of pattern variables is the idea that individuals interact in society based on the social role and their own needs-dispositions within a particular context. Each social institution must adapt as an organism, provide goals and motivations linked to the personality system to carry out its needs, integrate individuals, and create compatible values that relate to the particular institution and other interdependent social institutions; Parsons refers to this process as the AGIL (adaptation, goal attainment, integration, latency) model. This macro process associated with the micro actions of actors is premised on the idea that each social system must attend to diversity and differentiation concerning individuals and values. Parsons's aim in developing the interdependent relationships between the personality, social, and cultural systems is to demonstrate how individuals' needs-gratifications, social roles, and cultural values contribute to the functioning of social institutions and to society's stability.

A critical theory of Parsons's structural functionalism is termed *voluntaristic action*. Having been influenced by utilitarian thinkers and the works of Alfred Marshall, Vilfredo Pareto, Durkheim, and Max Weber, Parsons formed an action model that could account for the complexities of individuals' action processes in a way that integrated structure and agency in a mutually supportive manner. Parsons's theoretical undertaking was to show the voluntary aspects of individuals' action while accounting for structural conditions that influenced their agency. In developing the unit act, which is able to account for an action process that informs social systems, Parsons first had to reconcile the utilitarian dilemma. Utilitarian theorists tended to support ideas that individuals created social structure and social laws based on their active negotiation of exchange relations. The problem associated with this idea was neglecting to account for how individuals' subjective wants could align without the influence of certain constraints. Utilitarians also neglected to demonstrate how structure was formed based on exchange relations. Parsons illustrated the utilitarian dilemma as individuals' actions driven by hedonistic drives and subjective wants or action as structurally determined.

Parsons identifies that the unit act incorporates an actor, means, end, and a situation involving conditions and a normative orientation. These elements interrelate to account for action with regard to the actor taking into account structural conditions and cultural and social values in his or her process to use particular means to actualize a goal. Parsons does not directly displace the actor's agency because emphasis is placed on the ability of the actor to control means and use them to achieve a particular end. However, the actor consults structural constraints and social norms in selecting appropriate means to achieve his or her end. In connection to structural functionalism, Parsons's theory of action creates a mutually dependent relationship between structure and agency to integrate individuals' needs-dispositions with social and cultural norms of society. Parsons developed the unit act to be used as a frame of reference to theorize the interrelations between individual and society in an effort to explain social integration and the functional requisites necessary for social systems.

Social Change and Deviance

The functional components that characterize society as an equilibrium became subjected to critiques by conflict theorists concerning the role of social change and deviance. As such, this discussion leads to the issue of the degree of dynamic functions associated with individuals and societies and a central weakness associated with structural–functional theories. Durkheim received criticism that his idea of a society functioning based on the interdependent parts contributing to the whole lacked a fair discussion of conflict. Parsonian theory also experienced criticism in its attempt to see deviance as a function to society. Critics identify tautological and teleological problems in structural–functional theories due to circular theorizing of cause and effect and reducing society's components to function. Other critiques have challenged functional requisites of systems by indicating that social systems do not have needs.

However, Parsons approaches deviance by identifying how social institutions socially control deviance. Essentially from the macro side, Parsons claims that safety valve institutions are in place that socially condone minor forms of deviance to reduce strain on the system. For example, Halloween and high school dances offer socially appropriate forms of deviance to be enacted in a socially controlled context. Previously, Durkheim indicated that moral

norms upheld by individuals prevented deviance to an extent that authority was associated with the collective conscience against individuals' deviations. Parsons supports this idea in his discussion of anomie, but he also notes that in addition to anomie central to the social system and social roles, individuals experience alienation in terms of the personality system and their needs-dispositions. This micro and macro focus not only broadens understandings of deviance, but also addresses the interaction context of individuals. For example, the ego's potential deviation may be responded to by the alter's ability to either reframe his or her own desires and/or re-establish the interaction as a way to prevent deviance from fully emerging and disrupting the solidarity of the interaction. In this sense, Parsons takes a micro–macro approach to the interrelations of individuals and structural systems. Parsons also claims that strain emerges in society due to changes in role structure that cause society to restructure these situations toward equilibrium. In the case of the family, a child's role and relationship changes throughout time based on maturation and socialization. The family institution responds to these strains by restructuring the role relationship to establish reequilibrium. Thus, the social system is able to continue to function among the emergence of strain by attempting to restore the state of equilibrium.

Merton's Theory

Merton also conceptualized functional components of society, particularly developing concepts of manifest and latent functions. Manifest functions are defined as objective consequences, while latent functions refer to unintended consequences. This differentiation of terms enables Merton to avoid initial critiques of how function was illogically theorized. Theoretically, functionality has a more precise range by observing possibilities of diverse functions. For example, Merton illustrates that certain rituals may be interpreted as irrational and fail to bring about a particular consequence based on manifest functions; however, the use of latent functions may further pronounce the possibility of social members and collectivities to engender equilibrium. This effort prompts sociologists to be better apt to take on value-neutral, objective observations and conclusions.

Merton extends structural–functional theorizing to address the interactive relationship between cultural goals and legitimate means. A society establishes cultural goals that coincide with guidelines to achieve them. However despite an interactive component, deviance emerges when a particular combination of cultural goals fails to align with legitimate means. Merton develops a typology of adaptation (conformity, innovation, ritualist, rebellion, and retreatism) to examine the degree to which individuals engage in deviant action. Individuals may encounter strain with regard to internalizing cultural goals and attaining them through legitimate means. A form of conflict emerges when strain develops in the process of conforming. Equilibrium serves as a functional goal of society; however, institutions may involve conditions in which individuals fail to functionally adapt. Society can achieve stability when individuals conform to cultural expectations and corresponding means. In this sense, structural functionalism as a paradigm advances theories that suggest that social systems and actors have certain independent functions that participate in interdependent networks.

Erin Rider

See also Anomie Theory; General Strain Theory; Norms and Societal Expectations; Positive Deviance

Further Readings

Cole, R. (1966). Structural-functional theory, the dialectic, and social change. *Sociological Quarterly, 7*, 39–58.

McQuarie, D., & Denisoff, R. S. (1995). Functionalism and neofunctionalism. In D. McQuarie (Ed.), *Readings in contemporary sociological theory: From modernity to post modernity* (pp. 1–8). Englewood Cliffs, NJ: Prentice Hall.

Merton, R. (1938). Social structure and anomie. *American Sociological Review, 3*, 672–682.

Parsons, T. (1951). *The social system.* New York, NY: Free Press.

Parsons, T. (1968). *The structure of social action: Vol. 1. Marshall, Pareto, Durkheim.* New York, NY: Free Press.

Parsons, T. (1968). *The structure of social action: Vol. 2. Weber.* New York, NY: Free Press.

SUBCULTURE

From the very first time the concept was applied at the University of Chicago in the 1920s, subculture was described as a set of values, modes of behavior, and attitudes relating to the lifestyle and ritual of social groups that were different from the mainstream or the dominant culture of society. As a concept, subculture remains important within the disciplines of criminology and sociology because subculture represents a struggle over meaning and lived experience.

For almost a century, within criminology and sociology, the concept of subculture has been applied within different paradigms, including positivism, functionalism, behaviorism, symbolic interactionism, Marxism, and postmodernism. As a consequence, the concept of subculture has been used to define people in different ways, such as subnormal, dysfunctional, delinquent, resistant, and consumerist. The concept of subculture attracts attention because it is focused on deviance, and at the same time, each approach puts forward a definite answer to a social issue. As a result, for decades, there has been a cyclical debate where different paradigms have fought over ownership of the concept of subculture. Theoretically, one of the key issues within the subcultural debate relates to agency and constraint, whether the concept allows individuals to express meaning or whether the concept determines individuals rendering them passive.

Normality or Criminality

From its earliest usage, the concept of subculture has been associated with deviance and criminality, because the so-called deviant was assumed to be part of a subculture, which showed opposition to the dominant order. One sociological theory that has played a major role in understanding the social condition of deviance in society has been anomie. It was a concept that one of the founding figures of sociology, Émile Durkheim, first outlined in his study of suicide. While anomie gives an account of how we experience hopelessness, it is also concerned with normlessness in society. This means that as a concept, it is focused on explaining social action at the level of the individual and, at the same time, seeking to understand how a person's actions can be explained by the social structure. In contemporary society, young people are searching for meaning, and anomie is a measurement of the degree to which social solidarity or disintegration is experienced in communities. The Chicago school approach fought to understand the deviant within his or her social context rather than adopt a pathological understanding of deviance derived from biology. The early sociologists and criminologists at the University of Chicago looked at collective rituals within urban settings and put forward ways to empirically examine how individuals and groups construct and negotiate social and cultural meaning. As a result, subcultural deviance was explained as a form of behavior within the wider context of social normality.

During the early to mid-20th century, two dominant sociological approaches of social thought were the behavioralist and the functionalist paradigms. Both approaches defined subculture as a negative attribute that promoted delinquency and caused problems for order and consensus in society. Both the American and British theories of subculture located the cause of deviance in biology and psychology. In Britain, the eugenics movement saw the term *subculture* as a means to describe sets of young people defined as subnormal. This understanding was established through the Mental Deficiency Committee (the Wood Committee) in 1929. Policymakers and academics were heavily influenced by the hereditarian interpretation of the eugenics movement and saw subculture as a sign of mental deficiency or social evil. Working-class young people who became part of a subculture were described in depersonalized language as delinquents who were "shiftless" and "subnormal." In Britain, after the Second World War, this evolutionary theory of the delinquent subculture metamorphosed into a psychoanalytical theory of inadequate socialization. Here, psychoanalysis was the driving force behind this view of subculture as a sign of young people's inability to integrate into society, which accelerated their movement into a deviant subculture. Participation within a subculture was identified as a sign of an "affectionless personality," which was defined in social class terms of originating from a deprived culture suffering from psychological problems.

During the 1950s, the most popular and orthodox theory of subculture was developed within the American sociological school of structural functionalism. The general theory of subculture was shaped by two macro theories: first, Durkhiem's theory of anomie and, second, Sigmund Freud's theory of reaction formation. The functionalist theory of subculture placed at its center a theory of deviance, which asserted that delinquency resulted from the interplay between culture and structure caused by differential access to rewards between social classes. This structural strain of the social class system generated deviance due to different levels of access to opportunity. This was first theorized as individual adaptation toward acceptance or refusal of the institutional means to achieve social mobility.

Subsequently, individual adaptation changed to collective adaptation; here, the delinquent subculture is born, whereby movement along the matrix from normal to deviant became a marker of anomie and a sign of subcultural affiliation. It was not only social hierarchy, which created structural strain and the generation of the subcultural identity, it was identified that working-class young people experience status frustration at school.

At the center of the functionalist theory of subculture was a belief in the American Dream. It was argued that the deviant subculture inverts the legitimate aspirational goals of middle-class culture, through the creation of their own delinquent set of values, which then preoccupy young people offering an alternative reward system. Based on an inversion, the normal goals of society get replaced with a delinquent solution. This theory of subculture seeks to explain the motivation for joining a subculture on the basis of a psychoanalytical theory of deviance derived from Freud. The attraction of the functionalist theory of subculture is that it provides an answer for the origin of deviance and labels subcultural members as dysfunctional for society as a result of their inadequate socialization and failure to accept the values of society. A further attraction of this theory relates to its apparent common sense rationale that subcultures are the result of class conflict where working-class youth suffer status frustration because their avenue to social mobility is blocked. While this theory quickly became adopted in the United States and the United Kingdom to become the orthodox interpretation that specified that subculture was a causal link to deviance, a major weakness of the functionalist theory of subculture was its inherent class discrimination. As a theory, it could not explain middle-class deviance because the middle classes were already in possession of status. Only working-class youth became defined as pathological, thereby the model predicted too much proletarian deviance and could not explain middle- or upper-class deviance.

Resistance or Consumer Choice

In Britain, the functionalist theory of subculture became subject to criticism during the 1960s and 1970s from the British National Deviance Conference. In particular, the challenge came from the Centre of Contemporary Cultural Studies (CCCS) at the University of Birmingham, Britain. A range of the contemporary social and cultural approaches influenced the CCCS theory of subculture, including cultural and structural Marxism, literary theory, anthropology, the Chicago school, ethnography, post-structuralism, labeling theory, and psychoanalysis. At the center of the CCCS theory of subculture is resistance and dissent. For this subcultural theory to possess agency, it was linked to the idea of hegemony and placed in the center of the Marxist base and superstructure problematic.

Both the functionalist and the CCCS theory of subculture put great emphasis on social class as a determining factor in the formation and meaning of subculture. Subcultures were defined as working class and emerged from social and class struggle. During the post–Second World War period working-class young people within their communities sought to resolve the social problems and contradictions of change created by harsh material conditions. Within the world of leisure, young people's adoption of subcultural style gave expression and articulation to class experience and became the source of their attempt to resolve the social problems of class tension. The interpretation of subcultural activities by the CCCS theory gave agency to young people who were defined as engaged in counterhegemonic practices. So the theory saw subcultures through the lens of symbolic politics rather than criminality or deviance. A major contribution of the CCCS theory was to separate subculture from delinquency. This enabled youth subcultural style to operate on many platforms and to create identity and express imagination through do-it-yourself practices. Each subculture could demonstrate its own value and meaning through its dress and appearance, objects, music, image, and identity.

One of the problems with the CCCS theory is that while subcultures were engaged in re-creating new forms of class solidarity, this was at the expense of a focus on the role of women in subcultures, and hence, subcultural theory tended to be male centered or even repressive toward women. At the same time, the social issue of race tended to be seen as less relevant by the CCCS theory, although subsequently, through further work at the CCCS, race became identified as a key variable to explain how successive youth subcultures develop and articulate their stylistic practices. One of the reasons why the CCCS theory was less developed in terms of gender and race may be because the core case study ethnographies advanced on teds, mods, and skinheads occurred at the level of literary or textual ethnography rather than through direct empirical observation as in the

anthropological understanding of ethnography. This is not to say that the CCCS failed to undertake ethnographic studies because they clearly did, but in the examples selected to advance their theory of subculture, evidence did not derive from firsthand empirical research.

During the 1990s, an emergent critique of the CCCS theory of subculture developed among theories of postmodernism. By the start of the 21st century, this had turned into a rejection of the concept of subculture advanced under what was termed the *postsubcultural turn*. The criticism put forward of the CCCS theory of subculture included the lack of empirical evidence and the claim that the CCCS did not consider local variations in young people's responses to music and style. Furthermore, postsubculturalists claimed that not only was the CCCS approach theoretically driven, it was also too preoccupied with social class, modernism, and emancipation within a Marxist framework, making it irrelevant to the postmodern age. Thus, a series of new terms to replace *subculture* were proposed, including *tribe*, *neo-tribe*, *postsubculture*, *lifestyle*, and *scene*.

Postsubculturalist theory with its new focus on spatiality, locality, and fluid individual identity wants us to view subcultures more creatively, liberating identity from the subordination of oppression. The aim is to move away from models of social constraint and place increased emphasis on agency. The argument of this new approach to subculture was based on positioning the CCCS theory as a Marxist determinist approach that defined subculture within a totalizing perspective. The foundation of the postsubculturalist theory is based on Weberian concerns fused with contemporary postmodern theory, which argues against grand theory and claims that the social structure is unstable and fragmented. Hence, the postsubcultural position argues that style is expressed through individual consumption and lifestyle rather than its relations to production and struggle. The postmodern argument is focused on particularity and individualism where postsubculturalists assert that subcultural formation and practice are no longer articulated by the modernist structuring relations of class, gender, and race. Subculture is shaped by consumption and individual autonomy through choice. The emphasis of the postsubcultural argument based on individual consumer creativity enables individuals to forge their own identity. Here, subcultures appear to be cut adrift from the social structure, social divisions, and the collectivity of young people's identity. Subculture is reduced to a matter of choice without constraint. This represents an overemphasis on agency. Through seeking to move away from models of social constraints and increased emphasis on agency in subcultural action, the postsubculturalist position aligns with classical neo-liberal ideology; here, individuals pursue entrepreneurial freedom of choice in the subculture supermarket. With little focus on the material experiences of young people, postsubcultural studies tend to marginalize questions of social class and structural inequalities and appear to have little interest in examining social divisions that may generate deviance. In contrast, in the early 21st century, the increased levels of social disturbance by young people and young adults, from micro antisocial behavior to mass rioting, have shown that subcultural identities are shaped through material and social conditions.

The postsubculturalist critique of the CCCS theory has tended to be based on a series of assertions without evidence; for example, it has been claimed by postsubculturalist theorists that academics rather than young people created subcultures. It is ironic that postsubculturalists should argue that little empirical evidence exists to support the CCCS theory of subculture, when it is now admitted by postsubculturalists that few studies have been undertaken to support their own theoretical argument. Furthermore, it was claimed by postsubcultural theorists that subcultures are fragmented and possess no rules, making subcultures depoliticized. It is clear that the development of contemporary subcultural practices among groups of young people who identify with punk, goth, hip-hop, metal, mod, dance, and grime, whether at festivals, concerts, through the Internet, or on the street, reveal that subcultural activities have a strong collective and symbolic presence in culture and society. In contrast, the postsubculturalist advocacy for and take-up of postmodern theory has resulted in an interpretation of subculture that gives priority to the individual over the collective and fails to identify the collective and global basis to subcultures. The reluctance to focus on structural inequalities and material differences among young people in subcultures reduces the understanding of how the social structure influences the formation of subculture. In this sense, postsubculturalist analysis amounts to a mirror reflection of a consumer-driven ideology of neo-liberalism. The response to the postsubcultural critique of subculture has resulted in a defense of the concept, and in the United States and Britain, there have been a series of suggestions to fuse together elements of both approaches to the concept. But even those theorists who previously argued for the rejection of the concept of subculture have moved their argument to acknowledge that the likelihood is that subculture will remain significant as a concept within both criminology and sociology.

Conclusion

Subculture fits within a field of knowledge that is both historical and contemporary but also contested. It can be suggested that the different approaches to understanding subculture from each sociological paradigm are still in operation today both within the wider social community and within academic discourse. As a concept, subculture captures the popular imagination because it is most associated with young people and deviance through representations of the outsider. Because subcultures are often linked to fashion and style this guarantees attention, which gives them an appeal of immediacy and their association with deviance or alternative modes of life can be suggestive of danger. Thus, the concept is heavy with meaning, even excitement, because through the application of the concept, a certain group in society is labeled, identified, and put before us to be read.

Shane Blackman

See also Argot; Authenticity; Code of the Street; Focal Concerns Theory; Prison Culture/Inmate Code

Further Readings

Bennett, A. (2011). The post-subcultural turn: Some reflections 10 years on. *Journal of Youth Studies, 14*(5), 493–506.

Blackman, S. J. (2004). *Chilling out: The cultural politics of substance consumption, youth and drug policy.* New York, NY: McGraw-Hill.

Cohen, A. (1956). *Delinquent boys: The subculture of the gang.* London, England: Collier Macmillan.

Hall, S., & Jefferson, T. (Eds.). (2006). *Resistance through rituals.* London, England: Hutchinson and Centre for Contemporary Cultural Studies, University of Birmingham. (Original work published 1975)

Hart, C. (Ed.). (2010). *The legacy of the Chicago school of sociology.* Kingswinsford, England: Midrash.

Hebdige, D. (1979). *Subculture: The meaning of style.* London, England: Methuen.

Muggleton, D. (2000). *Inside subcultures: The postmodern meaning of style.* London, England: Berg.

Shildrick, T., & MacDonald, R. (2006). In defence of subculture: Young people, leisure and social divisions. *Journal of Youth Studies, 9*(2), 125–140.

Williams, P. (2011). *Subcultural theory.* Cambridge, England: Polity Press.

SUICIDE

The term *suicidal behavior* is used to categorize various forms of suicidal-related phenomena, including suicide attempt, suicidal ideation, and suicide. According to the Centers for Disease Control and Prevention, *suicide attempt* refers to nonfatal behavior with the potential to injure oneself with the intention of death. Such behaviors may or may not result in an individual being physically harmed. Consideration, thoughts of, or planning suicide attempts or suicide commonly describes *suicidal ideation*. *Suicide* is a form of self-directed violence, where death is the intended result of self-inflicted injury. Acts of suicide have been recorded in almost all cultures throughout history and contribute considerably to global mortality and morbidity rates. Globally, suicide remains an important issue of public interest and health policy. Suicide is commonly characterized as a taboo or stigmatized topic that is not often openly discussed. Despite the serious emotional impact that suicide has on the family, friends, and acquaintances of the deceased individual, societal and cultural attitudes concerning suicide vary. The purpose of this entry is to provide a broad overview of the topic of suicide. Specifically, it begins with an examination of the history and prevalence of suicidal behaviors. It then addresses associations between suicide and self-harm, risk and protective factors for suicidal behavior, media reporting of suicidal behavior, and individual- and population-focused approaches to suicide prevention.

History of Suicidal Behaviors

Historical evidence shows that acts of suicide have been practiced throughout recorded human history. Perhaps one of the earliest popular historical depictions of suicide involves the death of Cleopatra of Egypt, who, it was alleged, willed a venomous snake to bite her in an intentional act to end her life. Since that time, a number of historical figures, including military leaders and biblical figures, have reportedly died by acts of suicide (e.g., Hannibal, Judas Iscariot). In the modern age, the deaths of notable public figures, such as artists, scientists, and authors, have also been attributed to suicide (e.g., Vincent van Gogh, Sigmund Freud). More recently, the suicides of renowned musicians and actors have received extensive media coverage, leading to debate surrounding the media reporting of suicides. Philosophical discussions centering on the topic of suicide date back to the Ancient Greeks. In particular, both Plato and Aristotle expressed their opposition to suicide in their writings. Similarly, a range of influential scholars and philosophers, including Immanuel Kant and Émile Durkheim, have proposed arguments both for and against the act of suicide.

Prevalence of Suicidal Behaviors

Calculating the number of completed suicides each year is a challenging and often imprecise task. First, due to the nature of some suicide methods (e.g., motor vehicle accident or drowning) and in the absence of a suicide note, it is often difficult for authorities to determine whether a death was accidental or intentional. Second, social or cultural factors may encourage the underreporting of suicides, particularly in regions where suicide may be highly stigmatized. Making meaningful comparisons of suicide rates between countries can be difficult due to differences in procedures for classifying and reporting suicide and an absence of data from many regions. Nonetheless, the World Health Organization (WHO) estimates that nearly 1 million people complete suicide each year. Suicide is listed as one of the top three causes of mortality for youth in many nations. Historically, global rates of suicide fluctuate and appear to be influenced by a variety of major events (e.g., war, economic downturns, famine). The WHO estimates that worldwide suicide rates have increased by up to 60% within the past 45 years and that suicide will account for more than 2% of global disease burden by the second decade of the 21st century. The rate of nonfatal suicide attempts is believed to be far greater than completed suicides; however, as many survivors of suicide attempts will not subsequently seek medical or psychological treatment, precise numbers cannot be calculated. Nonetheless, the WHO reports that nonfatal suicide attempts may be 10 to 20 times more common than completed suicides. Based on this figure, it can be assumed that nonfatal suicide attempts contribute immensely to global morbidity through injury and permanent disablement.

Associations Between Self-Harm and Suicide

Self-harm or injury without lethal intent is a behavior often categorized alongside suicide due to its association with suicidal behavior. Self-harm refers to self-injuring behavior that may or may not involve suicidal intent. Another similar definition is intentional and self-inflicted injury where death is not the intended result, for example, self-mutilation. Self-harm often has its origins in early adolescence; however, patterns of self-harm commonly decrease during adulthood. Globally, self-harm is reportedly more common for females than for males. Self-harm is believed to be far more prevalent than suicide despite scarce statistics, owing to relatively few individuals presenting at hospital following self-harm behavior. Despite these two behaviors differing in many respects, they are by no means mutually exclusive, with many individuals engaging in both self-harm and suicidal behavior.

Risk Factors for Suicidal Behaviors

Factors contributing to suicidal behaviors have been studied by many researchers. A wide range of factors arising from within individual, family, school, and societal domains have been proposed to increase an individual's likelihood of attempting or completing suicide. However, the relationship between these factors and the outcome of suicide is complex. Importantly, these factors are not necessarily direct causes of suicidal behavior but rather may be associated with engagement in this behavior.

Individual factors of interest to suicide researchers include gender, age, ethnicity, and sexual orientation. In comparison to other individual factors, gender patterns of suicidal behavior appear to be relatively stable. Although females are more likely than males to *attempt* suicide, a greater number of males *complete* suicide annually. This pattern is explained in part by the methods chosen for these attempts, with males more likely to choose highly lethal methods in contrast to females who may choose methods offering a greater chance of survival. Similarly, the age at which most suicides occur has fluctuated over time. Recent data from the WHO demonstrates that men aged 15 to 45 years are at greatest risk of completing suicide. Other individual factors of interest include mental health and disorder, substance use, and some antisocial behaviors. For instance, numerous studies have shown a high prevalence of mental illness in individuals who attempt or complete suicide.

Family characteristics identified as potential contributors to suicidal behavior include social disadvantage, family history of suicidal behavior, childhood abuse, and poor family relationships. For example, vicarious exposure to suicide is reported to increase suicide risk. In particular, children of a parent who completed suicide are more likely to attempt or complete suicide themselves. Particularly for adolescents, family factors, such as poor emotional relationships with parents, parental separation and divorce, and parental mental disorder, have been cited as potential contributory factors for suicidal behavior. School factors are also recognized as potential influences for suicidal behavior in adolescents. Commonly described factors include low rates of school attendance, low levels of school achievement and performance, and lack of acceptance and support provided by peers. Unemployment, war, economic downturns, and drought or famine are commonly mentioned societal factors.

Protective Factors for Suicidal Behaviors

Some researchers have also studied factors that may decrease the likelihood of, or protect individuals from, engagement in suicidal behaviors. In particular, these factors include the following: higher levels of social cohesion, the development of positive coping and problem-solving skills, provision of health care services for mental disorders, access to avenues for help-seeking, and provision of ongoing health care. Studies examining protective factors are relatively rare, and so, it is unclear how specific risk and protective factors act in combination to reduce engagement in suicidal behavior.

Media Reporting of Suicidal Behavior

Media reporting of suicidal behavior is a contentious topic, given that research suggests the widespread reporting of suicide may serve to increase suicide rates. This is particularly relevant following the completed suicide of a public figure or celebrity. Increased suicide by readers of Johann Wolfgang von Goethe's *The Sorrows of Young Werther* in the late 18th century is widely believed to be the first documented instance of this phenomenon. Hence, when the media reports a death by suicide, details such as the location or method may not be disclosed. The media can sensationalize as well as inform the public of suicide methods. A number of studies have documented increased suicide rates using specific methods in the wake of detailed reporting of suicide methods. For this reason, many nations enforce strict media codes of ethics governing exactly what details can be reported in the event of a suicide. Modern approaches include providing information about support services following reports of suicide in media.

Preventing Suicidal Behavior

In comparison to many other causes of death such as illness or accidents, suicide is viewed as being largely preventable. The task of preventing and reducing suicide requires a multifaceted approach. Approaches to the prevention of suicide can generally be divided into two distinct types: public health and individual.

Public health approaches focus on the general population and aim to decrease suicide rates by reducing the ease with which members of the population are able to complete suicide. In particular, these approaches have focused on suicide methods deemed to be particularly lethal. Commonly known as means-restriction approaches, examples have included removing carbon monoxide from household gas supplies, constructing fences or barriers on bridges and train stations known to be suicide hotspots, stocking certain products (i.e., poisons or pharmaceuticals) behind the counter so that sales can be controlled, and placing restrictions and cooling-off periods on the sale of firearms. Despite the widely held belief that suicidal individuals will simply substitute their preferred method for another more accessible method, evidence suggests this is often not the case. For many individuals, intense thoughts of suicide are fleeting; thus, restricting access to highly accessible and lethal methods can reduce impulsive acts of suicide in many regions. Furthermore, restricting suicide methods proven to have a low survival rate may see individuals choose alternative methods that are less lethal than the restricted method, providing a greater chance of survival (e.g., some types of medication overdoses).

Individual approaches aim to identify individuals who may be at an increased risk of attempting suicide and intervene to reduce the likelihood of this outcome. Accurately identifying individuals who may be at an increased risk of suicide is challenging. Many people who experience suicidal thoughts may hide their feelings from others or plan their suicide in a covert manner to avoid raising the suspicion or concern of friends and family. Although the task of determining whether an individual is at risk of suicide is imprecise at best, a number of psychiatric screening tests have been designed for this purpose. Additionally, many countries provide 24-hour suicide prevention telephone services offering support and counseling to individuals who may be at risk of attempting suicide. Unfortunately, due to societal taboos and associated stigma, many nations neglect to make efforts to address this issue. However, online support services for at-risk individuals and persons bereaved by suicide are becoming more readily accessible.

Jessica A. Heerde, David Broderick, and Sheryl A. Hemphill

See also Mental Illness; Self-Injury

Further Readings

Crosby, A. E., Ortega, L., & Melanson, C. (2011). *Self-directed violence surveillance: Uniform definitions and recommended data elements* (Version 1.0) [Computer software]. Atlanta, GA: Centers for Disease Control and Prevention, National Center for Injury Prevention and Control.

Evans, E., Hawton, K., & Rodham, K. (2004). Factors associated with suicidal phenomena in adolescents: A systematic review of population-based studies. *Clinical Psychology Review, 24*, 957–979.

Owens, D., Horrocks, J., & House, A. (2002). Fatal and nonfatal repetition of self harm: Systematic review. *British Journal of Psychiatry, 181*, 193–199.

Pitman, A., Krysinska, K., Osborn, D., & King, M. (2012). Suicide in young men. *Lancet, 379*, 2383–2392.

Wagner, B. M. (1997). Family risk factors for child and adolescent suicidal behavior. *Psychological Bulletin, 121*(2), 246–298.

World Health Organization. (2012). *Public health action for the prevention of suicide: A framework*. Geneva, Switzerland: Author.

Yip, P. S., Caine, E., Yousuf, S., Chang, S., Wu, K. C., & Chen, Y. Y. (2012). Means restriction for suicide prevention. *Lancet, 379*, 2393–2399.

SUSPENSION

Flesh hook suspension involves the hanging of an individual from hooks that have been inserted either through the skin or existing body piercing. Suspensions take place in front of a small group or at a performance with a larger gathering. Although suspension rituals were customary in some cultures, in modern-day American culture, they are considered a deviation from the norm, practiced by a distinct subculture. This entry discusses the history of, explanations for, and the process and impacts of the practice of suspension.

History

This practice has a long and diverse history. Countries such as India, Sri Lanka, and Malaysia have histories that include suspension rituals. Over time, these customs have become less prevalent. Research also indicates that Native Americans had suspension practices. The Mandan tribe lived in what is now North Dakota and South Dakota. Their spirit-seeking O-Kee-Pa suspension ceremonies were part of a culture that viewed suffering and pain as a necessity. The ceremonies lasted for four days and were split into three main parts. The final ceremony was reserved for young men entering manhood. The object of this ceremony was to enter a state in which the young men would meet the "Great Spirit" to obtain healing or special knowledge. Although this practice could be viewed as torture, this ritual also had functional aspects. It was believed to harden the young men's muscles, teach them physical endurance, and allow tribal elders to compare the men's strength to see who would be the best leader of future war parties.

In a similar rite called the Sun Dance, Sioux Indian males were pierced much like those in the Mandan tribes; except, once they were pierced, they were attached to a tree. Their weight would pull against the tree until the piercings were pulled loose, and they were freed. Through this painful process, the men entered a trance where they received healing or special knowledge. Through this ritual, the men experienced "death." When one has completed this ceremony, he is "reborn." Today, these ancient rites of passage are used as a model for contemporary suspension rituals. For instance, the O-Kee-Pa suspension, a vertical suspension hooked from the chest, is one of the popular styles used in modern-day rituals. The mechanics of the suspension may have changed with new technology, but the behavior is rooted in Native American rituals.

Explanations

Contemporary research finds that there are many reasons for suspending. Many are drawn to suspending through contact with the body modification subculture. Through body modification, these individuals are exposed to a subculture where suspensions are regularly practiced, sometimes known as "modern primitives." This group engages in body modification that explicitly references primitive cultural practices. However, there are a variety of motivations behind suspending. Some want to push the boundaries of their bodies or to experience the pleasure and feelings of freedom described by their friends. Others believe that a suspension may help them gain insight and test their physical and mental abilities to prove to themselves that they can do anything. Curiosity and fascination have moved some into suspensions. Others attempt suspensions as a way to celebrate a specific turning point in their lives. They understand that they have overcome an important obstacle and want to express their gratitude by suspending. Some use suspensions as a coping mechanism. Others have gone so far as to professionalize suspensions, presenting it as performance art. They suspend for crowds and love the "rush" that they get when they perform.

Process

Preparation is critical for a successful suspension. Since suspensions have become more structured, more work goes into the preparation and performance of a suspension. Once a person has decided he or she wants to suspend, the person is expected to find a location for the event. The right amount of space is needed to fit the rig, which is the equipment that hoists the suspender in the air. In the past, the rigging was done with separate ropes attached to hooks that latched to a specific point on the body. However, a new system of rigging has been developed that is more reliable and safe. This new system employs a single rope through a system of links, eye bolts, and/or pulleys to allow the hooks to reach a state of equilibrium. There are two types of rigging: static and dynamic. Static rigging involves multiple ropes that secure to individual hooks, which allow the body to stay in a secure position. In dynamic rigging, there is one rope that is laced into several hooks, which allows for faster setup and more movement. The rig is built with specifications according to the individual's weight and height. Most suspenders are also expected to find people who are willing to build the rig for their suspension. Through the organization process, the suspender signals his or her commitment to others within the subculture. However, there are those who engage in a suspension only after viewed by a witness at a suspension event.

The suspender also must decide what kind of suspension he or she will do, how many hooks will be pierced into the skin, and where the hooks will be placed. There are many different types of suspension. They include the suicide suspension, which is a vertical suspension hooked from the upper back, named because it looks as if the person has been hanged. There is the coma suspension, which is a horizontal suspension hooked from the front of the body; the person floats on his or her back, as if in an isolation tank. The Superman suspension, where the hooks are placed on the back of the body, is made to look as though a person is flying. There is also the sitting suspension, where a person is pierced and hung in a sitting position, and the O-Kee-Pa suspension (described earlier). Each suspension requires a different number of piercings. The number of hooks can range from 1 to 30.

Another way that individuals prepare for a suspension is to develop the right frame of mind for the event. An air of excitement tends to surround the time leading up to the suspension. However, some postpone this stage of the process until the period immediately before they suspend. They then isolate themselves from the group, allowing themselves time and space to contemplate the event and to channel their anxieties. Fasting, abstinence, and hydration are common. Emotional or spiritual preparation through meditation is also customary.

Usually a team is assembled by the suspender to assist him or her with the suspension. The team includes friends, family, and/or acquaintances, if they are familiar with the process. A high level of trust is needed for those who assist with the suspension. Those with suspension experience help coach those who are being pierced, to alleviate the suspender's fear and anxiety. In addition, these individuals play an important part in reducing the medical risks that accompany this kind of endeavor. Safety precautions are taken seriously, so those who suspend are made aware of the risks for shock, seizures, and unconsciousness before the piercing begins. Once the suspender is ready, the hooks, which are usually 10-gauge stainless steel, are pierced throughout the body, including the arms, back, chest, and legs. The skin is cleaned and marked for the positioning of the hooks. Piercing the skin requires the insertion of a needle, such as a 10-gauge needle, and then the hooks replace the needle. Because of the risks, a kind of checks-and-balances system has been implemented. Suspenders are asked numerous times if they are ready and if they are sure they want to

go through with the experience. The suspension can last from 10 minutes to more than an hour. Physical tension and pain accompanies suspending because the skin is stretched as it latches on to the hooks to support the weight of the body. Even though great care is taken in sterilizing all of the materials used for the suspension, there are physical side effects that cannot be avoided. A team of experts has to be familiar with the early signs of shock, seizure, and nausea. These signs may develop during the piercing or the initial lifting of the body. The safety of those suspending is always a priority.

There are several elements that can enhance the intensity of the sensations during a suspension. Physical movement, such as spinning and swinging, allows the suspender to alter the physical sensation of the suspension, intensifying the pain as the suspender wishes. Music is another element that augments this ritual. Music can also help set the tone for the suspension. For some, music enables them to forget about the pain. Those who suspend are able to request songs to be played during the event. While the main goal is to achieve a feeling of freedom and happiness, many feel closer to those friends or family who are present or to those who assist during their suspension.

When he or she is ready, the individual is lowered, the hooks are removed, and the wounds are cleaned and bandaged. Air bubbles can become trapped under the stretched skin; therefore, the skin has to be massaged to release the air. Participants call these air pockets "rice krispies" (because of the crackling sounds made when trapped air is released). The suspension team squeezes the back and other pierced body parts to help prevent infection and soreness. Accompanying the rice krispies are bleeding, swelling, numbness, bruising, and itching.

Implications

Participants claim that suspensions can change a person both mentally and physically. After their suspension, people recount the physical pain their body went through and the mental images and feelings that developed. Some participants have a renewed outlook on life and look at their experience as an antidote for their problems. The involvement of both novices and regulars creates an atmosphere of encouragement and solidarity, which works to acculturate individuals into the subculture. Many acknowledge that the sense of unity they feel throughout the suspension process remains positive even after the suspension has ended.

After the suspension experience, many participants feel that they are now able to think on a "higher level." Many indicate feeling more positive and happier after the suspension. Because of the intense nature of the suspension experience, some participants lose the thrill they once received from the minor forms of body modification and begin to experiment further with more radical forms, such as tattooing, scarification, implants, plastic surgery, piercings, and so on. There are also physical reminders of the event. Scars may develop where the suspension hooks were inserted. Many look forward to this, hoping for a token from their experience. Like the ancient Mandan tribe, most wear these scars as a badge of honor.

Jessica Simpson Pearce

See also Body Modification; Tattooing

Further Readings

Atkinson, M. (2001). Neo primitives and the contemporary rediscovery of radical body modification. *Deviant Behavior, 22,* 117–146.

Atkinson, M. (2004). Figuring out body modification cultures: Interdependence and radical body modification processes. *Health, 8,* 373–379.

Becker, H. (1963). *Outsiders.* New York, NY: Free Press.

Forsyth, C. J., & Simpson, J. (2008). Everything changes once you hang: Flesh hook suspensions. *Deviant Behavior, 29*(4), 367–387.

Goode, E., & Vail, D. A. (2008). *Extreme deviance.* Thousand Oaks, CA: Pine Forge Press.

Lyng, S. (1990). Edgework: A social psychological analysis of voluntary risk taking. *American Journal of Sociology, 95,* 851–886.

Musafar, F. (1997). Flesh hooks: Some historical perspective. *Body Play and Modern Primitives Quarterly, 4,* 4–9.

Pitts, V. (2003). *In the flesh: The cultural politics of body modification.* New York, NY: Palgrave Macmillan.

Swinging

Swinging, or extradyadic sex, refers to a practice whereby committed partners engage in consensual sexual activities with other committed couples. The most common motivations for swinging include sexual variety and fantasy fulfillment. Swinging is contrasted with infidelity because it does not involve partner betrayal. In other words, partners mutually participate in sexual activities without dishonesty or secrecy. Compared with infidelity, swinging has more positive outcomes such as enhanced relational, sexual, and life satisfaction. Infidelity, by contrast, is associated with negative outcomes such as depression, anger, partner violence, relationship dissolution, and homicide. Although jealousy is associated with both swinging and infidelity, swingers are more likely to manage their jealousy and/or transfer it into positive sexual experiences. After describing the prevalence and characteristics of swinging, this entry discusses several theories that have been used to explain swinging and assess whether it is deviant.

Prevalence

Swinging has been enacted across historical periods but was not scientifically studied until the late 1960s. It is difficult to identify the current number of swingers in the U.S. population because of sampling bias (e.g., social stigma influencing reports), but estimates range from 2% to 15%, depending on the source. Researchers commonly report rates from 2% to 4%, whereas the North American Swing Club Association provides estimates closer to 15%. Swingers typically partake in extradyadic sex several times a year, and partners are most commonly located online and through swinger-specific clubs, vacation packages, and conventions. Swinging occurs in regions across the world and has been examined by researchers in North America, the United Kingdom, Europe, and Asia.

Characteristics of Swingers

On average, swingers tend to be middle aged (average age = 40 years), White, college educated, middle or upper class, and politically conservative (i.e., Republican). Apart from their political views, swingers hold liberal attitudes regarding sex, abortion, gender roles, and sexual orientation. A large percentage of swinging women are bisexual, whereas the majority of swinging men are heterosexual. In terms of psychological characteristics and emotional stability, swingers do not differ from the nonswinging population.

Theoretical Perspectives on Swinging

A variety of theories have been used to explain swinging. Here, three theories are presented with different foci: symbolic interaction, evolutionary psychology, and social exchange. Much research on mate selection and relationship patterns has been guided by these theories. Symbolic interaction is macro and cultural in its focus, assuming that individuals develop meanings and identities through socialization. Evolutionary psychology is more focused at the individual level and assumes that people are born with genetic predispositions that affect their beliefs and practices. Finally, social exchange is focused in between these perspectives at the dyadic level and assumes that individuals seek to maximize rewards and minimize costs in their relationships.

Symbolic Interaction

One of the best theories for investigating how cultural meanings influence social behavior is symbolic interaction. According to this theory, individuals develop meanings about themselves and relationships through socialization. The theory assumes that a person's self-concept, including his or her values and beliefs, guides behavior. However, human actions are often constrained by social norms, and in general, individuals choose behaviors that correspond with the values and norms of their culture. Finally, individuals do not passively respond to their environment. Instead, they interact with people on a daily basis and influence social settings through the subjective meanings they assign to their interactions.

From a symbolic interaction perspective, the practice of swinging is considered socially deviant. In North America, committed partners are expected to be monogamous. This shared meaning is derived from the norms and practices of the society, including religious prescriptions, which are transmitted through socialization. An examination of the wedding ritual helps illustrate how shared meaning systems are socially created and maintained. In North America, weddings typically involve a church and minister (representing the sanctity of marriage), a white dress (representing virginity and birth), wedding rings (representing eternal love), vows (representing promises to one's spouse, including monogamy), and a celebration (representing the importance of family and friends in the couple's life). When people attend weddings, they expect to see these symbols and recognize, whether consciously or not, the meanings associated with them. This example demonstrates the clash between societal expectations regarding committed relationships and the practice of swinging. Research supports the view that nonswingers judge swingers harshly. For instance, swingers are inaccurately perceived

as socially deviant not only with respect to sexual activity but also in terms of drug use, psychological problems, and history of abuse.

Evolutionary Psychology

Evolutionary psychology is different from symbolic interaction because it examines genetic, rather than cultural, influences on behavior. The genetic patterns that are prevalent in the population today have evolved over thousands of years and are thought to have been advantageous for humans who lived in hunter-gatherer societies. According to this theory, humans are primarily concerned with reproduction and passing on their genes to as many healthy offspring as possible. Men and women differ in the amount of time needed for this task. Men have a goal of dispersing their genes to numerous women in the hopes of producing maximal numbers of offspring. The amount of time needed for successful reproduction is small and might only involve a single occasion of intercourse. Women, on the other hand, generally have responsibilities for both bearing (9 months) and raising children (18+ years). Unlike men, parental certainty for women is guaranteed due to internal fertilization. Although DNA tests provide one means of determining biological relatedness, they have yet to be used as a common method of determining paternity. Therefore, women are more likely to focus on quality, rather than quantity in selecting their mates.

Traditionally, evolutionary psychologists assumed men would be more likely than women to engage in extradyadic sex because they have more to gain from promiscuous interactions. In other words, men who mate with numerous women would produce more offspring than men who mate with few women. However, birth control methods provide an example of how modern social norms interact with inherited traits to influence behavior, particularly for women. It is commonly assumed that due to their greater investment in offspring, women avoid risky sexual behaviors, such as swinging, for fear of pregnancy. Recently though, advances in contraception enable women to engage in sex without the risk of pregnancy that existed in the past. In addition, women who have multiple sex partners without using contraception experience an evolutionary advantage due to sperm competition. With more than one man's sperm competing for egg fertilization, the strongest sperm should win out, thereby producing the most genetically fit offspring.

Despite the genetic benefits of promiscuous sex for both men and women, factors that interfere with reproduction must be considered. The risks associated with contracting HIV/AIDS (human immunodeficiency virus/acquired immune deficiency syndrome), in particular, have caused individuals to become more conservative in their sexual practices. Another factor discouraging promiscuous sex relates to cultural norms. Individuals who opt for a swinging lifestyle risk social rejection. This is likely one reason why swingers have formed their own subculture, which includes an overarching association (North American Swing Club Association), online forums, and swinger-specific clubs, vacations, and events. Overall then, mating with multiple partners might be beneficial for reproductive fitness, but it is associated with potentially negative outcomes as well. Individuals who partake in this lifestyle must evaluate the benefits as well as the costs. A good theory for examining how romantic partners rationally weigh such pros and cons is social exchange.

Social Exchange

According to social exchange, individuals seek to maximize their rewards and minimize costs in intimate relationships. Rewards refer to the benefits obtained from a partner that fulfill one's needs and provide satisfaction and enjoyment. Needs are subjectively evaluated and vary depending on the person. For example, one person might consider sexual satisfaction to be important in maintaining happiness and fulfillment, whereas another person might place high importance on financial security. Individuals will feel satisfied if their partner is able to fulfill their important needs. Costs refer to expenditures or rewards that are unavailable due to one's involvement in a relationship. Satisfying relationships are ones in which the rewards exceed the costs. If an individual is responsible for the rewarding outcomes experienced by his or her partner, the partner will feel dependent on the individual. If both partners are responsible for the rewarding outcomes experienced by the other, a state of mutual dependency exists. Individuals who are in costly relationships and who have attractive alternative partners will be less dependent on the partner and more likely to commit infidelity or dissolve the partnership.

Social exchange principles have been used to explain relationship commitment. A predominant model explains commitment according to the collective influence of satisfaction, alternative partners, and relationship investments. As mentioned, satisfaction results from having a partner who exceeds one's expectations in terms of need fulfillment. Alternatives refer to individuals who may be able to provide greater rewards than a current partner. Investments refer to the amount of irretrievable resources put into a relationship and can include time, money, intimate disclosures, and linking one's identity to a partner. Investments strengthen commitment because they increase the costs of relationship dissolution. Therefore, a committed individual will perceive high levels of satisfaction and investments and few good alternatives to the relationship.

Using social exchange theory and the commitment model, it is possible to demonstrate how swinging benefits relationships. Swingers experience heightened satisfaction because partners are meeting each other's needs for intimacy and sexual variety. The quality of alternatives is low because people in the general population are typically unwilling to participate in swinging activities, which reduces the chances of finding a more well-suited partner. Swingers are also investing in their relationships in terms of time, money (e.g., vacation packages, convention attendance), intimate disclosures, and linking their identity to a relationship. Each of these factors bolsters relationship commitment and protects from dissolution.

Conclusion

In this entry, three theories were presented to illuminate distinct perspectives on swinging. Symbolic interaction identifies swinging as a socially deviant practice that violates North American cultural norms regarding committed relationships. Evolutionary psychology indicates that swinging is advantageous for maximizing the reproductive fitness of both men and women. However, deterrents such as HIV/AIDS, as well as cultural norms discouraging promiscuous sex, interfere with practices that may have been advantageous thousands of years ago. Today, promiscuous sex must be considered in conjunction with its costs. Social exchange theory describes swinging as a beneficial practice that enhances partners' satisfaction and commitment. This perspective is supported by research indicating that swingers tend to be happier than nonswingers in both their relationships and life.

Is swinging socially deviant? The only theory supporting this view is symbolic interaction, which demonstrates that North American cultural values conflict with a swinging lifestyle. Swingers have responded by developing their own communities within the broader culture. By identifying with this microculture, rather than society at large, swingers may reconcile feelings of deviance. If macrolevel cultural norms were to become less restrictive, swinging would no longer be perceived as a deviant practice. High rates of infidelity and divorce suggest that monogamy may not be in the genes, and given that swinging occurs in cultures all over the world, it appears to be a genetically motivated behavior. Therefore, it is important to examine the benefits associated with swinging and recognize that this lifestyle may be particularly advantageous if safe sex is practiced.

Kelly Campbell

See also Bisexuality; Fetishes; Intersexuality; Public Sex

Further Readings

Barash, D. P., & Lipton, J. E. (2001). *The myth of monogamy.* New York, NY: W. H. Freeman.

Barber, N. (2003). Divorce and reduced economic and emotional interdependence: A cross national study. *Journal of Divorce and Remarriage, 39,* 113–124.

Buss, D. M. (1998). Sexual strategies theory: Historical origins and current status. *Journal of Sex Research, 35,* 19–31.

Campbell, K., & Wright, D. W. (2010). Marriage today: Exploring the incongruence between Americans' beliefs and practices. *Journal of Comparative Family Studies, 41*(3), 329–345.

De Visser, R., & McDonald, D. (2007). Swings and roundabouts: Management of jealousy in heterosexual "swinging" couples. *British Journal of Social Psychology, 46*(2), 459–476.

Fernandes, E. M. (2009). The swinging paradigm: An evaluation of the marital and sexual satisfaction of swingers. *Electronic Journal of Human Sexuality, 12.*

Jenks, R. J. (1998). Swinging: A review of the literature. *Archives of Sexual Behavior, 27,* 507–521.

Rusbult, C. E., Martz, J. M., & Agnew, C. R. (1998). The investment model scale: Measuring commitment level, satisfaction level, quality of alternatives, and investment size. *Personal Relationships, 5,* 357–391.

Symbolic Crusade

The concept of the symbolic crusade comes from Joseph Gusfield's 1963 book of the same name, in which Gusfield advances the theory that the U.S. movement for Prohibition was not essentially a movement to stop the drinking of alcohol. Rather, it was a class conflict that took the form of a political assault on poor urban immigrants' way of life by the traditional Protestant middle class whose values had dominated the U.S. culture since the early 19th century. Although the book focuses on the temperance movement that supported Prohibition, it is applicable to other movements, social problems, and moral panics that present as crusades but may be a guise for mass social action. Movements supporting "blue laws" or abortion rights are masks for cultural wars; hence, the movements are symbolic.

The American temperance movement started in the 1820s, continued with the founding of the Women's Christian Temperance Union in 1874 and the Anti-Saloon League in 1896, and peaked in 1919 with the passage of the Eighteenth Amendment and the Volstead Act. Gusfield's theory, as applied to the temperance movement, concerns the relations between three main components: (1) temperance attitudes, (2) the organized temperance movement, and (3) the conflict between the different subcultures in American society.

Critical to understanding this historical theory is the difference between the instrumental and symbolic character of law. The instrumental function of law lies in its enforcement; without enforcement, law has little effect on people's behavior. The symbolic aspects of laws and government acts do not depend on enforcement for their effect. Rather, they affect the designation of public norms. A legal decision or legislative act is a gesture that often glorifies the values of one group and demeans those of another. Public affirmation of a moral norm directs the major institutions of the society to its support. Each act affects the status of one group over another. Those who support a current moral norm are seen as having higher status than those who support a moral norm that lacks the support of law.

In the 1820s, the United States was dominated by the old middle class—a white, orthodox Protestant, rural/agricultural culture. Members of the middle class adhered to a value system in which self-control, industriousness, and impulse denial were praised and deemed necessary. They respected temperance norms. Sobriety was considered virtuous and necessary in a community dominated by middle-class Protestants. The New England Federalists, who had held power since the nation was founded, were the political representation of the old middle class.

These cultural ideals/norms did not need the support of law because they were accepted without opposition. It is not until a group opposes the norm that the support of law becomes necessary.

Opposing this cultural/class domain were the Irish Catholic immigrants who began arriving in the 1820s, and in the decades that followed, there were successive waves of immigrants from the largely Catholic countries of southern and Eastern Europe. Mass immigration and rapid industrial growth led to a marked increase in the U.S. urban population and, thus, a demographic and political shift that presented a direct challenge to the prestige and power of the middle class. It is against this background that the increasing pressure toward legal prohibition of alcohol can perhaps best be understood.

Until 1920, when the sale and transportation of alcoholic beverages became prohibited by law in the United States, many urban immigrants would meet in taverns and saloons not only to socialize but also to discuss local political issues, organize campaigns and other political activities, and pursue political aims. Such establishments were of course where patrons drank alcohol, an essential component of their traditional culture. This cultural trait (i.e., drinking in public) stood in direct contrast to the Protestant middle class who supported a nondrinking norm by drinking—if at all—in private. In reaction, and fueled by anti-immigrant sentiment, moral entrepreneurs from the middle class founded the Anti-Saloon League, supporting the nondrinking norm by public adherence. Recent immigrants, however, did not support the norm. This became the proverbial line in the sand dividing the two groups. As Gusfield notes, the Anti-Saloon League, which strenuously advocated for Prohibition, was not so much against drinking as it was a response to a perceived threat to the political power of the middle class. Thus, urban immigrants became designated as deviants because they were disobeying the norms of the dominant culture. From this it can be seen that the analysis of any instance of the violation of a social norm (i.e., social deviance) requires a clear understanding of the symbolic character of the norm itself.

Assimilative and Coercive Reform

To force people to obey norms of which they do not approve, it is often necessary to dominate them. This can be accomplished by *assimilative reform* (i.e., by using prestige). In the first few decades of the 20th century, assimilative reform failed because the immigrants did not accept the status of the temperance supporters' culture. There is a paradox here. Although the temperance supporters appeared to want immigrants to stop drinking, in reality, they wanted them to fail. By failing to abstain from drinking, immigrants would have to admit their inferiority to those they were trying to emulate. Thus, according to Gusfield, the middle class were not true reformers. Alcohol reform was not just a political crusade; it was a morality that was misused.

In the 19th century, drinking *any* alcohol was viewed as a moral problem, not as a disease, as the *abuse* of alcohol often is seen today. In the U.S. society of that period, drinking alcohol signified flawed values that placed desire over reason, impulsivity over self-control, and immediate pleasure over delayed gratification. According to the Protestant ethic, any behavior that failed to improve and perfect man's ability to progress and better himself as a producer of goods and performer of services was sinful. If a man drank, he was often not given a good job or a loan because he was deemed unreliable. So if you drank, you were by definition low class. If, however, you deny anyone who is a drinker the avenues for success and then declare he is unsuccessful because he is a drinker, this is a self-fulfilling prophecy, which means the prediction will be the result. One way a man could "prove" he was not a drinker was to join the temperance movement and, of course, only drink in private. Alcohol reform, then, became a method by which the dominant class could further exert power over the urban immigrant class, whose culture clashed with their own.

If assimilative reform fails, then one can dominate by force and authority, or coercive reform. Coercive reform emerges when the object of reform is seen as an intractable defender of another culture; someone who rejects the reformers' values and in reality does not want to change. Coercive force means forcing morals or legislating morality; that is, coercing the public definition of what is moral and respectable through the use of laws. Laws against drinking were passed in every state; the apex of these laws is the Eighteenth Amendment.

Types of Deviants

The focal point of the idea of a symbolic crusade is that the designators of deviant behavior react differently to various norm-sustaining implications of an act. Gusfield classified deviant behavior from this standpoint. There are four types of norm violators or deviants: repentant, cynical, sick, and enemy. Each has implications for deviance behavior, in general. Specifically, repentant, sick, and enemy types can be applied to alcohol use.

1. *Repentant deviant:* A norm violator in this context admits that his or her acts are wrong. The norm he or she violates is unquestioned. The repentant deviant wants to be better and keeps trying to do so. Whether he succeeds or not, he supports the norm. There is a consensus between the designator of the norm and the deviant; repentance confirms the norm. The repentant deviant can be dealt with using assimilative reform. He is not a threat because he tries to obey the norm: He supports it; hence, he is assimilated.

2. *Cynical deviant:* A cynical deviant's behavior does not threaten the legitimacy of the norm, but it does call for repression, which is an instrumental function of law. The cynical deviant can be dealt with using assimilative reform, if the cynical deviant attempts to rehabilitate himself or herself.

3. *Sick deviant:* Neither the sick deviant nor the public see the sick deviant as responsible for his or her acts. The designation as sick neutralizes any conflict. If someone is sick, then it is not their fault.

4. *Enemy deviant:* The enemy deviant contradicts the cultural and institutional expectations of an opposing group. Neither group pays homage to the other's culture. The enemy deviant accepts his or her own behavior as proper and considers the public norm as illegitimate. The enemy deviant becomes an upholder of an opposite norm. The behavior of the enemy deviant is designated as neither repentant nor sick. The enemy deviant is publicly defined as deviant, with the reason for such definition depending on the notion of political power. If a violator is a member of a politically weak group, his or her actions are labeled deviant. One's deviance, then, becomes an issue of political conflict, with culture clashing against culture to determine whose morals are superior. This is dominance without a corresponding legitimacy; hence, cultural conflict.

When a group designated as deviant achieves enough political power, a change in the designation of deviance may occur. In 1933, with the repeal of Prohibition under President Franklin D. Roosevelt, there was such a shift, particularly with regard to alcohol drinkers. The definition of the drinker as an object of social shame (repentant drinker) began in the 19th century. By the 1870s, rural and small-town America defined middle-class morals to include the "dry attitude." This definition had little need for legal codes, as it was assumed that the drinkers shared the normative pattern of the ruling class and could be brought back into nondrinking by moral persuasion. The repentant deviant's error was a lapse from a shared moral virtue, and the repentant drinker was seen as an individual, not as part of a group. The demand for laws (enemy drinker) arose from a situation in which drinkers possessed power as a definitive political and social group. The temperance movement to develop laws emerged in reaction to cultural groups that did not accept the norms of abstinence and sobriety. The effort to turn informal norms into laws polarized the opposing groups and brought forth the symbolic importance of status politics. After the repeal of Prohibition, alcoholics became classified as sick persons. The temperance movement was against this designation, because if the deviant is sick, then there is no longer a cause to fight or support.

Issues of moral reform are one way through which a cultural group acts to preserve, defend, or enhance the dominance and prestige of its own style of living within the greater society. One indication that this movement for Prohibition was a symbolic rather than a moral crusade was that after the passage of the Eighteenth Amendment, the supporters of Prohibition had considerable political power but refused to use it. The Volstead Act was ineffective without funding to enforce it; although the "drys" had the power to increase appropriations, they made no effort to raise the funding needed for proper enforcement. In truth, the law could not be enforced. A large minority cannot be forced to absolutely accept a norm they think is illegitimate; it will cause a reaction (e.g., widespread flouting of a law) and become the focus of a massive group cause. A true moral crusade goes full force; politics would not be an obstacle. By stopping short of strong enforcement, the supporters of Prohibition showed acute political savvy. This also reinforces the notion of the old middle class as disinterested reformers: They wanted *their* norms in place but were not interested in reforming people.

A legal norm cannot be established and maintained in an area that does not support the norms.

Indeed, in the case of alcohol and Prohibition, the urban immigrants had counter norms. The drinking behavior that the temperance movement sought to end occurred in communities in which the temperance advocates were unlikely to live and the laws were not likely to be enforced. A norm cannot be effectively enforced in a location where the majority of people have counter norms and the norms are seen as illegitimate.

Laws regulating abortion and drugs and blue laws are examples of attempts to legislate morality and, for most of those involved with these attempts, symbolic crusades. The defeat of temperance was not caused by immigrants but by the defection of this status group's own members. Status groups are loose collectives. They are formed on the basis of sentiments rather than concrete objectified interests, as with economic groups. Commitment is less structured. The campaign for national prohibition had a polarizing effect on the temperance movement—it maximized the cultural differences between pro- and anti-Temperance forces while minimizing the class differences. Eventually, many who were originally pro-Prohibition became anti-Prohibition.

Factors contributing to the eventual repeal of the Eighteenth Amendment included the advent of the Great Depression and the need for tax revenue from the sale of alcohol and a growing urban voting block that did not support Prohibition.

Drinking is now a middle-class custom, as well as a custom among all classes. The Women's Christian Temperance Union and the Prohibitionist Party are still active today. Their aims are to bring back fundamentalist values, but their crusades have changed—they are antiabortion, support prayer in schools, and oppose the use of drugs and alcohol. What has occurred is a normative change in the designation of deviance; during the past 80 years, there has not been much change in American drinking patterns, generally, what have changed are the class backgrounds of those who support temperance. In 1885, the Women's Christian Temperance Union was composed of mostly professionals and managers, in a country with a small middle class. By 1950, with a growing middle class, the percentage of middle-class members had fallen to below 25% and has continued to drop. Hence, deviant drinking patterns may have shifted culturally, but the designator of deviance is still social class.

York A. Forsyth

See also Conflict Theory; Defining Deviance; Labeling Approach; Prohibition

Further Reading

Gusfield, J. R. (1963). *Symbolic crusade: Status politics and the American temperance movement*. Urbana: University of Illinois Press.

SYMBOLIC INTERACTIONISM

Symbolic interactionism (SI) is an approach to social science adopted by a variety of scholars, mostly from sociology, social psychology, and communications. The term *symbolic interactionism* unites two concepts: symbol and interaction. *Symbol* refers to any social object (e.g., a physical object, a gesture, or a word) that stands in place of, or represents, something else. Symbols are a uniquely human creation. No other species has the ability to arbitrarily assign meaning to objects, transforming them into elements of social action. *Interaction* highlights the significance of interpersonal communication in transmitting the meaning of symbols. Through interaction, culture arises. Interactionists understand culture to be a shared system of meaning that constitutes everyday life. The sociologist Howard Becker has noted that, on the one hand, culture preexists individuals' births and therefore structures their lives. On the other hand, people are autonomous, interpretive beings who have the ability to negotiate, modify, or reject the meanings they learn, thus actively renewing, shaping, or creating culture. From a symbolic interactionist perspective, then, human beings are unique in their active creation and manipulation of symbols and culture. This entry discusses the origins of SI as a sociological perspective, its epistemological premises, and methodological tradition and then examines the application of SI to deviance.

Origins

As a theoretical perspective, SI was originally developed in the early half of the 20th century by scholars at the University of Chicago and was grounded in the study of the meanings that people assigned to the objects and actions that surrounded their everyday experiences. SI was originally conceptualized by the University of Chicago philosopher George Herbert Mead, although he never used the term. The perspective was first given coherence after Mead's death in 1931 by his students at Chicago, who collected and in 1934 published their notes from his social psychology courses in a book titled *Mind, Self, and Society*. In 1937, Herbert Blumer, one of Mead's students, coined the term *symbolic interactionism* and subsequently consolidated much of Mead's work into a distinct sociological perspective. Blumer's 1969 book, *Symbolic Interactionism*, is a collection of his own essays, which is still widely acknowledged as a primary statement on the perspective.

Mead's own preferred description for his work was *social behaviorism*, which he contrasted with the radical behaviorist psychology of J. B. Watson. Watson argued that "mind" was a redundant metaphysical notion and that all action could be explained in terms of responses to stimuli. Mead objected that there was an important difference in the processing of incoming stimuli by humans compared with the animals studied by behaviorist psychologists. Animals treated stimuli as *signs*, information about the world that directly triggered behavioral responses. Humans mostly responded to stimuli as *symbols*, signals that required cognitive transformation before becoming the basis of action. Thus for Mead, "mind" represented the intervening process between the perception of a stimulus and a person's response to it. Further emphasizing a social, rather than psychological, dimension for the human mind, Mead also stressed the extent to which the meaning of acts was not derived from the actor's intention. An actor would design an act in *imagined* anticipation of the response of its projected recipient or audience. However, the meaning of that act would only emerge from the *actual* response and might be further revised by the producer's subsequent self-correction. The act of speech, for example, involves organizing utterances into blocks that stand for, or symbolize, the actor's imaginative projection of a hearer's response. For these blocks to function as potentially shareable communicative symbols, they must form part of an *intersubjective* cultural system, of which language is a familiar and oft-cited example. This system is socially constructed and is learned through the process of socialization. Many classic interactionist studies of deviance focused at least in part on the socialization process through which individuals learn new cultural systems and thereby how to attach unconventional meanings to social objects.

Epistemological Premises

During its emergence in the 1930s, SI offered a radical conceptualization of social theory in the face of macro-, structural, and positivist sociology and the biological and behavioral models of psychology. Dominant midcentury sociology and psychology were aligned with positivism, which assumed that the social sciences could be modeled after the biological and physical sciences to produce verifiable "facts" that explain social behavior and predict future behavior. SI, in contrast, is an interpretive perspective that allows for the agency inherent in human behavior and supports a methodology to study social behavior without demanding that it be definitively explained or predicted. Symbolic interactionists typically collect and analyze qualitative data from people's experiences in naturalistic settings, though some practitioners of the perspective, often called structural interactionists, do use quantitative methods and experimental designs. SI has tended to be labeled as distinctly micro-oriented, rather than macro-oriented, although this has changed in recent decades with the explicit push among some SI scholars toward mesolevel theorizing. Another difference that has emerged over the past few decades especially relates to the role of the researcher. Whereas positivist science has emphasized a value-neutral perspective—the social scientist's ability to separate one's values, beliefs, and interests from data collection and analysis—most symbolic interactionists embrace the notion that research is a situated, contextual practice from which the researcher cannot easily extricate herself or himself. Researchers must therefore identify how biases, values, interests, and other intersubjective phenomena affect the research process and acknowledge (if not highlight) that impact in their research questions, data collection and analysis techniques, and writing.

Three premises, as defined by Blumer, are considered foundational to the perspective. First, human beings act toward things based on the meaning they attribute to those things. Nothing has inherent meaning, rather all meaning is assigned. When a female student walking on campus hears footsteps behind her, she must attribute meaning to the footsteps, and to the larger social situation, before acting toward those footsteps. If she is in the middle of a crowded student center in the middle of the day, she may likely dismiss the footsteps as normal or unimportant. But if she is in a secluded part of campus at night and alone, she might attribute a menacing or dangerous meaning to the footsteps. Second, the meanings people attribute to things arise out of social interaction. The potential meanings a person assigns are not arbitrary, but are learned. People learn the meanings of things through face-to-face interaction with other people or with the thing itself, or through various forms of mediated interaction, such as televisions, magazines, music, or the Internet. Elijah Anderson's research on interracial interaction, for example, highlights how white people's fear of black males is socially learned and oftentimes unjustified. Many whites learn to fear black males without having any significant contact with them. Third, the meanings people attribute to things are handled through an interpretive process used by a person in specific situations. When a female student hears footsteps behind her at night, or when a white woman sees several black males walking toward her on an otherwise empty sidewalk, she will decide how to respond to them based on her own experiences and/or knowledge of similar situations. Reading about recent assaults or muggings may give her reason to feel afraid enough to cry for help. Or she may decide to ignore the "hype" surrounding such alleged threats and treat the footsteps or men as nonthreatening.

In addition to Blumer's three premises, interactionists have subsequently discussed a larger set of guiding principles for the perspective. One is the idea that all social life is *intersubjective*. Human experiences are inextricably social in nature. Symbolic interactionist research has studied how even a person's most private thoughts are learned and given meaning through group life. A similar idea highlights the centrality of emotions to social life. Symbolic interactionists do not define emotions solely in biological terms. Instead, they understand that people's bodies are made up of biological and physiological processes that are shaped by, and in turn shape, social action. Social action is itself another key term for interactionists; Blumer called it the fundamental unit of sociological analysis. Symbolic interactionists do not study individuals; they study the social actions in which individuals engage. Social actions are actions that take other people into account and include visible behaviors, as well as inner actions such as thoughts and emotions. Because most human actions take account of other people, SI provides an inductive explanation of the creation, maintenance, and change in society. Through the alignment of social action, society is created on a moment-by-moment basis by people acting socially.

In short, symbolic interactionists see society as interaction. It is this emphasis on social action that most obviously highlights SI as a sociological perspective. Finally, because symbolic interactionists study social action, they support the development of sociological methods that enable researchers to grasp the meanings that people come to attach to such action.

Methodological Traditions

As alluded to previously, most interactionists do not believe that conventional scientific methods such as large-scale surveys or experimental designs yield sufficient insight into the intersubjective construction of reality, the self or society, preferring instead naturalistic inquiry—research that focuses on people's behaviors in natural social settings. According to Blumer, naturalistic inquiry consists of two phases: exploration and inspection. During the exploration phase, the interactionist works to familiarize herself or himself with the topic at hand, generally by becoming an "insider" of a particular social world. Throughout the exploration phase, the goal is to learn to understand the topic being studied from the perspective of the people who are active participants of that world. What is sociologically significant about the data recorded becomes clearer in Blumer's second phase, inspection, which refers to the process of analyzing the data collected during exploration. Field notes, interview transcripts, documents, and other data sources are all scrutinized as the interactionist engages in the creative process of establishing sensitizing concepts: concepts that are grounded in what the interactionist thinks is most significant or relevant about the data and that offer an analytic frame for understanding the social phenomena being studied. Exploration and inspection are not temporally ordered but overlap as the researcher continuously inspects collected data and modifies the exploration process as necessary.

The findings of such an approach are often written and disseminated as ethnographic texts. Ethnography was developed within sociology, in parallel with its formulation in anthropology, by W. I. Thomas and Robert Park, who worked at the University of Chicago during the same time as Mead. The so-called Chicago school of sociology, referred to either as the spark behind SI or as the incarnation of SI itself, is best known for its legacy of ethnographic research on everyday urban life. While Mead's and Thomas's works offered a coherent interpretivist approach to sociological research, Park turned his training in journalism and philosophy into a methodology for describing lived experience. Often-cited examples of this tradition include, but are not limited to, Frederick Thrasher's (1927) *The Delinquent Gang*, Clifford Shaw's (1930) *The Jack Roller*, Paul Cressey's (1932) *The Taxi-Dance Hall*, and William Foote Whyte's (1943) *Street Corner Society*. With the exception of the former, these studies are also considered key classic texts in the study of deviance.

Symbolic Interactionism and Deviance

The studies just mentioned are representative of the so-called Chicago school tradition of American sociology, a tradition which spawned overlapping developments in both SI and the sociology of deviance. Perhaps the most significant theory to arise out of this tradition is labeling theory, which was coherently formulated in Becker's (1963) *Outsiders*. Utilizing data from interrelated studies of marijuana smoking and dance musicians (social worlds within which Becker was a self-acknowledged "insider"), labeling theory demonstrates the interactionist assumption that deviance is not objectively real but rather is a distinctly social phenomenon based on how people apply meaning to events, behaviors, or attributes and subsequently react to them. As Becker pointed out, the behaviors characteristic of many dance musicians in his day, including their preference for "negro" music, their use of recreational drugs, and their self-chosen isolation from mainstream others became deviant to the extent that they were labeled as such by those who held power over the musicians' lives and livelihood. More broadly, labeling theory posits that deviance is a social and moral process and that events, behaviors, or attributes are *constructed as* deviant through a series of steps. Each step is a necessary component of the labeling process, which is conceptualized in a fixed order. As such, labeling theory was an important part of the emergence of social constructionism as a sociological perspective in the 1960s along with books like Peter L. Berger and Thomas Luckmann's (1967) *The Social Construction of Reality*. SI and social constructionism share many common assumptions about deviance.

We can utilize an ambiguous example such as having sex—an event—to highlight the socially constructed rather than natural foundations of deviance. Similar examples could be used for a behavior (e.g., drinking alcohol) or an attribute (e.g., being obese).

First, certain events, behaviors, or attributes must be banned by agents of social control, either formally or informally. For example, some families, religions, and other institutions ban certain individuals from having sex. The ban is a necessary condition for deviance to arise, and without the ban in place, there could be no deviance to speak of. Second (i.e., once an event, behavior, or attribute has been banned), it must next be detected to be identified or categorized as a problem. A sexual encounter that is kept secret or hidden is not subject to moral judgment. If it were to be observed, then the potential would exist for it to be labeled deviant. Next, however, a specific meaning must be attributed to what has been detected. In other words, social actors will decide whether a particular event, behavior, or attribute is deviant or not. A married couple having sex with each other in the privacy of their bedroom is typically defined as normal, while a married couple having sex with a third person is more likely (though not necessarily) to be defined as deviant. Similarly, the meanings attached to consuming alcohol are not universal—some parents may find their teenager drinking and label the behavior as part of growing up, while other parents may define it as gross misconduct. Once these three steps—banning, detecting, and attributing intent—are complete, meaning has been successfully assigned to the event, behavior, or attribute and labeling has thus occurred. Subsequently, social actions can occur on the basis of such meanings.

Symbolic interactionists (and social constructionists more broadly) are interested in both the interpretive processes through which deviance is created and negotiated on the one hand and the social action that they facilitate on the other. Social reactions toward deviance come in many forms and degrees, depending on the type of deviance in question. Some social reactions are informal; for example, a simple look from a parent can communicate disappointment in a child's behavior and lead the child to feel shame or guilt. Other reactions are more organized or formalized, such as when communities throughout Europe and North America concertedly labeled some thousands of women as witches in the 14th and 17th centuries and enacted a variety of punishments on them, including execution. In both of these examples, social reaction represents attempts by those engaged in labeling to exert control over those labeled as deviant in order to restore the social or moral order. Interactionists argue that it is impossible to explain processes of social control without understanding the meanings relied on to construct the boundaries between normal and deviant behavior. The outcomes of labeling are keenly felt by those affected by both informal and formal methods of social control. Bullying and hazing among adolescents are at an all-time high, as is the number of individuals in U.S. federal prisons for drug-related crimes. A symbolic interactionist approach to these facts would emphasize that the victims of bullying, and those convicted of drug crimes are similar to the extent that they exhibit attributes or engage in behaviors that are defined as socially unacceptable. Drug offenders are not deviant because of drug use per se but rather because of the type of drug they use (there are many legal drugs, e.g., alcohol) or their behaviors as a result of using drugs. Bullying victims may be labeled because of their appearance, their social networks, or because of identification with a stigmatized racial, religious, or other group. Such "deviants," of course, may adopt various strategies to resist or subvert these labels, either by challenging the rights of the labeler to do so or by celebrating their deviance. One might think of how alternative-thinking youths get together and form subcultural groups as a form of collective resistance, or how gays and lesbians have successfully challenged psychiatrists to exclude their preferred sexuality from the list of mental disorders while simultaneously asserting their right to this orientation through "gay pride."

J. Patrick Williams and Robert Dingwall

See also Defining Deviance; Labeling Approach

Further Readings

Becker, H. (1963). *Outsiders: Studies in the sociology of deviance*. New York, NY: Free Press.

Blumer, H. (1969). *Symbolic interactionism*. Berkeley: University of California Press.

Lemert, E. M. (1967). *Human deviance, social problems and social control*. Englewood Cliffs, NJ: Prentice Hall.

Loseke, D. R. (2003). *Thinking about social problems*. New York, NY: Aldine de Gruyter.

TABOO

A taboo is any ritual prohibition of an action, including contact or associations with objects that are part of material culture. In its widest sense, taboo involves any action or thing considered culturally prohibited based on widespread norms. Some scholars believe that the term has lost its usefulness, but current research on taboo words in the social sciences and in neuroscience reflects its ongoing benefits.

History of Taboo

The concept of taboo emerged in the Western world after a British vessel commanded by Captain James Cook visited the Polynesian Islands in the late 1700s. In written reports, Cook noted that certain objects and actions in Polynesian culture were "tafoo," which he would later pronounce "taboo." This included anything natives considered forbidden or dangerous. Cook's party discovered that cultural standards disallowed women from eating certain forms of meat. Taboos kept women away from males while menstruating. If crops were unfit for consumption, priests would taboo them with magic wands. Interestingly, Cook created a constructionist analysis of deviance with his writings. The things he reported on were not taboo in and of themselves. As with the previous example, priests had the ability to decide which objects and actions were taboo, which gave them considerable political power. Historical accounts of Polynesian culture imply that revolts would take place when priests tabooed too many things. These revolts triggered

legitimation deficits for religious leaders. Tribes would sometimes remove priests from leadership positions when they abused tabooing powers.

Cook also believed that taboo included the idea of something being sacred. In one of his reports, he discusses a human sacrifice and references the person as "taboo" and "consecrated." Scholars are skeptical of Cook's interpretation because of its inconsistencies. For example, Christians using the same word to describe the holy cross and something detestable such as human excrement does not make sense. However, there are modern words, such as "bad" that carry multiple interpretations expressing opposite meanings. In some subcultures, something considered bad means that it is good.

By the late 1800s, the word *taboo* had become adopted as part of the English language. In the early to mid-20th century, scholars such as Sigmund Freud and Claude Lévi-Strauss used the term to identify anything strongly prohibited within a culture. They avoided Cook's premise of interchangeable meaning. At that time, popular topics relating to academic work on taboos involved sexual relations, specifically incest.

The Incest Taboo

Many scholars believe that incest is a universal taboo. There appears to be a common prohibition across cultural lines where norms disallow members of a nuclear family to engage in intercourse. Sibling sexual relations are the most common form of this taboo. The key term is *nuclear family;* there are cultures that do freely permit sexual relations between uncles and nieces, aunts and nephews, and first cousins. Moreover, limited knowledge of biological ties often supersedes the stigmatization of incestuous relationships involving distant relatives. Often taboo, however, are certain sexual relations *not* involving biological ties, such as stepfather and stepdaughter relationships.

Theoretical explanations for the incest taboo give insight into how taboos form. One theory is that incestuous relationships are known sometimes to produce offspring with genetic defects, so humans have a natural aversion to accepting them. Another theory proposes that women are sacred symbols of families, especially considering spiritual concepts related to fertility and the symbolism of blood that accompanies menstruation. Therefore, engaging in sexual contact with women within the family, especially during menstruation, came to carry a forbidden tone. Extending this concept, one theory argues encouraging marriage and sexual relations outside of the family ensures social bonds and cooperation needed for social order. Consider the case of arranged marriages facilitating political alliances.

In the contemporary United States, people did not even discuss the idea of incest openly until the 1980s. However, once the taboo barrier around public incest issues fell, research discovered that incest existed at higher rates than previously believed. With the topic breached, victims of incest felt more comfortable talking about their experiences, and advocacy groups argued that law enforcement should do more to investigate this once forbidden topic. The criminal justice system concentrated more resources on incestuous relationships, with a specific focus on issues such as child sexual abuse.

Forbidden Words

Some academicians have argued that the word *taboo* has outlived its usefulness. Indeed, in contemporary mainstream society, with many formerly prohibited behaviors now practiced openly, it may seem like nothing is taboo anymore. However, use of the taboo concept is still beneficial, specifically in terms of analyzing forbidden words. Forbidden words associated with taboos are just as important as the taboos themselves. Consider talking about death.

People will use an abundance of metaphors and euphemisms to avoid direct discussions of death. People say someone has "passed away" or is "no longer with us" and avoid directly stating that someone is dead. Groundbreaking research involving neurological responses to taboo words is taking place. One recent study used functional magnetic resonance imaging and found that internal inhibition for using taboo words involves a specific area of the brain scientists previously believed only responded to external social rules about word use. This implies that humans neurologically encode cultural norms for language use.

Jason S. Ulsperger

See also Child Sexual Abuse; Constructionist Theories; Incest; Norms and Societal Expectations

Further Readings

Durkheim, E. (1963). *Incest: The nature and origin of the taboo*. New York, NY: Lyle Stuart.

Freud, S. (1913). *Totem and taboo: Resemblances between the psychic lives of savages and neurotics*. London, England: Routledge.

Lévi-Strauss, C. (1969). *The elementary structures of kinship*. Boston, MA: Beacon Press.

Parsons, T. (1954). The incest taboo in relation to social structure and the socialization of the child. *British Journal of Sociology, 5,* 101–117.

Severens, E., Kuhn, S., Hartsuiker, R. J., & Brass, M. (2012). Functional mechanisms involved in the internal inhibition of taboo words. *Social Cognitive and Affective Neuroscience, 7,* 431–435.

Steiner, F. B. (1956). *Taboo*. London, England: Cohen & West.

Walter, T. (1991). Modern death: Taboo or not taboo? *Sociology, 25,* 293–310.

TATTOOING

Tattooing is the practice of permanently marking the body by injecting indelible ink into the deep layers of the skin. Like other forms of body modification (e.g., piercing, scarification), tattooing has a long history in Eastern and Western cultures, where tattoos were a means of ethnic identification and self-adornment. Although tattoos have commonly been associated with violence and crime, in contemporary Western societies their popularity is on the rise. According to the 2012 Harris Poll, a fifth of the adult population (18 to 65 years) in the United States have a tattoo, and this prevalence increases to close to a third in younger adults (25 to 29 years). Among adolescents, these figures rise to close to 40%.

The reasons for getting a tattoo are multiple and varied, and while they are related for the most part to self-identity, group allegiance, and/or a form of protest against parents and society, they also include a desire for beauty or distinction from others, maintaining one's self-identity, and testing endurance and one's threshold for pain. Whereas certain religious groups have specific laws about marking the body, some countries (e.g., Japan) have no formal laws about getting tattooed but strong cultural norms that forbid people to display their tattoos in public places. Behavioral studies routinely show that individuals with tattoos are more likely to engage in risk-taking behaviors than those without tattoos and, in particular, are more likely to exhibit socially deviant behavior. The literature on this topic demonstrates that both legal and illegal deviance is predicted by tattoos.

Tattoos and Legal Deviance

Studies conducted in Europe and the United States report that permanent tattoos are strongly associated with various forms of addiction. A U.S. survey of 6,072 adolescents between the ages of 11 and 21 years explored the association between permanent tattoos and alcohol consumption. In this group, episodes of binge drinking (five or more drinks in a row) during the last year were positively associated with tattoos. Several other studies report a similar association among American college students, where tattooed individuals show an increased propensity for binge drinking. It has also been found that weekly binge drinking increases with the number of tattoos. While most studies linking tattoos with increased risk-taking behavior use self-reporting surveys to collect data, a recent study conducted in France found the same positive correlation using a real measure of alcohol consumption. In a sample of 2,970 French men and women, bar goers were asked as they left an establishment selling alcohol (bars and discothèques) whether or not they had a tattoo. Respondents were then asked to breathe into a breathalyzer to measure their alcohol consumption. It was found that participants with tattoos had consumed more alcohol.

Research also shows that people with tattoos engage in other risk-taking behaviors with specific consequences for their health. Several studies report a positive correlation between tattoos and smoking behavior, cannabis use, and sexual promiscuity. A U.S. study found that 63% of tattooed adolescents report smoking in the past month compared with only 26% of their nontattooed peers. In a French study of smoking behavior in university students (1,168 females and 1,419 males), both men and women who wore tattoos were more likely to report smoking behavior. Tattooed students report smoking more cigarettes per day and claim to have begun smoking at an earlier age than their nontattooed peers.

Research also points to other indicators of legal deviance that are associated with tattoos. In a recent survey of Australian adults, tattooed individuals (both men and women) report having greater numbers of sexual partners and higher incidence of sexually transmitted diseases. Similarly, a survey of American college students reports a positive correlation between the presence of tattoos and the number of different sexual partners over the past year, a trend that has been routinely reported for both male and female students. In addition, among adolescents with tattoos, the number of sexual partners increases with the number of tattoos that are visible when the individual is fully clothed. In other studies, more than 80% of tattooed adolescents report having experienced sexual intercourse compared with only 36% of nontattooed adolescents. The age of first sexual intercourse is also positively correlated with tattoos in American students, where tattooed men report having sexual intercourse at a significantly earlier age than nontattooed men, though no statistical difference is reported for women. In France, this correlation between having a tattoo and experiencing sex for the first time was found in both male and female students. It has also been observed that individuals with tattoos report greater monthly use of pornography than those with no tattoo. Other studies have indicated that tattooed individuals are more likely to engage in unprotected sexual intercourse with strangers than are those without a tattoo.

Further studies of adolescent groups correlate tattoos with juvenile delinquency, truancy and school dropout rates, affective disorders, and suicide ideation. Overall, these studies strongly support the assumption that tattoos are positively associated with behaviors that go against established social norms and include use and abuse of alcohol, cannabis and other gateway drugs, pornography and tobacco, as well as sexual promiscuity. These behaviors fall within the realm of what is termed legal deviance, and a host of studies show that the presence of tattoos can have an important predictive value in determining risk-taking behavior, particularly in adolescents. It is not only the presence of a tattoo that may indicate deviant behavior but also the number and size of the tattoos, as well as their connotations. However, the presence of a tattoo is not correlated only with legally deviant behaviors, and a large body of research involving primarily street gangs and prison inmate populations confirms that tattoos can also serve as a predictor of illegal deviance.

Tattoos and Illegal Deviance

The use of illicit drugs, illegal firearms, and criminal violence are forms of illegal deviance that have been correlated with higher prevalence of tattoos. Research examining illegal substance use and tattoos reports the same positive relationship as with cigarettes and alcohol consumption. Tattooed American students were more likely to smoke cannabis each month than those without tattoos, and students with more than one tattoo reported greater drug use than those with a single tattoo. Indeed, adolescents with 2 to 3 tattoos report higher monthly cannabis use than those with only one tattoo. The number of other illegal drugs used per month by tattooed adolescents is also higher than in nontattooed adolescents. This relation between tattoos and illicit drug use has been confirmed in several studies conducted in different countries and cultural contexts. Overall, controlling for age, adolescents with tattoos would have 2.2 times greater odds of problem substance use compared with their nontattooed peers. As has been found with illegal substance use, a correlation between tattoos and violence and/or criminal behavior also exists. Among U.S. college students, 8.5% of those with no tattoo reported having been arrested for something other than a routine traffic violation compared with 18.7% of those with one tattoo and 70.6% of those with at least four tattoos. In a longitudinal survey of American adolescents, the presence of tattoos is associated with increased physical violence, such as involvement in serious fights, inflicting serious injuries that require subsequent medical treatment, and joining a named gang. This study showed that adolescents with tattoos were 2.5 times more likely to exhibit these violent behaviors than adolescents without tattoos. Furthermore, studies conducted with prison inmates show that as the popularity for tattoos increases within the general population, the number and size of tattoos within the prison population also increases.

Overall, the growing body of literature on behavioral correlates confirms that tattoos act as predictors of both legal and illegal deviance. Tattooed individuals have greater odds of abusing alcohol, cannabis, diverse other gateway and illicit drugs; having unprotected sexual intercourse and using pornography; participating in violence and joining street gangs—all potentially risky behaviors that have an important impact for health and well-being. The question that now remains is how to explain this relation. Several theoretical explanations are proposed to explain this intriguing relationship.

Tattoos and Subcultural Identity Theory

According to the subcultural identity theory, individuals get tattooed to demonstrate their allegiance to a specific group and to maintain and/or increase their desire to distance themselves from mainstream society. Initially, deviant behaviors such as alcohol consumption, drug use, and minor violence are more likely to be produced by individuals of such social groups as a way of resisting dominant social values and to demonstrate their dissociation from conventional social norms by displaying their distinctiveness. People who belong to a specific subculture try to maintain their distinctiveness not only with their everyday behaviors but also with their physical appearance. Thus, tattoos could be perceived by members of such groups as a good way of making their differences visible to everyone. Empirical evidence confirms this assertion. It has been shown that, as tattooing becomes increasingly widespread within the population, members of such distinctive groups increase the number and size of their tattoos, as well as the body area that is tattooed, so as to maintain their distinctive self-proclaimed identity. In the same way, a study examining individual motivations for getting tattooed confirms the association between tattoos and a desire to integrate oneself within a subcultural group/gang or certain social circle. Several surveys also report that allegiance to a group is often put forward by individuals as their reason for getting a tattoo. Gang members are among the most highly visible subcultural groups that frequently use the same tattoos to display their membership, and it has been found that gangs are habitually associated with high levels of behavioral and social deviance and, in particular, illegal deviance.

In addition, people with tattoos are generally poorly perceived by those who do not have tattoos, giving tattooing a bad reputation. Among those who do not have tattoos, tattooing is generally associated with delinquency and the refusal to comply with social norms, and tattoos are perceived negatively. Despite an increase in tattoos among role models with high public visibility (e.g., celebrities and athletes), the general perception of tattoos is still strongly associated with violence, delinquency, and crime.

Tattoos and Self-Identity

Because of the increasing popularity of tattoos in people of all walks of life, contemporary youth in Western societies have begun to view tattoos as a fashion accessory or as an expression of esthetic taste, enabling individuals to demonstrate their personal identity to others. This is particularly the case for individuals who may suffer from poor self-esteem and who need to project a particular image of themselves. In this sense, a tattoo would serve as a form of dressing or makeup, a sort of mask that could hide a person's defects or psychological wounds. Nonetheless, people with low self-esteem and who seek to distinguish themselves may already be prone to greater deviance and more likely to use drugs and alcohol and commit acts of violence whether they have a tattoo or not. One study of suicide in young Americans shows that more than 50% of young people who committed suicide were tattooed compared with only 26% of those who died accidentally. Another study of risk behavior in adolescents shows that higher numbers of tattooed adolescents reported having problems at school (truancy 60%, school failure 52%) compared with their nontattooed peers (truancy 26%; school failure 29%).

Conclusion

In contemporary Western society, tattooing has become an increasingly common behavior, particularly among adolescents and young adults, and has been strongly associated with a variety of legal and illegal deviant behaviors. In particular, tattoos have been positively correlated with premature sexual activity and sexual promiscuity, alcohol and drug use, interpersonal violence, and truancy, all of which are risk behaviors that are considered to be responsible for a large part of adolescent morbidity and mortality recorded in today's youth. The increasing incidence of tattooing among the younger members of the population has alerted educators, parents, and health professionals to the increased risk-taking behavior of young people in contemporary society and efforts are being made

to establish the usefulness of observing tattoos as predictive tags or markers.

Nicolas Guéguen and Andrea Bullock

See also Body Modification; Metal Culture; Punk Subculture; Stigma and Stigma Management

Further Readings

Burger, T. D., & Finkel, D. (2002). Relationships between body modifications and very high-risk behaviors in a college population. *College Student Journal, 36,* 203–213.

Guéguen, N. (2012). Tattoos, body piercing and alcohol consumption. *Alcoholism: Clinical and Experimental Research, 36,* 1253–1256.

Heywood, W., Patrick, K., Smith, A. M., Simpson, J. M., Pitts, M. K., Richters, J., & Shelley, J. M. (2012). Who gets tattoos? Demographic and behavioral correlates of ever being tattooed in a representative sample of men and women. *Annals of Epidemiology, 22,* 51–56.

Koch, J. R., Roberts, A. E., Armstrong, M. L., & Owen, D. C. (2005). College students, tattoos, and sexual activity. *Psychological Reports, 97,* 887–890.

Koch, J. R., Roberts, A. E., Armstrong, M. L., & Owen, D. C. (2010). Body art, deviance, and American college students. *Social Science Journal, 47,* 151–161.

Robert, T. A., & Ryan, S. A. (2002). Tattooing and high-risk behavior in adolescent. *Pediatrics, 110,* 1058–1063.

Wohlrab, S., Stahl, J., & Kappeler, P. M. (2007). Modifying the body: Motivations for getting tattooed and pierced. *Body Image, 4,* 87–95.

TEA PARTY MOVEMENT

On February 19, 2009, CNBC reporter Rick Santelli, while reporting at the Chicago Mercantile Exchange, launched into a rant about the newly elected president's plan to help homeowners refinance their mortgages, describing the homeowners who were at risk of losing their houses as "losers." This rant soon made its way onto YouTube and other virtual media outlets and has been credited with the beginning of the Tea Party movement. The Tea Party took its name from the historic Boston Tea Party, one of the events that launched the American Revolution. Many Tea Party members use the word *tea* as an acronym to mean "Taxed Enough Already." Principally the Tea Party movement can be seen as emphasizing a reduction in the deficit and national debt through an adherence to fiscally conservative principles of limited government and low taxes. Among the Tea Party, there was a strong animosity against the health care plan presented to Congress by the Democratic Party and President Barack Obama. The debate over the health care plan resulted in angry town hall meetings in August 2009, in which many members of Congress were shouted down by Tea Party members, and the defeat that many Tea Party members labeled "Obamacare" became a top priority within the party. After the passage of the Patient Protection and Affordable Care Act, signed into law on March 23, 2010, the repeal of the act has become a hot-button issue among representatives of the Tea Party.

Grassroots Movement or Not

The Tea Party is not a monolithic group. Instead, it consists of many groups that are all loosely organized under the umbrella that is called the Tea Party. Of these, the three largest ones are the Tea Party Express, the Tea Party Patriots, and the Tea Party Nation. However, The Tea Party has received help from groups such as Americans for Prosperity and FreedomWorks, which are national 501 C4 groups often aligned with highly conservative elements of the Republican Party and among whose principal funders are Charles and David Koch, who have given large amounts of money to conservative and libertarian causes. There has also been criticism of the extensive coverage, amounting to promotion, of certain Tea Party events by Fox News. Many Democrats, inside and outside of Congress, have called the Tea Party an arm of the Republican Party and an "Astroturf group," referring to a trade name for artificial grass.

The Tea Party and Social Deviance

The pioneering sociologist Émile Durkheim, writing about the legitimate functions of deviance, argued that social deviance in the form of collective action may be necessary to bring about change in a society. The Tea Party used forms of social deviance by disrupting town hall meetings and created collective action in response to the health care reform fight. Many in the Tea Party vented their frustrations with high government spending and professed a belief that government was attempting to do too much in U.S. society. Many may have been giving voice to frustrations with the economic downturn that occurred in 2007 and 2008. As Robert Merton would argue, one of the primary goals of an individual in our society is to accumulate material

wealth; because of the economic downturn, many people could not climb the economic ladder or fell to the bottom. This created a strain within society between people's goals and the legitimate means of attaining those goals. Many in the Tea Party view the use of many governmental services as an illegitimate means of attaining wealth or as a threat to their own wealth through taxation; thus, the desire to counteract these practices was the driving force behind the formation of the party.

Various characterizations have been applied to the Tea Party. Many on the left of the political spectrum have used the terms *racist, radical, right wing*, and *extremists* to describe it, while many on the political right have labeled the Tea Party as heroes, regular Americans, crusaders against unchecked government, and so on. Accordingly, opinion has become polarized, and its members are seen as either deviants or heroes. According to Howard Becker, the more people are labeled the more they *become* the deviant behavior. In response, Tea Party members have often issued harsh condemnations of Democrats and even of Republicans who are not seen as sufficiently conservative.

In the 2012 election, the Tea Party was instrumental in the Republicans taking back the U.S. House from the Democrats, but the Democrats retained a majority in the Senate. One clear goal the Tea Party had was to defeat Barack Obama in 2012; this did not occur. Many moderate conservative commentators, such as David Brooks and David Frum, have argued that Republicans would have done better without the Tea Party because they supported many candidates further right than the mainstream, such as Christine O'Donnell and Sharron Angle, in races that Republicans might otherwise have won. However, it is hard to argue that the Tea Party did not change the dynamics of debate in Washington. In 2011, there was a debt fight in which many Tea Party allies in Congress were unwilling to raise the debt ceiling unless serious cuts were made in the budget. In the end, cuts were made, but the political instability led to a reduction in America's credit rating by Standard & Poor's.

Derrick Shapley

See also Occupy Movement

Further Readings

O'Hara, J. M. (2010). *A new American Tea Party: The counterrevolution against bailouts, handouts, reckless spending, and more taxes* (Foreword by M. Malkin). Hoboken, NJ: Wiley.

Rasmussen, S., & Schoen, D. (2010). *Mad as hell: How the Tea Party Movement is fundamentally remaking our two-party system.* New York, NY: HarperCollins.

Skocpol, T., & Williamson, V. (2012). *The Tea Party and the remaking of Republican conservatism.* New York, NY: Oxford University Press.

Zernike, K. (2010). *Boiling mad: Inside Tea Party America.* New York, NY: Times Books.

TEAROOMS

Tearooms are public restrooms where men gather to have sex with other men. Tearooms are commonly found in public buildings, shopping malls and stores, on university campuses, and in hotels and gyms. Tearooms are one variety of the larger category of public places (including parks, public parking lots, and highway rest areas) known as erotic oases. These are locations men learn about by word of mouth, through subcultural publications and websites, or simply by accident. Public sex locations for men seeking to have sex with men are numerous, with some online listings reporting more than 6,000 sites in the United States.

Tearoom behavior involves men being present and waiting for other men to come into a restroom and "signal" a desire to engage in sex—typically by publicly displaying one's genitals to others or making subtle but overt attempts to observe another man's genitals, to make eye contact, or to "accidentally" touch another man. If the recipient of such behavior is interested in sex, he will signal back to the first man, and overt sexual acts will ensue. Most research has shown communications to be largely silent but do occur through gestures, gazes, and body language. However, more recent research suggests that in at least some types of public environments, there is significant verbal conversation between the men present.

The most well-known research on tearooms is Laud Humphreys's controversial *Tearoom Trade.* This classic work was based on Humphreys's observations of men's meetings and sexual encounters in a public park restroom followed by his conducting a "public health" survey with them while disguised. The ethics of Humphreys's work are staples in social science research debates. What Humphreys found was that these men are very "normal," regular, typically heterosexual, often married with children, community members who have no known deviant identity or behaviors.

In the more than 40 years since the original publication of *Tea Room Trade,* several scholars have attempted to replicate Humphreys's work. This line of research has largely validated his findings, across types of settings and time. Later scholars have focused more closely on the interactional dynamics of such encounters but otherwise have largely replicated his findings.

The first and best known of these efforts is Edward Delph's *The Silent Community* (1978). In this, Delph examines multiple settings where men engage in public sex. He outlines common physical structures, and the "taken for granted functions of these settings, as perceived by the population at large, (which) serve as a cloak of concealment for illicit activity" (p. 60). Others have looked at the same issues as Humphreys and Delph but drew on law enforcement generated data, typically surveillance video. Their findings largely echo those of Humphreys about who is involved, how sexual encounters are negotiated and consummated, and how physical structures can facilitate or inhibit sexual encounters. Research in other erotic oases, including public parks, has also shown similar processes and impacts of physical environments.

It is important to note that dangers may be associated with tearooms. Men who meet and engage in sex with other (almost always anonymous) men in any type of public sex environment run risks of sexually transmitted diseases, robbery, assault, and arrest. Interestingly, men who frequent public sex environments do recognize that there are dangers associated with their behaviors. While some engage in activities they believe may limit their risks/dangers, such as carrying defensive items/weapons, avoiding men who look "dangerous," or limiting the days/times they are present, these measures are not necessarily effective.

In the second decade of the 21st century, a decreased number of tearooms appear to be present, and the intensity of sexual activities taking place in such environments seems to be minimized. This may be due to safety concerns or police enforcement of laws banning sexual behavior in public places. A more suitable explanation may be the fact that traditional tearooms have largely been replaced with Internet-based connections between men. While an important difference is that such connections do not lead to sexual contact instantly, they are delayed only until connecting men can get to one another.

The trade-off is that there is a perceived (whether real or not) level of increased safety to meeting a "known" individual from a website in a private location. However, some tearooms and other erotic oases do still exist and function.

While more research and greater understanding of tearoom participants, their experiences, the aspects of environments seen as desirable and undesirable by participants, and other information would all be of value—whether to participants or those seeking to control such activities—it is unlikely that a plethora of research will be forthcoming. For the social scientist, there are personal and professional risks associated with studying such environments that appear to preclude at least some scholars undertaking such endeavors. However, in other fields, such as public health, where an HIV/STD (human immunodeficiency virus/sexually transmitted disease) prevention approach may be seen as more valuable and less stigmatizing than simply "wanting to know" about such activities, such efforts may be more likely to occur. In this regard, for understanding this topic, it may be more important to look outside of the traditional social sciences and to more applied disciplines.

Richard Tewksbury

See also Deviant Places; Normalization; Qualitative Methods in Studying Deviance; Quantitative Methods in Studying Deviance; Queer Theory; Stigma and Stigma Management

Further Readings

Brown, M. C. (2003). *Thanks, buddy: The personal aspects of public sex sites* (Unpublished doctoral dissertation). University of Colorado, Boulder.

Delph, E. (1978). *The silent community: Public homosexual encounters.* Beverly Hills, CA: Sage.

Humphreys, L. (1970). *Tearoom trade: Impersonal sex in public places.* New York, NY: Aldine de Gruyter.

Polley, N. M., & Tewksbury, R. (2007). Conversation at the erotic oasis. *Journal of Men's Studies, 15,* 147–159.

Tewksbury, R. (1995). Adventures in the erotic oasis: Sex and danger in men's same-sex, public, sexual encounters. *Journal of Men's Studies, 4,* 9–24.

Tewksbury, R. (2004). The intellectual legacy of Laud Humphreys: His impact on research and thinking about men's public sexual encounters. *International Journal of Sociology and Social Policy, 24,* 20–57.

Tewksbury, R. (2008). Finding erotic oases: Locating the sites of men's same-sex anonymous sexual encounters. *Journal of Homosexuality, 55,* 1–19.

TEEN PREGNANCY

While the concept of teen pregnancy explicitly draws attention to age, its application—by both social scientists and lay people alike—also implicitly emphasizes marital status: teenage pregnancies of concern are those involving individuals who are not married. Moreover, the prevailing sexual double standard means that the stigma of teen pregnancy tends to be associated with young women more so than with the men who impregnate them.

In the United States, teen births currently make up 23% of all nonmarital births, a historic low. Nevertheless, the United States continues to have the highest teen pregnancy, abortion, and birthrates of all industrial nations. The current teen pregnancy rate stands at 40 births per 1,000 teenage girls aged 15 to 19, which is nearly double the rate in Canada and 10 times the rate in Japan. Recent declines in teen pregnancies can be attributed to the widespread availability of contraception and the fact that young people are using it with regularity. When teen pregnancies do occur, however, teens are less likely to seek an abortion than in past decades. Today, pregnant teens are more likely to carry the baby to term and raise the child.

Social concern about teen pregnancy emerged during the 1960s. Compared with current figures, the rate of teen pregnancy was incredibly high. As this decade began, the teen birthrate was a 96.3 per 1,000 young women. Most of the teens that became pregnant at this time were either married or soon to be married. The rate continued to increase throughout the decade and into the next. Scholars attribute these increases to several factors. First, fertility rates among women over the age of 20 declined during this period. By comparison, teen births made up a larger percentage of births. Second, during this period, the large baby boom generation reached adolescence and sexual maturity. Simply put, teens became a larger percentage of the population, which gave the appearance of a surge in teen pregnancies. Third, fewer pregnant women decided to "remedy" their situation through marriage. As these factors converged, they produced a seeming teen pregnancy "epidemic."

Throughout the 1990s and early 2000s, the teen pregnancy rate decreased. This decline held across all racial groups, with particularly significant declines among African American teens. In 2005, the teen birthrate reached 81.5 for Latinas, 60.9 for African American, 52.5 for Native American, and

26.0 for whites. By the time scholars and the public recognized the teen pregnancy "epidemic," the trend was over, and teen pregnancies were already on the decline.

Americans continue to view teen pregnancy as a dangerous social problem not because of the amount that occurs, but rather, because of the perceived costs to the teen mothers, the children, and society in general. Early research based on data collected in the 1960s indicates that most teen mothers are single, and thus, they often lack the necessary economic support. In addition, they suffer from limited educational and career prospects. Thus, teen mothers hold a better than average chance of living in poverty. The children born to teen mothers tend to have a low birth weight. On average, they have lower academic achievements because of lack of resources and are more likely than other children to drop out of school. Boys are more likely to become criminal; girls are more likely to become teen mothers themselves. Moreover, these children are more likely than those born to older (and married) mothers to live in poverty. Estimates suggest the cost associated with teen pregnancy adds more than $9 billion annually to the nation's social service burden. Close to 50% of adults on welfare were teen parents at some point. Taken together, this body of research paints teen pregnancy as a costly social problem.

Research based on current data, however, indicates that outcomes associated with teen pregnancy are more varied and less pessimistic than previous studies have suggested. Currently, teens who become pregnant graduate from high school at rates similar to other students. This trend is—in part—the result of Title IX, which among other reforms, prevents schools from discriminating against pregnant teens or teen mothers. Moreover, research clearly indicates that teen motherhood does not necessarily lead to long-term welfare dependency. In short, the negative consequences identified in prior research are not as great as was once believed. Moreover, the negative consequences that do exist are largely the result of other enduring forms of inequality (social class, race, etc.). Rather than producing negative outcomes, teen pregnancy simply exacerbates those that already exist.

For the most part, pregnant teens are no longer sent away or forced to give up their child for adoption. Nevertheless, pregnant teens continue to face social disapproval. One reason for this stigma is the dominant discourse on motherhood that emphasizes a white, middle-class, heterosexual, married standard. This concept is layered on traditional gender expectations associated with an emphasized femininity and hegemonic masculinity—both of which regulate female and male sexuality and sexual behavior. Together, these standards problematize motherhood among groups that fail to meet these expectations. Given that a disproportionate number of teen mothers are women of color, this group faces multiple marginality. It is important to realize, however, that motherhood holds divergent and even contradictory meanings across subcultures. Although viewed by mainstream society as a social failing, teen pregnancy may be viewed as a badge of adulthood within communities where opportunities and conventional pathways into adulthood are blocked.

Daniel Renfrow

See also Changing Deviance Designations; Premarital Sex

Further Readings

Coontz, S. (2008). *American families.* New York, NY: Routledge.

Furstenberg, F. (2003). Teenage childbearing as a public issue and private concern. *Annual Review of Sociology, 29,* 23–39.

Gregson, J. (2009). *The culture of teenage mothers.* Albany: State University of New York Press.

McKay, A., & Barrett, M. (2010). Trends in teen pregnancy rates from 1996–2006: A comparison of Canada, Sweden, U.S.A., and England/Wales. *Canadian Journal of Human Sexuality, 19,* 43–52.

TOBACCO AND CIGARETTES

The practice of tobacco smoking dates back to between 3000 and 5000 BCE. The practice was believed to have started in South America and was a part of many early religious traditions. It was introduced to Europe and Asia in the 16th century. When Christopher Columbus and his crew arrived in the New World, they were given tobacco by the native inhabitants. Many in Europe believed that tobacco had healing powers. In the English colony of Virginia, John Rolfe cultivated tobacco and turned it into a cash crop in the 1600s. Tobacco helped finance the American Revolution because it was often tobacco products that were used as collateral on loans from France. In 1875, the R. J. Reynolds Company was established to produce chewing tobacco. However, it was not until the early 1900s that cigarette smoking became a dominant form of tobacco use, overtaking cigars and tobacco pipes in popularity. After World War I, the use of cigarette products began to sky-rocket. In the 1920s, women's smoking rates began to increase following the introduction of the Lucky Strike brand and its advertising campaign associating women's smoking with greater social equality and personal freedom.

There are many different ways to smoke tobacco products, including pipes, cigarettes, cigars, hookahs, vaporizers, and kreteks (clove-flavored cigarettes). There is also smokeless tobacco in the form of chewing tobacco and snuff. Chewing tobacco comes in three forms: (1) loose leaf (cured tobacco strips typically sweetened and packaged in foil pouches), (2) plug (cured tobacco leaves pressed together into a cake or "plug" form and wrapped in a tobacco leaf), and (3) twist (cured tobacco leaves, often flavored, twisted together to resemble rope). There are also three types of snuff: (1) moist (cured and fermented tobacco processed into fine particles and packaged in round cans), (2) dry (fire-cured tobacco processed into a powder), and (3) sachets (moist snuff packaged in ready-to-use pouches that resemble small tea bags).

Health Risks

The American Cancer Society estimates that each year tobacco use is directly or indirectly related to 443,000 deaths. This accounts for roughly one in five deaths each year, which makes smoking the leading preventable cause of death in the United States. Of all cancers of the larynx (voice box), at least 90% are partially attributed to cigarette smoking. Of all cases of lung cancer, 87% are at least partially attributed to cigarette smoking. Tobacco has also been linked to oral cancer, diabetes, high blood pressure, strokes, stomach cancer, and erectile dysfunction. Smoking is risky for pregnant women and newborn babies. Children whose mothers have smoked during pregnancy are at elevated risks for diabetes, obesity, and mental retardation. Also, smoking causes more low–birth weight babies and miscarriages. It is estimated that each year smoking is responsible for $50 billion in direct health care costs and $97 billion total in health care costs and lost productivity. Based on an analysis of U.S. Centers for Disease Control data collected from 1995 to 1999, adult male smokers lost an average of 13.2 years of life and women lost an average of 14.5 years of life.

Smoking affects the person smoking but also nonsmokers. There are two types of secondhand smoke: sidestream smoke and mainstream smoke. Sidestream smoke is the smoke released from the cigarette, pipe, cigar, or other type of tobacco device. Mainstream smoke is exhaled from the individual smoker. Sidestream smoke has higher concentrations of cancer-causing agents. Secondhand smoke has been linked to breast cancer, heart disease, respiratory tract infections, and asthma. Secondhand smoke has been a cause of some controversy in recent years over bans of smoking in public places. In addition to the many states and cities that have enacted ordinances or laws banning smoking in public places, many hospitals nationwide have enacted bans on smoking; many colleges have banned smoking on campus.

Smokeless tobacco also has its health risks. Some view smokeless tobacco as having fewer health risks than other forms of tobacco smoking; however, its use increases the risk of oral cancer and has been associated with recession of the gums, gum disease, and tooth decay. There is also some evidence that smokeless tobacco leads to smoking, because both products contain nicotine.

Other public policy initiatives have been enacted to try and prevent or eliminate cigarette smoking. Because cigarette smoking adds to increased health care costs and lost productivity, many governments at the state and local level in the United States as well as in other countries have levied "sin taxes" on tobacco in an effort to get people to stop smoking by making tobacco products more expensive. There has been some evidence of success in reducing tobacco smoking through increasing taxes for young, minority, and poor smokers. In 1971, tobacco ads were banned on TV and radio. All tobacco advertising has been banned in European Union countries since 1991. Many countries including the United States have restrictions on the selling of tobacco to minors.

Demographics

According to the American Cancer Society, 45.3 million adults are smokers, 21.5% of men are smokers compared with 17.3% of women. In all, 21% of whites smoke, 20.6% of African Americans smoke, 12.5% of Hispanics, 31.5% of Native Americans, 9.2% of Asians, and 25.9% of people who claim multiple races smoke. In the United States, 20% of all high school students smoke.

Fewer people use smokeless tobacco than the smokable kind; 3.5% of all adults use smokeless tobacco. In all, 7.0% of men, 0.3% of women, 1.0% of African Americans, 5.7% of American Indian/Alaska Natives, 0.5% of Asian Americans, 1.1% of Hispanics, and 4.5% of whites use some form of smokeless tobacco. Also 6.1% of all high school students and 2.6% of middle school students have used some form of smokeless tobacco.

Tobacco Lawsuit

In 1964, the U.S. Surgeon General's report on smoking and health was released. While linkages between smoking and various other problems had been reported since the 1920s, this was the first major report by a government institution in the United States detailing the linkage between smoking and disease. Many tobacco companies during the 1950s and 1960s were running advertisements trying to counter the claims of such reports and arguing that cigarettes had medical benefits. As recently as the 1990s, many tobacco company executives testified that they believed there was no linkage between cigarette smoking and lung cancer. In 1994, Michael Moore, attorney general of the state of Mississippi, filed suit on behalf of the state against the tobacco companies for reimbursements of health care cost as it related to Medicaid. Eventually, 46 other states followed suit. In 1998, a settlement was reached in which the tobacco companies agreed to pay $206 billion over 25 years, as well as agreed not to target youth in advertisements along with many other provisions.

Reasons for Smoking

Most people who start smoking do so at an early age, often in their teenage years. Among the main reasons why teenagers start smoking has been peer pressure. Young people are especially influenced by those who surround them. Although smoking is seen as more socially unacceptable or deviant in recent years, there are still segments of society that view smoking as acceptable. Some may grow up in households were parents, older siblings, or other relatives have smoked. Some may have friends who smoke and feel the need to join to be a part of the crowd. Also, adolescence is widely recognized as a time of experimentation and rebellion; it is not uncommon for teens to rebel against those in higher authority and to try things that others consider deviant. Teens may see their favorite musicians smoking at a concert, on television, or on the Internet, and countless vintage movies feature scenes in which an aura of glamour surrounds stars smoking on camera.

Many people who smoke argue that smoking relaxes them and calms their nerves; however, smoking does not really relax them. It merely calms and satisfies the urge to smoke. Some have argued that smoking may increase their concentration level, but once again, there is no direct linkage between smoking and concentration. It may be that the urge to smoke was interfering with their powers of concentration, and after smoking the cigarette, they regained their ability to concentrate. Cigarette smoking is a stimulant, which means it increases heart rate and blood pressure. Some smokers say that cigarette smoking eases their stress levels. Many people, especially women, are afraid to quit smoking for fear they will gain weight. While cigarette smoking often is a suppressant of hunger, one can maintain an active lifestyle and diet while maintaining a healthy weight. Furthermore, the effects of exercise are enhanced by the increase in lung capacity that results from quitting smoking. Perhaps the chief reason why people continue to smoke is because smoking itself is highly addictive.

Reasons to Quit Smoking

According to the American Cancer Society, one's heart rate and blood pressure, which are abnormally high from smoking, begin to return to normal levels once the smoker quits. The level of carbon monoxide in the blood begins to return to normal. Within a few weeks, smoking cessation results in improved blood circulation and less production of phlegm; lung function overall will improve within several months. Also widely reported is an improved sense of smell and taste. The skin may become less wrinkled, one's clothes will no longer smell of stale cigarette smoke, and both car and house will begin to lose the cigarette odor. For the smoker who has quit, a thorough cleaning of car and house is recommended. A smoker who quits before age 30 reduces his or her chance of dying prematurely by 90%; one who quits smoking at age 50 reduces one's chance of dying prematurely by 50%.

Derrick Shapley

See also Alcoholism; Drug Dependence Treatment; Legal Highs

Further Readings

Centers for Disease Control and Prevention. (2010). Tobacco use among middle and high school students—United States, 2000–2009. *Morbidity and Mortality Weekly Report, 59,* 1063–1068.

Djordjevic, M. V., & Doran, K. A. (2009). Nicotine content and delivery across tobacco products. *Handbook of Experimental Pharmacology, 192,* 61–82.

Hatsukami, D. K., Stead, L. F., & Gupta, P. C. (2008). Tobacco addiction. *Lancet, 371,* 2027–2038.

Henley, S. J., Thun, M. J, Chao, A., & Calle, E. E. (2004). Association between exclusive pipe smoking and mortality from cancer and other diseases. *Journal of the National Cancer Institute, 96,* 853–861.

Henningfield, J. E, Fant, R. V., Radzius, A., & Frost, S. (1999). Nicotine concentration, smoke pH and whole tobacco aqueous pH of some cigar brands and types popular in the United States. *Nicotine Tobacco Research, 1,* 163–168.

National Cancer Institute. (1992). *Smokeless tobacco or health: An international perspective.* Bethesda, MD: U.S. Department of Health and Human Services, National Institutes of Health, National Cancer Institute.

Smith-Simone, S., Maziak, W., Ward, K. D., & Eissenberg, T. (2008). Waterpipe tobacco smoking: Knowledge, attitudes, beliefs, and behavior in two U.S. samples. *Nicotine Tobacco Research, 10,* 393–398.

U.S. Department of Health and Human Services. (1994). *Preventing tobacco use among young people: A report of the surgeon general.* Atlanta, GA: U.S. Department of Health and Human Services, Public Health Service, Centers for Disease Control and Prevention, National Center for Chronic Disease Prevention and Health Promotion, Office on Smoking and Health.

TOTAL INSTITUTIONS

The sociologist Erving Goffman introduced the concept of total institutions in his 1968 work *Aslyums.* The phrase *total institution* was used to describe a selection of organizations or social entities that were unique in their capacity to isolate members from society, regulate their behavior, and have policies that pervaded the entirety of the life of a resident of that institution. A notable contribution to sociology, the concept has encouraged scholars to examine how organizations differ in their capacity to promote and monitor conformity of residents within the institutions to minimize the potential for disorder and deviance.

In crafting this concept and providing some archetypical examples, Goffman argued that the identification of a total institution would be contingent on the presence of several ascribed characteristics, including the dismantling of the barriers that allow individuals to compartmentalize different aspects of their life and the creation of barriers (social or physical) to distance residents of the institution from those of regular society. Residency within a total institution creates conditions that facilitate the disintegration of the purposeful separation between aspects of an individual's social life (rest, entertainment, and work), allowing the rules and authority of the institution to permeate every aspect of the individual's life. This disintegration and immersion occurs through four processes.

First, within a total institution, the entirety of the individual's routine activities is conducted within relatively close proximity and under the supervision and monitoring of those who operate the institution. This environment creates a rare convergence in which one authority has control over all segments of an individual's life, and consequences from one aspect (rest, work, or play) can be directly applied to another. This pervasiveness is unavoidable and inescapable.

Second, the institution takes an active role in the organization of routine activities of its members to create a tightly scheduled environment for convenience for either success in the institutional purpose, increased security, or to facilitate control. This regimentation is imposed on all phases of the person's life, and it primarily acts through policies or regulations directing that daily activities start and end at specified times to allow an orderly sequence of activities. For example, when members of that institution will eat, sleep, and be allowed to congregate with other members are the types of behaviors subject to control.

Third, this sequence is not experienced in isolation but rather in the presence of a larger cohort of fellow members. This cohort is treated similarly and is expected to comply with the same regulations, and its members are engaged in the same activities at the same time with one another. In essence, the individual is part of a grouped daily experience in which the institutional authority is treating everyone identically.

The final characteristic is that the activities offered by the institution, and the policies enforced by the institution, are neither random nor an unforeseen by-product. Rather, they are purposeful consequences of a rationally instituted plan designed to fulfill the institutional purpose. According to Goffman, the cumulative consequence of these characteristics is the devaluing of the members' individuality and dignity, with grave potential for dehumanization in their treatment as a group rather than as individuals.

In his original work, Goffman gave five examples of the types of total institutions. These are as follows:

1. Institutions created to care for individuals who are believed to be incapable of taking care of themselves and pose no threat to society, such as orphanages or nursing homes.

2. Institutions created to isolate individuals who need to be cared for, but their condition may pose an unintended threat to the general community, such as hospitals for contagious illnesses, leprosaria, and mental hospitals.

3. Institutions created to isolate individuals who are identified as a threat to the community and the isolation is for the safety of the community more than it is for the welfare of those isolated. This category includes prisons, jails, and enemy combatant camps.

4. Institutions established to better pursue a technical task and justify themselves only on these instrumental grounds. These institutional models do not protect the individuals or the community but rather serve an instrumental function by easing the completion of the institutional goal. This category includes work camps, boarding schools, ships and military training facilities.

5. Institutions that were created as a religious retreat with a purpose of self-reflection, meditation, or religious vocational training. This category includes convents, abbeys, and monasteries.

In addition to the process of institutionalization described above, these institutions are affected, to a varying degree, by a second type of isolation imposed by total institutions—restricted access to social connections outside the institution. Simply stated, the restricted access to communities outside the institution, which is incorporated in all of the foregoing examples of total institutions, permits these organizations to more readily manage security concerns, prioritize the concerns of those sequestered within the institution according to

concerns relevant to the institution, and minimize the distractions that might be caused by exposure to outside communities.

Contemporary Applications and Extensions

Along with defining the archetypes listed above, Goffman suggested that the concept was more inclusive than a mere listing of a few unique types of institutions. Subsequent scholars have attempted to extend the concept of total institutions by application to alternative circumstances (e.g., the dance conservatory) or by addressing perceived limitations in Goffman's original definition. One such extension by Christie Davies focused on the fact that there was considerable variation across institutions along dimensions not explicitly defined by Goffman's original work. First, institutions varied in the degree to which members volunteered, were obligated, or were involuntarily required to be part of the institution. The degree to which an individual is voluntary, a member of an institution can drastically alter the level of monitoring and social control the institution must utilize to complete its stated objectives. A boarding school and a prison will (and should) have different policies in place to fulfill their institutional objectives. Second, institutions vary both in the purpose of the institutions and the degree to which that mission is intentionally integrated into the day-to-day activities of its members. Although the prison and monastery are both identified as total institutions, the rationale behind the insulated lifestyle is fundamentally different. Finally, institutions vary considerably in the extent of social control used to achieve compliance within the institution.

Richard Lemke

See also Deviant Places; Informal Social Control; Prison Culture/Inmate Code; Social Control

Further Readings

Coser, L. (1974). *Greedy institutions: Patterns of undivided commitment.* New York, NY: Free Press.

Davies, C. (1989). Goffman's concept of the total institution: Criticisms and revisions. *Human Studies, 12,* 77–95.

Goffman, E. (1968). *Asylums.* Harmondsworth, England: Penguin Books.

Gordon, R., & Williams, B. (1977). *Exploring total institutions.* Champaign, IL: Stipes.

TRANSGENDER LIFESTYLES

Transgender is an umbrella term for people whose gender identities, gender expressions, and/or behaviors are different from those culturally associated with the sex to which they were assigned at birth. Transgender encompasses a wide variety of identities including, but not limited to, transsexual, genderqueer, bi-gender, third gender, cross-dresser, and drag king/queen. Despite a common misconception, transgender identity is not related to sexual orientation or erotic interests. Transgender individuals can identify as homosexual, heterosexual, bisexual, asexual, pansexual, or polysexual. Instead, transgender status is specifically related to gender, sex, gender identity, and gender expression.

Many transgender individuals feel as if their gender, the socially constructed roles and behaviors deemed culturally appropriate for males and females, does not align with their sex, the biological and physical category to which they were assigned at birth. To acknowledge their gender identity, their internal sense of being a man, a woman, or something else, many transgender individuals choose to alter their gender expression. This involves the way a person presents gender identity to others through dress, behavior, hairstyle, voice, makeup, or body language. This entry provides an overview of the status of transgender identities. Specifically, it addresses the various identities and expressions within this category, the process of gender transition, as well as the discrimination faced by transgender individuals because of the lack of acceptance of gender nonconformity in mainstream society.

Identities and Expressions

Although many people identify broadly as transgender, this category involves a wide range of more specific identities and behaviors, including transsexual, genderqueer, cross-dresser, and drag king/queen.

Transsexual

Transsexual is a term for people whose gender identity is different from the sex they were assigned at birth. Many transsexual people make the decision to undergo a gender transition for their gender expression to culturally align with their gender identity. For some people, part of this gender transition process involves what is known as sex reassignment surgery, or occasionally, gender affirmation surgery.

This process can involve a variety of medical interventions, which include, but are not limited to, hormone replacement therapy, sex reassignment surgery, and chest reconstruction surgery. People who were assigned a male sex at birth but who identify as women and wish to undergo a gender transition are known as male-to-female transsexuals, MTFs, transsexual women, or transwomen. People who were assigned a female sex at birth but who identify as men and wish to undergo a gender transition are known as female-to-male transsexuals, FTMs, transsexual men, or transmen. While some individuals readily acknowledge their transsexual identity, others prefer to be referred to simply as male or female.

Genderqueer

Genderqueer is a term for people who identify with a gender that is outside of the gender binary. Genderqueer can encompass a variety of identities including those who identify as both man and woman (bi-gender), somewhere in between man and woman (genderfluid), neither man nor woman, (nongendered), or other than man or woman (third gender). Recently, genderqueer identities have also been adopted by some individuals who hold radical political positions based on eschewing the binary gender system. Under the umbrella of genderqueer identities, gender expressions can vary greatly. While some individuals choose to express their identities by presenting as masculine or feminine, others present as androgynous, or change their presentations throughout their lives. Some genderqueer people do not specifically identify as transgender.

Cross-Dresser

Cross-dresser is a term for people who wear clothing typically associated with the opposite gender. Cross-dressers typically identify with the sex they were assigned at birth, subscribe to the gender identity typically associated with that sex, yet occasionally or always express the opposite gender by presenting themselves in clothing stereotypically worn by that gender. Cross-dressers generally do not desire to undergo a gender transition or medically change their bodies. Cross-dressers are also sometimes referred to as transvestites; however, many members of the cross-dressing community consider this term derogatory.

Drag King, Drag Queen

Drag king and *drag queen* are terms for people who dress in clothing typically associated with the opposite gender for purposes of entertainment or performance. *Drag king* specifically refers to women who dress up and perform as men, while *drag queen* specifically refers to men who dress up and perform as women. Generally, drag involves exaggerated or caricatured depictions of a feminine or masculine gender identity for comedic or theatrical purposes. Drag performers can identify with a wide range of gender and sex-based identities.

Gender Transitions

Based on specific identities within the category of transgender, some people may desire to undergo a gender transition to align their gender expression, behaviors, and/or physical sex with their gender identity. For many people, a gender transition begins by physically presenting as a different gender in certain situations. This can involve dress, makeup, or hairstyle. For some people, specifically transsexuals, the goal of this step is often to be able to "pass" as the opposite gender in public situations. However, for others, such as genderqueer individuals, passing may not be a desired goal.

Additionally, some people may slowly "come out," or tell other people they are transgender. This can involve telling friends and loved ones about their internal feelings about their gender identity and, possibly, their desire to transition. Furthermore, some people may request that others refer to them using alternate gender pronouns. For example, a transgender man may request that others refer to him as "he" and "him" instead of "she" and "her." For certain genderqueer individuals, this can involve requesting pronouns that are not based on the gender binary including "ze" and "hir." A gender transition may also involve legally changing one's name and/or gender on birth certificates, passports, and driver's licenses. For some, the goal of a gender transition is to eventually be able to pass in society as the other gender without other people realizing their transgender identity. However, others prefer to remain identifiable as transgender. For many people, transitioning is a lifelong process, instead of a single event. Their gender identity and gender expression may develop and change throughout their lives.

For some members of the transgender community, usually transsexuals, medical intervention and sex reassignment surgery can be part of their transition process. This process usually begins with a mandatory psychological evaluation by a mental health professional to address possible depression and anxiety issues that might arise during the gender reassignment process. After gaining medical approval, many transsexuals begin hormone replacement therapy, which usually involves transsexual men introducing testosterone and transsexual women introducing estrogen. This can lead to the development of certain secondary sexual characteristics including, but not limited to, breast growth, facial hair growth, distribution of muscle and body fat, and voice changes.

After hormone replacement therapy, some transsexuals decide to undergo chest reconstruction and sexual reassignment surgery (sometimes called sex affirmation surgery) for their bodies to align with their gender identities. For transsexual men, this can involve a mastectomy to remove breast tissue, a hysterectomy to remove the uterus, and/or a metoidioplasty or phalloplasty to create a penis. For transsexual women, this can involve breast augmentation to create breasts and/or a vaginoplasty to create a vagina. Additionally, some transsexual women also undergo facial feminization surgery to reduce typically masculine facial features. In light of the wide range of options available, some transgender individuals may choose to undergo none, some, or all of the aforementioned procedures. The process of gender transition and sex reassignment surgery is an individual and personal decision that varies greatly from person to person.

Transgender Experiences and Discrimination

It has been estimated that between 0.25% and 1% of all people are transgender. Transgender people have existed in many cultures and societies throughout history, but these people have been perceived differently based on time, cultural location, and social understanding. While some transgender individuals are able to lead normal lives in society today, many transgender people face severe discrimination due to lack of tolerance for gender nonconformity in today's society. This discrimination is often worse for people of color and those with limited financial resources. Research has shown that transgender individuals face discrimination in nearly every aspect of their lives including education, workplace, public settings, and their families.

Family

Frequently, transgender people disclose their transgender identity to their families and loved ones early in their gender transition process. Although family dynamics vary widely, in 2011, the National Transgender Discrimination Survey (NTDS) discovered that over half of all transgender individuals face some sort of familial rejection because of their gender nonconformity. This rejection can include the ending of spouse/partner relationships, domestic violence, and the loss of visitation with or custody of children. While research suggests that relationships with family members sometimes slowly improve postdisclosure, family rejection has been shown to lead to suicide attempts, homelessness, incarceration, and drug use.

Education

Studies have documented that transgender children, teenagers, and college students often face pervasive discrimination in the education system. When these individuals express a transgender or gender nonconforming identity, they often face bullying, violence, and even sexual assault, which prevent them from accessing equal educational opportunities. The NTDS reported that more than three fourths of respondents reported experiencing harassment in school. In addition to harassment by their peers, these individuals report incidents of discrimination by teachers and staff, including expulsion due to gender identity as well as denied access to resources such as on-campus housing in college.

Employment

According to the NTDS, transgendered people are more than twice as likely to be unemployed as nontransgendered people. Unemployment, as well as pervasive underemployment, can lead to extreme poverty for many transgendered individuals. When employed, these individuals face widespread discrimination in the workplace. The NTDS suggests that nearly half of all transgendered individuals have experienced being fired, being denied a promotion, or not being hired because of their transgender status. This workplace discrimination contributes to the overwhelming representation of transgender individuals in underground employment such as sex work.

Public Accommodations, Housing, and Health Care

In addition to discrimination in the family, in education, and in the workplace, transgender people face pervasive discrimination in the public sphere in their everyday lives. According to the NTDS, a majority of transgender individuals report being harassed in public places such as restaurants, retail stores, hotels, and airports, and more than 40% report being refused service or denied equal treatment in these locations. Furthermore, transgender individuals report being evicted or denied housing because of their transgender status in addition to being refused adequate medical care and being harassed in medical settings. This discrimination can lead to homelessness, delayed medical care, increased rates of HIV (human immunodeficiency virus) infection, and suicide attempts.

Kolbe Franklin

See also Drag Queens and Kings; Queer Theory; Transsexuals

Further Readings

Bullough, V., & Bullough, B. (1993). *Cross dressing, sex, and gender.* Philadelphia: University of Pennsylvania Press.

Califa, P. (1997). *Sex changes: The politics of transgenderism.* San Francisco, CA: Cleis Press.

Devor, H. (1997). *FTM: Female to male transsexuals in society.* Bloomington: Indiana University Press.

Girshick, L. (2009). *Transgender voices: Beyond women and men.* Lebanon, NH: University Press of New England.

Meyerowitz, J. (2002). *How sex changed: A history of transsexuality in the United States.* Cambridge, MA: Harvard University Press.

Nanda, S. (1998). *Neither man nor woman: The Hijras of India.* Belmont, CA: Wadsworth.

Nestle, J., Wilchins, R. A., & Howell, C. (2002). *Genderqueer: Voices from beyond the sexual binary.* Los Angeles, CA: Alyson Books.

Rupp, L., & Taylor, V. (2003). *Drag queens at the 801 cabaret.* Chicago, IL: University of Chicago Press.

Stryker, S., & Whittle, S. (Eds.). (2006). *The transgender studies reader.* New York, NY: Routledge.

TRANSNATIONAL TERRORISM

Transnational terrorism, sometimes called international terrorism, has become a major issue in the 21st century as an expanded version of domestic terrorism. Transformation of domestic terrorism to transnational terrorism has been accelerated by factors such as globalization, religious extremism, and advanced communication tools. Remarkable and revolutionary political events also sped up this process. Transnational terrorism is distinguished from domestic terrorism by its more complex organizational structure, the involvement of several states, and its use of high technology. Therefore, it requires international cooperation to combat it.

Defining transnational terrorism is difficult owing to the lack of a consensus on the issue. Political interpretations of terrorist activities and ideological concerns make it hard to reach a common definition accepted by all countries. However, some key elements of transnational terrorism are identified in the literature. Using violence, targeting not only military forces but also civilians and government officials, and having a political aim such as to instill fear to reach political and social change are defined as the key elements of transnational terrorism. One addition to this definition is that it must affect at least two states and involve nonstate actors.

In the previous century, transnational terrorist groups operated mainly for three reasons: (1) to foster and support national liberation, (2) to achieve radical left-wing goals, and (3) to serve the purposes of marginal religious movements. These groups committed kidnappings, hijackings, bombings, including suicide bombings, assassinations, and, recently, cyberattacks to reach their objectives. In addition to the aforementioned purposes, several motives such as opposition to abortion, protecting animal rights, and protesting globalization resulted in the creation of different terrorist organizations. In the past decade, however, religiously exploited motivations have become a more decisive factor in transnational terrorist activities.

History of Transnational Terrorism

The history of transnational terrorism in the past century reveals a rapid increase in such activities following historic events and dramatic changes in political environments. The First World War in 1914–1917, the fall of the Ottoman Empire in 1923, the creation of Israel in 1948, the Iranian Revolution and the invasion of Afghanistan by the Soviet Union in 1979, the opening of the Berlin Wall in 1990, disbanding of the Warsaw Pact in 1991, and the Gulf War in 1991 were all turning points in the history of transnational terrorism. Demands of people who were affected by these events, political turmoil, and lack of state authority fostered the escalation of transnational terrorism.

Early examples of transnational terrorism were seen during the late 1930s. In 1937, Zionist groups such as Lehi and Irgun committed sabotage of British installations in Palestine, then under the British Mandate, to protest restrictions on Jewish immigration. Whether the attacks by Irgun were terrorist activities are still disputed; however, several civilians were killed in Irgun's attacks. Thus, it is regarded as a terrorist organization mainly by the United Kingdom and even by some Jewish organizations. The state of Israel was founded in 1948. Palestinian nationalist groups founded Fatah in 1959. Israel gained a stronger control over the region after winning the 1967 Six Day War against surrounding Arab countries. In an effort to take back control over the region, Fatah joined the Palestinian Liberation Organization in 1967 to fight against Israel together.

Members of these groups were trained by the Soviet Union. Palestinians committed kidnappings, airline hijackings, and suicide bombings. They accused Israel of committing state terrorism by killing innocent people, assassinating Palestinian leaders, and destroying Palestinian dwellings. In turn, Israel accused them of committing terrorist attacks and killing civilians. Neither Israelis nor Palestinians considered their activities as terrorism; instead, they defined themselves as "freedom fighters." In 1968, the Palestinian Liberation Organization hijacked an Israeli flight to force Israel to release Palestinian prisoners. Israel accepted their demands and released prisoners in exchange for the hostages. In 1972, Al-Fatah committed the Munich Olympics kidnappings. During an unsuccessful rescue operation by German police, the kidnappers killed 11 hostages. These two cases attracted intensive media coverage, which was one of the main purposes of the attackers.

After World War II, nationalist groups used terrorism to achieve their independence. Several terrorist organizations were established mainly in the Middle East, North Africa, Asia, China, Palestine, and Cyprus. During the 1960s, terrorist groups arose throughout the world. Argentina and Brazil in Latin America and Germany and Italy in Europe faced terrorist attacks from groups located in those states. The activities of these terrorist groups were mainly domestic and demonstrated the characteristics of guerilla warfare. This pattern began to change after the Iranian Revolution in 1979. Hezbollah, created after the Revolution, carried out its attacks outside Iran in accordance with the aims of Iran's regime exportation. Operating mainly in the same area, the

Kurdistan Workers' Party (Partiya Karker Kurdistan, which was founded in the early 1980s and is still active) and the Kurdish Democratic Confederation (Koma Civaken Kurdistan) committed terrorist attacks in Turkey, Syria, Iraq, Iran, Germany, and England. It is held responsible for the deaths of approximately 30,000 people from all sides.

Another critical event happened in the same year. The invasion of Afghanistan in 1979 by the Soviet Union created an exploitable atmosphere for the sake of expanding transnational terrorism. After the invasion, thousands of young people from Algeria, Egypt, Saudi Arabia, and other Muslim countries went to Afghanistan to help the Afghans in the war against the Soviet Union. The United States supported these people, and the Central Intelligence Agency provided weapons and trained them. After a decade of war, the Soviets withdrew from Afghanistan. Those trained and equipped young people broadened their activities across Sudan, Algeria, Azerbaijan, Egypt, Yemen, and the United States. These people were members of a holy war, a *jihad*, against the Soviet Union, in their own eyes and in much of the world's during the Afghan invasion. However, after the Soviet withdrawal, they changed their targets, mainly to attack Western states, and became widely viewed as terrorists. Osama bin Laden was among these young soldiers. He first proved himself as the leader of militants in Afghanistan, and then organized al Qaeda, which committed one of the most shocking attacks of religiously motivated transnational terrorism on September 11, 2001, destroying the World Trade Center in New York City and a portion of the Pentagon, headquarters of the U.S. Department of Defense, in Washington, D.C., causing nearly 3,000 deaths.

This incident resulted in a dramatic change in the foreign policy of the United States. After 9/11, the United States launched *a war on transnational terrorism* especially against al Qaeda, with the support of the United Kingdom and member states of the North Atlantic Treaty Organization, resulting in the invasion of Iraq. The United States also targeted Syria, Iran, and North Korea as supporters of transnational terrorism. During this war, this coalition of states carried out military operations in Afghanistan, the Philippines, Somalia, Yemen, and Pakistan. The U.S.-led coalition invaded Afghanistan in 2001, claiming that Taliban was protecting Osama bin Laden. The coalition invaded Iraq in 2003 on the grounds that the Saddam Hussein regime was a major supporter of terrorist activities.

al Qaeda, on the other side, organized attacks in several countries especially against people, embassies, and soldiers of Israel and the United States. Despite concerted efforts by the U.S.-led coalition, al Qaeda succeeded in attacking Istanbul, Turkey, in 2003, and Madrid, Spain, in 2004. The attack by al Qaeda on a Muslim country, Turkey, resulted in widespread questioning of the real motives and aims of the organization, especially in Muslim countries. During the war, many casualties were suffered by the coalition forces, terrorists, and civilian people. The actual number of casualties is not known, but it is estimated that approximately 1 million people were either killed or wounded. Since 2001, al Qaeda has been the most notorious and effective figure of transnational terrorism.

In recent years, transnational terrorism has included cyberattacks. The rapid growth and extensive use of computer technology, Internet, and mobile communication tools provided opportunity for saboteurs and hackers to engage in terrorist acts. Attacking network systems of a country's government agencies or of a critical institution and making these systems not working to cause system failure or to steal secrets are their main purposes. Economies, government institutions, and almost every area involving computers have faced threats from cyberattacks. One of the best examples of these attacks is known as STUXNET. This was a highly sophisticated computer worm with the ability of harming not only the software but also hardware of computers. It was specifically designed to affect Siemens industrial equipment. In 2010, Iranian nuclear power facilities were harmed by a STUXNET attack. Some cybersecurity firms asserted that this level of sophistication and cyberattack could only be made with nation-state support. Year by year, internationally operating and anonymous groups have increased their attacks. One of these groups, Anonymous, uses BOTNETs (a large array of slave computers connected by worms and viruses) very effectively in their global-level attacks. In the next decade, cyberterrorism is expected to be among the biggest problems in international affairs.

Characteristics of Transnational Terrorism

There are some main characteristics of transnational terrorism we have faced in the past century. First, there is no strict hierarchy in these organizations. They have a horizontal structure. Subgroups do not necessarily need a command for action and can organize themselves autonomously. The networks between subgroups and members are hard to identify. Even though a top leader is not available, subunits continue to operate. Given all these factors, dangerousness of these organizations is much higher than domestic terrorist organizations.

Second, they do not operate in a specific region. They can attack their enemies wherever they are. Therefore, they have a decentralized structure in terms of location and their enemies.

Third, resulting from decentralized structure, loosely coupled networks, and use of advanced technology, their attacks are mostly unpreventable. In addition, they target all people in their target area without regard for their civilian, noncivilian, innocent, or actual enemy status. Their main aim is to attract as much attention as possible by massive attacks and massive killings.

Several factors helped the increase of transnational terrorism. The first and most influential factor is globalization. Defining factors of globalization are increased communication, sophisticated computer technology, prevalence of the Internet, and ease of transportation. As a result of these factors, cultural and economic relationships have dramatically increased between countries and states. Countries have loosened the procedures for interstate travel to allow transportation of goods, services, and people. Terrorists have also benefited from these regulations. While they freely traveled and were easily organized, they were hardly tracked. Ease of transportation provided some advantages to terrorist organizations. Transportation by plane or train between the states in the United States or in Europe was easy especially before 9/11, and terrorist organizations benefited from this situation. In addition, terrorist organizations have exploited the global availability of electronic communication devices. Even though antiterrorism agencies have plenty of tools to track electronic communications, agencies may lack the full capacity to monitor all such activities in a timely manner.

Second, increased religious extremism has played an important role in operations of several terrorist organizations especially in the past decade. Radically interpreted and deliberately distorted verses of the Qur'an were used by al Qaeda and others to justify their activities. Another religiously motivated terrorist organization, Aum Shinrikyo of Japan, professes beliefs that combine elements of Buddhism and Christianity.

Third, international politics, of course, was another factor feeding transnational terrorism. Even though it has never been officially accepted, several states have funded and supported terrorist organizations to harm their rival countries. Instead of waging a war against a country, supporting terrorist groups to target their enemies has always been preferred by some states.

Fourth, failure of states was highly important in the emergence and expansion of transnational terrorism. As detailed above, lack of state authority after such failures and the demands of people living in those areas were basic factors fueling terrorist activities. For example, in the years immediately following the collapse of Ba'ath regime and Saddam Hussein in Iraq, the Kurdistan Workers' Party seized a large number of weapons from the old Iraqi military forces and used it against Turkish people to gain control over the southeastern region of Turkey.

The War on Transnational Terrorism

The characteristics and history of transnational terrorism show clearly that efforts to combat it face many challenges. This fight necessitates transnational cooperation, use of advanced technology, and, above all, good leadership to manage all of the components in harmony. Of paramount importance is international cooperation, since borders are of no consequence for terrorists. Therefore, antiterrorism agencies from different countries must have agreements to be able to operate in other countries. To this end, International Security Assistance Force was established by the North Atlantic Treaty Organization in 2001 to fight in Afghanistan. This force performed several military operations. Another example of international cooperation is Joint Investigation Teams (JITs) built by the Organization for Security and Cooperation in Europe to deal with transnational terrorism in Europe. In the beginning, most countries supported JITs; however, JITs could not be used effectively owing to the lack of awareness of the availability of JITs, insufficient funding, and difficulties in negotiation for creating and operating JITs.

Several experiences have shown that cooperation in criminal issues at desired and expected levels is not without its challenges. Several factors play roles in the creation of good cooperation in criminal investigations, especially those of terrorist activities. Nations must show willingness, supported by politicians, for intensified cooperation on strategic issues. However, achieving this willingness is far from easy. Such cooperation takes time and patience and a basis of mutual trust to be effective. In contrast, transnational terrorists do not necessarily need such cooperation, and thus, they are capable of acting more quickly than states. This issue creates one of the biggest challenges in the fight against transnational terrorism: lack of sufficient cooperation among countries and law enforcement agencies. Few would disagree, however, that it is a must to achieve a high level of cooperation among all components to combat transnational terrorism effectively and to defeat it.

Serdar Yildiz and Erhan Beyhan

See also Anonymous; Cybercrime; Domestic Terrorism; Hacktivism; Organized Crime

Further Readings

Bakker, E., & Powderly, J. (2011). Dealing with transnational terrorism, the concept and practice of Joint Investigation Teams. *Security and Human Rights, 22*(1), 19–28.

Kushner, H. W. (2003). *Encyclopedia of terrorism.* Thousand Oaks, CA: Sage.

Ors, H., & Cetin, H. C. (2007). Characteristics of global terrorism. In S. Ozeren, I. D. Gunes, & M. D. Al-Badayneh (Eds.), *Understanding terrorism: Analysis of sociological and psychological aspects* (pp. 85–99). Amsterdam, Netherlands: IOS Press.

TRANSSEXUALS

Transgender phenomena include complex conditions such as transsexuality, transvestism, and cross-dressing. Apart from analysis based on the definition of medical and moral labels and their detrimental effects on identity constructions, the study of transsexuality and its theoretic construction reveals a history of discrimination of sexual differences within social science theories, both in terms of explicit reference to "deviant" or pathological practices and in terms of denial or concealment or simply nonrecognition. For example, in the American Psychiatric Association's *Diagnostic and Statistical Manual of Mental Disorders,* transsexualism is featured as a "syndrome" that is characterized by a strong and persistent identification with the opposite sex; by a persistent preoccupation, lasting at least two years, with removing one's primary and secondary sexual characteristics and acquiring the sexual characteristics of the opposite sex; and by persistent unease regarding one's sex,

leading to a sense of extraneousness toward the role of that sex, and to unease that becomes clinically significant and that notably compromises relationships, work, and social interactions.

Transsexual individuals are, according to medical descriptions, people who feel they have been born and trapped in the wrong body and belong to one of two main categories: (1) individuals who are born with male sex characteristics (penis and testicles) but whose gender identity does not correspond to their original sex characteristics but tends toward an elected female gender—this is the case with so-called MTFs (Male-to-Female); and (2) individuals born with female sex attributes (vagina and ovaries), whose gender identity does not correspond to these characteristics but rather to an elected male gender—FTMs (Female-to-Male). It is most common for transsexual individuals, once formally defined as "ill" by medical and psychiatric diagnoses, to turn to legal procedures of gender reassignment surgery.

Let us consider the aspects of interest to social scientists and scholars of phenomena perceived to be "pathological" and/or "abnormal"—how medico-surgical and legislative practices relating to transsexuality resort to formal (and informal) ceremonies of debasement and attribution of often pathologizing biomedical definitions and discriminatory sociolegal constructions. The process of attribution of the new sex status (both biological and in terms of vital statistics) can be divided into two main stages: (1) the medico-surgical adaptation to the elected sex and (2) related amendments to vital statistics. Some Western countries pathologize the individual, through the so-called diagnosis of gender dysphoria. Recently, there have been movements of opinion that profoundly criticize recourse to compulsory psychotherapy in transsexual adults, asking that they conform instead to protocols of the World Professional Association for Transgender Health.

The Medical Construction of Abnormality

This description of transsexuality and transsexuals has a pronounced effect on relationships, institutions, legal points, scientific beliefs, expectations, status and roles, norms, values, desires, emotions, pleasure, attraction and revulsion, abjection, and repression. Medical authority functions in a cultural system of descriptions in which heterosexual hegemony acts not as one of the possible sexual identities but as the "norm," the "ideal," the "standard," with some significant effects.

The traditional medical model defines two genders that are mutually exclusive. That is, it sees gender as an invariant property, and genitals are the essential indication of belonging to a gender. Any exception is not to be taken seriously. In fact, there are no forms of passage from one gender to another other than those which are socially "tolerated." These cultural definitions normalize and create standard and ideal sex citizens: Every individual can be male or female, but not a bit male and a bit female. The distinction between male and female is viewed as a natural fact, and belonging completely to one of the two categories is natural and normal. Thus, males have precise biological characteristics (a penis and testicles), have male characteristics and traits (gender), desire women (their sexual orientation is therefore heterosexual), think like males (adhering to gender identity), and have the ideal characteristics of the male *breadwinner* (regarding performance related to the role of gender). Women, on the other hand, are biologically endowed with a vagina, have traits and characteristics that are defined as female, desire men, think like females, and are principally seen (and imagined) to be occupied with looking after offspring. While these males and females are "normal," they are invisible because they are taken for granted or rather because they occupy, with the due differences, social hierarchies of being able to be "seen" and therefore "recognized." Anything else is not to be taken seriously.

Such a cultural description constructs a static idea of identity and an obligation to belong to one of the two genders, with repercussions for trans individuals in terms of personal rights to self-determination and civil status. Doctors and legislators, seen as moral entrepreneurs, define aspects of morality, whereby individuals who do not adapt to the normative division of the genders or sexes and who challenge sexual orientations are classed as deviates.

A case may arise in which individuals have made changes to their secondary sex characteristics, assuming a corresponding social role, and therefore acquiring psychic harmony while not wanting to turn to surgery. In some countries, legislation responds only to a dichotomised, heterosexist, and homophobic vision of gender, institutionalizing a necessary correspondence between name and sex according to vital statistics, psychosexual identity and external characteristics, biological sex, and sexual orientation. This means that protection of a transsexual person's right to identity is less guaranteed when the individual does not have a clear idea of which of the two genders the individual belongs to. In many countries, during the process of gender reassignment, individuals undergo a transition period (known as the Real Life Test) in which they live as their elected sex, maintaining the personal details of their original civil status and vital statistics until the reassignment surgery has been completed. This system makes obligatory proof that transsexuals can demonstrate that they "know" how to live suitably in their elected sex (gender), but it is unable to respond to social demands for legal and social recognition of all those who do not want to resort to surgery. It seems paradoxical that the law recognizes suitability for a sex change only according to consideration of variables ascribable to the physical-biological aspect, rather than also including the attitude of the individual and therefore the psychic and emotional aspect. It can therefore be affirmed that the medical profession has assumed the function of social control and normalization of individuals and that the entire professional system, customarily characterized by specialized knowledge off limits to patients, consists of interactions between different and conflicting systems of norms, specialized and "profane" knowledge. Medicalization is directly correlated with revocation of the rights of the "deviant." People of atypical sex and gender are recognized as transsexuals, and transsexualism becomes a specific syndrome about which professional knowledge is produced in the area of expertise of the doctor, the psychiatrist, and the endocrinologist. But what deserves particular emphasis here is that pathologization (and the consequent denial of rights) does not depend exclusively on the condition (of being transsexual) but rather on the forced standardization to "normal" categories of male and female. The doctor becomes a "moral entrepreneur" as medical activity leads to the creation of rules that define deviance, and medical practices observe such rules.

A Sociology of Transsexuality

A sociological research agenda on transgender cannot evade the consideration that for many people, the process of identity construction is often a fertile mass of creativity and survival strategies throbbing with a carnality that, if prohibited, discriminated against or suppressed, or simply not recognized, is unable to reveal its own emerging dimensions (properties). There are various subjects and processes that may be of interest to our discipline and our perspective that regard the transsexual as an individual capable of constructing meanings and resisting and negotiating labels and as one able to embody the figure of the social constructivist. It is useful to consider, for example, the shifts in status that transsexual individuals undergo. Doing so would allow us to understand how complex techniques of revelation and concealment and internal and interpersonal communicative processes shape and redefine transsexuals' bodies in the new gender form, according to what is perceived as authentic both by themselves and by others. It is therefore a matter of analyzing strategies of social mimicry or, alternatively, of devastating revelations of gender, their transformations within different social contexts, their negotiations within public space in both work settings and in intimate relationships.

The normative aspect of demonstrating recognition and legitimacy of the transgender individual and of social policies and interventions is one that requires particular attention, sensitivity, and urgency. The processes of victimization and the forms of specific violence against trans individuals (transphobia) are subjects that are perhaps more useful to discuss here. Most forms of violence and discrimination against transsexuals are firmly linked to definitions of public space and therefore to cultural sanctions of the "visibility" of gender identities. The risks of victimization will therefore be higher for people who do not conform to the normative dichotomy of gender as public spaces (and other specific spaces) can represent areas of risk of physical or verbal abuse or attacks. Research on victimization of trans individuals is extremely limited; however, it must be taken into account that transphobic positions are not limited. One study on a sample of individuals with a high level of education and residing in metropolitan settings with a reputation for liberal attitudes toward sex and gender has shown extremely intolerant attitudes toward gender variability. This result is corroborated by another study conducted in Great Britain that discovered that the ideology of gender conventionality based on biological arguments was strongly linked to opposition to civil rights of trans individuals.

The paradox of the invisibility of transgender individuals, or rather of those who will never wish to undergo gender reassignment surgery, lies in their being represented as eccentric, parodied, rhetorical figures, with the result that there is little research that critically aims to go beyond stereotypes and prejudices and that has the analytical aim of understanding the lives, bodies, and everyday experiences of transgender individuals. There are various research topics that can contribute to defining an agenda for sociological research on the everyday lives of trans individuals.

Currently, there are difficulties in estimating the number of trans individuals. This is because of methodological problems preventing access to precise estimates of this socially undesirable phenomenon. The subsequent lack of information makes it difficult for policy makers to plan social interventions and develop policies. This causes problems for trans individuals because they are unable to access social health care services, which makes their demands and health needs invisible. Moreover, safety in public places and in schools must be considered by policymakers. Various studies show the extremely high risk of victimization for trans individuals. This victimization includes harassment by strangers on the street and traumas suffered by children and adolescents in school settings. School experiences seem to be the most terrifying for trans individuals because they are often bullied by other students and staff at the school. Some studies report that there seems to be a higher level of violence toward trans individuals than toward gay or lesbian individuals of the same age. The same results overturn the widely held belief that there is less tolerance for "sissy boys" than for "tomboys," finding that females who then become trans men are subjected to a higher level of harassment and bullying. The trans youth category is among the most vulnerable, together with elderly trans and those who for health reasons, for example, cannot undergo reassignment surgery and are, therefore, subjected to the stress of the (nonexistent) changes to civil status and personal data.

The public space aspect, however, remains the most problematic. Foreign studies report that trans individuals make scarce use of public facilities (services, interventions, etc.) for fear of being discriminated against and harassed. The aspect of public visibility of trans individuals and provision of services (and elimination of obstacles to access to them) must be reconciled with diversification in the period of transition or permanence between the genders—for example, those who use private health care services and who then want to turn to public health care (which at least in Great Britain would seem to take between 6 and 10 years). It is therefore necessary to reflect on the various biographical transitions and on their impact on real life, when crossdressing starts, the period of the gender reassignment operation, and when these phases are shared with the family or peer groups. Moreover, FTM, the transition of biologically feminine individuals to the male gender, is extremely underestimated: If trans women are very frequently victims of discrimination because of their visibility, trans men are because of their invisibility.

Cirus Rinaldi

See also Abominations of the Body; Medicalization of Deviance; Normalization; Transgender Lifestyles

Further Readings

Halberstam, J. (1998). *Female masculinity.* Durham, NC: Duke University Press.

Hird, M. (2002). For a sociology of transsexualism. *Sociology, 36*(3), 577–595.

Namaste, V. K. (2000). *Invisible lives: The erasure of transsexual and transgendered people.* Chicago, IL: University of Chicago Press.

Rinaldi, C. (2012). *Generi e sessi non normativi. Riflessioni e prospettive di ricerca nell'analisi sociologica* [Non-normative genders and sexes. Interpretations and research approaches in sociological analysis]. In R. Vitelli & P. Valerio (Eds.), *Sesso e genere* [Sex and gender] (pp. 171–222). Napoli, Italy: Liguori.

Rubin, H. S. (2003). *Self-made men: Identity and embodiment among transsexual men.* Nashville, TN: Vanderbilt University Press.

Sharpe, A. (2002). *Transgender jurisprudence: Dysphoric bodies of law.* London, England: Cavendish.

Stryker, S., & Whittle, S. (Eds.). (2006). *The transgender studies reader.* New York, NY: Routledge.

Whittle, S. (2002). *Respect and equality: Transsexual and transgender rights.* London, England: Cavendish.

TRANSVESTISM

The term *transvestite* first appeared in the early 1900s to describe a male who dresses in female clothing. Today, the term transvestite is still used, but the more commonly used term is cross-dresser. *Transgender* describes individuals who live in a continuous state of dressing as the opposite sex without surgical or hormonal treatment to reassign sex characteristics, while *cross-dressing* is reserved for those who still identify themselves according to one sex but occasionally dress as a member of the opposite sex. *Transsexual* is the term used for a person who has gone through some form of reassignment procedure (surgical or hormonal).

The historical origins of transvestism or cross-dressing are not exactly known, but historians believe that this behavior has existed for centuries, if not longer. There is also evidence that cross-dressing is not isolated to the United States, Canada, and Western Europe. Studies of cross-dressing have been conducted in other parts of the world, but research on cross-cultural aspects of cross-dressing remains limited.

Most of the attention given to cross-dressing, transgender, and transsexual behaviors pertains to males cross-dressing as females. There are undoubtedly instances of female cross-dressing, but it is treated as less of a clinical issue than male cross-dressing. Generally speaking, females have more flexibility in gender bending behaviors than do males. Therefore, unless a female makes the transition to transsexual, cross-dressing behavior is likely to receive relatively little social attention. Males, on the other hand, are less free to deviate from the culturally accepted presentations of self as a masculine gender. Males who choose to wear female-assigned clothing subject themselves to criticism, psychiatric evaluation, and ostracism from families and friends.

There are two forms of cross-dressers: fetishist and transgenderist. Fetishist transvestites are males who are sexually aroused by wearing female clothing and seek sexual gratification from this behavior. Transgenderist transvestites are males who cross-dress for purposes of experiencing life as a female. There are cases of fetishist cross-dressers who develop a sense of transgender, but it is uncommon for a male to cross-dress for the purpose of the feminine identity and also gain sexual gratification from the act. It is possible that, over time, a fetish transvestite will gain more than sexual gratification from the behavior, and it is unclear whether sexual gratification remains a part of their cross-dressing or not. Masturbation is the typical sexual outlet for fetishist transvestites, but there are some who seek out partners (male or females) who are willing to allow for the cross-dressing to be part of their sex life. Also, prostitutes have been known to be a sexual outlet for some fetishist cross-dressers.

Among the many misunderstandings about cross-dressing behavior is the belief that cross-dressing is a parallel behavior with homosexuality. It is not uncommon for the cross-dresser himself to believe he is homosexual when he first engages in this behavior. However, most cross-dressers are heterosexual, especially those who don't progress to transgenderism or transsexuality. Homosexuals who do engage in cross-dressing are more often referred to as drag queens, and their cross-dressing is for the purpose of exhibition and entertainment of others. Furthermore, there is a difference between cross-dressers and drag queens in that the drag queen wants to be seen as a male wearing female clothing, while the heterosexual cross-dresser wants to pass as a female.

Another commonly held erroneous belief about cross-dressers is that their cross-dressing behavior is the result of sexual confusion. Although some cross-dressers do report gender dysphoria, many cross-dressing heterosexuals see themselves as males who desire to get in touch with their feminine side. Furthermore, these males do not wish to completely leave their male identity and do not wish to receive sex-change treatments or surgeries. However, there is a potential pattern in which a male begins cross-dressing and later decides to go further with hormone treatments or other procedures to resemble a female. Nevertheless, the cross-dresser who retains his male identity does wish to be seen temporarily as a female while engaged in cross-dressing.

Cross-dressing behaviors typically begin when the individual is a child or teenager. It often starts as an exhibition in front of parents or other relatives, or as a costume worn at Halloween, or while playing a part in a theatrical performance. These innocent behaviors sometimes produce a feeling of excitement or euphoria in the individual that he wishes to continue to experience. As cross-dressing becomes a part of the individual's persona, it is likely to be done exclusively in private, without an audience. However, these private experiences become less satisfying, and the desire to be seen by others eventually arises. Furthermore, many cross-dressers make a specific point of documenting their cross-dressing by taking pictures of themselves dressed in female clothing to share with other cross-dressers. The fetish transvestite usually has no desire to be seen in public dressed as a female.

The public presentation of the cross-dresser is often done with a strong desire to be seen as a female. The attempt to pass as a female includes cross-dressing as well as wearing wigs, makeup, and enhancements to give the appearance of the female physique. It is also common for these cross-dressers to either feminize their male name or make up a new female name while they are passing as female. It is possible that the first attempt to publicly display their female self is to a spouse, relative, or friend. There are also cross-dressing clubs and organizations

where a cross-dresser can satisfy his desire to be seen by an audience, which offers a safe environment where the cross-dresser can feel comfortable exposing his female persona.

Being discovered as a cross-dresser by friends and relatives is a major concern in the early career of a cross-dresser. The circumstance of wearing female clothing is only one part of the problem that the cross-dresser experiences in trying to keep his behavior a secret. Clothing must be kept hidden from significant others who are unaware of the individual's behavior. Having a spouse, parent, or other relative find female clothing that is unexplainable often becomes the first step in the process of being discovered as a cross-dresser. As questions are asked, and legitimate excuses are not forthcoming, the cross-dresser is often required to confess his secret behavior. Furthermore, the suspicious acquaintance can easily find information on the Internet regarding cross-dressing.

Many cross-dressers who are in committed relationships with females are more likely than not to have their behavior discovered by their partner at some point in time. Research on wives of cross-dressers has found that they are not likely to support this behavior (although some do) but tolerate or learn to live with this side of their husband. A spouse or girlfriend is more likely to accept the behavior if it is known before the relationship begins, or if it is disclosed early in the relationship. Those who find out much later on in the relationship have a more difficult time accepting the cross-dressing behavior. There are support groups and counseling for those who are spouses of cross-dressers. As is the case with the general population, spouses or girlfriends who discover the cross-dressing behavior are quick to assume that her husband or boyfriend is homosexual.

Research Findings

Two major research efforts have been undertaken to understand more about cross-dressers. The first was done in 1972. A second study with a larger sample was done in 1997. Neither study was based on a random sample, therefore, results may not be truly representative of the entire population of cross-dressers. Samples in these studies were gathered using advertisements in publications for cross-dressers and at conferences or other organizations for cross-dressers. Despite the limitations of these surveys, they do contain much information about the characteristics of cross-dressers as well as the feelings and attitudes they hold. Other studies have been done with clinical samples, which are also not representative of the true population of cross-dressers.

The results of these surveys show that cross-dressers are average individuals. The typical cross-dresser is male who has grown up in a family without distress, has an average to above-average level of education, and is employed in skilled labor or in a professional occupation. Some, but not a majority, see themselves as a female captured in a male's body. More often, the male cross-dresser sees himself as a male who enjoys certain aspects of being a female, namely, dressing in female clothing. Most cross-dressers in these samples did not see themselves becoming females at any point in the future. However, these and other surveys of cross-dressers do find counseling to be involved to some extent. It is unclear whether the counseling is a direct attempt to stop the cross-dressing behavior or to help in dealing with the social stigma they experience from being a cross-dresser. It is possible that a combination of stigma and compulsion to get counseling by significant others may explain the high rate of counseling among cross-dressers.

As mentioned earlier, there are support groups for friends and families of cross-dressers. There are also groups and organizations for cross-dressers as well. Many of these are social support systems that provide the cross-dresser with a network of individuals who engage in similar behavior. These organizations hold regular meetings for members. In addition, there are websites that provide information, chat rooms, picture galleries, and links to other sites such as online shopping. One of the most prominent social organizations for cross-dressers is called Tri-Ess. This is a worldwide organization with chapters in many locations. Tri-Ess has many local chapters, which provide members with meetings and informal get-togethers. Cross-dressers attend these functions to get information about the organization, share research, and enjoy the company of other cross-dressers.

John McMullen

See also Bisexuality; Gender and Drug Use; Homosexuality; Transgender Lifestyles; Transsexuals

Further Readings

Brown, G. R. (1994). Women in relationships with cross-dressing men: A descriptive study from a nonclinical setting. *Archives of Sexual Behavior, 23*, 515–530.

Ceglian, C., Penor, M., & Lyons, N. (2004). Gender type and comfort with cross-dressers. *Sex Roles, 50*, 539–546.

Docter, R. F. (1988). *Transvestites and transsexuals: Toward a theory of cross-gender behavior.* New York, NY: Plenum Press.

Docter, R. F., & Prince, V. (1997). Transvestism: A survey of 1032 cross-dressers. *Archives of Sexual Behaviors, 26*, 589–605.

Ekins, R. (1993). On male femaling: A grounded theory approach to cross-dressing and sex-change. *Sociological Review, 41*, 1–29.

Rosser, B. R., Oaks, J. M., Bockting, W. O, & Miner, M. (2007). Capturing the social demographics of hidden sexual minorities: An Internet study of the transgender population in the United States. *Sexuality Research & Social Policy: Journal of the NSRC, 4*, 50–64.

Talamini, J. T. (1981). Transvestitism: Expression of a second self. *Free Inquiry in Creative Sociology, 9*, 72–74.

Tewksbury, R. (1994). Gender construction and the female impersonator: The process of transforming "he" to "she." *Deviant Behavior, 15*, 27–43.

Wysocki, D. K. (1993). Construction of masculinity: A look in the lives of heterosexual male transvestites. *Feminism & Psychology, 3*, 374–380.

TRIANGULATION

Within the research arena, the term and concept of *triangulation* has been employed for approximately 45 years. The term originally referred to a strategy to improve the validity of research findings by seeking convergence among different methodological and data sources that are used to form interpretive themes or categories. According to this strategy, if two or more data collection methods, sources of data, or researchers converge on the same findings, then the findings and their eventual conclusions are more valid. Increasingly, there is an alternative conception of triangulation as well. This is the use of triangulation to assist in discovering inconsistent or contradictory findings that enable the researcher to consider additional data so that a richer and more contextualized explanation of the social phenomenon under investigation can be constructed. Using either of these conceptions should increase the credibility of findings.

The Origins of Triangulation

In their classic article on determining the construct validity of various measures of psychological traits, Donald Campbell and Donald Fiske wanted to provide a practical way to assist in determining whether a set of measures were, in fact, measuring actual formulated constructs (psychological traits). To accomplish this, these quantitative researchers conceptualized two new forms of validity—convergent and discriminant—as subcategories of construct validity. By employing different tools to measure different psychological traits and then employing correlational analyses, the independence of the methods and traits could be established. In effect, this enabled the researchers to determine if the variance obtained across the measurements was reflective of the actual trait(s) measured or of the methods employed to measure the trait. Campbell and Fiske suggested the application of a multitrait-multimethod matrix, wherein several different tests or measures of targeted psychological traits would be administered within the same time period. If the tests designed to measure the same construct (trait) correlated more highly among themselves than with those designed to measure a different construct, then convergent validity was established. If the construct being measured by a test did not correlate highly with different constructs—even if the measuring tools across the constructs employed the same methods of measurement (e.g., both employed multiple choice questions)—then discriminant or divergent validity was established. If more than one trait and more than one method was used so that both convergent and discriminant validity could be determined through correlational methods and the relative contributions of the trait or method-specific variance could be determined, then there could be a strong and defensible inference that the construct (trait) under consideration and the tools used to measure it possessed construct validity.

This article had profound implications for methods in the social sciences, and it was the first effective application of employing multiple methods to search for convergence in the same data set. Several years later, Campbell and colleagues coined the term *triangulation* for this strategy of trying to use multiple methods to look at the same data set so as to create valid results and interpretation of their results. The term *triangulation* is a metaphorical description for the research strategy taken from navigational or military practices wherein multiple reference points and the principles of geometry were used to locate an object's exact location. That is, as with navigators, researchers could improve the accuracy of their judgments and findings by collecting different kinds of data bearing on the same phenomenon.

While this approach emerged from quantitative research initially, the concept of triangulation—albeit under a different name—was also suggested in the initial descriptions of the qualitative method of inquiry known as *grounded theory*. When Barney Glaser and Anselm Strauss successfully provided specific methods and discussions for grounded theory, an important component of their description was the application of what they called the "constant comparative method." This method was employed during the coding process to determine what the data under scrutiny revealed about the targeted social phenomenon. Within the coding process—which is a key aspect of analyzing the data and developing an emergent theory of explication in qualitative research—data from one interview (or observation) were compared with data from another interview (or observation) to find similarities and differences. By comparing data across different interviews, participants, or methods during coding and interpretation, categories or properties of categories could be developed. This approach was parallel to the earlier triangulation suggestions from the quantitative realm. Several years after the term was coined by Eugene J. Webb and colleagues, Norman Denzin in his 1978 qualitative methods book *The Research Act: A Theoretical Introduction to Sociological Methods* provided further description of the process of triangulation. He defined it generally as the combining of different methodologies to study the same phenomenon, and he described four types of triangulation: (1) across data sources (e.g., participants), (2) across data collection methods (e.g., observations, interviews, document analyses), (3) across and among different data collectors (e.g., investigators), and (4) across different theoretical perspectives (e.g., behaviorist vs. constructivist). He stated that by providing corroborating evidence collected in any of these four types of triangulation, the data interpretation is more valid, since the researchers tend to rely on multiple forms of evidence rather than singular data points.

Purposes of Triangulation

As noted previously, the original and primary purpose suggested for employing triangulation was to increase *convergent validation* of research findings. Simply put, if findings from different methods (or participants) agree, it is assumed that the findings are more valid because triangulation aids in the elimination of bias in helping remove other plausible rival explanations. Within the original Campbell and Fiske statistical analyses where this "multiple operationism" was first proposed, this is generally correct; within the more descriptive qualitative realm, there are also instances where there *is* convergence on a single proposition about some social phenomenon, but this is not typically the case. More likely, other outcomes will result from triangulation. Why might this be the case?

The process of triangulation within the research enterprise is more complex and multifaceted when dealing with qualitative than quantitative data. Consequently, several problems arise with the application of triangulation as a method of convergence. One advantage of triangulation is that when using more than one version of data type (method, data source, or investigator) the weaknesses inherent in that version will be compensated by the counterbalancing strengths of another version of the data type. So, for example, using surveys may provide data that are too superficial for effective interpretation. To compensate, the researcher may also include interviews that assist in overcoming this limitation (though they have their own weaknesses). The problematic assumption is that while each version of a particular data type has its own strengths and weaknesses, triangulation will exploit the strengths and neutralize the weaknesses. However, there is no reason to assume such a convenient balancing out across data types. Additionally, if the researcher has to choose between putting a priority on one method over another, how do such decisions occur? Is all evidence equally useful? How should the researcher weigh one method and its data against another?

A second problematic assumption involves the potential biases that are considered. Since convergence depends on whether findings from different data types (methods, sources, investigators) agree, the assumption is that the findings are more likely to be valid since different data types (methods, sources, investigators) display different kinds of errors. However, if they had the same biases, combining them would just multiply the error. For example, if two investigators exhibit the same bias or the two data collection measures have a similar methodological flaw, then triangulation across these two investigators or using the two measures would only intensify the bias.

A third problematic assumption is that the process of data interpretation is straightforward. While this may be true in statistical analyses, when interpreting social phenomena, there are many more contextual variables that have to be considered so that a demonstration of convergence may only be an artifact of an unidentified variable. Some have referred to such as instance in the discussion of "bogus triangulation." For example, when employing a focus group to obtain opinions, the data could be biased if one person in the group was considered to be an expert or had higher status than the others. In such cases, there was a tendency to echo that person's opinion rather than one's own opinion. This resulted in high redundancy rather than a demonstration of convergence between independent sources. Perhaps the most damaging assumption involving triangulation is the belief that this research strategy will provide convergence to a single conclusion. In reality, it is far more likely that the data will yield inconsistent or even contradictory findings. These assumptions, especially the reality that convergence to a single finding is less likely, have resulted in an alternative conception of triangulation.

This second purpose for triangulation is to discover a *divergence* of findings or results; surprises and discrepancies that arise from the utilization of different data types effectively require the diligent researcher to reconcile these differences. This is an opportunity for enriching the interpretations and explanations of the social phenomenon under scrutiny. In her discussion of triangulation, Sandra Mathison effectively describes this second purpose of triangulation. She argues that the value in triangulation is that it can provide evidence for researchers to construct meaningful propositions about the social world. Mathison suggests that in this application of triangulation, the inconsistent and/or contradictory data are analyzed to construct different and plausible explanations based on several different layers of evidence. First, there are the actual findings from the study; here, all the data, both the similarities and differences, are considered. Second, there is an awareness of the project as a whole. This holistic level provides input about the actual context(s) within which the investigation has been developed and implemented. Third, there is the more general understanding of the background knowledge that has previously been revealed about the class of social phenomena under investigation. Each of these levels of data input—given expression initially through the divergent findings of triangulation— enable the researcher to create a richer description and a more defensible explanation of the phenomenon being studied. Whether the convergent or the divergent conception of triangulation is employed in qualitative research, the result in each case that applies should be an increase in the *credibility* of the findings.

A final purpose of triangulation is as a crucial element in the conceptualization of mixed methods designs in psychological and social research. Increasingly, mixed methods research is being advocated as a way to effectively complement the traditional qualitative and quantitative research paradigms. By employing the triangulation concept to include methods across the qualitative-quantitative divide, it is suggested that there is an integration of these two fundamental ways of thinking that will be beneficial to research in the social and psychological sciences. This integration should address the concerns discussed so many years ago by Lee Cronbach and Donald Campbell in experimental research and by Kenneth Howe—among others—in qualitative research.

As a research strategy, triangulation may serve several purposes for the researcher addressing the issue of deviant behavior. Regardless of which conceptualization of triangulation is employed, the ultimate result should be an increase in the credibility and the utility of one's research findings.

John A. Tetnowski and Jack S. Damico

See also Cross-Cultural Methodology; Ethnography and Deviance; Qualitative Methods in Studying Deviance; Quantitative Methods in Studying Deviance

Further Readings

Campbell, D. T. (1988). *Methodology and epistemology for social science: Selected papers*. Chicago, IL: University of Chicago Press.

Campbell, D. T., & Fiske, D. W. (1959). Convergent and discriminant validity by the multi-trait, multi-method matrix. *Psychological Bulletin, 56*, 81–105.

Cronbach, L. J. (1975). Beyond the two disciplines of scientific psychology. *American Psychologist, 30*, 116–127.

Denzin, N. K. (1978). *The research act: A theoretical introduction to sociological methods* (2nd ed.). New York, NY: McGraw-Hill.

Fielding, N. (2012). Triangulation and mixed methods designs data integration with new research technologies. *Journal of Mixed Methods Research, 6*, 124–136.

Glaser, B., & Strauss, A. L. (1967). *The discovery of grounded theory*. Chicago, IL: Aldine.

Howe, K. R. (1992). Getting over the quantitative-qualitative debate. *American Journal of Education, 100*(2), 236–256.

Jick, T. D. (1979). Mixing qualitative and quantitative methods: Triangulation in action. *Administrative Science Quarterly, 24*(4), 602–611.

Mathison, S. (1988). Why triangulate? *Educational Researcher, 17*(2), 13–17.

Webb, E. J., Campbell, D. T., Schwartz, R. D., & Secrest, L. (1966). *Unobtrusive measures: Nonreactive research in the social sciences*. Chicago, IL: Rand McNally.

TRIBAL STIGMA

Tribal stigma is a term coined by Erving Goffman, one of the most influential sociologists of the 20th century, to indicate types of stigma that are attached to the group rather than to the individual; this kind of stigma is also called a *collective stigma*. As Goffman used the term, tribal stigma refers to membership in devalued races, ethnicities, or religions. Lineage is a necessary element in tribal stigma as Goffman originally explained the term. By this, he meant that tribal stigma was a condition believed to be transmitted genetically by the stigmatized as well as the stigmatizer.

Goffman wrote about tribal stigma in the 1960s. Among the examples he used were being Jewish, Roman Catholic, or African American. Tribal stigmas are still a topic of interest, of course, and select tribal stigmas constitute their own area of study and research at universities, like Chicana/o American Studies and Asian American Studies. It is no surprise that the very term Goffman suggested has roots in language that stresses the depth and the permanence of this kind of stigma, while also evoking societal ability to incorporate multiple tribal stigmas.

Origins and Definition of Tribal Stigma

The English word *tribe* is derived from the Latin word *tribus* and referred to the three original tribes of Ancient Rome, whose number swelled to as many as 35 different entities in that one society. Goffman chose the word *stigma*, meaning mark, from the name for the brand used to identify slaves and criminals. He defined stigma as the phenomenon whereby an individual with an attribute is deeply discredited by his society. Stigmatization itself was the "process by which the reaction of others spoils normal identity." These crucial concepts guide researchers in stigma today.

Tribal stigma is one of the three types of stigma in the classification system Goffman suggests in *Stigma:*

Notes on the Management of Spoiled Identity (1963). The other two types are what Goffman referred to as "blemishes of moral character" and "abominations of the body" to be applied, respectively, to individuals known to have acted immorally and irregularly and to individuals who had physical characteristics believed to spoil the self. Unlike the other types of stigma, tribal stigma could not be completely eradicated, although it might be avoided, denied, hidden, or modified. Implicit in the origin of the term *tribal stigma*, then, is the assumption that a society will indeed feature multiple groups, perhaps shifting in number and identity, one or more of which could bear an intrinsic "mark" as serious as a tribal stigma. After Goffman, researchers of stigma suggested new groups capable of fitting the criteria for tribal stigma or other ways to modify the concept.

Identity and Career, Passing and Seeming

Writing in *Asylums: Essays on the Social Situation of Mental Patients and Other Inmates* (1961), Goffman described the situation of those stigmatized by the "spoiled" identity of people with mental illness who were committed to the mental hospital of the time and therefore suffered a character-blemishing stigma. In writing *Asylums*, Goffman coined the term *career* to describe common developments, events, and paths likely to be found in the stigmatized person's life in this role. The term *career* has also been applied to the experience of those with different tribal stigmas, for this situation—perhaps more so than incarceration in a mental hospital—affords even people who are not confined similar treatment and similar reactions. Of the varied possible landmark events and realizations that mark the career of the person with a tribal stigma, his or her experience with simultaneously being a member of the stigmatizing mainstream society is one of the most crucial.

With regard to the individual's identity in having a tribal stigma, Goffman noted that the possibility of passing and being taken as a member of the nonstigmatized mainstream was central. It was central to the person with a tribal stigma because, forbidden as he or she was from taking part in the general social life, to be tempted to do so was inevitable; it was central to the person without a tribal stigma because he or she would know best what was being kept from the stigmatized for no real reason at all.

In discussing the ramifications of these features, Goffman proposed two possibilities for the character

of a stigma. These two possibilities are related to how evident to others the stigma is and are crucial when discussing tribal stigma in particular. First is the possibility that a stigma is discrediting; that is, the person's identity is discredited because the stigma is evident and recognized. An example would be the person who is Jewish and is identified as Jewish by others; their knowledge could be based on expectations for the person's physiognomy. Of course, considering what Goffman described as the relatively loose standards for Jewish looks, the person might be or might not be recognized as Jewish, and this brings up the second possibility. It is possible that the stigma is discreditable, that is, the person's identity could be stigmatized but is not. An example of a modification would be the person, born Jewish, who chose to be a Reform Jew rather than taking on the practices and restrictions of an observant Orthodox Jew. By renouncing those features that would publicly identify him or her as Orthodox or require that he or she demand changes in a chosen lifestyle, the person could change his or her discredited identity to one that was merely discreditable.

Goffman considered individuals whose stigmatizing attributes are not immediately evident. In that case, the individual can encounter two distinct social atmospheres. In the first, he or she is discreditable—his or her stigma has yet to be revealed, but may be revealed either intentionally by the individual (in which case he or she will have some control over how it is revealed) or by some factor he or she cannot control. Of course, it also might be successfully concealed, as in "passing." In this situation, the analysis of stigma is concerned only with the behaviors adopted by the stigmatized individual to manage his or her identity: the concealing and revealing of information. In the second atmosphere, he or she is discredited—the stigma has been revealed, and thus, it affects not only his or her behavior but the behavior of others.

Goffman emphasizes that tribal stigmas are partly distinguished by an element of lineage; that is, those with a tribal stigma are born, not made. It is true, however, that the person born with a tribal stigma can attempt to renounce the group, either completely or by a series of smaller steps signaling disloyalty. For instance, there may be formal steps that allow the person to exchange his or her tribally stigmatized group for a nonstigmatized group; an example would be when a person undergoes religious instruction and conversion. The person can take these steps, of course; however, he or she can encounter people (from either the tribally stigmatized group or the adoptive group) who tell him or her that, no matter what he or she does, his or her tribal stigma will never be really erased.

In addition to religious instruction, the person with a tribal stigma can take steps to alter his or her physical appearance intended to make the stigmatized origin completely disappear or to moderate how evident it is. A person might have surgery, for instance, to change a nose that is "too African American" to one that either escapes or moderates the stereotypical nose associated with the tribal group.

The person with a tribal stigma sometimes chooses to make a clean break by lying, passing, and otherwise dissembling about his or her original group. There are sometimes physical changes to be made, sometimes a legal (or illegal) name change, a personal and family history to create and memorize, and original family members, friends, and others to manage or avoid. Sloughing the tribal stigma can be done with some success even in these days of abundant records, depending on how polished and plausible the deception is.

Sometimes members associated with a tribal group explain that what once was a shameful identity is shameful no more. Those who have amended and crafted their identity may agree, yet by having sought to deny his or her origins, such individuals have ironically provided proof that the tribal group is one that they too have devalued and rejected.

Conditions Described as Tribal Stigma

The term *tribal stigma* has been and still is cited when academics write about stigma. Novel groups and novel circumstances can profit from an analysis of tribal stigma, as was the case for the situation of nonnative immigrants to Sweden whose tribal stigma was reported to be partly eclipsed if a native Swedish spouse was found. In such a case, the immigrant's relative youth and educational attainments could effectively be bartered to an older, less well-educated Swedish spouse.

Other researchers have suggested that Goffman's original trio of race, religion, and ethnicity be altered and extended in other ways. Certain other kinds of situations, they argue, merit the term more permanently that in spousal barter. Elements of the experience of tribal stigma include a strong original attachment to the particular group or way of life, increasingly augmented by the attitude of the mainstream; that is, a simultaneous devotion to and antipathy toward the group that constitutes one's master status in the society. To balance the two attachments is part of the work of anyone with a social category membership that is also a master status. Tribal stigma additionally required a supposed physical basis due to lineage.

This physical or genetic basis, together with the judgment that the individual cannot alter the characteristic that pervades his or her identity, no doubt helps rationalize to the mainstream stigmatizer the extreme repulsion and rejection he or she claims. It is common to hear that the person with a tribal stigma can be detected because, to the mainstream individual, he or she is claimed to look, behave, perhaps even smell "different"; mainstream group members sometimes claim that they can always tell such a person even if others claim they detect no difference at all. In sum, a tribal stigma is a deeply felt identity mediated by an alleged physical basis passed on by parents or a parent—ineradicable, thoroughgoing, potentially lethal.

It is no surprise, then, that some argue that gender can constitute a tribal stigma, particularly feminine gender. After all, that stigma is also from birth and, apart from certain medical possibilities, is evident from birth and is permanent; it involves appearance; it has been taken to involve differences of behavior, emotion, intelligence, and cognition as well; and it is a circumstance that can engender hatred, violence, and disgust from mainstream stigmatizers. In addition, while both parents cannot bear this particular tribal stigma, one of them certainly did.

Some other suggested additions to the original three types of tribal stigma also involve feminine gender in addition to another characteristic. For example, more than one researcher has suggested that the sexually transmitted infections (STIs) that women can acquire mark them as tribally stigmatized; of course STIs are deeply discrediting, possibly engendering disgust. It is also true that STIs are not necessarily acquired at birth, but STIs can be transmitted to offspring and to others. If transmitted, those infected would metaphorically constitute successive generations.

With a greater knowledge of the different types of potential identities, it is possible to see the complexities of other situations that involve tribal stigmas and, often, a health status. Sometimes, for example, the physical and biological aspect of tribal identity is now carried in genetic predispositions to illness and disease, as is the case with Portuguese Americans of

Azorean lineage, whose young men are subject to Machado-Joseph disease. This disease, which cannot yet be detected using genetic testing, but will kill some adolescent boys after long and painful suffering, has in some ways created a tribally stigmatized subgroup within a tribally stigmatized community. The larger community of Aozeans is then faced with the task of dealing with a stigmatized group within their tribal membership. Their work is to assuage the fate of those already afflicted by the disease and prevent prejudice and discrimination toward those families who are known already to carry the condition.

Carol Gardner and William Gronfein

See also Stigma and Stigma Management

Further Readings

Behtoui, A. (2010). Marriage patterns of immigrants in Sweden. *Journal of Comparative Family Studies, 41*(3), 415–435.

Boutte, M. I. (1990). Waiting for the family legacy: The experience of being at risk for Machado-Joseph disease. *Social Science and Medicine, 30*(8), 839–847.

Cornish, F. (2006). Challenging the stigma of sex work in India: Material context and symbolic change. *Journal of Community & Applied Social Psychology, 16*(6), 462–471.

Goffman, E. (1961). *Asylums: Essays on the social situation of mental patients and other inmates.* Chicago, IL: Aldine de Gruyter.

Goffman, E. (1963). *Stigma: Notes on the management of spoiled identity.* Englewood Cliffs, NJ: Prentice Hall.

Gramling, R., & Forsyth, C. J. (1987). Exploiting stigma. *Sociological Forum, 2*(2), 401–415.

Nack, A. (2002). Bad girls and fallen women: Chronic STD diagnoses as a gateway to tribal stigma. *Symbolic Interaction, 25*(4), 463–485.

Sanchez, M. C., & Schlossberg, L. (2001). *Passing: Identity and interpretation in sexuality, race, and religion.* New York: New York University Press.

TWELVE-STEP PROGRAMS

Alcoholism and other addictions are generally considered aberrant or deviant behavior because they interfere with the individual's ability to make a full contribution to society. During the 20th century, a type of self-help program, known as 12-step recovery, arose to deal with a wide range of deviant or dysfunctional behaviors. Alcoholics Anonymous (http://www.aa.org) is the original 12-step program. Many others have since emerged.

Twelve-step programs are based on spiritual principles but have no particular religious doctrine. Based on the steps originally set forth by the organization Alcoholics Anonymous, a number of similar programs dealing with other problem behaviors have arisen. Although research on 12-step programs is limited due to the hidden nature of the population, some experts suggest that participation in 12-step programs is a strong predictor of recovery from addictions. However, such programs have also been criticized by some, and at times, they have been viewed as being deviant and cultlike.

Overview

The concept of 12-step recovery is that the individual must first admit that he or she cannot control addictive compulsions and obsessions. This is followed by finding something greater than the individual as a source of strength and surrendering to that power or entity. The individual is then required to repair, through a series of steps, relationships with other people and institutions. Finally, the individual is supposed to share his recovery with others seeking help. One of the key characteristics of 12-step programs is one individual helping another so that both can maintain abstinence from the compulsive behavior. This is most often carried out through a process referred to as sponsorship, wherein a more experienced member guides the newer member through the 12 steps. Today, there are dozens of different 12-step programs created to help individuals deal with a range of addictive and compulsive behaviors.

Early Influences on 12-Step Programs

The roots of 12-step programs are found in the Oxford Group, an evangelical Christian movement that began in Pennsylvania in the early 20th century. However, prior to the Oxford Group, two other movements emerged in the United States to deal with the problem of alcoholism; both contributed to the development of the original 12-step program, Alcoholics Anonymous. The Washington Temperance Society was a mid-19th-century group founded on the principle that individuals with drinking problems could help each other stay abstinent from alcohol. Distinct from the temperance movement of that era, this society focused on assisting the individual problem drinker. At its zenith, there were probably more than half a million members. However, the society was short lived because it shifted its focus to tackle other social ills, including slavery. Later 12-step programs learned the importance of maintaining a single focus from this mistake and have generally focused on one specific problem.

The second important movement was much smaller. Richard Peabody, a member of what was at one time among the wealthiest families in America, sought help for alcoholism in 1921 and began offering therapy to others suffering from alcoholism in New York City. However, he charged relatively high fees for his services, thus limiting them to the wealthy. He is credited with creating the concept that an alcoholic must abstain from alcohol the rest of his life, one of the key ideas later adopted by Alcoholics Anonymous and mirrored in other 12-step programs.

Simultaneously, the Oxford Group, an evangelical Christian movement, began gaining strength as a spiritual movement and started working with individuals suffering from alcoholism. Oxford Groups held "house parties" where their members experienced a spiritual conversion, surrendered to a higher power, and shared with others at the gathering about their deliverance from compulsive behaviors. Rowland Hazard III, a Rhode Island businessman and alcoholic, had sought help from Dr. Carl G. Jung, the noted psychotherapist, who told him that the only way he would achieve freedom from his addiction to alcohol would be through a vital spiritual experience. Rowland, thoroughly shaken by this seeming death sentence, joined the Oxford Group and was able to stop drinking. He then carried the Oxford Group message to another friend suffering from alcoholism, Edwin "Ebby" Thacher.

Oxford Groups believed that they could help the individual deal with alcoholism and other self-defeating behaviors using spiritual principles, especially their "four absolutes": (1) absolute honesty, (2) absolute purity, (3) absolute unselfishness, and (4) absolute love. Spiritual rebirth was thought to occur through engaging in the following spiritual practices: sharing one's failings and sins with a fellow member, surrendering one's entire life to God, making restitution for any wrongs committed, and engaging in spiritual contemplation. These four practices were later used as the basis for the Twelve Steps of Alcoholics Anonymous. Finally, Oxford Group members attempted to live their lives using five "C's": (1) confidence, (2) confession, (3) conviction, (4) conversion, and (5) continuance, also adapted by the program of Alcoholics Anonymous.

Ebby Thacher, an alcoholic who was facing permanent commitment, was able to establish a period of sobriety after being introduced to the principles of the Oxford Group. In November 1934, Thacher visited a friend, William Griffith Wilson, an unemployed stockbroker suffering from alcoholism. Wilson was at first uninterested in the methods Thacher had tried with seeming success. However, after a debilitating drinking spree, he soon checked himself into the Charles Towns Hospital for Drug and Alcohol Addiction, where he achieved sobriety that would last the remainder of his life. Wilson became one of the cofounders of Alcoholics Anonymous. Because of the principle of anonymity, Wilson is generally known in 12-step programs as "Bill W."

Birth of Alcoholics Anonymous

Wilson initially joined the Oxford Group and began trying to find other alcoholics to help. He had little success until he took a business trip to Akron, Ohio, in May 1935. After failing to complete his business transaction, he was close to drinking but instead called a local minister, explaining that he was a recovering alcoholic who needed to find another alcoholic to help. In Akron, a small but thriving Oxford Group had begun meeting. Reverend Tunks, the minister Wilson had called, put him into contact with Oxford Group members, who introduced him to Dr. Robert H. Smith, a local alcoholic whose wife had begun attending the Oxford Group meetings with a friend, Henrietta Seiberling. Wilson and Smith spent the entire day talking about how Bill Wilson had recovered from alcoholism, and "Doctor Bob," as he became known, decided to try the spiritual principles that Wilson had used. Smith did drink again a few weeks after this meeting, but he took his last drink on June 10, 1935, which is considered the birth date of Alcoholics Anonymous.

Wilson remained in Akron for several months living in the Smith household, and the two men began developing their own program to help alcoholics. They drew heavily at first from the principles of the Oxford Group, with one exception. While alcoholism was seen as sin and moral failing within the Oxford Groups, "Bill W." and "Doctor Bob" felt that they would have more success by utilizing the disease concept that Wilson had learned from Dr. Silkworth at Towns Hospital. The two men eventually attracted others into what would become the first Alcoholics Anonymous group. Wilson then returned to New York City, where he began locating alcoholics who wanted to stop drinking and formed a group there. For a few years, the Akron group remained part of the Oxford Group in that city, which welcomed those trying to stop drinking. However, the New York City Oxford Group was less receptive, and Wilson and his wife Lois left the group in 1937, along with the alcoholics Wilson had recently recruited. They formed their own separate group consisting solely of alcoholics. The Akron alcoholics eventually broke with the Oxford Group in 1939 to show support for the New York City alcoholics. Wilson then began campaigning with the members of the two fledgling groups to launch a larger program to help alcoholics. He envisioned missionaries, treatment centers, and a book about their experiences. The membership was not supportive of the idea of missionaries and treatment centers, but they did agree to allow Wilson to cowrite the book with other members. The book *Alcoholics Anonymous: The Story of How Many Thousands of Men and Women Have Recovered From Alcoholism* was released in 1939, giving its name to the fledgling movement, garnering publicity, and leading to the rapid growth of the program. Additionally, the 12 steps were expanded and codified with the publication of *Alcoholics Anonymous*. Today, Alcoholics Anonymous estimates that there are more than 2 million members in more than 170 countries worldwide. However, there are no membership rosters, so this remains only an estimate.

In 1946, Alcoholics Anonymous published what came to be known as the Twelve Traditions in its magazine, *The Grapevine*. The traditions were developed as guidelines for groups and their relationships both within and outside of the fellowship. Most 12-step programs have adopted some version of these traditions. The principle of anonymity is featured in the traditions as protection for both the individual and the group as a whole. Additionally, the traditions set forth the principles of service rather than leadership, singleness of purpose, self-support, and lack of structured organization that are defining characteristics of 12-step programs.

Other 12-Step Programs

There is a plethora of 12-step programs dealing with a wide range of emotional and behavioral problems. Although originally developed to deal with addictions, 12-step programs today also focus on mental illness (e.g., Depressed Anonymous), emotional problems (e.g., Codependents Anonymous), eating disorders (e.g., Overeaters Anonymous), compulsive behaviors (e.g., Debtors Anonymous, Gamblers Anonymous), and relationships with individuals with addictions (e.g., Al-Anon, Nar-Anon, Gam-Anon). Additionally, numerous programs have adopted modified versions of the 12 steps (e.g., Celebrate Recovery).

Al-Anon/Alateen is the oldest 12-step program after Alcoholics Anonymous. Al-Anon was founded in 1951 by the wives of Alcoholics Anonymous cofounders Bill Wilson and Bob Smith. The focus is on problems experienced by those close to an alcoholic and utilizes the 12 steps to change the family member or friend's reactions to the problems created by alcoholism.

The second largest 12-step program is Narcotics Anonymous, founded in 1953 by a narcotics addict, James Kinnon ("Jimmy K."), who had gotten off drugs in Alcoholics Anonymous. Like Alcoholics Anonymous, its roots were in several different organizations, including Alcoholics Anonymous, NARCO or Addicts Anonymous (in the federal prison in Lexington, Kentucky), and a brief program called Narcotics Anonymous in the New York state prison system. Narcotics Anonymous grew very slowly during its first 30 years, then published its "basic text" in 1983, leading to rapid expansions in the United States and throughout the world.

Criticisms and Controversies

Twelve-step programs also face a number of criticisms. First, while anonymity is the norm, there is no way to ensure that an individual's participation will remain confidential. Because 12-step programs have no therapists, there is no legal requirement to maintain the confidentiality of participants. Therefore, the individual may have his participation exposed, with no legal recourse.

Second, some critics express concerns that repeated self-identification as someone with a problem (i.e., an alcoholic, addict, overeater, compulsive gambler) reinforces the deviant identity and can lead to increased stigma. Similarly, 12-step programs have been viewed as being cultlike because members tend to all adopt the same philosophy and terminology, placing their identity as members of the 12-step programs ahead of other identities. Finally, because 12-step programs demand abstinence, the success rate is fairly low. Nor do the programs view a permanent cure as possible. This has been seen as reinforcing a deviant identity and poor self-image.

Nonetheless, 12-step programs have flourished, particularly in the Western world, despite limited evidence about their effectiveness.

Susan F. Sharp

See also Alcoholism; Drug Dependence Treatment; Gambling Addiction

Further Readings

Alcoholics Anonymous. (1984). *Pass it on: The story of Bill Wilson and how the A.A. message reached the world*. New York, NY: Alcoholics Anonymous World Services.

Alcoholics Anonymous. (n.d.). *A.A. fact file*. Retrieved from http://www.aa.org/en_pdfs/m-24_aafactfile.pdf

Alexander, F., & Rollins, M. (1984). Alcoholics Anonymous: The unseen cult. *California Sociologist, 17*, 33–48.

Doweiko, H. E. (2002). *Concepts of chemical dependency* (5th ed.). Pacific Grove, CA: Brooks/Cole.

Kurtz, E. (1979). *Not-God: A history of Alcoholics Anonymous*. Center City, MN: Hazelden.

Miller, M. M. (2003). Twelve step programs: An update. *Addictive Disorders & Their Treatment, 2*, 157–160.

UNDERAGE DRINKING

The dilemmas that surround underage drinking are complicated by our cultural notions of consuming alcohol. On the one hand, alcohol is widely consumed and is often present at celebrations and gatherings. On the other hand, out of control alcohol consumption is also associated with addiction and is one of the leading causes of accidental death. Reflecting this complicated landscape, alcohol is a legal and widely available intoxicant, but it is also highly regulated for minors below the age of 21. Surveys suggest that most Americans agree that underage drinking should continue to be illegal and that minors are incapable of responsibly consuming alcoholic beverages. This entry discusses the patterns and consequences of underage drinking and offers an overview of debates around laws and interventions for underage drinking.

Patterns of Underage Drinking

According to the Monitoring the Future Survey, an annual study of middle and high schoolers, approximately 70% of students will try alcohol by the time they reach 12th grade, and more than half of all 12th graders will report being drunk on alcohol at least once in their lives. These levels of consumption suggest that experimentation with alcohol is a kind of universal deviance: a deviant activity in which most people engage in spite of social disapproval (in this case, the fact that drinking underage is illegal).

While drinking alcohol underage is fairly common, we do know that some kinds of alcohol consumption are particularly risky. First, those who begin drinking before the age of 15 are at particularly high risk for developing drinking problems, particularly alcohol dependence. Those who experiment early also tend to have high rates of polydrug use, meaning that they are likely to use a variety of other intoxicating substances. In addition to early drug users, binge drinkers also have concerning patterns. Approximately 25% of high school students engage in binge drinking, or consuming more than five drinks in a single setting. Students who report binge drinking are more likely to report getting into fights, sexual assaults, driving or riding with a drunk driver, poor school performance, and attempting suicide. Finally, alcohol dependence tends to emerge in late adolescence and early adulthood. Prevalence rates for alcohol dependence peak around ages 18 to 20, notably before the legal drinking age of 21. Thus, those who will develop alcohol dependence tend to do so earlier in their lives.

To understand the patterns of underage drinking, it is important to understand the predictors of alcohol consumption. The strongest predictor of alcohol consumption is age. Rates of drinking increase gradually through adolescence, peaking at the age of 21. Alcohol consumption generally levels off around the age of 21 and stays steady until older adulthood (around age 50). While adolescents drink less often than young adults, they tend to drink more on a single occasion. Alcohol consumption is higher for boys than girls, although girls' alcohol consumption is on the rise. White adolescents and young adults drink at the highest rates, followed by Hispanics, African Americans, and finally Asian Americans. Alcohol consumption also tends to be higher for adolescents and young adults who come from families with a history of alcohol abuse and who have experienced maltreatment, neglect, and low levels of parental monitoring. On the other hand, those who have close, nurturing relationships with their parents are more likely to have nonusing friends and therefore are less likely to use. The youngest alcohol users tend to have personal histories of impulsivity, aggression, and early cognitive challenges.

The social settings of alcohol use tend to differ by age. Adolescents are more likely to drink with adults (most likely under supervision) and to drink at home. However, by later high school, young adults are less likely to drink in the company of adults and are more likely to drink at someone else's house and in groups where others are likely underage. By college, drinking is viewed as a social activity and alcohol consumption peaks in these years. Alcohol consumption is particularly high for college students involved in Greek organizations and athletics. According to the Core Alcohol and Drug Survey, an annual study of college students, alcohol is viewed as a kind of "social lubricant" in that alcohol makes social interactions easier and more fun. Notably, students of all ages tend to overestimate the alcohol consumption of their peers, meaning that students think their peers drink more than they actually do. In late high school and early college, it has been argued that this belief that peers drink heavily actually encourages young adults to drink more.

Consequences of Underage Drinking

The widely shared belief that underage drinking is a problem has led researchers to focus on the most serious consequences of underage drinking. Among people less than the age of 21, alcohol contributes to the three leading causes of death. Around 2,000 adolescents and young adults in the United States die annually from alcohol-related car accidents, and alcohol is often involved in homicides and suicides. Alcohol is also frequently a factor in sexual assaults for both the perpetrator and the victim. On college campus, alcohol consumption increases the risk of sexual assault by an acquaintance. Alcohol increases the likelihood of being involved in a physical assault. For men, the risk of assault is highest in public spaces, such as bars, while women are most likely to experience assault in private spaces, for example, at home.

The investigation of the serious consequences of underage drinking is important, but few people actually experience the most serious consequences of drinking. Heavy alcohol consumption has been linked with poor academic performance, particularly low grades, performing poorly on exams and papers, and missing classes. Heavy drinkers are also at higher risk of dropping out of school. Among college students who drink, about half report having a hangover or experiencing nausea. And about a third report getting into a fight or argument, regretting something that they did, or being criticized by others. These academic and social consequences are more widely shared, but less understood, than the serious consequences discussed above. For example, it is difficult to know if students experience academic problems because they drink or drink because they have academic problems.

Although understanding the consequences of underage drinking is important, it is also crucial not to overgeneralize the problems to all underage drinkers. The majority of college students report that they have not missed class or performed poorly due to alcohol use. Moderate drinkers report higher grades than their heavy-drinking counterparts. Although underage drinkers can experience serious consequences, most moderate their use and avoid serious consequences.

Age-Specific Drinking Laws

After the repeal of Prohibition in 1933, states were allowed to have their own drinking laws. Most states set the legal drinking age between 18 and 21, with most states opting for the older legal age of 21. After the adoption of the 26th Amendment in 1971 to lower the voting age to 18, there was a widespread movement to lower states' drinking ages to correspond to the voting age as a marker for adulthood. In the early 1980s, concern over drunk driving among underage drinkers propelled Mothers Against Drunk Driving to campaign for raising the drinking age to combat the problem. In 1984, the National Minimum Drinking Age Act was passed by Congress, which required all states to limit purchasing and public consumption of alcohol to persons 21 years of age or older. Seven states banned alcohol consumption for the underaged completely, while most other states allowed underage consumption under some circumstances.

The relationship between drinking-age laws and alcohol consumption is a difficult one to tease out. It is unclear whether the laws themselves actually decrease consumption. For example, during Prohibition, alcohol consumption among college students declined. But the decline in drinking rates occurred before the law was even passed. Similarly, underage drinking rates continued to decline after 1984, but the decline in underage drinking began before the law was passed. Thus, larger cultural shifts in the meaning of alcohol and drinking behavior may have as much or more to do with drinking rates than laws.

Conversely, some critics have argued that the current higher drinking age of 21 is fueling high rates of binge drinking among the underaged. Because alcohol is prohibited, it serves as an enticing "forbidden fruit" for young people who naturally try to challenge the boundaries of acceptability as they mature. Not only are young people more interested in trying alcohol because of its illegality, they are also forced to hide their drinking from adults who might otherwise encourage responsible consumption. This criticism led college presidents and chancellors across the nation to join the Amethyst Initiative, an organization that seeks the repeal of the National Minimum Drinking Age Act.

Underage Drinking Interventions

A variety of programs have been designed to either discourage underage drinking completely or, less commonly, to encourage responsible consumption. The strategies, design, and resources vary tremendously. But some very clear patterns have emerged about what works and what does not. The best programs are evidence based (meaning they rely on information we learn through research) and continually evaluated.

One of the most widely implemented programs in the nation is the Drug Abuse Resistance Education (DARE) program. This organization offers education on drugs, gangs, and violence generally, and one of their primary educational foci is alcohol. The DARE program operates in 75% of school districts across the nation. The program is well-known for using police officers as teachers and relying on information and scare tactics to discourage use. The DARE program claims to be evidence based, but evaluations of the program have often produced discouraging results. Substance use rates do not vary significantly between those who participate and those who do not. The problems with the DARE program are twofold. First, research suggests that

information alone is insufficient to discourage drinking behavior. Students need a variety of skills and social supports to develop responsible behaviors, so efforts to provide primarily facts and exemplar stories are unlikely to change behaviors. Second, DARE's emphasis on scare tactics is undermined by students' lived experiences. The DARE curriculum relies heavily on tragic or terrifying stories to demonstrate the dangers of drinking. But as discussed above, most students will drink alcohol underage and most will avoid serious consequences. Using their own and others' experiences, it makes sense that students will conclude that drinking alcohol, even underage, is unlikely to result in deleterious consequences.

Successful programs are more difficult to identify because none have reached the popularity level of the DARE program. However, researchers have identified some qualities of effective programs that paint a general picture of alternative programs that work. First, good programs are multidimensional, meaning that they address a variety of circumstances and strategies. For example, programs that integrate classroom learning with extracurricular activities and parental involvement fare better than programs that include only one of these dimensions. Second, effective programs are reality based, meaning that they acknowledge that experimentation is normal (rather than pathological) and they distinguish between drug use and abuse. Finally, community participation is important. For example, several studies have documented that organized efforts to reduce the sale of alcohol to minors are effective in reducing the availability of alcohol. Additionally, communities can have a crucial role in providing alternative activities for adolescents and young adults.

Conclusion

Most young adults will consume some alcohol before the age of 21. Although this behavior is formally illegal, its commonality suggests that underage drinking is to some degree normal. Drinking is more common for white males than other groups and often happens among groups of friends. Certainly, some underage drinkers experience serious consequences, but the majority of underage drinkers will experience only minor consequences and will manage their drinking responsibly. While organizations like Mothers Against Drunk Driving and DARE have advocated for harsher laws and complete abstinence, others like the Amethyst Initiative have argued for approaches that recognize that underage drinking is common. It is unlikely that underage drinking will be universally eliminated, but strategies to encourage responsibility and to avoid serious consequences are important for discouraging drinking problems.

Kimberly M. Baker

See also Alcohol and Crime; Alcoholism; Tobacco and Cigarettes

Further Readings

Beck, K. H., Scaffa, M., Swift, R., & Ko, M. (1995). A survey of parent attitudes and practices regarding underage drinking. *Journal of Youth and Adolescence, 24*, 315–334.

Bonnie, R. J., & O'Connell, M. E. (2004). *Reducing underage drinking: A collective responsibility.* Washington, DC: National Academies Press.

Forster, J. L., Mayer, R. R., Murray, D. M., & Wagenaar, A. C. (1998). Social settings and situations of underage drinking. *Journal of Studies on Alcohol, 59*, 207–215.

Furr-Holden, C. D. M., Ialongo, N. S., Anthony, J. C., Petras, H., & Kellam, S. G. (2004). Developmentally inspired drug prevention: Middle school outcomes in a school-based randomized prevention trial. *Drug and Alcohol Dependence, 73*, 149–158.

Grube, J. W. (1997). Preventing sales of alcohol to minors: Results from a community trial. *Addiction, 92*(Suppl. 2), S251–S260.

Masten, A. S., Faden, V. B., Zucker, R. A., & Spear, L. P. (2008). Underage drinking: A developmental framework. *Pediatrics, 121*(Suppl. 4), S235–S251.

Miller, J. W., Naimi, T. S., Brewer, R. D., & Jones, S. E. (2006). Binge drinking and associated health risk behaviors among high school students. *Pediatrics, 119*, 76–85.

Rosenbaum, M. (1999). *Safety first: A reality-based approach to teens, drugs, and drug education.* San Francisco, CA: Lindesmith Center.

Song, E., Beth, R. A., Foley, K. L., Kaltenbach, L. A., Wagoner, K. G., & Wolfson, M. (2009). Selected community characteristics and underage drinking. *Substance Use & Misuse, 44*, 179–194.

Uniform Crime Reports

The Uniform Crime Report (UCR) is a database of crime statistics managed by the Federal Bureau of Investigation (FBI). Information contained in the database is provided by police departments across the United States. The Department of Justice uses these data to publish yearly reports about crime and to analyze crime trends over several years. The UCR is a primary source of crime information for police agencies and academic researchers.

The UCR was conceptualized by the International Association of Chiefs of Police, and data collection began in 1929. Four hundred police agencies provided data during the initial collection effort. Now, approximately 18,000 police agencies voluntarily contribute to the data collection process every year. Agencies either submit their information to a state repository or directly submit the information to the FBI. Because every state has its own definitions for criminal behavior, all agencies use FBI guidelines and definitions for reporting, so that there is consistency in the data. There are three major reports published every year using UCR data. (1) *Crime in the United States* provides information about the violent and property crimes reported to the police. (2) *Law Enforcement Officers Killed and Assaulted* provides information about officers killed or assaulted while they are on duty. (3) *Hate Crime Statistics* provides information on hate crimes. The FBI also publishes reports on special topics on a periodic basis.

The UCR comprises several data collection efforts focused on specific crime information. The Summary Reporting System contains information about eight crimes that are known as *index crimes* or *Part 1 crimes.* These crimes are forcible rape, criminal homicide, aggravated assault, burglary, larceny/theft, motor vehicle theft, robbery, and arson. Arrest data are collected for a variety of offenses, including drug-related crimes and crimes committed by juveniles. The UCR also includes information about how crimes are cleared by the police. A case is cleared when either an arrest is made or when extenuating circumstances prevent a case from being prosecuted.

The National Incident Based Reporting System contains specific case information about crime victims, offenders, and characteristics of the crime from a limited number of agencies. This database includes differentiation between attempted and completed crimes and tracks arrests and clearances for specific cases. The Hate Crime Statistics database includes information about hate or bias crimes that are committed because of a victim's protected status, such as religion or race. Another database houses information about police employees, including incidents involving the injury or death of police officers while on duty. Information about cargo theft crimes has its own database, and the UCR also requires participating agencies to provide information about human trafficking and prostitution.

The UCR has several limitations that can affect the interpretation of the prevalence and incidence of crime. First, the UCR likely underestimates the number of crimes that occur because it only accounts for crimes reported to the police. Many crimes are not reported to the police, as indicated by other data sources such as the National Crime Victimization Survey. Second, some departments provide crime data sporadically, which makes it difficult to track crime in their jurisdictions in a consistent manner. A third limitation is that the Summary Reporting System uses a hierarchical classification system, which means that only the most serious crime is included in the database when more than one crime is committed as part of the same incident. This coding method can result in an underestimation of some crimes compared with others. A fourth limitation is that inclusion in the UCR data collection requires that crimes meet specific criteria. While using standardized definitions is the best practice and provides consistency in reporting, this can lead to the exclusion of some crimes that would be considered criminal by individual state statutes but cannot be included in the UCR.

One notable change to the UCR occurred in 2011 when the definition of forcible rape was amended. The former definition limited the inclusion of only cases of rape involving a female victim and involving vaginal penetration. The new definition includes male victims and acts of oral, anal, or vaginal penetration with an object. The new definition also states that the sex act must occur without the victim's consent, as opposed to occurring "forcibly and against her will." The FBI is currently reorganizing its data collection process to improve usability and storage of crime information.

UCR data are available publicly from the website of the U.S. Department of Justice. The provided data analysis tool can be used to generate a variety of reports about crime at the national and local levels. The tool includes data collected from cities with 10,000 or more people and from counties with 25,000 or more people. While the UCR does collect information from agencies that serve smaller populations, that information can only be accessed by contacting the FBI directly.

Wendy Perkins Gilbert

See also Crime Statistics; Index Crimes; National Crime Victimization Survey; Property Crime; Violent Crime

Further Readings

Gove, W., Hughes, M., & Geerken, M. (1985). Are Uniform Crime Reports a valid indicator of the index crimes? An affirmative answer with minor qualifications. *Criminology, 23,* 451–502.

Levitt, S. D. (1998). The relationship between crime reporting and police: Implications for the use of Uniform Crime Reports. *Journal of Quantitative Criminology, 14,* 61–81.

McCleary, R., Nienstedt, B. C., & Erven, J. M. (1982). Uniform Crime Reports as organizational outcomes: Three time series experiments. *Social Problems, 29,* 361–372.

Rosen, L. (1995). The creation of the Uniform Crime Report: The role of social science. *Social Science History, 19,* 215–238.

Urban Legends

An urban legend is a secondhand story of doubtful origins but nonetheless told as true. The story is, at first glance, plausible enough to be believed and usually deals with some embarrassing, ironic, or horrific event that purportedly happened to a real person. The term *urban legend* was coined by Jan Harold Brunvand and has appeared in print since 1968. Brunvand's primary contribution pointed out that legends and folklore are not relegated to "primitive" or "traditional" societies, but rather, they exist in contemporary culture and can help inform our understanding of modern society.

The term *urban legend* is not specific to urban areas. Rather, the term *urban* serves to classify the legend as modern as opposed to other legends in folklore, which generally refer to preindustrial times. These tales are presented as actual occurrences that happened recently and often provide context for the story that may include dates, names, places, or easily recognizable venues the listener may be familiar with. Some anthropologists and sociologists prefer the term *contemporary legend* to disambiguate the terms. Urban legends also differ from myths, although the terms are often used synonymously. The primary distinction rests in myths typically having some sort of supernatural or magical component dealing with creation or life origins, while legends relate to actual events that could have happened to ordinary people under ordinary circumstances. For example, explaining sunrise and sunset as the result of a turtle carrying the sun on its back would qualify as a myth, whereas Paul Bunyan's extraordinary strength would qualify as a legend.

What Distinguishes an Urban Legend?

Urban legends come in many forms but can be broadly classified as morality or cautionary tales. These tales may include common literary elements and themes in their construction such as humor, fear, intrigue, politics, love, and horror to name a few. These narratives serve to allay fears or anxieties or confirm some particular worldview. They caution humans to act or not act in specific ways to avoid harm or other calamity. Also, urban legends often focus on loss of social control or the imposing threat of some other overarching entity. These may include corporations or companies, drugs/intoxicants, technology, disease, governments, or otherwise "wicked people" or those with pernicious intentions.

It is important to emphasize that urban legends do not necessarily reference false or made-up events. Although urban legends are often informally referred to as false events, this is not always the case. From a sociological perspective, the veracity of the story has no bearing on its status as an urban legend. For example, an event may have occurred, but it is not likely that it occurred to countless "friends of friends." It is the legend's broad appeal that is rooted in supposed personal or near-personal experience that aides an urban legend's self-propagation and mutation over time.

Some legends are apocryphal, meaning they are of dubious origin or simply made up. Other legends fall into the category of *ostension*, which is a particular mechanism in folklore whereby parts or a whole of an urban legend do play out, but this occurs after the legend is established. If an actual event happens that mimics the legend, intentionally or not, it can be considered ostention. In cases of pseudo-ostension, events are reproduced or acted out and then presented as evidence of an urban legend's legitimacy. For example, the infamous tale in which seemingly pleasant people give away Halloween treats with needles or razor blades hidden within them qualifies as pseudo-ostension. The story began circulating in the late 1960s, but several reports can be found of actual sharp foreign objects being found in candy from 1972 to 1982. Virtually all of these incidents

have proven to be hoaxes perpetrated by parents or children. Almost every year, there are reports of this legend being "true" as new evidence shows that people are still contaminating candy. This legend also has tangible effects on people's behaviors. Each year, hospitals and police departments around the country offer free screening services to locate potentially deadly treats. In late September 1982, Chicago was plagued by a scare involving proprietary drug tampering, where seven people died after ingesting the pain killer Tylenol. It turned out that the capsules had been tainted with potassium cyanide. In the shadow of this event, in October of that year, the tampered candy scare reached a fever pitch and has somewhat subsided over the decades. Nonetheless, the legend remains a popular cautionary tale and a powerful driving force behind people's behavior, with countless individuals screening their children's candy for contraband.

Examples of Classic Urban Legends

There are literally hundreds of urban legends propagated throughout culture, but some are more popular and possess many of the folkloric and sociological mechanisms described above. The urban legend dealing with "snuff films" is a classic example that taps into several common themes. The basic premise behind a snuff film is that images or footage of murder and/or sexual torture were created by individuals for the prurient and base entertainment of others. Many persons have claimed to have seen or witnessed the creation of a snuff film, but so far, no verifiable footage of such a film has been found to exist. To be sure, there are many images and films that do depict the killing and abuse of individuals. Some of this footage is staged, while some depicts real events as they unfolded. With the accessibility of the Internet, such footage is easy to find and can be offered as evidence that snuff films do exist. What sets these documents apart from snuff films is that they were not created by a person solely for profit or to fill a market niche. Instead, these images are best described as ostensious or pseudo-ostensious in nature. The urban legend surrounding snuff films is perpetuated as a cautionary tale where a free-market economy produces motivations and social forces where nothing, including life, is sacred, and therefore, all vices and pleasures are up for sale. Furthermore, this legend promotes cultural ideals about female innocence and virtue. The snuff film legend most often involves a female victim and can be interpreted as a cautionary tale about waywardness, promiscuity, and filial disobedience.

Another classic example surrounds the legend of the mother who bakes her infant in an oven thinking it is a turkey. In the various versions of this tale, the mother is either high on LSD (D-lysergic acid diethylamide [psychedelic drug]) or some other drug and unwittingly prepares her offspring or a child in her care as dinner. Again, there have been cases where a parent or guardian has killed a child by putting the child in a microwave or otherwise exposing the child to extreme danger, but the key elements that set this legend apart are important. First it serves as a cautionary tale for those who may be tempted to experiment with psychoactive drugs. Second, it reaffirms society's traditional gender roles where it is always the mother or a female babysitter in the tale who is derelict in her child care duties and in turn brings about tragedy. Third, it feeds into the anxieties of working or absent parents who leave their children with caregivers whom they may not be able to trust. Finally it contains elements of dark humor that tackle taboos such as infanticide and cannibalism.

Contemporary Examples of Urban Legends

Not all urban legends are dark or sinister. Political urban legends are very popular especially in an age of facile communication. Many of these legends deal with fear of government or, more specifically, those in positions of power. Examples of these legends include President George W. Bush refusing to sell his home to African Americans or having the lowest IQ (intelligence quotient) of all presidents. During President Barack H. Obama's presidency, claims circulated that he refused to salute U.S. troops or the American flag or that he was sworn into office on the Qur'an. The truth behind these tales is irrelevant since the promoters and disseminators of such information are more concerned with believing that their worldview is valid rather than what is true. In essence, these examples point to fears of unpatriotic behavior, poor policy making, anti-Americanism, and moral collapse.

With the advent of cheap and easy mass communication, urban legends have taken on some new forms in the past decades. Examples of these contemporary urban legends include computer threats that may include viruses, malware, or scams in general. These stories most often include elements of technological threats, where the expanding and

seemingly "uncontrollable" nature of the Internet or technology can lead to peril. These cautionary tales provide advice on how to protect oneself from threat or point to others who have not heeded the warnings with disastrous results. These urban legends contain similar elements of classic urban legends but use new technology platforms for dissemination.

Another specific type of contemporary urban legend can be referred to as *slacktivism*. This term is used to describe a modern form of urban legend where one can seemingly do great good with little to no effort. The Internet abounds with examples of boycotts, donations, petitions, and requests to forward information or e-mails. Participants in such activities engage in this behavior because of a seemingly plausible notion that their efforts will have some tangible effect on reality. The desire to participate in altruistic behavior seems to override the obvious implausibility of the legends' claims. Examples include a dying child who needs a message forwarded to receive payment from a corporation or charity, prayer requests for real of fictional individuals suffering from a variety of harms, or the signing of petitions to ban anything from oil drilling to horse slaughter.

It is important to mention that these examples are different from mere symbolic support. For example, individuals who become involved in a "Walk for the Cure" campaign do not necessarily believe that walking will cure an ailment, but their actions raise awareness and require actual participation. In cases of slacktivism, the participation is symbolic at best and most often allows the participant to escape the guilt of doing nothing or arouses self-righteousness from having effectively done nothing.

A final contemporary example of an urban legend falls under the category of *glurge*. The etymology of the term is disputed, but it most likely originated from a contributor to the popular Snopes.com, a website dedicated to urban legends. The term refers to cloyingly oversentimental stories or object lessons that are spread through chain letters, e-mails, or during inspirational speeches and religious services. Glurge is not necessarily new, but its popularity has increased dramatically through easy communication. Glurge is most often spread with the best intentions in mind and is meant to inspire people who may be facing impossible odds. Furthermore, glurge serves as an object lesson for those who may feel like the complexities of modern life have robbed individuals of their humanity. In these examples, a child's wisdom or an individual's faith in the face of incredible odds are offered as inspirational tales.

As with other urban legends, glurge stories may be true or false but their desirability is almost universal. In one famous tale, a husband arranges for flowers to be delivered to his widowed wife long after he has passed away. In this particular tale, one can find themes of undying love, commitment, and sentimentality. In another example, a child is about to donate blood to her brother who is ill. Once the transfusion begins, she asks if it will hurt when she dies, apparently believing that the act of donating blood will be fatal to her. The child's courage and selflessness is designed to make the reader introspective about life in general. In the tale of Temple Baptist Church, a child's savings of 57 cents buys the congregation a new home. In some versions of the tale, the child is said to have been denied attendance at the church's Sunday school. This particular tale hits on elements of shaming, redemption, love, and God's affinity for a particular group. The tale also resembles "Lesson of the widow's mite" as presented in the Synoptic Gospels.

Filip Wiecko

See also Defining Deviance; Social Change and Deviance

Further Readings

Best, J., & Horiuchi, G. T. (1985). The razor blade in the apple: The social construction of urban legends. *Social Problems, 32*(5), 488–497.

Brunvand, J. H. (2002). *Encyclopedia of urban legends.* New York, NY: W. W. Norton.

Dégh, L., & Vázsonyi, A. (1983). Does the word "dog" bite? Ostensive action: A means of legend-telling. *Journal of Folklore Research, 20*(1), 5–34.

Donovan, P. (2004). *No way of knowing: Crime, urban legends, and the Internet.* New York, NY: Routledge.

Vandalism

Vandalism has numerous and diverse definitions, but most agree that it includes the intentional destruction of other people's property. The Federal Bureau of Investigation defines vandalism as follows:

> To willfully or maliciously destroy, injure, disfigure, or deface any public or private property, real or personal, without the consent of the owner or person having custody or control by cutting, tearing, breaking, marking, painting, drawing, covering with filth, or any other such means as may be specified by local law. (U.S. Department of Justice, 2009)

Most of the definitions emphasize three essential features: intentionality, destructiveness, and property ownership. Nowadays, the results of vandalism may be found on buildings, billboards, street signs, bus stops, vehicles, tunnels, many other public places, and even public or personal computers and websites by computer hacking.

Of French origin, the term *vandalisme* refers to a Germanic tribe, the Vandals, who conquered North Africa and Rome and looted the regions in the 5th century CE. Because of their acts of destruction of buildings and works of art, such behaviors began being referred to by their name. The term *vandalisme* was first used by Abbé Gregoire to denote barbaric behavior after the willful destruction of works of art during the French Revolution.

Although there are several ways to categorize vandalism, the most cited one was proposed by the sociologist Stanley Cohen. He categorizes vandalism into six types:

1. *Acquisitive vandalism:* Damage caused to acquire money or property, such as looting and petty theft.
2. *Tactical vandalism:* Damage as a means, such as breaking a window to be arrested and get a bed in a cell.
3. *Ideological vandalism:* Damage for an explicit ideological reason or to deliver a message.
4. *Vindictive vandalism:* Damage for revenge like arson.
5. *Play vandalism:* Destruction as a part of children's game.
6. *Malicious vandalism:* Damage as an expression of frustration and rage.

Another way to categorize vandalism is by specifying targets: public telephones, public transport, schools, and so on. Among these types of vandalism, school vandalism is the most common and most studied.

Traditionally, motivations for vandalism were explained by one of three theories. First, psychologists consider vandalism as a pathologic behavior. They suggested that juvenile delinquents have the same personality and social background as those who are pathologically ill. Second, sociologists understand vandalism, which is often committed to express feelings against authority figures, as a social behavior. Vandalism has been shown to be more common and more serious when unemployment is high. This theory suggests that vandalism is a malaise of modern society characterized by deindividuation (i.e., losing individual uniqueness), alienation, and meaninglessness. The third theory, developed by Oswald Newman, emphasizes environmental factors as a cause of vandalism. Architectural factors, including a building's location, size, design, materials, and associations with social lifestyles, affect vandals' choice of targets to attack. These classical theories of vandalism have been criticized, and most recent theories developed from newer research.

One of the major studies on vandalism, the Safe School Study, was done by U.S. Department of Health, Education, and Welfare in the mid-1970s. School size, age of the student population, teacher turnover, and parental support for the school's discipline policy were found to explain school vandalism. Other studies found that negative school climate and students' sense of belonging or not belonging to a school are important factors in vandalistic behavior.

Difficulties in determining the extent and the cost of vandalism have led to a minimization of the problem. For instance, it is often difficult to determine whether damage is the result of vandalism or burglary, which leads to an underreporting of vandalism. Also, victims of vandalism often fail to report these acts. Therefore, the prevalence and statistics on vandalism are often inadequate. The cost of vandalism is also underestimated due to hidden costs—some of these costs include the cost of the supervision of the workers, vehicles to transport workers and material for repair, preparation of work orders and materials, labor to clean up, and the security investigation of the act.

Controlling and preventing vandalism are the main objectives of researchers, especially those who work for government agencies. Although no single method may prevent vandalism, several strategies have been developed, and today a mixture of strategies tends to be applied to control or prevent vandalism. Those advocating a legal strategy seek to clarify definitions of the offense, increase prosecution, and strengthen penalties. But some studies suggest that increasing penalties may be ineffective for solving this problem.

Social strategies assert the importance of the community on creating a positive environment to change behaviors and to reduce vandalism. Effective social strategies include developing educational programs for parents, promoting antivandalism campaigns for public awareness, enhancing media publicity exclusively on prosecution and conviction of vandals, and

providing places where other activities are offered as attractive alternatives to vandalism.

Schools play a critical role in controlling and preventing vandalism by changing behaviors and attitudes through education. Schools as a target of vandalistic behavior, very often, have a chance to investigate the nature of vandalism. Research has emphasized a need for more personal and meaningful education programs for students to have better relationships with others. Some studies have shown that changing staff–student relationships, updating the curriculum, and encouraging students to take on more responsibility for their own lives and education are effective deterrents to vandalism.

Another important strategy that prevents vandalism is architectural design. The main idea of this strategy is to design buildings that are less likely to attract vandals and are better able to resist their attacks. This strategy begins with the selection of location, size, and appearance of the school buildings and the design of school grounds. Important design features include placing doors and windows in observable positions, avoiding dark spots by well-planned lighting, and having internal and external circulation of people. In addition to design features, the materials used in construction, furnishing, and finishing should be simple, durable, and damage resistant. Damages from acts of vandalism should be promptly repaired to discourage further attacks. Finally, security and surveillance systems are the most supportive and integrated strategy. These include (a) boundary security fencing, (b) security lighting, (c) alarm systems, and (d) use of security personnel.

Cihangir Baycan and Hilmi Seven

See also Broken Windows Thesis; Delinquency; Property Crime

Further Readings

Bural, P. (1979). *Designing against vandalism.* New York, NY: Van Nostrand Reinhold.

Cohen, S. (1971). Directions for research on adolescent group violence and vandalism. *British Journal of Criminology, 11*(4), 319–340.

Goldstein, A. P. (1996). *The psychology of vandalism.* New York, NY: Plenum Press.

Levy-Leboyer, C. (1984). *Vandalism: Behavior and motivations.* New York, NY: Elsevier Science.

Sykes, J. (1980). *Designing against vandalism.* New York, NY: Van Nostrand Reinhold.

U.S. Department of Justice, Federal Bureau of Investigation. (2009). *Offense definitions* (Uniform Crime Reporting). Retrieved from http://www2.fbi.gov/ucr/cius2009/about/offense_definitions.html

Ward, C. (1973). *Vandalism*. New York, NY: Van Nostrand Reinhold.

VEGETARIANISM AND VEGANISM

Vegetarians avoid eating any meat, including beef, poultry, fish, and other sea creatures. The most common form of vegetarianism is ovo-lacto vegetarianism, which includes eating dairy products and eggs. Vegans are strict vegetarians who, in addition to not eating meat, also avoid all animal products including dairy, eggs, and animal by-products for food, clothing, and other purposes. Instead of eating meat and eggs, vegetarians and vegans typically acquire protein from legumes, nuts, and many varieties of soy and vital wheat gluten products. Instead of dairy products, they derive calcium from leafy greens, tofu, and green vegetables such as broccoli.

This entry concentrates on the deviant social and cultural dimensions of vegetarianism and veganism, focusing primarily on societies that have significant vegetarian and vegan organizations and activism. The number of vegetarians, policy implications, and activism constitute some of the socially deviant aspects of vegetarianism, whereas the ideologies and style encompass some of its culturally deviant features. In general, avoiding meat and animal products would be seen as informal deviance, a departure from the traditional folkway of eating meat.

Characteristics of Vegetarians and Vegans

In certain societies, the practice of vegetarianism and veganism is not considered to be deviant, such as in India, where many Hindus practice vegetarianism. According to the European Vegetarian Union, 40% of India is vegetarian. Although vegetarianism and veganism may be more common than ever throughout the Western world, it still exists as a deviant practice in comparison to the broader population. A 2012 Gallup poll found that 5% of the U.S. population consider themselves to be vegetarian, and 2% identify as vegan. Various polls in the United Kingdom and Australia show similar results. Many Asian countries have a tradition of vegetarian dishes in their cuisine, though they have fewer people who identify as strictly vegetarian or vegan. The International Vegetarian Union reports particularly low percentages of people identifying as vegetarian or vegan throughout Latin America and Africa.

Various polls also indicate that there are about twice as many female than male vegetarians. Very little information has been gathered about the race and ethnicity of vegetarians other than the international comparisons noted above. Polls show the age of most self-identified vegetarians to be in early to late adulthood, with fewer children and elderly vegetarians.

Vegetarian and Vegan Ideologies

There is a wide array of ideological reasons for people becoming vegetarian or vegan. One of the most common reasons involves an opposition to animal cruelty and/or a belief in animal rights. Most animal protection organizations also promote vegetarianism, even mainstream organizations such as the Humane Society of the United States. The Humane Society has 11 million members, or one in every 28 people in the United States. They recently created a factory farming division to monitor and investigate the occurrence of animal cruelty, environmental impact, and the spread of disease (e.g., avian influenza), and they promote vegetarian food and recipes in their newsletters. With this belief, vegetarians say they avoid meat and animal products as a way to boycott cruel practices toward animals.

Another common reason for becoming vegetarian is health benefits. The American Dietetic Association (along with the Dietitians of Canada) published a position paper supporting vegetarianism and veganism at all stages of life. They outline the benefits of a vegetarian diet for preventing heart disease, obesity, hypertension, diabetes, osteoporosis, and many other diseases and illnesses. However, this support is not found everywhere. For example, the national association of dietitians in France (Association des Dieteticiens de Langue Française) has no such position paper and provides no information on vegetarianism. The French government also actively opposes vegetarianism. In October 2011, a governmental order declared that all meals served in school cafeterias must contain animal products for protein and calcium and that meat and fish should be served at certain minimum levels. Many vegetarian groups oppose this order, which they claim effectively outlaws vegetarianism and veganism in school-age children.

Vegetarians also cite environmental concerns among their reasons for avoiding meat. According to a 2006 report from the United Nations titled "Livestock's Long Shadow," the livestock sector produces more greenhouse gases than all forms of transportation combined, and it negatively affects the environment, especially in terms of land and water degradation. Related to this argument is the idea that eating vegetarian would reduce food scarcity. Instead of using vast amounts of grain and water to raise animals for food, humans could eat plant-based foods directly. However, not all environmental or famine-related organizations promote vegetarianism, and vegetarian advocates note its conspicuous absence from Al Gore's environmental call-to-action film *An Inconvenient Truth*.

Finally, religious ideologies can provide a foundation for vegetarianism. Nearly every religion has a vegetarian society, even if that religion does not prescribe vegetarianism as clearly as does Hinduism. Organizations such as the Christian Vegetarian Association, the Jewish Vegetarian Society, and the Muslim Vegetarian/Vegan Society use religious teachings to argue for vegetarianism. For example, many Christian societies believe in the concept of dominion, which many followers take to mean that humans can use animals to their own ends. The Christian Vegetarian Association, in contrast, promotes the idea of a "sacred stewardship," instead of human control over animals, as a way to promote vegetarianism.

Deviant and Mainstream Characteristics of Vegetarianism and Veganism

Although vegetarianism and veganism are still socially and culturally deviant in comparison with the wider society, many vegetarian and vegan organizations are attempting to make this diet and lifestyle more mainstream. Socially, this involves the increased availability of vegetarian food in restaurants and grocery stores, promoting campaigns such as Meatless Mondays, and engaging in activism to change policies and laws. Culturally, this involves highlighting famous vegetarians throughout history, promoting vegetarian and vegan fashion, and by incorporating vegetarianism into subcultures. However, these efforts do not always succeed.

One method of making vegetarianism and veganism more mainstream is to increase the availability of vegetarian foods in grocery stores and restaurants. In the United States, most supermarkets have a

"natural foods" section that carries many vegetarian foods. Marketing research from Datamonitor's Product Launch Analytics shows that the number of new food products labeled "vegetarian," "vegan," or "no animal products" has increased nearly 70 times since 1980, moving from four to five products per year in the late 1980s to more than 200 products per year in the early 2000s, and reaching nearly 300 new products in 2007. Even fast-food restaurants such as Burger King carry a veggie burger. Seeing this growing market, multinational corporations such as ConAgra, General Mills, Kraft Foods, and Kellogg have bought vegetarian companies such as Lightlife, Small Planet Foods, Boca Burgers, and Worthington Foods, respectively.

Another method is promoting the one-day-a-week vegetarian campaign called Meatless Mondays. In August 2012, the U.S. Department of Agriculture (USDA) distributed an internal memo called "Greening Headquarters Update," where the update mentioned the campaign as a way to reduce their employees' and headquarters' environmental impact. The memo cited the ways in which animal agriculture, and especially beef production, contributes to climate change by using extravagant amounts of water, fossil fuels, and other resources. The National Cattlemen's Beef Association condemned the USDA, and just two days after the internal report appeared, the USDA retracted it and claimed that it does not endorse Meatless Mondays. Scholars and activists point out the conflict within the USDA's mission, wherein they simultaneously represent the meat and dairy industries while putting out dietary guidelines promoting healthy eating by reducing saturated fats.

There also exists a backlash from the U.S. government, especially with the association of vegetarianism with the animal rights and environmental movements. The journalist Will Potter has dubbed this backlash the "Green Scare" and has written extensively about the U.S. government's attempts to intimidate and shut down these movements by redefining the term *terrorism* to include more basic forms of activism, by taking these activists to court and charging them as domestic terrorists, and by promulgating the specter of "eco-terrorism." For example, the 2006 Animal Enterprise Terrorism Act was created to amend the 1992 Animal Enterprise Protection Act by making the bill stronger, expanding its purview, and giving federal authorities the ability to increase penalties for offenders. The Animal Enterprise Terrorism Act expanded the term *terrorism* to include not only acts that interfere with but also acts that promote interfering with any animal enterprise. Thus, activists fear that encouraging people to become vegetarian or vegan—effectively interfering with animal enterprises by encouraging boycotts—would be considered terrorism under this new law.

Vegetarian organizations also attempt to make vegetarianism and veganism seem more culturally mainstream. For example, in an effort to show the illustrious lineage of vegetarianism, many organizations highlight famous vegetarians throughout history, going as far back as Pythagoras and Siddhartha Gautama, all the way up to Albert Einstein and Martina Navratilova. More recently, actors such as Joaquin Phoenix provide a public face for veganism, and the singer Morrissey proclaims his vegetarianism with his song (with his former band The Smiths) titled "Meat Is Murder."

High fashion often denotes fur, leather, and exotic animal skins, and many animal rights organizations target their campaigns against practices of raising and killing animals for fur. Additionally, vegetarian and vegan fashion designers attempt to make animal-free products more mainstream in the fashion world. Stella McCartney, a lifelong vegetarian, creates exclusively vegan high fashion as well as everyday fashion designs. Her Adidas jackets, for example, have a logo that reads "suitable for sporty vegetarians." Companies such as Vegetarian Shoes create shoes, belts, wallets, and handbags for consumers wishing to avoid leather products.

Another example of cultural mainstreaming is the ways in which certain subcultures promote vegetarianism and veganism through their music. Elizabeth Cherry studied how the punk subculture enabled punks to practice a stricter form of veganism than those not affiliated with the subculture by providing social support for becoming and staying vegan, opportunities to consume and create vegan cultural goods (e.g., holding vegan potlucks or writing pro-vegan music and zines), and embeddedness in a supportive social network to avoid backsliding. Many other subcultures, such as straight edge and hippies, are also associated with vegetarianism and veganism.

Vegetarians and vegans acknowledge their deviant cultural status, and they have devised supportive strategies for living in a nonvegetarian world. Many international and national vegetarian organizations seek to provide dietary information and recipes, such as the International Vegetarian Union or the Association Végétarienne de France, as well as

numerous local organizations. These organizations often coordinate potlucks or dinners so that vegetarians may meet one another. An Internet dating site, Veggie Date, seeks to narrow the dating pool to only those who are already vegetarian, vegan, or leaning that way. Carol Adams's book *Living Among Meat-Eaters* details philosophical and practical strategies for dealing with nonvegetarian friends, family, and coworkers, as does the North American Vegetarian Society's Vegetarian Summerfest, with sessions titled like "Vegan Empowerment: How to Have a Sustainable and Empowered Life as a Vegan in a Dominant, Meat-Eating Culture."

Although vegetarian campaigns have only slightly increased the numbers of vegetarians and vegans in recent years, studies show that meat consumption is decreasing, overall, from year to year. In a few decades, vegetarianism might be seen as less deviant and more mainstream.

Elizabeth Cherry

See also Positive Deviance; Straight Edge

Further Readings

Adams, C. J. (1990). *The sexual politics of meat: A feminist-vegetarian critical theory*. New York, NY: Continuum.

American Dietetic Association. (2003). Position of the American Dietetic Association and Dietitians of Canada: Vegetarian diets. *ADA Reports, 103*(6), 748–765.

Cherry, E. (2006). Veganism as a cultural movement: A relational approach. *Social Movement Studies, 5*(2), 155–170.

Fiddes, N. (1991). *Meat: A natural symbol*. London, England: Routledge.

Maurer, D. (2002). *Vegetarianism: Movement or moment?* Philadelphia, PA: Temple University Press.

Potter, W. (2011). *Green is the new red: An insider's account of a social movement under siege*. San Francisco, CA: City Lights Books.

Spencer, C. (1995). *The heretic's feast: A history of vegetarianism*. London, England: Fourth Estate.

VIOLENT CRIME

In 1929 the Uniform Crime Reporting (UCR) Program was begun by the Federal Bureau Investigation. It is the official crime data–gathering program covering the entire United States. The present UCR structure classifies Part I offenses (also referred to as index crimes) into eight major offenses. Index Crimes are subdivided into two categories: violent personal crime and property crime. Violent crime consists of murder and nonnegligent manslaughter, forcible rape, robbery, and assault. Violent crimes are defined in the UCR program as those offenses that involve force or the threat of force. Annual information about index crimes (both violent and property) appears each August in the UCR report *Crime in the United States.*

Murder and Nonnegligent Manslaughter. It is the willful (nonnegligent) killing of one human by another. The classification of this offense is based solely on the investigation by police. Any determination of a court, jury, medical examiner, or other judicial body does not change this classification.

Historically, murder is primarily an intraracial crime as the vast majority of black murder victims were murdered by black offenders and the vast majority of white murder victims were murdered by white offenders. Men are much more likely than women to murder and be murdered. Most homicides involve the use of handguns and other firearms and are among people who know each other. The dramatic rise in homicides in the United States from the 1980s to the early 1990s occurred due to murders in which both the killer and the victim were young black males. Scholars have offered a number of explanations for this peak in homicides, including (a) declining economic opportunities in inner cities are said to have increased despair; (b) increased drug trafficking in these areas because of declining economic opportunities; (c) the increased use of powerful firearms, which is associated with drug trafficking battles between gangs; and (d) a code of the street that arises from despair and encourages the use of violence in response to perceived disrespect.

Aggravated Assault. It is an unlawful attack by one person on another for the purpose of inflicting severe or aggravated bodily injury. This type of assault is usually accompanied by the use of a weapon or by other means likely to produce death or great bodily harm. Attempted aggravated assault that involves the display of or threat to use a gun, knife, or other weapon is included in this category because serious personal injury would likely result if the assault were completed. When aggravated assault and larceny/theft occur together, the offense falls under the category of robbery. The difference between murder and aggravated assault is a matter

of the degree of injury. If the victim dies then it becomes a homicide. The same events that precipitate homicide are thought to cause assault. The typical assault is a relatively spontaneous event arising from a quarrel that gets out of hand and escalates into violence.

When considering the facts regarding homicide and assault, the United States has the highest violent crime rate among industrialized nations. Researchers have tended to see our involvement with violence over the long sweep of our history as having become part of our value structure. The United States is a country of confrontation, born of rebellion against authority, with a Wild West tradition of settling differences with guns. The cruelty of displacing Native Americans, slavery, indentured servitude, and violence against labor did much to further the proclivity to violence in the United States and to develop what some have called a subculture of violence. This, combined with a high level of structural inequality in U.S. society, creates the conditions for violence.

Robbery. It is the taking or attempting to take anything of value from the care, custody, or control of a person or persons by force or threat of force or violence and/or by putting the victim in fear. There are various terms that are used to describe subtypes of robberies. The term *armed robbery* signifies that a weapon was used, usually a gun or knife. Armed robbery usually occurs when commercial establishments, such as service stations, banks, or convenience stores, are robbed. *Highway or street robbery* refers to any robbery that occurs in a public place, usually outdoors, and against citizens. Strong-arm robbery means that the robber(s) were unarmed and took the victim's possessions through brute physical force or intimidation. Strong-arm or street robbery is often perpetrated by a group of robbers working together, as when a gang preys on one or more victims.

Forcible Rape. For UCR purposes, the FBI defines rape as "penetration, no matter how slight, of the vagina or anus with any body part or object, or oral penetration by a sex organ of another person, without the consent of the victim." The UCR changed this definition for data collected in 2012, which will make annual comparisons of rape difficult. Attempts or assaults to commit rape by force or threat are also included; however, statutory rape (without force) and other sex offenses are excluded. Although most victims of homicide, assault, and robbery are men, the majority of victims of rape are women.

Victim–offender relationships for rape and sexual assaults indicate that only 18% were committed by strangers. Rape is the most underreported of the violent index crimes.

These four crimes taken together constitute the violent crime index. Although crimes against children and battering are not part of the violent crime index per se, they can be. Battering and the physical and sexual abuse of children can include assault, homicide, and/or rape. Crimes against children are vastly underreported, because it is almost always a third party reporting the crime. Battering is more common and more underreported than rape. Because rape and battering are so underreported, variation among social classes and ethnic groups remains unclear.

Craig J. Forsyth

See also Homicide; Property Crime; Rape; Robbery; Uniform Crime Reports

Further Readings

Federal Bureau of Investigation. (1930–2011). *Crime in the United States.* Washington, DC: U.S. Department of Justice.

Gurr, T. R. (1981). Historical trends in violent crime: A critical review of the evidence. *Crime and Justice: A Review of Research, 3*, 295–353.

LaFree, G. (1999). Declining violent crime rated in the 1990s: Predicting crime booms and busts. *Annual Review of Sociology, 25*, 145–168.

Luckenbill, D. (1977). Criminal homicide as a situated transaction. *Social Problems, 25*, 176–186.

Steffensmeier, D., Feldmeyer, B., Harris, C. T., & Ulmer, J. T. (2011). Reassessing trends in black violent crime, 1980–2008: Sorting out the Hispanic effect in Uniform Crime Reports arrests, National Crime Victimization Survey offender estimates, and U.S. prisoner counts. *Criminology, 49*, 197–251.

Weiner, N. A., Zahn, M. A., & Sagi, R. J. (Eds.). (1990). *Violence: Patterns, causes, public policy.* San Diego, CA: Harcourt Brace Jovanovich.

VOYEURISM

Voyeurism is typically defined as the viewing of people who are engaged in a variety of intimate behaviors such as undressing, sexual activity, or other private acts. Men who engage in such practices are colloquially referred to as "Peeping Toms" in reference to the Lady Godiva legend. According to the American Psychiatric Association, voyeurism is considered a paraphilia if the person has acted on these urges or if the urges cause distress or interpersonal problems.

While the act of viewing others is central to the definition of voyeurism, not all agree on precisely what behaviors should fall under this concept. Most agree that what constitutes voyeurism varies depending on the social and cultural situation in which the action takes place. Some believe that true voyeurs need an unknowing victim and are not satisfied unless they are violating someone's privacy. Others believe masturbation to orgasm at the time of peeping must also be present. Thus, clarifying what types of viewing or "peeping" constitutes voyeurism is difficult. Most would not consider a man visiting a strip show on a business trip away from home as voyeur. Most, however, would view someone who regularly peeps into bedroom windows and masturbates as one. Researchers label males in high-rise offices who bring binoculars to view women undressing in nearby buildings as not being true voyeurs. The assumption is that these men are not true voyeurs because their behavior is situational and they are not masturbating to orgasm. Some researchers distinguish voyeurism as perverse or abnormal when the voyeur has a preference for voyeurism over sexual intercourse. Clearly, the vagueness of behaviors that constitute voyeurism makes determining the prevalence of the activity difficult.

Another factor that complicates the definition of voyeurism is whether the person being watched knows he or she is being watched or objects to being watched. Nude sunbathing, for example, incorporates both types of voyeurism. That is, some go to nude beaches to be free of constraints (i.e., nonsexualized nudity), whereas others go simply to view others. According to Martin Weinberg, voyeurism poses a dilemma for the nude beach naturalists (i.e., those who share in some vague way the casual, nonsexualized vision of the nude beach). To these people, voyeurs have become the plague of the nude scene. While some who frequent nude beaches express disdain for the voyeur, a majority of nude sunbathers do not mind others peeping.

Many sexually deviant behaviors can be viewed as exaggerated versions of familiar components of ordinary sexuality. Thus, the boundary between normal and deviant is sometimes blurred. In tracing the history of the term *voyeurism*, Jonathon Metzl has shown that psychiatrists going back to the

1950s and continuing today have viewed voyeurism as pathological deviance. However, other researchers argue that some acts of voyeurism should be viewed as normal. For instance, William Feigelman suggests that voyeurism or peeping is endemic among construction workers. In fact, peeping while on the job was a means of constructing masculine sexuality. In addition, he argues that given the opportunity, most people will watch (i.e., "peep") others engaging in sexual behavior. He argues that watching sex on a movie screen is not much different, nor does it have any more or less erotic quality, than watching sex through someone's window. The emphasis on safe sex that emerged in the late 1980s (likely due to the AIDS [acquired immune deficiency syndrome] epidemic) has both suggested and encouraged the idea of viewing sex. In fact, there is a fairly well-developed body of literature on various sexual activities that involve what could be termed voyeurism. Indeed, vicarious sexual gratification has always been a replacement for physical sexual fulfillment. The ease at which we can now view others because of the Internet and other media may suggest that voyeurism is or may become endemic to our population.

Researchers have described the motivations of those who intentionally expose themselves to voyeurs. It is not uncommon for individuals to expose portions of or all of their body in the presence of others, even when it is in violation of social proscription. People may exhibit their bare anatomy out of pride, for economic purposes, to interest members of the opposite sex, to sexually stimulate the observer, or as a means of sexually arousing themselves. Depending on the social context, anatomical exposure, like voyeurism, can be conceptualized as erotic, pathological, or both. For example, Craig Forsyth studied women who expose themselves during Mardi Gras. He found that the women who exposed their breasts did so to secure beads and trinkets from those riding on parade floats. Interestingly, these women objected to some people viewing their actions, but not others. Such findings show the symbolic importance of viewing, which is illustrated in the defining of appropriate viewers.

Craig J. Forsyth

See also Bead Whores; Erotica Versus Pornography; Fetishes; Masturbation; Normal Deviance; Public Sex; Tearooms

Further Readings

Bergler, E. (1957). Voyeurism. *Archives of Criminal Psychodynamics, 2,* 211–225.

Bryant, C. (1977). *Sexual deviancy in social context.* New York, NY: New Viewpoints.

Feigelman, W. (1974). Peeping: The pattern of voyeurism among construction workers. *Urban Life and Culture, 3,* 35–49.

Forsyth, C. J. (1996). The structuring of vicarious sex. *Deviant Behavior, 17*(3), 279–295.

McKinstry, W. C. (1974). The pulp voyeur: A peek at pornography in public places. In J. Jacobs (Ed.), *Deviance: Field studies and self-disclosures* (pp. 30–40). Palo Alto, CA: National Press Books.

Metzl, J. M. (2004). Voyeur nation? Changing definitions of voyeurism, 1950–2004. *Harvard Review of Psychiatry, 12,* 127–131.

Smith, S. R. (1976). Voyeurism: A review of the literature. *Archives of Sexual Behavior, 5,* 585–608.

Yalom, I. (1960). Aggression and forbiddenness in voyeurism. *Archives of General Psychiatry, 3,* 309–319.

WHITE SUPREMACIST GROUPS

White supremacist groups have been a persistent feature of American society, in one form or another, since the 1840s. However, in the past 50 years, there has been an explosion in the number and diversity of these groups in response to a variety of stimuli: a more active and intrusive federal government, the civil rights movement, economic dislocation, social media (Internet), and recently, the election of Barack Obama. As this congeries of causes suggests, white supremacist groups differ a good bit from one another in membership, beliefs, and practices. Some groups are linked to the Ku Klux Klan (KKK), others to British Israelism in the 19th century, and still others to the Ska and Reggae music scene in England in the mid-1960s. While variety makes categorization difficult, most often, researchers delineate four types of white supremacist groups: (1) KKK, (2) Christian Identity (CI), (3) neo-Nazis, and (4) racist skinheads, which are discussed in some detail below.

All white supremacist groups see the world in racial terms, believing that the white or "Aryan" race is the chosen or master race. Some believe that whites have a special destiny to fulfill in the world. Groups with an apocalyptic or millenarian view believe that history is heading toward a crisis in which whites must coalesce to defeat the forces of evil, most often represented as being Jewish led. Jews are believed to have duped the "mud races" (nonwhites) into doing their bidding.

White supremacist groups employ a number of symbols and texts, some of which have broad meaning within the general culture (e.g., the Bible, the Confederate battle flag, and the swastika). Other symbols have meaning only to initiates, as in the graphic art and tattoos used to signify racist skinhead groups, or the letter symbols RAHOWA (racial holy war) or ZOG (Zionist occupied government) that function as shorthand for complicated subjects. Some symbols bridge several white supremacist groups, like the "14 words" created by Order member David Lane: "*We must secure the existence of our people and a future for white children.*

Whatever the ideology and symbols used, each group relies on a collective identity to bind members to the group, build solidarity, lower collective action costs, and increase the likelihood that members will participate in potentially risky activities. White supremacist groups also develop complex "frames." Frames tell members how to understand themselves and the world and indicate how members should think and behave. A general frame widely used by white supremacist groups emphasizes the supremacy of the white race over all other races and the violation of white "rights" by other races and peoples.

Several groups monitor, track, and investigate white supremacist groups, including the Southern Poverty Law Center (SPLC), which regularly publishes a "Hate Watch" newsletter, and the Anti-Defamation League of B'nai B'rith. Governmental agencies like the Department of Homeland Security and the Federal Bureau of Investigation regularly track, monitor, and infiltrate white supremacist groups to disrupt potential terrorist attacks. In March 2012, the Southern Poverty Law Center estimated that there were 1,018 "hate groups" in the United States, although not all of them were white supremacist. A report published by the Center for the Study of Hate and Extremism showed that neo-Nazi groups led the total with 170 active groups, followed by the KKK with 152, White Nationalists with 146, Racist Skinheads with 133, and CI with 55. White supremacist groups are found in every state in the United States, with 84 in California alone.

The researchers Betty Dobratz and Stephanie Shanks-Meile estimate the number of hard-core white supremacists in the United States to be around 25,000, with as many as 175,000 active sympathizers. The majority of white supremacist groups' members are working class, but several studies have suggested that the poor and middle class also make up a significant portion of participants. While most illegal actions by white supremacist groups have been attacks on individuals (6,624 hate crimes in 2010 in the United States), others have had wider effects, as when Timothy McVeigh bombed the Alfred P. Murrah Federal Building in Kansas City, killing 168 men, women, and children in hopes of starting a race war to remake American society.

The Major White Supremacist Groups

The KKK is the oldest and best known white supremacist group, emerging three times in the 100 years after the Civil War. Begun in Pulaski, Tennessee, in 1865 by six Confederate soldiers, the movement was a response to the freeing of the slaves and the general absence of law and order in the post–Civil War South. Adopting the name Ku Klux Klan and the familiar robes and hoods for secrecy, the movement quickly spread to Mississippi and Alabama, culminating in a national convention in Nashville, Tennessee, in 1867, where former Confederate general Nathan Bedford Forrest was elected "Grand Wizard." The convention called for the "maintenance of the supremacy of the white Race in this Republic." KKK members, estimated by Forrest at 550,000, fought blacks, carpetbaggers, vagrants, Republican officeholders, and sympathizers. Arson, whippings, night riding, lynching, murder, and intimidation were the chosen weapons of the vigilantes. Perhaps wishing to escape responsibility for these activities, Forrest disbanded the KKK in 1869, but it continued all across the South until the end of Reconstruction in 1876 sent the federal troops home.

The "second" KKK movement coincided with the release of D. W. Griffith's silent movie *The Birth of a Nation* in 1915. In this movie (based on a trilogy written by Thomas Dixon called *The Clansman*), KKK vigilantes save southern womanhood and honor from a horde of rapacious carpetbaggers, corrupt federal troops, and gullible freed slaves. Promoted by entrepreneur "Colonel William Summers," the success of *Birth* led to a revival of interest in the KKK. Estimates put this second KKK at 2 million, the majority of whom were not southerners. Interestingly, antiblack action and rhetoric took a backseat to anti-Semitism, anti-Catholicism, and anti-immigrant views in this second KKK incarnation, linking the movement to the Nativist, Know-Nothing parties of the 1840s and 1850s. In many states, the KKK of the 1920s had a populist "main street" flavor based on religious and racial homogeneity and anti-immigrant fervor. An oddity as a national movement because of the diverse nature of its ideology and membership, the second KKK faded in importance by the late 1930s.

The third period of major KKK activity came on the heels of the civil rights movement and the *Brown v. Board of Education* (1955) decision to integrate southern schools. With an activist federal government as a recruitment tool, membership in various state KKK organizations rose to 50,000 in 1960. Although attempts were made to create a strong national organization linking all the state KKKs, disputes over power, control, money, ideology, and activities served to keep the KKKs (mostly) separated from each other. In addition, the Justice Department and the Federal Bureau of Investigation moved aggressively during this period to destabilize and penetrate the KKK, placing as many as 2,000 informants in various state organizations. Occasionally making common cause with the KKK are a number of different neo-Nazi or national socialist groups.

Most neo-Nazi or national socialist groups are proto-fascist, use Nazi imagery and symbolism, and venerate former Nazis, including Adolf Hitler. Unlike the KKK and CI movements, neo-Nazi groups are not typically religious in orientation, rejecting Judaism and Christianity in favor of apocalyptic millenarianism. George Lincoln Rockwell is viewed as the father of the post–World War II, neo-Nazi or National Socialist Movement in America. Although he dabbled in right-wing politics with other organizations, Rockwell believed that a more robust approach was needed to counter the communists,

Jews, and blacks, who threatened the survival of American and the white race. Rockwell said,

> We must have a government which . . . preserves the right of White citizens to keep and to bear arms, [and a] government which maintains an eternal vigilance against the enemies, both internal and external, of a White America. (Internet, numerous sources)

Although Rockwell was assassinated in 1967, neo-Nazi groups are currently active in every state and have proliferated under names like White Aryan Resistance, American Aryan Reich, National Socialist Movement, Volkfront, and Aryan Nations 88.

One of the founders of the modern neo-Nazi movement in the United States was William Pierce, who led the National Alliance prior to his death. Pierce wrote an influential book called *The Turner Diaries* under the pen name Andrew MacDonald. In *Diaries*, the protagonist Earl Turner participates in a race war aimed at ridding the world of all nonwhites permanently. A copy of *The Turner Diaries* was in Timothy McVeigh's car when he was stopped outside Oklahoma City, lending credence to the theory that Pierce's book had provided a "manual" for revolution and race war.

Sometimes linked to neo-Nazis, skinheads, Hammerskins, and a plethora of other youth-oriented groups are also part of the white supremacist movement. White supremacist skinheads are often referred to as "racist skinheads" to distinguish them from those skinheads who are not racist. Skinheads are distinguished by their shaved heads and by the clothing they wear: Doc Martens (jackboots) and braces (suspenders). One of the distinguishing characteristics of the racist skinhead movement is the importance of music and other youth culture elements including graphic art and "zines." Rejecting such genres as reggae and ska, a number of skinhead bands with names like Skrewdriver, Brutal Attack, No Remorse, Extreme Hatred, Nordic Thunder, and RAHOWA began to create a variant of punk music devoted to articulating and advancing white supremacy. Current American groups include the Vinlanders, Aryan Terror Brigade, Volksfront, and AC skins.

Although established neo-Nazi organizations have attempted to align with or co-opt skinhead movements, these efforts have not been entirely successful, in part because of the extreme individualism of the skinheads themselves. The skinheads taken together are fairly few, although because of their propensity for violence and mayhem, their numbers are magnified compared with other white supremacist groups. Current estimates suggest the presence of between 1,500 and 3,000 hard-core racist skinheads in the United States.

A relatively recent group in the white supremacist movement is Christian Identity. Most CI adherents attend churches led by white supremacist ministers associated with the movement. Historically CI is a variant of Christianity, which has roots in British Israelism in the mid-19th century. CI doctrine holds that the 10 lost tribes of Israel migrated west to found the white European nations. In this view, white "Aryans," not Jews, are the true descendants of the Israelites of the Old Testament. Modern Jews, meanwhile, are children of the Devil, produced by the Devil's coupling with Eve as told in Genesis. In contrast, Anglo-Saxon, Scandinavian, and Germanic peoples are God's "chosen people" and heirs. Followers of CI look to a battle in the future between the children of light (Aryans) and the children of darkness (Jews), which will fulfill the biblical prophecies of the last days. Blacks and other nonwhite races are thought to be not-chosen and subhuman but not directly evil themselves. Currently, the CI movement is a hodgepodge of churches, splinter groups, charismatic leaders, and followers with minimal coherence. Although CI is not specifically violent, it has served as the basis for some particularly violent groups, including Posse Comitatus, the Order, and Aryan Nation, the group associated with the prominent pastor Richard Butler.

Conclusion

White supremacist groups expand and contract in response to changes in American society, the economy, immigration, and foreign policy. In contrast to a view that describes these groups as foreign to American culture, they are, despite their unsavory history and ambitions, quite American. They are creations of the broad American political culture, which has more often produced movements of the right than of the left. A constant presence since the Civil War, white supremacist groups promise to maintain themselves in the future, regardless of how far outside the mainstream they may appear to be.

G. Pearson Cross

See also Domestic Terrorism; Hate Crimes; Ku Klux Klan; Racism; Skinheads

Further Readings

Adams, J., & Roscigno, V. J. (2005). White supremacists, oppositional culture and the World Wide Web. *Social Forces, 84*(2), 759–778.

Barkun, M. (1994). *Religion and the racist right: The origins of the Christian identity movement.* Chapel Hill: University of North Carolina Press.

Berber, A. L. (Ed.). (2004). *Home-grown hate: Gender and organized racism.* New York, NY: Routledge.

Bertlet, C., & Vysotsky, S. (2006). Overview of U.S. white supremacist groups. *Journal of Political and Military Sociology, 34*(1), 11–48.

Dobratz, B. A., & Shanks-Meile, S. L. (1997). *"White power, white pride!" The white separatist movement in the United States.* New York, NY: Twayne.

MacDonald, A. (1978). *The Turner diaries.* New York, NY: Barricade Books.

McDermott, M., & Samson, F. L. (2005). White racial and ethnic identity in the United States. *Annual Review of Sociology, 31,* 245–261.

WHITE-COLLAR CRIME

The term *white-collar crime* was first introduced by Edwin Sutherland, in 1939, during his presidential address at the annual meeting of the American Sociological Society. He defined such a crime as one committed by a person of respectability and high social status in the course of his or her occupation. Within this definition, Sutherland also included crimes committed by corporations, organizations, and other legal entities. In contrast to sociologists and criminologists of the time, who focused their attention almost exclusively on the importance of poverty, broken families, and disturbed personalities as crime factors, he claimed that white-collar criminals did not fit the profiles of street offenders. Sutherland emphasized the social background of offenders and focused on nonviolent offenses committed in the course of employment.

In his book *White Collar Crime*, Sutherland pointed out that white-collar crimes were those illegal acts committed by people in higher-status occupations. John Braithwaite argues that the book became popular because it addressed crimes committed by America's 70 largest private companies and 15 public utility corporations. However, because of fear of libel suits, all the references to those companies were removed. He suggested that his aim with the book was to reform the theory of criminal behavior rather than reform criminal behavior itself. Since that time, research on white-collar crime has become more popular and has had a significant impact on public policy and public opinions.

Sutherland expressed concern over those criminologists and sociologists who focused exclusively on crime committed by persons of low socioeconomic status and on street crimes. According to him, white-collar criminals could be people with different socioeconomic backgrounds. Particularly, crime can be committed by persons working and operating in large and powerful organizations. Consequently, Sutherland recommended that criminologists and sociologists pay greater attention to crimes committed by people from the middle or upper socioeconomic groups in connection with their occupations. At the same time, however, he also noted that such cases should be charged and handled differently from cases involving criminal acts by those of low socioeconomic status.

Sutherland observed that white-collar crime can cause social harm. The financial cost of white-collar crime is greater in the aggregate than the combined economic impact of common crimes. The cost of white-collar crime ranges to $600 billion annually, while street crime ranges to $20 billion annually. Sutherland underlined three main objectives: (1) white-collar crime includes law-violative behavior, (2) poor people are not the only ones who commit crime, and (3) his theory of differential association could explain a general process characteristic of all criminality.

Among critics of Sutherland's work, Paul Tappan noted in 1947 that white-collar crimes are not "crimes" if they are not included in legal definitions. He argued that actions that were not literally against the law were not crimes, and that persons who had not been convicted of criminal charges were not criminals. Ernest Burgess also supported Tappan with the view that Sutherland failed to distinguish between civil and criminal law. Consequently, scholars divided into two groups. Tappan and his followers have proposed new concepts instead of crime, including white-collar illegality, white-collar law breaking, and elite deviance.

Susan Shapiro argues that white-collar criminals violate norms of trust, enabling them to rob without violence and without trespass. Albert Biderman and Albert Reiss examined white-collar crime as violations of law, to which penalties are attached, and that involve the use of a violator's position of significant power, influence, or trust in the legitimate economic or political institutional order for the purpose of illegal gain, or to commit an illegal act for personal or organizational gain. James Coleman defines white-collar crime as a violation of the law committed by a person or group of persons in the course of their otherwise respected and legitimate occupational or financial activity.

Critics of Sutherland's viewpoint pointed out that by definition white-collar offenders were not criminals, because such business offenses were treated as civil or administrative issues.

However, Sutherland had anticipated some of these criticisms by providing an alternative definition of crime as the legal description of an act that is socially injurious, while making a distinction between street crime and white-collar crime and provision for respective legal penalties for such acts, according to their different natures. In so doing, he wished to enable scholars and policymakers to break out of their traditional view of crime.

Thus, the use of this extended definition of crime allowed Sutherland and his followers to continue using the term *white-collar crime* precisely. Additionally, many criminologists and sociologists agreed with Sutherland's view that white-collar crime should include both civil and criminal violations.

Since that time, the definition of white-collar crime has been changing in many ways. The criminologist Herbert Edelhertz defines white-collar crime as an illegal act or series of illegal acts committed by nonphysical means and by concealment or guile to obtain money or property, to avoid payment or loss of money or property, or to obtain business or personal advantage. The Federal Bureau of Investigation (FBI) has adopted its own approach to white-collar crime in terms of the offense. The FBI has defined white-collar crime as those illegal acts that are characterized by deceit, concealment, or violation of trust and that are not dependent on the application or threat of physical force or violence. Individuals and organizations commit these acts to obtain money, property, or services; to avoid the payment or loss of money or services; or to secure personal or business advantage.

In 1981, the U.S. Department of Justice described white-collar crime as nonviolent crime for financial gain committed by means of deception by persons whose occupational status is entrepreneurial, professional, or semiprofessional, and who utilize their special occupational skills and opportunities. It also implies nonviolent crime for financial gain utilizing deception and committed by anyone having special technical and professional knowledge of business and government, irrespective of the person's occupation.

Perhaps the most notable definition was suggested by J. Kelly Strader. He believed that to distinguish white-collar crime from common or "street" crime, practitioners and judges should look into white-collar crime as crime that does not

a. necessarily involve force against a person or property;
b. directly relate to the possession, sale, or distribution of narcotics;
c. directly relate to organized crime activities;
d. directly relate to such national policies as immigration, civil rights, and national security; or
e. directly involve "vice crimes" or the common theft of property. (Strader, 2002, p. 2)

Others have pointed out that although the concept has changed and gained widespread popularity, it is still confusing and controversial in criminology. Still others propose that even if there are two divergent views about white-collar crime, both of them are reasonable and necessary. The main difference is that Sutherland and his followers are focused on the offender as the defining characteristic of white-collar crime, while Tappan and his followers treat the offense itself as the central feature.

Distinguishing White-Collar Crime From Other Crimes

For comparative purposes, white-collar crime has its own definition and distinctions from other crimes described as common crimes or conventional crimes. A number of distinctive features of white-collar crime have been identified. They could be a direct consequence of the location of offenses in occupational roles, while others could be associated with the class and status of offenders. From the perspective of occupational role, white-collar criminals offend during the course of their employment. For example, a particular business may place white-collar offenders within easy access to certain types of information. A consequent crime would be insider trading or embezzlement, in which the employee abuses the trust inherent in an occupational role.

According to Sutherland, the notable difference between the profile of white-collar criminals and ordinary criminals is that these criminals can be quite high in terms of social status: physicians, lawyers, advocates, and government officials.

Another characteristic of white-collar crime is the absence of violence. For example, white-collar criminals who have special skill can rob a bank through the Internet with a computer, while the street criminal may use a knife or gun to threaten the life of someone directly. Consequently, white-collar criminals can embezzle money from or defraud an organization where they work without resorting to killing or inflicting serious bodily harm.

Detection and Law Enforcement

For law enforcement agents, it is hard to catch white-collar criminals because they clean up after themselves and leave little trace of their crimes. Furthermore, white-collar crime is harder to detect because it takes more resources to build a case. In addition, white-collar crimes are usually committed in private places with no eyewitness. Because of lack of resources and expertise, it is sometimes hard for law enforcement agencies to identify white-collar criminals. The offenders may include several persons with different types of responsibility, and they may be highly organized. Even if they are caught, it may be difficult to charge them because of the spread of responsibility up or down the hierarchy.

Even when white-collar crime gets detected, the punishments and fines that are levied on criminals may not be tough. Consequently, it leads to little fear of sanction and deterrence. The victims of white-collar crimes are the entire community or even the whole nation; conversely, the victims of common crimes are mostly poor and vulnerable people. Three aspects of punishment are worth noting: first, the sanctions for white-collar criminals are increasing; second, enforcement has been given more resources in which to investigate and prosecute; third, part of the punishment for white-collar crime is the lost of honor and trust. Although this may seem intangible, it may be a real cost to the offender who despite years of training and educational costs can no longer work at his or her profession. This latter has been contentious as it assumes that other offenders have no such losses and/or that white-collar criminals deserve less of a sentence/fine due to these "intangible" penalties.

Types of White-Collar Crime

White-collar crime can be divided into three categories: (1) occupational crime, (2) corporate crime, and (3) political crime. Each category includes a variety of criminal acts committed in a business or professional setting to achieve financial gain and/or political power. For instance, in the 1950s and 1960s, FBI agents broke into the offices of several left-wing political organizations. The main objective was not financial but to ensure against a perceived threat to the maintenance of political power.

Occupational crime is defined as illegal or rule-breaking activities for personal gain at the expense of consumers, clients, or employers and is committed by individuals in connection with their occupations. It includes politicians, businessmen, lawyers, labor union leaders, doctors, or pharmacists who embezzle money from their employers or steal merchandise and tools. Occupational crime includes insider trading, fraud, embezzlement, and cybercrime.

Insider trading occurs when a person uses inside, confidential, or advance information to profit by trade in shares of publicly held corporations. Fraud can include the sale of counterfeit goods, false advertising, filing false insurance claims, or false billing. Embezzlement is committed when a person who has been entrusted with money or property (accountant, cashier, bookkeeper) misappropriates for his or her own use and/or benefit.

Corporate crime is also called organizational crime. This type of crime occurs when corporate executives or lower-level employees commit criminal acts to benefit their company. For example, corporate directors can use their inside knowledge to make money or accountants can manipulate the books to avoid taxes. Many of such crimes do not involve direct personal gain; persons may commit such crimes to enhance profitability or efficiency of a particular organization. Corporate crime includes any act committed on behalf of corporations that can be punished by the state.

Corporate crimes also can be divided into subcategories such as price fixing, false advertising, violation of labor laws, antitrust violations, and black market activities. It is very difficult to control such types of crime, because lower-level employees can claim that they were merely doing their jobs or carrying out orders from above. On the other hand, top executives can deny knowledge of such practice and blame their employees below. Since corporate crime often goes undetected, reliable estimates of the cost to the public are difficult to obtain. However, the savings and loan scandal of the 1980s cost American taxpayers at least $500 billion.

Political crime or governmental crime involves politicians accepting favors for their individual economic benefit or career advancement, as well as certain acts that can be perceived to be in the interests of the party or government. For example, if there is chaos or rebellion in a particular country, then the president or prime minister of that country, in acting to crush the chaos or rebellion, may not consider the issue of possible subsequent legal prosecution for those actions. White-collar crime of this type very rarely results in criminal prosecution, because the offense is both committed by and investigated by the same political organization. The termination of one's political career may be considered as punishment in lieu of fines and/or sentences (thereby fueling another debate over intangible punishment). Personal corruption and bribery of and by political officials represent another major type of government white-collar crime.

Ruslan Zholdoshbaev

See also Corporate Deviance; Fraud; Occupational Criminality

Further Readings

Braithwaite, J. (1985). White collar crime. *Annual Review of Sociology, 11*, 1–25.

Clinard, M. B., & Yeager, P. C. (1980). *Corporate crime.* New York, NY: Free Press.

Coleman, J. (1994). *The criminal elite: The sociology of white collar crime* (3rd ed.). New York, NY: St. Martin's Press.

Croall, H. (2001). *Understanding white-collar crime.* Buckingham, England: Open University Press.

Edelhertz, H. (1970). *The nature, impact and prosecution of white collar crime.* Washington, DC: Government Printing Office.

Green, G. S. (1990). *Occupational crime.* Chicago, IL: Nelson Hall.

Hagar, J., & Parker, P. (1985). White collar crime and punishment: The class structure and legal sanctioning of securities violations. *American Sociological Review, 50*, 302–316.

Poveda, T. (1994). *Rethinking white-collar crime.* Westport, CT: Praeger.

Schrager, L. S., & Short, J. P. (1978). Toward a sociology of organizational crime. *Social Problems, 25*, 407–419.

Shapiro, S. P. (1990). Collaring the crime, not the criminal: Reconsidering the concept of white collar-crime. *American Sociology Review, 55*, 346–365.

Strader, J. K. (2002). *Understanding white collar crime.* Dayton, OH: LexisNexis.

Sutherland, E. H. (1949). *White collar crime.* New York, NY: Dryden Press.

Wheeler, S. (1992). The problem of white collar crime motivation. In K. Schlegel & D. Weisbund (Eds.), *White collar crime reconsidered.* Boston, MA: Northeastern University Press.

WORKPLACE VIOLENCE

On August 20, 1986, Patrick H. Sherril, a part-time postal employee working at the U.S. Post Office in Edmond, Oklahoma, killed his 14 coworkers and himself because of disciplinary actions taken against him by his supervisors. This was not the first incident of its kind. In fact, the phrase "going postal" came into being in response to several incidents involving postal employees. However, the Edmond massacre attracted a great deal of public and media attention and raised the issue of workplace violence.

Tragic events such as the Edmond massacre; the destruction of the Alfred P. Murrah Federal Building in downtown Oklahoma City, and terrorist attacks by al Qaeda militants on the World Trade Center and Pentagon on September 11, 2001, have represented major turning points in the debates about violence in the workplace and have shown how people can be victims of violence while they are at work. As in these tragic events, many employees have been subject to various forms of violence by either fellow employees or civilians during their daily work activities, and no employee in any sector, public or private, is immune from the threat of workplace violence. According to the Bureau of Justice Statistics, in 2009, more than 500 employees were murdered at their place of employment and more than 572,000 people above16 years of age were victims of nonfatal violent crimes while they were working. Homicide is still the fourth leading cause of occupational death and the leading cause of death for female employees.

Additionally, organizations, employees, and their families incur substantial costs stemming from workplace violence. These costs include tangible costs (i.e., reduced productivity, medical and legal expenses, loss of workforce and income, and security expenses) and intangible costs (i.e., pain, suffering, fear, decreased efficiency and performance, loss of quality of life, and damaged public image) at the individual and organizational levels. Calculating the exact dollar cost of workplace violence is not an easy task because of the difficulties in quantifying the monetary value of intangible costs. Thus, estimates about the cost of workplace violence for employers have ranged somewhere between $5 billion and $300 billion a year.

Defining Workplace Violence

Workplace violence, also known as "occupational violence," refers to violence that occurs in the workplace. However, providing an exact definition of workplace violence is difficult. Scholars have proposed various overlapping definitions of workplace violence. The difference between these definitions stems from how scholars or practitioners define violence and the workplace.

When defining violence in the workplace, definitions of violence range from nonphysical acts, such as verbal, emotional, or psychological abuse, harassment, threats, and intimidation, to physical acts, such as assault, rape, and homicide. Most scholars have proposed a broad range of deviant behaviors that lie somewhere in between these two extremes. The spectrum of crimes considered workplace violence has expanded over time. For instance, after the September 11 attacks, terrorist acts have entered into the spectrum of violence in the workplace. Some scholars have even included deviant behaviors such as vandalism and sabotage targeting an employee's or employer's property under the umbrella of workplace violence.

Just as in defining violence, the term *workplace* has a broad meaning and includes the traditional workplace as well as situations away from offices in which the victim is at work or on duty. Work-related violence can occur in a specific location in which any work activities are performed. Yet violence is not limited to that specific locale and can arise while the victim undertakes his or her work-related duties without regard to that particular locale (i.e., a parole officer attacked during a parolee home visit or a police officer responding to a call and attacked by the suspects) or can arise due to the victim's particular work activities (i.e., a store manager attacked by a laid-off store cashier outside the store or an off duty police officer killed by a man who had been arrested before by the murdered officer).

In this framework, we can define *workplace violence* as any incident in which one or more employees are subject to any sort of nonphysical or physical violent acts in the course of their employment or as a direct result of their work. Workplace violence may also be inflicted on a person (i.e., customer, patient, visitor, or a member of the general public) or property (i.e., vandalizing a coworker's desk or a company vehicle) other than an employee. Perpetrators of workplace violence can include a fellow or former employee, family member, spouse or ex-lover, student, former student, customer, client, visitor, vendor, or a member of the general public.

Currently, neither federal nor state statutes specifically address the issue of workplace violence. However, federal and state statutes alike treat crimes committed against public employees more harshly. Namely, murdering a federal employee is an aggravating factor in determining whether an offense is punishable by capital punishment. For instance, according to the Texas Penal Code, though the act of assault is a Class A misdemeanor punishable by a fine up to $4,000, by jail time up to a year, or by both, it is considered as a felony of the third degree punishable by a prison term of 2 to 10 years, or a fine up to $10,000 if the victim is a public servant.

Types of Workplace Violence

Many typologies have been developed to categorize violence in the workplace. As in the definition of workplace violence, each scholar and practitioner has offered his or her own version of typology. However, consistent themes can be found in all of them. One commonly used typology comprises four types of workplace violence based on the relationship between the victim and the perpetrator.

Type I: Criminal intent. The perpetrator has no other connection with the workplace but to commit a crime from which violence arises (i.e., robbery, shoplifting, theft, and terrorism).

Type II: Customer or client violence. The perpetrator has a legitimate relationship with the business and becomes violent while receiving services or because of reasons stemming from the business transaction (i.e., clients, customers, patients, students, and inmates). This type of violence also encompasses staff violence to consumers, clients, or any other individuals for whom the business provides services.

Type III: Employee-on-employee violence. This type of violence generally occurs when a current or former employee commits violence against another employee(s) or former employee(s) in the workplace (i.e., employee vs. employee, past employee vs. supervisor, or manager vs. employee).

Type IV: Personal relationship. The perpetrator has no relationship with the workplace but has a personal relationship with the targeted employee (i.e., a spouse, relative, friend, or lover). The perpetrator assaults or threatens the victim while at work. Cases of domestic violence spilling over into the workplace generally fall under this category.

Some scholars have also included one more category called *organizational violence* into the aforementioned typology. In this type, the organization itself puts its staff or customers/clients in risky and violent situations by allowing such situations to grow within the organization. Such an organization constitutes a hostile and violent work environment for employees and customers alike, and violence is always likely.

Contributing Factors

Scholars have pointed to a number of contributing factors for workplace violence. Organizational factors also play a part in workplace violence (i.e., work overload, cutbacks, layoffs, lack of involvement, managerial policies, and supervisory styles). These factors could create such a hostile environment in the workplace that violence could erupt at any time. Besides organizational factors, social and cultural factors have a significant effect on the workplace. As argued by some scholars, we live in a society where violence abounds, and this societal violence is creeping into the workplace. Finally, the role of the media on aggressive and violent behavior has also been widely discussed in academic circles. Research shows that there is a relationship between the viewing of media violence and subsequent aggressive or violent behavior in the workplace.

Diversity is another factor that needs to be taken into consideration in the workplace. Today's workforce is more diverse than ever through federal laws governing equal opportunity, which is called Equal Employment Opportunity (EEO) laws. The purpose of the EEO laws is to make sure that all citizens have fair and equal opportunities in employment terms and conditions. Due to EEO laws, organizations employ diverse groups of people coming from different race, gender, religion, culture, national origin, and different age-group as well as persons with mental and physical disabilities. However, although EEO laws aim to achieve balance between certain groups of people making up the social fabric, such diversity has sometimes become a factor contributing to violence in the workplace (e.g., hate crimes).

Responsibility

Under the Occupational Safety and Health Act's (OSHA) general duty clause, employers are required to provide a safe and healthful workplace for all employees. Employers who fail to take necessary steps to prevent or decrease work-related violence are, therefore, liable under OSHA regulations. Thus, an employer who fails to comply with OSHA requirements can be given a citation or fine for workplace violence.

In addition to OSHA's general duty clause, employers may be held liable for workplace violence according to various negligence-based liability rules, such as negligent hiring, negligent retention, negligent training, negligent supervision, negligent recommendation or misinterpretation, and other general common law duties. There are many court cases based on these negligence claims. For instance, in *Deerings West Nursing Center v. Scott* (1990), a Texas court found a nursing home negligent in hiring an unlicensed nurse with a criminal record. The nursing home had hired the nurse without a background check, and the nurse later assaulted an elderly visitor. In another case, *Yunker v. Honeywell Inc.* (1993), Honeywell had fired one of its employees for attempting to strangle a coworker. After serving five years in prison for that offense, the former employee reapplied for a position in Honeywell and was rehired. However, this time the employee formed a romantic attachment with a female coworker who he harassed and ultimately killed. The victim's family filed a lawsuit against the company, claiming that the company was liable for negligent retention, and the court decided in favor of the plaintiff.

Conclusion

Workplace violence is a phenomenon that affects many employers, employees, and their families and brings about substantial tangible and intangible costs for all those involved. Workplace violence contains a broad spectrum of deviant employee behaviors, ranging from nonphysical acts (i.e., verbal, emotional, or psychological abuse; harassment; threats; and intimidation) to physical acts (i.e., assault, rape, and homicide). Personal, psychological, behavioral, and organizational factors together with diversity can contribute to violent behaviors in the workplace. Employers who fail to provide a violence-free workplace may be subject to monetary penalties and liability claims.

Halil Baltaci

See also Bullying; Violent Crime

Further Readings

Bowie, V., Fisher, B. S., & Cooper, C. L. (Eds.). (2005). *Workplace violence: Issues, trends, strategies.* Portland, OR: Willan.

Empie, K. M. (2002). *Workplace violence and mental illness.* New York, NY: LFB Scholarly.

Gill, M., Fisher, B., & Bowie, V. (Eds.). (2002). *Violence at work: Causes, patterns and prevention.* Portland, OR: Willan.

Harrell, E. (2011, March). *Workplace violence, 1993–2009* (Report No.: NCJ 233231). Washington, DC: U.S. Department of Justice, Bureau of Justice Statistics. Retrieved from http://www.bjs.gov/content/pub/pdf/wv09.pdf

Kelloway, E. K., Barling, J., & Hurrell, J. J. (Eds.). (2006). *Handbook of workplace violence.* Thousand Oaks, CA: Sage.

Kerr, K. M. (2010). *Workplace violence: Planning for prevention and response.* Burlington, MA: Butterworth-Heinemann.

Paludi, M. A., Nydegger, R. V., & Paludi, C. A. (2006). *Understanding workplace violence: A guide for managers and employees.* Westport, CT: Praeger.

Van Fleet, D. D., & Van Fleet, E. W. (2010). *The violence volcano: Reducing the threat of workplace violence.* Charlotte, NC: Information Age.

Warchol, G. (1998, July). *Workplace violence, 1992–96* (Report No. NCJ 168634). Washington, DC: U.S. Department of Justice, Bureau of Justice Statistics. Retrieved from http://bjs.ojp.usdoj.gov/content/pub/pdf/wv96.pdf

Index

Entry titles and their page numbers are in **bold**. Page numbers preceded by 1: are in volume 1, and page numbers preceded by 2: are in volume 2. Illustrative material is identified by (fig.) or (table).

types of, **1:**186–187
usage and physiological effects, **1:**188–189
Desistance, 1:189–190
Detoxification. *See* **Drug dependence treatment**
Devereux, George, **1:**161
Deviance (generally)
death of sociology of deviance, **1:**172–175
defined, **1:**127–128, 179–181
deviants, defined, **1:**131
as genetically encoded potentials, **1:**162 (*See also* **Culturally specific mental illnesses**)
normal deviance, **2:**467–468
primary and secondary, **1:**131–132, **2:**541–543
recognizing deviant identity, **1:**359 (*See also* **Identity work**)
Deviance in the academic profession, 1:190–193
academic deviance, **1:**5–8
consequence of teaching role performance, **1:**193
consequences of research role deviance, **1:**192
deviance in teaching role performance, **1:**192–193
generally, **1:**190–191
research role performance and, **1:**191–192
Deviant career, 1:193–196
continuing involvements, **1:**195–196
disinvolvement and reinvolvement, **1:**196
generally, **1:**193–194
initial involvements, **1:**194–195
sequential models of deviant involvements, **1:**194
Deviant places, 1:196–199
addressing issues of, **1:**198–199
examples of, **1:**197–198
generally, **1:**196–197
Deviant Society, The (Adler, Adler), **1:**394
Devil in Miss Jones, The (film), **2:**533
Dexter (TV program), **2:**630
Diagnostic and Statistical Manual, **1:**199–200
autism spectrum disorders, **1:**45–46
gambling addiction, **1:**291, 292
on gays and lesbians, **2:**692

mental illness, **2:**431
mental retardation, **2:**432–434
pedophilia, **2:**492–493
pica, **2:**516
pornography, **2:**534
sadism and masochism, **2:**610
serial murder and paraphilias, **2:**627
sexual addiction, **2:**638
transsexualism, **2:**746
Dialect contact theory, **2:**672
Dick, Lyle, **1:**160
Dieticians of Canada, **2:**771
Differences, **1:**345
Differential association theory, 1:200–203
drift theory and, **1:**223
generally, **1:**200–201
key principles of, **1:**201–203
social learning theory and, **2:**664–665
theory development, **1:**201
Differential reinforcement, **1:**217
Differential susceptibility perspective, **1:**60
Diff'rent Strokes (television), **1:**185
Digital Millennium Copyright Act, **1:**205
Digital piracy, 1:203–206
correlates and predictors, **1:**205–206
as cybercrime, **1:**166
enforcement strategies, **1:**205
generally, **1:**203–204
persistence of, **1:**204
Dinitz, Simon, **1:**134–135
Dirty Harry (film), **2:**523
Disabilities Education Act, **1:**45
Discipline and Punishment: The Birth of the Prison (Foucault), **1:**133
Discrimination, 1:206–209
discriminatory housing practices, **1:**207–208
gay bashing, **1:**297–299, **2:**572
generally, **1:**206
individual discrimination, **1:**208–209
obesity and, **2:**473–476
racial profiling, **1:**206–207
racism, **2:**578–581
sex discrimination, **2:**630–632
sexual harassment, **2:**640–642
transgender lifestyles, **2:**741–742

Disinvolvement, deviant career and, **1:**196
Dixon, Thomas, **2:**778
Dobratz, Betty, **2:**778
"Doctor shopping," **2:**540
Dogfighting, 1:209–212
in America, **1:**210
historical background, **1:**209–210
in 20th century, **1:**210–212
Dolu, Osman, **1:**30
Domestic terrorism, 1:212–215
defining, **1:**212–213
generally, **1:**212
hate crimes and, **1:**320–321
scope of, **1:**214–215
violent extremism versus, **1:**213–214
Domestic violence, 1:215–217
generally, **1:**215
historical background, **1:**215–216
military deviance and, **2:**443
risk factors for abuse, **1:**217
typologies of, **1:**216–217
Donald, Beulah Mae, **1:**392
Donald, Michael, **1:**392
Don't Ask Don't Tell, **2:**612
Dotter, Daniel, **1:**90
Douglas, Jack, **1:**180
Doyle, Sir Arthur Conan, **1:**110
Dracic, Sabaha, **1:**83
Drag queens and kings, 1:217–220
definitions and historical background, **1:**217–218
drag performance, **1:**218–220
generally, **1:**217
transgender lifestyles, **2:**740–741
Dramaturgy, 1:220–223
assumptions of (status, role, context), **1:**220
discrepant roles, **1:**221–222
generally, **1:**220
players, **1:**221
social drama, **1:**222–223
Dreier, Marc, **2:**530
Drew, Lori, **1:**165
Drexler, Melissa, **1:**370
Drift theory, 1:139–140, 223–224
Drug Abuse Warning Network, 1:12, 109, 224–226, 2:415, 568
Drug dependence treatment, 1:226–228
drug treatment approaches, **1:**227–228
drug treatment settings, **1:**226–227
generally, **1:**226